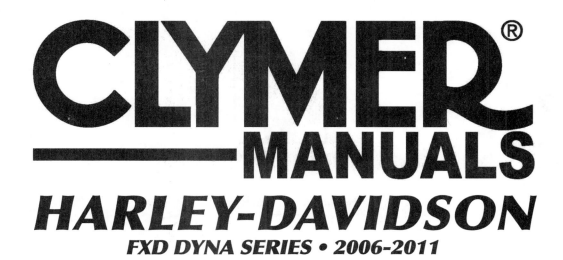

CLYMER® MANUALS

HARLEY-DAVIDSON
FXD DYNA SERIES • 2006-2011

WHAT'S IN YOUR TOOLBOX?

You Tube™

More information available at Clymer.com

Phone: 805-498-6703

Haynes Publishing Group
Sparkford Nr Yeovil
Somerset BA22 7JJ England

Haynes North America, Inc.
861 Lawrence Drive
Newbury Park
California 91320 USA

ISBN 10: 1-59969-536-7
ISBN-13: 978-1-59969-536-5
Library of Congress: 2011943233

Author: Ed Scott

M254, 9S1, 14-544   ABCDEFGHIJKLMNOPQRS

Chapter One
General Information

1

Chapter Two
Troubleshooting

2

Chapter Three
Lubrication, Maintenance and Tune-up

3

Chapter Four
Engine Top End

4

Chapter Five
Engine Lower End

5

Chapter Six
Clutch and Primary Drive

6

Chapter Seven
Transmission

7

Chapter Eight
Fuel System

8

Chapter Nine
Electrical System

9

Chapter Ten
Wheels, Hubs and Tires

10

Chapter Eleven
Front Suspension and Steering

11

Chapter Twelve
Rear Suspension

12

Chapter Thirteen
Brakes

13

Chapter Fourteen
Body and Frame

14

Index

15

Common spark plug conditions

NORMAL

Symptoms: Brown to grayish-tan color and slight electrode wear. Correct heat range for engine and operating conditions.

Recommendation: When new spark plugs are installed, replace with plugs of the same heat range.

WORN

Symptoms: Rounded electrodes with a small amount of deposits on the firing end. Normal color. Causes hard starting in damp or cold weather and poor fuel economy.

Recommendation: Plugs have been left in the engine too long. Replace with new plugs of the same heat range. Follow the recommended maintenance schedule.

CARBON DEPOSITS

Symptoms: Dry sooty deposits indicate a rich mixture or weak ignition. Causes misfiring, hard starting and hesitation.

Recommendation: Make sure the plug has the correct heat range. Check for a clogged air filter or problem in the fuel system or engine management system. Also check for ignition system problems.

ASH DEPOSITS

Symptoms: Light brown deposits encrusted on the side or center electrodes or both. Derived from oil and/or fuel additives. Excessive amounts may mask the spark, causing misfiring and hesitation during acceleration.

Recommendation: If excessive deposits accumulate over a short time or low mileage, install new valve guide seals to prevent seepage of oil into the combustion chambers. Also try changing gasoline brands.

OIL DEPOSITS

Symptoms: Oily coating caused by poor oil control. Oil is leaking past worn valve guides or piston rings into the combustion chamber. Causes hard starting, misfiring and hesitation.

Recommendation: Correct the mechanical condition with necessary repairs and install new plugs.

GAP BRIDGING

Symptoms: Combustion deposits lodge between the electrodes. Heavy deposits accumulate and bridge the electrode gap. The plug ceases to fire, resulting in a dead cylinder.

Recommendation: Locate the faulty plug and remove the deposits from between the electrodes.

TOO HOT

Symptoms: Blistered, white insulator, eroded electrode and absence of deposits. Results in shortened plug life.

Recommendation: Check for the correct plug heat range, over-advanced ignition timing, lean fuel mixture, intake manifold vacuum leaks, sticking valves and insufficient engine cooling.

PREIGNITION

Symptoms: Melted electrodes. Insulators are white, but may be dirty due to misfiring or flying debris in the combustion chamber. Can lead to engine damage.

Recommendation: Check for the correct plug heat range, over-advanced ignition timing, lean fuel mixture, insufficient engine cooling and lack of lubrication.

HIGH SPEED GLAZING

Symptoms: Insulator has yellowish, glazed appearance. Indicates that combustion chamber temperatures have risen suddenly during hard acceleration. Normal deposits melt to form a conductive coating. Causes misfiring at high speeds.

Recommendation: Install new plugs. Consider using a colder plug if driving habits warrant.

DETONATION

Symptoms: Insulators may be cracked or chipped. Improper gap setting techniques can also result in a fractured insulator tip. Can lead to piston damage.

Recommendation: Make sure the fuel anti-knock values meet engine requirements. Use care when setting the gaps on new plugs. Avoid lugging the engine.

MECHANICAL DAMAGE

Symptoms: May be caused by a foreign object in the combustion chamber or the piston striking an incorrect reach (too long) plug. Causes a dead cylinder and could result in piston damage.

Recommendation: Repair the mechanical damage. Remove the foreign object from the engine and/or install the correct reach plug.

CONTENTS

QUICK REFERENCE DATA IX

CHAPTER ONE
GENERAL INFORMATION 1

Manual organization
Warnings, cautions and notes
Safety
Serial numbers
Fasteners
Shop supplies

Tools
Measuring tools
Electrical system fundamentals
Service methods
Storage
Specifications

CHAPTER TWO
TROUBLESHOOTING 31

Operating requirements
Engine starting
Engine performance
Engine noises
Electrical testing
Starting system
Charging system
Ignition system
Fuel system

Engine lubrication
Clutch
Transmission
Lighting system
Vibration
Front suspension and steering
Brake system
Electronic diagnostic system
Specifications

CHAPTER THREE
LUBRICATION, MAINTENANCE AND TUNE-UP 60

Pre-ride inspection
Tires and wheels
Screamin' Eagle and CVO model lubricants
Engine oil and filter
Transmission oil
Primary chaincase oil
Front fork oil
Control cables (non-nylon lined cables)
Throttle control grip lubrication
Jiffy stand lubrication
Primary chain and drive belt
Brake system
Clutch system
Throttle cable adjustment
Fuel line inspection

Steering play inspection
Swing arm pivot bolt inspection
Shock absorber inspection
Engine mounts and stabilizer inspection
Exhaust system inspection
Fastener inspection
Electrical equipment and switches
Tune-up
Air filter element
Compression test
Spark plugs
Ignition timing
Idle speed adjustment
Motorcycle alignment
Specifications

CHAPTER FOUR
ENGINE TOP END 93

Engine service precautions
Rocker arms, pushrods and valve lifters
Cylinder head
Valves and valve components
Cylinder

Pistons and piston rings
Exhaust system
Active exhaust module
Specifications

CHAPTER FIVE
ENGINE LOWER END 146

Engine
Oil pump
Camshaft support plate
Crankcase and crankshaft

Crankcase bearing replacement
Engine break-in
Specifications

CHAPTER SIX
CLUTCH AND PRIMARY DRIVE 181

Primary chaincase cover
Primary chaincase housing
Clutch assembly
Clutch pushrod and release plate inspection
Primary drive assembly
Clutch shell, hub and sprocket
Primary chain and tensioner inspection
Compensating sprocket inspection
Clutch cable replacement
Clutch lever assembly

Clutch release cover
Hydraulic clutch service
Clutch master cylinder
Clutch release cover
Clutch secondary actuator
Clutch hydraulic hose replacement
Clutch system flushing
Clutch system draining
Clutch system bleeding
Specifications

CHAPTER SEVEN
TRANSMISSION 220

Shift assembly
External shift mechanism
Transmission top cover
Shift arm assembly
Shift forks and shift cam
Transmission side door assembly
Transmission shafts

Side door bearings
Main drive gear
Transmission drive sprocket
Transmission case
Oil pan
Specifications

CHAPTER EIGHT
FUEL SYSTEM 256

Air filter backplate
Backplate inspection
Depressurizing the fuel system
Fuel tank
Fuel supply check valve
Top plate
Fuel level sending unit
Fuel pump assembly
Fuel filter
Inlet strainer
Fuel pump
Fuel pressure regulator
Fuel pressure test

Fuel tank console
Electronic fuel injection (EFI)
Throttle and idle cables
Induction module
Fuel injectors
Intake air temperature (IAT) sensor
Throttle position (TP) sensor
Idle air control (IAC)
Manifold absolute pressure (MAP) sensor
Engine temperature (ET) sensor
Oxygen (O_2) sensor
Evaporative emission control system
Specifications

CHAPTER NINE
ELECTRICAL SYSTEM. 304

Electrical component replacement
Fuses
Maxi-Fuse
Ground wires and studs
Battery
Battery tray
Charging system
Alternator
Voltage regulator
Ignition system
Ignition coil
Electronic control module (ECM)
Side electrical caddy
Crankshaft position (CKP) sensor
Engine temperature (ET) sensor
Bank angle (BAS) sensor
Vehicle speed sensor (VSS)
Starting system
Starter

Lighting system
Headlight
Turn signals
Tail/brake light
Fuel tank console mounted instruments
Indicator lamps
Handlebar mounted instruments
Fuel gauge
Automatic compression release (ACR) solenoid
Switches
Jiffy stand interlock sensor (HDI)
Horn
Turn signal security modules
   (TSM, TSSM and HFSM)
Relays
Electrical connector service
Wiring diagrams
Specifications

CHAPTER TEN
WHEELS, HUBS AND TIRES 381

Motorcycle stands
Brake rotor protection
Front wheel
Rear wheel
Wheel inspection
Front and rear hubs
Driven sprocket
Drive sprocket

Drive belt
Laced wheel service
Wheel balance
Tire changing
Tire repairs
Tire runout
Specifications

CHAPTER ELEVEN
FRONT SUSPENSION AND STEERING 413

Handlebar
Handlebar wiring
Handlebar inspection
Lower clamp rubber bushing replacement
Front fork

Steering head and stem
Steering head bearing race replacement
Fork stem lower bearing replacement
Steering play inspection and adjustment
Specifications

CHAPTER TWELVE
REAR SUSPENSION 441

Shock absorbers
Shock absorber adjustment

Swing arm
Specifications

CHAPTER THIRTEEN
BRAKES 454

Brake service
Front brake pad replacement
Front brake caliper
Front master cylinder
Rear brake pad replacement
Rear brake caliper
Rear master cylinder

Brake hose and line replacement
Brake disc
Rear brake pedal
Brake bleeding
Flushing the brake system
Specifications

CHAPTER FOURTEEN
BODY AND FRAME 508

Seats
Front fender
Rear fender
Jiffy stand

Foot rest
Highway foot rest
Spoiler
Specifications

INDEX 525

WIRING DIAGRAMS . . . . .See CD

QUICK REFERENCE DATA

MODEL: _____ YEAR: _____

VIN NUMBER: _____

ENGINE SERIAL NUMBER: _____

THROTTLE BODY SERIAL NUMBER OR I.D. MARK: _____

TIRE INFLATION PRESSURE (COLD)*

	psi	kPa
Front wheel (all models except FXDF)		
Rider only	30	207
Rider and one passenger	30	207
Front wheel (FXDF models)		
Rider only	36	248
Rider and one passenger	36	248
Rear wheel		
Rider only	36	248
Rider and passenger	40	276

*Tire pressure for OE equipment tires. Aftermarket tires may require different inflation pressure.

FUEL, ENGINE AND DRIVE FLUID CAPACITIES

Item	Capacity	Item	Capacity
Fuel tank capacity (total)		Transmission (approximate)	32 U.S. oz (946 ml)
2006 models		Primary chaincase (approximate)	
FXD, FXDC	4.8 gal (18.17 L)	Wet	32 U.S. oz (946 ml)
FXDL, FXDB	4.7 gal (17.79 L)	Dry	40 U.S. oz (1.19L)
FXDWG, FXD35	5.1 gal (19.31 L)	Engine oil capacity	
2007 models		2006-2011 FXD, FXDB,	
FXD	4.8 gal (18.17 L)	FXDC, FXDL, FXDWG	
FXDL, FXDB	4.7 gal (17.79 L)	and FXD35 models	
FXDWG, FXDC	5.1 gal (19.31 L)	With oil change	2.5 qt. (2.4 L)
FXDSE	5.0 gal (18.93 L)	After engine rebuild	3.0 qt. (2.7 L)
2008-2011 models		2007 FXDSE	
FXD, FXDL, FXDB	4.8 gal (18.17 L)	and 2008 FXDSE2 models	
FXDWG, FXDC, FXDF	5.1 gal (19.31 L)	(oil tank w/filter)	3.5 qt. (3.3 L)
FXDSE2, FXDFSE	5.0 gal (18.93 L)	2009 FXDFSE	
		and 2010 FXDFSE2 models	
		(oil tank w/filter)	4.0 qt. (3.8 L)

RECOMMENDED ENGINE OIL

Type	Viscosity	H-D Rating	Ambient operating temperature
H-D Multi-grade	SAE 10W40	HD 360	Below 40° F (4° C)
H-D Multi-grade	SAE 20W50	HD 360	Above 40° F (4° C)
H-D Regular Heavy	SAE 50	HD 360	Above 60° F (16° C)
H-D Extra Heavy	SAE 60	HD 360	Above 80° F (16° C)
Screamin' Eagle and CVO models			
SYN3 Synthetic Motorcycle Lubricant	SAE 20W50	HD 360	Above 40° F (4° C)

RECOMMENDED LUBRICANTS AND FLUIDS

Brake fluid	DOT 4 hydraulic fluid
Clutch fluid (Screamin' Eagle models)	DOT 4 hydraulic fluid
Front fork oil	H-D Type E fork oil
Fuel	91 pump octane or higher
Transmission oil	
All models except Screamin' Eagle and CVO models	H-D Formula+ Transmission and Primary Chaincase Lubricant
	(continued)

RECOMMENDED LUBRICANTS AND FLUIDS (continued)

Transmission oil (continued)	
Screamin' Eagle and CVO models	Screamin' Eagle SYN3 Synthetic Motorcycle Lubricant
Primary chaincase oil	
All models except Screamin' Eagle and CVO models	H-D Formula+ Transmission and Primary Chaincase Lubricant
Screamin' Eagle and CVO models	Screamin' Eagle SYN3 Synthetic Motorcycle Lubricant

MAINTENANCE SPECIFICATIONS

Item	Specification
Brake pad minimum thickness	0.015 in. (0.38 mm)
Clutch cable free play	1/16-1/8 in. (1.6-3.2 mm)
Drive belt deflection	
FXD, FXDWG, FXDF models	1/4-5/16 in. (6.4-7.9 mm)
All other models	5/16-3/8 in. (7.9-9.5 mm)
Engine compression	
All models except Screamin' Eagle and CVO models	125 psi (862 kPa)
Screamin' Eagle and CVO models	
ACR valve connected	130-170 psi (896-1172 kPa)
ACR valve disconnected	200-220 psi (1379-1517 kPa)
Spark plugs	HD No. 6R12*
Gap	0.038-0.043 in. (0.97-1.09 mm)
Idle speed	950-1050 rpm
Ignition timing	Non-adjustable

*The manufacturer recommends that no other type of spark plug be substituted.

MAINTENANCE AND TUNE-UP TORQUE SPECIFICATIONS

Item	ft.-lb.	in.-lb.	N•m
Air filter (2007 FXDSE and 2008 FXDSE2 models)			
Breather bolts	22-24	–	29.8-32.5
Cover Allen screw	–	36-60	4.1-6.8
Element mounting screws	–	55-60	6.3-6.8
Standoff bolts	–	55-60	6.3-6.8
Trimplate Allen screw	–	27-32	3.1-3.6
Air filter hose clamp			
(2009 FXDFSE and 2010 FXDFSE2 models)	–	45-55	5.1-6.3
Air filter (all other models)			
Breather bolts	22-24	–	29.8-32.5
2006 models	10-12	–	13.6-16.3
2007-on models	22-24	–	29.8-32.5
Mounting bracket Torx screws	–	40-60	4.5-6.8
Cover Allen screw	–	36-60	4.1-6.8
Brake master cylinder reservoir cover			
(front and rear) screws	–	6-8	0.7-0.9
Clutch adjusting screw locknut	–	72-120	8.1-13.6
Clutch inspection cover screws	–	84-108	9.5-12.2
Clutch master cylinder reservoir cover			
screws (Screamin' Eagle and CVO models only)	–	6-8	0.7-0.9
Engine isolator bolt and nut	25	–	33.9
Engine oil drain plug			
2006 models	–	36-60	4.1-6.8
2007-on models	14-21	–	19-28.5
Primary chaincase			
Inspection cover screws	–	84-108	9.5-12.2
Drain plug	14-21	–	19.0-28.5
Jiffy stand leg stop bolt	12-15	–	16-20
Rear axle adjuster screw	–	96-120	10.8-13.6
Rear axle nut			
2006 models	60-65	–	81.4-88.1
2007 models	92-98	–	124.7-132.9
2008-2011 models	95-105	–	128.8-142.4
Spark plug	12-18	–	16.3-2.4
Transmission			
Dipstick	–	25-75	2.8-8.5
Drain plug	14-21	–	19-28.5

CHAPTER ONE

GENERAL INFORMATION

This detailed and comprehensive manual covers the 2006-2011 Harley-Davidson FXD Dyna series. The text provides complete information on maintenance, tune-up, repair and overhaul. Hundreds of photos and drawings guide the reader through every job. Each procedure is in step-by-step format and designed for the reader who may be working on the motorcycle for the first time.

MANUAL ORGANIZATION

A shop manual is a tool and, as in all Clymer manuals, the chapters are thumb tabbed for easy reference. Main headings are listed in the table of contents and the index. Frequently-used specifications and capacities from the tables at the end of each individual chapter are listed in the *Quick Reference Data* section located at the front of the manual. Specifications and capacities are provided in U.S. standard and metric units of measure.

During some of the procedures there will be references to headings in other chapters or sections of the manual. When a specific heading is called out in a step, it will be *italicized* as it appears in the manual. If a sub-heading is indicated as being "in this section", it is located within the same main heading. For example, the sub-heading *Handling Gasoline Safely* is located within the main heading *SAFETY*.

This chapter provides general information on shop safety, tools and their usage, service fundamentals and shop supplies. **Tables 1-10** at the end of the chapter provide general motorcycle, mechanical and shop information.

Chapter Two provides methods for quick and accurate diagnosis of problems. Troubleshooting procedures present typical symptoms and logical methods to pinpoint and repair the problem.

Chapter Three explains all routine maintenance necessary to keep the motorcycle running well. Chapter Three also includes recommended tune-up procedures, eliminating the need to constantly consult the chapters on the various assemblies.

Subsequent chapters describe specific systems such as engine, clutch, drive system, transmission, fuel system, suspension, brakes and body. Each disassembly, repair and assembly procedure is discussed in step-by-step form.

WARNINGS, CAUTIONS AND NOTES

The terms WARNING, CAUTION and NOTE each have specific meanings in this manual.

A WARNING emphasizes areas where injury or even death could result from negligence. Mechanical damage may also occur. WARNINGS are to be taken seriously.

A CAUTION emphasizes areas where equipment damage could result. Disregarding a CAUTION could cause permanent mechanical damage, though injury is unlikely.

A NOTE provides additional information to make a step or procedure easier or clearer. Disregarding a NOTE could

cause inconvenience, but would not cause equipment damage or injury.

SAFETY

Follow these guidelines and practice common sense to safely service the motorcycle.

1. Do not operate the motorcycle in an enclosed area. The exhaust gasses contain carbon monoxide, an odorless, colorless and tasteless poisonous gas. Carbon monoxide levels build quickly in small enclosed areas and can cause unconsciousness and death in a short time. Make sure to properly ventilate the work area or operate the motorcycle outside.

2. Never use gasoline or any extremely flammable liquid to clean parts. Refer to *Cleaning Parts and Handling Gasoline Safely* in this section.

3. Never smoke or use a torch in the vicinity of flammable liquids, such as gasoline or cleaning solvent.

4. If welding or brazing on the motorcycle, remove the fuel tank and take it at least 50 ft. (15 m) away from the motorcycle.

5. Use the correct type and size of tools to avoid damaging fasteners.

6. Keep tools clean and in good condition. Replace or repair worn or damaged equipment.

7. When loosening a tight fastener, be aware of what would happen if the tool slips.

8. When replacing fasteners, make sure the new fasteners are the same size and strength as the original ones.

9. Keep the work area clean and organized.

10. Wear eye protection anytime the safety of the eyes is in question. This includes procedures that involve drilling, grinding, hammering, compressed air and chemicals.

11. Wear the correct clothing for the job. Tie up or cover long hair so it does not get caught in moving equipment.

12. Do not carry sharp tools in clothing pockets.

13. Always have an approved fire extinguisher available. Make sure it is rated for gasoline (Class B) and electrical (Class C) fires.

14. Do not use compressed air to clean clothes, the motorcycle or the work area. Debris may be blown into the eyes or skin. Never direct a compressed air hose at anyone. Do

not allow children to use or play with any compressed air equipment.

15. When using compressed air to dry rotating parts, hold the part so it does not rotate. Do not allow the force of the air to spin the part. The air jet is capable of rotating parts at extreme speed. The part may disintegrate or become damaged, causing serious injury.

16. Do not inhale the dust created by brake pad and clutch wear. These particles may contain asbestos. In addition, some types of insulating materials and gaskets may contain asbestos. Inhaling asbestos particles is hazardous to health.

17. Never work on the motorcycle while someone is working under it.

18. When placing the motorcycle on a stand, make sure it is secure before walking away from it.

Handling Gasoline Safely

Gasoline is a volatile flammable liquid and is one of the most dangerous items in the shop. Because gasoline is used so often, many people forget it is hazardous. Only use gasoline as fuel for internal combustion gas engines. Keep in mind when working on the machine that gasoline is always present in the fuel tank, fuel line and throttle body. To avoid a disastrous accident when working around the fuel system, carefully observe the following precautions:

1. Never use gasoline to clean parts. Refer to *Cleaning Parts* in this section.

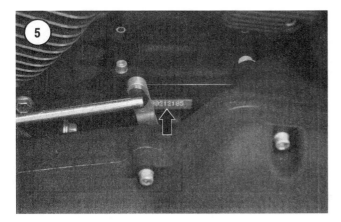

2. When working on the fuel system, work outside or in a well-ventilated area.

3. Do not add fuel to the fuel tank or service the fuel system while the motorcycle is near open flames, sparks or where someone is smoking. Gasoline vapor is heavier than air; it collects in low areas and is more easily ignited than liquid gasoline.

4. Allow the engine to cool completely before working on any fuel system component.

5. Do not store gasoline in glass containers. If the glass breaks, a serious explosion or fire may occur.

6. Immediately wipe up spilled gasoline with rags. Store the rags in a metal container with a lid until they can be properly disposed of, or place them outside in a safe place for the fuel to evaporate.

7. Do not pour water onto a gasoline fire. Water spreads the fire and makes it more difficult to put out. Use a class B, BC or ABC fire extinguisher to extinguish the fire.

8. Always turn off the engine before refueling. Do not spill fuel onto the engine or exhaust system. Do not overfill the fuel tank. Leave an air space at the top of the tank to allow room for the fuel to expand due to temperature fluctuations.

Cleaning Parts

Cleaning parts is one of the more tedious and difficult service jobs commonly performed in the home garage. Many types of chemical cleaners and solvents are available for shop

use. Most are poisonous and extremely flammable. To prevent chemical exposure, vapor buildup, fire and serious injury, observe each product warning label and note the following:

1. Read and observe the entire product label before using any chemical. Always know what type of chemical is being used and whether it is poisonous and/or flammable.

2. Do not use more than one type of cleaning solvent at a time. If mixing chemicals is required, measure the proper amounts according to the manufacturer.

3. Work in a well-ventilated area.

4. Wear chemical-resistant gloves.

5. Wear splash-resistant safety glasses or goggles.

6. Wear a vapor respirator if the instructions call for it.

7. Wash hands and arms thoroughly after cleaning parts.

8. Keep chemical products away from children and pets.

9. Thoroughly clean all oil, grease and cleaner residue from any part that must be heated.

10. Use a nylon brush when cleaning parts. Metal brushes may cause a spark.

11. When using a parts washer, only use the solvent recommended by the manufacturer. Make sure the parts washer is equipped with a metal lid that will lower in case of fire.

Warning Labels

Most manufacturers attach information and warning labels to the motorcycle. These labels contain instructions that are important to personal safety when operating, servicing, transporting and storing the motorcycle. Refer to the owner's manual for the description and location of all labels. Order replacement labels from the manufacturer if they are missing or damaged.

SERIAL NUMBERS

Serial numbers are stamped in various locations on the frame, engine and transmission.

The VIN number label (**Figure 1**) is located on the right side frame down tube.

The frame number label (**Figure 2**) is located on the right side of the steering head.

The engine serial number (**Figure 3**) is stamped on the raised pads found on the left side and right side (**Figure 4**) of the crankcase.

The transmission serial number (**Figure 5**) is stamped on a pad located on the left side of the transmission case, next to the shift lever.

Record these numbers in the *Quick Refernce Data* section in the front of this manual and have these numbers available when ordering parts.

FASTENERS

WARNING
Do not use replacement fasteners with a strength classification lower than the originals.

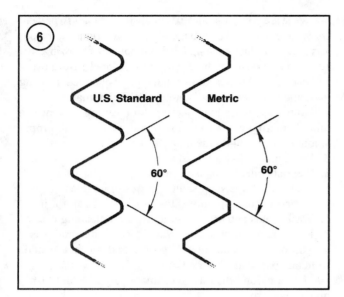

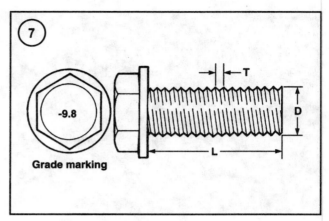

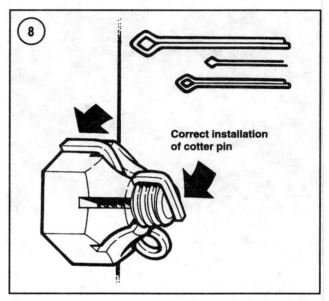

Make sure replacement fasteners meet all the same requirements as the originals; failure to do so may cause equipment failure and/or damage.

Threaded Fasteners

CAUTION
To ensure that the fastener threads are not mismatched or cross-threaded, start all fasteners by hand. If a fastener is hard to start or turn, determine the cause before tightening with a wrench.

Pay particular attention when working with unidentified fasteners; mismatched thread types can damage threads. Both U.S. and metric fasteners (**Figure 6**) are used on the engine and chassis.

Threaded fasteners secure most of the components on the motorcycle. Most fasteners are tightened by turning them clockwise (right-hand threads). If the normal rotation of the component being tightened would loosen the fastener, it may have left-hand threads. If a left-hand threaded fastener is used, it is noted in the text.

Two dimensions are required to match the thread size of the fastener: the number of threads in a given distance and the outside diameter of the threads.

The length (L, **Figure 7**), diameter (D) and pitch (T), or distance between thread crests, classify metric screws and bolts. A typical bolt may be identified by the numbers, 8—1.25 × 130. This indicates the bolt has a diameter of 8 mm, the distance between thread crests is 1.25 mm and the length is 130 mm. Always measure bolt length as shown in L, **Figure 7** to avoid purchasing replacements of the wrong length.

The numbers on the top of the fastener (**Figure 7**) indicate the strength of metric screws and bolts. The higher the number, the stronger the fastener is. Typically, unnumbered fasteners are the weakest.

Many screws, bolts and studs are combined with nuts to secure particular components. To indicate the size of a nut, manufacturers specify the internal diameter and the thread pitch.

The measurement across two flats on a nut or bolt indicates the wrench size.

Torque Specifications

The materials used in manufacturing the motorcycle may be subjected to uneven stresses if the fasteners of the various subassemblies are not installed and tightened correctly. Fasteners that are improperly installed or work loose can cause extensive damage. It is essential to use an accurate torque wrench as described in this chapter.

Specifications for torque are provided in Newton-meters (N•m), foot-pounds (ft.-lb.) and inch-pounds (in.-lb.). Refer to **Table 5** for general torque recommendations. To determine the torque requirement, first determine the size of the fastener as described in *Threaded Fasteners* (this section). Torque specifications for specific components are at the end of the appropriate chapters. Torque wrenches are covered in *Basic Tools* (this chapter).

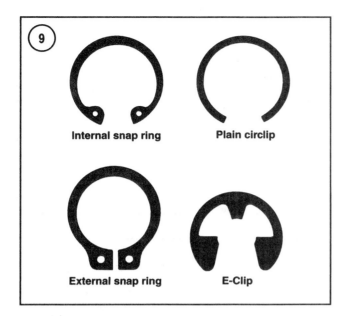

Internal snap ring   Plain circlip

External snap ring   E-Clip

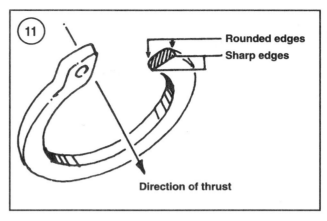

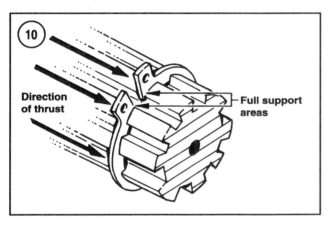

Self-Locking Fasteners

Several types of bolts, screws and nuts incorporate a system that creates interference between the two fasteners. Interference is achieved in various ways. The most common types are the nylon insert nut and a dry adhesive coating on the threads of a bolt.

Self-locking fasteners offer greater holding strength than standard fasteners, which improves their resistance to vibration. Self-locking fasteners cannot be reused. The materials used to form the lock become distorted after the initial installation and removal. Discard and replace self-locking fasteners after removing them. Do not replace self-locking fasteners with standard fasteners.

Washers

The two basic types of washers are flat washers and lockwashers. Flat washers are simple discs with a hole to fit a screw or bolt. Lockwashers are used to prevent a fastener from working loose. Washers can be used as spacers and seals, or can help distribute fastener load and prevent the fastener from damaging the component.

As with fasteners, when replacing washers make sure the replacement washers are of the same design and quality.

Cotter Pins

A cotter pin is a split metal pin inserted into a hole or slot to prevent a fastener from loosening. In certain applications, such as the rear axle on an ATV or motorcycle, the fastener must be secured in this way. For these applications, a cotter pin and castellated (slotted) nut is used.

To use a cotter pin, first make sure the diameter is correct for the hole in the fastener. After correctly tightening the fastener and aligning the holes, insert the cotter pin through the hole and bend the ends over the fastener (**Figure 8**). Unless instructed to do so, never loosen a tightened fastener to align the holes. If the holes do not align, tighten the fastener just far enough to achieve alignment.

Cotter pins are available in various diameters and lengths. Measure the length from the bottom of the head to the tip of the shortest pin.

Snap Rings and E-clips

Snap rings (**Figure 9**) are circular-shaped metal retaining clips. They are required to secure parts and gears in place on parts such as shafts, pins or rods. External type snap rings are used to retain items on shafts. Internal type snap rings secure parts within housing bores. In some applications, in addition to securing the component(s), snap rings of varying thickness also determine endplay. These are called selective snap rings.

The two basic types of snap rings used are either machined and stamped. Machined snap rings (**Figure 10**) can be installed in either direction, because both faces have sharp edges. Stamped snap rings (**Figure 11**) are manufactured with a sharp and a round edge. When installing a stamped snap ring in a thrust application, install the sharp edge facing away from the part producing the thrust.

E-clips are used when it is not practical to use a snap ring. Remove E-clips with a flat blade screwdriver by prying between the shaft and E-clip. To install an E-clip, center it over the shaft groove and push or tap it into place.

Observe the following when installing snap rings:

1. Remove and install snap rings with snap ring pliers. Refer to *Basic Tools* in this chapter.

2. In some applications, it may be necessary to replace snap rings after removing them.

3. Compress or expand snap rings just far enough to install them. If overly expanded, they lose their retaining ability.

4. After installing a snap ring, make sure it seats completely.

5. Wear eye protection when removing and installing snap rings.

SHOP SUPPLIES

Lubricants and Fluids

Periodic lubrication helps ensure a long service life for any type of equipment. Using the correct type of lubricant is as important as performing the lubrication service, although in an emergency the wrong type is better than not using one. The following section describes the types of lubricants most often required. Make sure to follow the manufacturer's recommendations for lubricant types.

Engine, transmission and primary chaincase oil recommendations for Screamin' Eagle and CVO models

Screamin'Eagle and CVO models use HD Screamin' Eagle SYN3 synthetic motorcycle lubricant. If additional oil must be added to correct oil level, and the SYN3 oil is not available, *temporarily* add HD-360 motor oil. Although both types of lubricant are compatible, it is recommended that the lubricant be changed as soon as possible. If the Screamin' Eagle SYN3 is not going to be used permanently, drain the engine, or transmission or primary chaincase oil and use the recommended oil in **Table 4** or **Table 5** of Chapter Three.

Engine oils

Engine oil for use in four-stroke motorcycle engines is classified by three standards: the American Petroleum Institute (API) service classification, the Society of Automotive Engineers (SAE) viscosity rating and the Japanese Automobile Standards Organization (JASO) T 903 Standard classification. Always use a oil with a classification and viscosity recommended by the manufacturer. Using oil with a different classification or viscosity can cause engine damage. The API service classification and the SAE viscosity index are not indications of oil quality.

The API service classification indicates that the oil meets specific lubrication standards. The first letter in the classification S indicates that the oil is for gasoline engines. The second letter indicates the standard the oil satisfies.

The JASO M classification is for oil manufactured specifically for motorcycle use.

Viscosity is an indication of the oil's thickness. Thin oils have a lower number while thick oils have a higher number. Engine oils fall into the 5- to 50-weight range for single-grade oils. The number or sequence of numbers and letter (10W-40 for example) is ht oil's viscosity rating.

Most manufacturers recommend multi-grade oil. These oils perform efficiently across a wide range of operating conditions. Multi-grade oils are identified by a W after the first number, which indicates the low-temperature viscosity.

Greases

Grease is lubricating oil with thickening agents added to it. The National Lubricating Grease Institute (NLGI) grades grease. Grades range from No. 000 to No. 6, with No. 6 being the thickest. Typical multipurpose grease is NLGI No. 2. For specific applications, manufacturers may recommend water-resistant type grease or one with an additive such as molybdenum disulfide (MoS_2).

Brake fluid

> *WARNING*
> *Use of the incorrect brake fluid may cause brake failure and component damage. Make sure the correct brake fluid is being used at all times.*

Brake fluid is the hydraulic fluid used to transmit hydraulic pressure (force) to the wheel brakes. Brake fluid is classified by the Department of Transportation (DOT) to meet particular specifications. The DOT classification, DOT 4 for example, appears on the brake fluid container.

When adding brake fluid, use only the brake fluid recommended by the manufacturer. All models covered in this manual require DOT 4 brake fluid for the brake system, and on Screamin' Eagle models, for the clutch system.

Do not intermix different types of brake fluid. Silicone-based (DOT 5) brake fluid is not compatible with any other types or for use in systems not designed for it and may cause brake failure if used.

Brake fluid will damage any plastic, painted or plated surface it contacts. Use extreme care when working with brake fluid and remove any spills immediately with soap and water.

Hydraulic brake and clutch systems require clean and moisture-free fluid. Keep containers and reservoirs properly sealed. Never reuse old brake fluid. Recycle used brake fluid properly.

Cleaners, Degreasers and Solvents

Many chemicals are available to remove oil, grease and other residue from the motorcycle. Before using cleaning solvents, consider how they will be used and disposed of, particularly if they are not water-soluble. Local ordinances may require special procedures for the disposal of many types of cleaning chemicals. Refer to *Safety* in this chapter.

Use brake parts cleaner to clean brake system components. Brake system parts cleaner leaves no residue. Use electrical contact cleaner to clean electrical connections and components without leaving any residue. Carburetor cleaner is a powerful solvent used to remove fuel deposits and varnish from fuel system components. Do *not* use this cleaner on any of the fuel injection components, as it may damage them.

Generally, degreasers are strong cleaners used to remove heavy accumulations of grease from engine and frame components.

Most solvents are designed to be used with a parts washing cabinet for individual component cleaning. For safety, use only nonflammable or high flash-point solvents.

Gasket Sealant

Sealant is used in combination with a gasket or seal. In other applications, such as between crankcase halves, only a sealant is used. Follow the manufacturer's recommendation when using a sealant. Use extreme care when choosing a sealant different from the type originally recommended. Choose a sealant based on its resistance to heat, various fluids and its sealing capabilities.

A common sealant is room temperature vulcanization sealant, or RTV. This sealant cures at room temperature over a specific time period. This allows the repositioning of components without damaging gaskets.

Moisture in the air causes the RTV sealant to cure. Always install the tube cap as soon as possible after applying RTV sealant. RTV sealant has a limited shelf life and will not cure properly if the shelf life has expired. Keep partial tubes sealed and discard them if they have surpassed the expiration date.

Removing RTV sealant

Silicone sealant is used on some engine gasket surfaces. When cleaning parts after disassembly, a single-sided razor blade or gasket scraper is required to remove silicone residue that cannot be pulled off by hand from the gasket surface. To avoid damaging gasket surfaces, use Permatex Silicone Stripper (part No.80647) to help soften the residue before scraping.

Applying RTV sealant

Clean all old gasket residue from the mating surfaces. Remove all gasket material from blind threaded holes to avoid inaccurate bolt torque. Spray the mating surfaces with an aerosol parts cleaner, and then wipe them off with a lint-free cloth. The area must be clean for the sealant to adhere.

Apply RTV sealant in a continuous bead 0.08-0.12 in. (2-3 mm) thick. Circle all the fastener holes unless otherwise specified. Do not allow any sealant to enter these holes. Assemble and tighten the fasteners to the specified torque within the time frame recommended by the sealant manufacturer.

Gasket Remover

Aerosol gasket remover can help remove stubborn gaskets. This product can speed up the removal process and prevent damage to the mating surface that may be caused by using a scraping tool. Most of these types of products are very caustic. Follow the gasket remover manufacturer's instructions for use.

Threadlock

> *CAUTION*
> *Threadlock is anaeroblc and damages plastic parts. Use caution when using these products in areas where there are plastic components.*

Threadlock is a fluid applied to the threads of fasteners. After tightening the fastener, the fluid dries and becomes a solid filler between the threads. This makes it difficult for the fastener to work loose from vibration or heat expansion and contraction. Some types of threadlock also provide a seal against fluid leaks.

Before applying threadlock, remove any residue from both thread areas and clean them with aerosol parts cleaner. Use the compound sparingly. Excess fluid can run into adjoining parts.

The manufacturer recommends the use of Loctite Threadlocker No. 222 (purple), Loctite Threadlocker 243 (blue), Loctite 246 Medium Strength/High Temperature Threadlocker and Loctite RC/620 (green) High Temperature Retaining Compound. Use these products, or equivalent threadlock, where called for in this manual.

Adhesives and Anti-Seize

The manufacturer recommends using Loctite Pipe Sealant with Teflon (part No. HD 99818-97) on all pipe threads, Loctite 420 Superbonder when installing wheel weights onto cast and disc wheels, and Loctite Anti-Seize in various applications. Use these products, or their equivalents, when called for in this manual.

TOOLS

Most of the procedures in this manual can be carried out with simple hand tools and test equipment familiar to the home mechanic. Always use the correct tools for the job at hand. Keep tools organized and clean. Store them in a tool chest with related tools organized together.

Quality tools are essential. The best are constructed of high-strength alloy steel. These tools are light, easy to use and resistant to wear. Their working surface is devoid of sharp edges and carefully polished. They have an easy-to-clean finish and are comfortable to use. Quality tools are a good investment.

If purchasing tools to perform the procedures covered in this manual, consider the tool's potential frequency of use

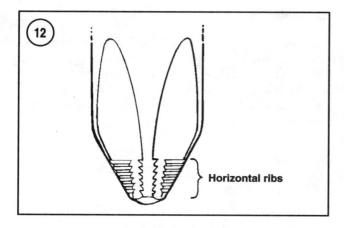

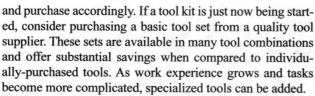

Horizontal ribs

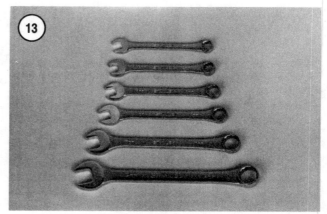

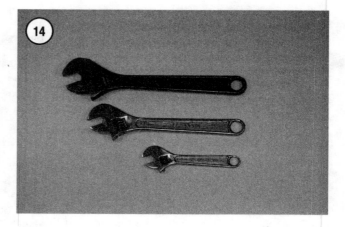

and purchase accordingly. If a tool kit is just now being started, consider purchasing a basic tool set from a quality tool supplier. These sets are available in many tool combinations and offer substantial savings when compared to individually-purchased tools. As work experience grows and tasks become more complicated, specialized tools can be added.

Some of the procedures in this manual specify special tools. These tools and their part numbers are listed with the individual procedures. The manufacturer's special tools are not available to the public.

The JIMS special tools are available directly from the company or from many aftermarket motorcycle part suppliers.

In many cases the tool is illustrated in use. Those with a large tool kit may be able to use a suitable substitute or fabricate a suitable replacement. However, in some cases, the specialized equipment or expertise may make it impractical for the home mechanic to attempt the procedure. When necessary, such operations come with the recommendation to have a dealership or specialist perform the task. It may be less expensive to have a professional perform these jobs, especially when considering the cost of necessary equipment.

Refer to **Table 10** at the end of this chapter for a list of tools, their manufacturer and part number. The tools throughout this manual are either Harley-Davidson (H-D), Motion Pro (MP) or JIMS tools. Motion Pro and JIMS tools are available from dealerships and many aftermarket tool suppliers. The publisher cannot guarantee tool availability now or in the future, or that the part numbering system will remain the same. Contact the tool manufacturer for additional information.

Screwdrivers

Screwdrivers of various lengths and types are mandatory for the simplest tool kit. The two basic types are the slotted tip (flat blade) and the Phillips tip. These are available in sets that often include an assortment of tip sizes and shaft lengths.

As with all tools, use a screwdriver designed for the job. Make sure the size of the tip conforms to the size and shape of the fastener. Use them only for driving screws. Never use a screwdriver for prying or chiseling metal. Repair or

replace worn or damaged screwdrivers. A worn tip may damage the fastener, making it difficult to remove.

Phillips-head screws are often damaged by incorrectly fitting screwdrivers. Quality Phillips screwdrivers are manufactured with their crosshead tip machined to precise specifications. Poor quality or damaged Phillips screwdrivers can back out (camout) and round out the screw head. In addition, weak or soft screw materials can make removal difficult.

An ACR Phillips II screwdriver, patented by the Phillips Screw Company, is available. ACR stands for the horizontal anti-camout ribs found on the driving faces or flutes of the screwdriver's tip (**Figure 12**). Designed specifically for ACR Phillips II screws, the also provide a superior grip on common Phillips screws.

Another way to prevent camout and to increase the grip of a Phillips screwdriver is to apply valve grinding compound or Permatex Screw & Socket Gripper onto the screwdriver tip. After loosening/tightening the screw, clean the screw recess to prevent engine oil contamination.

Wrenches

Open-end, box-end and combination wrenches (**Figure 13**) are available in a variety of types and sizes.

The number stamped on the wrench refers to the distance between the work areas or flat sides on the fasteners. This size must match the size of the fastener head.

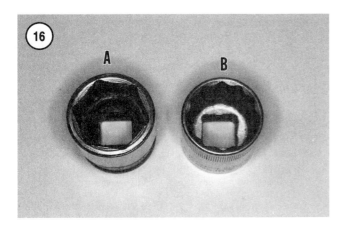

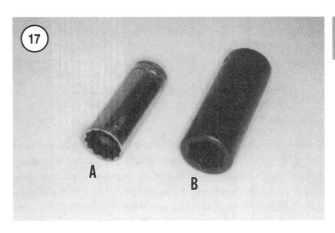

The box-end wrench is an excellent tool because it grips the fastener on all sides. This reduces the chance of the tool slipping. The box-end wrench is designed with either a 6 or 12-point opening. For stubborn or damaged fasteners, the 6-point provides superior holding because it contacts the fastener across a wider area at all six edges. For general use, the 12-point works well. It allows the wrench to be removed and reinstalled without moving the handle over such a wide arc.

An open-end wrench is fast and works best in areas with limited overhead access. It contacts the fastener at only two points and is subject to slipping if under heavy force, or if the tool or fastener is worn. A box-end wrench is preferred in most instances, especially when breaking loose a fastener and applying the final tightening force.

The combination wrench has a box-end on one end and an open-end on the other. This combination makes it a convenient tool.

Adjustable Wrenches

An adjustable, or Crescent, wrench (**Figure 14**) can fit nearly any nut or bolt head that has clear access around its entire perimeter. An adjustable wrench is best used as a backup wrench to keep a large nut or bolt from turning while the other end is being loosened or tightened with a box-end or socket wrench.

Adjustable wrenches contact the fastener at only two points, which makes them more subject to slipping off the fastener. Because one jaw is adjustable and may become loose, this shortcoming is aggravated. Make certain the solid jaw is the one transmitting the force.

Socket Wrenches, Ratchets and Handles

> *WARNING*
> *Do not use hand sockets with air or impact tools because they may shatter and cause injury. Always wear eye protection when using impact or air tools.*

Sockets that attach to a ratchet handle (**Figure 15**) are available with 6-point (A, **Figure 16**) or 12-point openings (B) and come in different drive sizes. The drive size indicates the size of the square hole that accepts the ratchet handle. The number stamped on the socket is the size of the work area, or flat sides on the fastener, and must match the fastener head.

As with wrenches, a 6-point socket provides superior-holding ability, while a 12-point socket needs to be moved only half as far if necessary to reposition it on the fastener.

Sockets are designated for either hand or impact use. Impact sockets are made of thicker material for more durability. Compare the size and wall thickness of a 19-mm hand socket (A, **Figure 17**) and the 19-mm impact socket (B). Use impact sockets when using an impact driver or air tools. Use hand sockets with hand-driven attachments.

Various handles are available for sockets. Use the speed handle for fast operation. Flexible ratchet heads in varying lengths allow the socket to be turned with varying force and at odd angles. Extension bars allow the socket setup to reach difficult areas. The ratchet is the most versatile. It allows the user to install or remove the nut without removing the socket.

Sockets combined with any number of drivers make them undoubtedly the fastest, safest and most convenient tool for fastener removal and installation.

Impact Drivers

> *WARNING*
> *Do not use hand sockets with air or impact tools because they may shatter and cause injury. Always wear eye protection when using impact or air tools.*

An impact driver provides extra force for removing fasteners by converting the impact of a hammer into a turning motion. This makes it possible to remove stubborn fasteners without damaging them. Impact drivers and interchangeable bits (**Figure 18**) are available from most tool suppliers. When using a socket with an impact driver, make sure the socket is designed for impact use. Refer to *Socket Wrenches, Ratchets and Handles* in this section.

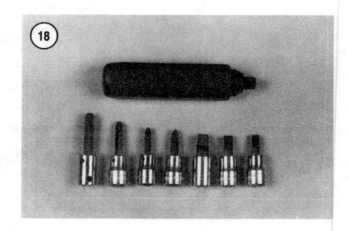

Allen Wrenches

Use Allen wrenches (**Figure 19**) on fasteners with hexagonal recesses in the fastener head. These wrenches are available in L-shaped bar, socket and T-handle types. A metric set is required when working on most motorcycles. Allen bolts are sometimes called socket bolts.

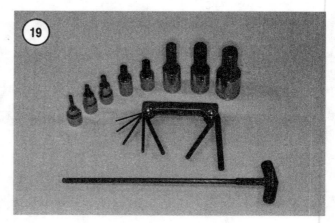

Torque Wrenches

Use a torque wrench with a socket, torque adapter or similar extension to tighten a fastener to a measured torque. Torque wrenches come in several drive sizes (1/4, 3/8, 1/2 and 3/4) and use various methods of displaying the torque value. The drive size indicates the size of the square drive that accepts the socket, adapter or extension. Common methods of displaying the torque value are the deflecting beam, the dial indicator and the audible click (**Figure 20**).

When choosing a torque wrench, consider the torque range, drive size and accuracy. The torque specifications in this manual provide an indication of the range required.

A torque wrench is a precision tool that must be properly cared for to remain accurate. Store torque wrenches in cases or separate padded drawers within a toolbox. Follow the tool manufacturer's instructions for their care and calibration.

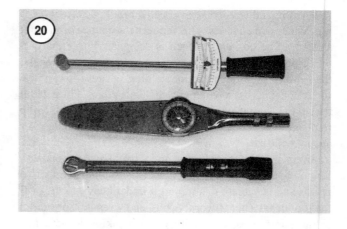

Torque Adapters

Torque adapters or extensions extend or reduce the reach of a torque wrench. The torque adapter is used to tighten a fastener that cannot be reached because of the size of the torque wrench head, drive and socket. If a torque adapter changes the effective lever length (**Figure 21**), the torque reading on the wrench will not equal the actual torque applied to the fastener. It is necessary to recalibrate the torque setting on the wrench to compensate for the change of lever length. When using a torque adapter at a right angle to the drive head, calibration is not required, because the effective length has not changed.

To recalculate a torque reading when using a torque adapter, use the following formula and refer to **Figure 21**.

$$TW = \frac{TA \times L}{L + A}$$

TW is the torque setting or dial reading on the wrench.

TA is the torque specification and the actual amount of torque that is applied to the fastener.

A is the amount that the adapter increases (or in some cases reduces) the effective lever length as measured along the centerline of the torque wrench.

L is the lever length of the wrench as measured from the center of the drive to the center of the grip.

The effective length is the sum of *L* and *A*.

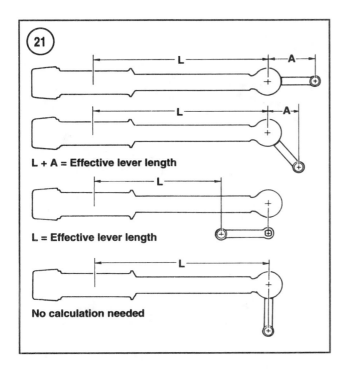

L + A = Effective lever length

L = Effective lever length

No calculation needed

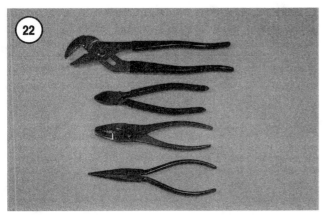

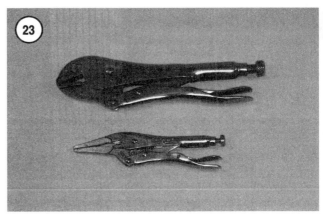

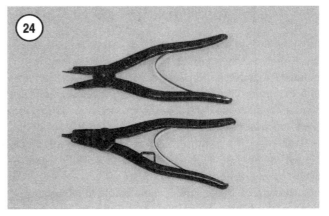

Example:
TA = 20 ft.-lb.
A = 3 in.
L = 14 in.
$$TW = \frac{20 \times 14}{14 + 3} = \frac{280}{17} = 16.5 \text{ ft.-lb.}$$

In this example, the torque wrench would be set to the recalculated torque value (TW = 16.5 ft.-lb.). When using a beam-type wrench, tighten the fastener until the pointer aligns with 16.5 ft.-lb. In this example, although the torque wrench is preset to 16.5 ft.-lb., the actual torque applied is 20 ft.-lb.

Pliers

Pliers come in a wide range of types and sizes. Pliers are useful for holding, cutting, bending and crimping. Do not use them to turn fasteners. **Figure 22** and **Figure 23** show several types of useful pliers. Each design has a specialized function. Slip-joint pliers are general-purpose pliers used for gripping and bending. Diagonal cutting pliers are needed to cut wire and can be used to remove cotter pins. Use needlenose pliers to hold or bend small objects. Locking pliers (**Figure 23**), sometimes called Vise-Grips, are used to hold objects very tightly. They have many uses ranging from holding two parts together, to gripping the end of a broken stud. Use caution when using locking pliers, as the sharp jaws will damage the objects they hold.

Snap Ring Pliers

WARNING
Snap rings can slip and fly off when removing and installing them. Also, the snap ring pliers' tips may break. Always wear eye protection when using snap ring pliers.

Snap ring pliers are specialized pliers with tips that fit into the ends of snap rings to remove and install them.

Snap ring pliers (**Figure 24**) are available with a fixed action (either internal or external) or convertible (one tool works on both internal and external snap rings). They may have fixed tips or interchangeable ones of various sizes and angles. For general use, select convertible type pliers with interchangeable tips (**Figure 24**).

Hammers

Various types of hammers (**Figure 25**) are available to fit a number of applications. Use a ball-peen hammer to strike another tool, such as a punch or chisel. Use soft-faced hammers when a metal object must be struck without damaging it. Never use a metal-faced hammer on engine and suspension components because damage occurs in most cases.

Always wear eye protection when using hammers. Make sure the hammer face is in good condition and the handle is not cracked. Select the correct hammer for the job and make sure to strike the object squarely. Do not use the handle or the side of the hammer to strike an object.

MEASURING TOOLS

The ability to accurately measure components is essential to perform many of the procedures described in this manual. Equipment is manufactured to close tolerances and obtaining consistently accurate measurements is essential to determine which components require replacement or further service.

Each type of measuring instrument (**Figure 26**) is designed to measure a dimension with a certain degree of accuracy and within a certain range. When selecting the measuring tool, make sure it is applicable to the task.

As with all tools, measuring tools provide the best results if cared for properly. Improper use can damage the tool and cause inaccurate results. If any measurement is questionable, verify the measurement using another tool. A standard gauge is usually provided with micrometers to check accuracy and calibrate the tool if necessary.

Precision measurements can vary according to the experience of the person performing the procedure. Accurate results are only possible if the mechanic possesses a feel for using the tool. Heavy-handed use of measuring tools produces less accurate results. Hold the tool gently by the fingertips to easily feel the point at which the tool contacts the object. This feel for the equipment produces more accurate measurements and reduces the risk of damaging the tool or component. Refer to the following sections for specific measuring tools.

Feeler Gauge

Feeler or thickness gauges (**Figure 27**) are required to measure the distance between two surfaces.

A feeler gauge set consists of an assortment of steel strips of graduated thickness. Each blade is marked with its thickness. Blades can be of various lengths and angles for different procedures.

A common use for a feeler gauge is to measure valve clearance. Use wire (round) type gauges to measure spark plug gap.

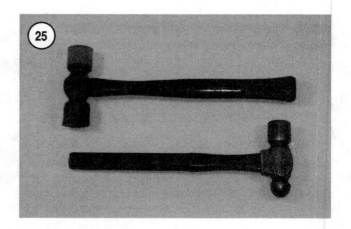

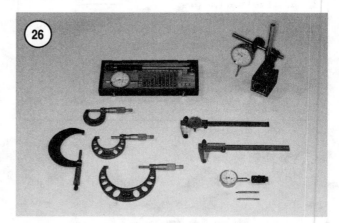

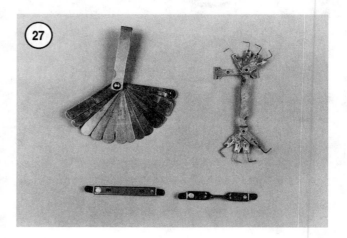

Calipers

Calipers (**Figure 28**) are excellent tools for obtaining inside, outside and depth measurements. Although not as precise as a micrometer, they allow reasonable precision, typically to within 0.001 in. (0.05 mm). Most calipers have a range up to 6 in. (150 mm).

Calipers are available in dial, vernier or digital versions. Dial calipers have a dial readout that provides convenient reading. Vernier calipers have marked scales that must be compared to determine the measurement. The digital caliper uses a liquid-crystal display (LCD) to show the measurement.

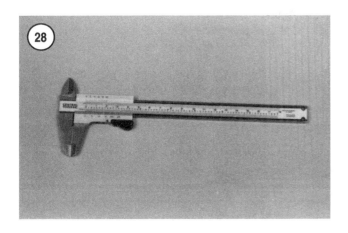

DECIMAL PLACE VALUES*

0.1	Indicates 1/10 (one tenth of an inch or millimeter)
0.010	Indicates 1/100 (one one-hundredth of an inch or millimeter)
0.001	Indicates 1/1,000 (one one-thousandth of an inch or millimeter)

*This chart represents the values of figures placed to the right of the decimal point. Use it when reading decimals from one-tenth to one one-thousandth of an inch or millimeter. It is not a conversion chart (for example: 0.001 in. is not equal to 0.001 mm).

Properly maintain the measuring surfaces of the caliper. There must not be any dirt or burrs between the tool and the object being measured. Never force the caliper to close around an object. Close the caliper around the highest point so it can be removed with a slight drag. Some calipers require calibration. Always refer to the tool manufacturer's instructions when using a new or unfamiliar caliper.

To read a metric vernier caliper, refer to **Figure 29**. The fixed scale is marked in 1-mm increments. Ten individual lines on the fixed scale equal 1 cm. The movable scale is marked in 0.05 mm (hundredth) increments. To obtain a reading, establish the first number by the location of the

0 line on the movable scale in relation to the first line to the left on the fixed scale. In this example, the number is 10 mm. To determine the next number, note which of the lines on the movable scale align with a mark on the fixed scale. A number of lines will seem close, but only one will align exactly. In this case, 0.50 mm is the reading to add to the first number. Adding 10 mm and 0.50 mm equals a measurement of 10.50 mm.

Micrometers

A micrometer is an instrument designed for linear measurement using the decimal divisions of the inch or meter (**Figure 30**). While there are many types and styles of micrometers, most of the procedures in this manual call for an outside micrometer. Use the outside micrometer to measure the outside diameter of cylindrical forms and the thickness of materials.

A micrometer's size indicates the minimum and maximum size of a part that it can measure. The usual sizes are 0-1 in. (0-25 mm), 1-2 in. (25-50 mm), 2-3 in. (50-75 mm) and 3-4 in. (75-100 mm).

Micrometers that cover a wider range of measurements are available. These use a large frame with interchangeable anvils of various lengths. This type of micrometer offers a cost savings, but its overall size may make it less convenient to use.

Adjustment

Before using a micrometer, check its adjustment as follows:
1. Clean the anvil and spindle faces.
2A. To check a 0-1 in. or 0-25 mm micrometer:
   a. Turn the thimble until the spindle contacts the anvil. If the micrometer has a ratchet stop, use it to ensure that the proper amount of pressure is applied.
   b. If the adjustment is correct, the 0 mark on the thimble will align exactly with the 0 mark on the sleeve line. If the marks do not align, the micrometer is out of adjustment.
   c. Follow the tool manufacturer's instructions to adjust the micrometer.
2B. To check a micrometer larger than 1 in. or 25 mm use the standard gauge supplied by the manufacturer. A standard gauge is a steel block, disc or rod that is machined to an exact size.
   a. Place the standard gauge between the spindle and anvil and measure its outside diameter or length. If the micrometer has a ratchet stop, use it to ensure that the proper amount of pressure is applied.
   b. If the adjustment is correct, the 0 mark on the thimble will align exactly with the 0 mark on the sleeve line. If the marks do not align, the micrometer is out of adjustment.
   c. Follow the tool manufacturer's instructions to adjust the micrometer.

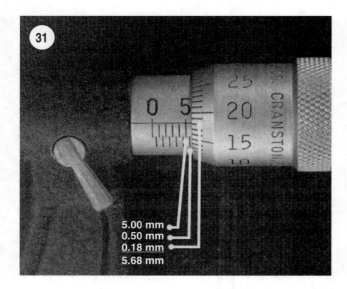

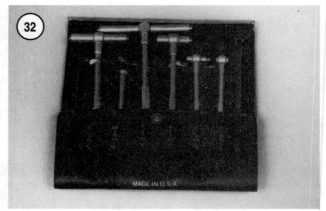

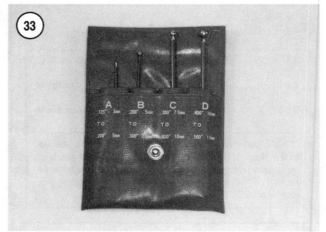

Care

Micrometers are precision instruments. They must be used and maintained with great care. Note the following:

1. Store micrometers in protective cases or separate padded drawers in a toolbox.

2. When in storage, make sure the spindle and anvil faces do not contact each other or an other object. If they do, temperature changes and corrosion may damage the contact faces.

3. Do not clean a micrometer with compressed air. Dirt forced into the tool will cause wear.

4. Lubricate micrometers to prevent corrosion.

Reading

When reading a micrometer, numbers are taken from different scales and added together. The following sections describe how to read the measurements of various types of outside micrometers.

For accurate results, properly maintain the measuring surfaces of the micrometer. There cannot be any dirt or burrs between the tool and the measured object. Never force the micrometer to close around an object. Close the micrometer around the highest point so it can be removed with a slight drag.

The standard metric micrometer (**Figure 31**) is accurate to one one-hundredth of a millimeter (0.01 mm). The sleeve line is graduated in millimeter and half millimeter increments. The marks on the upper half of the sleeve line equal 1.00 mm. Each fifth mark above the sleeve line is identified with a number. The number sequence depends on the size of the micrometer. A 0-25 mm micrometer, for example, will have sleeve marks numbered 0 through 25 in 5 mm increments. This numbering sequence continues with larger micrometers. On all metric micrometers, each mark on the lower half of the sleeve equals 0.50 mm.

The tapered end of the thimble has 50 lines marked around it. Each mark equals 0.01 mm. One complete turn

of the thimble aligns its 0 mark with the first line on the lower half of the sleeve line or 0.50 mm.

When reading a metric micrometer, add the number of millimeters and half-millimeters on the sleeve line to the number of one one-hundredth millimeters on the thimble. Perform the following steps while referring to **Figure 31**.

1. Read the upper half of the sleeve line and count the number of lines visible. Each upper line equals 1 mm.

2. See if the half-millimeter line is visible on the lower sleeve line. If so, add 0.50 mm to the reading.

3. Read the thimble mark that aligns with the sleeve line. Each thimble mark equals 0.01 mm.

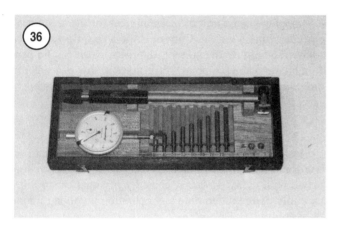

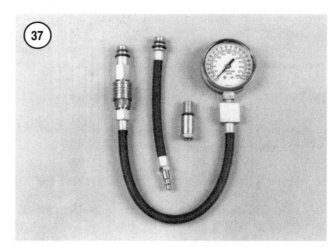

sion (**Figure 34**). Small bore gauges are typically used to measure valve guides.

Dial Indicator

A dial indicator (**Figure 35**) is a gauge with a dial face and needle used to measure variations in dimensions and movements. Measuring brake rotor runout is a typical use for a dial indicator.

Dial indicators are available in various ranges and graduations and with magnetic, clamp, or screw-in stud mounting bases.

Cylinder Bore Gauge

A cylinder bore gauge is similar to a dial indicator. The gauge set shown in **Figure 36** consists of a dial indicator, handle and different length adapters (anvils) to fit the gauge to various bore sizes. The bore gauge is used to measure bore size, taper and out-of-round. When using a bore gauge, follow the tool manufacturer's instructions.

Compression Gauge

A compression gauge (**Figure 37**) measures combustion chamber (cylinder) pressure, usually in psi or kg/cm^2. The gauge adapter is either inserted or screwed into the spark plug hole to obtain the reading. Disable the engine so it will not start and hold the throttle in the wide-open position when performing a compression test. An engine that does not have adequate compression cannot be properly tuned. Refer to procedure in Chapter Three, to perform a compression test.

Multimeter

A digital multimeter (**Figure 38**) is an essential tool for electrical system diagnosis. The voltage function indicates the voltage applied or available to various electrical components. The ohmmeter function tests circuits for continu-

4. If a thimble mark does not align exactly with the sleeve line, estimate the amount between the lines. For accurate readings in two-thousandths of a millimeter (0.002 mm), use a metric vernier micrometer.
5. Add the readings.

Telescoping and Small Bore Gauges

Use telescoping gauges (**Figure 32**) and small bore gauges (**Figure 33**) to measure bores. Neither gauge has a scale for direct readings. Use an outside micrometer (**Figure 34**) to determine the reading.

To use a telescoping gauge, select the correct size gauge for the bore. Compress the movable post and carefully insert the gauge into the bore. Carefully move the gauge in the bore to make sure it is centered. Tighten the knurled end of the gauge to hold the movable post in position. Remove the gauge and measure the length of the posts. Telescoping gauges are typically used to measure cylinder bores.

To use a small bore gauge, select the correct size gauge for the bore. Carefully insert the gauge into the bore. Tighten the knurled end of the gauge to carefully expand the gauge fingers to the limit within the bore. Do not overtighten the gauge because there is no built-in release. Excessive tightening can damage the bore surface and damage the tool. Remove the gauge and measure the outside dimen-

ity, or lack of continuity and measures the resistance of a circuit.

Some manufacturers' specifications for electrical components are based on results using a specific test meter. Results may vary if using a meter not recommended by the manufacturer. Such requirements are noted when applicable.

If an analog ohmmeter is used, it must be calibrated. Refer to the tester manufacturer's instructions.

ELECTRICAL SYSTEM FUNDAMENTALS

A thorough study of the many types of electrical systems used in today's motorcycles is beyond the scope of this manual. However, a basic understanding of electrical basics is necessary to perform simple diagnostic tests.

Refer to *Electrical Testing* in Chapter Two for typical test procedures and equipment. Refer to Chapter Nine for specific component test procedures.

Voltage

Voltage is the electrical potential or pressure in an electrical circuit and is expressed in volts. The more pressure (voltage) in a circuit, the more work can be performed.

Direct current (DC) voltage means the electricity flows in one direction. All circuits powered by a battery are DC circuits.

Alternating current (AC) means the electricity flows in one direction momentarily, and then switches to the opposite direction. Alternator output is an example of AC voltage. This voltage must be changed or rectified to direct current to operate in a battery-powered system.

Resistance

Resistance is the opposition to the flow of electricity within a circuit or component. It is measured in ohms. Resistance causes a reduction in available current and voltage.

Resistance is measured in an inactive circuit with an ohmmeter. The ohmmeter sends a small amount of current into the circuit and measures how difficult it is to push the current through the circuit.

An ohmmeter, although useful, is not always a good indicator of a circuit's actual ability under operating conditions. This is because of the low voltage (6-9 volts) the meter uses to test the circuit. The voltage in an ignition coil secondary winding can be several thousand volts. Such high voltage can cause the coil to malfunction, even though it tests acceptable during a resistance test.

Resistance generally increases with temperature. Perform all testing with the component or circuit at room temperature. Resistance tests performed at high temperatures may indicate high resistance readings and cause unnecessary replacement of a component.

Amperage

Amperage is the unit of measurement for the amount of current within a circuit. Current is the actual flow of electricity. The higher the current, the more work can be performed up to a given point. If the current flow exceeds the circuit or component capacity, it will damage the system.

SERVICE METHODS

Most of the procedures in this manual are straightforward and can be performed by anyone reasonably competent with tools. However, consider personal capabilities carefully before attempting any operation involving major disassembly.

1. In this manual, *Front* refers to the front of the motorcycle. The front of any component is the end closest to the front of the motorcycle. *Left* and *right* sides refer to the position of the parts as viewed by the rider sitting on the seat facing forward.

2. Whenever servicing an engine or suspension component, secure the motorcycle in a safe manner.

3. Tag all similar parts for location and mark all mating parts for position. Record the number and thickness of any shims when removing them. Identify parts by placing them in sealed and labeled plastic sandwich bags.

4. Label disconnected wires and hoses with masking tape and a marking pen. Electrical connectors must be reconnected to their mates. Do not rely on memory alone.

5. Protect finished surfaces from physical damage or corrosion. Keep gasoline and other chemicals off painted surfaces.

6. Use penetrating oil on frozen or tight bolts. Avoid using heat where possible. Heat can warp, melt or affect the temper of parts. Heat also damages the finish of paint and plastics.

7. When a part is a press fit or requires a special tool to remove, the information or type of tool is identified in the text. Otherwise, if a part is difficult to remove or install, determine the cause before proceeding.

8. To prevent objects or debris from falling into the engine, cover all openings.

9. Read each procedure thoroughly and compare the illustrations to the actual components before starting the procedure. Perform the procedure in sequence.

10. Recommendations are occasionally made to refer service to a dealership or specialist. In these cases, the work can be performed more economically by the specialist than by the home mechanic.

11. The term replace means to discard a defective part and replace it with a new part. Overhaul means to remove, disassemble, inspect, measure, renew and/or replace parts as required to recondition an assembly.

12. Some operations require using a hydraulic press. If a press is not available, have these operations performed by a shop equipped with the necessary equipment. Do not use makeshift equipment that may damage the motorcycle.

CAUTION
Do not direct high-pressure water at steering bearings, fuel hoses, wheel bearings, suspension and electrical components. Water may force grease out of the bearings and possibly damage the seals. This will also result in corrosion within electrical terminals.

13. Repairs are much faster and easier if the motorcycle is clean before starting work. Degrease the motorcycle with a commercial degreaser; follow the directions on the container for the best results. Clean all parts with cleaning solvent when removing them.

14. If special tools are required, have them available before starting the procedure. When special tools are required, they are described at the beginning of the procedure.

15. Make sketches or take pictures of similar-appearing parts. For instance, crankcase bolts are often not the same lengths. Do not rely on memory alone. Carefully laid out parts can become disturbed, making it difficult to reassemble the components correctly.

16. Make sure all shims and washers are reinstalled in the same location and position.

17. Whenever rotating parts contact a stationary part, look for a shim or washer.

18. Use new gaskets if there is any doubt about the condition of old ones.

19. If using self-locking fasteners, replace them with new ones. Do not install standard fasteners in place of self-locking ones.

20. Use grease to hold small parts in place if they tend to fall out during assembly. Do not apply grease to electrical or brake components.

Heating Components

WARNING
Wear protective gloves to prevent burns and injury when heating parts.

CAUTION
Do not use a welding torch when heating parts. A welding torch applies excessive heat to a small area very quickly, which can damage parts.

A heat gun or propane torch is required to disassemble, assemble, remove and install some parts and components in this manual. Read the safety and operating information supplied by the manufacturer of the heat gun or propane torch while also noting the following:

1. The work area should be clean and dry. Remove all combustible components and materials from the work area. Wipe up all grease, oil and other fluids from parts. Check for leaking or damaged fuel system components. Repair or remove these parts before beginning work.

2. Never use a flame near the battery, fuel tank, fuel lines or other flammable materials.

3. When using a heat gun, remember that the temperature can be in excess of 1000° F (540° C).

4. Have a fire extinguisher near the job.

5. Always wear protective goggles and gloves when heating parts.

6. Before heating a part installed on the motorcycle, check areas around the part and those parts hidden from view that could be damaged or possibly ignite. Do not heat surfaces than can be damaged by heat. Shield materials such as cables and wiring harnesses that are near the part or area to be heated.

7. Before heating a part, read the entire procedure to make sure the required tools are available. This allows quick work while the part is at its optimum temperature.

8. The amount of heat recommended to remove or install a part is typically listed in the procedure. However, before heating parts without a specific recommendation, consider the possible effects. To avoid damaging a part, monitor the temperature with heat sticks or an infrared thermometer, if possible. Another way, though not as accurate, is to place tiny drops of water on the part. When the water starts to sizzle, the part is hot enough. Keep the heat source in motion to prevent overheating.

Removing Frozen Fasteners

If a fastener cannot be removed, several methods may be used to loosen it. First, apply penetrating oil such as Liquid Wrench or WD-40. Apply it liberally and let it penetrate for 10-15 minutes. Rap the fastener several times with a small hammer. Do not hit it hard enough to cause damage. Reapply the penetrating oil if necessary.

For frozen screws, apply penetrating oil as described, and then insert a screwdriver in the slot and rap the top of the screwdriver with a hammer. This loosens the rust so the screw can be removed in the normal way. If the screw head is too damaged to use this method, grip the head with locking pliers and twist the screw out.

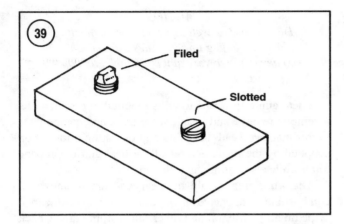

Avoid applying heat unless specifically instructed. Heat may melt, warp or remove the temper from parts. Most penetrating oils are also flammable.

Removing Broken Fasteners

If the head breaks off a screw or bolt, several methods are available for removing the remaining portion. If a large portion of the remainder projects out, try gripping it with locking pliers. If the projecting portion is too small, file it to fit a wrench or cut a slot in it to fit a screwdriver (**Figure 39**).

If the head breaks off flush, use a screw extractor. To do this, center punch (A, **Figure 40**) the exact center of the remaining portion of the screw or bolt. Drill a small hole (B, **Figure 40**) in the screw and tap the extractor (C) into the hole. Back the screw out with a wrench (D, **Figure 40**) on the extractor.

Repairing Damaged Threads

Occasionally, threads are stripped through carelessness or impact damage. Often the threads can be repaired by running a tap (for internal threads on nuts) or die (for external threads on bolts) through the threads (**Figure 41**). To clean or repair spark plug threads, use a spark plug tap.

If an internal thread is damaged, it may be necessary to install a Helicoil or some other type of thread insert. Follow the insert manufacturer's instructions when installing their part.

If it is necessary to drill and tap a hole, refer to **Table 8** for U.S. Standard tap and drill sizes or **Table 9** for metric tap and drill sizes.

Stud Removal/Installation

A stud removal tool is available from most tool suppliers. This tool makes the removal and installation of studs easier. If one is not available, thread two nuts onto the stud and tighten them against each other. Remove the stud by turning the lower nut (**Figure 42**).

1. Measure the height of the stud above the surface.

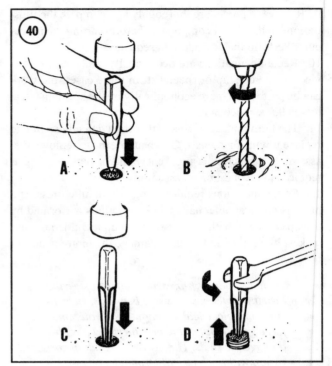

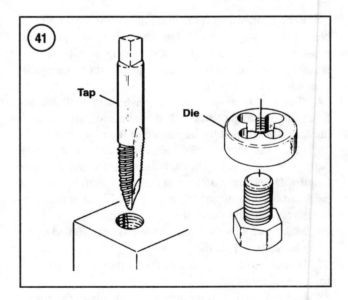

2. Thread the stud removal tool onto the stud and tighten it, or thread two nuts onto the stud.
3. Remove the stud by turning the stud remover or lower nut counterclockwise.
4. Remove any threadlock residue from the threaded hole. Clean the threads with a aerosol parts cleaner.
5. Install the stud removal tool onto the new stud or thread two nuts onto the stud.
6. Apply threadlock to the threads of the stud.
7. Install the stud and tighten with the stud removal tool or by turning the top nut clockwise.
8. Install the stud to the height noted previously or tighten to its torque specification.
9. Remove the stud removal tool or the two nuts.

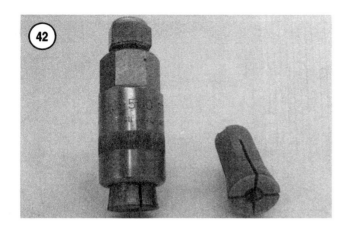

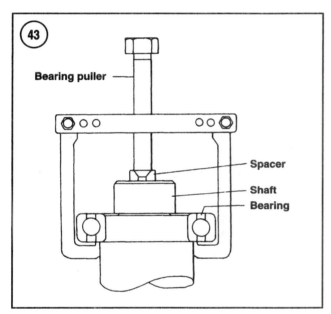

Bearing puller — Spacer — Shaft — Bearing

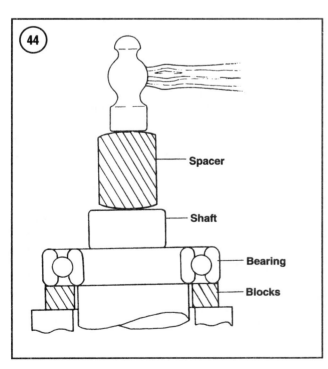

Spacer — Shaft — Bearing — Blocks

Removing Hoses

Do not exert excessive force on the hose or fitting when removing stubborn hoses. Remove the hose clamp and carefully insert a small screwdriver or pick tool between the fitting and hose. Apply a spray lubricant under the hose and carefully twist the hose off the fitting. Clean the fitting of any corrosion or rubber hose material with a wire brush. Clean the inside of the hose thoroughly. Do not use any lubricant when installing the new or old hose. The lubricant may allow the hose to come off the fitting, even with the clamp secure.

Bearings

Bearings are used in the engine and transmission assembly to reduce power loss, heat and noise resulting from friction. Because bearings are precision parts, they must be maintained with proper lubrication and maintenance. If a bearing is damaged, replace it immediately. When installing a new bearing, take care to prevent damaging it. Bearing replacement procedures are included in the individual chapters where applicable; however, use the following sections as a basic guideline.

NOTE
Unless otherwise specified, install bearings with the mark or number facing outward.

Removal

While bearings are normally removed only when damaged, there may be times when it is necessary to remove a bearing that is in good condition. However, improper bearing removal will damage the bearing and possibly the shaft or case. Note the following when removing bearings:
1. Before removing the bearings, note the following:
    a. Refer to the bearing replacement procedure in the appropriate chapter for any special instructions.
    b. Remove any seals that interfere with bearing removal. Refer to *Seal Replacement* (this section).
    c. When removing more than one bearing, identify the bearings before removing them. Refer to the bearing manufacturer's numbers on the bearing.
    d. Note and record the direction in which the numbers face for proper installation.
    e. Remove any set plates or bearing retainers before removing the bearings.
2. When using a puller to remove a bearing from a shaft, take care that the shaft is not damaged. Always place a spacer (**Figure 43**) or a piece of metal between the end of the shaft and the puller screw. In addition, place the puller arms next to the inner bearing race.
3. When using a hammer to remove a bearing from a shaft, do not strike the hammer directly against the shaft. Instead, use a brass or aluminum rod as a spacer (**Figure 44**) between the hammer and shaft. Make sure to support both bearing races with wooden blocks as shown.

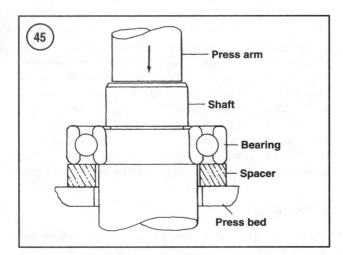

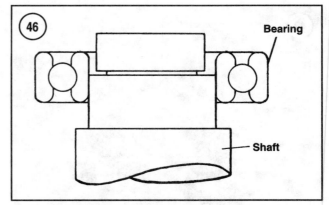

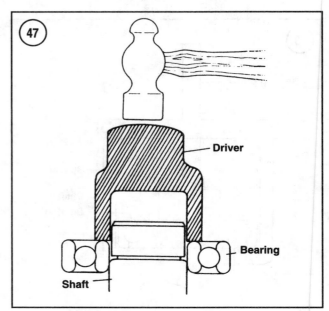

4. The ideal method of bearing removal is with a hydraulic press. Note the following when using a press:

    a. Always support the inner and outer bearing races with a suitable size wooden or aluminum spacer (**Figure 45**). If only the outer race is supported, pressure applied against the balls and/or the inner race will damage them.

    b. Always make sure the press arm (**Figure 45**) aligns with the center of the shaft. If the arm is not centered, it may damage the bearing and/or shaft.

    c. The moment the shaft is free of the bearing, it drops to the floor. Secure or hold the shaft to prevent it from falling.

    d. When removing bearings from a housing, support the housing with 4 × 4 in. wooden blocks to prevent damage to gasket surfaces.

Installation

1. When installing a bearing into a housing, apply pressure to the outer bearing race (**Figure 46**). When installing a bearing on a shaft, apply pressure to the inner bearing race (**Figure 46**).

2. When installing a bearing, some type of driver is required. Never strike the bearing directly with a hammer or it will damage the bearing. When installing a bearing, use a piece of pipe or a driver with a diameter that matches the bearing inner race. **Figure 47** shows the correct way to use a driver and hammer to install a bearing.

3. When installing a bearing over a shaft and into the housing at the same time, a tight fit is required for both outer and inner bearing races. In this situation, install a spacer underneath the driver tool (**Figure 48**) so that pressure is applied evenly across both races. If the outer race is not supported as shown, the balls will push against the outer bearing race and damage it.

Interference fit

1. Follow this procedure when installing a bearing over a shaft. When a tight fit is required, the bearing inside diam-

eter is smaller than the shaft. In this case, driving the bearing on the shaft using normal methods may cause bearing damage. Instead, heat the bearing before installation. Note the following:

    a. Secure the shaft so it is ready for bearing installation.

    b. Clean all residues from the bearing surface of the shaft. Remove burrs with a file or sandpaper.

    c. Fill a suitable pot or beaker with clean mineral oil. Place a thermometer rated above 248° F (120° C) in the oil. Support the thermometer so it does not rest on the bottom or side of the pot.

    d. Remove the bearing from its wrapper and secure it with a piece of heavy wire bent to hold it in the pot. Hang the bearing in the pot so it does not touch the bottom or sides of the pot.

    e. Turn the heat on and monitor the thermometer. When the oil temperature rises to approximately 248° F (120° C), remove the bearing from the pot and quickly install it. If necessary, place a socket on the inner bearing race and tap the bearing into place. As the bearing chills, it will tighten on the shaft, so installation must be done quickly. Make sure the bearing is installed completely.

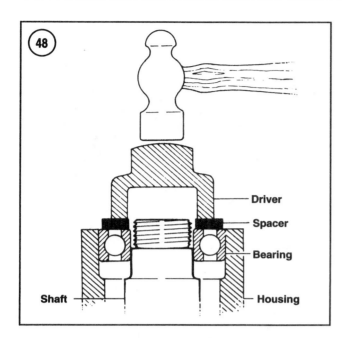

(48)

Driver

Spacer

Bearing

Shaft

Housing

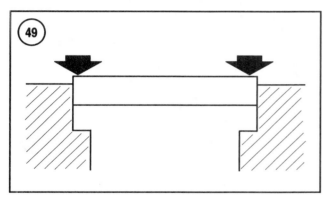

(49)

of water on the housing; if they sizzle and evaporate immediately, the temperature is correct. Heat only one housing at a time.

b. Remove the housing from the oven or hot plate and hold onto the housing with welding gloves. It is hot!

NOTE
Remove and install the bearings with a suitable size socket and extension.

c. Hold the housing with the bearing side down and tap the bearing out. Repeat for all bearings in the housing that will be replaced.

d. Before heating the bearing housing, place the new bearing in a freezer if possible. Chilling a bearing slightly reduces its outside diameter while the heated bearing housing assembly is slightly larger due to heat expansion. This makes bearing installation easier.

NOTE
Always install bearings with the mark or number facing outward.

e. While the housing is still hot, install the new bearing(s) into the housing. Install the bearings by hand, if possible. If necessary, lightly tap the bearing(s) into the housing with a driver placed on the outer bearing race (**Figure 49**). Do not install new bearings by driving on the inner-bearing race. Install the bearing(s) until seated completely.

Seal Replacement

Seals (**Figure 50**) contain oil, water, grease or combustion gasses in a housing or shaft. Improperly removing a seal can damage the housing or shaft. Improperly installing the seal can damage the seal. Note the following:

1. Prying is generally the easiest and most effective method of removing a seal from the housing. However, always place a rag underneath the pry tool to prevent damage to the housing. Note the seal's installed depth or if it is installed flush.

2. On small seals, carefully screw in a sheet metal screw (A, **Figure 51**) into the seal (B), being careful not to damage the bearing beneath it. Pull straight up and remove the seal.

3. Pack waterproof grease in the seal lips before the seal is installed.

4. In most cases, install seals with the numbers or marks facing out.

5. Install seals with a socket or driver placed on the outside of the seal as shown in **Figure 52**. Drive the seal squarely into the housing until it is to the correct depth or flush as noted during removal. Never install a seal by hitting against the top of it with a hammer.

STORAGE

Several months of non-use can cause a general deterioration of the motorcycle. This is especially true in areas of

2. Follow this procedure when installing a bearing in a housing. Bearings are generally installed in a housing with a slight interference fit. Driving the bearing into the housing using normal methods may damage the housing or cause bearing damage. Instead, heat the housing before the bearing is installed. Note the following:

CAUTION
Before heating the housing in this procedure, wash the housing thoroughly with detergent and water. Rinse and rewash the cases as required to remove all traces of oil and other chemical deposits.

CAUTION
Do not heat the housing with a propane or acetylene torch. Never bring a flame into contact with the bearing or housing. The direct heat will destroy the case hardening of the bearing and will likely warp the housing.

a. Heat the housing to approximately 212° F (100° C) in an oven or on a hot plate. An easy way to check that it is the proper temperature is to place tiny drops

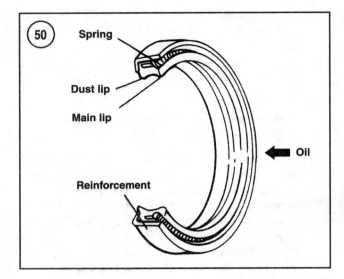

Figure 50

Spring
Dust lip
Main lip
Reinforcement
Oil

Figure 51

Figure 52

extreme temperature variations. This deterioration can be minimized with careful preparation for storage. A properly stored motorcycle is much easier to return to service.

Storage Area Selection

When selecting a storage area, consider the following:
1. The storage area must be dry. A heated area is best, but not necessary. It should be insulated to minimize extreme temperature variations.
2. If the building has large window areas, cover or mask them to keep sunlight off the motorcycle.
3. Avoid buildings in industrial areas where corrosive emissions may be present. Avoid areas close to saltwater.
4. Consider the area's risk of fire, theft or vandalism. Check with an insurer regarding motorcycle coverage while in storage.

Preparing the Motorcycle for Storage

The amount of preparation a motorcycle should undergo before storage depends on the expected length of non-use, storage area conditions and personal preference. Consider the following list the minimum requirement:
1. Wash the motorcycle thoroughly. Make sure all dirt, mud and road debris are removed.
2. Fill the fuel tank with a mixture of fuel and fuel stabilizer. Mix the fuel with a stabilizer in the ratio recommended by the stabilizer manufacturer. Run the engine for a few minutes so the stabilized fuel can enter the fuel system. If the motorcycle will be stored for a long period, consider draining the fuel system.
3. Start the engine and allow it to reach operating temperature. Drain the engine oil regardless of the riding time since the last service. Fill the engine with the recommended type of oil.
4. Fill the fuel tank completely. There is no need to try to empty the fuel delivery or return lines since they are not vented to the atmosphere.

5. Remove the spark plugs and pour a teaspoon of engine oil into the cylinders. Place a rag over the openings and slowly turn the engine over to distribute the oil. Reinstall the spark plugs.
6. Remove the battery. Store the battery in a cool and dry location. Charge the battery once a month.
7. Cover the exhaust and intake openings.
8. Apply a protective substance to the plastic and rubber components. Make sure to follow the protectant manufacturer's instructions for each type of product being used.
9. Place the motorcycle on blocks with the wheels off the ground.
10. Cover the motorcycle with old bed sheets or something similar to light canvas that can breathe. Do not cover it with any plastic material that will trap moisture.

Returning the Motorcycle to Service

The amount of service required when returning a motorcycle to service after storage depends on the length of non-use and storage conditions. In addition to reversing the storage procedure, make sure the brakes, clutch, throttle and engine stop switch all work properly before operating the motorcycle. Refer to Chapter Three and evaluate the service intervals to determine which areas require service.

Table 1 MODEL DESIGNATIONS

FXD Dyna Super Glide	(2006-2010)
FXDC Dyna Super Glide Custom	(2006-2011)
FXDL Dyna Low Ride	(2006-2009), (2010-2011: Japan only)
FXDWG Dyna Wide Glide	(2006-2008), (2010-2011)
FXDB Street Bob	(2006-2011)
FXD35 35th Anniversary Super Glide	(2006)
FXDF Fat Bob	(2008-2011)
FXDSE Screamin' Eagle Dyna	(2007)
FXDSE2 Screamin' Eagle Dyna	(2008)
FXDFSE CVO Dyna Fat Bob	(2009)
FXDFSE2 CVO Dyna Fat Bob	(2010)

Table 2 GENERAL DIMENSIONS

Item/model	in.	mm
Wheel base		
FXDWG	68.3	1735.0
FXDF	63.77	1619.76
FXDSE	65.5	1663.7
FXDFSE	63.66	1616.96
All other models	63.5	1612.9
Overall length		
FXD, FXDB		
2006-2011 models	92.80	2357
FXDC		
2006-2011 models	92.90	2360
FXDL		
2006-2011 models	93.1	2364
FXDWG		
2006-2008	97.5	2477
FXD35 (2006 models)	92.90	2360
FXDF (2008-2011 models)	91.7	2329
FXDSE (2007 models)	95.0	2413
FXDSE2 (2008 models)	92.4	2347
FXDFSE and FXDFSE2 (2009-2010 models)	91.7	2329
Overall width		
FXD (2006-2011 models)	36.7	932
FXDC		
2006 models	34.9	886
2007-2011 models	38.9	988
FXDL (2006-2011 models)	36.3	922
FXDWG (2006-2008 models)	36.0	914
FXD35 (2006 models)	38.9	988
FXDB (2006-2011 models)	37.5	953
FXDF (2008-2011 models)	35.0	890
FXDSE (2007 models)	35.0	890
FXDSE2 (2008 models)	37.0	940
FXDSE and FXDFSE2 (2009-2010 models)	36.69	931.93
Road clearance		
FXD, FXDC		
2006-2008 models	6.0	152
2009 models	5.32	135.13
FXDL, FXDB		
2006-2008 models	5.6	142
2009 models	4.92	125
FXDWG (2006-2008 models)	6.2	158
FXD35 (2006 models)	6.0	152
FXDF (2008-2011 models)	4.92	125
FXDSE (2007 models)	5.6	142
FXDSE2 (2008 models)	4.6	117
FXDFSE and FXDFSE2 (2009-2010 models)	4.33	109.98
Overall height		
FXD (2006-2011 models)	46.8	1188.72
FXDC (2006-2011 models)	47.7	1211.58
FXDL (2006-2011 models)	47.07	1195.6
FXDWG (2006-2008)	49.3	1252

(continued)

Table 2 GENERAL DIMENSIONS (continued)

Item/model	in.	mm
Overall height (continued)		
FXD35 (2006 models)	47.07	1193.80
FXDB (2006-2011 models)	50.4	1280
FXDF (2008-2011 models)	44.6	1133
FXDSE (2007 models)	51.4	1306
FXDSE2 (2008 models)	45.6	1158
FXDFSE and FXDFSE2 (2009-2010 models)	45.55	1156.97
Saddle height*		
FXD		
2006-2007 models	27.6	701
2008 models	26.60	675.64
FXDC		
2006-2007 models	27.8	706
2008-2011 models	26.8	681
FXDL		
2006-2008 models	26.8	681
2009 models	25.8	655.32
FXDWG (2006-2008 models)	28.5	724
FXD35 (2006 models)	27.8	706
FXDB		
2006-2007 models	26.8	681
2008-2011 models	26.1	663
FXDSE (2007 models)	27.1	688
FXDSE2 (2008 models)	26.5	673
FXDFSE and FXDFSE2 (2009-2010 models)	25.20	640.08

*Saddle height with 180 lb. (81.6 kg) rider on seat.

Table 3 MOTORCYCLE WEIGHT

Model	Dry weight lb. (kg)	Gross vehicle weight lb. (kg)	Gross axle weight front lb. (kg)	Gross axle weight rear lb.(kg)
FXD (2006-2011 models)	632 (287)	1085 (492)	390 (177)	695 (316)
FXDC				
2006 models	641 (291)	1085 (492)	390 (177)	695 (316)
2007-2011 models	645 (293)	1085 (492)	390 (177)	695 (316)
FXDL (2006-2011 models)	641 (291)	1085 (492)	390 (177)	695 (316)
FXDWG (2006-2008 models)	650 (295)	1085 (492)	390 (177)	695 (316)
FXD35 (2006 models)	645 (293)	1085 (492)	390 (177)	695 (316)
FXDB (2006-2011 models)	634 (288)	1085 (492)	390 (177)	695 (316)
FXDF (2008-2011 models)	670 (304)	1085 (492)	390 (177)	695 (316)
FXDSE (2007 models)	668 (303)	1085 (492)	390 (177)	695 (316)
FXDSE2 (2008 models)	678 (308)	1085 (492)	390 (177)	695 (316)
FXDFSE and FXDFSE2 (2009-2010 models)	701 (317.97)	1085 (492)	390 (177)	695 (316)

Table 4 DECIMAL AND METRIC EQUIVALENTS

Fractions	Decimal in.	Metric mm	Fractions	Decimal in.	Metric mm
1/64	0.015625	0.39688	33/64	0.515625	13.09687
1/32	0.03125	0.79375	17/32	0.53125	13.49375
3/64	0.046875	1.19062	35/64	0.546875	13.89062
1/16	0.0625	1.58750	9/16	0.5625	14.28750
5/64	0.078125	1.98437	37/64	0.578125	14.68437
3/32	0.09375	2.38125	19/32	0.59375	15.08125
7/64	0.109375	2.77812	39/64	0.609375	15.47812
1/8	0.125	3.1750	5/8	0.625	15.87500
9/64	0.140625	3.57187	41/64	0.640625	16.27187
5/32	0.15625	3.96875	21/32	0.65625	16.66875
11/64	0.171875	4.36562	43/64	0.671875	17.06562
3/16	0.1875	4.76250	11/16	0.6875	17.46250

(continued)

Table 4 DECIMAL AND METRIC EQUIVALENTS (continued)

Fractions	Decimal in.	Metric mm	Fractions	Decimal in.	Metric mm
13/64	0.203125	5.15937	45/64	0.703125	17.85937
7/32	0.21875	5.55625	23/32	0.71875	18.25625
15/64	0.234375	5.95312	47/64	0.734375	18.65312
1/4	0.250	6.35000	3/4	0.750	19.05000
17/64	0.265625	6.74687	49/64	0.765625	19.44687
9/32	0.28125	7.14375	25/32	0.78125	19.84375
19/64	0.296875	7.54062	51/64	0.796875	20.24062
5/16	0.3125	7.93750	13/16	0.8125	20.63750
21/64	0.328125	8.33437	53/64	0.828125	21.03437
11/32	0.34375	8.73125	27/32	0.84375	21.43125
23/64	0.359375	9.12812	55/64	0.859375	22.82812
3/8	0.375	9.52500	7/8	0.875	22.22500
25/64	0.390625	9.92187	57/64	0.890625	22.62187
13/32	0.40625	10.31875	29/32	0.90625	23.01875
27/64	0.421875	10.71562	59/64	0.921875	23.41562
7/16	0.4375	11.11250	15/16	0.9375	23.81250
29/64	0.453125	11.50937	61/64	0.953125	24.20937
15/32	0.46875	11.90625	31/32	0.96875	24.60625
31/64	0.484375	12.30312	63/64	0.984375	25.00312
1/2	0.500	12.70000	1	1.00	25.40000

Table 5 TORQUE RECOMMENDATIONS

Thread size	N•m	ft.-lb.	in.-lb.
Bolt			
5 mm	4.5-6	–	40-53
6 mm	8-12	6-9	–
8 mm	18-25	13-18	–
10 mm	30-40	22-29	–
12 mm	50-60	36-44	–
Nut			
5 mm	4.5-6	–	40-53
6 mm	8-12	6-9	–
8 mm	18-25	13-18	–
10 mm	30-40	22-29	–
12 mm	50-60	36-44	–
Screw			
5 mm	3.5-5	–	31-44
6 mm and SH type bolt with 8 mm head	7-11	–	61-97
6 mm flange bolt/nut	10-14	7-10	–
8 mm flange bolt/nut	24-30	17-22	–
10 mm flange bolt/nut	35-45	25-33	–

*Use these torque values for fasteners not individually listed.

Table 6 CONVERSION FORMULAS

Multiply:	By:	To get the equivalent of:
Length		
Inches	25.4	Millimeter
Inches	2.54	Centimeter
Miles	1.609	Kilometer
Feet	0.3048	Meter
Millimeter	0.03937	Inches
Centimeter	0.3937	Inches
Kilometer	0.6214	Mile
Meter	3.281	Mile
Fluid volume		
U.S. quarts	0.9463	Liters

(continued)

Table 6 CONVERSION FORMULAS (continued)

Multiply:	By:	To get the equivalent of:
Fluid volume (continued)		
U.S. gallons	3.785	Liters
U.S. ounces	29.573529	Milliliters
Imperial gallons	4.54609	Liters
Imperial quarts	1.1365	Liters
Liters	0.2641721	U.S. gallons
Liters	1.0566882	U.S. quarts
Liters	33.814023	U.S. ounces
Liters	0.22	Imperial gallons
Liters	0.8799	Imperial quarts
Milliliters	0.033814	U.S. ounces
Milliliters	1.0	Cubic centimeters
Milliliters	0.001	Liters
Torque		
Foot-pounds	1.3558	Newton-meters
Foot-pounds	0.138255	Meters-kilograms
Inch-pounsd	0.11299	Newton-meters
Newton-meters	0.7375622	Foot-pounds
Newton-meters	8.8507	Inch-pounds
Meters-kilograms	7.2330139	Foot-pounds
Volume		
Cubic inches	16.387064	Cubic centimeters
Cubic centimeters	0.0610237	Cubic inches
Temperature		
Fahrenheit	(F – 32°) × 0.556	Centigrade
Centigrade	(C × 1.8) + 32°	Fahrenheit
Weight		
Ounces	28.3495	Grams
Pounds	0.4535924	Kilograms
Grams	0.035274	Ounces
Kilograms	2.2046224	Pounds
Pressure		
Pounds per square inch	0.070307	Kilograms per square centimeter
Kilograms per square centimeter	14.223343	Pounds per square inch
Kilopascals	0.1450	Pounds per square inch
Pounds per square inch	6.895	Kilopascals
Speed		
Miles per hour	1.609344	Kilometers per hour
Kilometers per hour	0.6213712	Miles per hour

Table 7 TECHNICAL ABBREVIATIONS

A	Ampere
AC	Alternating current
ACC	Accessory position of ignition switch
ACR	Automatic compression release
A.h	Ampere hour
BAS	Bank angle sensor
C	Celsius
cc	Cubic centimeter
CDI	Capacitor discharge ignition
CKP sensor	Crankshaft position sensor
cid	Cubic inch displacement
cm	Centimeter
cu. in.	Cubic inch and cubic inches
cyl.	Cylinder
DC	Direct current
DOM	Domestic models
DTC	Diagnostic trouble code
ECM	Electronic control module
ECU	Electronic control unit
EFI	Electronic fuel injection

(continued)

Table 7 TECHNICAL ABBREVIATIONS (continued)

ET sensor	Engine temperature sensor
F	Fahrenheit
fl. oz.	Fluid ounces
ft.	Foot
ft.-lb.	Foot pounds
gal.	Gallon and gallons
H/A	High altitude
HDI	Harley-Davidson international models
hp	Horsepower
HFSM	Hands free security module
Hz	Hertz
IAC	Idle air control
IAT sensor	Intake air temperature sensor
ICM	Ignition control module
ID	Inside diameter
in.	Inch and inches
in.-lb.	Inch-pounds
in. Hg	Inches of mercury
k	One-thousand ohms (2k = 2000 ohms)
kg	Kilogram
kg/cm²	Kilogram per square centimeter
kgm	Kilogram meter
km	Kilometer
km/h	Kilometer per hour
kPa	Kilopascals
kW	Kilowatt
L	Liter and liters
L/m	Liters per minute
lb.	Pound and pounds
m	Meter
MAP sensor	Manifold absolute pressure sensor
mL	Milliliter
mm	Millimeter
N•m	Newton meter
O_2 sensor	Oxygen sensor
OD	Outside diameter
oz.	Ounce and ounces
P&A	Parts and accessories
psi	Pounds per square inch
pt.	Pint and pints
qt.	Quart and quarts
rpm	Revolution per minute
TDC	Top dead center
TP sensor	Throttle position sensor
TSM	Turn signal module
TSSM	Turn signal and security module
V	Volt
VSS	Vehicle speed sensor
W	Watt

Table 8 U.S. STANDARD TAP AND DRILL SIZES

Tap thread	Drill size	Tap thread	Drill size
#0-80	3/64	1/4-28	No. 3
#1-64	No. 53	5/16-18	F
#1-72	No. 53	5/16-24	I
#2-56	No. 51	3/8-16	5/16
#2-64	No. 50	3/8-24	Q
#3-48	5/64	7/16-14	U
#3-56	No. 46	7/16-20	W
		(continued)	

Table 8 U.S. STANDARD TAP AND DRILL SIZES (continued)

Tap thread	Drill size	Tap thread	Drill size
#4-40	No. 43	1/2-13	27/64
#4-48	No. 42	1/2-20	29/64
#5-40	No. 39	9/16-12	31/64
#5-44	No. 37	9/16-18	33/64
#6-32	No. 36	5/8-11	17/32
#6-40	No. 33	5/18-18	37/64
#8-32	No. 29	3/4-10	21/32
#8-36	No. 29	3/4-16	11/16
#10-24	No. 25	7/8-9	49/64
#10-32	No. 21	7/8-14	7/8
#12-24	No. 17	1-8	7/8
#12-28	No. 15	1-4	15/16
1/4-20	No. 8		

Table 9 METRIC TAP AND DRILL SIZES

Metric size	Drill equivalent	Decimal fraction	Nearest fraction
3 × 0.50	No. 39	0.0995	3/32
3 × 0.60	3/32	0.0937	3/32
4 × 0.70	No. 30	0.1285	1/8
4 × 0.75	1/8	0.125	1/8
5 × 0.80	No. 19	0.166	11/64
5 × 0.90	No. 20	0.161	5/32
6 × 1.00	No. 9	0.196	13/64
7 × 1.00	16/64	0.234	15-64
8 × 1.00	J	0.277	9/32
8 × 1.25	17/64	0.265	17/64
9 × 1.00	5/16	0.3125	5/16
9 × 1.25	5/16	0.3125	5/16
10 × 1.25	R	0.339	11/32
11 × 1.50	3/8	0.375	3/8
12 × 1.50	13/32	0.406	13/32
12 × 1.75	13/32	0.406	13/32

Table 10 SPECIAL TOOLS

Tool Description	Part No.	Manufacturer
Alternator rotor puller	HD-41771	H-D
ACR solenoid socket		
2007-2008 models	HD-48498	H-D
2009-2011 models	HD-48498-A	H-D
Bearing removal tool (expanding-collet type)	08-0410	Motion Pro
Belt tension gauge	HD-355381	H-D
2007-2011 models	969	JIMS
Bushing reamer tool	1726-3	JIMS
Camshaft assembly tool	990	JIMS
	HD-47956	H-D
Camshaft bearing puller	1280	JIMS
Camshaft locking tool	994	JIMS
	HD-47941	H-D
Camshaft chain tensioner tool	1283	JIMS
Camshaft inner bearing installer	991	JIMS
Camshaft inner bearing remover tool	993	JIMS
Camshaft inner bearing remover/installer tool	HD-42325A	H-D
Camshaft remove and installer	1277	JIMS
Camshaft/crankshaft sprocket lock tool	1285	JIMS
	HD-42314	H-D
Center stand jack	904	JIMS
Connecting rod bushing tool	1051	JIMS
Connecting rod bushing hone	HD-422569	H-D
Connecting rod clamping tool	1284	JIMS
	HD-95952-33C	H-D
Crankcase bearing snap ring remover and installer	1710	JIMS

(continued)

Table 10 SPECIAL TOOLS (continued)

Tool Description	Part No.	Manufacturer
Crankshaft bearing support tube	HD-42720-5	H-D
Crankshaft bearing support tube pilot/driver	HD-B-45655	H-D
Crankshaft bearing remover and installer	1146	JIMS
Crankshaft bushing tool	1281	JIMS
	HD-42315	H-D
	08-0148	Motion Pro
Crankcase stud installation tool	HD-42315	H-D
Crankshaft bushing reamer tool	1101	JIMS
	HD-42316	H-D
Crankshaft bearing support tube	HD-42720-5	H-D
Crankcase disassembly/removing tool	995	JIMS
	HD-42316	H-D
Crankshaft guide	1288	JIMS
Crankshaft hard cap	1048	JIMS
Crankshaft seal installation tool	39361-69	JIMS
Crankshaft sprocket locker	1285	JIMS
	HD-42314	H-D
Crankshaft support fixture	HD-44358	H-D
Cylinder chamfering cone	2078	JIMS
Cylinder head support stand	HD-39782-A	H-D
Cylinder head holding fixture	HD-39786-A	H-D
Cylinder stud steel ball	HD-8860	H-D
Cylinder torque plates	1287	JIMS
Driver handle and remover	HD-34740	H-D
Electrical connector terminal remover (Molex)	HD-48114	H-D
Electrical pin terminal tool (AMP)	HD-39621-28	H-D
Electrical receptacle extractor	1764	JIMS
Electrical socket terminal tool (AMP)	HD-39621-27	H-D
Electrical terminal block remover (Deutch)	114008	Deutsh
Electrical terminal pick (Autofuse)	GA500A	Snap-on
Electrical terminal remover (Packard)	HD-45928	H-D
Engine stand/Twin Cam 88		
Base stand	1138	JIMS
Engine stand	1142	JIMS
Exhaust seat adapter		
Screamin' Eagle and all 2007-2011 models	HD-39782-4	H-D
Final drive sprocket locker	2260	JIMS
	HD-46282	H-D
Final drive sprocket shaft bearing cone installer	HD-997225-55C	H-D
Final drive sprocket shaft bearing installation tool	97225-55	JIMS
Final drive sprocket shaft seal installer	39361-69	JIMS
Flywheel support fixture	HD-44358	H-D
Fork oil level gauge	08-0121	Motion Pro
Fork seal/cap installer	2046	JIMS
Fork tube holder	41177	H-D
Fuel pressure gauge	HD-41182	H-D
Fuel pressure gauge adapters	HD-44061	H-D
Hose clamp pincer tool	1171	JIMS
Hose clamp pliers	1171	JIMS
	HD-97087-65B	H-D
Hydraulic brake bleeder	MV8020	Mityvac
Hydraulic tensioner compression tool	HD-44063	H-D
Hydraulic tensioner retainer	HD-44408	H-D
Ignition switch alignment tool	943	JIMS
	HD-45962	H-D
Ignition switch connector remover	HD-45961	H-D
Ignition switch/fork lock wrench	HD-47853	H-D
Intake manifold wrench	35-3975	K&L
	HD-47250	H-D
Intake seat adapter		
2006 models except Screamin' Eagle and CVO	HD-39782A-3	H-D
Screamin' Eagle, CVO and all 2007-2011 models	HD-39782-3	H-D
Motor sprocket shaft seal installer tool	39361-69	JIMS
Oxygen sensor socket	969	JIMS
	HD-48262	H-D

(continued)

Table 10 SPECIAL TOOLS (continued)

Tool Description	Part No.	Manufacturer
Piston ring compressor		
2006-2007 models	HD-96333-51D	H-D
2008-2011 models	HD-96333-51E	H-D
Primary drive locking tool	2312	JIMS
	HD-47977	H-D
Push rod tool	08-0225	Motion Pro
Retaining ring pliers	J-5586	H-D
Rocker arm shaft reamer	94804-57	JIMS
Scissor jack	904	JIMS
Shift fork shaft remover	985	JIMS
Socket–hand drive	HD-43643	H-D
Snap ring pliers	HD-J-5586	H-D
Spark tester	08-0122	Motion Pro
Snap ring remover and installer	1710	JIMS
Steering stem bearing race remover	1414	JIMS
Steering head bearing race installer	1725	JIMS
Swing arm bearing installer	HD-45327	H-D
Threaded cylinders	HD-95952-1	H-D
Timken bearing race installer	2246	JIMS
Transmission bearing and race installer tool handle	33416-80	JIMS
Transmission drive sprocket locker tool	2260	JIMS
	HD-46282	H-D
Transmission mainshaft bearing race remove/install	34902-84	JIMS
Transmission mainshaft pulley locknut socket	989	JIMS
	HD-47910	H-D
Transmission mainshaft pulley locknut sprocket wrench pilot	HD-94660-2	H-D
Transmission side door puller	984	JIMS
Transmission mainshaft bearing race puller/installer	34902-84	JIMS
	HD-34902-C	H-D
Transmission mainshaft sprocket pulley locknut socket	94660-37A	JIMS
Transmission main drive gear installer	981	JIMS
Transmission main drive gear/bearing remover and installer	HD-35316-C	H-D
Transmission main drive gear bearing installer	987	JIMS
Transmission main drive gear seal installer	972	JIMS
	HD-47856	H-D
Transmission main drive gear wedge attachment	HD-95637-46B	H-D777
Transmission main drive gear bearing and seal installer	986	JIMS
	HD-47932	H-D
Transmission shaft installer	2189	JIMS
Valve guide driver		
All models except Screamin' Eagle and CVO	B-45524-1	H-D
Screamin' Eagle and CVO models	HD-34740	H-D
Valve guide installer sleeve		
All models except Screamin' Eagle and CVO	B-45524-2A	H-D
Screamin' Eagle and CVO models	HD-48628	H-D
Valve guide reamer		
All models except Screamin' Eagle and CVO	B-45523	H-D
Screamin' Eagle and CVO models	HD-39932	H-D
Valve guide reamer T-handle	HD-39847	H-D
Valve guide reamer and honing lubricant	HD-39964	H-D
Valve guide hone		
All models except Screamin' Eagle and CVO	B-45525	H-D
Screamin' Eagle and CVO models	HD-34723	H-D
Valve guide cleaning brush	HD-34751	
Valve guide seal installer		
Screamin' Eagle and CVO models	HD-48644	H-D
Vacuum hose identifier kit	74600	Lisle
Valve seat cutter set, Neway	HD-35758-C	H-D
Valve seat installation tool	HD-34643A	H-D
Valve seat driver handle	HD-34740	H-D
Valve spring compressor	HD-34736-B	H-D
Valve spring tester	HD-96796-47	H-D
Wheel bearing race remover and installer	33461	JIMS
Wheel (rear) compensator bearing remover/installer	HD-48921	H-D
Wrist pin bushing reamer tool	1726	JIMS

CHAPTER TWO

TROUBLESHOOTING

The troubleshooting procedures described in this chapter provide typical symptoms of a problem and logical methods for isolating its causes. There may be several ways to solve a problem, but only a systematic approach will successfully avoid wasted time and unnecessary parts replacement.

Begin troubleshooting by gathering as much information as possible and precisely describing the symptoms of the problem. Never assume anything, and do not overlook the obvious. For example, make sure there is fresh fuel in the tank, that the engine stop switch is in the RUN position, or that the spark plug wires are securely connected to the plugs.

If a quick check does not resolve the problem, find the troubleshooting procedure in this chapter that best describes the symptoms being experienced. Perform the listed tests to isolate the problem to a particular system (fuel, electrical, mechanical, etc.), and then further isolate it to a particular component. Repair or replace that component, and test ride the motorcycle to confirm the problem has been corrected.

In most cases, expensive and complicated test equipment is not needed to determine whether repairs can be performed at home. A few simple checks could prevent an unnecessary repair charge and lost time while the motorcycle is at a dealership's service department. On the other hand, be realistic and do not attempt repairs beyond individual abilities. Many service departments will not take work that involves the reassembly of damaged or abused equipment. If they do, expect the cost to be high.

If the motorcycle does require the attention of a professional, describe the symptoms, conditions and previous repair attempts accurately and fully. The more information a technician has, the easier it is to diagnose the problem.

By following the maintenance schedule described in Chapter Three, the need for troubleshooting can be reduced by eliminating many potential problems before they occur. However, even with the best of care a motorcycle may require troubleshooting.

Tables 1-5 at the end of this chapter contain electrical specifications, diagnostic trouble codes and other troubleshooting reference materials.

The diagnostic flow charts referenced in this chapter are located on the CD inserted into the back cover of the manual.

NOTE
*On models with an optional security siren, disarm the security system (TSSM/HFSM) before disconnecting the battery or before pulling the Maxi-Fuse so the siren will not sound. Refer to **Turn Signal and Security Module** in Chapter Nine.*

OPERATING REQUIREMENTS

An engine needs three basic conditions met in order to run properly: correct air/fuel mixture, compression and a spark all at the proper time. If one of these requirements is missing, the engine will not run.

ENGINE STARTING

NOTE
On fuel-injected models, do not open the throttle when starting either a cold or warm engine. The electronic control module (ECM) interprets this action during the starting procedure and it may affect starting.

Engine Fails to Start (Spark Test)

1. Shift the transmission into neutral and confirm that the engine stop/run switch (**Figure 1**) is in the run position.
2. Disconnect the fuel pump fuse (Chapter Eight).

NOTE
After removing each spark plug, shake it to see if the insulator slides down over the center electrode. Insulators can be broken when the spark plugs are mishandled or when a plug wrench is used incorrectly.

3. Disconnect the spark plug wire and remove the spark plug (Chapter Three).
4. Cover the spark plug hole with a clean shop cloth to lessen the chance of gasoline vapors being emitted from the hole.

WARNING
Mount the spark plug, or tester, away from the spark plug hole in the cylinder so that the spark or tester cannot ignite the gasoline vapors in the cylinder. If the engine is flooded, do not perform this test. The firing of the spark plug can ignite fuel that is ejected through the spark plug hole.

NOTE
*A spark tester (**Figure 2**) is a useful tool for testing spark output. This tool is inserted in the spark plug cap and its base is grounded against the cylinder head. The tool's air gap is adjustable, and it allows the visual inspection of the spark while testing the intensity of the spark. This tool is available through motorcycle repair shops.*

5. Insert the spark plug (**Figure 3**), or a spark tester (**Figure 4**), into its plug cap and ground the spark plug base against the cylinder head. Position the spark plug so the electrode is visible.
6. On 2007-2011 models, pull the clutch lever in even with the transmission in neutral

WARNING
*Do **not** hold the spark plug, wire or connector, or a serious electrical shock may result.*

7. Turn the engine over with the starter. A crisp blue spark should be evident across the spark plug electrode or spark tester terminals. Repeat test for the remaining cylinder.
8. If the spark is good, check for one or more of the following possible malfunctions:
   a. Faulty fuel system component.
   b. Low engine compression or engine damage.
   c. Flooded engine.
   d. Incorrect ignition timing. If the engine backfires during starting, the ignition timing may be incorrect due to a damaged ignition component. Refer to *Ignition Timing* (Chapter Three).

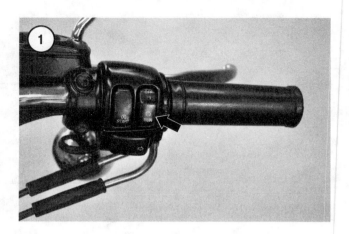

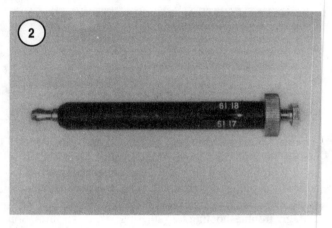

9. If the spark is weak or if there is no spark, refer to *Engine is Difficult to Start* (this section).
10. Install the spark plugs as described in Chapter Three.
11. Connect the fuel pump fuse (Chapter Eight).

Engine is Difficult to Start

1. After attempting to start the engine, remove one of the spark plugs (Chapter Three) and check for the presence of fuel on the plug tip. Note the following:
   a. If there is no fuel visible on the plug, remove the other spark plug. If there is no fuel on this plug, go to Step 2.
   b. If there is fuel present on the plug tip, go to Step 4.
   c. If there is an excessive amount of fuel on the plug, check for an air filter blockage or incorrect throttle valve operation (stuck open).
2. Perform the *Fuel Pump Pressure Test* (Chapter Eight). Note the following:
   a. If the fuel pump pressure is correct, go to Step 3.
   b. If the fuel pump pressure is incorrect, replace the fuel pump and retest the fuel system.
3. Inspect the fuel injectors (Chapter Eight).
4. Check for a clogged fuel line and/or contaminated fuel system.
5. Perform the spark test (this section). Note the following:
   a. If the spark is weak or if there is no spark, go to Step 6.
   b. If the spark is good, go to Step 7.

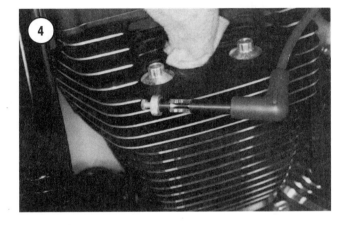

2

6. If the spark is weak or if there is no spark, check the following:
   a. Fouled spark plug(s).
   b. Damaged spark plug(s).
   c. Loose or damaged ignition coil wire(s).
   d. Damaged electronic control module (ECM).
   e. Damaged crankshaft position sensor.
   f. Damaged ignition coil.
   g. Damaged engine stop/run switch.
   h. Damaged ignition switch.
   i. Damaged clutch interlock switch (2007-2011 models).
   j. Dirty or loose-fitting terminals.

7. If the engine turns over but does not start, the engine compression is probably low. Check for the following possible malfunctions:
   a. Leaking cylinder head gasket(s).
   b. Bent or stuck valve(s).
   c. Incorrect valve timing. Worn cylinders and/or pistons rings.

8. If the spark is good, try starting the engine by following normal starting procedures. If the engine starts but then stops, check the following conditions:
   a. Leaking or damaged rubber intake boot.
   b. Contaminated fuel.
   c. Incorrect ignition timing due to a damaged ignition component.

Engine Will Not Crank

Check for one or more of the following possible malfunctions.
1. Ignition switch turned off or a defective switch.
2. Engine stop/run switch turned off or a defective switch.
3. Loose or corroded starter and battery cables (solenoid chatters).
4. A discharged or defective battery.
5. A defective starter or starter solenoid.
6. A defective starter shaft pinion gear.
7. Overrunning clutch assembly is slipping.
8. Seized piston(s).
9. Seized crankshaft bearing(s).
10. A broken connecting rod.
11. Bank angle sensor activated. Cycle ignition switch off and back to IGN.
12. Security system activated (on models so equipped).
13. Jiffy stand down and transmission in gear (HDI models).

ENGINE PERFORMANCE

If the engine runs, but performance is unsatisfactory, refer to the following procedure(s) that best describes the symptom(s).

NOTE
The ignition timing is not adjustable. If incorrect ignition timing is suspected as being the cause of a malfunction, a damaged ignition system component is indicated. Refer to **Ignition System** *(this chapter).*

Engine Will Not Idle

1. Clogged air filter element.
2. Poor fuel flow.
3. Fouled or improperly gapped spark plug(s).
4. Leaking head gasket(s) or vacuum leak.
5. Leaking or damaged rubber intake boot(s).
6. Incorrect ignition timing: damaged electronic control module (ECM), or crankshaft position sensor.
7. Obstructed or defective fuel injector(s).
8. Low engine compression.

Poor Overall Performance

1. Support the motorcycle with the rear wheel off the ground. Then, spin the rear wheel by hand. If the wheel spins freely, go to Step 2. If the wheel does not spin freely, check for the following conditions:
   a. Dragging rear brake.
   b. Damaged rear axle/bearing holder assembly.
   c. Damaged drive belt.
   d. Damaged drive or driven sprockets.
2. Check the clutch operation. If the clutch slips, refer to *Clutch* (this chapter).

3. If Step 1 and Step 2 did not locate the problem, test ride the motorcycle and accelerate lightly. If the engine speed increases according to throttle position, go to Step 4. If the engine speed does not increase, check for one or more of the following problems:
   a. Clogged air filter.
   b. Restricted fuel flow.
   c. Clogged or damaged muffler(s).
4. Check for one or more of the following problems:
   a. Low engine compression.
   b. Worn spark plug(s).
   c. Fouled spark plug(s).
   d. Incorrect spark plug heat range.
   e. Clogged or defective fuel injector(s).
   f. Incorrect oil level (too high or too low).
   g. Contaminated oil.
   h. Worn or damaged valve train assembly.
   i. Engine overheating. Refer to *Engine Overheating* (this section).
   j. Incorrect ignition timing: damaged electronic control module (ECM) or crankshaft position sensor.
5. If the engine knocks when it is accelerated or when running at high speed, check for one or more of the following possible malfunctions:
   a. Incorrect type of fuel.
   b. Lean fuel mixture.
   c. Advanced ignition timing: damaged electronic control module (ECM) or crankshaft position sensor.
   d. Excessive carbon buildup in combustion chamber.
   e. Worn pistons and/or cylinder bores.

Poor Idle or Low Speed Performance

1. Check for damaged intake rubber boots, a loose throttle body, or loose air filter housing hose clamps.
2. Check the fuel flow and the fuel injectors (Chapter Eight).
3. Perform the spark test in this section. Note the following:
   a. If the spark is good, test the fuel system (this chapter).
   b. If the spark is weak, test the ignition system (this chapter).

Poor High Speed Performance

1. Check the fuel flow and the fuel injectors (Chapter Eight).
2. Incorrect valve timing and worn or damaged valve springs can cause poor high-speed performance. If the camshafts were timed just prior to the motorcycle experiencing this type of problem, the cam timing may be incorrect. If the cam timing was not set or changed, and all of the other inspection procedures in this section failed to locate the problem, remove the cylinder heads and inspect the camshafts and valve assembly.

Engine Overheating

1. Improper spark plug heat range.
2. Oil not circulating properly.
3. Valves leaking.
4. Heavy engine carbon deposits in combustion chamber(s).
5. Dragging brake(s).
6. Clutch slipping.
7. Vacuum leak(s).
8. Lean fuel mixture.
9. Advanced ignition timing: damaged electronic control module (ECM) or crankshaft position sensor.

Engine Backfires

1. Incorrect ignition timing (due to loose or damaged ignition system component).
2. Incorrect throttle body adjustment.

Engine Misfires During Acceleration

1. Incorrect ignition timing (due to loose or damaged ignition system component).
2. Incorrect throttle body adjustment.

ENGINE NOISES

1. *Knocking or pinging during acceleration* can be caused by using a lower octane fuel than recommended or a poor grade of fuel. Check for excessive carbon buildup in the combustion chamber or on the piston crown. Incorrect (hot) spark plug heat range can also cause pinging. Refer to *Spark Plug Heat Range* in Chapter Three.
2. *Slapping or rattling noises at low speed or during acceleration* can be caused by excessive piston-to-cylinder wall clearance. Check also for a bent connecting rod(s) or worn piston pin and/or piston pin hole in the piston(s).
3. *Knocking or rapping while decelerating* is usually caused by excessive rod bearing clearance.
4. *Persistent knocking and vibration or other noises* are usually caused by worn main bearings. If the main bearings are in good condition, consider the following:
   a. Loose engine mounts.
   b. Cracked frame.
   c. Leaking cylinder head gasket(s).
   d. Exhaust pipe leakage at cylinder head(s).
   e. Stuck or broken piston ring(s).
   f. Partial engine seizure.
   g. Excessive connecting rod bearing clearance.
   h. Excessive connecting rod side clearance.
   i. Excessive crankshaft runout.
5. *Rapid on-off squeal* indicates a compression leak around the cylinder head gasket or spark plug.
6. *Valve train noise* can be caused by the following:
   a. Bent pushrod(s).
   b. Defective lifter(s).

c. Valve sticking in guide.

d. Worn cam gears and/or cam.

e. Damaged rocker arm or shaft. Rocker arm may be binding on shaft.

ELECTRICAL TESTING

This section describes general test procedures and equipment use. Subsequent sections break the electrical system down further into starting, charging and ignition systems for troubleshooting.

After determining which system requires testing, start with the first inspection in the list and perform the indicated test(s). Each test presumes that the component tested in the prior steps is working properly. The test can yield invalid results if they are performed out of sequence. If a test indicates that a component is working properly, reconnect the electrical connections and proceed to the next step. Systematically work through the procedure until the problem is found. Repair or replace faulty parts as described in the appropriate section of this manual.

If necessary, refer to the wiring diagrams located on the CD inserted into the back cover of the manual for component and connector identification. Trace the current paths from the power source through the circuit components to ground. Check any circuits that share the same fuse, ground or switch. If the other circuits work properly and the shared wiring is good, the cause must be in the wiring used only by the suspect circuit. If all related circuits are faulty at the same time, the probable cause is a poor ground connection or a blown fuse(s).

Electrical connections are often the weak link in the electrical system. Dirty, loose-fitting and corroded electrical connectors cause numerous electrical-related problems, especially on high-mileage motorcycles. When troubleshooting an electrical problem, carefully inspect the connectors and wiring harness.

As with all troubleshooting, analyze typical symptoms in a systematic manner. Never assume anything, and do not overlook the obvious, like a blown fuse or an electrical connector that has become separated.

Electrical Component Replacement

Most motorcycle dealerships and parts suppliers will not accept the return of any electrical part. Consider any test results carefully before replacing a component that tests only slightly out of specification, especially for resistance. A number of variables can affect test results dramatically. These include: the testing meter's internal circuitry, the ambient temperature and the conditions under which the machine has been operated. All instructions and specifications have been checked for accuracy; however, successful test results depend to a great degree upon individual accuracy. If the exact cause of any electrical system malfunction cannot be determined, have a dealership retest that specific system or component to verify the test results before purchasing a non-returnable part.

Preliminary Checks and Precautions

Prior to starting any electrical troubleshooting procedure perform the following:

1. Check the Maxi-Fuse as described in Chapter Nine. If the Maxi-Fuse is blown, replace it.

2. Check the individual fuses mounted in the fuse box (Chapter Nine). Remove the suspected fuse and replace if blown.

3. Inspect the battery as described in Chapter Nine. Make sure it is fully charged, and that the battery leads are clean and securely attached to the battery terminals.

4. Disconnect each electrical connector in the suspect circuit and check that there are no bent metal terminals on the male side of the connector. A bent male pin will not connect to the female receptacle, causing an open circuit.

5. Make sure all electrical terminals within the connector are clean and free of corrosion. Clean, if necessary, and pack the connectors with dielectric grease.

6. Make sure the terminals are pushed all the way into the connector. If not, carefully push them in with a narrow-bladed screwdriver.

7. Check the wires where they enter the individual connectors.

8. Push the connectors together and make sure they are fully engaged and locked together.

9. Never pull on the electrical wires when disconnecting an electrical connector.

Test Light or Voltmeter

Use a test light to check for voltage in a circuit by attaching one lead to ground and the other lead to various points along the circuit. Where battery voltage is present the light bulb will light.

Use a voltmeter in the same manner as the test light to determine if battery voltage is present in any given circuit. When using a voltmeter, attach the positive lead to the component or wire to be checked and the negative lead to a good ground (**Figure 5**).

Voltage Test

Make all voltage tests with the electrical connectors still connected unless otherwise specified. Insert the test leads into the backside of the connector and make sure the test lead touches the electrical wire or metal terminal within the connector housing. Touching the wire insulation will yield a false reading.

Always check both sides of the connector as one side may be loose or corroded thus preventing electrical flow through the connector. This type of test can be performed with a test light or a voltmeter. A voltmeter gives the best results.

NOTE
When using a test light, either lead can be attached to ground.

1. Attach the voltmeter negative test lead to a good ground. Make sure the part used for ground is not insulated with a rubber gasket or rubber grommet.
2. Attach the voltmeter positive test lead to the point (electrical connector, etc.) to be checked.
3. Turn the ignition switch to IGN. When using a test light, the test light will come on if voltage is present. When using a voltmeter, note the voltage reading. The reading should be within 1 volt of battery voltage. If the voltage is significantly less than battery voltage, there is a problem in the circuit.

Voltage Drop Test

Since resistance causes voltage to drop, a voltmeter can be used to determine resistance in an active circuit. This is called a voltage drop test. A voltage drop test measures the difference between the voltage at the beginning of the circuit and the available voltage at the end of the circuit while the circuit is operating. If the circuit has no resistance, there is no voltage drop so the voltmeter indicates 0 volts. The greater the resistance in the circuit will result in a greater the voltage drop reading. A voltage drop of 1 or more volts indicates that a circuit has excessive resistance.

Remember a 0 reading on a voltage drop test is good. Battery voltage, on the other hand, indicates an open circuit. A voltage drop test is an excellent way to check the condition of solenoids, relays, battery cables and other high-current electrical components.
1. Connect the voltmeter positive test lead to the end of the wire or device closest to the battery.
2. Connect the voltmeter negative test lead to the ground side of the wire or device (**Figure 6**).
3. Turn the components on in the circuit.
4. The voltmeter should indicate 0 volts. If there is a drop of 1 volt or more, there is a problem within the circuit. A voltage drop reading of 12 volts indicates an open in the circuit.

Ammeter

An ammeter measures the flow of current (amps) in a circuit (**Figure 7**). When connected in series in the circuit, the ammeter determines whether current is flowing in the circuit, and whether the current flow is excessive because of a short in the circuit. This current flow is usually referred to as current draw. Comparing actual current draw in the circuit or component to the manufacturer's specified current draw rating provides useful diagnostic information.

Ohmmeter

CAUTION
Never connect an ohmmeter to a circuit that has power applied to it. Always disconnect

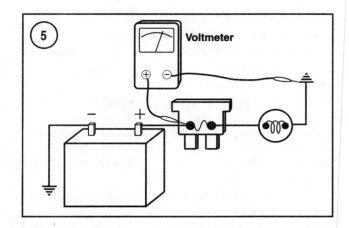

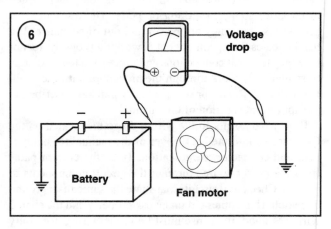

the negative battery cable before using the ohmmeter.

An ohmmeter reads resistance in ohms to current flow in a circuit or component. Ohmmeters may be an analog type (needle scale) or a digital type (LCD or LED readout). Both types of ohmmeters have a switch that allows the selection of different ranges of resistance for accurate readings. The analog ohmmeter also has a set-adjust control which is used to zero or calibrate the meter needle for accurate adjustments. Digital ohmmeters do not require calibration.

Use an ohmmeter by connecting its test leads to the terminals or leads of the circuit or component being tested. When using an analog meter, calibrate it by crossing the test leads and turning the set-adjust knob until the meter needle reads zero. When the leads are uncrossed, the needle should move to the other end of the scale, indicating infinite resistance.

During a continuity test, a reading of infinite indicates that there is an open (or break) in the circuit or component. A reading of zero indicates continuity, which means there is no measurable resistance in the circuit or component being tested. If the meter needle falls between the two ends of the scale, this indicates the actual resistance to current flow that is present. To determine the resistance, multiply the meter reading by the ohmmeter scale. For example, a meter reading of 5 multiplied by the R × 1000 scale is 5000 ohms of resistance

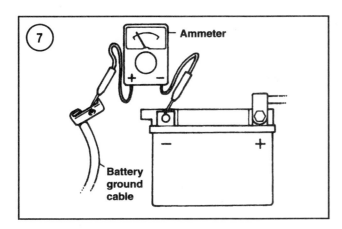

Self-Powered Test Light

CAUTION
Never use a self-powered test light on circuits that contain solid-state devices. The solid-state device may be damaged.

A self-powered test light can be constructed of a 12-volt light bulb, a pair of test leads and a 12-volt battery. When the test leads are touched together, the light bulb illuminates.

Use a self-powered test light as follows:
1. Touch the test leads together to make sure the light bulb goes on. If not, correct the problem prior to using it in a test procedure.
2. Disconnect the motorcycle's battery or remove the fuse(s) that protects the circuit to be tested. Refer to Chapter Nine.
3. Select two points within the circuit that should have continuity.
4. Attach one lead of the self-powered test light to each point.
5. If there is continuity, the self-powered test light bulb will come on.
6. If there is no continuity, the self-powered test light bulb will not come on. This indicates an open circuit.

Continuity Test

A continuity test is used to determine the integrity of a circuit, wire or component. A circuit has continuity if it forms a complete circuit; if there are no opens (or breaks) in either the electrical wires or components within the circuit. A circuit with an open has no continuity.

This type of test can be performed with a self-powered test light or an ohmmeter. An ohmmeter gives the best results. When using an analog ohmmeter, calibrate the meter by touching the leads together and turning the set-adjust knob until the meter needle reads zero.
1. Disconnect the battery negative cable.
2. Attach one test lead (test light or ohmmeter) to one end of the part of the circuit to be tested.
3. Attach the other test lead to the other end of the part or the circuit to be tested.

4. The self-powered test light comes on if there is continuity. An ohmmeter reads 0 or very low resistance if there is continuity. A reading of infinite resistance indicates no continuity; the circuit has an open or a break in it.

Jumper Wire

A jumper wire is a simple way to bypass a potential problem and isolate it to a particular point in a circuit. If a faulty circuit works properly with a jumper wire installed, an open or break exists between the two jumper points in the circuit.

To troubleshoot with a jumper wire, first use the wire to determine if the problem is on the ground side or the load side of a device. Test the ground by connecting the wire between the device and a good ground. If the device comes on, the problem is the connection between the device and ground. If the device does not come on with the jumper installed, the device's connection to ground is good so the problem is between the device and the power source.

To isolate the problem, connect the jumper between the battery and the device. If it comes on, the problem is between these two points. Next, connect the jumper between the battery and the fuse side of the switch. If the device comes on, the switch is good. By moving the jumper from one point to another, the problem can be isolated to a particular place in the circuit.

Note the following when using a jumper wire:
1. A jumper wire is a temporary test measure only. Do not leave a jumper wire installed as a permanent solution. This creates a severe fire hazard that could easily lead to complete loss of the motorcycle.
2. Never use a jumper wire across any load (a component that is connected and turned on). This would result in a direct short and will blow the fuse(s).
3. Install an inline fuse/fuse holder (available at most automotive supply stores or electronic supply stores) to the jumper wire.
4. Make sure the jumper wire gauge (thickness) is the same as that used in the circuit being tested. Smaller gauge wire will rapidly overheat and could melt.
5. Install insulated boots over alligator clips. This prevents accidental grounding, sparks or possible shock when working in cramped quarters.

Testing for a Short with an Ohmmeter

1. Disconnect the battery negative cable.
2. Remove the blown fuse from the fuse panel.
3. Connect one test lead of the ohmmeter (or self-powered test light) to the load side (battery side) of the fuse terminal in the fuse panel.
4. Connect the other test lead to a good ground. Make sure the part used for a ground is not insulated with a rubber gasket or rubber grommet.
5. With the ohmmeter attached to the fuse terminal and ground, wiggle the wiring harness of the suspect circuit at

6 in. (15.2 cm) intervals. Start next to the fuse panel and work away from the fuse panel.

6. Watch the ohmmeter as you progress along the harness. If the ohmmeter moves when the harness is wiggled, there is a short-to-ground at that point in the harness.

Testing For a Short with a Test Light

1. Remove the blown fuse from the fuse panel.
2. Connect the test light (or voltmeter) across the fuse terminals in the fuse panel. Turn the ignition switch to IGN. and check for battery voltage.
3. With the test light attached to the fuse terminals, wiggle the wiring harness of the suspect circuit at 6 in. (15.2 cm) intervals. Start next to the fuse panel and work away from the panel.
4. Watch the test light as you progress along the harness. If the test light blinks or if the needle on the voltmeter moves when the harness is wiggled, there is a short-to-ground at that point in the harness.

Wiggle Test

Locate intermittent problems within a circuit by performing the following:

1. Connect a digital volt/ohmmeter between two points within a suspected circuit.
2. State the engine, let it idle and note the voltage.
3. Wiggle or shake the harness while observing the meter. If a large change in voltage occurs, an intermittent short or break in the circuit exists between the two tested points.
4. To narrow the search, move one test probe closer to the other test point and repeat the test until the intermittent has been isolated to a place in the circuit.

STARTING SYSTEM

The starting system consists of the battery, starter, starter relay, solenoid, start switch, starter mechanism and related wiring.

When the ignition switch is turned to IGN. and the start button is pushed, current is transmitted from the battery to the starter relay. When the relay is activated, it allows electricity to flow from the battery to the starter. Refer to Chapter Nine for starter service.

Troubleshooting Preparation

Before troubleshooting the starting system, check for the following:

1. The battery is fully charged.
2. Battery cables are the proper size and length. Replace damaged or undersized cables.
3. All electrical connections are clean and tight. High resistance caused from dirty or loose connectors can affect voltage and current levels.

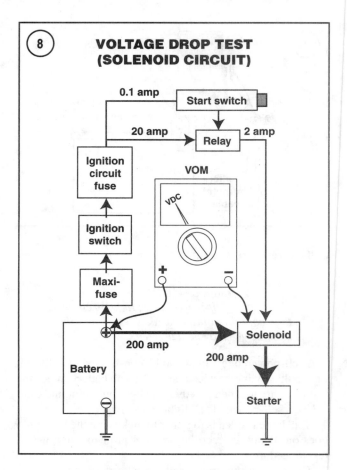

VOLTAGE DROP TEST (SOLENOID CIRCUIT)

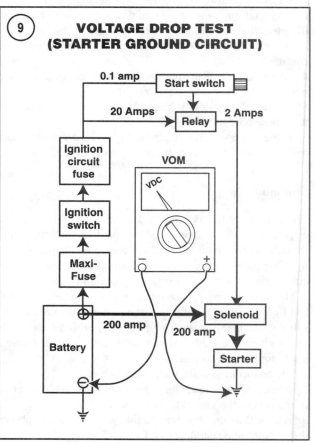

VOLTAGE DROP TEST (STARTER GROUND CIRCUIT)

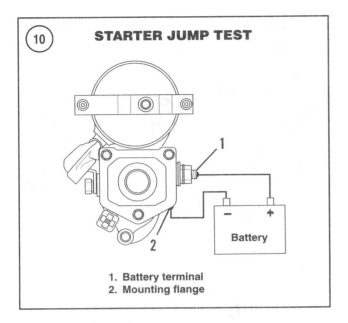

STARTER JUMP TEST

10

1. Battery terminal
2. Mounting flange

4. The wiring harness is in good condition with no worn or frayed insulation or loose harness sockets.
5. The fuel tank is filled with an adequate supply of fresh gasoline.
6. The spark plugs are in good condition and properly gapped.
7. The ignition system is working correctly.

Voltage Drop Test

Before performing the *Troubleshooting* steps (this section), perform this voltage drop test. These steps will help find weak or damaged electrical components that may be causing the starting system problem.
1. To check the solenoid circuit, connect the positive voltmeter lead to the positive battery terminal; connect the negative voltmeter lead to the solenoid (**Figure 8**). The voltmeter lead must not touch the starter-to-solenoid terminal.
2. Shift the transmission into neutral. On 2007-2011 models, pull the clutch lever in, even with the transmission in neutral.
3. Turn the ignition switch to IGN. and push the starter button while reading the voltmeter scale. Note the following:
   a. The circuit is operating correctly if the voltmeter reading is 2 volts or less. A voltmeter reading of 12 volts indicates an open circuit.
   b. A voltage drop of more than 2 volts shows a problem in the solenoid circuit.
   c. If the voltage drop reading is correct, continue the procedure.

NOTE
Also check the voltage on the starter ground circuit. To check any ground circuit in the starting circuit, repeat this test, but leave the negative voltmeter lead connected to the battery; connect the positive voltmeter lead to the ground in question.

4. To check the starter ground circuit itself, connect the negative voltmeter lead to the negative battery terminal; connect the positive voltmeter lead to the starter housing (**Figure 9**).
5. Turn the ignition switch to IGN. and push the starter button while reading the voltmeter scale. The voltage drop must not exceed 0.2 volts. If it does, check the ground connections between the meter leads.
6. If the problem is not located, refer to *Troubleshooting* (this section).

Troubleshooting

The basic starter-related troubles are:
1. Starter does not spin.
2. Starter spins but does not engage.
3. The starter will not disengage after the start button is released.
4. Loud grinding noise when starter turns.
5. Starter stalls or spins too slowly.

CAUTION
Never operate the starter for more than 30 seconds at a time. Allow the starter to cool before reusing it. Failure to allow the starter to cool after continuous starting attempts can damage the starter.

Starter does not spin

1. Turn the ignition switch to IGN. and push the starter button while listening for a click at the starter relay in the electrical panel. Turn the ignition switch off and note the following:
   a. If the starter relay clicks, test the starter relay as described in this section. If the starter relay test readings are correct, continue the procedure.
   b. If the solenoid clicks, go to Step 3.
   c. If there was no click, go to Step 5.
2. Check the wiring connectors between the starter relay and solenoid. Note the following:
   a. Repair any dirty, loose fitting or damaged connectors or wiring.
   b. If the wiring is good, remove the starter (Chapter Nine) and perform the bench tests (this section).
3. Perform a voltage drop test between the battery and solenoid terminals as described in *Voltage Drop Test* (this section). The normal voltage drop is less than 2 volts. Note the following:
   a. If the voltage drop is less than 2 volts, continue the procedure.
   b. If the voltage drop is more than 2 volts, check the solenoid and battery wires and connections for dirty or loose fitting terminals; clean and repair as required.
4. Remove the starter as described in Chapter Nine. Momentarily connect a fully charged 12-volt battery to the starter. Refer to **Figure 10**. If the starter is operational, it will turn over when connected to the battery. Disconnect the battery and note the following:

a. If the starter turns, perform the solenoid pull-in and solenoid hold-in bench tests (this section).

b. If the starter does not turn, disassemble the starter as described in Chapter Nine, and check for opens, shorts and grounds.

5. If there is no click when performing Step 1, measure voltage between the starter button and the starter relay. The voltmeter must read battery voltage. Note the following:

a. If battery voltage is present, continue the procedure.

b. If there is no voltage, go to Step 7.

6. Check the starter relay ground at the starter relay. Note the following:

a. If the starter relay is properly grounded, test the starter relay (this section).

b. If the starter relay is not grounded, check the ground connection. Repair the ground connection, and then retest the starter relay (this section).

7. Check for voltage at the starter button. Note the following:

a. If there is voltage at the starter button, test the starter relay (this section).

b. If there is no voltage at the starter button, check continuity across the starter button. If there is voltage leading to the starter button but no voltage leaving the starter button, replace the button switch and retest. If there is no voltage leading to the starter button, check the starter button wiring for dirty or loose-fitting terminals or damaged wiring; clean and/or repair as required.

Starter spins but does not engage

If the starter spins but the pinion gear does not engage the ring gear, perform the following:

1. Remove the outer primary cover as described in Chapter Six.

2. Inspect the starter pinion gear (**Figure 11**). If the teeth are chipped or worn, inspect the clutch ring gear (**Figure 12**) for the same problems.

a. If the pinion gear and ring gear are damaged, service these parts.

b. If the pinion gear and ring gear are not damaged, continue with Step 3.

3. Remove and disassemble the starter as described in Chapter Nine. Then, check the overrunning clutch assembly for:

a. Roller (**Figure 13**) damage.

b. Compression spring (A, **Figure 14**) damage.

c. Excessively worn or damaged pinion teeth.

d. Pinion does not run in overrunning direction.

e. Damaged clutch shaft splines (B, **Figure 14**).

4. Replace worn or damaged parts as required.

Starter will not disengage after the start button is released

1. A sticking solenoid, caused by a worn solenoid compression spring (A, **Figure 14**), can cause this problem. Replace the solenoid if damaged.

2. Check the start switch and starter relay for internal damage. Test the starter button as described in *Switches* (Chapter Nine). Test the starter relay as described in this section.

Loud grinding noises when the starter turns

Incorrect pinion gear and clutch ring gear engagement or a broken overrunning clutch mechanism (**Figure 15**) can

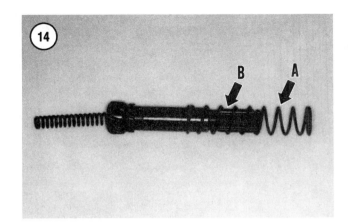

cause this problem. Remove and inspect the starter as described in Chapter Nine.

Starter stalls or spins too slowly

1. Perform a voltage drop test between the battery and solenoid terminals as described in *Voltage Drop Test* (this section). The normal voltage drop is less than 2 volts. Note the following:
   a. If the voltage drop is less than 2 volts, continue the procedure.
   b. If the voltage drop exceeds 2 volts, check the solenoid and battery wires and connections for dirty or loose-fitting terminals; clean and repair as required.
2. Perform a voltage drop test between the solenoid terminals and the starter as described in *Voltage Drop Test* (this section). The normal voltage drop is less than 2 volts. Note the following:
   a. If the voltage drop is less than 2 volts, continue the procedure.
   b. If the voltage drop exceeds 2 volts, check the solenoid and starter wires and connections for dirty or loose-fitting terminals; clean and repair as required.
3. Perform a voltage drop test between the battery ground wire and the starter as described in *Voltage Drop Test* (this section). The normal voltage drop is less than 2 volts. Note the following:

a. If the voltage drop is less than 2 volts, continue the procedure.
b. If the voltage drop exceeds 2 volts, check the battery ground wire connections for dirty or loose-fitting terminals; clean and repair as required.

4. Perform the *Current Draw Test* (this section) with the starter still installed. Note the following:
   a. If the current draw is excessive, check for a damaged starter or starter drive assembly. Remove the starter as described in Chapter Nine and perform the *Free-Running Current Draw Test* (this section).
   b. If the current draw reading is correct, continue the procedure.
5. Remove the outer primary cover as described in Chapter Six. Check the clutch ring gear (**Figure 12**). If the teeth are chipped or worn, service these parts as described in Chapter Six. Disassemble the starter and check the starter pinion gear (**Figure 11**). If the teeth are chipped or worn, service these parts as described in Chapter Nine.
6. Remove and disassemble the starter as described in Chapter Nine. Check the disassembled starter for opens, shorts and grounds.

Starter Relay
Removal/Testing/Installation

Check the starter relay operation with an ohmmeter, jumper wires and a fully charged 12-volt battery.
1. Pull straight out on the electrical caddy cover (**Figure 16**) and remove it.

> *NOTE*
> *Refer to **Figure 17** for fuse and relay description and location.*

2. Pull straight out and remove the starter relay (**Figure 18**) from the rear fuse block.

> *CAUTION*
> *The battery negative lead must be connected to relay terminal No. 85 to avoid internal diode damage.*

3. Connect an ohmmeter and 12-volt battery between the relay terminals as shown in **Figure 19**. This will energize the relay for testing.

4. Check for continuity through the relay contacts while the relay coil is energized using an ohmmeter as shown (**Figure 19**). The correct reading is 0 ohm. If resistance is excessive or if there is no continuity, replace the relay.

5. If the starter relay passes this test, re-install the starter relay into the rear fuse block. Press it in until it bottoms.

6. Install the electrical caddy and press it in until it locks in place.

Starter Current Draw Tests

The battery must be fully charged for this test. Refer to *Battery* in Chapter Nine. An inductive ammeter is required to perform this test.

Loaded current draw test (starter installed)

1. Shift the transmission into neutral.

2. Disconnect the spark plug caps from both spark plugs, and ground the plug caps with two extra spark plugs. *Do not* remove the spark plugs from the cylinder heads.

3. Connect an inductive ammeter (A, **Figure 20**) between the starter terminal (B) and positive battery terminal. Connect a jumper cable from the negative battery terminal to ground.

> *NOTE*
> *The current draw is high when the starter button is first pressed, and then it will drop and stabilize at a lower reading. Refer to the lower stabilized reading during this test.*

4. Turn the ignition switch to IGN. and press the start button for approximately 10 seconds. Note the ammeter reading.

5. If the current draw exceeds the current draw specification in **Table 1**, check for a defective starter or starter drive mechanism. Remove, inspect and service these components as described in Chapter Nine.

6. Disconnect the ammeter and jumper cables.

Free-running current draw test (starter removed)

A jumper wire (14 gauge minimum) and 3 jumper cables (6-gauge minimum) is required for this test.

1. Remove the starter as described in Chapter Nine.

> *NOTE*
> *The solenoid must be installed on the starter during the following tests.*

2. Mount the starter in a vise with soft jaws.

3. Connect the 14-gauge jumper wire between the positive battery terminal and the solenoid relay terminal (A, **Figure 21**).

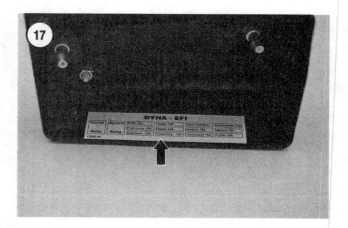

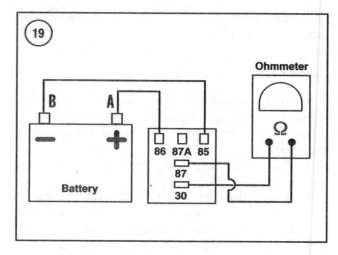

4. Connect the first jumper cable between the starter terminal (B, **Figure 21**) and the ammeter.

5. Connect the second jumper cable between the ammeter and the solenoid relay (A, **Figure 21**).

6. Connect the third jumper cable between the battery ground terminal and the starter mounting flange (C, **Figure 21**).

7. Read the ammeter; the correct ammeter reading is 90 amps. A damaged pinion gear assembly will cause an excessively high current draw reading. If the current draw reading is low, check for an undercharged battery or an open field winding or armature in the starter.

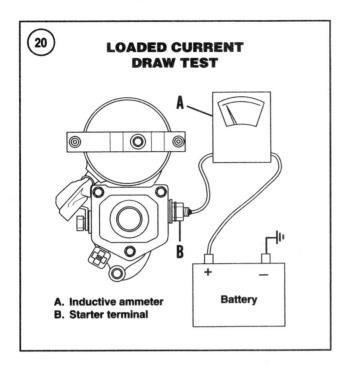

LOADED CURRENT DRAW TEST

A. Inductive ammeter
B. Starter terminal

Battery

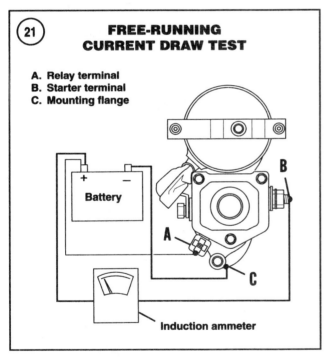

FREE-RUNNING CURRENT DRAW TEST

A. Relay terminal
B. Starter terminal
C. Mounting flange

Battery

Induction ammeter

Solenoid Testing (Bench Tests)

The battery must be fully charged for this test. Refer to *Battery* in Chapter Nine. Three jumper wires are also required.

1. Remove the starter (A, **Figure 22**, typical) as described in Chapter Nine.

NOTE
The solenoid (B, Figure 22) must be installed on the starter during the following tests. Do not remove it.

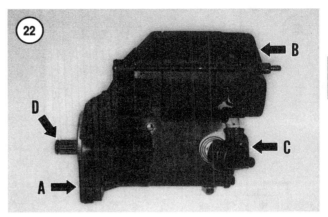

2. Disconnect the field wire terminal (C, **Figure 22**) from the solenoid before performing the following tests. Insulate the end of the wire terminal so that it cannot short out on any of the test connectors.

CAUTION
Battery voltage is being applied directly to the solenoid and starter in the following tests. Do not leave the jumper cables connected to the solenoid for more than 3-5 seconds; otherwise, the solenoid will be damage.

NOTE
Thoroughly read and understand the following procedure to test the connections. Perform the tests in the order listed, without interruption.

3. Perform the solenoid pull-in test as follows:
   a. Connect a jumper wire from the negative battery terminal to the solenoid motor terminal (A, **Figure 23**).
   b. Connect a jumper wire from the negative battery terminal to the solenoid housing ground (B, **Figure 23**).
   c. Touch a jumper wire from the positive battery terminal to the starter relay terminal (C, **Figure 23**). The pinion shaft (D, **Figure 22**) must pull into the housing.
   d. Leave the jumper wires connected and continue the procedure.

4. To perform the solenoid hold-in test, perform the following:
   a. With the pinion shaft retracted, disconnect the solenoid motor terminal jumper wire from the negative battery terminal and connect it to the positive battery terminal (**Figure 24**). The pinion shaft will remain in the housing. If the pinion shaft returns to its normal position, replace the solenoid.
   b. Leave the jumper wires connected and continue the procedure.

5. To perform the solenoid return test, perform the following:

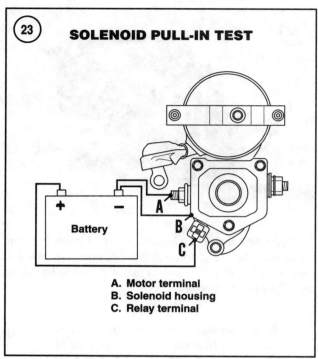

(23) SOLENOID PULL-IN TEST

A. Motor terminal
B. Solenoid housing
C. Relay terminal

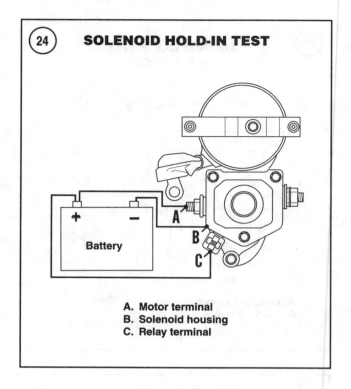

(24) SOLENOID HOLD-IN TEST

A. Motor terminal
B. Solenoid housing
C. Relay terminal

a. Disconnect the jumper wire from the starter relay terminal (**Figure 25**); the pinion shaft must return to its original position.

b. Disconnect all of the jumper wires from the solenoid and battery.

6. Replace the solenoid (Chapter Nine) if the starter shaft failed to operate properly during any of these tests.

CHARGING SYSTEM

The charging system consists of the battery, alternator and a solid state voltage regulator/rectifier.

The alternator generates alternating current (AC) which the rectifier converts to direct current (DC). The regulator maintains the voltage to the battery and loads (lights, ignition and accessories) at a constant voltage despite variations in engine speed and load.

A malfunction in the charging system generally causes the battery to remain undercharged.

Precautions

When servicing the charging system, note the following precautions to prevent damage to charging system components.

1. Never reverse battery connections.
2. Do not short across any connection.
3. Never start the engine with the alternator disconnected from the voltage regulator/rectifier unless instructed to do so during a test.
4. Never attempt to start or run the engine with the battery disconnected.

5. Never attempt to use a high-output battery charger to help start the engine.
6. Before charging the battery, remove it from the motorcycle as described in Chapter Nine.
7. Never disconnect the voltage regulator/rectifier connector with the engine running.
8. Do not mount the voltage regulator/rectifier unit in another location.
9. Make sure the negative battery terminal is securely connected to the engine and frame.

Milliamp Draw Test

1. Turn the ignition switch off. Make sure all accessories are in the off position.
2. Disconnect the Maxi-Fuse as described in Chapter Nine.

> *CAUTION*
> *Before connecting the ammeter into the circuit, set the meter to its highest amperage scale. This prevents a large current flow from damaging the meter or blowing the meter's fuse.*

> *NOTE*
> *Even with the ignition in the off position, an initial current draw of up to 200 mA will occur directly after connecting the ammeter. This should drop to the values shown in **Table 1** within one minute.*

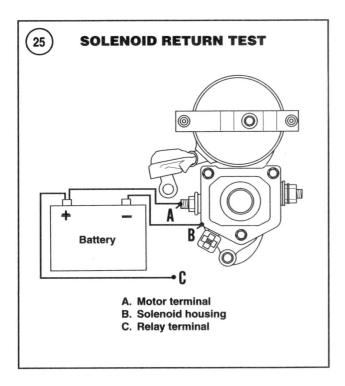

25 **SOLENOID RETURN TEST**

Battery
+ −

A
B
C

A. Motor terminal
B. Solenoid housing
C. Relay terminal

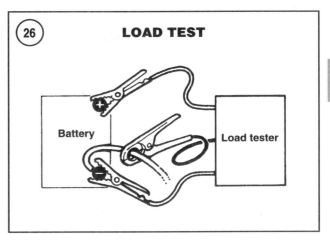

26 **LOAD TEST**

Battery

Load tester

3. Connect an ammeter between both red wire terminals of the Maxi-Fuse socket terminals. Note the meter reading after the initial one minute interval as follows:

a. Add the current draw (0.5 mA) to the approximate values of the TSM/TSSM/HFSM/ECM and other components listed in **Table 1**. If this total is less than the ammeter reading noted, then the current draw is within limits.

b. If the ammeter reading is higher, this indicates an excessive draw. All accessories must be checked for excessive current drain.

4. Dirt and/or electrolyte on top of the battery or a crack in the battery case can create a path for battery current to flow. If excessive current draw is noted, remove and clean the battery (Chapter Nine). Then, repeat the test.

5. If the current draw is still excessive, consider the following probable causes:

a. Faulty voltage regulator.

b. Damaged battery.

c. Short circuit in the system.

d. Loose, dirty or faulty electrical connectors in the charging circuit.

6. To find the short circuit that is causing excessive current draw, refer to the wiring diagrams located on the CD inserted into the back cover of the manual. Then, continue to measure the current draw while disconnecting different connectors in the electrical system one by one. If the current draw returns to an acceptable level, the circuit is indicated. Test the circuit further to find the fault.

7. Disconnect the ammeter.

8. Connect the Maxi-Fuse as described in Chapter Nine.

Total Current Draw Test

This test, requiring a load tester, measures the total current load of the electrical system and any additional accessories while the engine is running. Perform this test if the battery is repeatedly discharged, yet the charging system output is within specifications.

If aftermarket accessories have been installed, to the motorcycle, the increased current demand may exceed the charging systems capacity and result in a discharged battery.

CAUTION
When using a load tester, refer to the tester manufacturer's instructions. To prevent tester damage caused by overheating, do not leave the load switch on for more than 20 seconds at a time.

1. Connect a load tester to the battery as shown in **Figure 26**.

2. Turn the ignition switch to IGN., but do not start the engine. Then, turn on *all* electrical accessories and switch the headlight beam to high.

3. Note the ampere reading (current draw) on the load tester and compare it to the test results obtained in the *Current Output Test* (this section). The current output test results (current reading) must exceed the current draw by 3.5 amps for the battery to remain sufficiently charged.

4. If aftermarket accessories have been added to the motorcycle, disconnect them and repeat the test. If the current draw is not within specification, the problem is with the additional accessories.

5. If no accessories have been added to the motorcycle, a short circuit may be causing the battery to discharge.

Current Output Test

This test requires a load tester.

1. The battery must be fully charged for this test. Refer to *Battery* in Chapter Nine.

CAUTION
When using the load tester, read and follow the tester manufacturer's instructions. To prevent tester damage from overheating, do not leave the load switch on for more than 20 seconds at a time.

2. Connect the load tester negative and positive leads to the battery terminals. Then, place the induction pickup of the load tester around the positive voltage regulator wire (**Figure 27**).

3. Start the engine and bring the speed up to 3000 rpm while reading the load tester scale. With the engine running at 3000 rpm, operate the load tester switch until the voltage scale reads 13.0 volts. The correct reading is listed in **Table 1**.

4. Turn the engine off and disconnect the load tester.

5. Perform the *Stator Tests* (this section). If the stator tests acceptable, a defective voltage regulator/rectifier or a wiring short circuit is indicated.

6. Make sure to eliminate the possibility of a poor connection or damaged wiring before replacing the voltage regulator/rectifier.

Stator Tests

Grounded stator

1. Turn the ignition switch off.

2. Depress the tabs and open the front electrical caddy cover (**Figure 28**).

3. Release the latch and disconnect the round 3-pin connector (**Figure 29**) from the left side of the regulator.

4. Insert one of the ohmmeter probes into one of the stator connector terminals and connect the other probe to ground. The correct reading is infinity. Any other reading indicates a grounded stator. Repeat this test for the other two terminals in the stator connector. Again, the correct ohmmeter reading is infinity.

5. If resistance is not as specified, replace the stator assembly (Chapter Nine).

6. Reconnect the stator connector, and close the caddy door firmly until it locks in place.

Open stator

1. Turn the ignition switch off.

2. Depress the tabs and open the front electrical caddy cover (**Figure 28**).

3. Release the latch and disconnect the round 3-pin connector (**Figure 29**) from the left side of the regulator.

4. Insert the ohmmeter probes between all possible terminal combinations (1-2, 2-3, 1-3). The correct reading should be less than 1 ohm (typically 0.1-0.2 ohm). If resistance is not as specified, replace the stator assembly as described in Chapter Nine.

5. Reconnect and install the voltage regulator, and close the caddy door firmly until it locks in place.

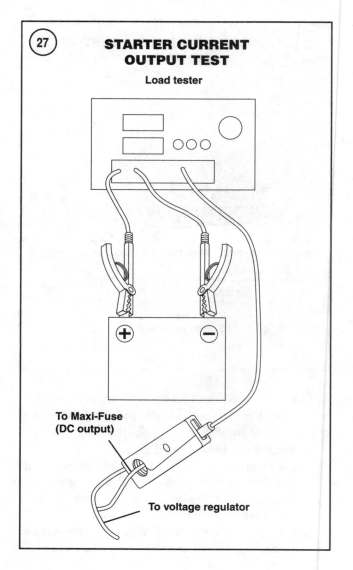

(27) STARTER CURRENT OUTPUT TEST

Load tester

To Maxi-Fuse (DC output)

To voltage regulator

AC Output Test

1. Turn the ignition switch off.

2. Depress the tabs and open the front electrical caddy cover (**Figure 28**).

3. Release the latch and disconnect the round 3-pin connector (**Figure 29**) from the left side of the regulator.

4. Connect an AC voltmeter across any two terminals.

5. Start the engine and slowly increase engine speed until the engine is running at 1000 rpm. The AC output should be as listed in **Table 1**.

6. If the AC voltage output reading is below the specified range, replace the stator assembly as described in Chapter Nine.

7. Reconnect the regulator/rectifier connector.

Voltage Regulator Ground Test

1. Connect one ohmmeter lead to a good engine or frame ground and the other ohmmeter lead to the regulator base. Read the ohmmeter scale. The correct reading is 0 ohm. Note the following:

a. If there is low resistance (0 ohm), the voltage regulator is properly grounded.

b. If there is high resistance, remove the voltage regulator and clean its frame mounting points.

2. Remove the voltage regulator and check the connectors on the backside of the voltage regulator. They must be tight and free of corrosion.

IGNITION SYSTEM

Ignition System Precautions

Before testing the ignition system, observe the following precautions to prevent damage to protect the system:

1. Never disconnect any of the electrical connectors while the engine is running.

2. Apply dielectric grease to all electrical connectors prior to reconnecting them. This will help seal out moisture.

3. Make sure all electrical connectors are free of corrosion and are completely coupled to each other.

4. The electronic control module (ECM) must always be mounted securely within the electrical caddy and the connector (**Figure 30**) must be securely fastened.

Troubleshooting

1. Refer to the wiring diagrams located on the CD inserted into the back cover for the specific model.

2. Check the wiring harness for visible signs of damage.

3. Make sure all connectors are properly attached to each other and locked in place.

4. Check all electrical components for a good ground to the engine.

5. The electronic control module (ECM) must always be mounted securely within the electrical caddy and the connector (**Figure 30**) must be securely fastened.

6. Check all wiring for short circuits or open circuits.

7. To check for a blown fuse, perform the following:

a. Pull straight out on the electrical caddy cover (**Figure 16**) and remove it.

NOTE
*Refer to **Figure 17** for fuse description and location.*

b. Locate the blown fuse and install a *new* fuse with the *same* amperage.

8. Make sure the fuel tank has an adequate supply of fresh gasoline.

9. Check the spark plug cable routing and the connections at the spark plugs. If there is no spark or only a weak one, repeat the test with new spark plugs. If the condition remains the same with new spark plugs and if all external wiring connections are good, the problem is most likely in the ignition system. If a strong spark is present, the problem is probably not in the ignition system. Check the fuel system.

10. Remove and examine the spark plugs as described in Chapter Three.

Ignition Coil Testing

Use an ohmmeter to check the ignition coil secondary and primary resistance. Test the coil twice: first when it is cold (room temperature) and then at normal operating temperature. If the engine will not start, heat the coil with a hair dryer, and test with the ohmmeter.

1. Remove the seat as described in Chapter Fourteen.

2. Remove the fuel tank as described in Chapter Eight.

3A. On FXDL and FXDWG models, perform the following:

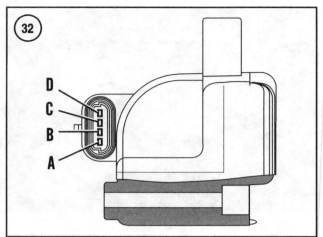

a. Remove the two long screws, washers and coil cover from the electrical caddy.
b. Remove the ignition coil and secondary cables from the side electrical caddy.
c. Disconnect the 4-pin connector from the backside of the ignition coil.
d. Do not lose the two screw spacers within the cover.
3B. On all other models, perform the following:
a. Remove the two screws (A, **Figure 31**) securing the ignition coil to the electrical caddy.
b. Remove the ignition coil and secondary cables from the side electrical caddy.
c. Disconnect the 4-pin connector from the backside of the ignition coil.
4. Disconnect the secondary wires (B, **Figure 31**) from the ignition coil.
5. Measure the primary coil resistance between terminals (**Figure 32**) as follows:
a. Front coil: Terminal A and D.
b. Rear coil: Terminal A and C.

NOTE
The manufacturer does not provide a procedure for checking secondary coil resistance.

6. Compare the test results to the specification in **Table 1**.
7A. If the resistance values are less than specified, this likely indicates a short in the coil windings. Replace the coil.
7B. If the resistance values are more than specified, this indicates possible corrosion or oxidation of the coil's terminals. Thoroughly clean the terminals, and spray with an aerosol electrical contact cleaner. Repeat Step 5 and if the resistance value is still high, replace the coil.
8. If the coil resistance does not meet (or come close to) specifications, the coil must be replaced. If the coil exhibits visible damage, it should be replaced as described in this chapter.
9. Reconnect the 4-pin connector onto the ignition coil.
10. Connect the secondary wires (B, **Figure 31**) onto the ignition coil.
11. Mount the ignition coil and cover. Install and tighten the mounting (A, **Figure 31**) screws to 50 in.-lb. (5.6 N•m).
12. Install the fuel tank as described in Chapter Eight.
13. Install the seat as described in Chapter Fourteen.

Spark Plug Wire and Plug Cap Inspection

1. Disconnect the high tension wires from the spark plugs (A, **Figure 33**) and ignition coil (B).
2. Measure the resistance of each wire from end to end.
3. Compare the reading to the specification listed in **Table 1**. Replace the plug wire(s) if the reading is not within specification.
4. Inspect the spark plug wires for:
a. Corroded or damaged connector ends.
b. Breaks in the wire insulation that could allow arcing.
c. Split or damaged plug caps that could allow arcing to the cylinder heads.
5. Connect the wires onto the correct spark plugs and ignition coil terminal(s).

FUEL SYSTEM

Start troubleshooting the fuel system at the fuel tank and work throughout the fuel system reserving the fuel injecting system to the final point. Most fuel system problems result from an empty fuel tank, a plugged filter, fuel pump failure, sour fuel or a clogged air filter element. Refer to *Starting The Engine* and *Engine Performance* (this chapter).

The fuel injection system is controlled by the electronic control module component of the engine management system.

ENGINE LUBRICATION

An improperly operating engine lubrication system will quickly lead to serious engine damage. Check the engine oil level weekly as described in Chapter Three. Oil pump service is covered in Chapter Five.

Low Oil Warning Light

The low oil warning light, mounted in the indicator lamp assembly, will come on when the ignition switch is

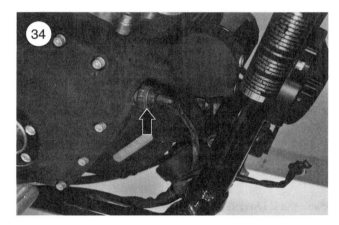

turned to IGN before starting the engine. After the engine is started, the oil light will turn off when the engine speed is above idle.

The low oil warning light, mounted on the indicator light panel, should come on when the ignition switch is turned ON before the engine is started. After the engine is started, the oil light should turn off when the engine speed is above idle.

If the low oil warning light does not come on when the ignition switch is turned ON and engine is not running, the LED indicator lamp assembly may be damaged and must be replaced as described in Chapter Nine. If the LED is working, check the oil pressure switch, or sensor (Figure 34) (Chapter Nine).

If the oil light remains on when the engine speed is above idle, turn the engine off and check the oil level (Chapter Three). If the oil level is correct, check for clogged or damaged oil pump (Chapter Five).

Oil Consumption High or Engine Smokes Excessively

1. Worn valve guides.
2. Worn valve guide seals.
3. Worn or damaged piston rings.
4. Oil pan overfilled.
5. Oil filter restricted.
6. Leaking cylinder head surfaces.

Oil Fails to Return to Oil Pan

1. Oil pump damaged or operating incorrectly.
2. Oil pan empty.
3. Oil filter restricted.

Engine Oil Leaks

1. Clogged air filter breather hose.
2. Loose engine parts.
3. Damaged gasket sealing surfaces.
4. Oil pan overfilled.
5. Restricted oil filter.
6. Plugged air filter-to-breather system hose.

CLUTCH

All clutch troubles, except adjustments, require partial clutch disassembly to identify and cure the problem. Refer to Chapter Six for clutch service procedures. Refer to Chapter Three for clutch cable adjustment procedures.

Clutch Chatter or Noise

This problem is usually caused by worn or warped friction and plain plates.

Clutch Slip

1. Incorrect clutch adjustment.
2. Worn friction plates.
3. Weak or damaged diaphragm spring.
4. Damaged pressure plate.
5. Air in hydraulic clutch system.

Clutch Dragging

1. Incorrect clutch cable adjustment (except Screamin' Eagle and CVO models).
2. Warped clutch plain plates.
3. Worn or damaged clutch shell or clutch hub.
4. Worn or incorrectly assembled clutch ball and ramp mechanism.
5. Incorrect primary chain alignment.
6. Weak or damaged diaphragm spring.

TRANSMISSION

Transmission symptoms are sometimes hard to distinguish from clutch symptoms. Refer to Chapter Seven for transmission service procedures.

Gears Will Not Stay Engaged

1. Worn or damaged shifter parts.
2. Incorrect shift rod adjustment.

3. Incorrect shift cam adjustment.
4. Severely worn or damaged gears and/or shift forks.

Difficult Shifting

1. Worn or damaged shift forks.
2. Worn or damaged shifter clutch dogs.
3. Weak or damaged shifter return spring.
4. Clutch drag.

Excessive Gear Noise

1. Worn or damaged bearings.
2. Worn or damaged gears.
3. Excessive gear backlash.

LIGHTING SYSTEM

If bulbs burn out frequently, check for excessive vibration, loose connections that permit sudden current surges, or the wrong type of bulb.

Most light and ignition problems are caused by loose or corroded ground connections. Check these prior to replacing a bulb or electrical component.

VIBRATION

Excessive vibration is usually caused by loose engine mounting hardware. A bent axle shaft or loose suspension component will cause high-speed vibration problems. Vibration can also be caused by the following conditions:
1. Cracked or broken frame.
2. Severely worn primary chain.
3. Tight primary chain links.
4. Loose, worn or damaged engine stabilizer link.
5. Loose or damaged rubber mounts.
6. Improperly balanced wheel(s).
7. Defective or damaged wheel(s).
8. Defective or damaged tire(s).
9. Internal engine wear or damage.
10. Loose or worn steering head bearings.
11. Loose swing arm pivot shaft nut.

FRONT SUSPENSION AND STEERING

Poor handling may be caused by improper tire inflation pressure, a damaged or bent frame, damaged steering components, worn wheel bearings or dragging brakes. Possible causes for suspension and steering malfunctions are listed below.

Irregular or Wobbly Steering

1. Loose wheel axle nut.
2. Loose or worn steering head bearings.
3. Excessive wheel bearing play.

4. Damaged cast wheel.
5. Laced wheel out of alignment.
6. Unbalanced wheel assembly.
7. Incorrect wheel alignment.
8. Bent or damaged steering stem or frame at steering neck.
9. Tire incorrectly seated on rim.
10. Excessive front end loading from non-standard equipment.

Stiff Steering

1. Low front tire air pressure.
2. Bent or damaged steering stem or frame.
3. Loose or worn steering head bearings.

Stiff or Heavy Fork Operation

1. Incorrect fork springs.
2. Incorrect fork oil viscosity.
3. Excessive amount of fork oil.
4. Bent fork tubes.
5. Incorrect fork air pressure.

Poor Fork Operation

1. Worn or damage fork tubes.
2. Fork oil capacity low due to leaking fork seals.
3. Bent or damaged fork tubes.
4. Contaminated fork oil.
5. Incorrect fork springs.
6. Heavy front end loading from non-standard equipment.

Poor Rear Shock Absorber Operation

1. Weak or worn springs.
2. Damper unit leaking.
3. Shock shaft worn or bent.
4. Incorrect rear shock springs.
5. Rear shocks adjusted incorrectly.
6. Heavy rear end loading from non-standard equipment.
7. Incorrect loading.
8. Incorrect rear shock air pressure.

BRAKE SYSTEM

All models are equipped with front and rear disc brakes. Good brakes are vital to the safe operation of any vehicle. Perform the maintenance specified in Chapter Three to minimize brake system problems. Brake system service is covered in Chapter Thirteen. When refilling the front and rear master cylinders, only use DOT 4 brake fluid.

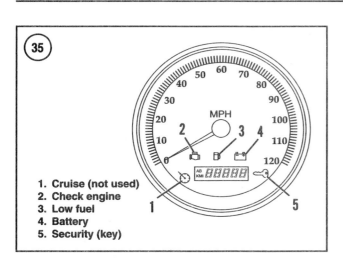

1. Cruise (not used)
2. Check engine
3. Low fuel
4. Battery
5. Security (key)

Insufficient Braking Power

Worn brake pads or a worn disc, air in the hydraulic system, glazed or contaminated pads, low brake fluid level, or a leaking brake line or hose can all reduce brake effectiveness. Brake drag will also result in excessive heat and brake fade. Refer to *Brake Drag* (this section). Check for worn brake pads. Visually check for leaks. Check also for a leaking or damaged primary cup seal in the master cylinder(s) Rebuild or replace a leaking master cylinder or brake caliper. Bleed and adjust the brakes.

Spongy Brake Feel

This problem is generally caused by air in the hydraulic brake system. Bleed and adjust the brakes.

Brake Drag

Check the brake adjustment, while checking for insufficient brake pedal and/or hand lever free play. Also check for worn, loose or missing parts in the brake calipers. Check the brake disc for excessive runout.

Brakes Squeal or Chatter

Check brake pad thickness and disc condition. Check that the caliper anti-rattle springs are properly installed and in good condition. Clean off any dirt on the pads. Loose components can also cause this. Check for the following:
1. Warped brake disc
2. Loose brake disc.
3. Loose caliper mounting bolts.
4. Loose front axle nut.
5. Worn wheel bearings.
6. Damaged hub.

ELECTRONIC DIAGNOSTIC SYSTEM

All models are equipped with an electronic diagnostic system that monitors the operating condition of the starting system, charging system, instruments, TSM/TSSM/HFSM, and engine management components. A serial data bus connects these components. If a malfunction occurs, a diagnostic trouble code (DTC) may be generated.

The DTC identifies an anomaly detected in a monitored component. The trouble code is stored in the memory of the ECM, the TSM/TSSM/HFSM and the speedometer.

A current DTC identifies a problem that presently affects motorcycle operation. A historic DTC identifies a problem that has been resolved either through servicing or a changed condition. Historic DTC's are retained to provide information should an intermittent problem exist. A historic DTC is retained in memory until fifty start/run cycles have occurred at which time the DTC is erased.

Not all malfunctions generate a DTC. Refer to **Table 4**.

Startup Check

The diagnostic system indicates a normal condition or an operating problem each time the ignition key is turned on.
1. During normal startup, the following occurs after the key is turned on:
   a. The *check engine* lamp (**Figure 35**) illuminates for four seconds, and then goes out.
   b. The *security* lamp (**Figure 35**) illuminates for four seconds, and then goes out.
2. Note the following indications of potential problems during startup:
   a. If the check engine lamp or security lamp does not illuminate, the speedometer may be faulty. Refer to the *Initial Diagnostic Check* DTC flowchart (**Figure 40**) located on the CD inserted into the back cover of the manual.
   b. If the check engine lamp or security lamp illuminates after 8 seconds, a serial data bus problem may exist. Check for a DTC.
   c. If the check engine lamp or security lamp stays on, the speedometer may be faulty or a DTC exists. Refer to the *Initial Diagnostic Check* DTC flowchart (**Figure 40**) located on the CD inserted into the back cover of the manual.

DTC Retrieval

Trouble codes consist of a letter prefix followed by four numbers.

NOTE
*The message **BusEr** is a trouble code which may appear during diagnostic troubleshooting. **BusEr** indicates a problem in the serial bus data circuit.*

NOTE
Make sure the engine stop switch in the RUN position.

1. Push and hold in the trip odometer reset switch on the back of the speedometer.

2. Turn the ignition key to IGNITION or IGN (**Figure 36**). The following should occur:

   a. The speedometer backlighting comes on.

   b. The speedometer needle rotates fully to its maximum position.

NOTE
*The security lamp (**Figure 35**) may come on even though the motorcycle is not equipped with a security system.*

   c. The indicator lamps controlled by the serial bus (battery, security and check engine) should illuminate.

3. The message *diag* appears in the odometer window on the speedometer.

4. Press and release the trip odometer reset switch. The letters *PSSPtb* will appear in the odometer window. DTCs are stored for several devices; each device is represented by a letter or letters. A flashing letter identifier indicates that a particular device has been selected. For example, a flashing *P* indicates the ECM has been selected. Continuing retrieval will provide further information about the ECM.

The letters *PSSPtb* identify the following components:

   a. The letter *P* identifies the ECM.

   b. The letter *S* identifies the TSM/TSSM/HFSM.

   c. The letter *SP* identify the speedometer.

   d. The letter *t* identifies the tachometer (models so equipped).

   e. The letter *b* identifies the ABS system (models so equipped).

5. To toggle through the *PSSPtb* letter identifiers, push and quickly release the trip odometer reset switch. The selected letter identifier will flash.

6. To obtain a DTC, select a component (identifier letter will flash). Then, push and hold in the trip odometer reset switch for more than 5 seconds. Release the switch. The DTC or *none* will appear in the odometer window. Record the DTC and the device (ECM, speedometer or TSM/TSSM/HFSM) where the DTC was triggered.

NOTE
Press and release the odometer reset switch just long enough to retrieve the next code. Holding in the odometer reset switch for more than 5 seconds will erase the codes.

7. Press and release the odometer reset switch as needed to read additional trouble codes until *end* appears.

8. If *none* appears, pushing and releasing the odometer reset switch causes the speedometer to display the part number of the selected device. For instance, the display may read *Pn 32534-05B*, or *34246-08A* (typical), for the ECM.

9. Push and release the odometer reset switch to return to the *PSSPtb* display.

10. Turn the ignition switch off to exit the diagnostic mode.

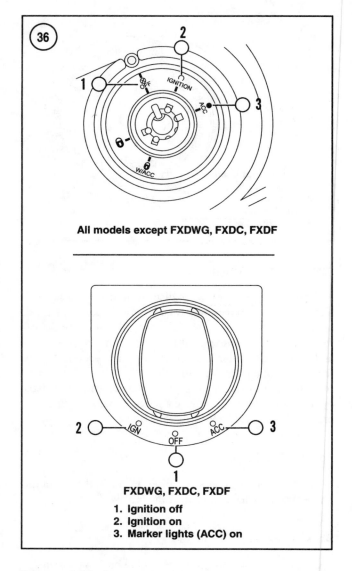

All models except FXDWG, FXDC, FXDF

FXDWG, FXDC, FXDF
1. **Ignition off**
2. **Ignition on**
3. **Marker lights (ACC) on**

Diagnostic Tools

The troubleshooting steps in some of the DTC flowcharts (located on the CD inserted into the back cover of the manual) require two different H-D breakout boxes. Refer to **Figure 37** for part No. HD-43876, or **Figure 38** for part No. HD-42682. H-D breakout box, part No. HD-42682 (**Figure 38**), is separated into two panels marked black and gray. The panel colors relate to the colors of the box connectors: one pair black; one pair gray.

A harness connector test kit (part No. HD-41404-A, -B or -C) is required for some of the DTC flowchart procedures. This test kit allows inserting the test lead probes into the various terminals without damaging them. Several additional adapters are also available including part No. HD-46601.

The Harley-Davidson digital technician (part No. HD-44750), or digital technician II (part No. HD-48650), and various cartridges are needed to obtain or erase historic DTCs and to reprogram a new ECM or new TSM/TSSM/HFSM. At the time of publication, these tools are not available to the general public. However, many of the test procedures can be performed without the H-D digital technician.

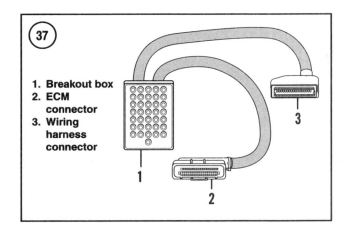

1. Breakout box
2. ECM connector
3. Wiring harness connector

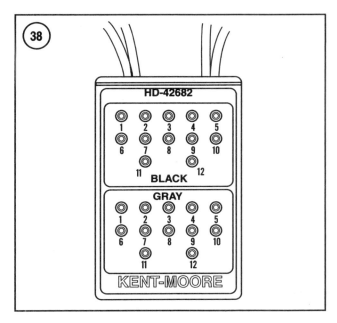

A number of aftermarket devices are available; however, we did not test them nor are the procedures written for their use. The wiring checks can be made performed with commercial pin connectors that connect to terminals and VOM meter leads. Use caution to prevent damage to the connectors.

Data Link Connector

The data link connector provides access to the data bus and provides a testing terminal when troubleshooting. Pull straight out and remove the electrical caddy cover (**Figure 16**). Slide the data link connector (A, **Figure 39**) forward and release it from the mounting bracket. Remove the cover (B, **Figure 39**) from the data link connector.

DTC Troubleshooting

NOTE
*The DTC flowcharts (**Figures 40-165**) are located on the CD inserted into the back cover of the manual.*

A list of DTCs is found in **Table 3** at the end of this chapter. The table identifies the possible problem and the related diagnostic flowchart for each DTC. Refer to the applicable DTC flowchart in **Figures 40—165** and perform the indicated procedures. Note the following before beginning troubleshooting:

1. Before retrieving DTCs, read the information in *Initial Diagnosis* (this section).
2. Not all malfunctions set a DTC. If the motorcycle is not operating properly and no DTC has been set, refer to **Table 4**. Select the symptom that best describes the problem, and turn to the indicated diagnostic flowchart.
3. Check for obvious causes before undertaking what may be a complicated troubleshooting procedure. Look for loose or disconnected connectors, damaged wiring, etc.
4. The DTCs are prioritized according to importance based upon the particular DTC and the device (ICM or ECM, speedometer or TSM/TSSM/HFSM) where that DTC is stored. It is possible for one fault to trigger more than one DTC. If multiple DTCs occur, turn to **Table 5** to determine which code has the highest priority, and troubleshoot that code first.
5. Refer to the wiring diagrams located on the CD inserted into the back cover of this manual to identify connectors referred to in the charts. Refer to the appropriate sections in this chapter and Chapter Nine for additional component testing.

No-DTC fault

Some malfunctions, such as fuel and starting system problems, will not trigger the generation of a DTC. In those cases, the troubleshooting guidelines found in this chapter will serve to locate the problem. However, there are faults that can be diagnosed using the procedures implemented when diagnosing a DTC. The following faults may not generate a DTC, but the specified flow chart will help identify the problem. Refer to **Table 4** for a list of symptoms that do not set fault codes.

Speedometer DTC Display Inspection

Because the speedometer displays the DTCs, it may be necessary to troubleshoot it before initiating a diagnostic sequence. Check speedometer operation as described in this section, and then follow the *Initial Diagnostic Check* flowchart (**Figure 40**).

> *NOTE*
> *Be sure the engine stop/run switch is in the RUN position.*

Check the speedometer as follows:

1. During normal operation, when the ignition key is turned to IGN, the speedometer should operate as follows:
   a. The speedometer backlighting comes on.

> *NOTE*
> *The security symbol may come on even though the motorcycle is not equipped with a security system.*

   b. The check engine and security symbols illuminate.
   c. The odometer display illuminates.
2. If the speedometer operates abnormally, perform a WOW test (this section). Then, refer to **Figure 41** and follow the *Speedometer Self-Diagnosis* DTC flow chart.

WOW Test

To ensure the speedometer is functioning correctly, perform the following procedure:
1. Push in the odometer reset button on the back of the speedometer.
2. Turn the ignition switch to IGN, and release the odometer reset switch. Check for the following:
   a. The speedometer backlighting should come on.
   b. The speedometer needle should rotate to the full deflection position.

> *NOTE*
> *The security symbol may come on even though the motorcycle is not equipped with a security system.*

   c. The check engine, battery and security symbols should illuminate.
   d. The message *diag* should appear in the odometer window on the speedometer.
3. If the speedometer fails this test, check the wiring for battery, ground, ignition, odometer reset switch and accessories.

FIGURES 40-165 CONTAINING DTC FLOWCHARTS LOCATED ON CD INSERTED INTO BACK COVER OF MANUAL.

Table 1 ELECTRICAL SYSTEM SPECIFICATIONS

Item	Specification
Current draw	
ECM	1.0 milliamperes
Speedometer	
2006-2007 models	0.5 milliamperes
2008-2011 models	1.0 milliamperes
Starter	
Loaded	160-200 amperes
Free-running	90 amperes
Maximum	250 amperes
Tachometer	
2006-2007 models	0.5 milliamperes
2008-2011 models	1.0 milliamperes
TSM (non-security models)	
2006-2007 models	0.5 milliamperes
2008-2011 models	1.0 milliamperes
TSSM/HFSM—disarmed	
2006, 2010-2011 models	3.0 milliamperes
2007 models	0.1 milliamperes
2008-2009 models	1.0 milliamperes
TSSM/HFSM—armed	
2006, 2010-2011 models	3.0 milliamperes
2007 models	0.6 milliamperes
2008-2009 models	1.0 milliamperes
TSSM/HSFM—storage mode	
2006 models	0.5 milliamperes
2007-2011 models	0.1 milliamperes
HFSM	1.0 milliamperes
Security siren—optional	20.0 milliamperes
Voltage regulator	2.0 milliamperes
2006-2007 models	0.5 milliamperes
2008-2011 models	1.0 milliamperes
(continued)	

Table 1 ELECTRICAL SYSTEM SPECIFICATIONS (continued)

Item	Specification
Alternator AC voltage output	
2006 models	16-20 VAC per 1000 rpm
2007-2011 models	16-23 VAC per 1000 rpm
Ignition coil resistance (2006-2009 models)	
Primary resistance	0.5-0.7 ohm
Secondary resistance	5500-7500 ohms
Ignition coil resistance (2010-2011 models)	
Primary resistance	0.3-0.5 ohm
Secondary resistance	3500-4500 ohms
Spark plug wire resistance	
Front cylinder	
2006-2009 models	4750-11,230
2010-2011 models	5475-14,941
Rear cylinder	
2006-2009 models	1812-4375
2010-2011 models	1813-5003
ET sensor (2006-2009)*	
-4° F (-20° C)	28,144 ohms, 4.4 volts
14° F (-10° C)	15,873 ohms, 4.0 volts
32° F (0° C)	9255 ohms, 3.5 volts
50° F (10° C)	5571 ohms, 3.0 volts
68° F (20° C)	3457 ohms, 2.4 volts
77° F (25° C)	2750 ohms, 2.1 volts
86° F (30° C)	2205 ohms, 1.8 volts
104° F (40° C)	1442 ohms, 1.3 or 4.1 volts
122° F (50° C)	965 ohms, 1.0 or 3.7 volts
140° F (60° C)	661 ohms, 3.3 volts
158° F (70° C)	462 ohms, 2.9 volts
176° F (80° C)	329 ohms, 2.5 volts
194° F (90° C)	238 ohms, 2.1 volts
212° F (100° C)	175 ohms, 1.7 volts
IAT sensor (2006-2008 models)	
-4° F (-20° C)	29,121 ohms, 4.9 volts
14° F (-10° C)	16,599 ohms, 4.8 volts
32° F (0° C)	9750 ohms, 4.6 volts
50° F (10° C)	5970 ohms, 4.3, volts
68° F (20° C)	3747 ohms, 4.0 volts
77° F (25° C)	3000 ohms, 3.8 volts
86° F (30° C)	2417 ohms, 3.6 volts
104° F (40° C)	1598 ohms, 3.1 volts
122° F (50° C)	1080 ohms, 2.6 volts
140° F (60° C)	746 ohms, 2.2 volts
158° F (70° C)	526 ohms, 1.7 volts
176° F (80° C)	377 ohms, 1.4 volts
194° F (90° C)	275 ohms, 1.1 volts
212° F (100° C)	204 ohms, 0.9 volts
IAT sensor (2009 models)*	
-4° F (-20° C)	28,582 ohms, 4.9 volts
14° F (-10° C)	16,120 ohms, 4.8 volts
32° F (0° C)	9399 ohms, 4.6 volts
50° F (10° C)	5658 ohms, 4.3, volts
68° F (20° C)	3511 ohms, 4.0 volts
77° F (25° C)	2795 ohms, 3.8 volts
86° F (30° C)	2240 ohms, 3.5 volts
104° F (40° C)	1465 ohms, 3.0 volts
122° F (50° C)	980 ohms, 2.5 volts
140° F (60° C)	671 ohms, 2.0 volts
158° F (70° C)	469 ohms, 1.6 volts
176° F (80° C)	334 ohms, 1.3 volts
194° F (90° C)	241.8 ohms, 1.0 volts
212° F (100° C)	178 ohms, 0.8 volts

*The manufacturer does not provide service information for 2010-2011 models.

2

Table 2 TYPICAL ENGINE SCAN VALUES

Item	Minimum value	Maximum value	Hot idle
MAP sensor	3 in. Hg (10 kPa)	31 in. Hg (104 kPa)	10-13 in. Hg (35-45 kPa)
	0 volts	5.1 volts	–
TP sensor	0%	100%	0%
	0.2 volts	4.5 volts	0.2-1.0 volts
IAC pintle	0	155	20-50 steps
RPM	800	5600	1000
ECT sensor	3° F (-16° C)	464° F (240° C)	230-300° F (110-150° C)
	0 volts	5.0 volts	0.5-1.5 volts
IAT sensor	3° F (-16° C)	248° F (120° C)	104-140° F (40-60° C)
	0 volts	5.1 volts	2.2-3.5 volts
Front injector pulse width	0	50 millisecond	2-4 millisecond
Rear injector pulse width	0	50 millisecond	2-4 millisecond
Ignition timing			
Advance-front cylinder	0	50°	10-15°
Advance-rear cylinder	0	50°	10-15°
VSS	0	6 volts	0 mph
Battery voltage	10 volts	15 volts	13.4 volts
Idle speed	800	1250	1000

Table 3 DIAGNOSTIC TROUBLE CODES

DTC	Problem	Diagnostic Flow Chart
BUS Er	Serial data bus fault	Figures 61-63
B0563	Battery voltage high	Replace the TSM/TSSM/HFSM[1]
B1004	Fuel level sending unit low (2006-2011 models)	Figures 46-48
B1005	Fuel level sending unit high/open (2006-2011 models)	Figures 49-51
B1006	Accessory line over voltage	Figure 52
B1007	Ignition line over voltage	Figure 52
B1008	Odometer reset switch closed	Figure 53
B1121	Left turn signal output fault; (2006-2011 models)	
	Left turn signal open circuit	Figures 71-74, Figures 76-77
B1122	Right turn signal output fault; (2006-2011 models)	
	Right turn signal open circuit	Figures 71-74, Figures 76-77
B1121, B1122	Turn signal short to ground (2010-2011 TSM/TSSM models)	Figure 78
B1123	Left or right turn signal short to ground	Figures 79-80
B1124	Left or right turn signal short to ground	Figures 79-80
B1125	Left or right turn signal short to voltage (2006-2011 models)	Figures 81-82
B1126	Left or right turn signal short to voltage (2006-2011 models)	Figures 81-82
B1131, B1132	Alarm output low or high (2006-2009 models)	Figure 83
B1131	Alarm output low (2010-2011 models)	Figure 84
B1132	Alarm output high (2010-2011 models)	Figure 85
B1134	Starter output high	Figure 86
B1141	Turn signal will not flash, 4-way flashers inoperable (2006-2011 models)	Figures 71-72, Figure 75
B1142	Internal fault	Replace the HFSM[1]
B1143	Security antenna short to ground	Figure 87
B1144	Security antenna short to voltage (HFSM models)	Figure 88
B1145	Security antenna open (2006-2009 HFSM models)	Figure 89
B1145	Security antenna open (2010-2011 HFSM models)	Figure 90
B1154	Clutch switch short to ground (2007-2011 models)	Figure 91
B1155	Neutral switch short to ground (2007-2011 models)	Figure 92
P0107, P0108	MAP sensor error, failed open/low or high (2006-2009 models)	Figure 97
P0107	MAP sensor open/shorted to ground (2010-2011 models)	Figure 98
P0108	MAP sensor high (2010-2011 models)	Figure 99
P0112	IAT sensor voltage low (2006-2011 models)	Figures 126-127
P0113	IAT sensor open/high (2006-2011 models)	Figure 126, Figure 128
P0117	ET sensor voltage low (2006-2011 models)	Figures 129-130
P0118	ET sensor open/high (2006-2011 models)	Figure 129, Figure 131
P0122	TP sensor open/low (2006-2011 models)	Figures 132-133
P0123	TP sensor high (2006-2011 models)	Figure 132, Figure 134
P0131	Front O2 sensor low or engine running lean (2006-2009 models)	Figure 138
P0131, P0151	Front O2 sensor low or engine running lean (2010-2011 models)	Figure 139
P0132	Engine running rich (2006-2009 models)	Figure 138
P0132, P0152	Engine running rich (2010-2011 models)	Figure 141
P0134	Front O2 sensor open/not responding/high (2006-2009 models)	Figure 138

(continued)

Table 3 DIAGNOSTIC TROUBLE CODES (continued)

DTC	Problem	Diagnostic Flow Chart
P0134, P0154	Sensor open/not responding/high (2010-2011 models)	Figure 140
P0151	Rear O2 sensor low or engine running lean (2006-2009 models)	Figure 138
P0152	Engine running lean or rich (2006-2009 models)	Figure 138
P0154	Rear O2 sensor open/not responding/high (2006-2009 models)	Figure 138
P0261	Front fuel injector open/low (2006-2009 models)	Figure 135
P0261, P0263	Fuel injectors open/low (2010-2011 models)	Figure 136
P0262	Front fuel injector high (2006-2009 models)	Figure 135
P0262, P0264	Fuel injectors high (2010-2011 models)	Figure 137
P0263	Rear fuel injector open/low (2006-2009 models)	Figure 135
P0264	Rear fuel injector high (2006-2009 models)	Figure 135
P0373	CKP sensor intermittent (2006-2009 models)	Figure 100
P0374	CKP sensor synchronize error (2006-2009 models)	Figure 100
P0373, P0374	CKP sensor intermittent or synchronize error (2010-2011 models)	Figure 101
P0501	VSS sensor low or high (2006-2009 models)	Figure 102
P0501	VSS sensor low (2010-2011 models)	Figure 103
P0502	VSS sensor high/open (2006-2009 models)	Figure 102
P0502	VSS sensor high (2010-2011 models)	Figure 104
P0505	Loss of idle speed control (2006-2009 models)	Figure 121
P0505	Loss of idle speed control (2010-2011 models)	Figure 122
P0562, P0563	Battery voltage low or high (2006-2009 models)	Figure 105
P0562, P0563	Battery voltage low or high (2010-2011 models)	Figure 106
P0603	EE-PROM error	Replace the ECM[1]
P0605	Flash memory error	Replace the ECM[1]
P0661	Active intake solenoid open/low (2006-2009 HDI models)	Figure 142
P0662	Active intake solenoid high/shorted (2006-2009 HDI models)	Figure 142
P0661, P0662	Active intake solenoid open/low or high/shorted (2010-2011 HDI models)	Figure 143
P1001	System relay coil open/low (2006-2009 models)	Figure 114
P1001, P1002	System relay coil open/low, high/shorted (2010-2011 models)	Figure 115
P1002	System relay coil high/shorted (2006-2009 models)	Figure 117
P1003	System relay contacts open (2006-2009 models)	Figure 114
P1003	System relay contacts open (2010-2011 models)	Figure 116
P1004	System relay contacts closed (2006-2009 models)	Figure 118
P1004	System relay contacts closed (2010-2011 models)	Figure 119
P1009, P1010	Incorrect or missing password (2006-2009 models)	Figure 107
P1009, P1010	Incorrect password (2010-2011 models)	Figure 108
P1351	Front ignition coil open/low (2006-2009 models)	Figure 109
P1352	Front ignition coil high/shorted (2006-2009 models)	Figure 109
P1354	Rear ignition coil open/low (2006-2009 models)	Figure 109
P1355	Rear ignition coil high/shorted (2006-2009 models)	Figure 109
P1351, P1354	Ignition coil open/low (2010-2011 models)	Figure 110
P1352, P1355	Ignition coil high/shorted (2010-2011 models)	Figure 111
P1353, P1356	Combustion absent (2006-2011 models)	Figures 123-124
P1357, P1358	Combustion intermittent (2006-2011 models)	Figure 123, Figure 125
P1475	Exhaust actuator position error (2007-2009 models)	Figure 144
P1477	Exhaust actuator open/low (2007-2009 models)	Figure 144
P1478	Exhaust actuator high (2007-2009 models)	Figure 144
P1475	Exhaust actuator position failure (2010-2011 HDI models)	Figure 145
P1477	Exhaust actuator open/low (2010-2011 HDI models)	Figure 146
P1478	Exhaust actuator high (2010-2011 HDI models)	Figure 147
P1501	Jiffy stand sensor low (2008-2009 HDI models)	Figure 149
P1501	Jiffy stand sensor low (2010-2011 HDI models)	Figure 150
P1502	Jiffy stand sensor high (2008-2009 HDI models)	Figure 151
P1502	Jiffy stand sensor high (2010-2011 HDI models)	Figure 152
U1016	Loss of ECM serial data (2006-2009 models)	Figure 54
U1016	Loss of ECM serial data (2010-2011 models)	Figure 55
U1064, U1255	Loss of TSM/TSSM/HFSM serial data (2006-2009 models)	Figure 56
U1064, U1255	Loss of TSM/TSSM/HFSM serial data or data error (2010-2011 models)	Figure 57
U1097	Loss of speedometer serial data (2006 models)	Figure 58
U1097	Loss of speedometer serial data (2007-2009 models)	Figure 59
U1097, U1255	Loss of speedometer serial data or error (2010-2011 models)	Figure 60
U1255	ECM serial data error/missing (2006-2009 models)	Figure 54, Figures 58-59
U1300, U1301	Engine starts then stalls (2006-2007 models)	Figure 61
U1300, U1301	Engine starts then stalls (2008-2009 models)	Figure 62
U1300, U1301	Engine starts then stalls (2010-2011 models)	Figure 63

1. The code indicates a failure that requires replacement of this device.

Table 4 SYMPTOMS THAT DO NOT SET DTC CODES

Item	Diagnostic Flow Chart
ACR Diagnostics (on models so equipped)	Figure 164, Figure 165
Charging system test: battery discharged	Figure 153
Engine cranks but will not start	Figure 96
Fuel pressure check	Figure 120
Fuel system electrical test	Figure 112, Figure113
HFSM fails to disarm (HFSM Models only)	Figure 67
High beam or turn signal indicator does not function	Figure 44, Figure 45
Initial diagnostic check	Figure 40
Misfire at idle or under load	Figure 95
No ECM power	Figure 93, Figure 94
Oil pressure or neutral indicator does not function	Figure 42, Figure 43
Security lamp on continuously (2006 models)	Figure 65
Security symbol does not light when ignition key is turned on (2006 models)	Figure 64
SidE StAnd displayed in odometer (2008-2011 HDI models)	Figure 148
Speedometer self diagnosis	Figure 41
Starter Test 1: initial test	Figure 154
Starter Test 2: solenoid clicks	Figure 155
Starter Test 3: relay clicks	Figure 156
Starter Test 4: nothing clicks	Figures 157-160
Starter Test 5: starter spins, but does not engage	Figures 161
Starter Test 6: starter stalls or spins too slowly	Figure 162
Tachometer inoperative (on models so equipped)	Figure 163
Turn signals cancel erratically or do not cancel upon completion of a turn	Figures 68, Figure 69
Turn signals flash at double normal rate; all bulbs work.	Figure 70
Weak or no key fob signal to TSM/TSSM/HFSM (2006 models)	Figure 66

Table 5 MULTIPLE DTC PRIORITY

Ranking	Speedometer	TSM	TSSM/HFSM	ECM
1	BUS Er	BUS Er	U1300	P0605
2	U1300	U1300	U1301	P0603
3	U1301	U1301	U1016	BUS Er
4	U1016	U1016	U1255	U1300 (ECM serial data low)
5	U1064	–	B1142	U1301 (ECM serial data open/high)
6	U1255	U1255	–	U1300 (TSM/TSSM/ HFSM serial data low)
7	B1007	–	–	U1301 (ignition line over voltage, serial data open/high)
8	B1006	–	B1154	U1300 (Speedometer serial data low)
9	B1008	–	B1154	U1301 (Speedometer serial data open/high)
10	B1004	–	B1134	U1064 (Loss of TSM/TSSM/ HFSM serial data at ECM)
11	B1005	B1134	B1121	U1064 (Loss of TSM/TSSM/ HFSM serial data at speedometer)
12		B1121	B1122	U1016
13		B1122	B1123	U1097
14		–	B1124	U1255 (Missing response at TSSM/HFSM)
5		B1131	B1125	U1255 (Missing response at speedometer)
16		B1132	B1126	P1003
17		B1141	B1143	P1002
18			B1144	P1001
19			B1145	P1004
20			–	P1009

(continued)

Table 5 MULTIPLE DTC PRIORITY (continued)

Ranking	Speedometer	TSM	TSSM/HFSM	ECM
21			B1131	P1010
22			B1132	P0373
23			B1141	P0374
24				P0122
25				P0123
26				P0107
27				P0108
28				P1501
29				P1502
30				P0117
31				P0118
32				P0112
33				P0113
34				P1351
35				P1354
36				P1352
37				P1355
38				P1357
39				P1358
40				P0261
41				P0263
42				P0262
43				P0264
44				P0562
45				P0563
46				P0501
47				P0502
48				P1353
49				P0505
50				P1475
51				P1477
52				P1478
53				P0661
54				P0662
55				P0131
56				P0151
57				P0132
58				P0152
59				P0134
60				P0154

Table 6 DEVICE PART NUMBERS

Device	2006	2007	2008	2009	2010-2011
TSM/HFSM	68921-01C	68920-07	68920-07	68920-07	68921-07
TSSM (HDI)					
Japan	68924-00C	68924-07	68924-07	68922-07	68922-07
Other than Japan		68922-07	68922-07	68924-07	68925-07
Remote control fob					
Japan	68926-00	68926-07	68926-07	68926-07	68926-07
Other than Japan	–	–	–	–	68939-007
Remote control fob (HDI)	68927-00	68926-07	68939-00	68939-00	–
Security system	68922-00C	68922-07	68924-07	68926-07	68956-07
Siren (HDI) 2006-2009	68958-00	68958-00	68958-07A	68958-07A	
2010	–	–	–	–	68958-07B
2011	–	–	–	–	68958-07C
ECM					
2006-2009	32534-05A	32534-05B	34246-08	34246-08A	–
2010	–	–	–	–	32534-05C
2011	–	–	–	–	32534-11

CHAPTER THREE

LUBRICATION, MAINTENANCE AND TUNE-UP

This chapter covers lubrication, maintenance and tune-up procedures. If a procedure requires more than minor disassembly, a reference is given to the appropriate chapter. Maintenance intervals, capacities, recommendations and specifications are in **Tables 1-7** at the end of this chapter.

Performing periodic inspections and maintenance maximizes the service life, safety and performance of the motorcycle. Minor problems found during routine service can be corrected before they develop into major ones.

Consider the maintenance schedule a guide. If the motorcycle is ridden harder than normal or exposed to mud, water or high humidity; perform most of these maintenance items more frequently than indicated.

> *NOTE*
> *On models with an optional security siren, disarm the security system (TSSM/HFSM) before disconnecting the battery or before pulling the Maxi-Fuse so the siren will not sound. Refer to **Turn Signal and Security Module** in Chapter Nine.*

PRE-RIDE INSPECTION

1. Check wheel and tire condition. Check tire pressure. Refer to *Tires and Wheels* (this chapter).
2. Make sure all lights work.
3. Check engine for oil leakage. If necessary, add oil as described in this chapter.
4. On models so equipped, check brake and clutch fluid level and condition. If necessary, add fluid as described in this chapter.
5. Check the operation of the front and rear brakes.
6. Check clutch operation. If necessary, adjust the clutch cable as described in this chapter. On models with hydraulic clutch, if necessary, bleed the system as described in Chapter Six.
7. Check the throttle operation. The throttle should move smoothly and return quickly when released. If necessary, adjust throttle cable free play as described in this chapter.
8. Inspect the front and rear suspension. They should have a solid feel with no looseness.
9. Check the exhaust system for leaks or damage.
10. Inspect the fuel system for leakage.
11. Check drive belt tension as described in this chapter.
12. Turn the ignition switch on, and check the following:
    a. Pull the front brake lever in and make sure the brake light works.
    b. Push the rear brake pedal down and check that the brake light comes on soon after the pedal has been depressed.
    c. Make sure the headlight (high and low beam) and taillight both work.

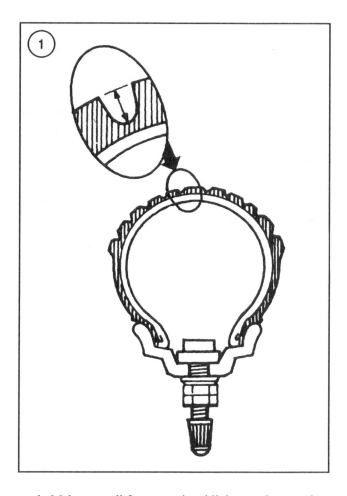

3

d. Make sure all four turn signal lights work properly.
e. Make sure all accessory lights work properly, if so equipped.
f. Check horn operation.

TIRES AND WHEELS

Tire Pressure

Check the tire pressure often to maintain tire performance and prevent unnecessary tire wear.

Refer to **Table 2** for original equipment tire pressure.

Tire Inspection

Inspect the tires periodically for excessive wear, deep cuts and imbedded objects such as stones or nails. If a nail or other object is found in a tire, mark its location with a light crayon prior to removing it. This will help locate the hole for repair.

Measure the tread depth (**Figure 1**) with a gauge or a small ruler. As a guideline, replace tires when the tread wear indicator bars appear on the tread surface and when the tread depth is 1/32 in. (0. 8 mm.) or less. Locate the arrows on the sidewall indicating the location of the tread wear indicators. Refer to Chapter Ten for tire changing and repair information.

Spoke Tension

Check the laced wheels for loose or damaged spokes, on models so equipped. Refer to Chapter Ten for laced wheel service.

Rim Inspection

On both cast and laced wheels, check the wheel rims for cracks and other damage. If damaged, a rim can make the motorcycle handle poorly. Refer to Chapter Ten for wheel service.

SCREAMIN' EAGLE AND CVO MODEL LUBRICANTS

Screamin' Eagle and CVO models use H-D Screamin' Eagle SYN3 synthetic motorcycle lubricant for the engine, transmission and primary chaincase. If additional oil must be added to correct oil level, and SYN3 oil is not available, *temporarily* add HD-360 motor oil. Although both types of lubricant are compatible, it is recommended that the lubricant be changed as soon as possible. If Screamin' Eagle SYN3 is not going to be used permanently, drain the engine, transmission or primary chaincase oil and use the oil recommended in **Table 4** or **Table 5** (this chapter).

ENGINE OIL AND FILTER

Engine Oil Level Check

Check the engine oil level using the dipstick/oil filler cap located in the transmission/oil tank case cover.

> *NOTE*
> *Oil level cannot be accurately measured on a cold engine. Do not add oil to bring the oil level to the FULL HOT mark on the dipstick on a cold engine. For the best results, perform the Cold Check, followed by the Hot Check.*

Cold check

1. Place the motorcycle on a level surface and park it on its jiffy stand.
2. Wipe the area around the oil filler cap with a clean rag. Unscrew the oil filler cap/dipstick (**Figure 2**) from the transmission case. Wipe the dipstick off with a clean rag, reinsert the oil filler cap/dipstick into the fill spout, and tighten completely.
3. Unscrew and withdraw the oil filler cap/dipstick again and check the oil level on the dipstick. The oil level should be between the two arrows (ADD QUART and FULL HOT) on the dipstick (**Figure 3**). If the oil level is below the lower arrow (ADD QUART) mark, add just enough of

the recommended oil (**Table 4**) to bring the level *between the two arrows*.

4. Check the O-ring (**Figure 4**) for cracks or other damage. Replace the O-ring if necessary.

5. Reinstall the oil filler cap/dipstick into the fill spout and tighten completely.

6. Perform *Hot Check* (this section).

Hot check

1. Ride the motorcycle until engine is at normal operating temperature.

> *CAUTION*
> *Holding the motorcycle straight up will result in an incorrect oil level reading.*

2. Place the motorcycle on a level surface and park it on the jiffy stand. Allow the engine to idle for 1-2 minutes, and then turn off the engine.

3. Wipe the area around the oil filler cap with a clean rag. Unscrew the oil filler cap/dipstick (**Figure 2**) from the transmission case. Wipe the dipstick off with a clean rag, reinsert the oil filler cap/dipstick into the fill spout, and tighten completely.

4. Unscrew and withdraw the oil filler cap/dipstick again and check the oil level on the dipstick. The oil level should be at the FULL HOT mark on the dipstick (**Figure 3**). If the oil level is below the FULL HOT mark, adjust the oil level as described in this section.

5. To correct the oil level, add the recommended engine oil (**Table 4**) to bring the oil to the FULL HOT mark on the dipstick.

6. Check the O-ring (**Figure 4**) for cracks or other damage. Replace the O-ring if necessary.

7. Reinstall the oil filler cap/dipstick into the fill spout and tighten completely.

Oil and Filter Change

Regular oil and filter changes will contribute more to engine longevity than any other maintenance performed. **Table 1** lists the recommended oil and filter change interval. This assumes that the motorcycle is operated in moderate climates. If the motorcycle is operated under dusty conditions, the oil becomes contaminated more quickly and should be changed more frequently.

Use a motorcycle oil with an API classification of *SF* or *SG*. The classification is printed on the container. Always try to use the same brand of oil at each change. Refer to **Table 4** for correct oil viscosity to use under anticipated ambient temperatures, not engine oil temperature. Using oil additives is not recommended as they may cause clutch slippage.

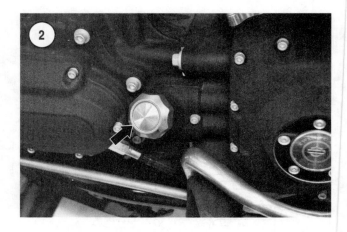

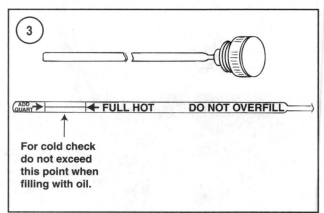

For cold check do not exceed this point when filling with oil.

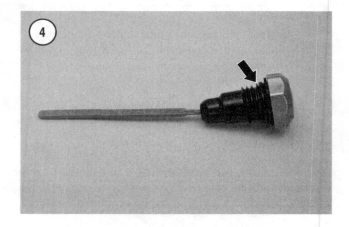

> *WARNING*
> *Contact with oil may cause skin cancer. Wash oil from hands with soap and water as soon as possible after handling engine oil.*

> *CAUTION*
> *Do not use SH and SJ automotive oils in motorcycle engines. Automotive oils may contain friction modifiers that reduce frictional losses on engine components. Specifically-designed for automotive engines, these oils can cause damage to motorcycle engines and clutches.*

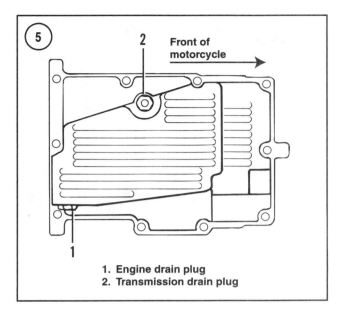

1. Engine drain plug
2. Transmission drain plug

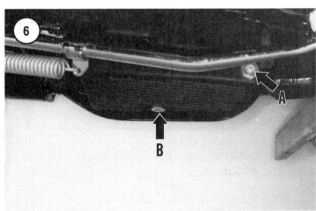

NOTE
Never dispose of motor oil in the trash, on the ground or down a storm drain. Many service stations and oil retailers will accept used oil for recycling.

1. Ride the motorcycle until engine is at normal operating temperature.

2. Turn off the engine and allow the oil to settle in oil pan. Support the motorcycle on level ground on a swing arm stand.

3. Wipe the area around the oil filler cap with a clean rag. Unscrew the oil filler cap/dipstick (**Figure 2**) from the transmission case.

NOTE
*The transmission/oil pan is equipped with two drain plugs. Only remove the engine oil drain plug (1, **Figure 5**). Do not remove the transmission drain plug (2, **Figure 5**).*

4. Place a drain pan underneath the oil pan. Remove the engine oil drain plug and O-ring (A, **Figure 6**) from the side of oil pan.
5. Allow the oil to drain completely.
6. To replace the oil filter (**Figure 7**), perform the following:
   a. Temporarily install the O-ring and drain bolt and finger-tighten the bolt. Then, move the drain pan underneath the oil filter. Place a shop cloth under the oil filter to catch any residual oil after the filter is removed.
   b. Install a socket-type oil filter wrench squarely over the oil filter (**Figure 7**) and loosen it *counterclockwise*. Quickly remove the oil filter as oil will begin to run out.
   c. Position the oil filter so the open end faces up.
   d. Turn the filter over the drain pan and pour out the remaining oil. Place the filter in a plastic bag, seal it and dispose of it properly.
   e. Remove the shop cloth and dispose of it properly. Wipe off all spilled oil from the surrounding area.
   f. Coat the new oil filter gasket with clean engine oil.

CAUTION
Tighten the oil filter by hand. Do not over-tighten.

   g. Screw the oil filter onto its mount by hand and tighten until the filter gasket just touches the sealing surface. Then, tighten the filter by hand an additional 1/2 to 3/4 turn.

7. Install a *new* O-ring (**Figure 8**) onto the engine oil drain plug.

8. Lubricate the O-ring with clean engine oil before installing it. Install the O-ring and drain plug. Tighten the drain plug to 14-21 ft.-lb. (19.0-28.5 N•m).

9. While the engine is drained of oil, inspect the pipe plug at the front right side of the crankcase for leakage. If leakage has occurred, remove the pipe plug, clean the threads thoroughly in solvent and dry. Apply Loctite Pipe Sealant, or an equivalent, to the threads. Then, reinstall the pipe plug, and tighten it securely.

10. Add the correct viscosity (**Table 4**) and quantity (**Table 3**) of oil into the oil pan.

11. Reinstall the oil filler cap/dipstick and tighten completely into the fill spout.

NOTE
*After oil has been added, the oil level will register above the FULL HOT dipstick mark (**Figure 3**) until the engine runs and the filter fills with oil. To obtain a correct reading after adding oil and installing a new oil filter, continue with the procedure.*

12. After changing the engine oil and filter, check the oil level as follows:
   a. Start and run the engine for 1 minute. Then, shut it off.
   b. Check the oil level on the dipstick as described in this section.
   c. If the oil level is correct, it will register in the dipstick's safe operating level range. If so, *do not* top off or add oil to bring it to the FULL HOT level on the dipstick.
   d. Ride the motorcycle until engine is at normal operating temperature.
   e. Place the motorcycle on a level surface and park it on its jiffy stand. Allow the engine to idle for 1-2 minutes. Turn off the engine and recheck the oil level; adjust if necessary.

13. Check the oil filter and drain plug for leaks.

14. Dispose the used oil properly.

TRANSMISSION OIL

Oil Level Check

Table 1 lists the recommended transmission oil level inspection intervals. When checking the transmission oil level, do not allow any dirt or debris to enter the transmission case opening.

WARNING
Contact with oil may cause skin cancer. Wash oil from hands with soap and water as soon as possible after handling transmission oil.

1. Ride the motorcycle for approximately 10 minutes and shift through all gears until the transmission oil has reached normal operating temperature. Turn the engine off

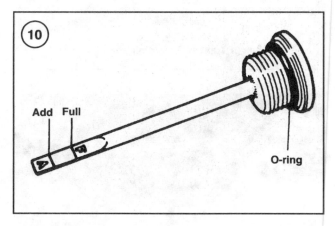

and allow the oil to settle. Park the motorcycle on a level surface on the jiffy stand.

CAUTION
Do not check the oil level with the motorcycle supported on its jiffy stand or the reading will be incorrect.

2. Clean the area around the transmission filler cap/dipstick (**Figure 9**) on top of the transmission case and unscrew it.

3. Wipe the dipstick and reinsert it back into the clutch release cover housing, or transmission case; do not screw the cap/dipstick into place. Rest it on the opening and then withdraw it. The oil level is correct when it registers between the two dipstick marks (**Figure 10**).

CAUTION
*Do not add engine oil. Add only the recommended type of transmission oil (**Table 5**).*

4. If the oil level is low, add the recommended type of H-D Transmission Oil, or equivalent (**Table 5**). Do not overfill.

5. Inspect the filler cap O-ring. Replace it if worn or damaged.

6. Install the transmission oil filler cap/dipstick and tighten it to 25-75 in.-lb. (2.8-8.5 N•m).

7. Wipe any spilled oil off the clutch release cover housing or transmission case.

Oil Change

Table 1 lists the recommended transmission oil change intervals.

1. Ride the motorcycle for approximately 10 minutes and shift through all gears until the transmission oil has reached normal operating temperature. Turn off the engine and allow the oil to settle in the tank. Park the motorcycle on a level surface and have an assistant support it in an upright position.

2. Clean the area around the transmission filler cap/dipstick (**Figure 9**) on top of the transmission case and unscrew it.

NOTE
*The oil pan is equipped with two drain plugs. Make sure to remove the transmission oil drain plug (2, **Figure 5**) and not the engine oil drain plug (1).*

3. Place a drain pan underneath the transmission/oil pan. Loosen and remove the transmission oil drain plug and O-ring (B, **Figure 6**) from the lower flat portion of the oil pan.

4. Check the drain plug O-ring (**Figure 8**) for damage and replace if necessary.

5. The drain plug is magnetic. Check the plug for metal debris that may indicate transmission damage, and wipe the plug off. Replace the plug if damaged.

6. Install the transmission drain plug (B, **Figure 6**) and O-ring. Tighten the drain plug to 14-21 ft.-lb. (19.0-28.5 N•m).

CAUTION
*Do not add engine oil. Add only the recommended type of transmission oil (**Table 5**). Make sure to add the oil to the correct oil filler hole.*

7. Refill the transmission through the oil filler cap/dipstick hole with the recommended quantity (**Table 3**) and type (**Table 5**) of transmission oil.

8. Install the oil filler cap/dipstick and tighten it to 25-75 in.-lb. (2.8-8.5 N•m).

9. Wipe any spilled oil off the clutch release cover housing or transmission case.

10. Dispose the used oil properly.

11. Ride the motorcycle until the transmission oil reaches normal operating temperature. Then, shut the engine off.

12. Check the transmission oil drain plug for leaks.

13. Check the transmission oil level as described in this section. Readjust the level if necessary.

PRIMARY CHAINCASE OIL

Oil Level Check

The primary chaincase oil lubricates the clutch, primary chain and sprockets. **Table 1** lists the intervals for checking the primary chaincase oil level. When checking the primary chaincase oil level, do not allow any dirt or debris to enter the housing.

CAUTION
Do not check the oil level with the motorcycle supported on its jiffy stand. The reading will be incorrect.

1. Ride the motorcycle for approximately 10 minutes and shift through all gears until the primary chaincase oil has reached normal operating temperature. Turn off the engine and allow the oil to settle in the case. Park the motorcycle on a level surface and have an assistant support it in an upright position. Do not support it on the jiffy stand.

2. Remove the Torx (T27) screws securing the clutch inspection cover (**Figure 11**) and seal ring. Then, remove the cover.

3. The oil level is correct when it is even with the bottom of the clutch opening (**Figure 12**) or at the bottom of the clutch diaphragm spring.

CAUTION
*Do not add engine oil. Add only the recommended type of primary chaincase lubricant (**Table 5**).*

4. If necessary, add H-D Primary Chaincase Lubricant, or equivalent, through the opening (**Figure 13**) to correct the level.

5. Refer to *Oil Change* (this section) to install the seal ring and inspection cover.

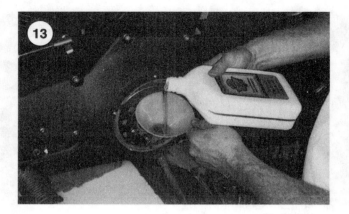

6. Install the clutch inspection cover seal ring (**Figure 14**) onto the primary chaincase cover.

7. Install the clutch inspection cover and tighten the screws to 84-108 in.-lb. (9.5-12.2 N•m).

Oil Change

Table 1 lists the recommended primary chaincase lubricant replacement intervals.

1. Ride the motorcycle for approximately 10 minutes and shift through all gears until the primary chaincase oil has reached normal operating temperature. Turn off the engine and allow the oil to settle in the case. Park the motorcycle on a level surface.

2. Place a drain pan under the chaincase and remove the drain plug (**Figure 15**).

3. Allow the oil to drain for at least 10 minutes.

4. The drain plug is magnetic. Check the plug for metal debris that may indicate drive component or clutch damage, and then wipe the plug off. Replace the plug if damaged.

5. Reinstall the drain plug. On 2006 models, tighten to 36-60 in.lb. (4.1-6.8 N•m). On 2007-on models, tighten to 14-21 ft.-lb. (19.0-28.5 N•m).

6. Remove the Torx (T27) screws securing the clutch inspection cover (**Figure 11**) and seal ring, and then remove the cover.

CAUTION
Do not add engine oil. Add only the recommended type of primary chaincase lubricant listed in Table 5.

7. Position a funnel (**Figure 13**) into the clutch opening, and refill the primary chaincase with the recommended quantity (**Table 3**) and type (**Table 5**) of primary chaincase oil. Do not overfill. The oil level must be even with the bottom of the clutch opening (**Figure 12**) or at the bottom of the clutch diaphragm spring.

NOTE
All lubricant must be removed from the seal ring and the groove prior to installation. If any lubricant remains, there will be temporary lubricant seepage around the inspection cover.

8. Remove the seal ring from the inspection cover. Wipe all lubricant from the seal ring and inspect it for cuts or deterioration; replace if necessary. Wipe all lubricant from the seal ring groove and install the seal ring onto the cover. Push the nibs into the ring groove walls.

9. Install the clutch inspection cover and seal ring (**Figure 14**) onto the primary chaincase cover.

10. Install the clutch inspection cover and tighten the screws to 84-108 in.-lb. (9.5-12.2 N•m).

11. Ride the motorcycle until the primary chaincase oil reaches normal operating temperature. Then, shut the engine off.

12. Check the primary chaincase drain plug for leaks.

FRONT FORK OIL

Oil Change

The front fork must be removed and partially disassembled in order to change the oil. Refer to Chapter Eleven.

CONTROL CABLES
(NON-NYLON LINED CABLES)

Lubricate the control cables at the intervals specified in **Table 1**, or when they become stiff or sluggish. When lubricating the control cables, inspect each cable for fraying and cable sheath damage. Cables are relatively inexpen-

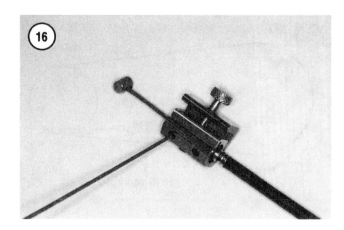

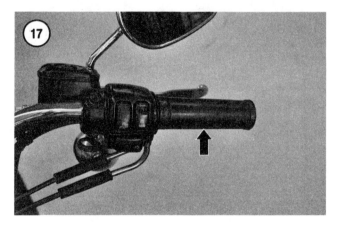

sive and should be replaced if they are faulty. Lubricate the cables with a cable lubricant.

CAUTION
If the original equipment cables have been replaced with nylon-lined cables, do not lubricate them as described in this procedure. Oil and most cable lubricants will cause the cable liner to expand, pushing the liner against the cable sheath. Nylon-lined cables are normally used dry. If servicing nylon-lined and other aftermarket cables, follow the cable manufacturer's instructions.

CAUTION
Do not use chain lubricant to lubricate control cables.

1. On all models except Screamin' Eagle and CVO, disconnect the clutch cable ends as described in *Clutch Cable Replacement* (Chapter Six).
2. Disconnect both throttle cable ends as described in *Throttle and Idle Cables* (Chapter Eight).
3. Attach a lubricator tool (**Figure 16**) to the cable following its manufacturer's instructions.

NOTE
Place a shop cloth at the opposite end of the cable to catch all excess lubricant.

NOTE
If the lubricant does not flow out of the other end of the cable, check the cable for fraying, bending or other damage. Replace damaged cables.

4. Insert the lubricant nozzle tube into the lubricator, press the button on the can and hold it down until the lubricant begins to flow out of the other end of the cable. If the lubricant squirts out from around the lubricator, it is not clamped it to the cable properly. Loosen and reposition the cable lubricator.
5. Remove the lubricator tool and wipe off both ends of the cable.
6. On all models except Screamin' Eagle and CVO, reconnect the clutch cable ends as described in *Clutch Cable Replacement* (Chapter Six).
7. Reconnect both the throttle cable ends as described in *Throttle and Idle Cable Replacement* (Chapter Eight).
8. Adjust the cables as described in this chapter.

THROTTLE CONTROL GRIP LUBRICATION

Table 1 lists the recommended throttle control grip lubrication intervals. To remove and install the throttle grip (**Figure 17**), refer to *Throttle and Idle Cable Replacement* in Chapter Eight. Lubricate the throttle control grip with graphite where it contacts the handlebar.

JIFFY STAND LUBRICATION

1. Support the motorcycle on a stand or floor jack with the rear wheel off the ground. Refer to *Motorcycle Stands* in Chapter Ten.
2. Wipe the pivot area clean of all road debris.
3. Move the jiffy stand back and forth, and check for ease of movement.
4. If the leg stop is covered with mud and debris, perform the following:
   a. Raise the jiffy stand and disconnect the return spring from the jiffy stand and anchor plate.
   b. Remove the cotter pin and washer from the pivot pin. Discard the cotter pin.
   c. Withdraw the pivot pin from between the frame tubes.
   d. Lower the jiffy stand and pivot block assembly from the frame.
   e. Thoroughly clean all parts in solvent and dry.
   f. Apply an anti-seize lubricant (Loctite aerosol), or an equivalent, onto the leg stop and the pivot area. Move the jiffy stand back and forth to work in the lubricant.
   g. Install the jiffy stand and pivot block assembly onto the frame.
   h. Insert the pivot pin from the backside through the frame tubes and pivot block. Install a *new* cotter pin and bend the ends over completely.

   i. Position the return spring with the hook facing up-
     ward and attach it to the jiffy stand. Hook the other
     end of the spring onto the anchor plate.

5. Move the jiffy stand back and forth, and check for ease
of movement.

PRIMARY CHAIN AND DRIVE BELT

Primary Chain Adjustment

The primary chain is automatically adjusted on all models.

Drive Belt Deflection and Alignment

Inspect drive belt deflection and rear axle alignment at
the intervals specified in **Table 1**. If the drive belt is severely worn, or if it is wearing incorrectly, refer to Chapter
Ten for inspection and replacement procedures.

The drive belt deflection can be inspected with the rear
wheel off the ground or with the motorcycle resting on the
jiffy stand without rider or luggage. A belt tension gauge
(JIMS part No. 923 or H-D part No. HD-35381), or an
equivalent, is required for this procedure.

NOTE
Check the drive belt deflection and axle align-
ment when the belt is at room temperature.

1. Support the motorcycle with the rear wheel off the
ground.
2. Shift the transmission into neutral.
3. Turn the rear wheel and check the drive belt for its tight-
est point. When this point is located, turn the wheel so that
the belt's tight spot is on the lower belt run, midway between the front and rear sprockets.
4. Slide the O-ring on the gauge toward the 0 lb. (0 kg)
mark on the gauge.
5. Position the gauge on the lower belt strand halfway between the transmission drive and rear wheel driven sprocket.
6. Push up on the gauge until the O-ring slides to the 10
lb. (4.5 kg) mark while measuring the belt deflection at the
same point (**Figure 18**).
7. Rotate the rear wheel and measure the deflection at different locations on the belt.
8. Compare the belt deflection measurement with the
specification in **Table 6**. If the deflection measurement is
incorrect, adjust it as described in this section.
9. On Screamin' Eagle or CVO models so equipped, loosen
the set screw and remove the trim cap from the rear axle nut.
10. Remove the e-clip (A, **Figure 19**) and loosen the rear
axle nut (B).
11. Support the motorcycle with the rear wheel off the
ground.
12. To adjust belt deflection while maintaining rear wheel
alignment, turn each axle adjuster screw (C, **Figure 19**) in

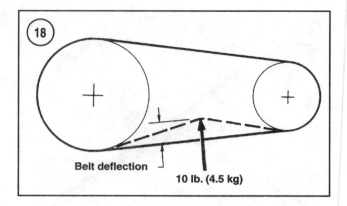

Belt deflection
10 lb. (4.5 kg)

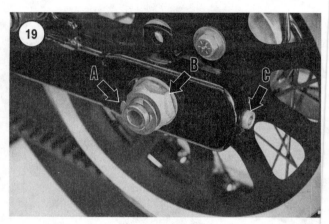

equal amounts. Recheck drive belt deflection as described
in this section.
13. After the drive belt deflection measurement is correct,
check axle alignment as follows:
   a. Place a vernier caliper (A, **Figure 20**) against the
     end of the swing arm and the rear axle washer (B).
     Record the measurement.
   b. Repeat the measurement on the opposite side, against
     the rear axle flange.
   c. The dimensions must be the same for both sides; re-
     adjust if necessary.
14. When the drive belt deflection and axle alignment adjustments are correct, secure the left side axle nut and tight-
en the right side axle nut (B, **Figure 19**) to the specification

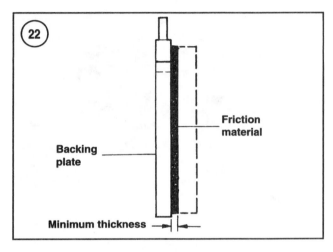

in **Table 7**. Position the e-clip (A, **Figure 19**) with the flat side facing out and install it onto the rear axle groove.
15. Tighten both rear axle adjuster screws to 96-120 in.-lb. (10.8-13.6 N•m).
16. Lower the rear wheel to the ground.

BRAKE SYSTEM

WARNING
Use only DOT 4 brake fluid. Do not intermix DOT 4 with DOT 5 brake fluids, as they are not compatible. DOT 5 is silicone-based and the mistaken use of silicone brake fluid in these models can cause brake failure.

WARNING
If the brake fluid level is low enough to allow air in the hydraulic system, bleed the brakes as described in Chapter Thirteen.

Front Brake Lever Pivot Pin Lubrication

Lubriate the front brake lever pivot pin with light weight oil at the intervals specified in **Table 1**. To service the pivot pin, refer to *Front Master Cylinder* in Chapter Thirteen.

Pad Inspection

1. Without removing the front or rear brake calipers, inspect the brake pads (**Figure 21**) for damage.
2. If the pad material appears excessively worn, remove the brake pads as described in Chapter Thirteen.
3. Measure the thickness of each brake pad lining (**Figure 22**) with a ruler. If worn to the minimum thickness in **Table 6**, replace both brake pads as described in Chapter Thirteen.

Fluid Level Check

Front master cylinder

1. Support the motorcycle on level ground using a swing arm stand.
2. Block the front wheel so the motorcycle will not roll in either direction while on the swing arm stand.
3. Turn the handlebars to the straight ahead position to level the front master cylinder.
4A. On 2006-2010 models, perform the following:
    a. Remove the screws (A, **Figure 23**), cover (B) and diaphragm from the master cylinder.
    b. The brake fluid level should be 1/8-1/4 in. (3.2-6.4 mm) from the top edge of the master cylinder body (**Figure 24**).
4B. On 2011 models, perform the following:
    a. Observe the brake fluid level by looking at the sight glass (C, **Figure 23**) on the master cylinder reservoir top cover. If the fluid level is incorrect, the sight glass will be dark. If the fluid level is low, sight glass will have a lightened, clear appearance.
    b. If the brake fluid level is low, remove the screws (A, **Figure 23**), cover (B), diaphragm plate, and diaphragm from the master cylinder.
    c. The brake fluid level should be 1/4 in. (6.4 mm) from the top edge of the master cylinder body (**Figure 24**).
5. Add fresh DOT 4 brake fluid to correct the level. Reinstall the diaphragm and top cover. Tighten the reservoir cover screws to 6-8 in.-lb. (0.7-0.9 N•m).

Rear master cylinder

1. Support the motorcycle on level ground.
2A. On 2006-2010 models, perform the following:
    a. Insert a long Phillips screwdriver (**Figure 25**) between the muffler bracket and frame. Remove the screws, cover (A, **Figure 26**), and diaphragm from the master cylinder.
    b. The brake fluid level should be 1/8-1/4 in. (3.2-6.4 mm) from the top edge of the master cylinder body.
2B. On 2011 models, perform the following:
    a. Observe the brake fluid level by looking at the sight glass (B, **Figure 26**) on the master cylinder reservoir top cover. If the fluid level is incorrect, the sight glass will be dark. If the fluid level is low, sight glass will have a lightened, clear appearance.

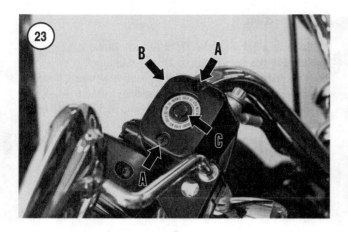

b. If the brake fluid level is low, remove the screws, cover (A, **Figure 26**), and diaphragm from the master cylinder.

c. The brake fluid level should be 1/4 in. (6.4 mm) from the top edge of the master cylinder body

3. Add fresh DOT 4 brake fluid to correct the level. Reinstall the diaphragm and top cover. Tighten the reservoir cover screws to 6-8 in.-lb. (0.7-0.9 N•m).

Disc Inspection

Visually inspect the front and rear brake discs for scoring, cracks or other damage. Measure the brake disc thickness, and if necessary, service the brake discs as described in Chapter Thirteen.

Brake Lines and Seals

Check the brake lines between each master cylinder and each brake caliper. If there are any leaks, tighten the connections and bleed the brakes as described in Chapter Thirteen.

Fluid Change

Every time the reservoir cover is removed, a small amount of dirt and moisture enters the brake fluid. The same thing happens if a leak occurs or if any part of the hydraulic system is loosened or disconnected. Dirt can clog the system and cause unnecessary wear. Water in the fluid vaporizes at high temperatures, impairing hydraulic function and reducing brake performance.

To change brake fluid, follow the brake bleeding procedure in Chapter Thirteen. Continue adding new fluid to the master cylinder until the fluid leaving the caliper is clean and free of contaminants and air bubbles.

CLUTCH SYSTEM

Clutch Lever Pivot Pin Lubrication

Lubricate the clutch lever pivot pin with light weight oil at the intervals specified in **Table 1**. To service the pivot pin, refer to *Clutch Cable Replacement* in Chapter Six.

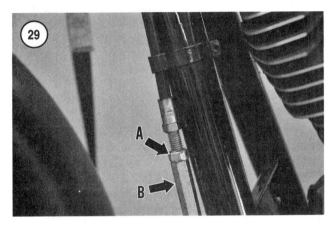

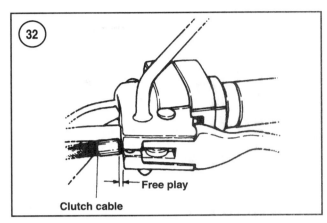

Free play

Clutch cable

Clutch Adjustment (All Models Except Screamin' Eagle and CVO)

> *CAUTION*
> *Because the clutch cable adjuster clearance increases with engine temperature, adjust the clutch when the engine is cold. If the clutch is adjusted when the engine is hot, insufficient pushrod clearance can cause the clutch to slip.*

1. Remove the Torx (T27) screws securing the clutch inspection cover (**Figure 27**) and seal ring, and then remove the cover.

2. Slide the rubber boot (**Figure 28**) off the clutch in-line cable adjuster.

3. Loosen the adjuster locknut (A, **Figure 29**) and turn the adjuster (B) to provide maximum cable slack.

4. Check that the clutch cable seats squarely in its perch (**Figure 30**) at the handlebar.

5. At the clutch mechanism, loosen the clutch adjusting screw locknut (A, **Figure 31**) and turn the adjusting screw (B) *clockwise* until it is lightly seated.

6. Apply the clutch lever three times to verify the clutch balls are seated in the ramp release mechanism located behind the transmission side cover.

7. Back out the adjusting screw (B, **Figure 31**) *counterclockwise* 1/2 to 1 turn. Then, hold the adjusting screw (B, **Figure 31**) and tighten the clutch adjusting screw locknut (A) to 72-120 in.-lb. (8.1-13.6 N•m).

8. Once again, apply the clutch lever to its maximum limit three times to set the clutch ball and ramp release mechanism.

9. Check the free play as follows:
   a. At the in-line cable adjuster, turn the adjuster away from the locknut until slack is eliminated at the clutch hand lever.
   b. Pull the clutch cable sheath away from the clutch lever, and then turn the clutch cable adjuster to obtain a free play clearance gap (**Figure 32**) of 1/16-1/8 in. (1.6-3.2 mm).
   c. When the adjustment is correct, tighten the in-line cable adjuster locknut (A, **Figure 29**) and slide the rubber boot (**Figure 28**) over the cable adjuster.

NOTE
All lubricant must be removed from the seal ring and the groove prior to installation. If any lubricant remains there will be temporary lubricant seepage around the inspection cover.

10. Remove the seal ring (**Figure 33**) from the inspection cover. Wiper all lubricant from the seal ring and inspect for cuts or deterioration, replace if necessary. Wipe all lubricant from the seal ring groove and install the seal ring onto the cover. Push the nibs into the ring groove walls.

11. Install the clutch inspection cover (**Figure 27**) and seal ring onto the primary chaincase cover.

12. Install the clutch inspection cover screws. Tighten the cover screws to 84-108 in.-lb. (9.5-12.2 N•m).

Fluid Level Check (Screamin' Eagle and CVO Models)

1. Turn the handlebar straight ahead so the master cylinder is level.

2. Clean any dirt from the master cylinder cover prior to removing it.

3. Remove the screws and top cover (**Figure 34**). Lift the diaphragm out of the reservoir.

NOTE
If the clutch fluid level is low enough to allow air in the hydraulic system, bleed the clutch system as described in the Chapter Six.

4. The clutch fluid level should be flush with the top of the inner ledge cast at the front of the clutch master cylinder body.

WARNING
Use only DOT 4 brake fluid in the clutch system. Do not intermix DOT4 with DOT 5 brake fluids, as they are not compatible. DOT 5 is silicone-based and the mistaken use of silicone brake fluid in these models can cause brake failure.

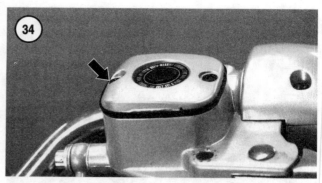

CAUTION
Be careful when handling brake fluid. Do not spill it on painted or plastic surfaces, as it damages them. Avoid getting brake fluid on the tires as well. Wash the area immediately with soap and water, and thoroughly rinse it.

NOTE
To control the flow of brake fluid, punch a small hole in the seal of a new container of brake fluid next to the edge of the pour spout. This helps prevent the fluid spillage, especially while adding fluid to the small reservoir.

5. If the clutch fluid level is low, perform the following:

  a. Add sufficient DOT4 brake fluid to bring the clutch fluid level up so it is flush with the top of the inner ledge (**Figure 35**) cast at the front of the clutch master cylinder body.

  b. Reinstall the diaphragm and top cover. Tighten the reservoir cover screws to 6.8 in.-lb. (0.7-0.9 N•m).

Line and Hose Inspection (Screamin' Eagle and CVO Models)

Check the clutch hose between the master cylinder and the release cylinder. If there are any leaks, tighten the connections and bleed the clutch system (Chapter Six). If this does not stop the leak or if a line is obviously damaged, cracked, or chafed, replace the hose and/or the master cylinder or release cylinder(s). Then, bleed the clutch as described in Chapter Six.

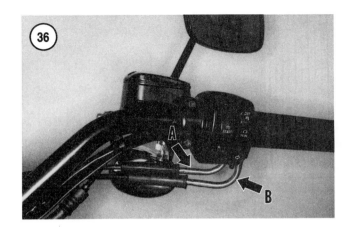

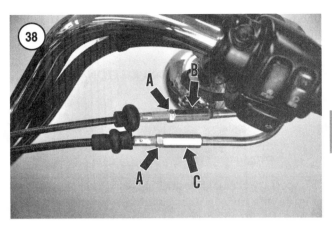

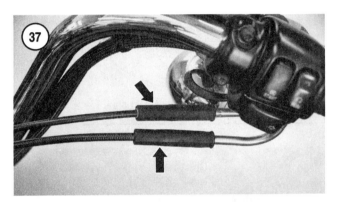

Clutch Fluid Change
(Screamin' Eagle and CVO Models)

A small amount of dirt and moisture enters the clutch fluid each time the reservoir cap is removed. The same thing happens if a leak occurs or when any part of the hydraulic system is loosened or disconnected. Dirt can clog the system and cause unnecessary wear. Water in the fluid vaporizes at high temperatures, impairing hydraulic function and reducing brake performance.

To change the clutch fluid, drain the fluid from the clutch system as described in Chapter Six. Add new fluid to the master cylinder, and bleed the clutch at the release cylinder until the fluid leaving the release cylinder is clean and free of contaminants and air bubbles. Then, bleed the clutch as described in Chapter Six.

THROTTLE CABLE ADJUSTMENT

WARNING
Do not ride the motorcycle until the throttle cables are properly adjusted. The cables must not catch or pull when the handlebar is turned from side to side. Improper cable routing and adjustment can cause the throttle to stick open. This could cause loss of control and a possible crash. Recheck this adjustment before riding the motorcycle.

There are two different throttle cables. At the throttle grip, the front cable is the throttle control cable (A, **Figure 36**) and the rear cable is the idle control cable (B).

1. Remove the air filter and backplate as described in Chapter Eight.
2. At the handlebar, roll the rubber boots (**Figure 37**) off both cable adjusters.
3. At the handlebar, loosen both throttle cable adjuster locknuts (A, **Figure 38**). Then, turn both cable adjusters *clockwise* as far as possible to increase cable slack.
4. Turn the handlebars so the front wheel points straight ahead. Then, turn the throttle grip to open the throttle completely and hold it in this position.
5. At the handlebar, turn the throttle cable adjuster (B, **Figure 38**) *counterclockwise* until the throttle cam (A, **Figure 39**) just touches the cam stop (B) on the throttle body. Then, tighten the throttle cable adjuster locknut and release the throttle grip.
6. Turn the front wheel all the way to the full right lock position and hold it there.
7. Turn the idle cable adjuster (C, **Figure 38**) until the lower end of the idle control cable housing (C, **Figure 39**) just contacts the spring (D) in the cable support sleeve. Tighten the idle cable locknut.
8. Install the backplate and air filter as described in Chapter Eight.
9. Shift the transmission into neutral and start the engine.
10. Increase engine speed several times. Release the throttle and make sure the engine speed returns to idle. If the engine speed does not return to idle, loosen the idle cable adjuster locknut at the handlebar, and turn the cable adjuster *clockwise* as required. Tighten the idle cable adjuster locknut.
11. Allow the engine to idle in neutral. Then, turn the handlebar from side to side. Do not operate the throttle. If the engine speed increases when the handlebar assembly is turned, the throttle cables are routed incorrectly or damaged. Turn off the engine. Recheck cable routing and adjustment.
12. Carefully rotate the throttle control *counterclockwise* to the wide open position and release it. The throttle must return to the idle position freely. If it does not, check for

improper cable routing, a damaged cable, or a binding throttle control.

FUEL LINE INSPECTION

> *WARNING*
> *A damaged or deteriorated fuel line can cause a fire or explosion if fuel spills onto a hot engine or exhaust pipe.*

Inspect the fuel tank-to-fuel injection module fuel lines (**Figure 40**), and the fuel tank crossover fuel lines (A, **Figure 41**). Replace any leaking or damaged fuel lines. Make sure the hose clamps (B, **Figure 41**) are securely in place. Check the hose fittings for looseness.

STEERING PLAY INSPECTION

Check the steering head play as described in Chapter Eleven at the intervals specified in **Table 1**.

SWING ARM PIVOT BOLT INSPECTION

Check the rear swing arm pivot bolt tightness as described in Chapter Twelve at the intervals specified in **Table 1**.

SHOCK ABSORBER INSPECTION

Check the rear shock absorbers for oil leakage or damaged bushings. Check the shock absorber mounting bolts and nuts for tightness. Refer to *Shock Absorbers* in Chapter Twelve for procedures.

ENGINE MOUNTS AND STABILIZER INSPECTION

Check the stabilizer link and the engine and frame isolators for loose or damaged parts at the intervals specified in **Table 1**. Refer to Chapter Five for procedures.

EXHAUST SYSTEM INSPECTION

Check all fittings for exhaust leaks, including the crossover pipe connections, at the intervals specified in **Table 1**. Tighten all bolts and nuts to specification (Chapter Four). Replace gaskets if necessary as described in Chapter Four.

FASTENER INSPECTION

> *CAUTION*
> *Specific procedures must be used when tightening the cylinder head mounting bolts. To check these bolts for tightness, refer to* ***Cylinder Head, Installation*** *in Chapter Four. Tightening these bolts incorrectly can cause an oil leak or cylinder head damage.*

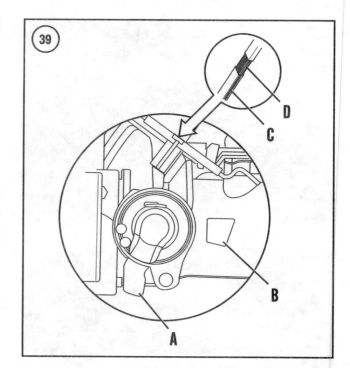

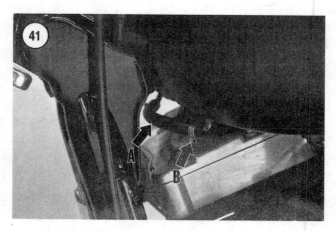

Check the tightness of all fasteners at the intervals specified in **Table 1**. Pay special attention to the following:
1. Engine mounting hardware.
2. Engine and primary covers.
3. Handlebar and front fork.

3

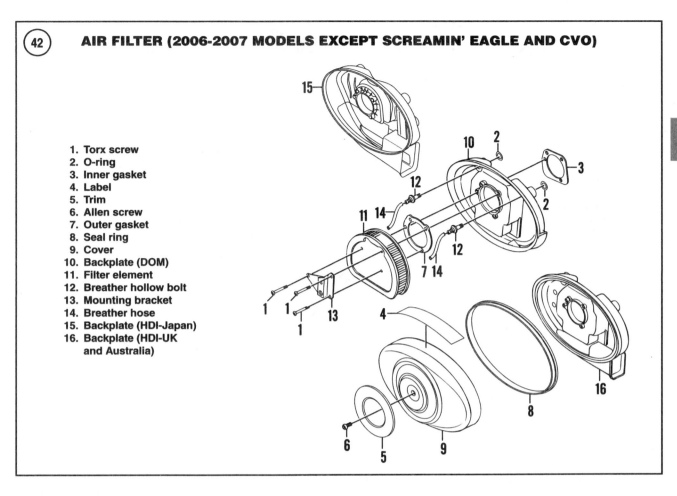

(42) AIR FILTER (2006-2007 MODELS EXCEPT SCREAMIN' EAGLE AND CVO)

1. Torx screw
2. O-ring
3. Inner gasket
4. Label
5. Trim
6. Allen screw
7. Outer gasket
8. Seal ring
9. Cover
10. Backplate (DOM)
11. Filter element
12. Breather hollow bolt
13. Mounting bracket
14. Breather hose
15. Backplate (HDI-Japan)
16. Backplate (HDI-UK
    and Australia)

4. Gearshift lever.
5. Sprocket bolts and nuts.
6. Brake pedal and lever.
7. Exhaust system.
8. Lighting equipment.

ELECTRICAL EQUIPMENT AND SWITCHES

Check all electrical equipment and switches for proper operation. Refer to Chapter Nine.

TUNE-UP

The following sections describes tune-up procedures. Perform the tasks at the intervals in **Table 1** and in the following order.
1. Clean or replace the air filter element.
2. Check engine compression.
3. Check or replace the spark plugs.

AIR FILTER ELEMENT

WARNING
Do not clean the air filter in any type of solvent. Never clean the air filter element in gas-oline or any type of low flash point solvent. The residual solvent or vapors left by these chemicals may cause a fire or explosion after the filter is reinstalled.

CAUTION
Do not tap or strike the air filter element on a hard surface to dislodge dirt. Doing so will damage the element.

The air filter removes dust and abrasive particles before the air enters the fuel injection module, and the engine. Without the air filter, very fine particles could enter into the engine and cause rapid wear of the piston rings, cylinder bores and bearings. Never run the motorcycle without the element installed.

Remove and clean the air filter at the interval in **Table 1**. Replace the element at the interval in **Table 1** or whenever it is damaged or starts to deteriorate.

Removal/Installation (All 2006-2007 Models, 2007-2008 FXDSE and 2009 FXDFSE CVO HDI Models)

Refer to **Figure 42** and **Figure 43**.

1A. On Screamin' Eagle and CVO models, perform the following:

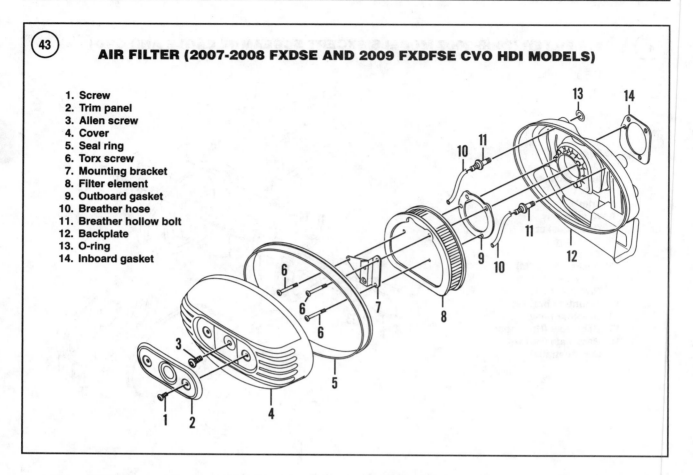

(43)

AIR FILTER (2007-2008 FXDSE AND 2009 FXDFSE CVO HDI MODELS)

1. Screw
2. Trim panel
3. Allen screw
4. Cover
5. Seal ring
6. Torx screw
7. Mounting bracket
8. Filter element
9. Outboard gasket
10. Breather hose
11. Breather hollow bolt
12. Backplate
13. O-ring
14. Inboard gasket

a. Remove the screws and the trim panel from the cover.

b. Remove the air filter cover Allen screw and remove the cover.

1B. On all other models, remove the air filter cover Allen screw (A, **Figure 44**) and remove the cover (B).

2. Remove the Torx (T27) screws and bracket (A, **Figure 45**) from the air filter element (B).

3. Gently pull the air filter element away from the backplate and disconnect the two breather hoses (A, **Figure 46**) from the breather hollow bolts on the backplate. Remove the air filter element (B, **Figure 46**).

4. Remove the outboard gasket (**Figure 47**) from the inboard side of the element. Discard the gasket.

5. Clean the air filter as described in this section.

6. Inspect the breather hoses (**Figure 48**) for tears or deterioration. Replace if necessary.

7. Inspect the seal ring (**Figure 49**) on the air filter cover for hardness or deterioration. Replace if necessary.

8. Install a *new* gasket (**Figure 47**) on the inboard side of the element.

9. Position the element with the flat side facing down and insert the breather hoses (A, **Figure 50**) into the element (B).

10. Move the element into position and install the mounting bracket (**Figure 45**). Install the Torx screws through the mounting bracket and element. Align the screw holes

(44)

(45)

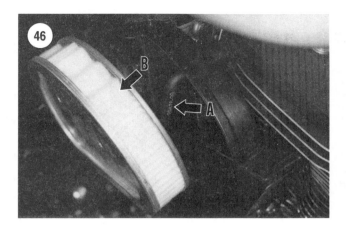

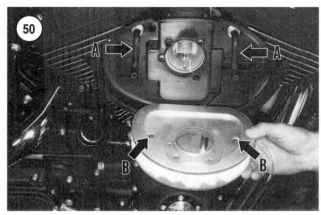

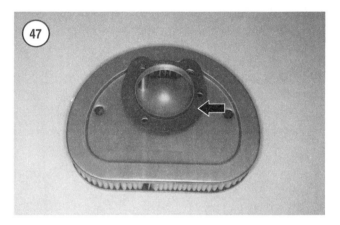

3

and tighten the Torx screws to 40-60 in.-lb. (4.5-6.8 N•m).

11. Apply a drop of Loctite 243 (blue), or an equivalent, threadlock to the cover screw prior to installation.

12A. On Screamin' Eagle and CVO models, perform the following:

    a. Install the air filter cover and Allen screw. Tighten the Allen screw to 36-60 in.-lb. (4.1-6.8 N•m).

    b. Install the trim panel onto the cover and tighten the screws securely.

12B. On all other models, install the air filter cover (B, **Figure 44**) and Allen screw (A). Tighten the Allen screw to 36-60 in.-lb. (4.1-6.8 N•m).

Removal/Installation (2008-2011 Models Except Screamin' Eagle and CVO)

Refer to **Figure 51**.

1. Remove the Allen screw (A, **Figure 52**) and remove the cover (B).

2. Gently disconnect the breather hoses (A, **Figure 53**) from the air filter element.

3. Slide the speed nut (B, **Figure 53**) to the left to access the bolt behind it.

4. Remove the Torx (T27) screws (A, **Figure 54**) and bracket (B) from the air filter element.

5. Remove the air filter element (C, **Figure 54**) from the backplate.

6. Remove the outboard gasket (**Figure 55**) from the inboard side of the element. Discard the gasket.

7. Clean the air filter as described in this section.

8. Inspect the breather hoses (**Figure 56**) for tears or deterioration. Replace if necessary.

9. Inspect the seal ring on the air filter cover for hardness or deterioration. Replace if necessary.

10. Install a *new* outboard gasket (**Figure 55**) onto the inboard side of the element.

11. Position the element with the flat side facing down and guide it into position on the backplate.

12. Install the mounting bracket (B, **Figure 54**). Then, install the Torx screws (A, **Figure 54**) through the mounting bracket and element. Align the screw holes and tighten the Torx screws to 40-60 in.-lb. (4.5-6.8 N•m).

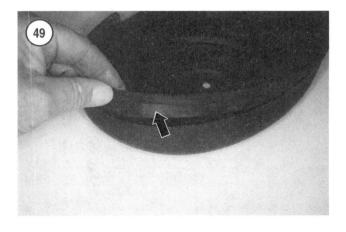

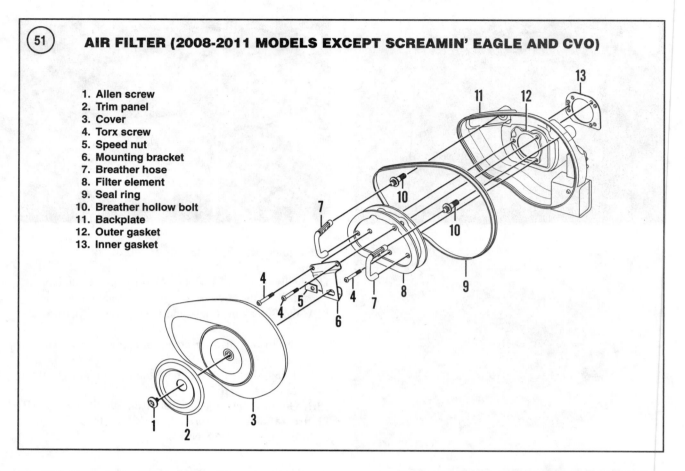

51 **AIR FILTER (2008-2011 MODELS EXCEPT SCREAMIN' EAGLE AND CVO)**

1. Allen screw
2. Trim panel
3. Cover
4. Torx screw
5. Speed nut
6. Mounting bracket
7. Breather hose
8. Filter element
9. Seal ring
10. Breather hollow bolt
11. Backplate
12. Outer gasket
13. Inner gasket

13. Slide the speed nut (**Figure 57**) to the right.

14. Insert both breather hoses. Insert one end into the element (A, **Figure 58**) and attach the other end to the backplate (B).

15. Ensure that the cover seal ring (**Figure 59**) is in place.

16. Apply a drop of Loctite 243 (blue), or an equivalent, threadlock to the cover screw prior to installation.

17. Install the air filter cover (B, **Figure 52**) and Allen screw (A). Tighten the Allen screw to 36-60 in.-lb. (4.1-6.8 N•m).

**Removal/Installation
(2007 FXDSE and 2008 FXDSE2 Screamin' Eagle Models)**

Refer to **Figure 60**.

1. Remove the trim plate Allen screws and trim plate. Remove the air filter cover Allen screw and remove the cover.

2. Remove the screws (A, **Figure 61**) from the air filter element (B).

3. Gently pull the air filter element away from the backplate and remove it.

4. Clean the air filter as described in this section.

5. On models so equipped, inspect the seal ring on the air filter cover for hardness or deterioration. Replace if necessary.

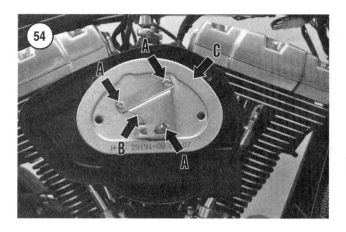

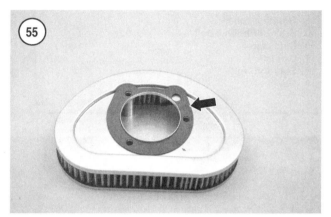

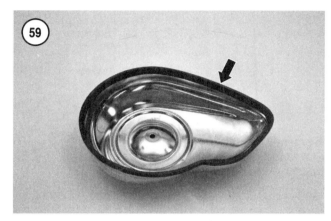

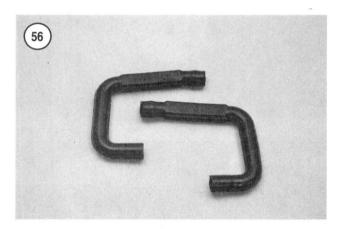

6. Check the tightness of the standoff bolts (**Figure 62**). If loose, tighten to 55-60 in.-lb. (6.3-6.8 N•m).

7. Install the element onto the backplate and align the screw holes

8. Install screws through the air filter element, and then tighten the screws to 55-60 in.-lb. (6.2-6.8 N•m).

9. Apply a drop of Loctite 243 (blue), or an equivalent, threadlock to the cover screw prior to installation.

10. Install the air filter cover and Allen screw. Tighten the cover Allen screw to 36-60 in.-lb. (4.1-6.8 N•m).

11. Install the trim plate and Allen screws. Tighten the screws to 27-32 in.-lb. (3.1-3.6 N•m).

Removal/Installation
(2009 FXDFSE CVO Models)

Refer to **Figure 63**.

1. Loosen the hose clamp and slide the air filter element assembly off the intake tube.

2. Clean the air filter as described in this section.

3. Install the air filter element onto the intake tube, and rotate it so the seam faces toward the engine.

4. Position the hose clamp with the screw at the bottom and just forward of the intake tube. Tighten the hose clamp screw to 45-55 in.-lb. (5.1-6.3 N•m).

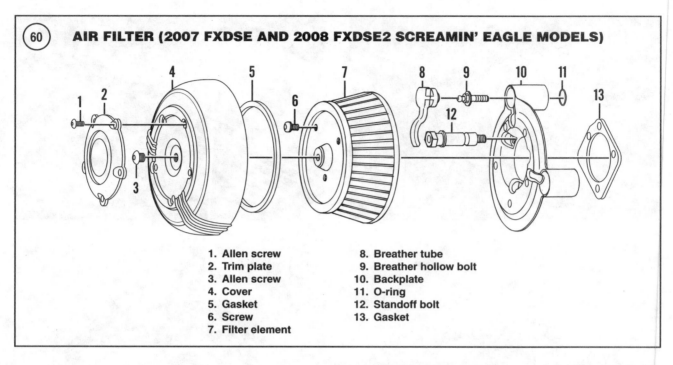

60 **AIR FILTER (2007 FXDSE AND 2008 FXDSE2 SCREAMIN' EAGLE MODELS)**

1. Allen screw
2. Trim plate
3. Allen screw
4. Cover
5. Gasket
6. Screw
7. Filter element
8. Breather tube
9. Breather hollow bolt
10. Backplate
11. O-ring
12. Standoff bolt
13. Gasket

Element Cleaning
(All Models Except 2009 FXDFSE
and 2010 FXDFSE2)

> *WARNING*
> *Do not clean the air filter in any type of sol-*
> *vent. Never clean the air filter element in gas-*
> *oline or any type of low flash point solvent.*
> *The residual solvent or vapors left by these*
> *chemicals may cause a fire or explosion after*
> *the filter is reinstalled.*

1. Remove the air filter element as described in this section.
2. Place the air filter in a pan filled with lukewarm water and mild detergent. Move the air filter element back and forth to help dislodge trapped dirt. Thoroughly rinse in low-pressure clean water to remove all detergent residue.
3. Remove the air filter from the cleaning solution and hold it up to a strong light. Check the filter pores for dirt and oil. Repeat cleaning process until there is no longer dirt and oil in the filter pores. If the air filter cannot be cleaned, or if the filter is saturated with oil or other chemicals, replace it.

> *CAUTION*
> *Do not blow compressed air through the outer*
> *surface of the air filter element. Doing so can*
> *force dirt trapped on the outer filter surface*
> *deeper into the air filter element, restricting*
> *airflow and damaging the air filter element.*

4. Gently apply compressed air through the inside surface of the air filter element to remove loosened dirt and dust trapped in the filter.
5. Inspect the air filter element. Replace if torn or damaged. Do not ride the motorcycle with a damaged filter ele-

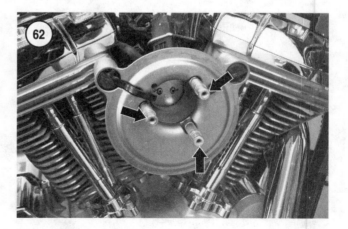

ment as it may allow dirt to enter the fuel injectors and engine.
6. Clean the breather hoses in the same lukewarm water and mild detergent solution. Make sure both hoses are clean and clear. Clean out with a pipe cleaner if necessary.

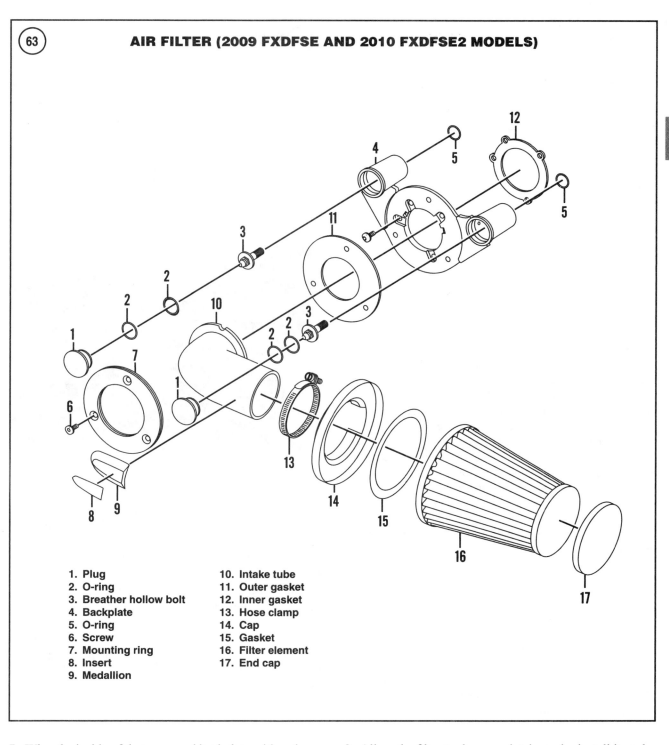

63 **AIR FILTER (2009 FXDFSE AND 2010 FXDFSE2 MODELS)**

1. Plug
2. O-ring
3. Breather hollow bolt
4. Backplate
5. O-ring
6. Screw
7. Mounting ring
8. Insert
9. Medallion
10. Intake tube
11. Outer gasket
12. Inner gasket
13. Hose clamp
14. Cap
15. Gasket
16. Filter element
17. End cap

7. Wipe the inside of the cover and backplate with a clean, damp shop rag.

CAUTION
Air will not pass through a wet or damp filter. Make sure the filter is dry before installing it.

CAUTION
Do not use high air pressure to dry the filter, as this will damage it.

8. Allow the filter to dry completely, and reinstall it as described in this section.

Element Cleaning
(2009 FXDFSE and 2010 FXDFSE2 Models)

WARNING
Do not clean the air filter in any type of solvent. Never clean the air filter element in gasoline or any type of low flash-point solvent.

The residual solvent or vapors left by these chemicals may cause a fire or explosion after the filter is reinstalled.

1. Remove the air filter element as described in this section.
2. Replace the air filter if damaged.
3. Carefully tap air filter element to dislodge dirt, and gently brush with a soft bristle brush.
4. Spray a liberal amount of K&N Air Filter Cleaner over the entire surface of the element, and let it soak in for about 10 minutes.
5. Thoroughly rinse filter in low-pressure clean water to remove all cleaner residue.

CAUTION
Do not apply low-pressure air or heat gun to the element as it will be damaged.

6. Carefully shake off excess water and allow the element to dry.
7. Remove the air filter and hold it up to a strong light. Check the filter pores for dirt and oil. Repeat cleaning process until there is no longer dirt and oil in the filter pores. If the air filter cannot be cleaned, or if the filter is saturated with oil or other chemicals, replace it.
8. Apply K&N Air Filter Oil onto each pleat of the element. Hold the spry nozzle approximately 3 in. (76 mm) from the element.
9. Carefully apply air from a squeeze bottle to spread the filter oil along each element pleat. Perform this step only once.
10. Allow the filter oil to penetrate the filter element for 20 minutes. Afterwards, inspect each pleat and apply filter oil to any visible white spots on the filter element. Wait an additional 20 minutes to allow the just-applied oil to absorb into the element.
11. Reinstall the air filter element as described in this section.

COMPRESSION TEST

A compression check is one of the most effective ways to check the condition of the engine. If possible, check the compression at each tune-up, record the results and compare with the readings at subsequent tune-ups. This will help spot any developing problems.

All Models Except Screamin' Eagle and CVO

1. Prior to starting the compression test, verify the following:
   a. The cylinder head bolts (**Figure 64**) are tightened to the proper torque specification. Refer to Chapter Four for specific tightening procedure.
   b. The battery is fully-charged to ensure proper engine cranking speed. Refer to Chapter Nine.
2. Ride the motorcycle until engine is at normal operating temperature.

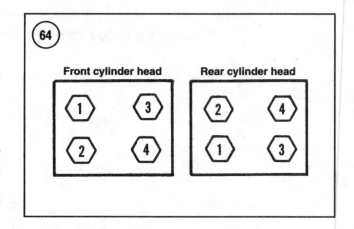

3. Place the motorcycle on a level surface and park it on its jiffy stand. Turn off the engine.
4. Shift the transmission into neutral.
5. Remove the spark plugs (**Figure 65**) as described in this chapter. Reinstall the caps onto the spark plugs and place them against the cylinder heads to ground them.
6. Connect a compression tester (**Figure 66**) to the front cylinder following the tester manufacturer's instructions.
7. Rotate the throttle to the wide-open position and keep it in this position.
8. Crank the engine over continuously through 5-7 full revolutions until there is no further rise in pressure.
9. Record the highest reading and remove the tester.
10. Repeat procedure for the rear cylinder.
11. Reinstall the spark plugs and reconnect their caps.

Screamin' Eagle and CVO Models

1. Prior to starting the compression test, verify the following:
   a. The cylinder head bolts (**Figure 64**) are tightened to the proper torque specification. Refer to Chapter Four for specific tightening procedure.
   b. The battery is fully-charged to ensure proper engine cranking speed. Refer to Chapter Nine.
2. Ride the motorcycle until engine is at normal operating temperature.

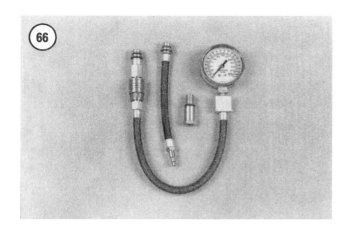

Results

Table 6 lists the standard engine compression reading. Pressure must not vary between the cylinders by more than 10 percent. Greater differences indicate worn or broken rings, leaky or sticky valves, blown head gasket or a combination of all.

If compression readings are within specification and do not differ between cylinders by more than 10 percent, the rings and valves are in good condition. A low reading (10 percent or more) on one cylinder indicates valve or ring trouble. To determine which, pour about a teaspoon of engine oil into the spark plug hole. Then, take another compression test and record the reading. If the compression increases significantly, the valves are good but the rings are defective on that cylinder. If compression does not increase, the valves require further inspection.

SPARK PLUGS

Removal

> *CAUTION*
> *Whenever the spark plug is removed, dirt around it can fall into the plug hole. This can cause serious engine damage.*

1. Blow away any loose dirt or debris that may have accumulated around the base of the spark plug that could fall into the cylinder head.
2. Grasp the spark plug lead (**Figure 67**), and twist from side to side to break the seal loose. Then pull the cap off the spark plug. If the cap is stuck to the plug, twist it slightly to break it loose.

> *NOTE*
> *Use a special spark plug socket equipped with a rubber insert that holds the spark plug. This type of socket is necessary for both removal and installation since the spark plugs are recessed in the cylinder head.*

3. Install the spark plug socket onto the spark plug. Make sure it is correctly seated and install an open-end wrench or socket handle and remove the spark plug. Mark the spark plug with which cylinder number it was removed from.
4. Repeat for the remaining spark plug.
5. Thoroughly inspect each plug. Look for broken center porcelain, excessively-eroded electrodes and excessive carbon or oil fouling.
6. Inspect the spark plug caps and secondary wires for damage, or hardness. If any portion is damaged, the cap and secondary wire must be replaced as an assembly. The front and rear cylinder assemblies have different part numbers.

3. Place the motorcycle on a level surface and park it on its jiffy stand. Turn off the engine.
4. Shift the transmission into neutral.
5. Remove the spark plugs (**Figure 65**) as described in this chapter. Reinstall the caps onto the spark plugs and place them against the cylinder heads to ground them.
6. Connect a compression tester (**Figure 66**) to the front cylinder following the tester manufacturer's instructions.
7. Rotate the throttle to the wide-open position and keep it in this position.
8. Crank the engine over continuously through 5-7 full revolutions until there is no further rise in pressure. Record the highest reading and remove the tester. The standard compression pressure is 130-170 psi (896-1173 kPa).
9. Repeat procedure for the rear cylinder.
10. Disconnect the 2-pin automatic compression release (ACR) connector (one yellow/green wire and one violet/grey wire) from the main harness adjacent to the front cylinder head. Repeat for the identical 2-pin ACR connector at the rear cylinder head.
11. Repeat the testing with the ACR disconnected. The standard compression pressure is 200-220 psi (1379-1517 kPa) with the ACR disconnected.
12. Reinstall the spark plugs and reconnect their caps.
13. Connect both 2-pin automatic compression release (ACR) connectors to the main harness.
14. Reinstall the spark plugs and reconnect their caps.

Gap and Installation

Carefully gap the spark plugs to ensure a reliable, consistent spark. A special spark plug gapping tool and a wire feeler gauge must be used.

1. Insert a wire feeler gauge between the center and side electrode of the plug (**Figure 68**). If the gap is correct, a slight drag will be felt as the wire gauge is pulled through. If there is no drag, or the gauge will not pass through, bend the side electrode with a gapping tool (**Figure 69**) to adjust the gap to the proper specification listed in **Table 6**.

2. Install the terminal nut (A, **Figure 70**).

3. Apply a *light coat* of antiseize lubricant on the threads of the spark plug before installing it. Do *not* use engine oil on the plug threads.

> *CAUTION*
> *The cylinder head is aluminum and the spark plug hole is easily damaged by cross-threading the spark plug.*

4. Slowly screw the spark plug into the cylinder head by hand until it seats. Very little effort is required. If force is necessary, the plug is cross-threaded; unscrew it and try again.

> *CAUTION*
> *Do not overtighten the spark plug.*

5. Finger-tighten the plug until it seats against the cylinder head. Then, tighten the plug to 12-18 ft.-lb. (16.3-24.4 N•m).

6. Install the spark plug cap and lead to the correct spark plug. Rotate the cap slightly in both directions and make sure it is attached to the spark plug.

7. Repeat procedure for the other spark plug.

Heat Range

Spark plugs are available in various heat ranges, hotter or colder than the plugs originally installed by the manufacturer.

Select a plug with a heat range designed for the loads and conditions under which the motorcycle will be operated. A plug with an incorrect heat range can foul, overheat and cause piston damage.

In general, use a hot plug for low speeds and low temperatures. Use a cold plug for high speeds, high engine loads and high temperatures. The plug should operate hot enough to burn off unwanted deposits, but not so hot that it is damaged or causes preignition. To determine if plug heat range is correct, remove each spark plug and examine the insulator.

Do not change the spark plug heat range to compensate for adverse engine or fueling conditions.

When replacing plugs, make sure the reach (B, **Figure 70**) is correct. A longer-than-standard plug could interfere with the piston, causing engine damage.

Refer to **Table 6** for recommended spark plugs.

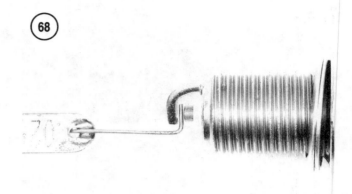

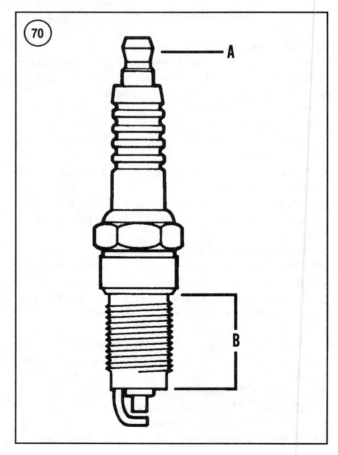

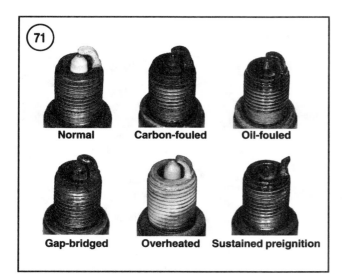

Normal   Carbon-fouled   Oil-fouled

Gap-bridged   Overheated   Sustained preignition

Reading

Reading the spark plugs can provide information regarding engine performance. Reading plugs that have been in use indicates spark plug operation, air/fuel mixture composition and engine conditions (such as oil consumption or pistons). Before checking the spark plugs, operate the motorcycle under a medium load for approximately 6 miles (10 km). Avoid prolonged idling before shutting off the engine. Remove the spark plugs as described in this section. Examine each plug and compare it to those in **Figure 71**. Refer to the descriptions in this section to determine the operating conditions.

Normal condition

If the plug has a light tan- or gray-colored deposit and no abnormal gap wear or erosion, good engine, air/fuel mixture and ignition conditions are indicated. The plug in use is of the proper heat range and may be serviced and returned to use.

Carbon fouled

Soft, dry, sooty deposits covering the entire firing end of the plug are evidence of incomplete combustion. Even though the firing end of the plug is dry, the plug's insulation decreases when in this condition. An electrical path is formed that bypasses the electrodes, resulting in a misfire condition. Carbon fouling can be caused by one or more of the following:
1. Cold spark plug heat range.
2. Clogged air filter.
3. Improperly-operating ignition component.
4. Ignition component failure.
5. Low engine compression.
6. Prolonged idling.

Oil-fouled

The tip of an oil-fouled plug has a black insulator tip, a damp, oily film over the firing end and a carbon layer over the entire nose. The electrodes are not worn. Oil-fouled spark plugs may be cleaned in an emergency, but it is better to replace them. It is important to correct the cause of fouling before the engine is returned to service. Common causes for this condition are:
1. Low idle speed or prolonged idling.
2. Ignition component failure.
3. Cold spark plug heat range.
4. Engine still being broken in.
5. Valve guides worn.
6. Piston rings worn or broken.

Gap bridging

Plugs with this condition exhibit gaps shorted out by combustion deposits between the electrodes. If this condition is encountered, check for excessive carbon or oil in the combustion chamber. Be sure to locate and correct the cause of this condition.

Overheating

Badly worn electrodes and premature gap wear are signs of overheating, along with a gray or white blistered porcelain insulator surface. The most common cause for this condition is using a spark plug of the wrong heat range (too hot). If spark plug is the correct heat range and is overheated, consider the following causes:
1. Improperly-operating ignition component.
2. Engine lubrication system malfunction.
3. Cooling system malfunction (clogged cooling fins).
4. Engine air leak.
5. Improper spark plug installation (over-tightening).
6. No spark plug gasket.

Worn out

Corrosive gases formed by combustion and high voltage sparks have eroded the electrodes. A spark plug in this condition requires more voltage to fire under hard acceleration. Replace with a new spark plug.

Preignition

If the electrodes are melted, preignition is almost certainly the cause. Check for intake air leaks at the manifold, or throttle body, and for advanced ignition timing. It is also possible that a plug of the wrong heat range (too hot) is being used. Find the cause of the preignition before returning the engine to service.

IGNITION TIMING

The engine ignition system is controlled by the electronic control module (ECM). There is no means of adjusting ignition timing. The manufacturer does not provide any ignition timing procedures. If an ignition-related problem is suspected, inspect the ignition components as described in Chapter Nine.

Incorrect ignition timing can cause a drastic loss of engine performance and efficiency. It may also cause overheating.

IDLE SPEED ADJUSTMENT

Idle speed adjustment must be performed with the H-D digital technician, or an equivalent.

MOTORCYCLE ALIGNMENT

This procedure checks the alignment of the rear axle with the swing arm pivot shaft. It also checks the engine stabilizer adjustment that aligns the engine in the frame. These checks determine the condition and alignment of the components that hold the motorcycle together: steering stem, front axle, engine, swing arm pivot shaft and rear axle. If any of these items are out of alignment, the motorcycle will not handle properly. Bad handling will increase the motorcycle's vibration level while reducing its overall performance and stability.

Preliminary Inspection

Before checking vehicle alignment, make the following checks to spot problems caused from normal wear. Adjust, repair or replace any component as required.
1. The top stabilizer, (**Figure 72**) mounted between the cylinder heads and upper frame weldment (**Figure 73**), aligns the top portion of the engine in the frame.
2. Check the engine stabilizer for loose or damaged parts at the intervals specified in **Table 1**. To service or replace the engine stabilizer, refer to Chapter Four. To adjust the engine stabilizer, perform the *Alignment* procedure in this section.

3. Check the steering head bearing adjustment as described in *Steering Play Inspection and Adjustment* (Chapter Eleven).
4. Check the runout of each wheel as described in Chapter Twelve.
5. Check the tightness of the engine mounting bolts; tighten if necessary as described in Chapter Four.

Alignment

Refer to **Figure 74**.

Each alignment inspection and adjustment, affects the next one. Work carefully, orderly and accurately when performing the following steps.
1. Perform all of the checks listed in *Preliminary Inspection* (this section). When all of the checks are within the specifications, continue the procedure. If the motorcycle has been involved in a crash, refer frame alignment to a dealership or motorcycle frame alignment specialist.

> *NOTE*
> *Always disarm the optional TSSM/HFSM security system prior to disconnecting the battery or pulling the Maxi-Fuse so the siren will not sound.*

2. On Screamin' Eagle and CVO models, remove the rear axle nut cover as described in Chapter Ten.
3. Support the motorcycle on level ground with the rear wheel off the ground. Refer to *Motorcycle Stands* in Chapter Ten.
4. Check axle alignment as follows:
  a. Place a caliper (A, **Figure 75**) against the end of the swing arm and the rear axle washer (B). Record the measurement.
  b. Repeat measurement on the opposite side, against the rear axle flange.
  c. The dimensions must be the same for both sides.
  d. If the alignment is incorrect, perform the drive belt adjustment procedure (this chapter). When the drive belt adjustment is correct, continue the procedure.

> *NOTE*
> *Make sure the rear wheel is off the ground for the remainder of the procedure.*

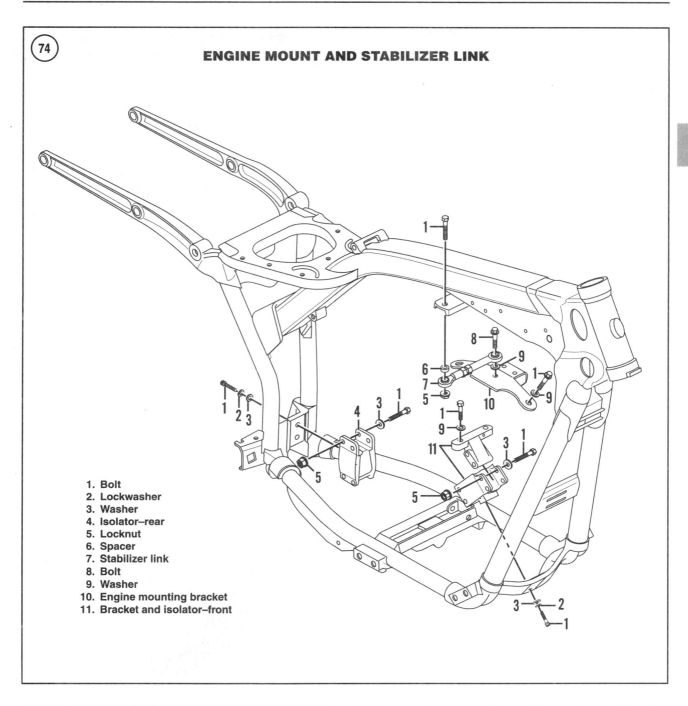

ENGINE MOUNT AND STABILIZER LINK

1. Bolt
2. Lockwasher
3. Washer
4. Isolator–rear
5. Locknut
6. Spacer
7. Stabilizer link
8. Bolt
9. Washer
10. Engine mounting bracket
11. Bracket and isolator–front

5. Remove the bolt (A, **Figure 76**) securing stabilize link eyelet to the engine mounting bracket (B).

6. Place an inclinometer on the front brake disc. Position the front wheel so the brake disc is vertical (90°), note the reading. This position must be maintained when performing Steps 7 and 8.

7. Align the stabilizer link hole with the engine mounting bracket and install the stabilizer link bolt (A, **Figure 76**). Do not force the bolt into position. Note the following:

   a. If the bolt holes do not align, adjust the stabilizer, starting with Step 8.

   b. If the holes align, proceed to Step 12.

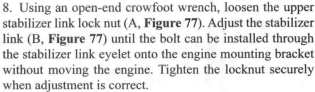

8. Using an open-end crowfoot wrench, loosen the upper stabilizer link lock nut (A, **Figure 77**). Adjust the stabilizer link (B, **Figure 77**) until the bolt can be installed through the stabilizer link eyelet onto the engine mounting bracket without moving the engine. Tighten the locknut securely when adjustment is correct.

9. Place the inclinometer on the rear brake disc and compare its position with the front brake disc noted in Step 6. If the readings are not within 1° of each other, continue to Step 10.

10. Readjust the stabilizer link (Step 8) until the rear brake disc is within 1° of the front brake disc. Note the following:

   a. If the adjustment cannot bring the brake discs within 1° of each other, inspect the swing arm, frame steering head and front forks for damage. If necessary, take the motorcycle to a dealership for further inspection.

   b. If the adjustment can bring the brake discs to within 1° of each other, but it takes more than five turns of the stabilizer link nut to do so, perform the chassis inspections described in this section. If a problem cannot be found with the chassis component, go to Step 11.

   c. If the adjustment cannot bring the brake discs within 1° of each other, and it takes less than five turns of the stabilizer link nut, tighten the stabilizer link locknut and go to Step 12.

11. If it takes more than five turns to align the brake discs, follow this procedure to center the frame and engine mounts. Read through the substeps, and then perform the following:

   a. Loosen but do not remove the front and rear engine isolator mounting bolts. Refer to **Figures 78-80**.

   b. Lower the motorcycle to the ground so that both wheels are on the ground.

   c. Shift the transmission into neutral, start the engine and let it idle for approximately 5 seconds. Turn off the engine.

   d. Tighten all isolator bolts and nuts to 25 ft.-lb. (34 N•m).

12. Securely tighten the bolt (A, **Figure 76**) securing stabilize link eyelet to the engine mounting bracket (B).

13. On Screamin' Eagle and CVO models, install the rear axle nut cover as described in Chapter Ten.

14. Test ride the motorcycle.

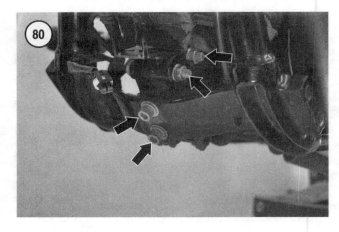

Table 1 MAINTENANCE AND LUBRICATION SCHEDULE[1]

Pre-ride check
  Check tire condition and inflation pressure.
  Check wheel rim condition.
  Check all lights and horn operation.
  Check engine oil level; add oil if necessary.
  Check brake fluid level and condition; add fluid if necessary.
  Check clutch fluid level and condition (Screamin' Eagle and CVO™ models); add fluid if necessary.
  Check the operation of the front brake lever and rear brake pedal.
  Check the throttle operation.
  Check clutch lever operation.
  Check fuel level in fuel tank; top off if necessary.
  Check fuel system for leaks.
First Service (1000 miles, 1600 km)
  Change engine oil and filter.
  Check the oil lines, brake lines, and clutch lines (Screamin' Eagle and CVO™ models) for leaks.
  Inspect air filter element.
  Check tire condition and inflation pressure.
  Check the wheel spokes; tighten as necessary.
  Change the primary chaincase lubricant.
  Change transmission lubricant.
  Check clutch operation; adjust if necessary.
  Check drive belt tension; adjust if necessary.
  Check condition of drive belt and sprockets.
  Check battery condition; clean cable connections if necessary.
  Check front and rear brake pads and discs for wear.
  Check brake fluid level and condition; add fluid if necessary.
  On Screamin' Eagle and CVO™ models, check clutch fluid level and condition; add fluid if necessary.
  Inspect spark plugs.
  Lubricate front brake and clutch lever pivot pins.
  Check throttle cable operation. Adjust and lubricate the cable as necessary.
  Check the clutch cable operation. Adjust and lubricate the cable as necessary (except Screamin' Eagle models).
  On Screamin' Eagle models, check the clutch release system.
  Check engine idle speed; adjust if necessary.
  Check fuel system for leaks.
  Check electrical switches and equipment for proper operation.
  Check the jiffy stand. Lubricate as necessary.
  Adjust the steering head bearings.
  Lubricate the hinges and latches on the fuel door.
  Check the exhaust system for leaks, cracks or loose fasteners.
  Check all fasteners for tightness[2].
  Road test the motorcycle.
Every 5000 miles (8000 km)
  Change engine oil and filter.
  Check the oil lines, brake lines, and clutch lines (Screamin' Eagle and CVO™ models) for leaks.
  Inspect and clean air filter element. Replace as necessary.
  Check tire condition and inflation pressure.
  Check the wheel spokes; tighten as necessary.
  Check clutch operation; adjust if necessary.
  Check primary chain deflection; adjust if necessary.
  Check drive belt tension; adjust if necessary.
  Check throttle cable operation. Adjust and lubricate the cable and throttle grip as necessary.
  Check the clutch cable operation. Adjust and lubricate the cable as necessary.
  On Screamin' Eagle and CVO™ models, check the clutch release system.
  Check fuel system for leaks.
  Check brake fluid level and condition; add fluid if necessary.
  Check clutch fluid level and condition (Screamin' Eagle and CVO™ models); add fluid if necessary.
  Inspect spark plugs.
  Check lubricant level in transmission and primary chaincase.
  Lubricate front brake and clutch lever pivot pins.
  Check battery condition; clean cable connections if necessary.
  Check electrical switches and equipment for proper operation
  Check engine idle speed; adjust if necessary.
  Lubricate the hinges and latches on the fuel door.
  Check the exhaust system for leaks, cracks or loose fasteners.
  Road test the motorcycle.

(continued)

Table 1 MAINTENANCE AND LUBRICATION SCHEDULE[1] (continued)

Every 5000 miles (8000 km) (continued)
  Lubricate throttle grip.
  Check steeing play; adjust if necessary.
Every 10,000 miles (16,000 km)
  Change engine oil and filter.
  Check the oil lines, brake lines, and clutch lines (Screamin' Eagle and CVO™ models) for leaks.
  Inspect and clean air filter element. Replace as necessary.
  Check tire condition and inflation pressure.
  Change the primary chaincase lubricant.
  Check clutch operation; adjust if necessary.
  Check drive belt tension; adjust if necessary.
  Check drive belt and sprockets condition.
  Check battery condition; clean cable connections if necessary.
  Check throttle cable operation. Adjust and lubricate the cable and throttle grip as necessary.
  Check the clutch cable operation. Adjust and lubricate the cable as necessary.
  On Screamin' Eagle and CVO models, check the clutch release system.
  Check fuel system for leaks.
  Check electrical switches and equipment for proper operation
  Check the jiffy stand. Lubricate as necessary.
  Check front and rear brake pads and discs for wear.
  Check brake fluid level and condition; add fluid if necessary.
  Check clutch fluid level and condition (Screamin' Eagle and CVO™ models); add fluid if necessary.
  Lubricate and adjust the steering head bearings.
  Check all fasteners for tightness[2].
  Check engine mounts and stabilizer links.
  Check tightness of swing arm pivot bolt.
  Road test the motorcycle.
Every 20,000 miles (32,000 km)
  Replace spark plugs.
  Clean and repack the swing arm bearings.
  Change the transmission lubricant.
  Change the primary chaincase lubricant.
  Disassemble, inspect, and lubricate the steering head bearings.
  Check the wheel spokes; tighten as necessary.
Every 25,000 miles (40,000 km)
  Adjust the steering head bearings.
Every 50,000 miles
  Change front fork oil.
Every year
  Check battery condition; clean cable connections if necessary.
  Check the exhaust system for leaks, cracks, broken heat shields and/or loose fasteners.
Every 2 years
  Flush and replace the hydraulic fluid in the brake system.
  Flush and replace the hydraulic fluid in the clutch system (Screamin' Eagle and CVO™ models).

1. Consider this maintenance schedule a guide to general maintenance and lubrication intervals. If the motorcycle is ridden harder than normal or if it is exposed to mud, water or high humidity, perform most of these maintenance items more frequently than indicated.
2. Except cylinder head bolts. Cylinder head bolts must be tightened following the procedure listed in Chapter Four. Improper tightening of the cylinder head bolts may cause cylinder gasket damage and/or cylinder head leakage.

Table 2 TIRE INFLATION PRESSURE (COLD)*

	PSI	kPa
Front wheel (all models except FXDF)		
Rider only	30	207
Rider and one passenger	30	207
Front wheel (FXDF models)		
Rider only	36	248
Rider and one passenger	36	248
Rear wheel		
Rider only	36	248
Rider and passenger	40	276

*Tire pressure for original equipment tires. Aftermarket tires may require different inflation pressure.

Table 3 FUEL, ENGINE AND DRIVE FLUID CAPACITIES

Item	Capacity	Item	Capacity
Fuel tank capacity (total)		Transmission (approximate)	32 U.S. oz (946 ml)
2006 models		Primary chaincase (approximate)	
FXD, FXDC	4.8 gal (18.17 L)	Wet	32 U.S. oz (946 ml)
FXDL, FXDB	4.7 gal (17.79 L)	Dry	40 U.S. oz (1.19L)
FXDWG, FXD35	5.1 gal (19.31 L)	Engine oil capacity	
2007 models		2006-2011 FXD, FXDB,	
FXD	4.8 gal (18.17 L)	FXDC, FXDL, FXDWG	
FXDL, FXDB	4.7 gal (17.79 L)	and FXD35 models	
FXDWG, FXDC	5.1 gal (19.31 L)	With oil change	2.5 qt. (2.4 L)
FXDSE	5.0 gal (18.93 L)	After engine rebuild	3.0 qt. (2.7 L)
2008-2011 models		2007 FXDSE	
FXD, FXDL, FXDB	4.8 gal (18.17 L)	and 2008 FXDSE2 models	
FXDWG, FXDC, FXDF	5.1 gal (19.31 L)	(oil tank w/filter)	3.5 qt. (3.3 L)
FXDSE2, FXDFSE	5.0 gal (18.93 L)	2009 FXDFSE	
		and 2010 FXDFSE2 models	
		(oil tank w/filter)	4.0 qt. (3.8 L)

Table 4 RECOMMENDED ENGINE OIL

Type	Viscosity	H-D Rating	Ambient operating temperature
H-D Multi-grade	SAE 10W40	HD 360	Below 40° F (4° C)
H-D Multi-grade	SAE 20W50	HD 360	Above 40° F (4° C)
H-D Regular Heavy	SAE 50	HD 360	Above 60° F (16° C)
H-D Extra Heavy	SAE 60	HD 360	Above 80° F (26.6° C)
Screamin' Eagle and CVO™ models			
SYN3 Synthetic Motorcycle Lubricant	SAE 20W50	HD 360	Above 40° F (4° C)

Table 5 RECOMMENDED LUBRICANTS AND FLUIDS

Brake fluid	DOT 4 hydraulic fluid
Clutch fluid (Screamin' Eagle models)	DOT 4 hydraulic fluid
Front fork oil	H-D Type E fork oil
Fuel	91 pump octane or higher
Transmission oil	
All models except Screamin' Eagle and CVO™ models	H-D Formula+ Transmission and Primary Chaincase Lubricant
Screamin' Eagle and CVO™ models	Screamin' Eagle SYN3 Synthetic Motorcycle Lubricant
Primary chaincase oil	
All models except Screamin' Eagle and CVO™ models	H-D Formula+ Transmission and Primary Chaincase Lubricant
Screamin' Eagle and CVO™ models	Screamin' Eagle SYN3 Synthetic Motorcycle Lubricant

Table 6 MAINTENANCE SPECIFICATIONS

Item	Specification
Brake pad minimum thickness	0.015 in. (0.38 mm)
Clutch cable free play	1/16-1/8 in. (1.6-3.2 mm)
Drive belt deflection	
FXD, FXDWG, FXDF models	1/4-5/16 in. (6.4-7.9 mm)
All other models	5/16-3/8 in. (7.9-9.5 mm)
	(continued)

Table 6 MAINTENANCE SPECIFICATIONS (continued)

Item	Specification
Engine compression	
All models except Screamin' Eagle and CVO models	125 psi (862 kPa)
Screamin' Eagle and CVO models	
ACR valve connected	130-170 psi (896-1172 kPa)
ACR valve disconnected	200-220 psi (1379-1517 kPa)
Spark plugs	HD No. 6R12*
Gap	0.038-0.043 in. (0.97-1.09 mm)
Idle speed	950-1050 rpm
Ignition timing	Non-adjustable

*The manufacturer recommends that no other type of spark plug be substituted.

Table 7 MAINTENANCE AND TUNE-UP TORQUE SPECIFICATIONS

Item	ft.-lb.	in.-lb.	N•m
Air filter (2007 FXDSE and 2008 FXDSE2 models)			
Breather bolts	22-24	–	29.8-32.5
Cover Allen screw	–	36-60	4.1-6.8
Element mounting screws	–	55-60	6.3-6.8
Standoff bolts	–	55-60	6.3-6.8
Trimplate Allen screw	–	27-32	3.1-3.6
Air filter hose clamp (2009 FXDFSE and 2010 FXDFSE2 models)	–	45-55	5.1-6.3
Air filter (all other models)			
Breather bolts	22-24	–	29.8-32.5
2006 models	10-12	–	13.6-16.3
2007-on models	22-24	–	29.8-32.5
Mounting bracket Torx screws	–	40-60	4.5-6.8
Cover Allen screw	–	36-60	4.1-6.8
Brake master cylinder reservoir cover (front and rear) screws	–	6-8	0.7-0.9
Clutch adjusting screw locknut	–	72-120	8.1-13.6
Clutch inspection cover screws	–	84-108	9.5-12.2
Clutch master cylinder reservoir cover screws (Screamin' Eagle and CVO models only)	–	6-8	0.7-0.9
Engine isolator bolt and nut	25	–	33.9
Engine oil drain plug	14-21	–	19-28.5
Primary chaincase			
Inspection cover screws	–	84-108	9.5-12.2
Drain plug			
2006 models	–	36-60	4.1-6.8
2007-on models	14-21	–	19.0-28.5
Jiffy stand leg stop bolt	12-15	–	16-20
Rear axle adjuster screw	–	96-120	10.8-13.6
Rear axle nut			
2006 models	60-65	–	81.4-88.1
2007 models	92-98	–	124.7-132.9
2008-2011 models	95-105	–	128.8-142.4
Spark plug	12-18	–	16.3-2.4
Transmission			
Dipstick	–	25-75	2.8-8.5
Drain plug	14-21	–	19-28.5
Vehicle alignment			
Isolator mounting bolt	25	–	33.9

CHAPTER FOUR

ENGINE TOP END

The air-cooled, four-stroke, overhead-valve, V-twin engine consists of three major assemblies: top end/cylinder, crankcase and gearcase. Viewed from the engine's right side, engine rotation is clockwise. A dual counterbalancing system rotates in the opposite direction to minimize vibration.

Both cylinders fire once in 720° of crankshaft rotation. The rear cylinder fires 315° after the front cylinder. The front cylinder fires again in another 405°. Note that one cylinder is always on its exhaust stroke when the other fires on its compression stroke.

Complete overhaul procedures for the engine top end and exhaust components are covered in this chapter. Refer to Chapter Five for lower end engine procedures. Refer to **Tables 1-5** at the end of the chapter for specifications.

ENGINE SERVICE PRECAUTIONS

Before servicing the engine, note the following:

1. Review *Service Methods* and *Measuring Tools* in Chapter One. Accurate measurements are required to successfully rebuild the engine.

2. The text frequently mentions the left and right side of the engine. This refers to the engine as it is mounted in the frame not how it may sit on the workbench.

3. Always replace worn or damaged fasteners with those of the same size, type and strength requirements. Clearly identify each bolt before replacing it. Lubricate bolt threads with engine oil, unless otherwise noted, before tightening them. If a specific torque value is not listed in **Table 5**, refer to the general torque recommendations in Chapter One.

4. Use special tools where noted. These tools and their part numbers are listed for individual procedures and in

Chapter One. Refer to *Tools* in Chapter One for additional information.

5. Store parts in boxes, plastic bags and containers. Use masking tape and a permanent, waterproof marking pen to label parts as they are removed from the motorcycle.

6. Use a box of assorted size and color vacuum hose identifiers (Lisle part No. 74600) to mark and help identify hoses and fittings during engine removal and disassembly.

7. Use a vise with protective jaws to hold parts.

8. Use a press or special tools when force is required to remove and install parts. Do not try to pry, hammer or otherwise force them on or off.

9. Replace all gaskets, O-rings and oil seals during reassembly. Lubricate new O-rings with the lubricant that is being sealed. Apply a small amount of grease to the inner lips of each new seal to prevent damage when the engine is first started. Thoroughly clean all gasket, O-ring or seal mating surfaces before installation.

10. Record the location, position and thickness of all shims as they are removed.

11. When disconnecting the battery is called for, on models with an optional security siren, disarm the security system (TSSM/HFSM) before disconnecting the battery or pulling the maxi-fuse so the sire will not sound. Refer to *Turn Signal* and *Security Module* in Chapter Nine.

12. The following components can be serviced while the engine is mounted in the frame:

   a. Rocker arm cover and rocker arms.
   b. Cylinder heads.
   c. Cylinders and pistons.
   d. Camshafts.
   e. Gearshift mechanism.
   f. Clutch and primary drive assembly.

g. Transmission.

h. Throttle body or fuel injection induction module.

i. Starter and gears.

j. Alternator and electrical systems.

ROCKER ARMS, PUSHRODS AND VALVE LIFTERS

Refer to **Figure 1** and **Figure 2**.

The rocker arm, pushrod and valve lifter procedures shown here are performed on the rear cylinder. The same procedures also apply to the front cylinder. Any differences are noted.

The rear cylinder head is closer to the frame backbone than the front cylinder. In some cases it may be possible to completely remove some of the rocker arm mounting bolts on the front cylinder that cannot be removed on the rear cylinder.

Removal

1. If the engine is mounted in the frame, perform the following:
   a. Securely support the motorcycle on a level surface. Refer to *Motorcycle Stands* in Chapter Ten.
   b. Thoroughly clean the engine of all dirt and debris.
   c. Remove the seat and right footrest as described in Chapter Fourteen.
   d. Disconnect the negative battery cable, and then the positive cable as described in Chapter Nine.
   e. Drain the engine oil and remove the spark plugs as described in Chapter Three.
   f. Remove the fuel tank as described in Chapter Eight.
   g. Remove the air filter and housing as described in Chapter Eight.
   h. Remove the exhaust system as described in this chapter.
   i. Remove the fuel induction module as described in Chapter Eight.

2. Following the sequence shown in **Figure 3**, evenly loosen the rocker arm cover bolts. Remove each bolt and its captive washer.

3. Remove the rocker arm cover and gasket. Discard the gasket.

4. Remove both spark plugs as described in Chapter Three to make it easier to rotate the engine by hand.

5A. Use a pushrod tool (Motion Pro part No. 08-0255) and compress the upper and lower pushrod covers (A, **Figure 4**). Insert a screwdriver and pry the spring cap retainer (B, **Figure 4**) free and remove it.

5B. If the pushrod tool is not available, using a screwdriver, pry the spring cap retainer (**Figure 5**) from between the cylinder head and spring cap. Compress the upper (A, **Figure 6**) and lower (B) push rod covers.

CAUTION
The piston must be at top dead center (TDC) on the compression stroke to avoid damage to the pushrods and rocker arms.

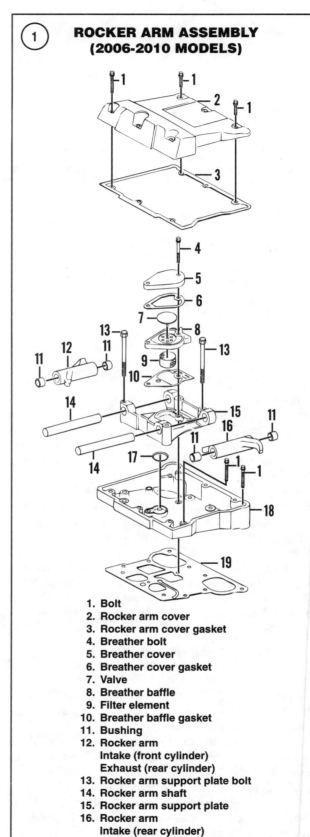

① ROCKER ARM ASSEMBLY (2006-2010 MODELS)

1. Bolt
2. Rocker arm cover
3. Rocker arm cover gasket
4. Breather bolt
5. Breather cover
6. Breather cover gasket
7. Valve
8. Breather baffle
9. Filter element
10. Breather baffle gasket
11. Bushing
12. Rocker arm
    Intake (front cylinder)
    Exhaust (rear cylinder)
13. Rocker arm support plate bolt
14. Rocker arm shaft
15. Rocker arm support plate
16. Rocker arm
    Intake (rear cylinder)
    Exhaust (front cylinder)
17. O-ring
18. Rocker arm housing
19 Rocker arm housing gasket

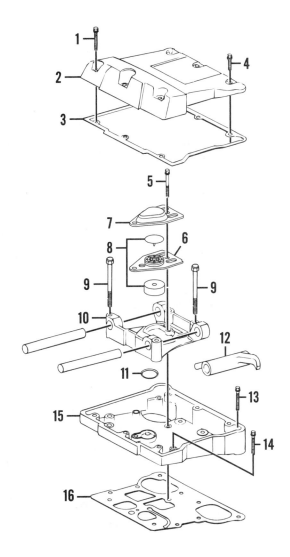

**ROCKER ARM ASSEMBLY
(2011 MODELS)**

1. Bolt
2. Rocker arm cover
3. Rocker arm cover gasket
4. Bolt
5. Breather bolt
6. Breather baffle plate
7. Breather cover
8. Baffle and cover
9. Rocker arm support plate bolt
10. Rocker arm support plate
11. O-ring
12. Rocker arm
   Intake-front cylinder
   Exhaust-rear cylinder
13. Bolt
14. Bolt
15. Rocker arm housing
16. Rocker arm housing gasket

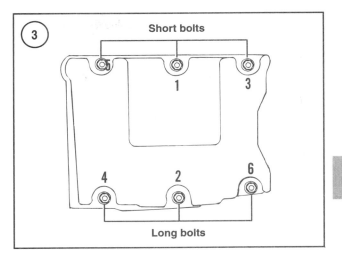

6A. *With the primary chain cover in place*, position the piston for the cylinder being worked on at top dead center (TDC) on the compression stroke as follows:

   a. Support the motorcycle on a stand with the rear wheel off the ground. Refer to *Motorcycle Stands* in Chapter Ten.

   b. Shift the transmission into sixth gear.

   c. Rotate the rear wheel in the direction of normal rotation.

   d. Stop rotating the rear wheel when the intake and exhaust valves are closed.

e. Look into the spark plug hole with a flashlight and verify that the piston is at TDC.

f. Wiggle both rocker arms. There should be free play that indicates that both valves are closed and the piston is at top dead center (TDC) on the compression stroke. Also, verify the push rods are in the unloaded position.

6B. *With the primary chaincase cover removed,* position the piston for the cylinder being worked on at top dead center (TDC) on the compression stroke as follows:

a. Remove the primary chaincase cover as described in Chapter Six.

b. Shift the transmission into NEUTRAL.

c. Place a socket or wrench on the compensating sprocket shaft nut.

d. Rotate the compensating sprocket shaft *counterclockwise* until the intake and exhaust valves are closed.

e. Look into the spark plug hole with a flashlight and verify that the piston is at TDC.

f. Wiggle both rocker arms. There should be free play that indicates that both valves are closed and the piston is at top dead center (TDC) on the compression stroke. Also, verify the push rods are in the unloaded position.

7. Using a crossing pattern, completely loosen the four bolts (A, **Figure 7**) securing the rocker arm support plate. The bolts cannot be removed at this time.

8. Completely loosen the bolts securing the breather assembly (B, **Figure 7**).

9. Remove the two *right side* rocker arm support bolts (A, **Figure 8**) and the *right side* breather assembly bolt (B).

NOTE
The two left side rocker arm support bolts and left side breather assembly bolt can not be removed until the rocker arm housing is removed from the cylinder head.

10. Lift the right side of the rocker arm support plate (A, **Figure 9**) sufficiently to clear the push rods (B).

11. Carefully slide the rocker arm support plate out through the right side and remove it from the cylinder head,

12. Remove the two *left side* rocker arm support bolts (A, **Figure 10**) and the *left side* breather assembly bolt (B).

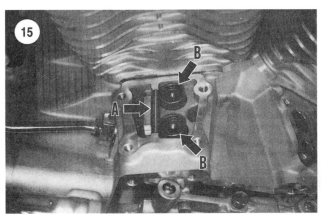

4

Remove the breather assembly (C, **Figure 10**) from the rocker arm support plate.

13. Remove the O-ring seal (A, **Figure 11**) from the rocker arm housing.

NOTE
When removing the pushrods, do not mix the parts from each set. When reinstalling the original pushrods, install them so each end faces in its original operating position. The pushrods develop a set wear pattern and installing them upside down may cause rapid wear to the pushrod, lifter and rocker arm.

14. Lift the silver intake (B, **Figure 11**) and black exhaust (C) pushrods from the cylinder head. Mark the top and bottom of the pushrods, and mark its operating position in the cylinder head.

15. Remove the pushrod covers as follows:
   a. Slide the upper cover (A, **Figure 12**) down, and remove the pushrod cover assembly (B) from the cylinder head and the lifter cover. Do not lose the O-rings.
   b. Label the cover assembly so it can be reinstalled in its original location.
   c. Repeat the process to remove the remaining pushrod cover.

NOTE
*To clear the cylinder's lower cooling fins, loosen the lifter cover's two inner Allen bolts with a short 90° Allen wrench (**Figure 13**).*

16. Remove the lifter cover mounting bolts (**Figure 14**) and captive washers. Then, remove the cover.

17. Remove and discard the lifter cover gasket.

CAUTION
Do not mix the valve lifters when removing them. Mark them so they can be installed in their original positions.

18. Remove the anti-rotation pin (A, **Figure 15**), and then remove both valve lifters (B). If the lifters will not be inspected as described in this section, store them upright in a container filled with clean engine oil until installation.

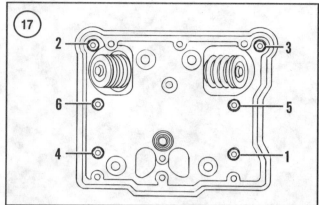

19. Cover the crankcase opening with duct tape (**Figure 16**) to prevent the entry of debris.

20. Loosen the six rocker arm housing bolts in 1/8-turn increments following the sequence shown in **Figure 17**. Remove the rocker arm housing bolts and their captive washers. Note that the two bolts on the left side of the engine are longer than the other four interior bolts.

21. Tap the rocker arm housing loose with a rubber mallet, and then lift it off the cylinder head.

22. Remove and discard the rocker arm housing gasket.

23. Disassemble and inspect the rocker arm assembly, pushrod covers or breather as needed (this section).

Installation

NOTE
Figure 18 and Figure 19 are shown with the engine removed to clearly illustrate the steps.

1. Position a *new* rocker arm housing gasket so it covers the breather channel (**Figure 18**), and install the gasket (**Figure 19**).

2. Install the breather assembly onto the rocker arm support plate, if removed.

3. Apply Loctite Threadlocker 243 (blue), or an equivalent, to the bolt threads. Then, install the two left side bolts (A, **Figure 10**) and left side breather assembly bolt (B) onto the rocker arm housing.

4. Install the rocker arm housing onto the cylinder head.

5. Apply Loctite Threadlocker 243 (blue), or an equivalent, to the bolt threads. Then, install the right side rocker arm housing bolts (A, **Figure 9**) along with their captive washer, and the right side breather assembly bolt (B).

6. Finger-tighten all bolts until snug. Following the sequence shown in **Figure 17**, evenly tighten the rocker arm housing bolts in 1/8-turn increments to 120-168 in.-lb. (13.6-19.0 N•m).

CAUTION
The valve springs must not contact any part of the rocker arm housing.

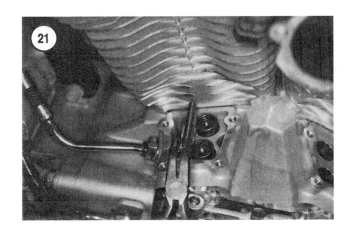

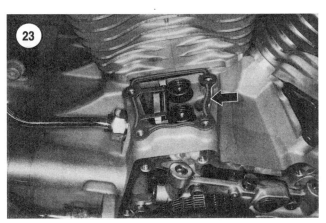

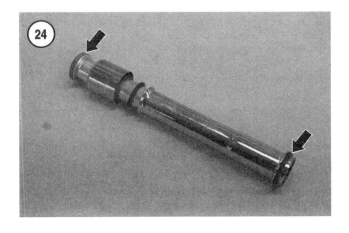

7. On Screamin' Eagle and CVO models, use a feeler gauge to check for clearance between each valve spring and the rocker arm housing. If necessary, loosen the housing bolts, and adjust the position of the rocker arm housing. Retighten the bolts as described in this section.

8. Install a *new* O-ring seal (**Figure 11**) onto the rocker arm housing. Apply a light coat of clean engine oil to the O-ring.

9. Remove the duct tape from the crankcase openings.

10. Install each valve lifter into the correct crankcase bore. The oil hole of each lifter must face the inboard side of its bore and the lifter flats must face the front and rear of the engine (**Figure 20**). This is necessary for installation of the anti-rotation pin in the next step.

CAUTION
Failure to install the anti-rotational pin will allow the lifter to rotate off the camshaft lobe and cause severe internal engine damage.

11. Completely seat the anti-rotation pin (**Figure 21**) within the crankcase slot so the pin rests against the flats (A, **Figure 15**) of both hydraulic lifters.

12. If the engine's position has been disturbed since the rocker arm components were removed, rotate the engine until both lifters for the cylinder being serviced sit on the lowest point (base circle) of the cam. The lifter's top surface should be flush with the top surface of the crankcase surface as shown in **Figure 22**.

13. Install a *new* lifter cover gasket (**Figure 23**) onto the crankcase.

NOTE
To clear the cylinder's lower cooling fins, tighten the two inner Allen bolts on the lifter cover with a short 90° Allen wrench.

14. Install the lifter cover and the mounting bolts (**Figure 14**). Tighten the bolts to 90-120 in.-lb. (10.2-13.6 N•m).

15. Install a *new* O-ring (**Figure 24**) onto each end of the pushrod covers. Apply a light coat of clean engine oil to each O-ring.

16. If the pushrod cover assembly was disassembled, reassemble it as described in *Pushrods* (this section).

CAUTION
*The pushrod covers and the pushrods must be installed in the correct locations (**Table 4**) in the cylinder head and lifter cover.*

17. Install the pushrod covers by performing the following:
   a. Compress the pushrod cover assembly, and fit the lower cover into the correct lifter cover bore (**Figure 25**).
   b. Slide the upper cover (**Figure 26**) up into the cylinder head bore. Do not install the spring cap retain at this time.
   c. Repeat the process to install the remaining pushrod cover.

18. Install the pushrods as follows:

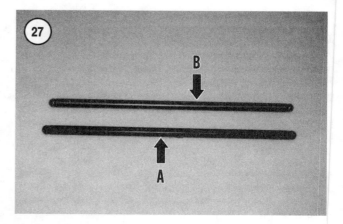

CAUTION
Two different length pushrods are used. The black exhaust pushrods (A, Figure 27) are longer than the silver intake pushrods (B).

a. When installing the existing pushrods, install each pushrod in its original position (A, **Figure 28**; intake) and with the correct orientation (B; exhaust). New pushrods can be installed with either end facing up

b. Make sure the pushrod is centered in its respective lifter.

19. Check the piston in the cylinder being serviced to confirm that it is still at top dead center on the compression stroke. If necessary, set the piston to TDC as described in *Installation* (this section). Watch the intake pushrod (B, **Figure 11**) while rotating the engine. When the intake rod rises and then comes down, the cylinder's piston is at TDC on the compression stroke.

20A. If the breather was disassembled, assemble it as described in *Breather Disassembly/Inspection/Assembly* (this section).

20B. Make sure the left breather bolt (B, **Figure 10**) and breather cover (C) are in place in the housing. Refer to *Breather Disassembly/Inspection/Assembly* (this section).

21. Install the two *left side* rocker arm support bolts (A, **Figure 10**).

22. From the right side, slide the rocker arm housing (A, **Figure 29**) onto the cylinder head cover, past the pushrods (B).

CAUTION
To avoid damaging a pushrod, rocker arms or valves, follow a crossing pattern and evenly tighten the rocker arm support plate bolts in 1/4 –turn increments. When tightening the mounting bolts, frequently spin each pushrod by hand to ensure the rocker arm support plate is being tightened evenly. If one or both pushrods cannot be rotated, loosen the mounting bolts and determine the cause.

23. Following a crossing pattern, evenly tighten the rocker arm support plate bolts in 1/4 turn increments to 18-22 ft.-lb. (24.4-29.8 N•m).

32

Short bolts

5   1   3

4   2   6

Long bolts

24. Evenly tighten the breather cover bolts to 90-120 in.-lb. (10.2-13.6 N•m).

CAUTION
If the valve lifters remained pumped up during disassembly, the pushrods may be under pressure and will not spin when checked. If this occurs, confirm that the cylinder is set to top dead center. If it is, wait. The pressure from pushrods will cause the lifters to bleed out. Do not rotate the engine while the pushrods are under pressure. If one or both pushrods cannot be rotated after a couple of

hours, remove the rocker arm support plate and determine the cause of the problem.

25. Lift each lower pushrod cover and confirm that each pushrod rotates freely.

26. Make sure the pushrod cover O-rings (**Figure 24**) are correctly seated in the cylinder head and lifter cover.

27. Install a *new* rocker arm cover gasket (**Figure 30**). Then, install the rocker arm cover (**Figure 31**).

NOTE
*There are two different length bolts (**Figure 32**) securing the rocker arm cover.*

28. Install each rocker arm cover bolt with its captive washer. Apply Loctite Threadlocker 243 (blue), or an equivalent, to the bolt threads. Following the sequence shown in **Figure 32**, tighten the rocker arm cover bolts in 1/8-turn increments to 15-18 ft.-lbs (20.3-24.4 N•m).

29A. Use a pushrod tool (Motion Pro part No. 08-0255) to compress the upper and lower pushrod covers (**Figure 33**) and install the spring cap retainer (**Figure 34**). Repeat for the remaining pushrod cover.

29B. If the pushrod tool is not available, compress the spring cap with a thin, open-end wrench (A, **Figure 35**) or an equivalent, and install the spring cap retainer (B). Make sure the spring cap retainer is positioned correctly on both the upper cover and the spring cap. Repeat for the remaining pushrod cover.

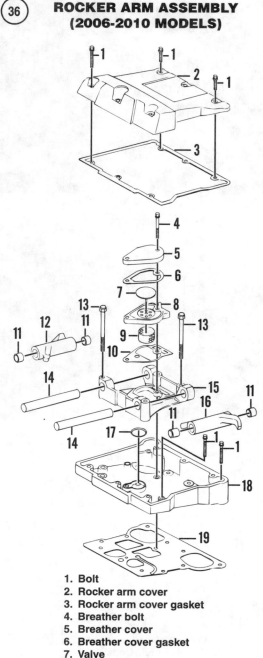

**ROCKER ARM ASSEMBLY
(2006-2010 MODELS)**

30. If the engine is mounted in the frame, perform the following:

   a. Install the fuel induction module as described in Chapter Eight.

   b. Install the exhaust system as described in this chapter.

   c. Install the air filter and housing as described in Chapter Eight.

   d. Install the fuel tank as described in Chapter Eight.

   e. Refill the engine oil and install the spark plugs as described in Chapter Three.

   f. Connect the negative, and then the positive battery cable as described in Chapter Nine.

   g. Install the seat and right footrest as described in Chapter Fourteen.

Rocker Arm Disassembly/Assembly

Refer to **Figure 36** and **Figure 37**.

1. Before removing the rocker arms, measure the rocker arm end clearance as follows:

   a. Insert a feeler gauge between the rocker arm and the inside rocker arm support plate (**Figure 38**).

   b. Record the measurement.

   c. Repeat for each rocker arm.

   d. Replace the rocker arm and/or the rocker arm support if the end clearance exceeds the service limit.

2. Prior to disassembling the rocker arms, mark each one with IN (A, **Figure 39**), for intake, or EX (B), for exhaust, to ensure they are installed in their original positions.

3. Use a hammer and drift to tap the left side of each rocker shaft so the notched ends come out first. Remove the rocker arm shafts (A, **Figure 40**) and the rocker arms (B).

4. Clean all parts in solvent, blow compressed air through all oil passages, and inspect the components this section.

5. Install the rocker arm shaft (A, **Figure 41**) in it's original position by inserting it part way into the rocker arm support plate (B).

6. Install a rocker arm (C, **Figure 41**) into its original position and push the shaft (A) part way through the rocker arm.

7. Align the notch (A, **Figure 42**) in the rocker arm shaft with the mating bolt hole (B) in the support and install the shaft all the way. Check for correct alignment (**Figure 43**).

1. Bolt
2. Rocker arm cover
3. Rocker arm cover gasket
4. Breather bolt
5. Breather cover
6. Breather cover gasket
7. Valve
8. Breather baffle
9. Filter element
10. Breather baffle gasket
11. Bushing
12. Rocker arm
   Intake (front cylinder)
   Exhaust (rear cylinder)
13. Rocker arm support plate bolt
14. Rocker arm shaft
15. Rocker arm support plate
16. Rocker arm
   Intake (rear cylinder)
   Exhaust (front cylinder)
17. O-ring
18. Rocker arm housing
19 Rocker arm housing gasket

4

ROCKER ARM ASSEMBLY (2011 MODELS)

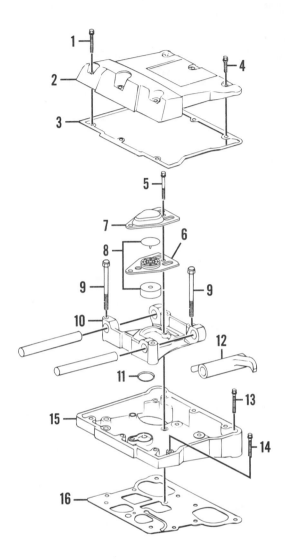

1. Bolt
2. Rocker arm cover
3. Rocker arm cover gasket
4. Bolt
5. Breather bolt
6. Breather baffle plate
7. Breather cover
8. Baffle and cover
9. Rocker arm support plate bolt
10. Rocker arm support plate
11. O-ring
12. Rocker arm
    Intake-front cylinder
    Exhaust-rear cylinder
13. Bolt
14. Bolt
15. Rocker arm housing
16. Rocker arm housing gasket

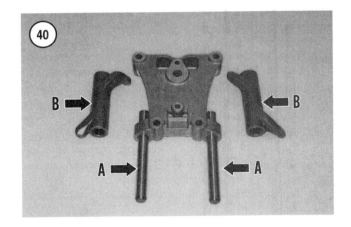

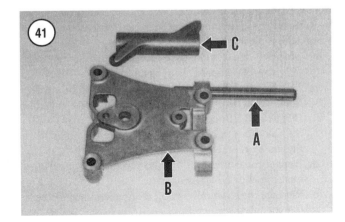

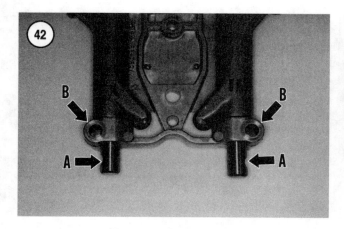

8. Repeat assembly procedure for the remaining rocker arm and shaft.

Rocker Arm Component Inspection

During inspection, compare any measurements to the specifications listed in **Table 2** or **Table 3**. Replace any part that is worn, damaged or out of specification.

1. Inspect the rocker arm pads (A, **Figure 44**) and ball sockets (B) for pitting and excessive wear.

2. Examine the rocker arm shaft (**Figure 45**) for scoring, ridge wear or other damage. If these conditions are present, replace the rocker arm shaft.

3. Check the rocker arm bushing (**Figure 46**) for wear or scoring.

4. Perform the following to determine the shaft-to-rocker arm support clearance.

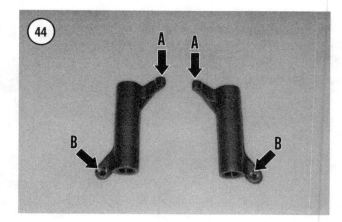

   a. Measure the inside diameter of each rocker arm support bore (**Figure 47**). Record the measurement.

   b. Measure the outside diameter of the rocker arm shaft at each end where it contacts the rocker arm support bore (**Figure 48**). Record the measurement.

   c. Subtract the rocker arm shaft outside diameter (**Figure 48**) from the rocker arm support bore inside diameter (**Figure 47**). The difference equals the shaft-to-rocker arm support clearance.

   d. Repeat measurements for the remaining rocker arm support bore and remaining rocker arm shaft.

   e. Replace the shaft or rocker arm support plate if any calculated clearance exceeds the service limit.

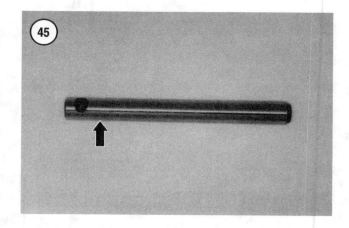

5. Perform the following to determine the shaft-to-rocker arm bushing clearance:

   a. Measure the rocker arm bushing inside diameter (**Figure 49**). Record the measurement.

   b. Measure the diameter of the rocker arm shaft outside diameter where it contacts the rocker arm bushing (**Figure 48**). Record the measurement.

   c. Subtract the rocker arm shaft outside diameter from the inside diameter of the bushing.

   d. Repeat measurements for the remaining rocker arm bushing and rocker arm shaft.

   e. Replace the shaft or bushing if any clearance exceeds the specified service limit.

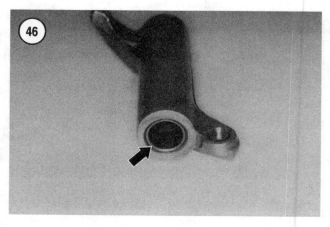

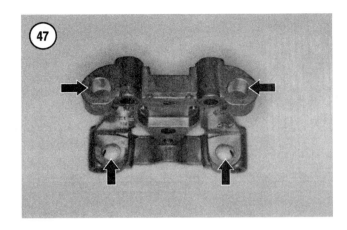

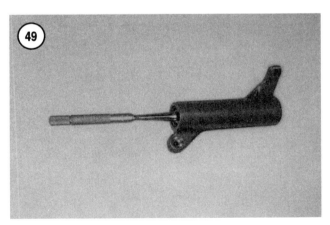

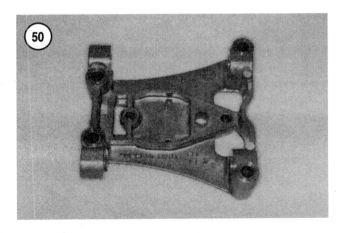

6. Inspect the rocker arm support bores (**Figure 47**) for wear or elongation.

7. Inspect the gasket surface of the rocker arm cover for damage or warp.

8. Inspect the rocker arm support plate (**Figure 50**) for damage or warp.

9. Inspect both gasket surfaces of the rocker arm housing for damage or warp.

Rocker Arm Bushing Replacement

Each rocker arm is equipped with two bushings (**Figure 46**). Replacement bushings must be reamed after installation. Use a rocker arm bushing reamer (JIMS part No. 94804-57) or an equivalent, to ream the replacement bushings. If the correct size reamer is unavailable, have the bushings replaced by a dealership.

NOTE
Since the new bushings must be reamed, remove one bushing at a time. The opposite bushing is then used as a guide to ream the first bushing.

1. Press one bushing (**Figure 46**) out of the rocker arm. Do not remove the second bushing. If the bushing is difficult to remove, perform the following:

    a. Thread a 9/16 × 18 tap into the bushing.

    b. Support the rocker arm in a press so the tap is at the bottom.

    c. Insert a mandrel through the top of the rocker arm and seat it on top of the tap.

    d. Press on the mandrel to force the bushing and tap out of the rocker arm.

    e. Remove the tap from the bushing and discard the bushing.

2. Position the new bushing with the split portion facing toward the top of the rocker arm.

3. Press the new bushing into the rocker arm until the bushing's outer surface is flush with the end of rocker arm bore.

4. Ream the new bushing with a bushing reamer as follows:

    a. Mount the rocker arm in a vise with soft jaws so the new bushing is at the bottom.

CAUTION
Only turn the reamer clockwise. Do not rotate the reamer counterclockwise or the reamer and bushing will be damaged.

    b. Mount a tap handle on top of the reamer and insert the reamer into the bushing. Turn the reamer *clockwise* until it passes through the new bushing and remove it from the bottom side.

5. Remove the rocker arm from the vise and repeat the procedure to replace the opposite bushing. The first bushing now serves as a guide to ream the second bushing.

6. After installing and reaming both bushings, clean the rocker arm assembly in solvent. Then, clean it with hot,

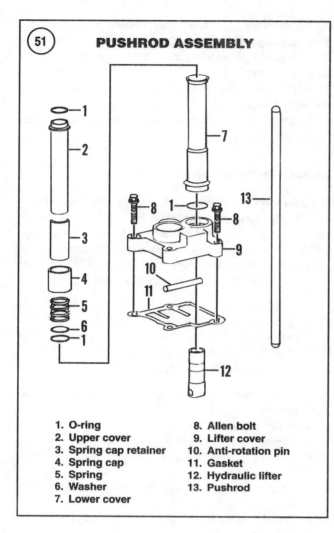

PUSHROD ASSEMBLY

1. O-ring
2. Upper cover
3. Spring cap retainer
4. Spring cap
5. Spring
6. Washer
7. Lower cover
8. Allen bolt
9. Lifter cover
10. Anti-rotation pin
11. Gasket
12. Hydraulic lifter
13. Pushrod

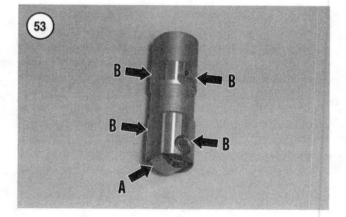

soapy water and rinse it with clear, cold water. Dry it with compressed air.

7. Calculate the shaft-to-rocker arm bushing clearance at each end of the rocker arm as described in *Rocker Arm Component Inspection* (this section). Each clearance must be within specification.

Valve Lifter Inspection

Figure 51 shows a valve lifter in relation to its pushrod and valve lifter cover. The valve lifters and covers are installed on the right side of the engine. During engine operation, the lifters are pumped full of engine oil, thus taking up all play in the valve train. When the engine is turned off, the lifters leak down after a period of time as some of the oil drains out. When the engine is started, the lifters click until they completely refill with oil. The lifters are working properly when they stop clicking after the engine is run for a few minutes. If the clicking persists, a problem may exist with the lifter(s).

CAUTION
Place the lifters on a clean, lint-free cloth during inspection.

1. Check the pushrod socket (**Figure 52**) in the top of the lifter for wear or damage.
2. Check the lifter roller (A, **Figure 53**) for pitting, scoring, galling or excessive wear. If the roller is excessively worn, check the mating cam lobe for the same condition.
3. Clean the lifter roller. Measure the roller clearance on the pin and the roller end clearance. Replace the lifter if either measurement clearance exceeds the wear limit.
4. Determine the lifter-to-bore clearance as follows:
   a. Use inside micrometers to measure the inside diameter of the lifter bore in the crankcase.
   b. Use outside micrometers to measure the lifter outside diameter (B, **Figure 53**).

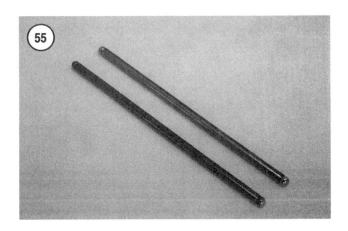

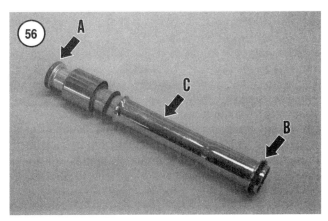

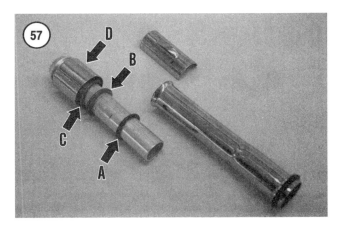

c. Calculate the lifter-to-bore clearance by subtracting the lifter outside diameter from the lifter bore inside diameter.

d. Replace the lifter and/or crankcase half if the lifter-to-bore clearance exceeds the service limit.

5. If a lifter does not show visual damage, it may be contaminated with dirt or have internal damage. If so, replace it. The lifters are not serviceable and must be replaced as a unit.

6. After inspecting the lifters, store them in a container filled with clean engine oil until installation.

7. If most of the oil has drained out of the lifter, refill it with a pump-type oil can through the oil hole in the side of the lifter.

8. Clean all gasket material from the mating surfaces of the crankcase and the lifter cover.

9. Inspect the lifter cover (**Figure 54**) for cracks or damage.

Pushrod Inspection

1. Clean the pushrods in solvent and dry them with compressed air.

2. Check the pushrods (**Figure 55**) for cracks and worn or damaged ball heads.

3. Roll the pushrods on a surface plate or on a piece of glass, and check for bending.

4. Replace any damaged pushrods.

Pushrod Cover Disassembly/Inspection/Assembly

Refer to **Figure 51**.

1. Remove and discard the O-ring from the seat (A, **Figure 56**) on the upper pushrod cover and from the seat (B) on the lower cover.

2. Pull the lower pushrod cover C, (**Figure 56**) from the upper cover.

3. Slide the O-ring (A, **Figure 57**), washer (B), spring (C) and spring cap (D) from the upper pushrod cover. Discard the O-ring.

4. Clean all parts in solvent, and blow them dry with compressed air. Make sure the O-ring seats and contact surfaces of the covers are clean.

5. Check the pushrod cover assembly as follows:

a. Check the spring for sagging or cracking.

b. Check the washer for deformation or damage.

c. Check the pushrod covers for cracking or damage.

6. Replace all worn or damaged parts.

7. Assembly is the reverse of disassembly. Install new O-rings. Lubricate each O-ring with clean engine oil.

Breather Disassembly/Inspection/Assembly

Refer to **Figure 36** and **Figure 37**.

1. Remove the left breather bolt (A, **Figure 58**), and lift the breather cover (B) from the rocker arm support plate.

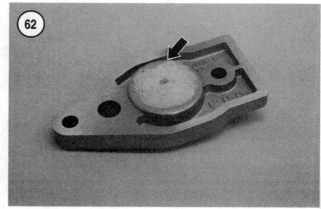

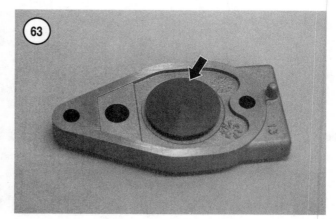

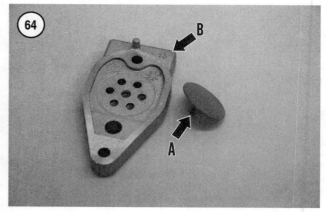

2. On 2006-2010 models, remove and discard the breather cover gasket (**Figure 59**).

3A. On 2006-2010 models, remove the baffle plate (**Figure 60**) and its gasket (**Figure 61**) from the rocker arm support plate. Discard the gasket.

3B. On 2011 models, remove the breather baffle plate from the rocker arm support plate.

4. Remove the filter element (**Figure 62**) from the breather baffle, and then remove the umbrella valve (A, **Figure 63**). Discard both.

5. Clean all parts in solvent. Blow them dry with compressed air.

6. Inspect the breather by performing the following:

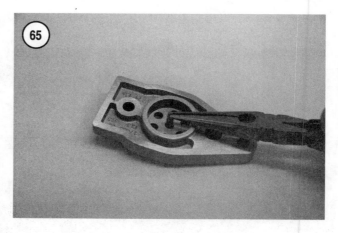

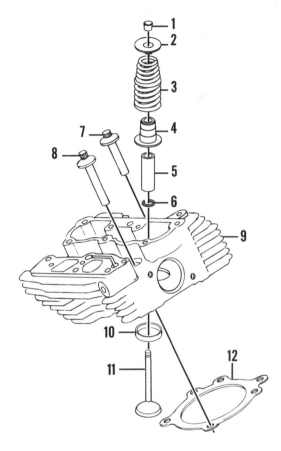

66

**CYLINDER HEAD
(ALL MODELS EXCEPT
SCREAMIN' EAGLE AND CVO)**

1. Valve keeper
2. Spring retainer
3. Spring
4. Valve stem seal/spring
   seat assembly
5. Valve guide
6. Retaining ring (exhaust
   valve only on 2006 and
   2007 models; exhaust
   valve and intake valves
   on 2008-2009 models)
7. Cylinder head bolt, short
8. Cylinder head bolt, long
9. Cylinder head
10. Valve seat
11. Valve
12. Gasket

a. Place a straightedge diagonally across the breather cover so the straightedge crosses opposite corners of the cover.

b. Check the breather cover warp by inserting a feeler gauge at several places between the straightedge and the cover.

c. Repeat procedure to check the warp across the opposite diagonal.

d. Replace the breather cover if any measurement exceeds the specified service limit.

e. Repeat procedure, and check the breather baffle warp.

7. Assemble the breather by performing the following:

a. Install the stem of the umbrella valve (A, **Figure 64**) into the breather baffle (B). Lubricate the valve stem with denatured alcohol or glass cleaner, insert the stem through the center hole in the top of the breather baffle and pull the stem through from the other side (**Figure 65**) to seat the valve.

b. Align the hole in a new filter element with the valve stem, and press the filter into the bore on the bottom of the baffle (**Figure 62**).

c. On 2006-2010 models, install a *new* breather baffle gasket (Figure 59) into the rocker arm support plate.

d. Hold the filter element in place and install the breather baffle (Figure 60, typical).

e. On 2006-2010 models, install a *new* cover gasket (Figure 59) onto the breather baffle.

f. Install the breather cover (B, Figure 58) and *left side* breather bolt (A).

CYLINDER HEAD

The cylinder head procedures are shown performed on the rear cylinder (**Figure 66** and **Figure 67**). The same procedures apply to the front cylinder. Any differences are noted.

NOTE
The following procedures are shown with the engine removed to clearly illustrate the steps.

Removal

1. Remove the rocker arm support plate, rocker arm housing and pushrods as described in this chapter.

2. Disconnect the engine temperature sensor (**Figure 68**) connector.

3. Remove the fuel induction module as described in Chapter Eight.

4. Disconnect the breather hose from the fitting on the cylinder head.

5. On Screamin' Eagle and CVO models, disconnect the 2-pin automatic compression release (ACR) connector.

6. Following the sequence shown in **Figure 69**, loosen the cylinder head bolts (**Figure 70**) in 1/4-turn increments until they are loose. Remove the four bolts. Note the position of the short and long bolts.

7. Tap the cylinder head with a rubber mallet to free it, and lift it off the cylinder.

8. Remove the cylinder head gasket.

9. Remove the cylinder head dowels (**Figure 71**) and O-rings. Discard each dowel's O-ring.

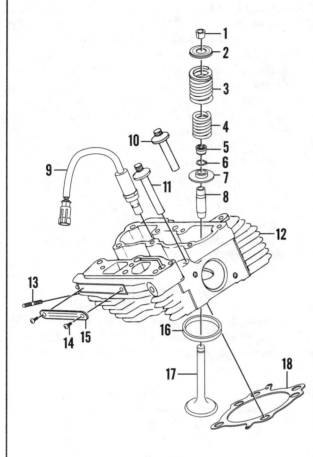

CYLINDER HEAD (SCREAMIN' EAGLE AND CVO MODELS)

1. Valve keepers
2. Upper retainer
3. Valve spring (outer)
4. Valve spring (inner)
5. Oil seal
6. Retaining ring (2009 models)
7. Lower retainer
8. Valve guide
9. Automatic compression release solenoid (2007-on)
10. Short bolt (1 7/8 in. internal threads)
11. Long bolt (3 3/16 in. internal threads)
12. Cylinder head
13. Stud (exhaust port)
14. Screw
15. Medallion
16. Valve seat
17. Valve
18. Gasket

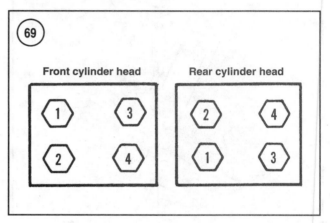

Front cylinder head   Rear cylinder head

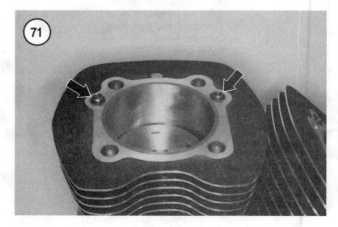

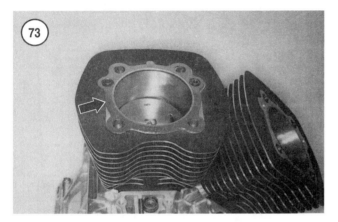

10. Repeat procedure to remove the opposite cylinder head.

Installation

1. If removed, install the piston and cylinder as described in this chapter.

2. Lubricate the cylinder studs and cylinder head bolts (**Figure 72**) as follows:

    a. Clean the cylinder head bolts in solvent and dry with compressed air.

    b. Apply clean engine oil to the cylinder head bolt threads and to the flat shoulder surface on each bolt. Wipe excess oil from the bolts; leave only an oil film on these surfaces.

3. Install the dowels (**Figure 71**) into the top of the cylinder.

4. Install a *new* O-ring over each dowel. Apply a light coat of clean engine oil to the O-rings.

> *CAUTION*
> *Because the O-rings center the head gasket on the cylinder, install them before installing the head gasket.*

5. Install a *new* cylinder head gasket (**Figure 73**) onto the cylinder.

> *CAUTION*
> *Do not use sealer on the cylinder head gasket. For an aftermarket head gasket, follow the gasket manufacturer's instructions for installation.*

> *NOTE*
> *The cylinder heads are **not** identical. Refer to the **FRONT** or **REAR** (**Figure 74**) cast into top surface of the cylinder head.*

6. Lower the cylinder head (**Figure 75**) onto the cylinder and the dowels. Position the head carefully to avoid moving the head gasket out of alignment.

7. Lightly apply clean engine oil to the threads and to the bottom of the bolt flange of each cylinder head bolt. Install the cylinder head bolts finger-tight. Make sure the short bolts are on the spark plug side of the head.

> *CAUTION*
> *Failure to follow the torque sequence may cause cylinder head distortion and gasket leakage.*

8. Following the torque sequences shown in **Figure 69**, tighten the cylinder head bolts as follows:

    a. Starting with bolt No. 1, finger-tighten the cylinder head bolts evenly, and in order.

    b. Initially, tighten each bolt, in order, to 10-12 ft.-lb. (13.6-16.3 N•m).

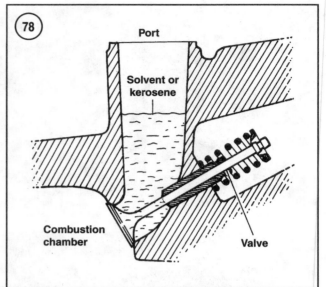

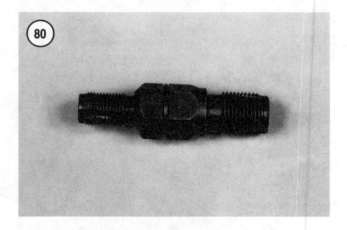

c. Next, tighten each bolt in order to 15-17 ft.-lb. (20.3-23.0 N•m).

d. Make a vertical mark with a permanent marker on each bolt head (A, **Figure 76**). Make another mark on the cylinder head (B, **Figure 76**) at a 90° angle or 1/4-turn from the mark on the bolt head.

e. Following the torque sequence, tighten each bolt a final 90° or 1/4-turn using the marks as a guide (**Figure 77**).

9. Connect the breather hose to its fitting.

10. Install the rocker arm assemblies and pushrods as described in this chapter.

Leak Test

Before removing the valves or cleaning the cylinder head, perform a cylinder head leak test.

1. Position the cylinder head so the exhaust port faces up. Pour solvent or kerosene into each exhaust port opening (**Figure 78**).

2. After at least ten seconds, turn the head over slightly and check each exhaust valve area on the combustion chamber side. If the valves and seats are in good condition, no leaks past the valve seats will be found. If any area is wet, the valve seat is not sealing correctly. The valve seat or face may be damaged or the valve may be bent or damaged. Remove the valve, and inspect the valve and seat.

3. Pour solvent into the intake port and check the intake valve in the same manner.

Inspection

During inspection, compare any measurements to the specifications in **Table 2** or **Table 3**. Replace any part that is worn, damaged or out of specification.

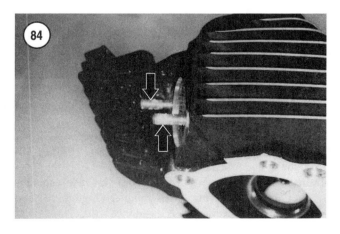

1. Perform the *Cylinder Head Leak Test* (this section).

2. Thoroughly clean the outside of the cylinder head. Use a stiff brush, soap and water to remove all debris from the cooling fins (**Figure 79**). If necessary, use a piece of wood and scrape away any lodged dirt. Clogged cooling fins can cause overheating and lead to engine damage.

CAUTION
Cleaning the combustion chamber with the valves removed can damage the valve seat surfaces. A damaged or even slightly scratched valve seat will cause poor valve seating.

3. *Without removing the valves*, use a wire brush to remove all carbon deposits from the combustion chamber. Use a fine wire brush and dip it in solvent or make a scraper from hardwood. Be careful not to damage the head, valves or spark plug threads.

CAUTION
When using a tap to clean spark plug threads, coat the tap with cutting fluid or kerosene.

CAUTION
Aluminum spark plug threads are commonly damaged due to galling, cross-threading and over-tightening. To prevent galling, apply an antiseize compound to the plug threads before installation and do not overtighten the plugs.

4. Examine the spark plug threads in the cylinder head for damage. If there is minor damage or if the threads are dirty or clogged with carbon, use a spark plug thread tap (**Figure 80**) to clean the threads following the tap manufacturer's instructions. If there is severe thread damage, restore the threads by installing a steel thread insert. Purchase a thread insert kit at an automotive supply store or have the insert installed by a dealership or machine shop.

5. After all carbon is removed from the combustion chambers and valve ports, and if the spark plug thread hole has been repaired, clean the entire head in solvent. Dry it with compressed air.

6. Examine the crown on the piston (**Figure 81**). The crown should show no signs of wear or damage. If the crown appears pecked or spongy-looking, also check the spark plug, valves and combustion chamber for aluminum deposits. If these deposits are found, the cylinder has overheated. Check for a lean fuel mixture or other conditions that could cause preignition.

7. Check for cracks in the combustion chamber, the intake port (**Figure 82**) and the exhaust port (**Figure 83**). Replace a cracked head if welding can not repair it.

8. Inspect the exhaust pipe mounting studs (**Figure 84**) for damage. Repair the threads with a die if they are damaged.

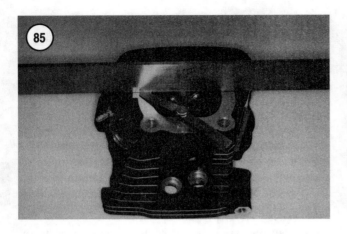

NOTE
If the cylinder head is bead-blasted, clean the head thoroughly with solvent, and then with hot soapy water. Residual grit seats in small crevices and other areas, and can be hard to get out. Also, run a tap through each exposed thread to remove grit from the threads. Any grit left in the engine will cause premature wear.

9. Thoroughly clean the cylinder head.

10. Measure for warp by placing a straightedge across the gasket surface at several points and attempting to insert a feeler gauge between the straightedge and cylinder head at each location (**Figure 85**). Distortion or nicks in the cylinder head surface could cause an air leak and overheating. If warp exceeds the specified service limit (**Table 2** or **Table 3**), replace the cylinder head.

11. Check the rocker arm housing mating surfaces (**Figure 86**) for warp in the same manner.

12. Make sure the breather channel (**Figure 87**) is clear at each end.

13. Check the valves and valve guides as described in *Valves and Valve Components* (this chapter).

VALVES AND VALVE COMPONENTS

Complete valve service requires a number of special tools. The following procedures describe how to check for valve component wear and to determine what type of service is required.

Refer to **Figure 66** and **Figure 67**.

Tools

The following tools, or their equivalents, are needed for valve removal and installation:

1. Valve spring compressor (H-D part No. HD-34736-B).
2. Valve guide cleaning brush (H-D part No. HD-34751).
3. Valve guide seal installer (H-D part No. HD-48644) – Screamin' Eagle and CVO models only.
4. ACR solenoid socket (H-D part No. HD-48498) – Screamin' Eagle and CVO models only.

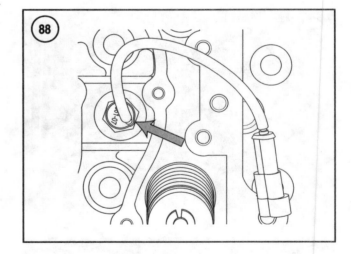

Valve Removal

1. Remove the cylinder head as described in this chapter.
2. If using the cylinder head holding fixture (H-D part No. HD-39786), install the 12-mm end into the spark plug hole. Secure the fixture in a vise.
3. On Screamin' Eagle and CVO models, use the ACR solenoid socket and remove the ACR solenoid (**Figure 88**) from the cylinder head.
4. Install the valve spring compressor (**Figure 89**) squarely over the valve spring upper retainer (**Figure 90**) and against the valve head.

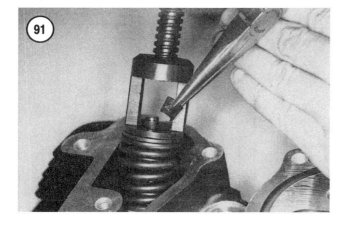

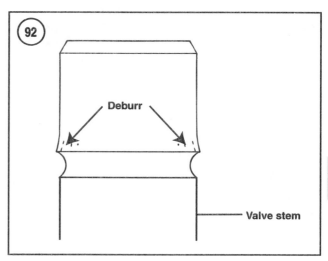

CAUTION
*Remove any burrs (**Figure 92**) from the valve stem groove before removing the valve; otherwise the valve guide will be damaged as the valve stem passes through it.*

8. Remove the valve from the cylinder head while rotating it slightly.

9A. On all models except Screamin' Eagle and CVO models, use needlenose pliers to carefully twist and remove the valve stem seal/spring seat assembly from the valve guide. Discard the valve stem seal/spring seat assembly.

9B. On Screamin' Eagle and CVO models:

    a. Use needlenose pliers to carefully twist and remove the valve seal from the valve guide. Discard the seal.

    b. Remove the spring seat from the cylinder head.

CAUTION
Keep the components of each valve assembly together by placing each set into separate small boxes or small plastic bags. Identify the components as either an intake or exhaust valve. If both cylinders are disassembled, also label the components as front and rear. Do not mix components from the valve assemblies. Excessive wear may result.

10. Repeat procedure to remove the remaining valve.

Valve Installation

1. Run the valve cleaning brush through the valve guide to assure it is clean.

2. Coat a valve stem with Torco MPZ, molybdenum-disulfide paste, or an equivalent lubricant. Install the valve part way into the guide. Slowly turn the valve as it enters the oil seal and continue turning it until the valve is installed all the way.

3. Work the valve back and forth in the valve guide to ensure the lubricant is distributed evenly within the valve guide.

CAUTION
To avoid loss of spring tension, compress the spring just enough to remove the valve keepers.

5. Tighten the valve spring compressor until the valve keepers separate from the valve stem. Lift the valve keepers out through the valve spring compressor with a magnet or needlenose pliers (**Figure 91**).

6. Gradually loosen the valve spring compressor and remove it from the cylinder head.

7. Remove the valve spring upper retainer and the valve spring. On Screamin' Eagle and CVO models, remove the outer and inner springs.

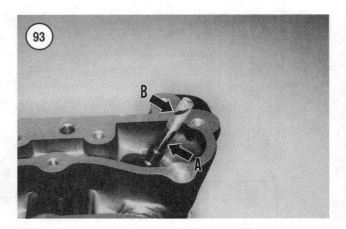

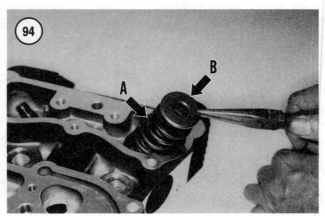

4. Withdraw the valve and apply an additional coat of lubricant.

5A. On all models except Screamin' Eagle and CVO, perform the following:

    a. Reinstall the valve into the valve guide, and push the valve (A, **Figure 93**) all the way into the cylinder head until it bottoms.

> *CAUTION*
> *The valve seal will be torn as it passes the valve stem keeper groove if the plastic capsule is not installed. The capsule is included in the new top end gasket set.*

    b. Hold the valve in place and install the plastic capsule (B, **Figure 93**) onto the end of the valve stem. Apply a light coat of clean engine oil to the outer surface of the capsule.

> *NOTE*
> *On all models except Screamin' Eagle and CVO, the valve seal/spring seat assembly is sold as a unit. Always install a new valve seal/spring seat assembly.*

    c. Hold the valve in place, and slowly slide the valve seal/spring seat assembly onto the valve stem. Push the assembly down until it bottoms on the machined surface of the cylinder head.

    d. Remove the plastic capsule (B, **Figure 93**) from the valve stem, and retain it. The capsule will be used to install the remaining valves.

    e. Install the valve spring (A, **Figure 94**) with the tapered end facing up.

    f. Install the valve spring retainer (B, **Figure 94**) on top of the spring.

5B. On Screamin' Eagle and CVO models, perform the following:

    a. Install the spring seat (**Figure 95**) over the valve guide and into the cylinder head.

    b. Reinstall the valve into the valve guide, but do not push the valve past the top of the valve guide.

    c. Use isopropyl alcohol or its equivalent to thoroughly clean all grease from the outside surface of the valve guide.

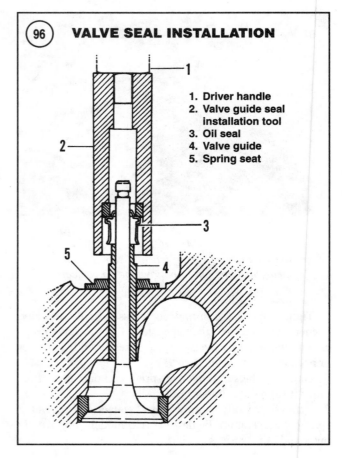

VALVE SEAL INSTALLATION

1. Driver handle
2. Valve guide seal installation tool
3. Oil seal
4. Valve guide
5. Spring seat

CAUTION
Do not apply any retaining compound to the top or inside of the valve guide.

d. Carefully apply Loctite RC/620 (green) High Temperature Retaining Compound, or an equivalent, to the valve seal seating surface on the outside of the valve guide.

e. Push the valve (A, **Figure 93**) all the way into the cylinder head until it bottoms.

CAUTION
The valve seal will be torn as it passes the valve stem keeper groove if the plastic capsule is not installed. The capsule is included in the new top end gasket set.

f. Hold the valve in place and install the plastic capsule (B, **Figure 93**) onto the end of the valve stem. Apply a light coat of clean engine oil to the outer surface of the capsule.

g. Slide a new valve seal over the capsule and down the valve stem until the seal contacts the valve guide.

h. Remove the plastic capsule from the valve stem, and retain it. The capsule will be used to install the remaining valves.

i. Slide the valve guide seal installer over the seal (**Figure 96**). Use a small hammer to gently tap the seal installer until the valve seal lightly bottoms on the valve guide.

j. Install the inner valve spring (**Figure 97**) and make sure it is properly seated on the lower spring retainer.

k. Install the outer valve spring (**Figure 98**) and make sure it is properly seated on the lower spring retainer. The larger diameter flange on the retainer must separate the inner and outer springs

l. Install the valve spring upper retainer (**Figure 99**).

CAUTION
To avoid loss of spring tension, compress the springs just enough to install the valve keepers.

6. Compress the valve spring with a valve spring compressor (**Figure 89**) and install the valve keepers (**Figure 91**).

7. Make sure both keepers are seated around the valve stem prior to releasing the compressor.

8. Slowly release tension from the compressor and remove it. After removing the compressor, inspect the valve keepers to make sure they are properly seated (**Figure 100**). Tap the end of the valve stem with a *soft-faced* hammer to ensure the keepers are properly seated.

9. Repeat the procedure to install the remaining valves.

10. On Screamin' Eagle and CVO models, install the ACR solenoid as follows:

a. Make sure the copper washer is in place on the ACR solenoid.

b. Apply three dots of Loctite 246 Threadlocker Medium Strength/High Temperature, or an equivalent thread-

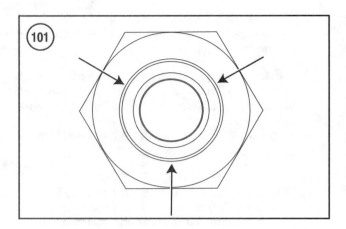

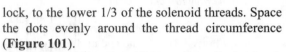

lock, to the lower 1/3 of the solenoid threads. Space the dots evenly around the thread circumference (**Figure 101**).

   c. Install the ACR solenoid into the cylinder head. Using the ACR solenoid socket, tighten the ACR solenoid to 11-15 ft.-lb. (14.9-20.3 N•m).

11. Install the cylinder head as described in this chapter.

Valve Inspection

During inspection, compare any measurements to the specifications in **Table 2** or **Table 3**. Replace any part that is worn, damaged or out of specification.

1. Clean valves in solvent. Do not gouge or damage the valve seating surface.

2. Inspect the valve face. Minor roughness and pitting (**Figure 102**) can be removed by lapping the valve as described in this section Excessive unevenness to the contact surface indicates the valve is not serviceable.

3. Inspect the valve stem for wear and roughness. Then, measure the valve stem outside diameter with a micrometer (**Figure 103**).

4. Remove all carbon and varnish from the valve guides with a stiff spiral wire brush before measuring wear.

5. Measure the valve guide inside diameter with a small bore gauge (**Figure 104**) at the top, center and bottom positions. Then, measure the small bore gauge with a micrometer.

6. Determine the valve stem-to-valve guide clearance by subtracting the valve stem outside diameter from the valve guide inside diameter.

7. If a small bore gauge is not available, insert each valve into its guide. Attach a dial indicator to the valve stem next to the head (**Figure 105**) hold the valve slightly off its seat and rock it sideways in both directions 90° to each other. If the valve rocks more than slightly, the guide is probably worn. Take the cylinder head to a dealership or machine shop and have the valve guides measured.

8. Check the valve spring as follows:

   a. Inspect the valve springs for visible damage.

   b. Use a square to visually check the spring for distortion or tilt (**Figure 106**).

   c. Measure the valve spring free length with a caliper (**Figure 107**).

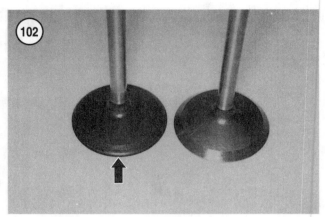

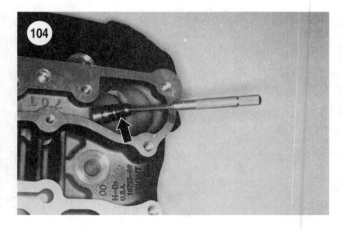

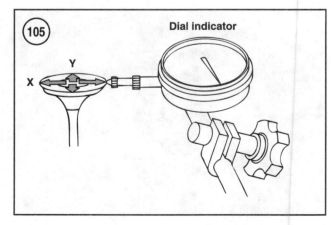

Dial indicator

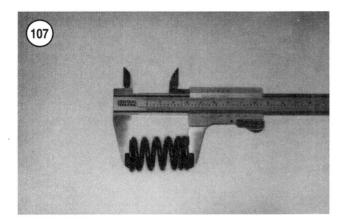

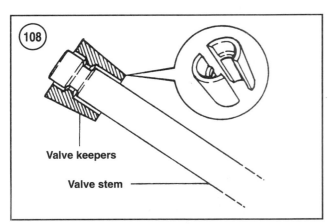

Valve keepers

Valve stem

d. Repeat the inspection process for each valve spring. Replace worn or defective springs.

9. Check the valve spring retainer and seat for cracks or other damage.

10. Check the fit of the valve keepers on the valve stem end (**Figure 108**). They should index tightly into the valve stem groove.

11. Inspect the valve seats (**Figure 109**) in the cylinder head. If they are worn or burned, they can be reconditioned as described in this section. Seats and valves in near-perfect condition can be reconditioned by lapping with fine Carborundum paste as described in this section.

Valve Guide Replacement

Tools

The following tools, or their equivalents, are required to replace the valve guides.

1. Cylinder head stand (H-D part No. HD-39782-A).
2. Valve guide driver (All models except Screamin Eagle and CVO models; H-D part No. B-45524-1; Screamin' Eagle models: H-D part No. HD-34740).
3. Valve guide installer sleeve (All models except Screamin' Eagle and CVO models; H-D part No. B-45524-2A); Screamin' Eagle and CVO models: H-D part No. HD-48628).
4. Valve guide cleaning brush (H-D part No. HD-34751-A).
5. Valve guide reamer (All models except Screamin' Eagle and CVO models; H-D part No. B-45523; Screamin' Eagle and CVO models: H-D part No. HD-39932).
6. T-handle (H-D part No. HD-39847).
7. Valve guide reamer honing lubricant (H-D part No. HD-39964).
8. Valve guide hone (All models except Screamin' Eagle models and CVO; H-D part No. B-45525; Screamin' Eagle and CVO models: H-D part No. HD-34723).
9. Hydraulic press.

Procedure

> *CAUTION*
> *The valve guides must be removed and installed using the proper tools to avoid damage to the cylinder head. Use the correct size of valve guide removal tool to remove the valve guides or the tool may expand the end of the guide. An expanded guide will widen and damage the guide bore in the cylinder head as it passes through it.*

1. Remove the old valve guide (**Figure 110**) as follows:
   a. Install the intake (A, **Figure 111**) or exhaust (B) valve seat adapter into the tube at the top of the cylinder head support stand (C).
   b. Set the support stand onto a hydraulic press table.

c. Install the cylinder head (A, **Figure 112**) onto the support stand (B). Center the cylinder head valve seat on the seat adapter.

d. Insert the valve guide driver (C, **Figure 112**) into the valve guide bore until the driver stops on the valve guide shoulder.

e. Center the valve guide driver under the press ram. Make sure the driver is perpendicular to the press table.

f. Support the cylinder head, slowly apply ram pressure and drive valve guide out through the combustion chamber. Discard the valve guide.

g. Remove the cylinder head and tools from the press bed.

NOTE
A retaining ring is used for the exhaust valve guide only on all models except Screamin' Eagle and CVO.

h. When removing an exhaust valve guide on all models except Screamin' Eagle and CVO, remove the retaining ring from the top of the cylinder head.

i. Repeat the process to remove the remaining valve guides.

2. Clean the valve guide bores in the cylinder head.

3. Because the valve guide bores in the cylinder head may enlarged during removal of the old guides, measure each valve guide bore. Purchase the new valve guides to match their respective bore diameters. Determine the bore diameter as follows:

a. Measure the valve guide bore diameter in the cylinder head with a bore gauge or small-hole gauge. Record the bore diameter.

b. The outside diameter of the *new* valve guide must be 0.0020-0.0033 in. (0.051-0.084 mm) larger than the guide bore in the cylinder head. When purchasing new valve guides, measure the new guide's outside diameter with a micrometer. If the new guide's outside diameter is not within this specification, install oversize valve guide(s). Refer to a dealership for available sizes and part numbers.

4. Apply a thin coat of Vaseline to the entire outer surface of the new valve guide before installing it in the cylinder head.

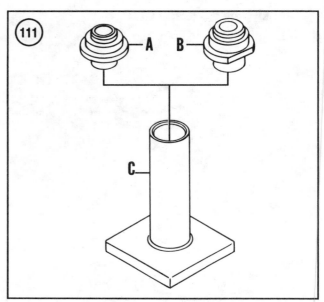

CAUTION
When installing oversize valve guides, make sure to match each guide to its respective bore in the cylinder head.

5. Install the *new* valve guide as follows:

a. Install the intake (A, **Figure 111**) or exhaust (B) seat adapter into the tube at the top of the cylinder head support stand (C).

b. Install the support stand onto the hydraulic press table.

c. Install the cylinder head (A, **Figure 113**) onto the support stand (B). Center the cylinder head valve seat on the seat adapter.

d. Install the valve guide onto the cylinder head bore. On guides that use retaining rings, make sure the valve guide groove faces out away from the cylinder head.

e. Install the valve guide installer sleeve (C, **Figure 113**) over the valve guide, and insert the tapered end of the valve guide driver (D) into the installer sleeve.

f. Center the valve guide driver under the press ram. Make sure the driver is perpendicular to the press table.

g. Support the cylinder head, apply ram pressure and slowly start to drive the valve guide into the cylinder head receptacle. Stop and back off the press ram to allow the valve guide to center itself.

h. Verify that the support stand (B, **Figure 113**) and valve guide driver (D) are square with the press table.

i. Apply ram pressure and continue to drive the valve guide part way into the cylinder head receptacle. Once again, stop and back off the press ram to allow the valve guide to center itself.

j. Again apply ram pressure and drive the valve guide into the bore until the installer sleeve (C, **Figure 113**) contacts the machined surface of the cylinder head. Remove the valve guide driver and installer sleeve.

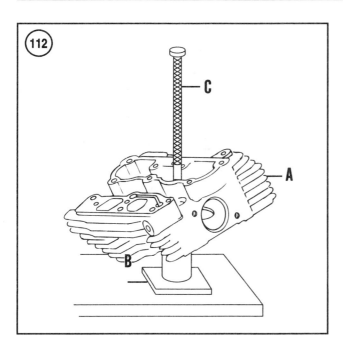

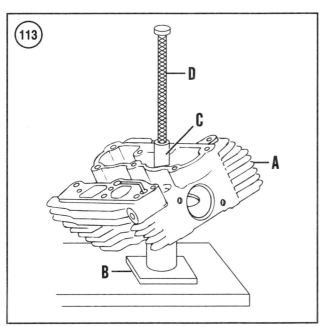

NOTE
A retaining ring is used for the exhaust valve guide only on all models except Screamin' Eagle and CVO.

k. On all models except Screamin' Eagle and CVO, install a *new* retaining ring into the groove of a exhaust valve guide. Make sure the retaining ring is completely seated in the valve guide groove.

l. Remove the cylinder head and tools from the press bed.

m. Repeat process to install the remaining valve guides.

6. Replacement valve guides are sold with a smaller inside diameter than the valve stem. Ream the guide to within

0.0005-0.0001 in (0.013-0.0025 mm) of its finished size as follows:

a. Install the valve guide reamer onto the T-handle.

b. Apply a liberal amount of reamer lubricant to the reamer bit and to the valve guide bore.

c. Start the reamer straight into the valve guide bore at the top of the cylinder head.

CAUTION
Only apply pressure to the end of the drive socket. If pressure is applied to the T-handle, the bore will be uneven, rough cut and tapered.

d. Apply thumb pressure to the end of the drive socket portion of the T-handle while rotating the T-handle *clockwise*. Only *light* pressure is required. Apply additional lubricant to the reamer and into the valve guide while rotating the reamer.

e. Continue to rotate the reamer until the entire bit has traveled through the valve guide and the shank of the reamer rotates freely.

CAUTION
Never back the reamer out through the valve guide as the guide will be damaged.

f. Remove the T-handle from the reamer. Remove the reamer from the combustion chamber side of the cylinder head.

g. Apply low-pressure compressed air to remove the small shavings from the valve guide bore. Clean the valve guide bore with the valve guide brush.

7. Hone the valve guide as follows:

a. Install the valve guide hone into a high-speed electric drill.

b. Lubricate the valve guide bore and hone stones with the reamer lubricant—*do not use engine oil.*

c. Carefully insert the hone stones into the valve guide bore.

d. Start the drill and move the hone back and forth in the valve guide bore for 10 to 12 complete strokes to obtain a 60° crosshatch pattern.

8. Repeat the reaming and honing procedure for each new valve guide.

9. Soak the cylinder head in a container filled with hot, soapy water. Then, clean the valve guides with a valve guide brush or an equivalent bristle brush. *Do not use a steel brush.* Do not use cleaning solvent, kerosene or gasoline as these chemicals will not remove all of the abrasive particles produced during the honing operation. Repeat this step until all of the valve guides are thoroughly cleaned. Then, rinse the cylinder head and valve guides in clear, cold water and dry them with compressed air.

10. After cleaning and drying the valve guides, apply clean engine oil to the guides to prevent rust.

11 Resurface the valve seats as described in *Valve Seat Reconditioning* (this section).

Valve Seat Inspection

1. Remove all carbon residue from each valve seat. Then, clean the cylinder head as described in *Valve Inspection* (this section).
2. Check the valve seats in their original locations with machinist's dye as follows:
   a. Thoroughly clean the valve face and valve seat with contact cleaner.
   b. Spread a thin layer of machinist's dye evenly on the valve face.
   c. Insert the valve into its guide.
   d. Support the valve by hand (**Figure 114**) and tap the valve up and down in the cylinder head. Do not rotate the valve or the reading will be false.
   e. Remove the valve and examine the impression left by the machinist's dye. The impressions on the valve and the seat should be even around their circumferences. The valve seat width (**Figure 115**) should be within the specification in **Table 2** or **Table 3**. If the width is beyond the specification or if the impression is uneven, recondition the valve seats.
3. Closely examine the valve seat in the cylinder head (**Figure 109**). It should be smooth and even with a polished seating surface.
4. If the valve seat is in good condition, install the valve as described in this section.
5. If the valve seat is not correct, recondition the valve seat as described in this section.

Valve Seat Reconditioning

Valve seat reconditioning requires considerable expertise and special tools. In most cases, it is more economical and practical to have these procedures performed by an experienced machinist.

The following procedure is provided for those equipped to perform the task. A valve seat cutter set (H-D part No HD-35758-C), or its equivalent, is required. Follow the tool manufacturer's instructions.

Refer to **Figure 116** for valve seat angles.
1. Clean the valve guides as described in *Valve Inspection* (this section).
2. Measure the valve stem protrusion by performing the following:
   a. Insert the valve stem into the valve guide from the combustion chamber side of the cylinder head.
   b. Use a caliper to measure the distance from the top of the valve stem to the cylinder head's machined surface.
   c. If the measured valve stem protrusion exceeds the service limit (**Table 2** or **Table 3**), replace the valve seat or cylinder head as necessary.
3. Carefully rotate and insert the solid pilot into the valve guide. Make sure the pilot is correctly seated.

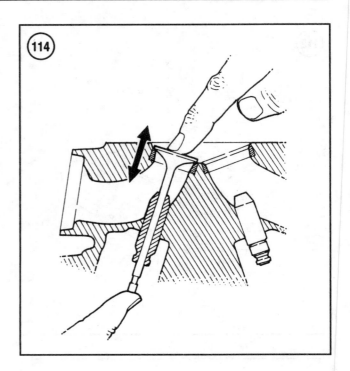

CAUTION
Valve seat accuracy depends on a correctly sized and installed pilot.

CAUTION
*Measure the valve seat contact area in the cylinder head (**Figure 116**) after each cut to make sure its size and area are correct. Overgrinding will lower the valves into the cylinder head and off the valve seat far enough that the seat will have to be replaced.*

4. Using the proper 46° cutter (intake or exhaust), descale and clean the valve seat with one or two turns.
5. If the seat is still pitted or burned, turn the cutter until the surface is clean. Work slowly and carefully to avoid removing too much material from the valve seat.
6. Remove the pilot from the valve guide.
7. Apply a small amount of valve lapping compound to the valve face and install the valve. Rotate the valve against the valve seat using a valve lapping tool. Remove the valve.
8. Measure the valve seat with a caliper as shown in **Figure 116** and **Figure 115**. Record the measurement to use as a reference point when performing the following steps.

CAUTION
The 31° cutter removes material quickly. Work carefully and check progress often.

9. Reinsert the solid pilot into the valve guide. Make sure the pilot is properly seated. Install the 31°cutter onto the solid pilot and lightly cut the seat to remove 1/4 of the existing valve seat.
10. Install the 60° cutter onto the solid pilot and lightly cut the seat to remove the lower 1/4 of the existing valve seat.

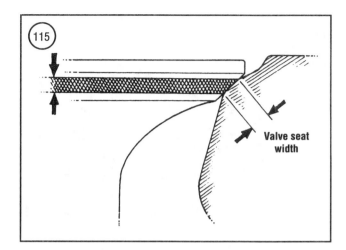

Valve seat width

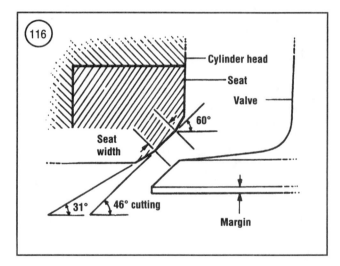

Cylinder head

Seat

Valve

60°

Seat width

31°   46° cutting

Margin

11. Measure the valve seat width with a caliper. Fit the 46° cutter onto the solid pilot, and cut the valve seat to the seat width specified in **Table 2** or **Table 3**.

12. Remove the solid pilot from the cylinder head.

13. Inspect the valve seat-to-valve face impression as described in *Valve Seat Inspection* (this section).

14. If the contact area is too high or too wide on the valve, cut the seat with the 31° cutter. This will remove part of the top valve seat area to lower or narrow the contact area.

15. If the contact area is too low or too wide on the valve, use the 60° cutter and remove part of the lower area to raise and widen the contact area.

16. After obtaining the desired valve seat position and angle, use the 46° cutter and *lightly* clean off any burrs caused by the previous cuts.

17. When the contact area is correct, lap the valve as described in this chapter.

18. Repeat the reconditioning procedure for the remaining valve seats.

19. Thoroughly clean the cylinder head and all valve components in solvent, wash them with detergent and hot water, and then rinse them in cold water. Dry them with compressed air. Apply a light coat of engine oil to all non-aluminum surfaces to prevent rust formation.

Valve Lapping

If valve wear or distortion is not excessive, attempt to restore the valve seal by lapping the valve to the seat.

1. Smear a light coat of fine grade valve-lapping compound on the seating surface of the valve.

2. Insert the valve into the head.

3. Wet the suction cup of the lapping tool, and stick it onto the head of the valve. Lap the valve to the seat by spinning the tool between both hands while lifting and moving the valve around the seat 1/4 turn at a time.

4. Wipe off the valve and seat frequently to check progress. Lap only enough to achieve a precise seating ring around the valve head.

5. Closely examine the valve seat in the cylinder head. The seat must be smooth and even with a polished seating ring.

6. Thoroughly clean the valves and cylinder head in solvent to remove all grinding compound residue. Compound left on the valves or the cylinder head will cause rapid engine wear.

7. After installing the valves into the cylinder head, test each valve for proper seating as described in this chapter. If solvent leaks past any valve, disassemble the leaking valve and repeat the lapping procedure or recondition the valve seat as described in this section.

Valve Seat Replacement

Valve seat replacement requires considerable experience and equipment. Refer this work to a dealership or machine shop.

CYLINDER

Refer to **Figure 117**.

Removal

1. Remove the cylinder head as described in this chapter.

2. Remove all dirt and debris from the cylinder base.

3. Remove the dowels (**Figure 118**) and O-rings from the top of the cylinder if they are still in place.

4. Turn the crankshaft until the piston is at bottom dead center (BDC).

NOTE
The front and rear cylinders are identical (same part number). Mark each cylinder so it can be reinstalled in its original position.

5. Pull the cylinder straight up and off the piston and cylinder studs. If necessary, tap around the perimeter of the cylinder with a rubber or plastic mallet to loosen it.

6. Place clean shop rags (A, **Figure 119**) into the crankcase opening to prevent objects from falling undetected into the crankcase.

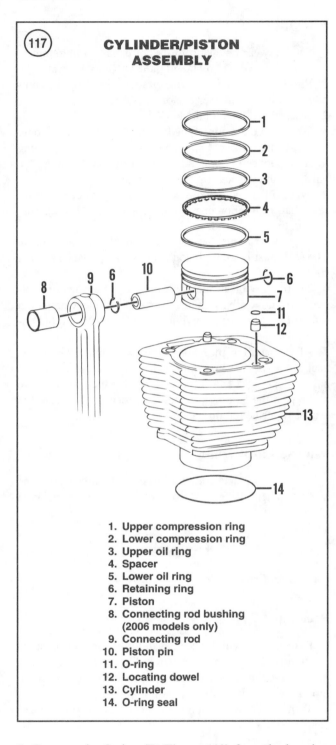

CYLINDER/PISTON ASSEMBLY

1. Upper compression ring
2. Lower compression ring
3. Upper oil ring
4. Spacer
5. Lower oil ring
6. Retaining ring
7. Piston
8. Connecting rod bushing (2006 models only)
9. Connecting rod
10. Piston pin
11. O-ring
12. Locating dowel
13. Cylinder
14. O-ring seal

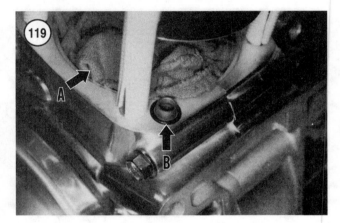

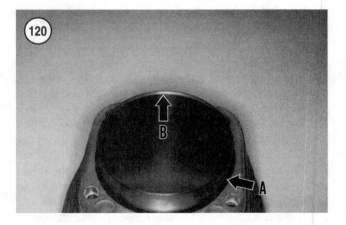

7. Remove the O-ring (B, **Figure 119**) from the locating dowel in the crankcase. Leave the dowels in place unless they are loose.

8. Remove and discard the O-ring (A, **Figure 120**) from the base of the cylinder.

9. Install a vinyl or rubber hose (**Figure 121**) over each stud. This protects both the piston and the studs from damage. After removing the cylinder, be careful when working around the cylinder studs to avoid bending or damaging them. The slightest bend could cause the stud to fail.

10. Repeat the procedure to remove the other cylinder.

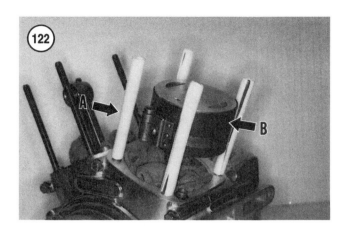

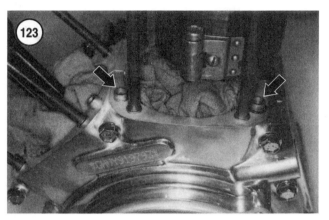

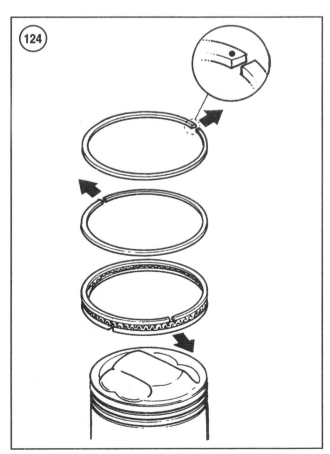

Installation

NOTE
When a cylinder has been bored oversize, the inner lead-in angle at the base of the bore skirt (B, Figure 120) has been eliminated. This lead-in angle is necessary for the piston rings to safely enter the cylinder bore. If necessary, use a cylinder chamfering cone (JIMS part No. 2078) or a hand grinder with a fine stone to make in a new lead-in angle. The finished surface must be smooth so will not catch and damage the piston rings during installation.

1. If removed, install the pistons and rings as described in this chapter.
2. Remove gasket residue and clean the cylinder as described in *Inspection* in this section.
3. Remove the vinyl or rubber hose (A, **Figure 122**) from each stud.
4. Install a *new* O-ring (A, **Figure 120**) into the base of the cylinder. Apply a light coat of clean engine oil to the O-ring.
5. If removed, install the dowels (**Figure 123**) into the crankcase.
6. Install a *new* O-ring (B, **Figure 119**) onto each dowel. Apply a light coat of clean engine oil to each O-ring.
7. Turn the crankshaft until the piston is at top dead center (TDC).
8. Lubricate the cylinder bore, piston and piston rings liberally with clean engine oil.
9. Position the top compression ring gap so it is facing the intake port. Then, stagger the remaining piston ring end gaps as shown in **Figure 124**.
10. Compress the piston rings with a ring compressor (B, **Figure 122**).

NOTE
Install the cylinder in its original position as noted during removal.

11. Position the cylinder so the indents in the cooling fins face the right side (front facing forward). Align the cylinder with the studs, and carefully slide the cylinder down (**Figure 125**) the studs until it sits over the top of the pis-

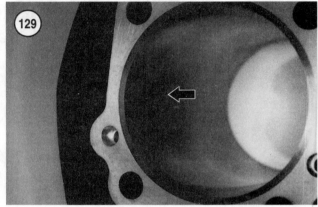

ton. Continue sliding the cylinder down past the rings. Remove the ring compressor (**Figure 126**) once the piston rings enter the cylinder bore. Remove the shop rag from the crankcase opening.

12. Continue to slide the cylinder down until it bottoms out on the crankcase.

13. Repeat procedure to install the other cylinder.

14. Install the cylinder heads as described in this chapter.

Inspection

During inspection, compare any measurements to the specifications in **Table 2** or **Table 3**. Replace any part that is worn, damaged or out of specification.

To obtain an accurate cylinder bore measurement, the cylinder must be tightened between cylinder torque plates (JIMS part No. 1287), or an equivalent. Measurements made without the torque plates will be inaccurate and may vary by as much as 0.001 in. (0.025 mm). Refer this procedure to a shop equipped and experienced with this procedure if the tools are not available. The cylinder bore must be thoroughly clean and at room temperature to obtain accurate measurements. Do not measure the cylinder immediately after it has been honed as it will still be warm. Measurements can vary by as much as 0.002 in. (0.051 mm) if the cylinder block is not at room temperature.

1. Thoroughly clean the outside of the cylinder. Use a stiff brush, soap and water to clean all debris from the cool-

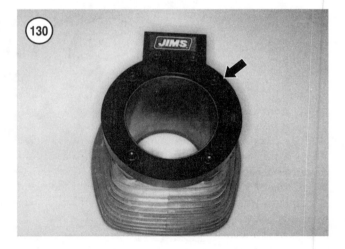

ing fins (**Figure 127**). If necessary, use a piece of wood to scrape away lodged dirt. Clogged cooling fins can cause overheating and lead to possible engine damage.

2. Carefully remove all gasket residue from the top and bottom cylinder gasket surfaces.

3. Thoroughly clean the cylinder with solvent, and dry it with compressed air. Lightly oil the cylinder block bore to prevent rust.

4. Check the top and bottom cylinder gasket surfaces for warp using a straightedge and feeler gauge (**Figure 128**).

5. Check the cylinder bore (**Figure 129**) for scuff marks, scratches or other damage.

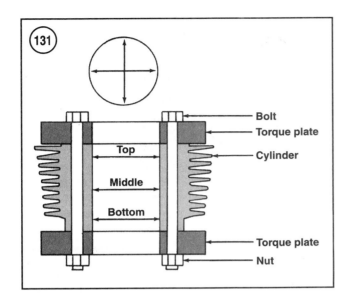

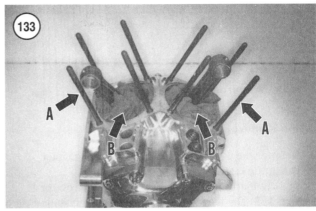

6. Install the cylinder torque plates (**Figure 130**) onto the cylinder following the tool manufacturer's instructions.

7. Measure the cylinder bore inside diameter with a bore gauge or inside micrometer at positions indicated in **Figure 131**. Perform the first measurement 0.500 in. (12.7 mm) below the top of the cylinder (**Figure 132**). Do not measure areas where the rings do not travel.

8. Measure the bore in two axes aligned with the piston pin and at 90° to the pin. If the taper or out-of-round measurements exceed the service limits (**Table 2** or **Table 3**), bore both cylinders to the next oversize and install oversize pistons and rings. Confirm the accuracy of all measurements and consult with a parts supplier on the availability of replacement parts before having the cylinder serviced.

9. Remove the torque plates.

CAUTION
Only hot, soapy water will completely clean the cylinder bore. Solvents or kerosene cannot wash fine grit out of the cylinder crevices. Abrasive grit left in the cylinder will cause premature engine wear.

10. If the cylinders were serviced, wash each cylinder in hot, soapy water to remove the fine grit material left from the boring or honing process. Run a clean white cloth through the cylinder bore. If the cloth shows traces of grit or oil, the bore is not clean. Wash the cylinder until the cloth passes through cleanly.

11. When the bore is clean, dry it with compressed air, and then lubricate it with clean engine oil to prevent rust.

Studs and Bolt Cleaning

The cylinder studs and cylinder head bolts must be in good condition and properly cleaned before the cylinder and cylinder heads are installed. Damaged or dirty studs may cause cylinder head distortion and gasket leaks.

CAUTION
The cylinder studs, cylinder head bolts and washers consist of hardened material. Do not substitute them with parts made of a lower grade material. If replacement is required, purchase the parts from the manufacturer.

1. Inspect the cylinder head bolts. Replace any that are damaged.

2. Examine the cylinder studs (A, **Figure 133**) for bending, looseness or damage. Replace studs as described in *Cylinder Stud Replacement* (Chapter Five). If the studs are in good condition, continue the procedure.

3. Cover both crankcase openings with shop rags (B, **Figure 133**) to prevent debris from falling into the engine.

4. Remove all carbon residue from the cylinder studs and cylinder head bolts as follows:

   a. Apply solvent to the cylinder stud and mating cylinder head bolt threads, and install the bolt onto the stud.

   b. Turn the cylinder head bolt back and forth to loosen and remove the carbon residue from the threads. Remove the bolt from the stud. Wipe off the residue with a shop rag moistened in cleaning solvent.

   c. Repeat process until both thread sets are free of carbon residue.

   d. Spray the cylinder stud and cylinder head bolt with an aerosol parts cleaner and allow them to dry.

   e. Set the clean bolt aside and install it on the same stud when installing the cylinder head.

4

5. Repeat the cleaning procedure for each cylinder stud and cylinder head bolt set.

PISTONS AND PISTON RINGS

Refer to **Figure 134**.

Piston Removal

1. Remove the cylinder as described in this chapter.
2. Cover the crankcase with clean shop rags.
3. Lightly mark the pistons with F for the front or R (A, **Figure 135**) for the rear so they can be reinstalled onto their original connecting rods.

> *WARNING*
> *The piston pin retaining rings may spring out of the piston during removal. Wear safety glasses when removing them.*

4. Using an awl, pry the piston pin retaining rings (A, **Figure 136**) out of the piston. Place a thumb over the hole to help keep the rings from flying out during removal.
5. Support the piston and push out the piston pin (B, **Figure 135**). If the piston pin is difficult to remove, make a piston pin removal tool (**Figure 137**) to remove the pin.
6. Remove the piston from the connecting rod. Keep the connecting rod upright so it does not strike the crankcase.
7. Fit a long piece of foam-type pipe insulation (B, **Figure 136**) over each crankcase stud so it will not be damaged.
8. If necessary, remove the piston rings as described in this section.
9. Inspect the pistons, piston pins and pistons rings as described in this section.

Piston Installation

1. Cover the crankcase openings to avoid dropping a retaining ring into the engine.
2. If removed, install the piston rings as described in this section.
3. Install a *new* piston pin retaining ring into one groove in the piston. Make sure the ring seats in the groove completely.
4. Coat the connecting rod bushing and piston pin with clean engine oil.
5. Slide the piston pin into the piston until its end is flush with the piston pin boss (**Figure 138**).
6. Place the piston over the connecting rod with its arrow mark (C, **Figure 135**) facing toward the front of the engine. Seat a used piston onto its original connecting rod. Refer to the F or R marks made on the pistons during removal.
7. Push the piston pin (B, **Figure 135**) through the connecting rod bushing and into the other side of the piston. Push the piston pin in until it bottoms against the retaining ring.
8. Install the other *new* piston pin retaining ring (**Figure 139**) into the opposite piston groove. Make sure it seats properly in the piston groove (**Figure 140**).

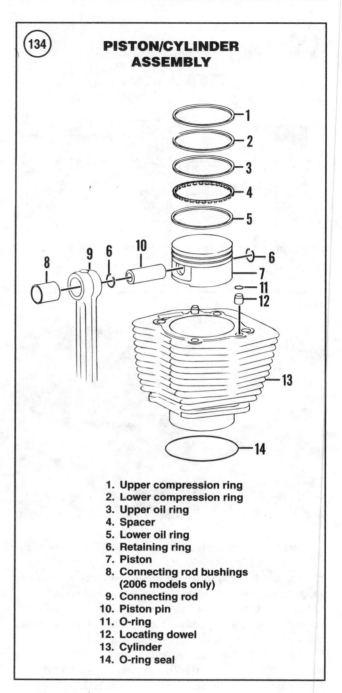

134

PISTON/CYLINDER ASSEMBLY

1. Upper compression ring
2. Lower compression ring
3. Upper oil ring
4. Spacer
5. Lower oil ring
6. Retaining ring
7. Piston
8. Connecting rod bushings (2006 models only)
9. Connecting rod
10. Piston pin
11. O-ring
12. Locating dowel
13. Cylinder
14. O-ring seal

135

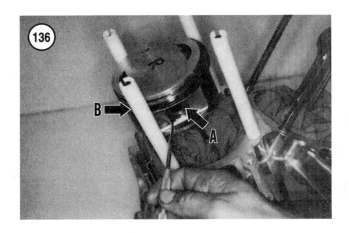

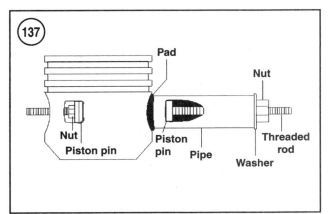

9. Repeat procedure to install the remaining piston.

10. Remove the foam-type insulation pieces from the crankcase studs.

11. Install the cylinders as described in this chapter.

Piston Inspection

During inspection, compare any measurements to the specifications in **Table 2** or **Table 3**. Replace any part that is worn, damaged or out of specification.

1. If necessary, remove the piston rings as described in this section.

> *CAUTION*
> *Be very careful not to gouge or otherwise damage the piston when removing carbon. Never use a wire brush to clean the piston ring grooves. Do not attempt to remove carbon from the sides of the piston above the top ring or from the cylinder bore near the top. Removal of carbon from these two areas may cause increased oil consumption.*

> *CAUTION*
> *The pistons have a special coating on the skirt (**Figure 141**). Do not scrape or use any type of abrasive on this surface as it will be damaged.*

2. Carefully clean the carbon from the piston crown (**Figure 142**) with a soft scraper. Large carbon accumulations reduce piston cooling and cause detonation and piston damage. Make sure the piston remains properly identified.

3. After cleaning the piston, examine the crown. The crown should show no signs of wear or damage. If the crown appears pecked or spongy-looking, check the spark plug, valves and combustion chamber for aluminum deposits. If aluminum deposits are found, the engine is overheating.

4. Remove all carbon buildup and oil residue from the ring grooves with a section of broken piston ring. Do not gouge or remove any aluminum from the ring grooves as this will increase side clearance. Replace the piston if necessary.

5. Examine each ring groove for burrs, dented edges or other damage. Pay particular attention to the top compression ring groove as it usually wears more than the others. The oil rings and grooves generally wear less than compression rings and their grooves. If the of oil ring groove is worn or if the oil ring assembly is tight and difficult to remove, the piston skirt may have collapsed due to excessive heat and is permanently deformed. Replace the piston.

6. Check the oil control holes (**Figure 143**) in the piston for carbon or oil sludge buildup. Clean the holes with wire and blow them out with compressed air.

7. Check the piston skirt (**Figure 142**) for cracks or other damage. If a piston shows signs of partial seizure such as aluminum build-up on the piston skirt, replace the piston to reduce the possibility of engine noise and further piston seizure. If the piston skirt is worn or scuffed unevenly from side-to-side, the connecting rod may be bent or twisted.

8. Check the circlip groove (**Figure 144**) on each side for wear, cracks or other damage. If the grooves are questionable, check the circlip fit by installing a new circlip into each groove, and then attempt to move the circlip from side-to-side. If the circlip has any side play, the groove is worn and the piston must be replaced.

9. Measure piston-to-cylinder clearance as described in *Piston Clearance* (this section).

10. If the piston needs to be replaced, select a new piston as described in *Piston Clearance* (this section). If the piston, rings and cylinder are not damaged and are within specification, they can be reused.

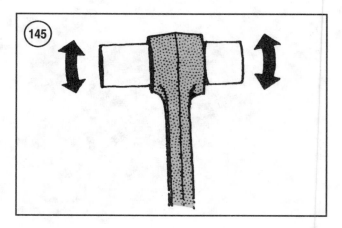

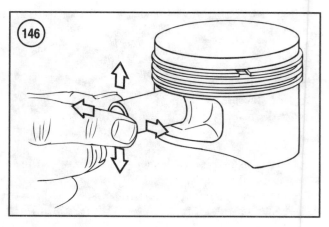

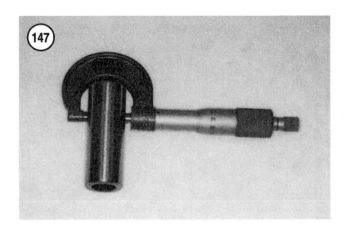

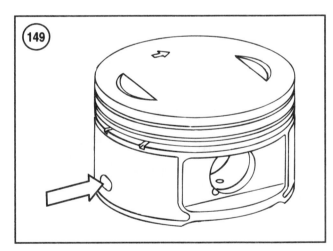

Piston Pin Inspection

1. Clean the piston pin in solvent and dry it thoroughly.
2. Inspect the piston pin for chrome flaking or cracks. Replace if necessary.
3. Oil the piston pin and install it in the connecting rod (**Figure 145**). Slowly rotate the piston pin and check for radial play.
4. Oil the piston pin and install it in the piston (**Figure 146**). Check the piston pin for excessive play.
5. To measure piston pin-to-piston clearance, perform the following:

    a. Measure the piston pin outside diameter with a micrometer (**Figure 147**).
    b. Measure the inside diameter of the piston pin bore (**Figure 148**) with a small bore gauge. Measure the small bore gauge with a micrometer.
    c. Subtract the piston pin outside diameter from the piston pin bore to obtain the piston pin clearance.

6. If the piston pin-to-piston clearance exceeds the service limit (**Table 2** or **Table 3**), replace the piston and/or the piston pin.

Piston Clearance

The piston has a small oval-shaped opening on the piston skirt coating. This opening is used to locate the micrometer for an accurate outer diameter measurement. This small oval-shaped opening is too small for the standard flat anvil micrometer to obtain an accurate measurement. Use a 3-4 inch blade or ball anvil-style micrometer, or a 4-5 inch micrometer with spherical ball adapters to achieve a correct measurement.

1. Make sure the piston skirt (**Figure 141**) and cylinder bore (**Figure 129**) are clean and dry.
2. Measure the cylinder bore inside diameter (**Figure 132**) as described in *Cylinder Inspection* (this chapter).
3A. On all models except Screamin' Eagle and CVO, measure the piston diameter with a micrometer as follows:

    a. Use the special micrometer and correctly position it on the bare aluminum spot on each side of the piston as shown in **Figure 149**.
    b. Measure the piston at this location only.

3B. On Screamin' Eagle and CVO models, measure the piston diameter with a micrometer as follows:

    a. Set the piston on a flat surface.
    b. Mark the center of each side of the skirt at a point 0.394 in. (10 mm) up from the skirt bottom (**Figure 150**).
    c. Fit a micrometer onto these marks, and measure the piston diameter.

4. Subtract the piston diameter from the largest bore inside diameter; the difference is piston-to-cylinder clearance. If the clearance exceeds the service limit in **Table 2** or **Table 3**, the pistons should be replaced with the cylinders bored oversize, and then honed. Purchase the new pistons first. Measure their diameter and add the specified clearance to determine the proper cylinder bore diameter for machining.

Piston Pin Bushing Inspection

The piston pin bushings are reamed to provide correct piston pin-to-connecting rod clearance. This clearance is critical in preventing pin knock and engine top end damage.

1. Inspect the piston pin bushings (**Figure 151**) for excessive wear or damage such as pit marks, scoring or wear grooves. Then, make sure the bushing is not loose. The bushing must be a tight fit in the connecting rod.

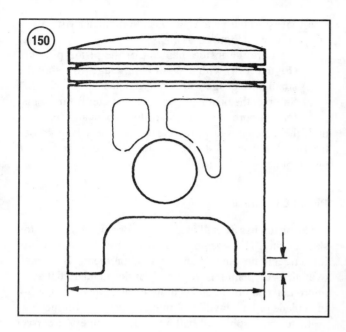

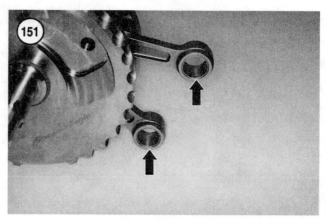

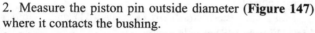

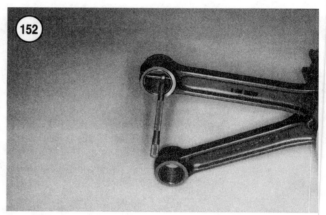

2. Measure the piston pin outside diameter (**Figure 147**) where it contacts the bushing.

3. Measure the piston pin bushing inside diameter using a small bore gauge (**Figure 152**).

4. Subtract the piston pin outer diameter from the bushing inner diameter to determine piston pin-to-connecting rod clearance.

5A. On all 2006 models, replace the piston pin and bushing if the pin-to-rod clearance equals or exceeds the service limit (**Table 2**).

5B. On all 2007-2011 models, the connecting rod bushing in not serviceable. Replace the piston pin and/or crankshaft assembly if the pin-to-rod clearance equals or exceeds the service limit (**Table 2** or **Table 3**).

Piston Pin Bushing Replacement (2006 Models Only)

Tools

The following tools, or their equivalents, are required to replace and ream the piston pin bushings. The clamp tool is only required if the bushing is being replaced with the crankcase assembled. If these tools are not available, have a shop with the proper equipment perform the procedure.

1. Connecting rod clamping tool (JIMS part No. 1284) or (H-D part No. HD-95952-33C).

2. Connecting rod bushing tool and threaded cylinders (JIMS part No. 1051).

3. Bushing reamer tool (JIMS part No. 1726-3).

4. Connecting rod bushing hone (H-D part No. HD-42569).

Procedure

1. Remove two of the pieces of foam-type pipe insulation protecting the cylinder studs.

2. Install the connecting rod clamping tool as follows:

a. Install the clamp portion of the connecting rod clamping tool over the connecting rod so the slots engage the cylinder head studs. Do not scratch or bend the studs.

b. With the knurled end of the threaded cylinder facing up, and turn the threaded cylinders onto the studs. Tighten them securely against the clamp.

c. Alternately tighten the thumbscrews on the side of the connecting rod. Do not turn only one thumbscrew, as this will move the connecting rod off center and tightening the other thumbscrew will cause the connecting rod to flex or bend.

3. Cover the crankcase opening to keep bushing particles from falling into the engine.

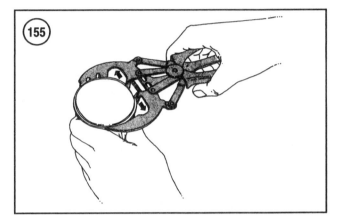

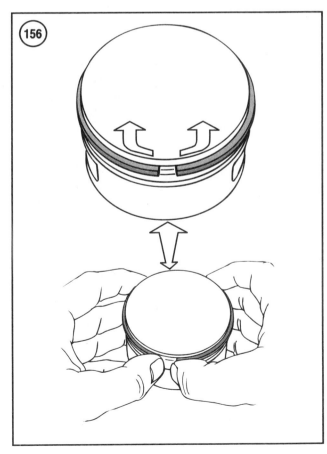

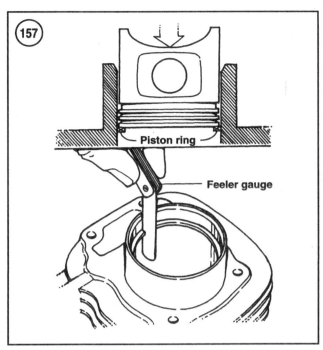

4

NOTE
When installing the new bushing, align the oil slot in the bushing with the oil hole in the connecting rod.

4. Replace the bushing using the connecting rod bushing tool (**Figure 153**) following the tool manufacturer's instructions. The new bushing must be flush with both sides of the connecting rod.

5. Ream the piston pin with the bushing reamer tool (**Figure 154**) following the tool manufacturer's instructions.

6. Hone the new bushing to obtain the specified piston pin-to-connecting rod clearance (**Table 2**). Use honing oil, not engine oil, when honing the bushing to size.

7. Install the piston pin through the bushing. The pin should move through the bushing smoothly. Confirm piston pin-to-connecting rod clearance using a micrometer and small bore gauge.

8. Carefully remove all metal debris from the crankcase.

Piston Ring Removal/Inspection

During inspection, compare any measurements to the specifications in **Table 2** or **Table 3**. Replace any part that is worn, damaged or out of specification.

1. Remove the piston rings using a ring expander tool (**Figure 155**) or spread them by hand (**Figure 156**).

2. Clean the piston ring grooves as described in *Piston Inspection* (this section).

3. Inspect the ring grooves for burrs, nicks, or broken or cracked lands. Replace the piston if necessary.

4. Insert one piston ring into the top of its cylinder, and tap it down approximately 1/2 in. (12.7 mm), using the piston to square it in the bore. Measure the ring end gap (**Figure 157**) with a feeler gauge and compare it with the specifica-

tion in **Table 2** or **Table 3**. Replace the piston rings as a set if any one ring end gap measurement is excessive. Repeat measurement process for each ring.

5. Roll each compression ring around its piston groove as shown in **Figure 158**. The ring should move smoothly with no binding. If a ring binds in its groove, check the groove for damage. Replace the piston if necessary.

Piston Ring Installation

Each piston is equipped with three piston rings: two compression rings (**Figure 159**) and one oil ring assembly (**Figure 160**). The upper and lower compression rings are each marked with a dot (**Figure 161**).

The manufacturer recommends that *new* piston rings be installed every time the piston is removed. Always lightly hone the cylinder before installing new piston rings.

1. Wash the piston in hot, soapy water. Rinse it with cold water, and then dry it with compressed air. Make sure the oil control holes in the lower ring groove are clear.

2. Install the oil ring assembly as follows:

   a. The oil ring consists of three rings: a ribbed spacer ring (A, **Figure 160**) and two steel rings (B).

   b. Install the spacer ring into the lower ring groove. Butt the spacer ring ends together. Do not overlap the ring ends.

   c. Insert one end of the first steel ring into the lower groove so it is below the spacer ring. Then, spiral the other end over the piston crown and into the lower groove. To prevent the ring end from scratching the side of the piston, place a piece of shim stock or a thin, flat feeler gauge between the ring end and piston.

   d. Repeat the process to install the other steel ring above the spacer ring.

> *NOTE*
> *To install the compression rings, use a ring expander as shown in **Figure 155**. Do not expand the rings any more than necessary to install them.*

3. Install the *new* lower compression ring with the dot (**Figure 161**) facing up.

4. Install the *new* top compression ring with the dot (**Figure 161**) facing up.

5. Check the ring side clearance with a feeler gauge as shown in **Figure 162**. Check side clearance in several spots around the piston. If the side clearance is larger than the service limit in **Table 2** or **Table 3**, replace the piston.

6. Stagger the ring gaps around the piston as shown in **Figure 163**.

EXHAUST SYSTEM

Removal

Refer to **Figure 164** and **Figure 165**.

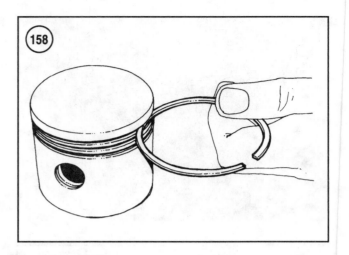

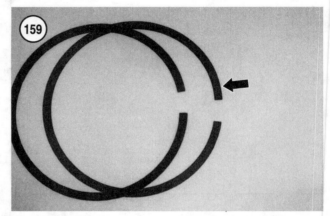

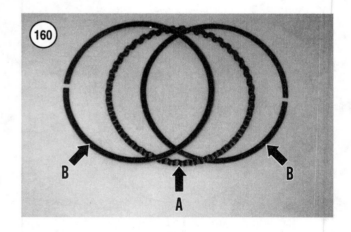

> *NOTE*
> *If the system joints are corroded or rusty, spray all connections with penetrating oil, and allow it to soak in sufficiently to free the rusted joints.*

1. Turn the ignition switch off.

2. Support the motorcycle on a work stand. Refer to *Motorcycle Stands* in Chapter Ten.

3. Remove the seat as described in Chapter Fourteen.

4. On HDI models, disconnect the cable from the active exhaust valve actuator as described in this chapter.

5. Disconnect the front oxygen sensor as follows:

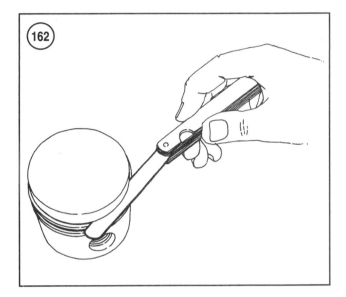

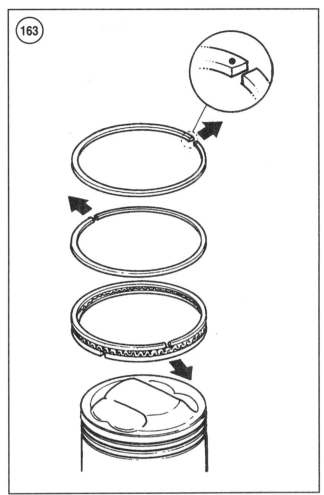

4

a. Depress the tabs and open the front electrical caddy cover (**Figure 166**).

b. Release the connector directly below the voltage regulator from the electrical caddy.

c. Disconnect the 2-pin front oxygen sensor connector (**Figure 167**).

d. Note the path of the sensor wiring harness though the frame as it must be routed in the same path during installation.

6. Disconnect the rear oxygen sensor as follows:

a. In the frame opening under the seat area, disconnect the 2-pin rear oxygen sensor connector (**Figure 168**).

b. Note the path of the sensor wiring harness though the frame as it must be routed in the same path during installation.

7. Remove the heat shields as follows, if necessary:

a. Identify the heat shields prior to removal as this will aid during installation. They look very similar but all have slight differences. Refer to these parts in **Figure 164** and **Figure 165**.

b. Loosen the clamps securing the exhaust pipe heat shields. Remove the front cylinder heat shield and the rear cylinder heat shield.

8. At front cylinder head, loosen and remove the two flange nuts securing the front exhaust flange (**Figure 169**) to the cylinder head.

9. At rear cylinder head, loosen and remove the two flange nuts securing the rear exhaust flange (**Figure 170**) to the cylinder head.

10. Remove the locknut and bolt (**Figure 171**) securing the front exhaust pipe clamp to the frame bracket.

11. Remove the locknut and bolt (**Figure 172**) securing the rear exhaust pipe clamp to the rear exhaust bracket.

12. Carefully pull the front and rear exhaust pipe assembly (**Figure 173**) free from the cylinder head studs and remove the assembly.

13. Remove the snap ring and gasket from each cylinder head exhaust port. Discard the gaskets.

14. Remove the mounting bolts (A, **Figure 174**) and nut (B) securing the rear bracket (C) to the crankcase, and then remove the bracket, if necessary.

15. Loosen the Torca clamp nut (**Figure 175**) and separate the muffler from the exhaust pipe, if necessary. Discard the Torca clamp.

16. Inspect the exhaust system as described in this section.

17. Store the exhaust system components in a safe place until they are reinstalled.

(164) **EXHAUST SYSTEM (ALL MODELS EXCEPT FXDF, FXDFSE AND FXDFSE2)**

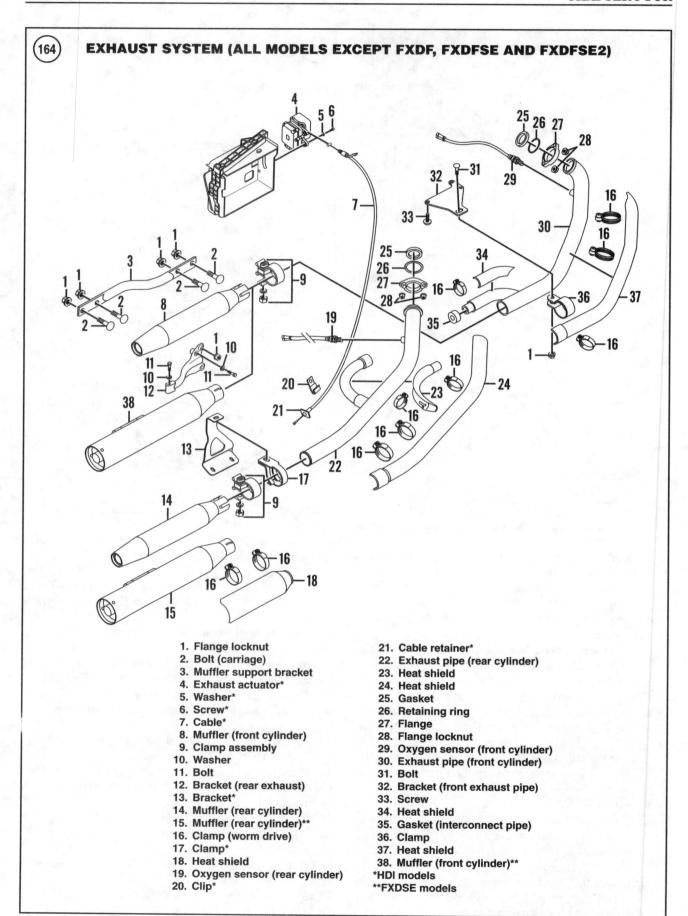

1. Flange locknut
2. Bolt (carriage)
3. Muffler support bracket
4. Exhaust actuator*
5. Washer*
6. Screw*
7. Cable*
8. Muffler (front cylinder)
9. Clamp assembly
10. Washer
11. Bolt
12. Bracket (rear exhaust)
13. Bracket*
14. Muffler (rear cylinder)
15. Muffler (rear cylinder)**
16. Clamp (worm drive)
17. Clamp*
18. Heat shield
19. Oxygen sensor (rear cylinder)
20. Clip*

21. Cable retainer*
22. Exhaust pipe (rear cylinder)
23. Heat shield
24. Heat shield
25. Gasket
26. Retaining ring
27. Flange
28. Flange locknut
29. Oxygen sensor (front cylinder)
30. Exhaust pipe (front cylinder)
31. Bolt
32. Bracket (front exhaust pipe)
33. Screw
34. Heat shield
35. Gasket (interconnect pipe)
36. Clamp
37. Heat shield
38. Muffler (front cylinder)**
*HDI models
**FXDSE models

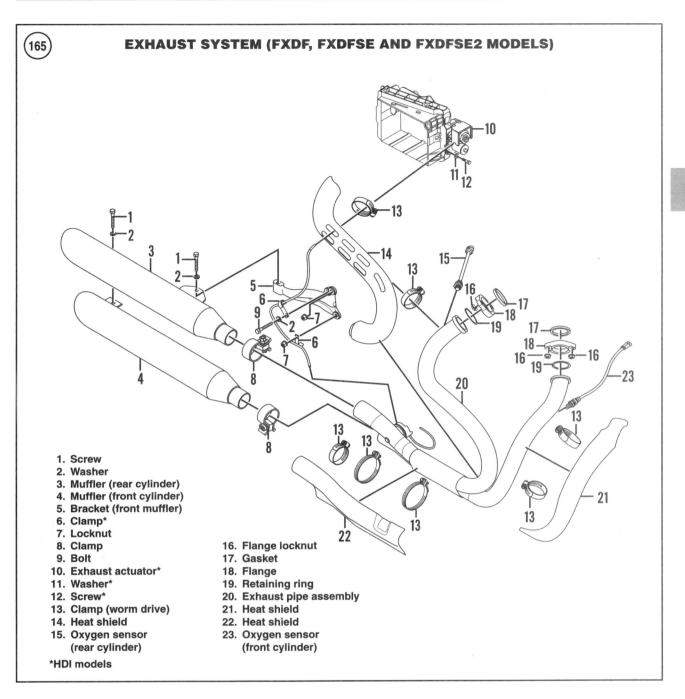

165 **EXHAUST SYSTEM (FXDF, FXDFSE AND FXDFSE2 MODELS)**

1. Screw
2. Washer
3. Muffler (rear cylinder)
4. Muffler (front cylinder)
5. Bracket (front muffler)
6. Clamp*
7. Locknut
8. Clamp
9. Bolt
10. Exhaust actuator*
11. Washer*
12. Screw*
13. Clamp (worm drive)
14. Heat shield
15. Oxygen sensor
   (rear cylinder)

*HDI models

16. Flange locknut
17. Gasket
18. Flange
19. Retaining ring
20. Exhaust pipe assembly
21. Heat shield
22. Heat shield
23. Oxygen sensor
   (front cylinder)

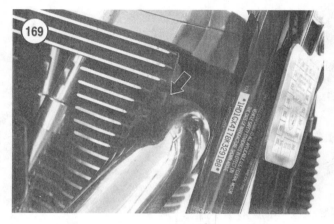

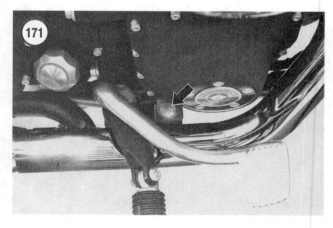

Installation

> *NOTE*
> *New Torca clamps must be installed to ensure correct sealing integrity. The new Torca clamps eliminate the need for graphite or silicone tape during installation of the mufflers.*

> *NOTE*
> *To eliminate exhaust leaks, do not tighten any of the mounting bolts and nuts or the Torca clamps until all of the exhaust components are in place.*

1. Install the rear muffler support bracket (C, **Figure 174**), if removed. Tighten the mounting bolts (A, **Figure 174**) and nut (B) to 15-19 ft.-lb. (20.3-25.8 N•m).

2. Install a *new* Torca clamp (**Figure 175**) onto the muffler, and install the muffler onto the exhaust pipe, if removed. Do not tighten the Torca clamp nut at this time.

3. Before installing the *new* exhaust port gaskets, scrape the exhaust port surfaces to remove all carbon residue—removing the carbon will ensure a good gasket fit. Then, wipe the port clean with a rag.

4. Install a *new* exhaust port gasket (**Figure 176**) into each exhaust port with the tapered thin side facing out. Install the snap ring and secure the gasket in place.

a. Install the front cylinder heat shield and the rear cylinder heat shield.

b. Securely tighten the clamps securing the exhaust pipe heat shields.

10. Correctly align the mufflers and exhaust pipes and tighten the fasteners in the following steps.

11. Tighten the front cylinder flange nuts as follows:

a. Finger-tighten the lower nut.

b. Tighten the upper nut to 9-18 in.-lb. (1-2 N•m).

c. Tighten the lower nut to 100-120 in.-lb. (11.3-13.6 N•m).

d. Tighten the upper nut to 100-120 in.-lb. (11.3-13.6 N•m).

12. Tighten the rear cylinder flange nuts as follows:

a. Finger-tighten the upper nut.

b. Tighten the lower nut to 9-18 in.-lb. (1-2 N•m).

c. Tighten the upper nut to 100-120 in.-lb. (11.3-13.6 N•m).

d. Tighten the lower nut to 100-120 in.-lb. (11.3-13.6 N•m).

13. Tighten the muffler support bracket bolts and nuts to 15-19 in.-lb. (20.3-25.8 N•m).

14. Tighten the muffler Torca clamp nuts (**Figure 175**) to 45-50 ft.-lb. (61.0-67.8 N•m).

15. Install all heat shields removed and tighten clamps securely.

16. Connect the rear oxygen sensor as follows:

a. Correctly route the sensor wiring harness though the frame as noted during removal.

b. Connect the 2-pin rear oxygen sensor connector (**Figure 168**).

17. Connect the front oxygen sensor as follows:

a. Correctly route the sensor wiring harness though the frame as noted during removal.

b. Connect the 2-pin front oxygen sensor connector (**Figure 167**).

c. Close the front electrical caddy cover (**Figure 166**) and snap the tabs into place.

18. On HDI models, connect the cable from the active exhaust valve actuator as described in this section.

19. Install the seat as described in Chapter Fourteen.

Exhaust System Inspection (All Models)

1. Replace rusted or damaged exhaust system components.

2. Inspect all pipes for rust or corrosion (**Figure 177**).

3. Remove all rust from exhaust pipes and muffler mating surfaces.

4. The Torca muffler clamps are not reusable and must be replaced whenever the muffler(s) is disconnected from the exhaust pipe.

5. Replace damaged exhaust pipe retaining rings.

6. Replace worn or damaged heat shield worm drive clamps (**Figure 178**) as required.

7. On all models except FXDF, FXDFSE and FXDFSE2, check the muffler mounting bracket bolts and nuts (**Figure 179**) for tightness.

5. Carefully install the front and rear exhaust pipe assembly (**Figure 173**) onto the cylinder head studs.

6. Slide the exhaust flange onto the cylinder head studs, and install the two flange nuts. Finger-tighten the nuts at this time.

7. Install the locknut and bolt (**Figure 171**) securing the front exhaust pipe clamp to the frame bracket. Finger-tighten the fasteners at this time.

8. Install the locknut and bolt (**Figure 172**) securing the rear exhaust pipe clamp to the rear exhaust bracket. Finger-tighten the fasteners at this time.

9. Install the heat shields as follows, if removed:

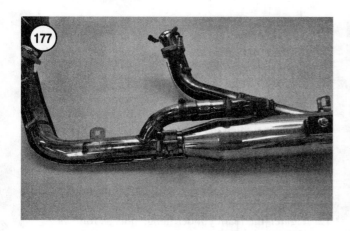

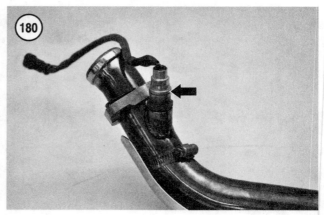

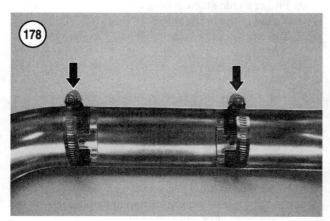

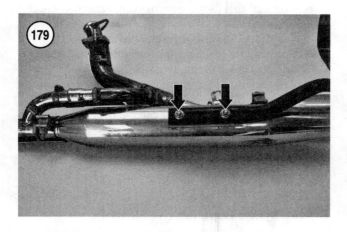

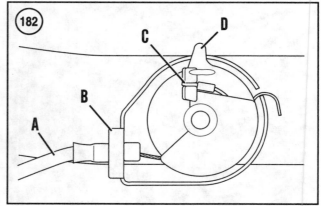

8. To replace an oxygen sensor (**Figure 180**), perform the following:

   a. Disconnect the 2-pin connector from the sensor.
   b. Carefully cut all cable clamps securing the sensor wiring harness to the frame.

NOTE
Figure 181 *is shown with the exhaust pipe removed for photo clarity.*

   c. Carefully install an oxygen sensor socket (JIMS part No. 969), or an equivalent, over the sensor (**Figure 181**). Using a socket extension, turn the sensor sock-et *counterclockwise* to loosen the sensor from the exhaust pipe.
   d. Remove the sensor socket and unthread the sensor from the exhaust pipe by hand.
   e. Install the oxygen sensor into the exhaust pipe by hand. Attach the sensor socket, and tighten the sensor to the specification in **Table 5**.

ACTIVE EXHAUST MODULE
(UK AND AUSTRALIA HDI MODELS)

Refer to **Figures 164**, **165**, and **182**.

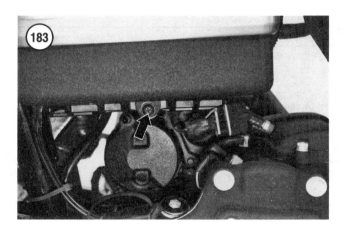

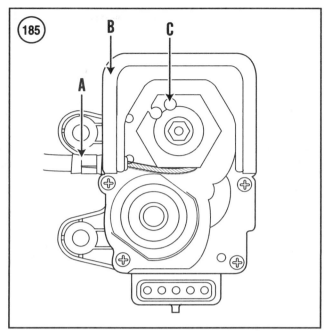

Removal/Installation

1. Release the cable from the rear exhaust pipe as follows:
   a. Release the cable from the groove in the bellcrank.
   b. Remove the cable and retainer from the bellcrank.
   c. Remove the ferrule from the bellcrank.

2. Remove the lower screw (**Figure 183**) securing the battery cover. Pull out on the bottom of the battery cover and release it from the two index tabs (**Figure 184**) at the top. Remove the battery cover.

3. Disconnect the 5-pin connector from the active exhaust module attached to the front side of the battery tray.

4. Remove the cable housing (A, **Figure 185**) from the notch in the exhaust module shroud (B).

5. Disconnect the cable end (C, **Figure 185**) from the module wheel, and remove the cable from the module.

6. Remove the screws and washers securing the module to the front side of the battery box, and remove the module.

7. Disconnect the cable (A, **Figure 182**) and retainer (B) from the exhaust pipe. Remove the ferrule (C, **Figure 182**) from the bellcrank (D), and remove the cable from the exhaust pipe.

8. Release the cable housing from the cable clips on the frame.

9. On FXDF and FXDFSE models, remove the screw and washer securing the cable to the muffler bracket.

10. Note the path of the cable through the frame, and remove the cable from the frame.

11. Install by reversing the removal steps. Note the following:
   a. Correctly route the cable through the frame. Keep the cable away from the exhaust system, battery cover and transmission case.
   b. Install the screws securing the module to the frame and tighten to 36-60 in.-lb. (4.1-6.8 N•m).

Tables 1-5 are on the following pages.

Table 1 GENERAL ENGINE SPECIFICATIONS

Item	Specifications
Engine type	4-stroke, 45°, OHV V-twin, Twin Cam 88, 96, and 110
Bore and stroke	
88 models	3.75 × 4.00 in. (95.25 × 101.60 mm)
96 models	3.75 × 4.375 in. (95.25 × 111.13 mm)
110 models	4.00 × 4.375 in. (101.60 × 111.13 mm)
Displacement	
88 models	88 cubic inch (1450 cc)
96 models	96 cubic inch (1584 cc)
110 models	110 cubic inch (1800 cc)
Compression ratio	
88 models	9.0:1
96 models	
2007-2008 models	9.0:1
2009 models	9.2:1
110 models	9.3:1
Torque	
88 models	
Standard exhaust system	85 ft.-lb. (115.2 N•m) @ 3000 rpm
Short, dual exhaust system	115 ft.-lb. (155.9 N•m) @ 3000 rpm
96 models	
Standard exhaust system	91 ft.-lb. (123.4 N•m) @ 3000 rpm
Short, dual exhaust system	123 ft.-lb. (166.7 N•m) @ 3000 rpm
110 models	
2007-2008 models	105 ft.-lb. (142.4 N•m) @ 3000 rpm
2009 models	114 ft.-lb. (154.6 N•m) @ 3500 rpm
Maximum sustained engine speed	5500 rpm
Idle speed	950-1050 rpm
Cooling system	Air-cooled

Table 2 ENGINE TOP END SPECIFICATIONS (ALL MODELS EXCEPT SCREAMIN' EAGLE AND CVO)

Item	New In. (mm)	Service limit In. (mm)
Breather cover warp	–	0.005 (0.13)
Breather baffle warp	–	0.005 (0.13)
Cylinder		
Taper	–	0.002 (0.051)
Out of round	–	0.002 (0.051)
Warp		
At top (cylinder head)	–	0.006 (0.152)
At base (crankcase)	–	0.004 (0.102)
Cylinder bore		
Standard	3.7500-3.7505 (95.250-95.263)	3.752 (95.301)
Oversize 0.005 in	3.7550-3.7555 (95.377-95.390)	3.757 (95.428)
Oversize 0.010 in.	3.7600-3.7605 (95.504-95.517)	3.762 (95.555)
Cylinder head		
Flatness limit	–	0.006 (0.15)
Valve guide fit in head	0.0020-0.0033 (0.051-0.084)	0.002 (0.051)
Valve seat fit in head	0.003-0.0045 (0.076-0.114)	0.002 (0.051)
Hydraulic lifters		
Lifter-to-bore clearance	0.0008-0.0020 (0.020-0.051)	0.0030 (0.076)
Roller clearance on the pin	–	0.0015 (0.038)
Roller end clearance	–	0.026 (0.660)
Piston-to-cylinder clearance	0.0014-0.0025 (0.036-0.064)	0.003 (0.076)
Piston pin-to-connecting rod clearance	0.0007-0.0012 (0.018-0.031)	0.002 (0.051)
Piston pin-to-piston clearance (fit in piston)	0.0002-0.0005 (0.005-0.013)	0.0008 (0.020)

(continued)

Table 2 ENGINE TOP END SPECIFICATIONS (ALL MODELS EXCEPT SCREAMIN' EAGLE AND CVO) (continued)

Item	New In. (mm)	Service limit In. (mm)
Piston rings		
End gap		
Top ring	0.010-0.020 (0.254-0.508)	0.003 (0.076)
Second ring	0.014-0.024 (0.356-0.610)	0.034 (0.864)
Oil control ring	0.010-0.050 (0.254-1.27)	0.050 (1.27)
Side clearance		
Top ring	0.0012-0.0037 (0.031-0.094)	0.0045 (0.114)
Second ring	0.0012-0.0037 (0.031-0.094)	0.0045 (0.114)
Oil control ring	0.0031-0.0091 (0.079-0.231)	0.010 (0.254)
Rocker arm		
Bushing fit in rocker arm	0.002-0.004 (0.051-0.102)	–
End clearance	0.003-0.013 (0.076-0.330)	0.025 (0.635)
Shaft-to-rocker arm bushing clearance	0.0005-0.0020 (0.013-0.051)	0.0035 (0.089)
Shaft-to-rocker arm support clearance	0.0007-0.0022 (0.018-0.056)	0.0035 (0.089)
Valves		
Valve stem-to-guide clearance		
Intake	0.001-0.003 (0.0254-0.0762)	0.0038 (0.0965)
Exhaust	0.001-0.003 (0.0254-0.0762_	0.0038 (0.0965)
Seat width	0.040-0.062 (1.02-1.58)	–
Valve stem protrusion from cylinder head boss	2.012-2.032 (51.11-51.61)	2.069 (52.55)
Valve springs		
Free length	2.325 (59.1)	–
Spring rate		
Closed	135 lbs. @ 1.850 in. (61.2 kg @ 47.0 mm)	–
Open	312 lbs. @ 1.300 in. (141.5 kg @ 33.0 mm)	–

4

Table 3 ENGINE TOP END SPECIFICATIONS (SCREAMIN' EAGLE AND CVO MODELS)

Item	New In. (mm)	Service limit In. (mm)
Breather cover warp	–	0.005 (0.13)
Breather baffle warp	–	0.005 (0.13)
Cylinder		
Taper	–	0.002 (0.051)
Out of round	–	0.002 (0.051)
Warp		
At top (cylinder head)	–	0.006 (0.152)
At base (crankcase)	–	0.004 (0.102)
Cylinder bore		
Standard	4.0000-4.0005 (101.6-101.613)	4.002 (101.65)
Oversize 0.005 in	4.0050-4.0055 (101.727-101.740)	4.007 (101.78)
Oversize 0.010 in.	4.0100-4.0105 (101.854-101.867)	4.012 (101.91)
Cylinder head		
Flatness limit	–	0.006 (0.15)
Valve guide fit in head	0.0020-0.0033 (0.051-0.084)	0.002 (0.05)
Valve seat fit in head		
Intake and exhaust	0.004-0.0055 (0.102-0.140)	0.002 (0.05)
Hydraulic lifters		
Lifter-to-bore clearance	0.0008-0.0020 (0.020-0.051)	0.0030 (0.076)
Radial play	–	0.0015 (0.038)
Roller end clearance	–	0.026 (0.660)
Piston-to-cylinder clearance	0.0018-0.0027 (0.046-0.069)	0.003 (0.076)
Piston pin-to-connecting rod clearance	0.0006-0.0012 (0.015-0.031)	0.002 (0.051)
Piston pin-to-piston clearance (fit in piston)	0.0005-0.0009 (0.013-0.023)	0.0009 (0.023)

(continued)

Table 3 ENGINE TOP END SPECIFICATIONS (SCREAMIN' EAGLE AND CVO MODELS) (continued)

Item	New In. (mm)	Service limit In. (mm)
Piston rings		
End gap		
Top ring	0.016-0.024 (0.406-0.610)	0.034 (0.864)
Second ring	0.014-0.024 (0.356-0.610)	0.034 (0.864)
Oil control ring	0.010-0.030 (0.254-0.762)	0.030 (0.762)
Side clearance		
Top ring	0.00098-0.0024 (0.025-0.061)	0.0032 (0.081)
Second ring	0.00098-0.0024 (0.025-0.061)	0.0032 (0.081)
Oil control ring	0.002-0.004 (0.051-0.102)	0.004 (0.102)
Rocker arm		0.002 (0.05)
Bushing fit in rocker arm	0.002-0.004 (0.051-0.102)	–
End clearance	0.003-0.013 (0.08-0.330)	0.025 (0.635)
Shaft-to-rocker arm bushing clearance	0.0005-0.0020 (0.013-0.051)	0.0035 (0.089)
Shaft-to rocker arm support clearance	0.0007-0.0022 (0.018-0.056)	0.0035 (0.089)
Valves		
Valve stem-to-guide clearance		
Intake and exhaust	0.0011-0.0029 (0.028-0.074)	0.02 (0.051)
Seat width	0.034-0.062 (0.86-1.57)	–
Valve stem protrusion from cylinder		
head boss	1.990-2.024 (50.55-51.41)	–
Valve springs		
Free length	2.210 (56.13)	–
Spring rate		
Closed	175 lbs @ 1.800 in (79 kg @ 45.72 mm)	–
Open	432 lbs @ 1.250 in. (196 kg @ 31.75 mm)	–

N.A. Specification not available from the manufacturer.

Table 4 PUSH ROD AND LIFTER LOCATION

Cylinder	Lifter bore	Cylinder head/rocker housing
Front		
Intake	Inside	Rear
Exhaust	Outside	Front
Rear		
Intake	Inside	Front
Exhaust	Outside	Rear

Table 5 ENGINE TOP END AND EXHAUST TORQUE SPECIFICATIONS

Item	ft.-lb.	in.-lb.	N•m
Active exhaust module screw	–	36-60	4.1-6.8
Automatic compression release (ACR) solenoid			
(Screamin' Eagle and CVO models)	11-15	–	14.9-20.3
Breather cover bolts	–	90-120	10.2-13.6
Cylinder head bolts			
Initial	10-12	–	13.6-16.3
Secondary	15-17	–	20.3-23.0
Final	additional 90°		
Cylinder head stabilizer link bracket bolts	35-40	–	47.5-54.2
Cylinder stud	10-20	–	13.6-27.1
	(continued)		

Table 5 ENGINE TOP END AND EXHAUST TORQUE SPECIFICATIONS (continued)

Item	ft.-lb.	in.-lb.	N•m
Exhaust system fasteners			
Crossover hanger nut (2009 models)	14-18	–	18.9-24.4
Cylinder head flange nuts			
Upper nut			
Preliminary	–	9-18	1-2
Final	–	100-120	11.3-13.6
Lower nut	–	100-120	11.3-13.6
Muffler support bracket nut/bolt	15-19	–	20.3-25.8
Muffler Torca clamp nut	45-50	–	61.0-67.8
Oxygen sensor			
2006-2009 models	29-44	–	39.3-59.7
2010-2011 models	29-34	–	39.3-46.1
Lifter cover bolts	–	90-120	10.2-13.6
Rocker arm cover bolt	15-18	–	20.3-24.4
Rocker arm housing bolt	10-14	–	13.6-19.0
Rocker arm support plate bolts	18-22	–	24.4-29.8
Spark plug	12-18	–	16.3-24.4

4

CHAPTER FIVE

ENGINE LOWER END

This chapter provides service and overhaul procedures for the lower end, including engine removal and installation.

Refer to **Tables 1-3** at the end of the chapter for specifications.

ENGINE

Removal

Refer to **Figure 1**.

> *WARNING*
> *Due to the weight of the engine assembly, a minimum of two people are required to safely remove the engine from the frame.*

> *NOTE*
> *On models with security system, disarm system before disconnecting the battery or pulling the Maxi-Fuse so the siren will not sound. Refer to **Turn Signal and Security Modules** in Chapter Nine.*

1. Thoroughly clean all dirt and debris from the engine.
2. Support the motorcycle on a stand or jack. Refer to *Motorcycle Stands* in Chapter Ten. Note the following:
   a. The motorcycle has almost a 50:50 weight distribution at the center of the engine location on the frame. Position the stand or jack so that the motorcycle is stable after being lifted off the ground.
   b. Use additional wooden blocks to ensure that the motorcycle is stable.
   c. Tie the motorcycle down for additional stability.
3. Remove the seat as described in Chapter Fourteen.
4. Remove the fuel tank as described in Chapter Eight.
5. Remove the air filter and backplate as described in Chapter Eight.
6. Remove the fuel induction module as described in Chapter Eight.
7. Remove the rear brake pedal as described in Chapter Thirteen.
8. Remove both foot rests as described in Chapter Fourteen.
9. Remove the pinch bolt (A, **Figure 2**), and remove the shift lever (B) from the primary chaincase.
10. Remove the exhaust system as described in Chapter Four.
11. Drain the engine oil and remove the oil filter as described in Chapter Three.
12. Remove the engine oil dipstick (**Figure 3**).
13. Remove the crankshaft position sensor bolt (A, **Figure 4**) and the sensor (B) from the crankcase.
14. Remove the voltage regulator as described in Chapter Nine.
15. Disconnect the following connectors:
    a. Oil pressure switch (**Figure 5**).
    b. Engine temperature sensor (**Figure 6**).
    c. Speed sensor (**Figure 7**).
    d. Neutral indicator switch (**Figure 8**).
16. Remove the horn assembly (A, **Figure 9**) as described in Chapter Nine.
17. Remove the primary chain case assembly, including the inner housing, as described in Chapter Six.
18. Remove the alternator rotor and stator as described in Chapter Nine.

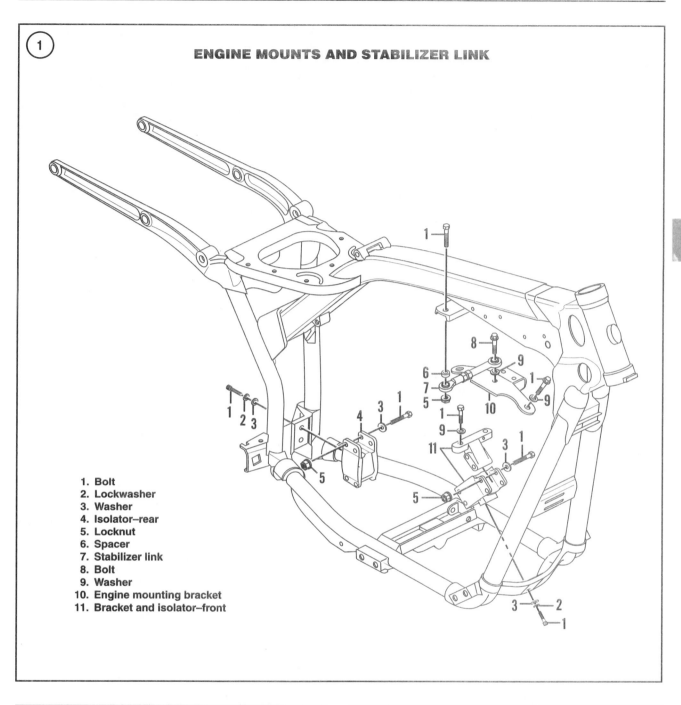

ENGINE MOUNTS AND STABILIZER LINK

1. Bolt
2. Lockwasher
3. Washer
4. Isolator–rear
5. Locknut
6. Spacer
7. Stabilizer link
8. Bolt
9. Washer
10. Engine mounting bracket
11. Bracket and isolator–front

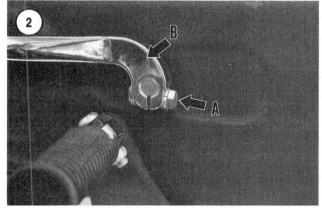

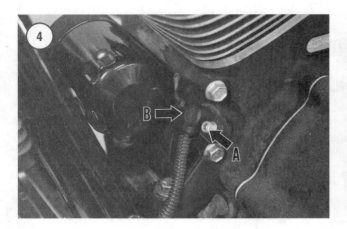

19. Remove the ignition coil assembly (**Figure 10**) as described in Chapter Nine.

20. Disconnect the hose (**Figure 11**) from the transmission breather cover and move the hose behind the transmission flange.

21A. On all models, except Screamin' Eagle and CVO, remove the clutch cable (**Figure 12**) from the lower portion of the crankcase as described in Chapter Six.

21B. On Screamin' Eagle and CVO, models, disconnect the hydraulic fluid line from the clutch release cover as described in Chapter Six.

22. Support the engine with a floor jack or scissor jack (JIMS part. No. 904) placed under the oil pan. Be sure to protect the oil pan with a piece of wood.

23. Apply enough jack pressure on the oil pan to support it prior to removing the engine mounting bolts.

24. On the right side, remove the bolt (A, **Figure 13**) and nut (B) securing the inboard end of the upper stabilizing link (C) to the frame weldment. Do not lose the spacer (D, **Figure 13**) between the frame weldment and stabilizer link.

25. On the left side, remove the two bolts (B, **Figure 9**) and washers securing the top stabilizer link mounting bracket to the cylinder heads. Note the location of the horn ground strap on the front cylinder.

26. Remove the stabilizer link and upper mounting bracket assembly (C, **Figure 9**) from the frame and engine.

5

27. Wrap the frame front down tubes and lower tubes in protective foam padding to protect the finish from damage.

28. Cover both rocker covers with foam padding to protect the finish.

29. Secure all loose ends of wiring out of the way so they will not get snagged during engine removal.

30. Secure the transmission to the frame with a ratchet strap so it will not shift after the engine is removed.

31. Remove the two short (1/2 in.) upper (**Figure 14**) and the long (9/16 in.) lower (**Figure 15**) bolts and washers on each side securing the engine to the transmission.

32. Remove the two bolts and washers (A, **Figure 16**) securing the engine to the front mounting bracket (B).

33. Check the engine to make sure all electrical wiring, hoses and other related components have been disconnected from the engine. Make sure nothing will interfere with the removal of the engine from the right side of the frame.

34. Move the engine far enough forward to clear the clear the locating dowels on the front of the transmission. The dowels stick out approximately 1/2 in. (12.7 mm). Slightly rotate the engine *counterclockwise* to disengage the locating dowels, if necessary.

35. Raise the engine up, and slightly rotate it toward the right side. Remove the engine from the right side of the frame carefully to avoid the rear brake line and reservoir and the main wiring harness.

36. Carry the engine to the workbench and mount the engine (**Figure 17**) in the Twin Cam 88 engine base stand (JIMS part No.1138) and engine stand (JIMS part No.1142), or an equivalent.

37. Remove and discard the engine-to-transmission gasket.

38. Remove the locating dowels either from the engine or transmission (**Figure 18**) mounting surface.

39. Clean all engine mounting bolts and washers in solvent and dry thoroughly.

Installation

> *WARNING*
> *Due to the weight of the engine assembly, a minimum of two people are required to safely install the engine into the frame.*

1. Remove engine from engine stand, if installed.

2. Cover both rocker covers with foam padding to protect the finish.

3. Secure the transmission to the frame with a ratchet strap, if the strap was removed.

4. If removed, install the two lower locating dowels into the transmission case (**Figure 18**).

5. Thoroughly clean the gasket mating surface of the transmission case.

6. Install a *new* gasket onto the transmission case making sure the gasket openings align with those on the transmission.

7. Make sure all electrical wiring, hoses and other related components are out of the way and will not interfere with engine installation.

8. Correctly position a stand or jack under the frame to support the frame when the engine is installed into the frame.

9. Install the engine from the right side of the frame and place it on a piece of wood and the jack. Apply enough jack pressure on the crankcase to support it prior to installing the engine mounting bolts.

10. Slide the engine toward the rear and onto the two transmission locating dowels. The engine may have to be rotated slightly to engage the dowels.

11. Install the two short (1/2 in.) upper (**Figure 14**) and the long (9/16 in.) lower (**Figure 15**) bolts and washers on each side that secure the engine to the transmission.

12. Install the two bolts (A, **Figure 16**) and washers securing the engine to the front mounting bracket (B). Finger-tighten the bolts at this time.

13. Using a crossing pattern, tighten the engine-to-transmission bolts to the following sequence:
   a. Initial: 15 ft.-lb. (20.3 N•m).
   b. Final: 34-39 ft.-lb. (46.1-52.9 N•m).

14. Tighten the two front mounting bracket bolts (A, **Figure 16**) to 25-30 ft.-lb. (33.9-40.7 N•m).

15. Install the stabilizer link and upper mounting bracket assembly onto the engine and frame.

> *NOTE*
> *If the bolt cannot be installed without pushing the engine to either side, refer to **Vehicle Alignment** in Chapter Three.*

16. On the right side, place the spacer (D, **Figure 13**) between the frame weldment and stabilizer link, and install the bolt (A) and nut (B) securing the inboard end of the upper stabilizing link (C) to the frame weldment. Do not tighten the bolt at this time.

17. On the left side, install the top mounting bracket (C, **Figure 9**) onto the cylinder heads. Install the two bolts and washers (B, **Figure 9**) securing bracket. Install the horn ground strap on the front cylinder.

18. Tighten the top mounting bolts as follows:
   a. Stabilizer link bolt: 18-22 ft.-lb. (24.4-29.8 N•m).
   b. Top mounting bracket padding bolts: 35-40 ft.-lb. (47.5-54.2 N•m).

19. Remove the floor jack.

20. Remove the protective padding from the frame front down tubes.

21. Remove the foam padding from the rocker covers.

22A. On all models, except Screamin' Eagle and CVO, attach the clutch cable to the lower portion of the crankcase as described in Chapter Six.

22B. On Screamin' Eagle and CVO, models, connect the hydraulic fluid line to the clutch release cover as described in Chapter Six.

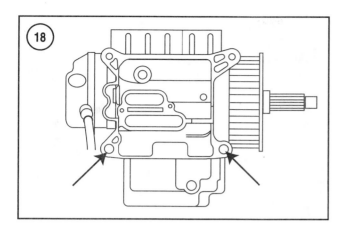

23. Connect the hose (**Figure 11**) onto the transmission breather cover.

24. Install the ignition coil assembly (**Figure 10**) as described in Chapter Nine.

25. Install the alternator rotor and stator as described in Chapter Nine.

26. Install the primary chain case assembly, including the inner housing, as described in Chapter Six.

27. Install the horn assembly as described in Chapter Nine.

28. Connect the following connectors:
   a. Oil pressure switch (**Figure 5**).
   b. Engine temperature sensor (**Figure 6**).
   c. Speed sensor (**Figure 7**).
   d. Neutral indicator switch (**Figure 8**).

29. Install the voltage regulator as described in Chapter Eleven.

30. Install the crankshaft position sensor (B, **Figure 4**) and bolt (A) onto the crankcase. Tighten the bolt to 90-120 in.-lb. (10.2-13.6 N•m).

31. Refill the engine with oil and install a new oil filter as described in Chapter Three.

32. Install the engine oil dipstick (**Figure 3**).

33. Install the exhaust system as described in Chapter Four.

34. Install the shift lever (B, **Figure 2**) onto the primary chaincase, and then install the pinch bolt (A). Tighten pinch bolt securely.

35. Install both foot rests as described in Chapter Fourteen.

36. Install the rear brake pedal as described in Chapter Thirteen.

37. Install the fuel induction module as described in Chapter Eight.

38. Install the air filter and backplate as described in Chapter Eight.

39. Install the fuel tank as described in Chapter Eight.

40. Install the seat as described in Chapter Fourteen.

41. Start the engine and check for leaks.

Cleaning and Inspection

1. Remove any corrosion from the engine mount bolts with a wire wheel.

2. Clean and dry the engine mount bolts.

3. Clean and inspect the engine mounting bolt threads and the threads in the frame for damage. Replace any damaged fasteners.

4. Inspect the jiffy stand bracket for cracks and fractures.

5. Check the wire harness routing in the frame. Check the harness cover and wires for chafing or other damage. Replace harness cable guides and clips as required.

6. Clean the connectors with contact cleaner.

7. On Screamin' Eagle models, check the clutch hydraulic line and fasteners for kinks or damage

OIL PUMP

The oil pump mounts onto the right side of the crankcase under the camshaft support plate. The oil pump consists of two sections: a feed pump (narrow rotors) which supplies oil under pressure to the engine components and a scavenger pump (wide rotors) which returns the oil from the engine to the oil pan in the base of the transmission case. The oil travels directly from the engine to the transmission case via oil flow channels within both components. There are no external oil lines.

Disassembly/Removal

The oil pump can be removed with the engine in the frame. Refer to **Figure 19**.

1. Drain the engine oil as described in Chapter Three.

2. Remove the camshaft support plate assembly as described in this chapter.

3. Remove the feed pump outer (A, **Figure 20**) and inner (B) rotors.

4. Remove the outer separator plate (**Figure 21**), wave washer (**Figure 22**), and the inner separator plate (**Figure 23**).

5. Remove the scavenger pump outer (A, **Figure 24**) and inner (B) rotors.

6. Carefully pull the oil pump body (**Figure 25**) straight off the crankshaft.

7. Remove the O-ring (A, **Figure 26**) from the backside of the oil pump.

8. Remove the oil screen (**Figure 27**) and O-ring from the chain guide oil passage.

Assembly/Installation

NOTE
Position both inner and outer rotor sets with the punch marks facing out. If the rotor set is not marked, position the rotors in either direction.

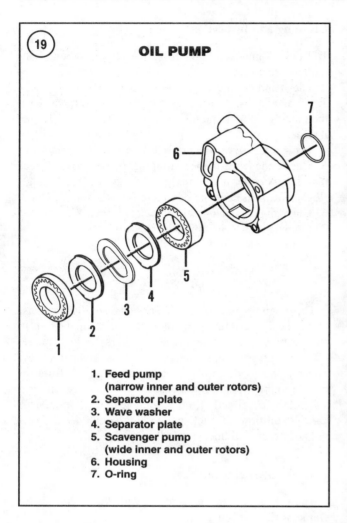

OIL PUMP

1. **Feed pump**
   (narrow inner and outer rotors)
2. **Separator plate**
3. **Wave washer**
4. **Separator plate**
5. **Scavenger pump**
   (wide inner and outer rotors)
6. **Housing**
7. **O-ring**

1. Install a new O-ring (A, **Figure 26**) onto the backside of the oil pump. Apply clean engine oil to the O-ring.

2. Carefully push the oil pump body (**Figure 25**) straight onto the crankshaft. Align the O-ring and fitting to the crankcase recess (B, **Figure 26**). Push the pump body on until it bottoms. Make sure the O-ring seats correctly in the crankcase recess.

3. Align the flat on the scavenger inner rotor with the flat on the crankshaft, and install the inner rotor (**Figure 28**).

4. Install the scavenger pump outer rotor (A, **Figure 24**) over the crankshaft and onto the inner rotor (B). Push the rotor assembly into the housing until it bottoms.

5. Align the tangs on the inner separator plate with the oil pump slots, and install the inner separator plate (**Figure 23**).

6. Install the wave washer (**Figure 22**).

7. Align the tangs on the outer separator plate with the oil pump grooves, and install the outer separator plate (**Figure 21**).

8. Align the flat on the feed pump inner rotor with the flat on the crankshaft and install the inner rotor (**Figure 29**).

9. Install the feed pump outer rotor (A, **Figure 20**) over the crankshaft and onto the inner rotor (B).

10. Install the oil screen (**Figure 27**) and O-ring into the chain guide oil passage.

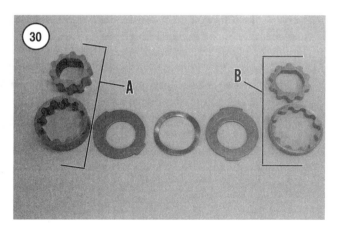

11. Install the camshaft support plate assembly as described in this chapter.

12. Refill the engine oil as described in Chapter Three.

Inspection

1. Clean all parts thoroughly in solvent and place them on a clean, lint-free cloth (**Figure 30**).

2. Inspect the scavenger pump (A, **Figure 30**) and the feed pump (B) inner and outer rotors for scratches and abrasion.

3. Inspect the oil pump housing (**Figure 31**) for scratches caused by the rotors.

4. Inspect the interior passageways of the oil pump housing. Make sure all oil sludge and debris are removed. Blow low-pressure compressed air through all passages in the pump housing.

5. Install one of the inner rotors into the outer rotor. Use a flat feeler gauge to measure the clearance (**Figure 32**) between the tips of the inner and outer rotors. Replace the rotors as a set if the clearance exceeds the service limit (**Table 1**). Also measure the other set of rotors.

6. Measure the thickness of the feed pump inner (**Figure 33**) and outer (**Figure 34**) rotors. Compare the two measurements. If the difference exceeds 0.001 in. (0.025 mm), replace the rotors as a complete set. Also measure the scavenger pump set of rotors.

7. Perform the following to check the feed rotor height:
   a. Assemble the oil pump (**Figure 19**).
   b. Set the pump on the bench with the feed rotors facing up.

   c. Place a straightedge across the feed rotors. Use a feeler gauge to measure the distance from the pump housing to the bottom of the straightedge (**Figure 35**).
   d. If this measurement is less than the service limit (**Table 1**), replace the wave washer.
   e. Assemble the pump with the new wave washer, and measure the feed rotor height. If it is still out of specification, replace the pump.

CAMSHAFT SUPPORT PLATE

A camshaft locking tool (JIMS part No. 994 or H-D part No. HD-47941). or equivalent, is required to remove and install the camshaft support plate.

Refer to **Figure 36**.

Removal

1. Remove the exhaust system as described in Chapter Four.
2. Drain the engine oil as described in Chapter Three.
3. Remove the rocker arm support plate, pushrods, pushrod covers as described in Chapter Four.

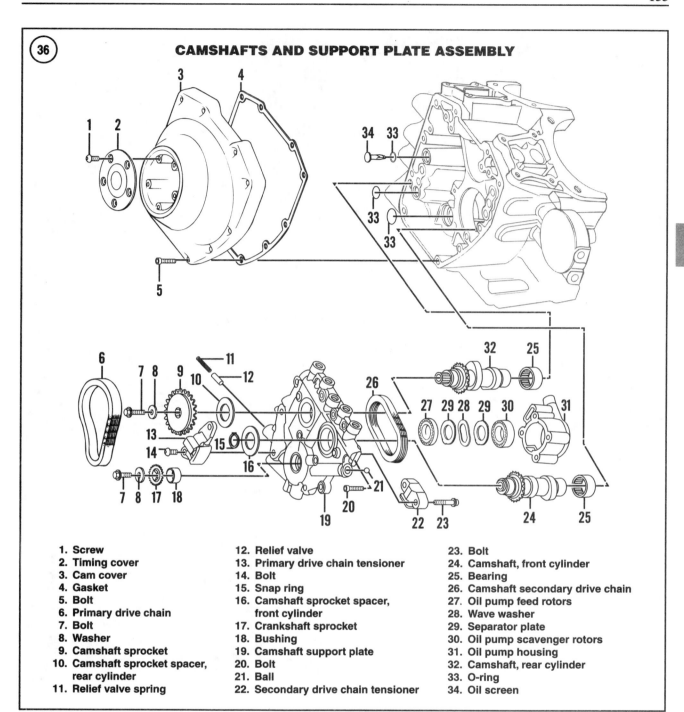

36 **CAMSHAFTS AND SUPPORT PLATE ASSEMBLY**

1. Screw
2. Timing cover
3. Cam cover
4. Gasket
5. Bolt
6. Primary drive chain
7. Bolt
8. Washer
9. Camshaft sprocket
10. Camshaft sprocket spacer, rear cylinder
11. Relief valve spring
12. Relief valve
13. Primary drive chain tensioner
14. Bolt
15. Snap ring
16. Camshaft sprocket spacer, front cylinder
17. Crankshaft sprocket
18. Bushing
19. Camshaft support plate
20. Bolt
21. Ball
22. Secondary drive chain tensioner
23. Bolt
24. Camshaft, front cylinder
25. Bearing
26. Camshaft secondary drive chain
27. Oil pump feed rotors
28. Wave washer
29. Separator plate
30. Oil pump scavenger rotors
31. Oil pump housing
32. Camshaft, rear cylinder
33. O-ring
34. Oil screen

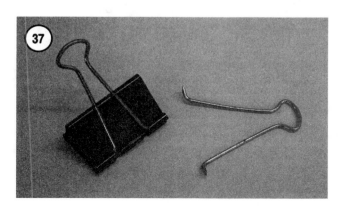

37

4. Make a lifter holder to hold the valve lifters so they will not fall from their bore once when the camshafts are removed. Perform the following:

   a. Purchase a large binder clip from an office supply store.

   b. Press each arm from the binder clip (**Figure 37**). Bend the end of the arms as needed so they will engage the valve lifters.

   c. Compress the lifter holder, and insert it into the lifter bores (**Figure 38**) so the holder presses each lifter against the walls of its bore.

5. Using a crossing pattern, evenly loosen and remove the ten camshaft cover bolts (A, **Figure 39**) along with their captive washers. Remove the cover (B, **Figure 39**) and its gasket. Discard the gasket.

6. To ensure the camshaft primary drive chain is reinstalled in its original direction of travel, mark one of the link plates with a permanent marking pen or a scribe.

7. Remove the primary chain tensioner as follows:

   a. Press the primary chain tensioner shoe into the housing, and insert a wire or paper clip into the hole (A, **Figure 40**) in the housing and through the hole in the shoe.

   b. Slowly release the shoe to confirm that that tensioner parts are locked in place.

   c. Remove the primary chain tensioner bolts (B, **Figure 40**), and remove the chain tensioner (C) from the support plate.

   d. Install the camshaft locking tool (A, **Figure 41**) so it engages the teeth of the rear camshaft sprocket and the crankshaft sprocket.

8. Loosen the crankshaft sprocket bolt (B, **Figure 4l**).

NOTE
Do not apply too much force when removing the rear camshaft sprocket bolt. It is assembled with threadlocking compound. If it is difficult to remove, use heat to break the compound. To not use impact tools. Excessive force can damage the sprockets.

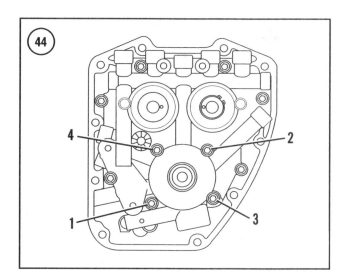

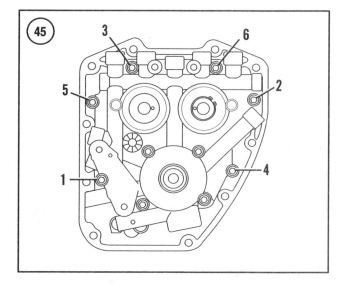

9. Loosen the rear camshaft sprocket bolt (C, **Figure 41**).
10. Remove the locking tool (A, **Figure 41**).
11. Remove the crankshaft (B, **Figure 41**) and camshaft (C) sprocket bolts along with their washers.

NOTE
If it is difficult to loosen either sprocket from its respective shaft, use a small pry bar to gently loosen the sprocket.

12. Remove the rear camshaft drive sprocket (A, **Figure 42**), the crankshaft sprocket (B) and the primary camshaft drive chain (C) as an assembly. Pull the assembly straight off the shafts.

NOTE
Mark the sprocket spacer on each camshaft. They look similar but are not identical. Only the rear camshaft spacer is removed in this procedure.

13. Remove the sprocket spacer (**Figure 43**) from the rear camshaft.

14. Remove the camshaft support plate bolts in the following sequence:
   a. Evenly loosen the four oil pump mounting bolts in the sequence shown in **Figure 44**, and remove the bolts.
   b. Evenly loosen the six camshaft support plate bolts in the order shown in **Figure 45**, and remove the bolts.
15. Withdraw the camshaft support plate assembly from the crankcase. If necessary, carefully pry the plate loose from the crankcase in the vicinity of the dowels (A, **Figure 46**).
16. Remove the dowels (A, **Figure 47**).
17. Remove the lower O-ring (B, **Figure 47**) from the left crankcase flange.
18. Remove the oil screen (C, **Figure 47**).
19. If necessary, disassemble and remove the camshafts as described in this section.

Installation

1. Press the oil pump assembly to make sure it is correctly seated against the crankcase.
2. Install the oil screen (C, **Figure 47**), and install a new a new lower O-ring (B). Apply a light coat of clean engine oil to each O-ring.
3. Lubricate the camshaft needle bearings (D, **Figure 47**) in the crankcase and the camshaft journals (**Figure 48**) with clean engine oil.

4. Use a straightedge to confirm that the timing marks (**Figure 49**) on the camshafts align with each other. If the marks are not aligned, reposition the camshafts before installing the assembly into the crankcase.

5. If removed, install the two locating dowels (A, **Figure 47**) onto the crankcase.

> *CAUTION*
> *Do not force the camshaft support plate assembly into the crankcase. During installation the camshaft ends may not be correctly aligned with the needle bearings. If force is applied, the needle bearing(s) will be damaged.*

6. Slowly install the camshaft support plate assembly (A, **Figure 50**) into the crankcase. Guide the camshaft ends into the crankcase needle bearings (B, **Figure 50**). If necessary, slightly rotate and/or wiggle the end of the rear cylinder camshaft to assist in the alignment.

> *CAUTION*
> *When properly aligned, the camshaft support plate assembly fits snugly against the crankcase mating surface. If they do not meet correctly, do not attempt to pull the parts together with the mounting bolts. Remove the camshaft support plate assembly and determine the cause of the interference.*

7. Push the camshaft support plate assembly into the crankcase until it engages the dowels and bottoms against the crankcase mating surface.

8. Make sure the timing marks (B, **Figure 46**) on the camshaft ends still align. If they are not aligned, correct the problem at this time.

9. Install the six camshaft support plate bolts by performing the following:
   a. Install and loosely tighten the six bolts (**Figure 45**).
   b. Following in the sequence shown in **Figure 45**, evenly tighten the bolts to 90-120 in.-lb. (10.2-13.6 N•m).

10. Install the four oil pump mounting bolts by performing the following:
   a. Loosely install the four bolts around the oil pump housing (**Figure 44**). Evenly tighten the bolts until they just contact the support plate, and then back them out 1/4 turn.
   b. Rotate the engine until the oil pump finds its neutral center with no load on it.
   c. Tighten the bolts 1 and 2 until they are snug against the support plate.
   d. Tighten bolts 3 and 4 until each is snug against the support plate.
   e. Following the sequence shown in **Figure 44**, initially tighten the bolts, to 40-45 in.-lb. (4.5-5.1 N•m), and then tighten them, in sequence, to a final torque of 90-120 in.-lb. (10.2-13.6 N•m).

11. Check the perimeter of the support plate to make sure it is seated against the crankcase mating surface.

> *NOTE*
> *Alignment is not necessary if the original camshaft support plate, both camshafts, rear camshaft sprocket, crankshaft drive sprocket and the crankshaft assembly are reused. If any of these components have been replaced, alignment is necessary to ensure correct alignment between the rear camshaft sprocket and the crankshaft drive sprocket. If the alignment is incorrect, the primary drive chain and both sprockets will bind and cause premature wear.*

12. If new parts been installed, perform the alignment procedure described in *Rear Camshaft Sprocket and*

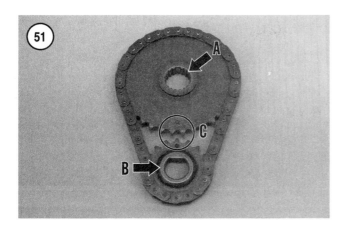

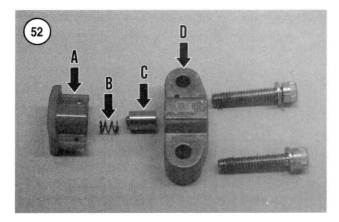

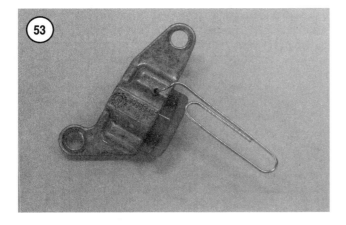

Crankshaft Drive Sprocket Alignment (this section). If all original parts have been installed, continue procedure.

13. Install the sprocket spacer (**Figure 43**) onto the rear camshaft with the manufacturer's marks facing the crankcase.

NOTE
Refer to the mark made before removal and position the camshaft primary drive chain so it will travel in the same direction. If it is installed incorrectly, the drive chain will wear prematurely.

14. Install the rear camshaft sprocket (A, **Figure 51**) and the crankshaft drive sprocket (B) into the primary drive

chain on the workbench. Make sure the index marks on the sprockets align as shown in C, **Figure 51**.

15. Install the rear camshaft sprocket (A, **Figure 42**), the crankshaft drive sprocket (B), and the primary camshaft drive chain (C) as an assembly. Align the flat on the crankshaft drive sprocket with the flat on the crankshaft, and seat each sprocket on its shaft. Check the alignment of the index mark on both sprockets. They must still face each other as shown in D, **Figure 42**. If necessary, remove the chain/sprocket assembly, and realign the sprockets.

NOTE
Before tightening the camshaft and crankshaft sprocket bolts, manually install the bolts to make sure the threads are clean. Chase the bolt or shaft threads as needed so the proper torque will be applied when the bolts are tightened to specification.

16. Install new crankshaft and rear-camshaft sprocket bolts as follows:
   a. Apply clean engine oil beneath the flange of each sprocket bolt.

NOTE
If new sprocket bolts are unavailable, oil the flange of the bolts and apply a small amount of Loctite Threadlocker 262, or an equivalent threadlock, to the threads of each sprocket bolt.

   b. Install the correct flat washer onto each sprocket bolt. The washers are not interchangeable.
   c. Install the rear camshaft sprocket bolt and crankshaft drive sprocket bolt. Finger-tighten the bolts at this time.

17. Install the locking tool (A, **Figure 41**) between the camshaft and crankshaft sprockets.

18. Tighten both sprocket bolts as follows:
   a. Tighten both bolts initially to 15 ft.-lb. (20.3 N•m).
   b. Loosen both bolts one complete revolution (360°).
   c. Tighten the rear camshaft sprocket bolt (C, **Figure 41**) to 34 ft.-lb. (46.1 N•m).
   d. Tighten the crankshaft drive sprocket bolt to (B, **Figure 41**) 24 ft.-lb. (32.5 N•m).

19. Remove the locking tool (A, **Figure 41**).

20. Install the primary chain tensioner (C, **Figure 40**) by performing the following:

NOTE
Figure 52 shows a disassembled secondary chain tensioner. The primary and secondary tensioners are internally the same. The housings are the only parts that differ.

   a. If disassembled, fit the plunger (A, **Figure 52**), spring (B), and shoe (C) into the housing (D).
   b. Press the shoe into the housing, and lock the assembly by installing a paper clip or small wire through the hole in the housing (**Figure 53**) and shoe.

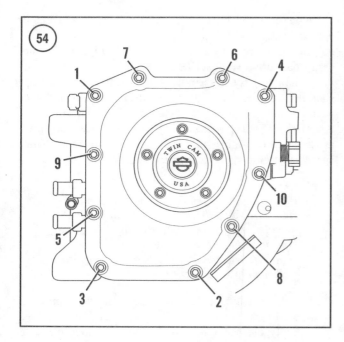

c. Install the primary chain tensioner (C, **Figure 40**) against the camshaft support plate, and tighten the cam chain tensioner bolts (B) to 100-120 in.-lbs. (11.3-13.6 N•m).

d. Remove the paper clip or wire to release the tensioner.

21. Install the camshaft cover (B, **Figure 39**) and a *new* cover gasket onto the crankcase. Install the cover bolts (A, **Figure 39**). Following the sequence shown in **Figure 54**, tighten the camshaft cover bolts to 125-155 in.-lb. (14.1-17.5 N•m)

22. Install the rocker arm support plate, pushrods and pushrod covers as described in Chapter Four.

23. Install the exhaust system (Chapter Four.)

24. Refill the engine with oil as described in Chapter Three.

Rear Camshaft Sprocket and Crankshaft Drive Sprocket Alignment

If alignment between the rear camshaft sprocket and the crankshaft drive sprocket is incorrect, the primary drive chain and both sprockets will bind and cause premature wear.

NOTE
This procedure is only required if the camshaft support plate, one or both camshafts, the rear camshaft sprocket, the crankshaft drive sprocket and/or the crankshaft assembly has been replaced.

1. Install the sprocket spacer (**Figure 43**) onto the rear camshaft with the manufacturer's marks facing the crankcase.

2. Apply clean engine oil to the camshaft splines and to the rear camshaft sprocket splines.

3. Install the rear camshaft sprocket onto the rear camshaft. Install the used camshaft sprocket bolt and flat washer (A, **Figure 55**). Finger-tighten the bolt at this time.

NOTE
Use a washer with a smaller outside diameter than the original washer installed on the crankshaft sprocket bolt. This creates room for a straightedge to be placed against the flat surface of the crankshaft sprocket face.

4. Install the crankshaft drive sprocket (B, **Figure 55**) onto the crankshaft. Install the *used* crankshaft sprocket bolt and a washer with a smaller outside diameter than the original washer. Finger-tighten the bolt at this time.

5. Install the locking tool (A, **Figure 41**) between the camshaft and crankshaft sprockets.

6. Tighten both crankshaft and rear camshaft sprocket bolts to 15 ft.-lb. (20.3 N•m). Remove the locking tool from between the sprockets.

7. If the engine was not removed from the frame, install the compensating sprocket (Chapter Six) to pull the crankshaft to the left side.

8. Press the crankshaft and rear camshaft into the crankcase to eliminate any end play.

9. Place a straightedge (C, **Figure 55**) against the face (D) of both sprockets.

10. Try to insert a 0.010 in. (0.254 mm) feeler gauge (E, **Figure 55**) between the straightedge and each sprocket face.

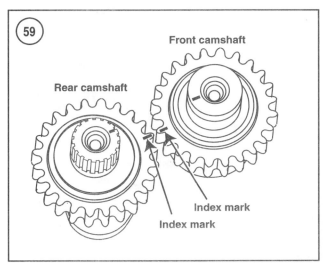

11A. If the 0.010 in. (0.254 mm) feeler gauge cannot be inserted at either location, the sprockets are correctly aligned. Remove both sprockets and continue *Camshaft Support Plate Installation* (this section).

11B. If a different thickness feeler gauge can be inserted, indicating a height difference other than 0.010 in. (0.254 mm), change the rear camshaft spacer. Continue to insert feeler gauges of different thicknesses until the offset dimension is determined. Record this dimension. It will be used to choose a new spacer.

12. Remove the rear camshaft sprocket bolt, washer and sprocket.

13. Remove the existing sprocket spacer (**Figure 43**) from the rear camshaft. Compare the part number stamped onto the spacer with the part numbers in **Table 2** to determine its thickness.

14A. If the crankshaft sprocket sits more than 0.010 in. (0.254 mm) above the rear camshaft sprocket, install the next thicker size spacer behind the camshaft sprocket.

14B. If the rear camshaft sprocket sits more than 0.010 in. (0.254 mm) above the crankshaft sprocket, install the next *thinner* size spacer behind the rear camshaft sprocket.

15. Install a new spacer and repeat this procedure until the sprockets are correctly aligned.

16. After the correct spacer thickness is established, remove the sprockets from the rear camshaft and crankshaft, and continue *Camshaft Support Plate Installation* (this section).

Camshaft Removal

1. Remove the camshaft support plate as described in this section.
2. Remove the secondary chain tensioner by performing the following:
   a. Press the shoe into the housing, and insert a paper clip or small wire into the hole (A, **Figure 56**) to lock the parts in place.
   b. Remove the tensioner bolts (B, **Figure 56**), and remove the secondary chain tensioner.
3. Remove the snap ring (A, **Figure 57**) and spacer (B) from the front cylinder camshaft. Mark the spacer (C, **Figure 57**) so it will not be confused with the rear camshaft spacer. They are not interchangeable.
4. Pull the camshafts (C, **Figure 56**) and secondary chain (D) assembly from the camshaft support plate.
5. Use a permanent marker to mark a link (A, **Figure 58**) on the outboard side of the secondary cam chain so the chain can be installed with the same orientation.
6. Remove each camshaft from between the runs of the secondary chain.

Camshaft Installation

The camshaft assembly tool (JIMS part No. 990 or H-D part No. HD-47956), or an equivalent, is needed for this procedure.

NOTE
*On some models, the index marks are lines as shown in **Figure 59**. On other models, these marks are dots (B, **Figure 58**).*

1. Position the camshafts so the index marks (**Figure 59**) on the sprockets face directly opposite each other.
2. Position the secondary chain with the marked link plate (A, **Figure 58**) facing up, and install the secondary chain onto both camshafts.
3. Rotate the camshafts in either direction several times, and check the alignment of the index marks. If necessary,

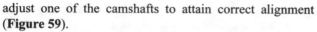

adjust one of the camshafts to attain correct alignment (**Figure 59**).

4. Set the inboard end of each camshaft into the camshaft assembly tool base. Use a straightedge to confirm that the timing marks on the shaft ends align (**Figure 60**).

5. Place the small guide (A, **Figure 61**) onto the rear camshaft and the large guide (B) over the front camshaft.

6. Apply engine oil to the camshaft bores in the camshaft support plate (A, **Figure 62**), and lower the support plate over the two guides (B), and onto the camshafts.

7. Remove the guides (B, **Figure 62**), and base from the assembly.

8. Use a straightedge to confirm that the camshaft index marks are still correctly aligned (**Figure 63**). If necessary, remove the camshafts and realign the index marks.

9. Install the front camshaft spacer (B, **Figure 57**) onto the front camshaft, and install a new snap ring (A) so its sharp edge faces out. Make sure the snap ring is completely seated in the camshaft groove.

10. Rotate the camshafts (C, **Figure 56**) through several complete revolutions and check for binding.

11. Compress the shoe into the secondary chain tensioner, and install a wire through the hole (A, **Figure 56**) to lock the tensioner. Set the secondary chain tensioner onto the support plate. Install the cam chain tensioner bolts (B, **Figure 56**) and tighten to 100-120 in.-lb. (11.3-13.6 N•m).

Camshaft and Sprocket Inspection

Visually inspect the camshafts to determine if they require replacement. The manufacturer does not provide camshaft specifications.

1. Check the camshaft lobes (A, **Figure 64**) on each shaft for wear. The lobes should not be scored and the edges should be square.

2. Inspect the camshaft secondary sprocket (B, **Figure 64**) on each shaft for broken or chipped teeth. Also check the teeth for cracking or rounding. If a sprocket is damaged or severely worn, replace the camshaft.

3. If the camshaft secondary sprockets are worn, check the camshaft secondary drive chain (C, **Figure 64**) for damage.

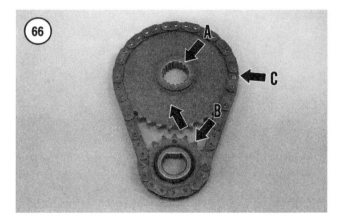

4. Inspect the external splines (A, **Figure 65**) on the rear cylinder camshaft and the internal splines on the rear camshaft sprocket (A, **Figure 66**). Check for worn or damaged splines and replace either or both parts as necessary. The sprocket must fit tightly on the camshaft.

5. Inspect the crankshaft sprocket (B, **Figure 66**) and rear camshaft drive sprocket (A) for broken or chipped teeth. Also check the teeth for cracking or rounding. Replace a damaged or severely worn sprocket, and inspect the primary drive chain (C, **Figure 66**) for damage.

6. Check the snap ring groove (B, **Figure 65**) on the front cylinder camshaft for wear or damage.

7. Inspect the crankshaft bushing (**Figure 67**) for wear or damage.

Camshaft Support Plate Inspection

1. Check the support plate bolt holes for cracks or fractures; replace the plate as necessary. Refer to A, **Figure 68** for the flange bolts and B, **Figure 68** for the oil pump bolts.

2. Check the crankcase mating surface (**Figure 69**) for warp and/or surface damage, replace as necessary.

Camshaft Bearing Replacement

The camshaft inner bearing installer (JIMS part No. 991) and camshaft inner bearing remover (JIMS part No. 993), or equivalent tools, are required for this procedure.

NOTE
*The camshaft needle bearings (**Figure 70**) can be removed with the engine mounted in the frame after the camshaft support plate has been removed.*

NOTE
Replace both needle bearings as a set even if only one bearing requires replacement.

1. Remove the camshaft support plate assembly from the engine as described in this section.

2. Install the puller portion of the tool set (A, **Figure 71**) part way into the needle bearing. Install a small hose clamp

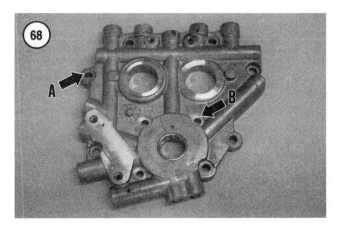

(B) onto the end that is closest to the needle bearing and tighten it. This closes the end of the tool so it can pass through the needle bearing. Push the puller all the way through the needle bearing, and remove the hose clamp.

3. Assemble the remainder of the tool components onto the puller (**Figure 72**) following the tool manufacturer's instructions.

4. Place a 5/8 in. wrench (A, **Figure 73**) onto the flats of the puller.

5. Place a 1 1/8 in. wrench, or an adjustable wrench (B, **Figure 73**), on the large nut of the puller.

CAUTION
Do not turn the 5/8 in. wrench as this will damage the tool and the crankcase receptacle.

6. Hold the 5/8 in. wrench (A, **Figure 73**) to keep the puller from rotating. Turn the 1 1/8 in. wrench (B) *clockwise* to tighten the large nut and pull the needle bearing out of the crankcase bore.

7. Disassemble the tool, and remove the needle bearing from it. Discard the old needle bearing.

8. Repeat the procedure to remove the other needle bearing.

9. Apply a light coat of clean engine oil, or press lube, to the outer surface of the new needle bearings and to the crankcase needle bearing bore (**Figure 74**).

NOTE
The following photographs are shown with the crankcase disassembled to clearly illustrate the steps.

10. Apply a light coat of clean engine oil to the threads of the screw portion and to the installer plate.

11. Insert the screw portion of the tool part way into the installer plate.

12. Push the installer onto the screw until it locks into place.

13. Position the new bearing (**Figure 75**) on the installer with the manufacturer's marks facing away from the installer.

14. Position the installer plate onto the crankcase, aligning the tool (A, **Figure 76**) to the bearing bore.

15. Install the thumb screws through the installer plate (B, **Figure 76**) and into the crankcase threaded holes. Tighten the thumb screws securely.

16. Slowly tighten the installer screw until the bearing starts to enter the crankcase bore. Continue to tighten the screw until the installer contacts the crankcase surface. This correctly positions the needle bearing within the crankcase.

17. Remove the tools.

18. Repeat the procedure to install the other needle bearing.

Oil Pressure Relief Valve
Removal/Inspection/Installation

If experiencing abnormally high or low oil pressure, confirm that the valve body is moving freely within the entire length of its bore.

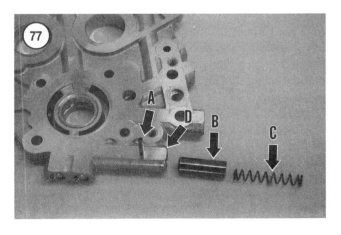

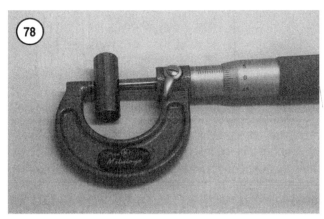

NOTE
This procedure is shown with the camshafts removed to clearly illustrate the steps.

1. Remove the camshaft support plate assembly from the engine as described in this section.

2A. If the camshafts are still in place, secure the camshaft support plate in a vise with soft jaws.

2B. If the camshafts have been removed, place the camshaft support plate on a piece of soft wood.

3. Before disassembling the valve, measure the seated depth of the valve body in the bore by performing the following:

    a. With the valve body fully seated in the bore, insert a stiff wire through the valve spring until it bottom inside the valve body, which is a cylinder.

    b. Mark the wire where it aligns with the outside edge of the bore.

    c. Remove the wire and measure the distance from the wire's end to the mark. It should approximately equal the valve seated depth (**Table 1**).

    d. If the measurement is out of specification, the spring is fatigued and should be replaced.

4. Use a 1/8 in. punch and drive the roll pin (A, **Figure 77**) from the camshaft support plate. Discard the roll pin.

5. Remove the valve body (B, **Figure 77**) and spring (C) from the relief-valve port of the camshaft support plate.

6. Inspect the spring for signs of stretching, cracks or wear. Replace if worn.

7. Inspect the valve body and bypass port (D, **Figure 77**) for burrs, scoring or metal chips. If found, replace the valve body and the support plate.

8. Determine the running clearance by performing the following:

    a. Measure the outside diameter of the valve body (**Figure 78**).

    b. Measure the inside diameter of the bypass port bore in the camshaft support plate (**Figure 79**).

    c. Subtract the valve body outside diameter from the bypass port bore inside diameter. This difference is the running clearance.

    d. If running clearance exceeds specification (**Table 1**), replace the valve body. Measure the outside diameter of the new valve body, and recalculate the running clearance. If the running clearance still exceeds specification, replace the valve body and camshaft support plate.

9. Apply a light coat of clean engine oil to the bypass port and to the valve body.

10. Install the valve body (B, **Figure 77**) so its closed end goes into the bypass port (D) first.

11. Install the spring (C, **Figure 77**) into the valve body.

12. Push the valve body and spring into the bypass port. Hold them in place and install a *new* roll pin (A, **Figure 77**). Tap the roll pin in until it sits flush with the support plate.

Chain Tensioner Inspection

> *NOTE*
> *Figure 80 shows a secondary chain tensioner. It also applies to the primary chain tensioner.*

1. Visually inspect the tensioner shoe (A, **Figure 80**). Replace the tensioner(s) if the contact surface of the shoe is less than 0.060 in. (1.52 mm) thick.

2. If tensioner was disassembled, assemble it by performing the following:

   a. Insert the piston (B, **Figure 80**) and spring (C) into the tensioner housing (D).

   b. Align the shoe (A, **Figure 80**) with the cutouts in the housing, and press the shoe into the housing.

   c. Insert a wire through the hole in the tensioner housing to hold the assembly together.

CRANKCASE AND CRANKSHAFT

Crankcase Disassembly

A twin cam 88 engine stand (JIMS part No. 1022), base stand (JIMS part No. 1138) and crankcase assembly removing tool (JIMS part No. 995) are used in some of the following procedures.

Refer to **Figure 81**.

1. Remove the engine as described in this chapter.

> *CAUTION*
> *Do not lift the crankcase assembly by the cylinder studs. Bent or damaged cylinder studs may cause the engine to leak oil.*

2. Remove the following components:

   a. Rocker arms, pushrods and valve lifters as described in Chapter Four.

   b. Cylinder heads, pistons and cylinders as described in Chapter Four.

   c. Camshaft support plate and oil pump as described in this chapter.

   d. Alternator rotor and stator assembly as described in Chapter Nine.

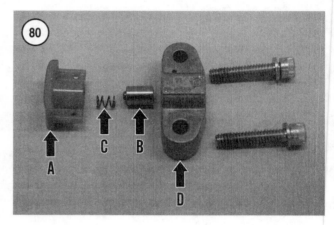

> *NOTE*
> *Leave the bolts for the left side off so the crankcase halves can be separated in the following steps.*

3. If the tool is available, attach the crankcase assembly to an engine stand (**Figure 82**), following the tool manufacturer's instructions.

4. Secure the engine stand to the workbench.

5. Following the sequence shown in **Figure 83**, loosen the bolts from the left side of the crankcase (**Figure 84**) in two to three stages. Then, remove the bolts.

6. Place the crankcase assembly on wooden blocks with the camshaft cover facing up. Use wooden blocks thick enough so the crankshaft (**Figure 85**) clears the workbench surface.

7. Tap around the perimeter of the crankcase with a plastic mallet and remove the right crankcase half (**Figure 86**).

8. If the crankcase halves will not separate easily, perform the following:

   a. Install a flywheel press (A, **Figure 87**) onto the left side crankcase half, following the tool manufacturer's instructions.

   b. Make sure the right side engine stand bolts (A, **Figure 88**) are *not* installed onto the crankcase half.

   c. Apply clean engine oil, or press lube, to the end of the center screw and install it into the tool.

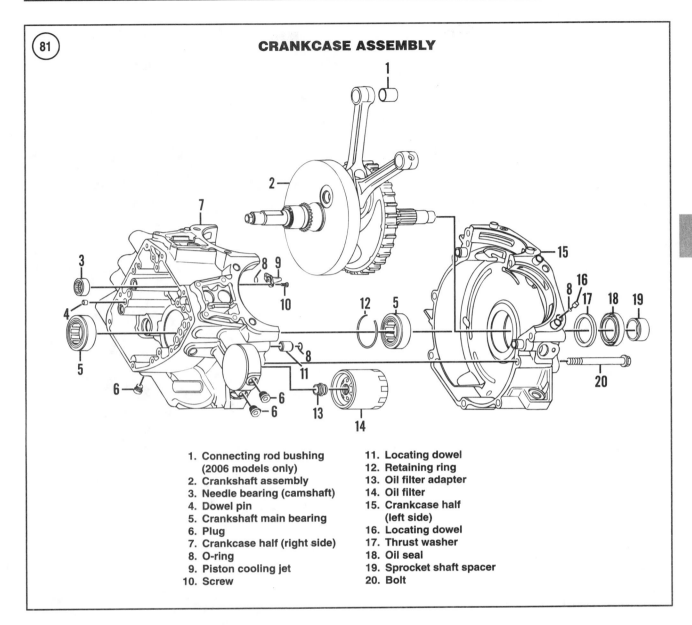

81

CRANKCASE ASSEMBLY

1. Connecting rod bushing
   (2006 models only)
2. Crankshaft assembly
3. Needle bearing (camshaft)
4. Dowel pin
5. Crankshaft main bearing
6. Plug
7. Crankcase half (right side)
8. O-ring
9. Piston cooling jet
10. Screw

11. Locating dowel
12. Retaining ring
13. Oil filter adapter
14. Oil filter
15. Crankcase half
    (left side)
16. Locating dowel
17. Thrust washer
18. Oil seal
19. Sprocket shaft spacer
20. Bolt

5

82

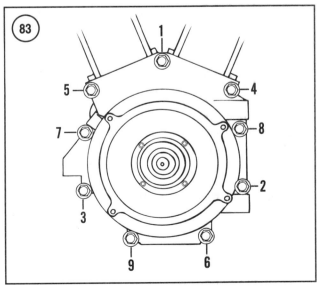

83

> *CAUTION*
> *Do not use a hand impact driver or air impact wrench on the center screw. These tool(s) will damage the crankcase halves and the tool(s)*

d. Slowly turn the center screw with a wrench (B, **Figure 87**) 1/2 turn at a time. After each turn, tap on the end of the center screw with a brass mallet to relieve the stress on the center screw and the tool.

e. Repeat process until the center screw turns freely and the crankcase halves begin to separate (B, **Figure 88**).

f. Remove the crankcase from the engine stand.

g. Remove the right side crankcase half (**Figure 89**).

h. Remove the tool from the left side crankcase half unless the crankshaft is going to be removed.

9. Remove the locating dowels (**Figure 90**) and O-rings from the right side crankcase half.

> *CAUTION*
> *Do not drive the crankshaft out of the crankcase half with a hammer.*

10A. If a hydraulic press is available, press the crankshaft out of the left crankcase half as follows:

a. Support the right crankcase half in a press on wooden blocks with the outer surface facing up.

b. Center the press ram onto the end of the crankshaft, and then press the crankshaft out of the left crankcase half. Have an assistant support the crankshaft as it is being pressed out.

c. Remove the crankshaft.

d. Remove the left crankcase half from the press bed and move it to workbench for further service.

10B. If a hydraulic press is not available, perform the following:

a. Install a flywheel press (A, **Figure 91**) onto the left side crankcase half, following the tool manufacturer's instructions.

b. Apply clean engine oil, or ram lube, to the end of the center screw and install it into the tool.

> *CAUTION*
> *Do not use a hand impact driver or air impact wrench on the center screw, as these tool(s) will damage the crankcase and the tool(s).*

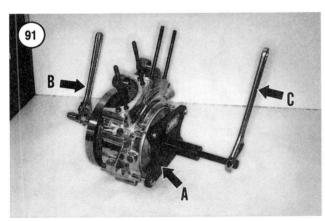

c. Secure the right side of the crankshaft with a wrench (**B, Figure 91**) to prevent it from rotating in the following step.

d. Slowly turn the center screw with a wrench (**C, Figure 91**) 1/2 turn at a time. After each turn, tap on the end of the center screw with a brass mallet to relieve the stress on the center screw and the tool.

e. Repeat process until the center screw pushes the crankshaft out of the left side crankcase half.

f. Remove the tool from the left side crankcase half.

11. To remove the left side crankshaft outer roller bearing and oil seal assembly, perform the following:

a. Place the left side crankcase half on the workbench with the outer surface facing up.

b. Carefully pry the sprocket shaft spacer out of the oil seal.

c. Carefully pry the oil seal out of the crankcase using a wide-bladed screwdriver. Support the screwdriver with a rag to prevent damage to the crankcase surface.

d. Lift the outer roller bearing from the crankcase.

Crankcase Assembly

A crankshaft guide (JIMS part No. 1288), or an equivalent tool, is required to assemble the crankcase halves.

1. Perform Steps 1-9 of *Crankcase Cleaning and Inspection* (this section).

2. Support the left crankcase half on wooden blocks so its inboard side faces up (**Figure 92**). Make sure the blocks are thick enough so the crankshaft will clear the workbench surface.

3. Install the locating dowels (**Figure 93**) and *new* O-rings in both locations (**Figure 94**) on the right crankcase half. Apply clean engine oil to the O-rings.

4. Fit the crankshaft guide (**Figure 95**) onto the crankshaft sprocket shaft (left side), and install the crankshaft into the left crankcase half. Make sure each connecting rod sits in the correct cylinder cutout.

5. Thoroughly clean and dry the crankcase gasket surface of each crankcase half.

6. Apply a thin coat of a non-hardening gasket sealant to the crankcase mating surfaces. Use High Performance Sealant, Gray (H-D part No. HD-99650-02), or an equivalent.

5

7. Align the crankcase halves and carefully lower the right crankcase half (**Figure 96**) over the crankshaft and onto left crankcase half. Press it down until it is seated correctly on the locating dowels. If necessary, carefully tap the perimeter of the right crankcase half until it is completely seated on the left half (**Figure 97**).

CAUTION
When properly aligned, the crankcase halves will fit snugly against each other around the entire perimeter. If they do not meet correctly, do not attempt to pull the crankcase halves together with the mounting bolts. Separate the crankcase assembly and investigate the cause of the interference.

8. Pull the crankshaft guide from the crankshaft.
9. If available, place the crankcase assembly in an engine stand (A, **Figure 98**). Secure the engine stand to the workbench.
10. Install the crankcase bolts into the left crankcase half (B, **Figure 98**) and tighten them as follows:
    a. Alternately finger-tighten the bolts.
    b. Following the sequence shown in **Figure 83**, tighten the bolts to an initial torque of 10 ft.-lb. (13.6 N•m).
    c. Following the same sequence, tighten the crankcase bolts to a final torque of 15-19 ft.-lb. (20.3-25.8 N•m).

5

11. Apply clean engine oil to the outer surface of the sprocket shaft spacer (**Figure 99**) and install it onto the crankshaft and into the new oil seal.

12. Install the following components:

    a. Alternator rotor and stator assembly (Chapter Eleven).

    b. Camshaft support plate and oil pump (this chapter).

    c. Cylinder heads, pistons and cylinders (Chapter Four).

    d. Rocker arms, pushrods and valve lifters (Chapter Four).

Crankcase Cleaning and Inspection

1. Clean both crankcase halves in solvent and dry with compressed air.

2. Apply a light coat of oil to the races to prevent rust.

3. Inspect the right side (**Figure 100**) and left side (**Figure 101**) crankcase halves for cracks or other damage.

4. Inspect the case studs (**Figure 102**) for bending, cracks or other damage. If necessary, replace studs as described in *Cylinder Stud Replacement* (this section).

5. Inspect the left and right side main roller bearings (**Figure 103**) for wear or damage. The bearing must turn smoothly with no roughness. If damaged, replace the bearing assembly as described in this chapter.

6. Inspect the camshaft needle bearings (**Figure 104**) in the right side crankcase half for damage. To replace these bearings, refer to *Camshaft Support Plate* in this chapter.

7. Inspect the valve lifter bore receptacles (**Figure 105**) for wear or damage (Chapter Four).

NOTE
If the original piston cooling jets are being reinstalled, apply Loctite No. 222 (purple), or an equivalent, threadlock to the screw threads prior to installation.

8. Make sure the piston cooling jets (**Figure 106**) are clear. If necessary, remove the Torx (T20) mounting screws, and then remove the cooling jets and O-rings. Clean the oil jets

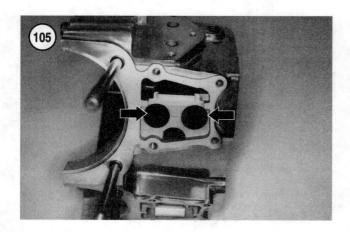

thoroughly with compressed air. Install *new* O-rings and tighten the screws securely.

Crankshaft and Connecting Rods
Cleaning and Inspection

If any portion of the crankshaft and/or connecting rods are worn or damaged, replace both as one assembly. If necessary, have the crankshaft overhauled by a dealership.

1. Clean the crankshaft assembly in solvent and dry thoroughly with compressed air.

2. Hold the shank portion of each connecting rod where it attaches to the crankshaft (**Figure 107**). Pull up and down on each connecting rod. Any slight amount of up and down movement indicates excessive rod bearing wear. If there is any movement, have a dealership overhaul the crankshaft.

3. Measure connecting rod side play with a feeler gauge (**Figure 108**). Check measurement against the service limit in **Table 2**.

4. Inspect the pinion shaft (**Figure 109**) and the sprocket shaft (**Figure 110**) surfaces for excessive wear or damage.

5. Support the crankshaft on a truing stand or in a lathe and check runout at the flywheel outer rim (A, **Figure 111**) and at the shaft adjacent to the flywheel (B) with a dial indicator. If the runout exceeds the service limit in **Table 2**, have the crankshaft trued or overhauled.

6. Inspect the crankshaft position sensor timing teeth (C, **Figure 111**) on the left side flywheel for damaged or missing teeth.

7. Inspect the connecting rod bushings (**Figure 112**) for wear. If necessary, replace the bushings on 2006 models as described in *Piston Pin Bushing Replacement* (Chapter Four). The bushings are not serviceable on 2007-2011 models.

Cylinder Stud Replacement

Replace bent or otherwise damaged cylinder studs (A, **Figure 113**) to prevent cylinder block and cylinder head leaks.

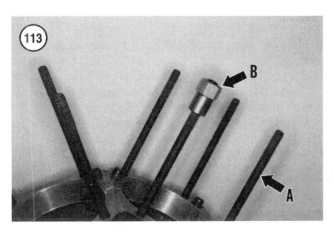

1. If the engine lower end is assembled, block off the lower crankcase opening with clean shop cloths.

2A. If the stud has broken off with the top surface of the crankcase, remove it with a stud remover. Refer to Chapter One.

2B. If the stud is still in place, perform the following:

    a. Thread a 3/8 in.-16 nut onto the top of the stud.

    b. Thread an additional nut onto the stud and tighten it against the first nut so that they are locked.

    c. Turn the bottom nut *counterclockwise* and unscrew the stud.

3. Clean the stud threads in the crankcase with a spiral brush, and then clean them with an aerosol parts cleaner. If necessary, clean the threads with an appropriate size tap.

> *NOTE*
> *The cylinder studs have a shoulder on one end. Install the shoulder end next to the crankcase surface.*

4A. Install a stud installation tool (Motion Pro part No. 08-0148) onto the stud (B, **Figure 113**).

4B. Place a 0.313 in. (7.95 mm) diameter steel ball (H-D part No. HD-8860) into a cylinder head bolt, and then thread the bolt onto the end of the new stud without the collar.

5. Position the stud with its shouldered end going in first, and hand-thread the new stud into the crankcase.

> *CAUTION*
> *Do not use a breaker bar, ratchet or similar tool to install the studs. These tools may bend the stud and cause the engine to leak oil.*

6. Hold the air impact wrench directly in-line with the stud. *Slowly* tighten the new stud with an air impact wrench until the stud shoulder just contacts the top surface of the crankcase (**Figure 114**)

7. Use hand tools to tighten the cylinder stud to 10-20 ft.-lb. (13.6-27.1 N•m).

8. Remove the cylinder head bolt and steel ball from the cylinder stud.

9. Repeat the procedure to install any additional studs.

⑮ **CRANKCASE ASSEMBLY**

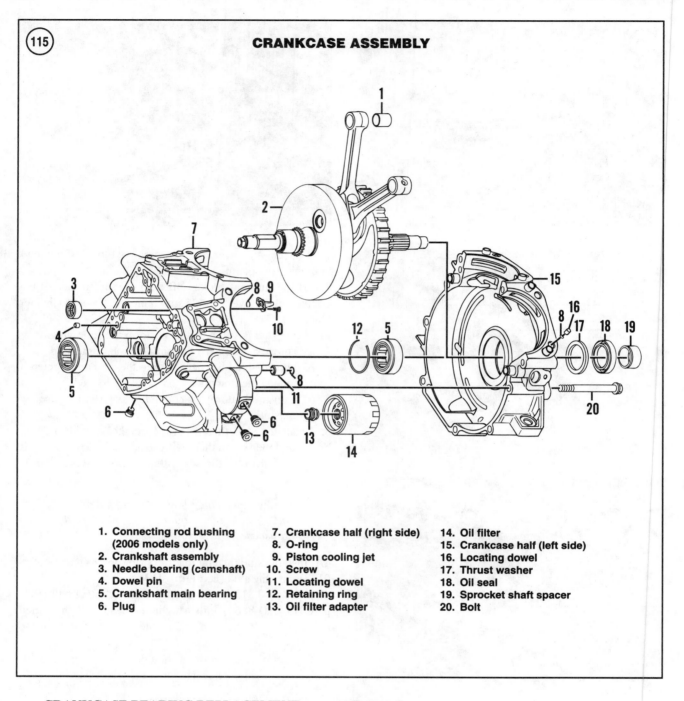

1. Connecting rod bushing
   (2006 models only)
2. Crankshaft assembly
3. Needle bearing (camshaft)
4. Dowel pin
5. Crankshaft main bearing
6. Plug
7. Crankcase half (right side)
8. O-ring
9. Piston cooling jet
10. Screw
11. Locating dowel
12. Retaining ring
13. Oil filter adapter
14. Oil filter
15. Crankcase half (left side)
16. Locating dowel
17. Thrust washer
18. Oil seal
19. Sprocket shaft spacer
20. Bolt

CRANKCASE BEARING REPLACEMENT

Right Side Main Bearing Replacement

Refer to **Figure 115**.

Tools

The following tools, or their equivalents, are required to remove and install the right side main bearing:
1. Hydraulic press.
2. Crankshaft bearing support tube (H-D part No. HD-42720-5) marked with either *A* or *B*.
3. Pilot/driver (H-D part No. HD-B-45655).

Removal

1. Place the support tube with the *A* side facing up on the press bed.
2. Position the right side crankcase half with the outboard surface facing up and position the bearing directly over the support tube on the press bed.
3. Install the pilot/driver shaft (A, **Figure 116**) through the bearing and into the support tube.
4. Center the press ram (B, **Figure 116**) over the pilot/driver shaft.
5. Hold the crankcase half parallel to the press bed and have an assistant slowly apply ram pressure on the pilot shaft until the bearing is free from the crankcase half.

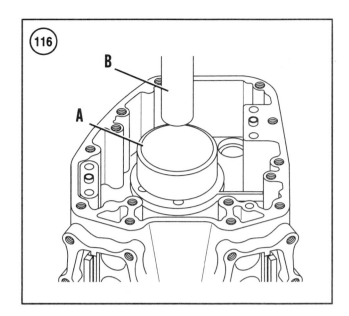

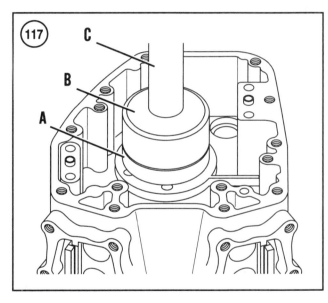

6. Remove the crankcase half and tools from the press bed.

Installation

1. Apply a light coat of clean engine oil to the outer surface of the *new* bearing and to the crankcase receptacle.
2. Place the support tube with the *B* side facing up on the press bed.
3. Position the right side crankcase half with the outboard surface facing up onto the press bed. Position the crankshaft's bearing bore over the support tube. Correctly align the two parts.
4. Position the new *bearing (A, **Figure 117**)* with the manufacturer's marks facing up and place it over the crankcase receptacle.
5. Install the pilot/driver (B, **Figure 117**) through the bearing and into the support tube.

6. Center the press ram (C, **Figure 117**) over the pilot driver.
7. Slowly apply ram pressure on the pilot driver, pressing the bearing into the crankcase. Apply pressure until resistance is felt and the bearing bottoms in the support tube. This will correctly locate the bearing within the crankcase. Remove the pilot driver.
8. Remove the crankcase and the support tube from the press bed.
9. Check on each side of the crankcase to make sure the bearing is centered within the receptacle. If not, reposition the bearing until it is centered correctly.
10. Spin the bearing to make sure it rotates smoothly with no binding.

Left Side Main Bearing Assembly Replacement

Refer to **Figure 115**.

Tools

The following tools or their equivalents are required to remove and install the right side main bearing:
1. Hydraulic press.
2. Crankshaft bearing support tube (HD part No. HD-42720-5).
3. Pilot/driver (HD part No. HD-B-45655).

Removal

1. Place the crankcase on the workbench with the inboard surface facing up.
2. If still in place, remove the crankshaft spacer from the bearing bore.
3. Carefully pull the thrust washer from the outboard surface of the crankcase past the oil seal.
4. Place the support tube on the workbench with the *A* side facing up.
5. Position the crankcase with the inboard surface facing up and place the bearing bore over the support tube.
6. Use a suitable size drift and tap the oil seal out of the bearing bore. Discard the oil seal.
7. Turn the crankcase over with the inboard surface facing up.

CAUTION
Do not damage the crankcase retaining ring groove with the screwdriver. The groove must remain sharp to correctly seat the retaining ring.

8. The roller bearing (A, **Figure 118**) is secured in the crankcase with a retaining ring (B) on the inner surface of the bearing bore. Remove the retaining ring as follows:
   a. Use a flat-tipped screwdriver (C, **Figure 118**) and place it under the retaining ring. Carefully lift the edge of the retaining ring up and out of the crankcase groove.

b. Slide the tip of the screwdriver around the edge of the bearing and continue to lift the retaining ring out of the crankcase groove.

c. Remove the retaining ring.

9. Position the support tube (A, **Figure 119**) on the press bed with the *A* side facing up.

10. Position the left side crankcase half with the outboard surface facing up onto the press bed. Position the crankshaft's bearing bore over the support tube. Correctly align the two parts.

11. Slide the pilot/driver (B, **Figure 119**) through the crankcase bearing and into the support.

12. Center the press ram (C, **Figure 119**) directly over the pilot/driver (B) and slowly press the bearing out of the crankcase.

13. Remove the crankcase and tools from the press bed.

14. Clean the crankcase half in solvent and dry it with compressed air.

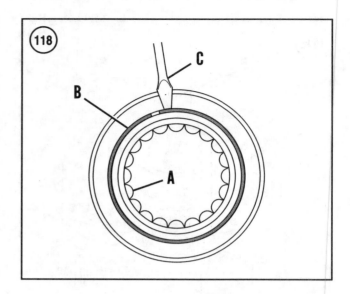

Installation

1. Apply clean engine oil, or press lube, to the bearing receptacle in the crankcase and to the outer race of the *new* bearing.

2. Position the support tube (A, **Figure 120**) on the press bed with the *A* side facing up.

3. Position the crankcase half with the inboard side facing up and position the crankshaft's bearing bore over the support tube. Correctly align the two parts.

4. Correctly position the *new* bearing (B, **Figure 120**) over the crankcase bore with the manufacturer's marks facing down.

5. Slide the pilot/driver (C, **Figure 120**) through the new bearing and the crankcase and into the support.

6. Center the press ram (D, **Figure 120**) directly over the pilot/driver (C) and slowly press the bearing into the crankcase until it *lightly* bottoms in the crankshaft bearing bore.

7. Remove the crankcase and tools from the press.

8. Make sure the bearing has been pressed in past the retaining ring groove. If the groove is not visible above the bearing, repeat the process until the groove is visible.

9. Position the crankcase on the workbench with the inboard surface facing up.

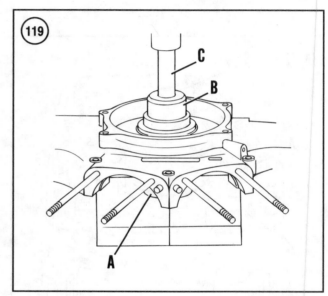

CAUTION
Do not damage the crankcase retaining ring groove with the screwdriver. The groove must remain sharp to correctly seat the retaining ring.

NOTE
If the retaining ring will not correctly seat in the crankcase groove, the bearing is not correctly seated in the crankcase bore. Repeat the installation process until the groove is accessible.

10. Install a *new* bearing retaining ring as follows:

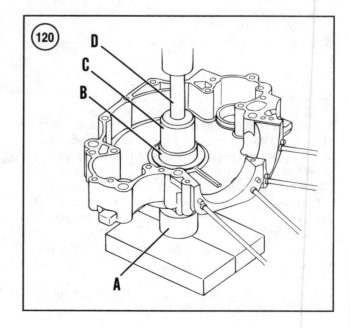

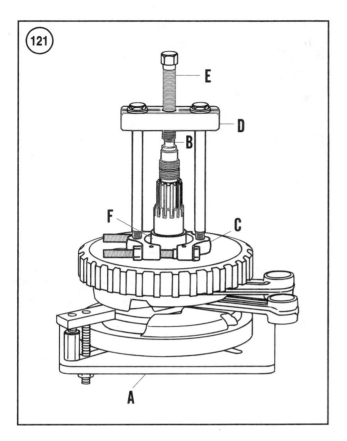

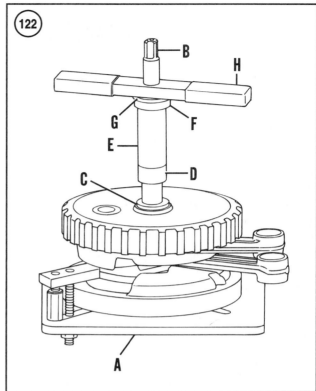

a. Work the retaining ring into the crankcase groove being careful not to damage the crankcase groove.

b. Use a flat-tipped screwdriver and push in the retaining ring. Continue to push the retaining ring into the
crankcase groove and make sure it is correctly seated
in the groove.

**Crankshaft Left Side Main Bearing Assembly Inner
Race Replacement**

Refer to **Figure 115**.

Removal

1. Support the crankshaft in a support fixture (H-D part
No. HD-44358), or an equivalent, with the bearing side
facing up (A, **Figure 121**).

2. Place a hardened plug (B, **Figure 121**) between the
bearing puller and the end of the crankshaft.

3. Install the bearing splitter (C, **Figure 121**) under the
bearing inner race.

4. Apply graphite lubricant to the bearing puller center
screw, and attach a bearing puller (D, **Figure 121**) to the
splitter.

> *WARNING*
> *Never use the heat gun in conjunction with
> penetrating oil. The heat from the gun may
> ignite the oil, resulting in a fire.*

5A. Use an industrial heat gun and apply heat uniformly to
the bearing inner race for approximately 30 seconds.

5B. If a heat gun is not available, apply penetrating oil to
the inner race and crankshaft and allow the oil to penetrate
for 30 minutes.

6. Make sure the bearing puller is square to the crankshaft
so the bearing inner race is not out of alignment with the
crankshaft shoulder.

7. Slowly tighten the center screw (E, **Figure 121**) and
withdraw the bearing inner race (F) from the crankshaft
shoulder.

8. Remove the bearing puller, the bearing splitter and the
inner bearing race from the crankshaft.

9. Remove the thrust washer from the crankshaft. Discard
the thrust washer; it cannot be re-used.

10. Clean the sprocket shaft with contact cleaner. Check
the sprocket shaft for cracks or other damage. If it is damaged, refer service to a dealership.

Installation

A final drive sprocket shaft bearing cone installer (H-D
part No. HD-997225-55B), or its equivalent, is required to
install the sprocket shaft bearing inner race.

1. Support the crankshaft in a support fixture (H-D part
No. HD-44358), or an equivalent, with the bearing side
facing up (A, **Figure 122**).

2. Thread the pilot shaft (B, **Figure 122**) onto the crankshaft until it contacts the crankshaft.

3. Slide the *new* thrust washer (C, **Figure 122**) over the
sprocket shaft.

WARNING
Never use the heat gun in conjunction with penetrating oil. The heat from the gun may ignite the oil, resulting in a fire.

4A. Place the new bearing race on the workbench. Use a heat gun and uniformly heat the bearing race for approximately 60 seconds. Wear heavy duty gloves and install the new inner race (D, **Figure 122**) onto the crankshaft.

4B. If a heat gun is not available, apply penetrating oil to the inner surface of the bearing race and to the crankshaft shoulder. Install the new inner race (D, **Figure 122**) onto the crankshaft.

5. Apply graphite lubricant to the threads of the pilot shaft and flat washer

6. Slide the sleeve (E, **Figure 122**) onto the crankshaft until it contacts the bearing inner race.

7. Slide the radial bearing (F, **Figure 122**) and flat washer (G) over the pilot shaft until it contacts the top of the sleeve.

8. Thread the tool handle (H, **Figure 122**) onto the pilot shaft (B).

9. Slowly tighten the handle *clockwise* until the bearing inner race bottoms on the crankshaft shoulder.

10. Unscrew and remove all parts of the installer tool.

Crankcase Left Side Oil Seal Replacement

Refer to **Figure 115**.

Tools

The following tools, or their equivalents, are required to install the oil seal.

1. Final drive sprocket shaft seal installer tool (JIMS part No. 39361-69).

2. Final drive sprocket shaft bearing installation tool (JIMS part No. 97225-55).

Removal

1. Remove the sprocket shaft spacer (**Figure 123**) from the crankshaft and the oil seal.

2. Carefully pry the old oil seal out of the bearing bore and discard it. If the thrust washer comes out with the oil seal, mark the washer side that faces the oil seal. Inspect the washer for deterioration. If it is in good condition, reinstall the thrust washer so the marked side faces the oil seal. If the washer is worn, install a new thrust washer, so the side marked OUT faces outboard. This places the washer's chamfered side inboard.

3. Position the new oil seal so the open side faces out.

4. Install the oil seal (**Figure 124**) onto the crankshaft, and center it within the bearing bore.

5. Apply clean engine oil or press lube to the installer tool threads, both washers and the radial bearing.

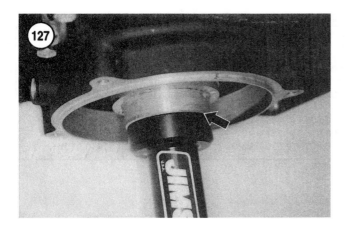

6. Install the tool's main body (**Figure 125**) onto the crank-shaft and screw it on until it stops.

7. Install the shaft seal installer tool following the tool manufacturer's instructions.

8. Hold the handle (A, **Figure 126**) of the main body and slowly tighten the large nut (B) with a wrench. Make sure the oil seal (C, **Figure 126**) enters straight into the bearing bore.

9. Tighten the large nut until the shaft seal installer tool contacts the crankcase surface (**Figure 127**).

10. Remove the tools.

11. Apply clean engine oil to the outer surface of the sprocket shaft spacer (**Figure 123**), and install it onto the crankshaft and into the oil seal.

ENGINE BREAK-IN

Following cylinder service (boring, honing, new rings) and major lower end work, operate the engine during the break-in period as though it were new. The service and performance life of the engine depends on a careful and sensible break-in.

1. For the first 50 mi. (80 km), maintain engine speed below 2500 rpm in any gear. However, do not lug the engine. Do not exceed 50 mph (80 km/h) during this period.

2. From 50-500 mi. (80-805 km), vary the engine speed. Avoid prolonged steady running at one engine speed. During this period, increase engine speed to 3000 rpm. Do not exceed 55 mph (89 km/h) during this period.

3. After the first 500 mi. (804 km), the engine break-in is complete.

5

Table 1 ENGINE LOWER END SPECIFICATIONS

Item	New In. (mm)	Service limit In. (mm)
Breather assembly		
Cover warp	–	0.005 (0.13)
Baffle warp	–	0.005 (0.13)
Camshaft support plate		
Camshaft chain tensioner shoe	–	0.060 (1.524)
Camshaft bushing fit (2006 models)	–	0.0008 (0.020)
Camshaft bushing maximum inside diameter		
(2007-on models)	–	0.08545 (2.1704)
Connecting rod		
Connecting rod-to-crankpin clearance	0.0004-0.0017 (0.0102-0.0432)	0.002 (0.051)
Piston pin clearance in connecting rod		
All models except Screamin' Eagle and CVO	0.0007-0.00012 (0.018-0.031)	0.002 (0.051)
Screamin' Eagle and CVO models	0.0006-0.0012 (0.015-0.031)	0.002 (0.051)
Side play	0.005-0.015 (0.13-0.38)	0.020 (0.508)
Oil pump pressure		
(at 230° F [110° C])	30-38 psi (207-262 kPa) @ 2000 rpm	
Oil pump rotor tip-to-tip clearance	–	0.004 (0.10)
Oil pump feed rotor height	0.015-0.025 (0.38-0.64)	0.015 (0.38)
Oil pressure relief valve		
Running clearance	0.003 (0.076)	–
Seated depth	2.25 (57.15)	–
	(continued)	

Table 1 ENGINE LOWER END SPECIFICATIONS (continued)

Item	New In. (mm)	Service limit In. (mm)
Crankshaft		
End Play	0.003-0.010 (0.076-0.254)	0.010 (0.254)
Runout		
Measured in truing stand	0.000-0.004 (0.0-0.102)	0.005 (0.127)
Crankshaft/sprocket shaft bearings		
Roller bearing fit (loose)	0.0002-0.0015 (0.005-0.038)	greater than 0.0015 (0.038)
Bearing in crankcase	0.0038-0.0054 (0.097-0.137)	less than 0.0038 (0.097)
Crankshaft to inner face clearance	0.0004-0.0014 (0.010-0.036)	less than 0.0004 (0.010)

Table 2 REAR CAMSHAFT SPROCKET SPACERS

Part No.	in.	mm
25729-06	0.100	2.54
25731-06	0.110	2.79
25734-06	0.120	3.05
25736-06	0.130	3.30
25737-06	0.140	3.56
25738-06	0.150	3.81

Table 3 ENGINE LOWER END TORQUE SPECIFICATIONS

Item	ft.-lb.	in.-lb.	N•m
Breather cover bolts	–	90-120	10.2-13.6
Camshaft cover bolts	–	125-155	14.1-17.5
Camshaft support plate bolt			
Outer six bolts	–	90-120	10.2-13.6
Inner four bolts (adjacent to oil pump)			
Initial		40-45	4.5-5.1
Final	–	90-120	10-2-13.6
Sprocket bolts			
Initial	15	–	20.3
Rear camshaft sprocket bolt (final)	34	–	46.1
Crankshaft drive sprocket bolt (final)	24	–	32.5
Camshaft cover bolts	–	125-155	14.1-17.5
Camshaft primary chain tensioner bolts	–	100-120	11.3-13.6
Camshaft secondary chain tensioner bolts	–	100-120	11.3-13.6
Crankshaft position sensor bolt	–	90-120	10.2-13.6
Crankcase bolts			
Initial	10	–	13.6
Final	15-19	–	20.3-25.8
Cylinder studs	10-20	–	13.6-27.1
Engine mounting fasteners			
Engine-to-transmission bolts			
Initial	15	–	20.3
Final	34-39	–	46.1-52.9
Cylinder head stabilizer link			
Top mounting bracket bolts	35-40	–	47.5-54.2
Stabilizer link bolt	18-22	–	24.4-29.8
Front mounting bracket bolts	25-30	–	33.9-40.7

CLUTCH AND PRIMARY DRIVE

This chapter describes service procedures for the clutch and primary drive assemblies.

Refer to **Table 1** and **Table 2** at the end of this chapter for specifications.

NOTE
*On models with the optional security system, disarm system before disconnecting the battery or pulling the Maxi-Fuse so the alarm will not sound. Refer to **Turn Signal and Security Modules** in Chapter Nine.*

PRIMARY CHAINCASE COVER

Removal

Refer to **Figure 1**.

WARNING
Disconnect the negative battery cable or pull the Maxi-Fuse before working on the clutch or any primary drive component to avoid accidentally activating the starter.

1. Disconnect the negative battery cable or remove the Maxi-Fuse as described in Chapter Nine.
2. On all models except FXDF and FXDWG, perform the following:
   a. Remove the left side footrest assembly (A, **Figure 2**) as described in Chapter Fourteen.
   b. Make an alignment mark on the outer shift lever and the end of the inner shift lever shaft.

c. Remove the clamping bolt (B, **Figure 2**), and then remove the outer gear shift lever (C).
3. Drain the primary chaincase oil as described in Chapter Three.

CAUTION
*Two different length bolts secure the primary chaincase cover. Note the location of the short and long bolts (**Figure 3**). They must be reinstalled in the correct location.*

NOTE
*The primary chaincase cover (D, **Figure 2**) can be removed with the clutch inspection cover (E) in place.*

4. Evenly loosen the primary chaincase cover bolts.
5. Remove the cover bolts along with their washers, and then remove the chaincase cover (**Figure 4**) and gasket (A, **Figures 5**). Do not lose the dowel pins (B, **Figure 5**) behind the cover.

Installation

1. On FXDWG and FXDF models, if the bolt and sleeve (A, **Figure 6**) were removed, perform the following:
   a. Apply two drops of Loctite Threadlocker 262 (red), or an equivalent threadlock, to the bolt threads.
   b. Install the bolt and sleeve (A, **Figure 6**) and tighten to 15-19 ft.-lb. (20.3-25.6 N•m).

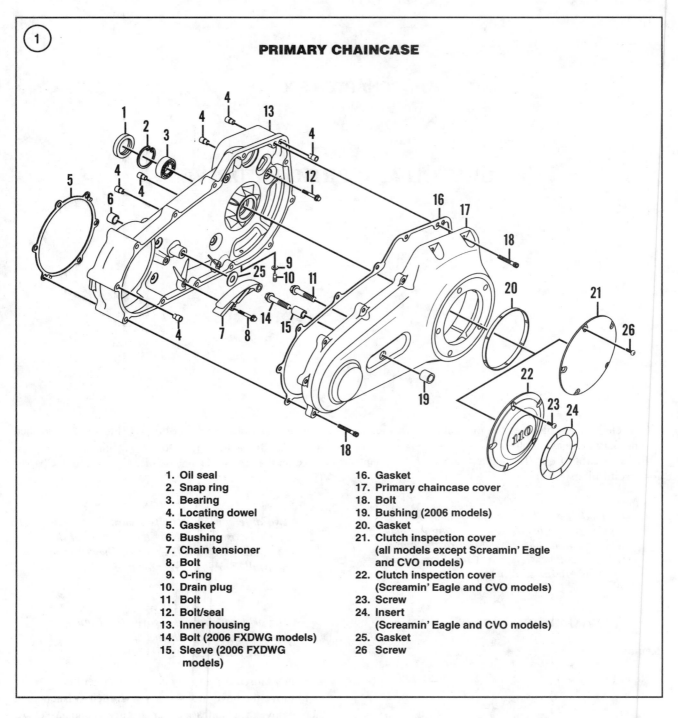

PRIMARY CHAINCASE

1. Oil seal
2. Snap ring
3. Bearing
4. Locating dowel
5. Gasket
6. Bushing
7. Chain tensioner
8. Bolt
9. O-ring
10. Drain plug
11. Bolt
12. Bolt/seal
13. Inner housing
14. Bolt (2006 FXDWG models)
15. Sleeve (2006 FXDWG models)
16. Gasket
17. Primary chaincase cover
18. Bolt
19. Bushing (2006 models)
20. Gasket
21. Clutch inspection cover (all models except Screamin' Eagle and CVO models)
22. Clutch inspection cover (Screamin' Eagle and CVO models)
23. Screw
24. Insert (Screamin' Eagle and CVO models)
25. Gasket
26. Screw

2. If removed, install the dowels (B, **Figure 5**) into the primary chaincase housing.

NOTE
The gasket sealing surface is very thin and the overall size of the gasket is very large, so it may shift prior to installation of the cover bolts.

3. Apply a couple of small dabs of gasket sealer to the backside of the gasket to help hold it in place on the dowels.

CAUTION
*The manufacturer specifies that a **new** gasket must be installed every time the primary chaincase cover is removed.*

4. Install a *new* gasket (B, **Figure 6**) over the dowels, and seat it against the gasket surface of the chaincase housing (A, **Figure 5**).

5. Slide the primary cover over the dowels, and set it against the gasket.

6. Insert the short and long bolts, with their washers into the locations noted during removal. Following the torque

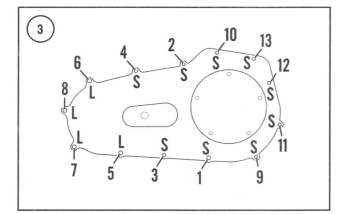

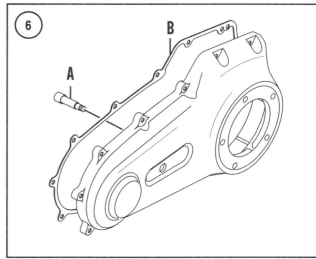

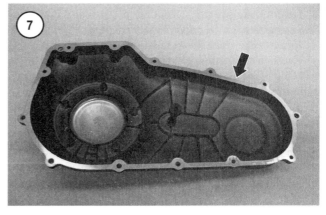

sequence shown in **Figure 3**, tighten the primary chaincase cover bolts to 108-120 in.-lb. (12.2-13.6 N•m). Make sure the gasket seats flush around the cover.

7. Fill the primary chaincase with the specified type and quantity of oil as described in Chapter Three.

8. Connect the negative battery cable or install the Maxi-Fuse as described in Chapter Nine.

Inspection

1. Remove all gasket residue from the primary chaincase cover and chaincase housing gasket surfaces (**Figure 7**).

2. Clean the primary chaincase cover in solvent. Dry it with compressed air.

3. Inspect the primary chaincase cover (**Figure 8**) for cracks or damage.

PRIMARY CHAINCASE HOUSING

The primary chaincase housing mounts to both the engine and transmission. It houses the primary drive assembly, alternator rotor, and the mainshaft oil seal and bearing assembly.

Refer to **Figure 1**.

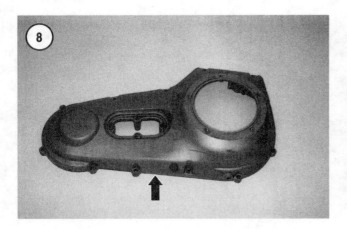

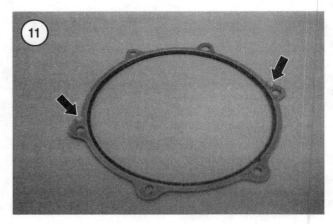

Removal

1. Disconnect the negative battery cable or remove the Maxi-Fuse as described in Chapter Nine.
2. Remove the primary chaincase cover and the primary drive assembly as described in this chapter.
3. Remove the starter as described in Chapter Nine.
4. Remove the primary housing bolts (**Figure 9**) along with the captive rubber washers. Discard the bolts as they cannot be reused.
5. Tap the housing loose and remove it from the crankcase, transmission and gearshift shaft.
6. Remove the gasket (**Figure 10**) from the crankcase flange and discard it.
7. If still in place, remove the gasket locating pins (**Figure 11**) from the crankcase flange or old gasket.
8. If still in place, remove the two locating dowels from the transmission case.

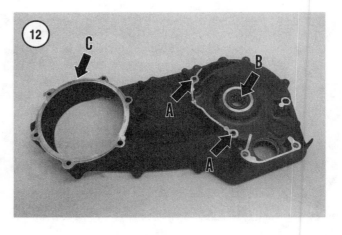

Installation

1. Confirm that the swing arm pivot shaft is properly tightened. Refer to Chapter Twelve.
2. Thoroughly clean the *outer surface* of the five bolt holes of the primary chaincase housing. Also, clean all threadlock residue from the blind bolt holes in the transmission and crankcase.
3. Thoroughly clean the mating gasket surfaces of the transmission and crankcase.
4. Install the dowels (A, **Figure 12**) into the transmission case or into the inboard side of the primary chaincase housing.
5. Ensure the two gasket locating pins (**Figure 11**) are in place on the new crankshaft gasket. Apply engine oil to the rubber portion of the gasket.
6. Install the *new* gasket (**Figure 10**) onto the crankcase flange so the locating pins engage the crankcase flange holes.
7. To prevent the transmission mainshaft splines from damaging the oil seal in the housing, wrap the mainshaft splines (A, **Figure 13**) with tape. Apply clean primary crankcase oil to the tape and to the lips of the oil seal (B, **Figure 12**).

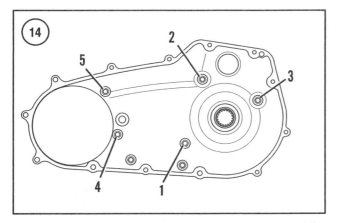

8. If removed, install the drive belt before installing the housing.

9. Align the housing dowels (A, **Figure 12**) with their mating holes in the transmission case. Then, install the housing and press it against the crankcase and transmission case. Remove the tape from the mainshaft splines.

10. Install five *new* primary chaincase bolts and finger-tighten the bolts. Do not apply lubricant to the captive rubber seal on the bolts.

11. Following the torque sequence shown in **Figure 14**, evenly tighten the bolts in two-to-three stages as follows:

    a. 2006 models; 15-19 ft.-lb. (20.3-25.8 N•m).

    b. 2007-2011 models; 25-27 ft.-lb. (33.9-36.6 N•m).

12. Install the starter as described in Chapter Nine.

13. Install the primary drive assembly and the chaincase cover as described in this chapter.

14. Connect the negative battery cable or install the Maxi-Fuse as described in Chapter Nine.

Inspection

1. Remove all gasket residue from the housing gasket surfaces on the outboard side (**Figure 15**) and inboard side (C, **Figure 12**) of the primary chaincase housing.

2. Clean the inner housing in solvent. Dry it thoroughly.

3. Check the housing for cracks or other damage.

4. Turn the mainshaft bearing (**Figure 16**) by hand. It must turn smoothly with no roughness. If necessary, replace the bearing as follows:

    a. Remove the oil seal (**Figure 17**) as described in this section.

    b. Remove the bearing snap ring (A, **Figure 18**) that sits beneath the oil seal.

    c. Support the housing in a press with the clutch side facing up and press the bearing (**Figure 16**) from the housing.

    d. Apply engine oil to the new bearing and the bearing bore in the primary chaincase housing.

    e. Support the housing in the press so the transmission side faces up.

    f. Position the bearing so the side with the manufacturer's marks face up, and then press the bearing in until it bottoms in the bearing bore. Use a driver or socket that matches the outside diameter of the bearing.

   g. Install a *new* snap ring (A, **Figure 18**) so it is completely seated within the groove in the housing. Position the ring so it does not block the oil hole (B, **Figure 18**).

   h. Install a *new* oil seal as described in this section.

5. If necessary, replace the mainshaft bearing inner race (B, **Figure 13**) as described in Chapter Seven.

6. Inspect the oil seal (**Figure 17**) for excessive wear, tearing or other damage. To replace the oil seal, perform the following:

   a. Use a wide-bladed screwdriver to pry the oil seal from the transmission side (inboard) of the housing.

   b. Clean the oil seal bore.

   c. Pack the oil seal lip with a waterproof bearing grease.

   d. Position the oil seal so the side marked *OIL SIDE* faces the bearing. Using a driver (**Figure 19**) or socket that matches the outside edge of the seal, press the *new* oil seal into the housing until its outer surface sits flush with the edge of the bearing bore.

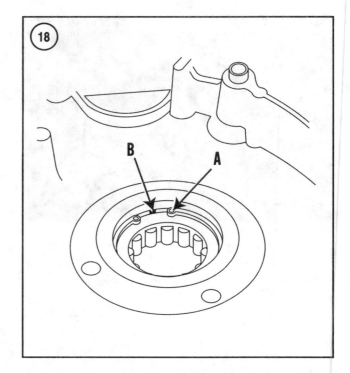

CLUTCH ASSEMBLY

This section describes removal, inspection and installation of the clutch plates. If the clutch requires additional service, refer to *Clutch Shell, Hub and Sprocket* in this chapter.

Refer to **Figure 20** and **Figure 21**.

Removal

1. Disconnect the negative battery cable as described in Chapter Nine.

2. Remove the primary chaincase cover as described in this chapter.

3A. On all models except Screamin' Eagle and CVO, perform the following at the clutch:

   a. Loosen the clutch adjusting screw locknut (A, **Figure 22**) and turn the adjusting screw (B) *counterclockwise* to allow slack against the diaphragm spring.

   b. Remove the snap ring (C, **Figure 22**), and remove the release plate/adjusting screw assembly (D).

3B. On Screamin' Eagle and CVO models, perform the following:

   a. Remove the large snap ring (A, **Figure 23**) securing the release bearing plate.

   b. Pull the bearing plate (B, **Figure 23**) and the pushrod (C) as an assembly.

   c. Remove the small snap ring (D, **Figure 23**). If necessary, pull the push rod from the release bearing.

4. Using a crossing pattern, evenly loosen the diaphragm spring retainer bolts (A, **Figure 24**). Remove the bolts and the spring retainer (B, **Figure 24**).

5. Remove the diaphragm spring (**Figure 25**) and pressure plate (**Figure 26**).

6. Remove each friction disc and plain plate from the clutch shell, keeping them in the order of removal (**Figure 27**).

7. Remove the damper spring (**Figure 28**) and damper spring seat (**Figure 29**) from the clutch shell.

8. Inspect the parts as described in this section.

Installation

> *NOTE*
> *The clutch (**Figure 27**) has nine friction discs, eight plain plates, one damper spring and one damper spring seat. Make sure each part is installed. When installing an aftermarket clutch plate assembly, follow the clutch manufacturer's instructions.*

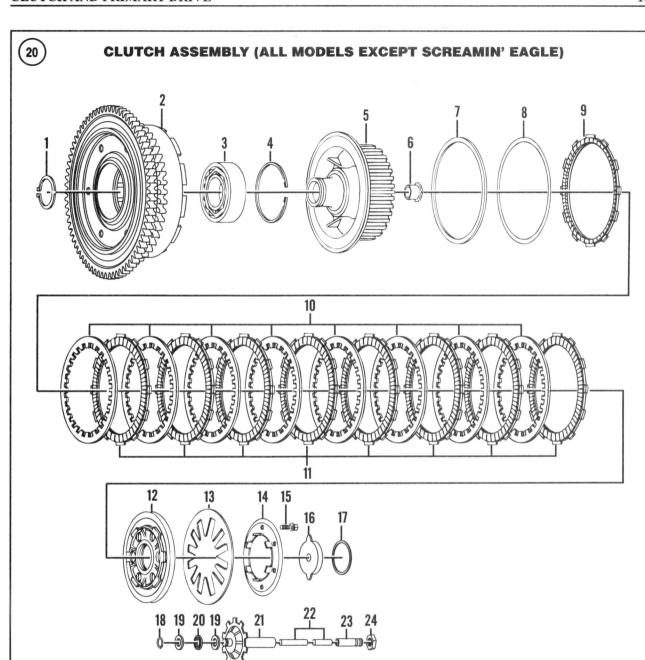

CLUTCH ASSEMBLY (ALL MODELS EXCEPT SCREAMIN' EAGLE)

1. Snap ring
2. Clutch shell and sprocket
3. Bearing
4. Snap ring
5. Clutch hub
6. Clutch nut
7. Damper spring seat
8. Damper spring
9. Friction disc B
10. Plain plates
11. Friction disc A
12. Pressure plate
13. Diaphragm spring
14. Diaphragm spring retainer
15. Bolt
16. Release plate
17. Snap ring
18. Snap ring
19. Thrust washer
20. Radial bearing
21. Oil slinger
22. Pushrod (right side)
23. Adjust screw
24. Locknut

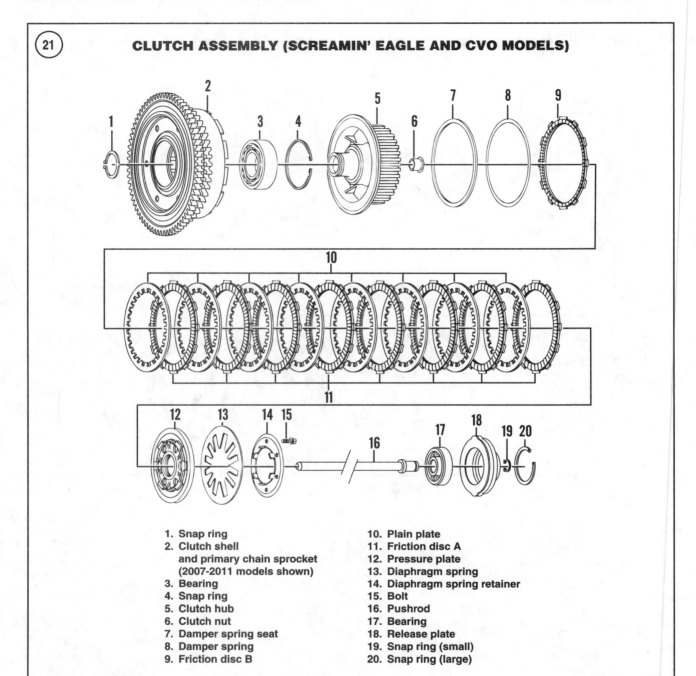

CLUTCH ASSEMBLY (SCREAMIN' EAGLE AND CVO MODELS)

1. Snap ring
2. Clutch shell
   and primary chain sprocket
   (2007-2011 models shown)
3. Bearing
4. Snap ring
5. Clutch hub
6. Clutch nut
7. Damper spring seat
8. Damper spring
9. Friction disc B
10. Plain plate
11. Friction disc A
12. Pressure plate
13. Diaphragm spring
14. Diaphragm spring retainer
15. Bolt
16. Pushrod
17. Bearing
18. Release plate
19. Snap ring (small)
20. Snap ring (large)

NOTE
*The clutch uses two different types of friction discs (**Figure 30**). Friction disc A (A, **Figure 30**) is the normal width disc. The narrower friction disc B (B, **Figure 30**) is installed first, as it works in conjunction with the damper spring and damper spring seat.*

1. Soak the clutch friction discs and plain plates in new primary drive oil for approximately 5 minutes before installing them.
2. Install friction disc B (**Figure 31**) so the tangs engage the slots in clutch shell. Push the disc all the way in until it bottoms within the clutch hub.

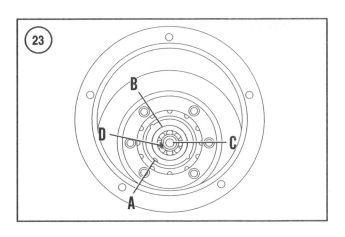

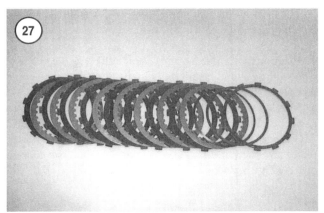

6

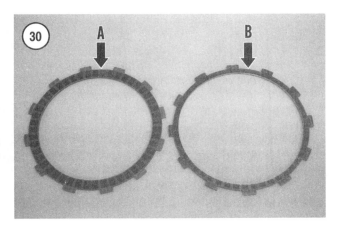

3. Install the damper spring seat (**Figure 29**) onto the clutch hub and push it in until it seats within friction disc B.

4. Position the damper spring (**Figure 28**) with the concave side facing out and install it onto the clutch hub against the damper spring seat.

5. Install a plain plate (**Figure 32**) so its inner teeth engage the clutch hub, and then install a wide friction disc A (**Figure 33**). Continue to alternately install the clutch plates and friction discs. The last part installed is a friction disc A (**Figure 34**).

6. Install the pressure plate (**Figure 26**) onto the clutch hub.

7. Position the diaphragm spring (**Figure 25**) with its concave side facing in, and seat it onto the pressure plate.

8. Install the diaphragm spring retainer (B, **Figure 24**) so its tabs sit between the fingers of the diaphragm spring, and thread in the retainer bolts (A).

9. Using a crossing pattern, evenly tighten the diaphragm spring retainer bolts to 90-110 in.-lb. (10.2-12.4 N•m).

10A. On all models except Screamin' Eagles and CVO, perform the following:

    a. Install the release plate/adjuster assembly (D, **Figure 22**) so the ears of the release plate engage the cutouts (**Figure 35**) in the pressure plate. Make sure the side of the release plate marked OUT faces out.

    b. Install a *new* snap ring (C, **Figure 22**) and make sure it is seated correctly.

10B. On Screamin' Eagle and CVO models, refer to **Figure 21** and perform the following:

    a. Press a new bearing into the release plate.

    b. Install the pushrod into the bearing, and install a new small snap ring into the pushrod groove.

    c. Slide the pushrod/release plate assembly into the mainshaft bore so the ears of the release plate engage the cutouts in the pressure plate.

    d. Install a new large snap ring.

11. Install the primary chaincase cover as described in this chapter.

12A. On all models except Screamin' Eagles and CVO, adjust the clutch as described in Chapter Three.

12B. On Screamin' Eagle and CVO, models, check the clutch pushrod and release plate movement as described in this chapter.

NOTE
All lubricant must be removed from the seal ring and groove prior to installation. If any lubricant remains there will be temporary lubricant seepage around the inspection cover.

13. Remove the seal ring from the inspection cover. Wipe all lubricant from the seal ring and inspect it for cuts or deterioration; replace if necessary. Wipe all lubricant from the seal ring groove and install the seal ring (**Figure 36**) into the cover. Push the nibs into the ring groove walls.

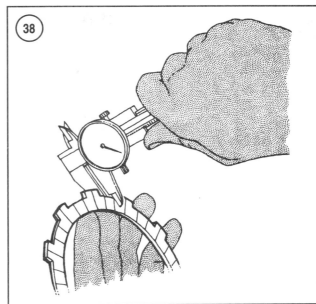

14. Install the clutch inspection cover and seal ring (**Figure 37**) onto the primary chain case cover.

15. Install the clutch inspection cover and tighten the screws to 84-108 in.-lb. (9.5-12.2 N•m).

16. Connect the negative battery cable as described in Chapter Nine.

Inspection

Compare any measurements to the specifications in **Table 1** when inspecting clutch components. Replace parts that are worn, damaged or out of specification.

1. Clean all parts in solvent. Thoroughly dry them with compressed air.

2. Inspect the friction discs as follows:

> *NOTE*
> *If any friction disc need replacing, replace* ***all nine friction discs*** *as a set. Never replace only one or two discs.*

> *NOTE*
> *If the disc tangs are damaged, inspect the clutch shell fingers carefully as described later in this section.*

a. Inspect the friction material (**Figure 30**) for excessive or uneven wear, cracks and other damage. Check the disc tangs for surface damage. The sides of the disc tangs must be smooth where they contact the clutch shell slots; otherwise, the discs cannot engage and disengage correctly.

b. Measure the thickness of each friction disc with a caliper (**Figure 38**) at several places around the disc.

3. Inspect the plain plates (**Figure 39**) as follows:

a. Inspect the plain plates for cracks, damage or color change. Overheated clutch plates have a blue discoloration.

b. Check the plain plates for oil glaze buildup. Remove any glaze by lightly sanding both sides of each plate with a piece of 400 grit sandpaper placed on a surface plate or piece of glass.

c. Place each plain plate on a flat surface, and check for warp with a feeler gauge (**Figure 40**).

> *NOTE*
> *If the clutch plate teeth are damaged, inspect the clutch hub splines carefully as described later in this section.*

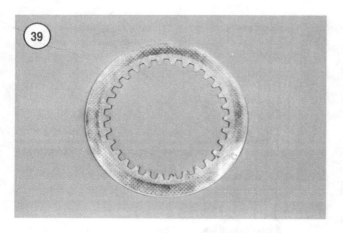

d. The clutch plate inner teeth mesh with the clutch hub splines. Check the clutch plate teeth for any roughness or damage. The teeth contact surfaces must be smooth; otherwise, the plates cannot engage and disengage correctly.

4. Inspect the diaphragm spring (**Figure 41**) for cracks or damage.

5. Inspect the diaphragm spring retainer for cracks or damage. Check also for bent or damaged fingers (**Figure 42**).

6. Inspect the pressure plate contact surface (**Figure 43**) for cracks or other damage.

7. Inspect the outer surfaces (**Figure 44**) of the pressure plate for wear caused by contact with the diaphragm spring.

8. On all models except Screamin' Eagle and CVO, perform the following:

a. Inspect the release plate, left pushrod and locknut for wear or damage.

b. Inspect the pressure-plate snap ring groove (**Figure 45**) for damage.

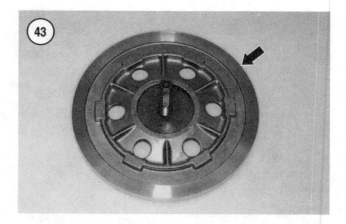

CLUTCH PUSHROD AND RELEASE PLATE INSPECTION (SCREAMIN' EAGLE AND CVO MODELS)

1. Remove the clutch inspection cover from the primary chaincase cover.

2. Mount a dial indicator to one of clutch inspection cover bolt holes or to a suitable stationary stand.

(45)

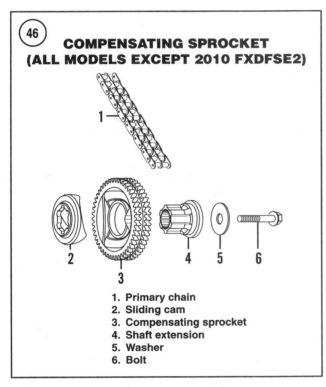

(46)

COMPENSATING SPROCKET (ALL MODELS EXCEPT 2010 FXDFSE2)

1. Primary chain
2. Sliding cam
3. Compensating sprocket
4. Shaft extension
5. Washer
6. Bolt

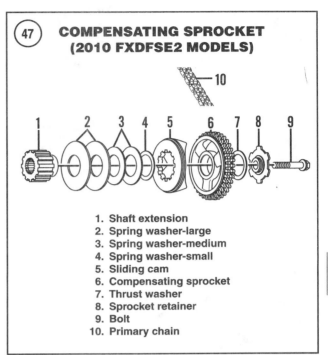

(47)

COMPENSATING SPROCKET (2010 FXDFSE2 MODELS)

1. Shaft extension
2. Spring washer-large
3. Spring washer-medium
4. Spring washer-small
5. Sliding cam
6. Compensating sprocket
7. Thrust washer
8. Sprocket retainer
9. Bolt
10. Primary chain

6

3. Position the dial indicator anvil against the end of the pushrod (C, **Figure 23**).

4. Fully apply the clutch lever, and note the pushrod movement.

5. The pushrod must move a minimum of 0.0065 in. (1.65 mm) to guarantee complete clutch disengagement.

NOTE
Correcting the clutch fluid level and properly bleeding the clutch results in pushrod movement greater than 0.0065 in. (0.165 mm).

6. If the push rod movement is less than specified, the clutch fluid level is low and/or the clutch system must be bled as described in this chapter.

NOTE
All lubricant must be removed from the seal ring and groove prior to installation. If any lubricant

remains there will be temporary lubricant seepage around the clutch inspection cover.

7. Remove the seal ring from the clutch inspection cover. Wipe all lubricant from the seal ring and inspect for cuts or deterioration, replace if necessary. Wipe all lubricant from the seal ring groove and install the seal ring into the cover. Push the nibs into the ring groove walls.

8. Install the clutch inspection cover and seal ring onto the primary chain case cover.

9. Install the clutch inspection cover and tighten the screws to 84-108 in.-lb. (9.5-12.2 N•m).

PRIMARY DRIVE ASSEMBLY

The primary drive assembly consists of the clutch shell, compensating sprocket and primary chain. These must be removed and installed as an assembly.

A primary drive locking tool (JIMS part No. 2312 or H-D part No. HD-47977) is needed to removal and install the primary drive assembly.

Removal

Refer to **Figure 46** and **Figure 47**.

1. Disconnect the negative battery cable as described in Chapter Nine.

2. Remove the primary chaincase cover as described in this chapter.

3A. On all models except Screamin' Eagles and CVO models, perform the following:11

   a. Loosen the clutch adjusting screw locknut (A, **Figure 48**) and turn the adjusting screw (B) *counterclockwise* to allow slack against the diaphragm spring.

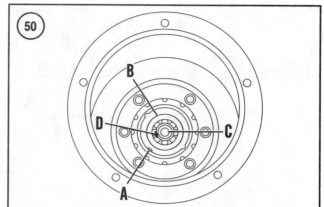

b. Remove the snap ring (C, **Figure 48**).

c. Make sure the locknut is still on the adjusting screw, and remove the release plate/adjuster assembly (**Figure 49**).

3B. On Screamin' Eagle and CVO models, perform the following:

a. Remove the large snap ring (A, **Figure 50**) securing the release bearing plate.

b. Remove the bearing plate (B, **Figure 50**) and the pushrod (C) as an assembly.

c. If necessary, remove the small snap ring (D, **Figure 50**), and then remove the pushrod from the release bearing.

CAUTION
Failure to secure the tensioner in the compressed position will result in damage to the last 2-3 threads of the primary chain tensioner bolts during removal.

4. Secure the tensioner assembly in the compressed position with a cable tie (A, **Figure 51**). Insert the cable tie under the tensioner and over the top of the tensioner shoe, leaving the tail of the tie in place. It serves as a reminder to remove the cable tie during installation.

5. Remove the primary chain tensioner bolts (B, **Figure 51**), and remove the tensioner assembly.

6. Install the primary drive locking tool between the teeth of the primary chain sprocket on the clutch hub and the

compensating sprocket teeth as shown in A, **Figure 52**. This will prevent the clutch hub from rotating when the clutch nut is loosened.

CAUTION
*The clutch nut has **left-hand threads**. Turn the clutch nut clockwise to loosen it.*

7. Loosen the clutch nut (B, **Figure 52**) by turning it *clockwise* with an impact wrench. Remove the clutch nut.

8. Reposition the primary drive locking tool as shown in A, **Figure 53**. This will prevent the compensating sprocket from rotating when the sprocket bolt is loosened.

9. Loosen the compensating sprocket bolt (B, **Figure 53**) with an impact wrench.

10. Use a permanent marker pen or scribe to mark an outboard link on the primary chain. The primary chain should be reinstalled so it rotates in its original direction to prolong chain life. Refer to these marks during installation.

11A. On all models except 2010 FXDFSE2 models, perform the following:
    a. Remove the compensating sprocket bolt (**Figure 54**), washer and shaft extension (**Figure 55**).
    b. Remove the compensating sprocket (**Figure 56**), primary chain and clutch shell assembly (**Figure 57**) at the same time.
    c. Remove the sliding cam (A, **Figure 58**) from the behind the compensating sprocket (B).

11B. On 2010 FXDFSE2 models, perform the following:
    a. Remove the compensating sprocket bolt, sprocket retainer and the thrust washer.
    b. Remove the compensating sprocket (**Figure 56**), primary chain and clutch shell assembly (**Figure 57**) together as a unit.
    c. Remove the sliding cam (A, **Figure 58**) from the behind the compensating sprocket (B).
    d. Remove the small spring washer, two medium spring washers and two large spring washers from the engine sprocket shaft.
    e. Remove the shaft extension from the engine sprocket shaft.

12. Inspect the various components as described in this chapter.

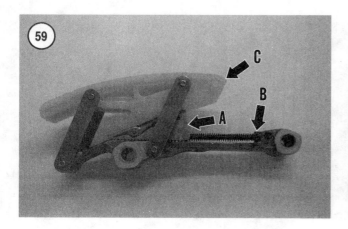

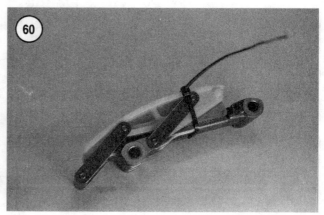

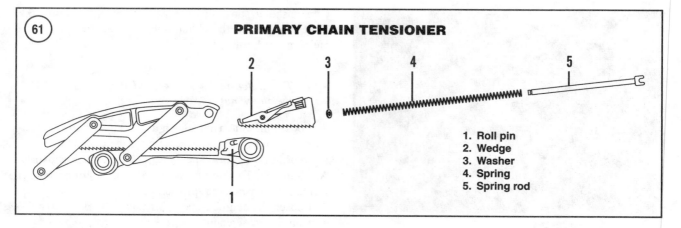

PRIMARY CHAIN TENSIONER

1. Roll pin
2. Wedge
3. Washer
4. Spring
5. Spring rod

Installation

1. Remove all threadlock residue from the threads of the crankshaft, mainshaft, compensating sprocket bolt and the clutch nut.

2. Remove all gasket residue from the primary housing gasket surfaces.

3A. If reinstalling the old primary chain tensioner, compress the tensioner as follows:

  a. Cut and remove the cable tie installed during tensioner removal. Let the tensioner decompress slowly.

  b. Lift the wedge (A, **Figure 59**) and release it from the serrations in the tensioner.

  c. Compress the spring, and slide the wedge to the very end of the spring rod (B, **Figure 59**).

  d. Lower the wedge so its rear-most tooth engages the rear-most tooth on the tensioner serrations. Hold the wedge in this position.

  e. Push the tensioner shoe (C, **Figure 59**) down against the wedge. Hold it in this position.

  f. Use a cable tie to secure the tensioner in this compressed position (**Figure 60**). The cable tie end must sit on the outboard side of the tensioner so it can be cut and removed after tensioner installation.

NOTE
*The chain tensioner is sold as an assembly, but it may become disassembled during shipment. Refer to **Figure 61** to assemble the tensioner.*

3B. If installing a new chain tensioner, assemble the tensioner, if necessary, and then compress it as follows:

  a. Install the spring rod through the spring and washer.

  b. Compress the spring rod into the wedge, and seat the end of the spring rod onto the roll pin.

  c. Slide the wedge (A, **Figure 59**) to the very end of the spring rod (B).

  d. Lower the wedge so its rear-most tooth engages the rear-most tooth on the tensioner serrations. Hold the wedge in this position.

  e. Push the tensioner shoe (C, **Figure 59**) down against the wedge. Hold it in this position.

  f. Use a cable tie to secure the tensioner in this compressed position (**Figure 60**). The cable tie end must sit on the outboard side of the tensioner so it can be cut and removed after tensioner installation.

4. Apply a light coat of primary chaincase oil to the bore of the compensating sprocket and to the splines (C, **Figure 58**) of the shaft extension.

5A. On all models except 2010 FXDFSE2 models, perform the following:

  a. Lubricate the ramps of the sliding cam (A, **Figure 58**) and fit the sliding cam on back of the compensating sprocket (B).

  b. Slide the washer onto the compensating sprocket bolt.

  c. Refer to the marks made on the primary chain during removal to ensure it will rotate in the original

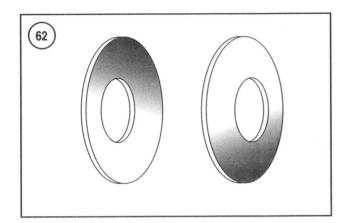

direction. Fit the primary chain onto compensating sprocket and onto the primary chain sprocket on the clutch shell.

   d. Install the compensating sprocket (**Figure 56**), primary chain and clutch assembly (**Figure 57**) at the same time. Rotate the compensating sprocket and clutch hub slightly to ease installation.

   e. Install the shaft extension (**Figure 55**) into the compensating sprocket.

5B. On 2010 FXDFSE2 models, perform the following:

   a. Position the bearing journal side of the shaft extension going on last and install the shaft extension onto the engine sprocket shaft.

   b. Position the two large washers so the convex side of the washers face each other (**Figure 62**) and install the two large washers and install them onto shaft extension.

   c. Position the two medium washers so the convex side of the washers face each other (**Figure 62**) and install the two large washers and install them next to the two large washers on the shaft extension.

   d. Install the small spring washer onto the shaft extension.

   e. Install the sliding cam onto the shaft extension.

   f. Install the compensating sprocket (**Figure 56**), primary chain and clutch shell assembly (**Figure 57**) together as a unit.

   g. Install the thrust washer, sprocket retainer and the compensating sprocket bolt.

> *CAUTION*
> *If the primary chain tensioner is not installed, the primary chain could be pinched against the primary chain housing when the compensating sprocket bolt is tightened.*

6. Insert the primary chain tensioner under the primary chain, and seat it against its mounting boss. Install and finger-tighten the tensioner mounting bolts (B, **Figure 51**).

7. Apply two drops of Loctite Threadlocker 262 (red), or an equivalent threadlock, to the threads of the *new* compensating sprocket bolt. Install the bolt (A, **Figure 54**) and washer (B). Finger-tighten the bolt.

8. Position the primary drive locking tool as shown in A, **Figure 52** to keep the compensating sprocket from rotating.

9A. On 2006-2008 models, tighten the compensating sprocket bolt to 155-165 ft-lb. (210.1-223.7 N•m).

9B. On 2009-2011 models, perform the following:

   a. Tighten the compensating sprocket bolt to 100 ft.-lb. (135.6 N•m).

   b. Loosen the bolt one full turn (360°).

   c. Re-tighten the compensating sprocket bolt to 140 ft.-lb. (189.8 N•m).

10. Position the primary drive locking tool as shown in A, **Figure 53** keep the clutch from rotating.

11. Apply two drops of Loctite Threadlocker 262 (red), or an equivalent threadlock, to the clutch nut.

> *NOTE*
> *The clutch nut has **left-hand threads**. Turn the nut counterclockwise to tighten it.*

12. Install the clutch nut (B, **Figure 52**), and tighten it to 70-80 ft.-lb. (94.9-108.5 N•m).

13. Remove the locking tool.

14. Tighten the primary chain tensioner bolts (B, **Figure 51**) to 15-19 ft.-lb. (20.3-25.8 N•m).

> *NOTE*
> *The tensioner will not completely release and adjust the primary chain until the motorcycle has been ridden.*

15. Cut and remove the cable tie (A, **Figure 51**). Make sure no portion of the tie to remains in the primary chaincase.

16A. On all models except Screamin' Eagle and CVO, perform the following:

   a. Install the release plate/adjuster assembly (**Figure 63**) so the ears of the release late engage the cutouts (**Figure 64**) in the pressure plate. Make sure the side of the release plate marked OUT faces out.

   b. Install a *new* snap ring (C, **Figure 22**) and make sure it is seated correctly.

16B. On Screamin' Eagle and CVO models, perform the following:

a. Press a *new* bearing into the release plate.

b. Install the pushrod into the bearing, and install a *new* small snap ring into the pushrod groove.

c. Slide the pushrod/release plate assembly into the mainshaft bore to the ears of the release plate engage the cutouts in the pressure plate.

d. Install a *new* large snap ring, and make sure it is correctly seated.

17. If removed, install the clutch plain plates, friction discs, pressure plate and diaphragm spring as described in *Clutch Assembly* (this chapter).

18. Install the primary chaincase cover as described in this chapter.

19. On all models except Screamin' Eagle and CVO, models, adjust the clutch as described in Chapter Three.

20. Connect the negative battery cable as described in Chapter Nine.

CLUTCH SHELL, HUB AND SPROCKET

Inspection (All Models)

The clutch shell is a subassembly consisting of the clutch shell, the clutch hub, the bearing and two snap rings. Refer to **Figure 65** and **Figure 66**.

1. Remove the primary drive assembly as described in this chapter. Remove the clutch shell assembly from the primary drive chain.

2. Hold the clutch shell and rotate the clutch hub by hand. The bearing is damaged if the clutch hub binds or turns roughly.

3. Check the primary chain sprocket (A, **Figure 67**) and the starter gear (B) on the clutch shell for cracks, deep scoring, excessive wear or heat discoloration.

4. If the sprocket or the gear are worn or damaged, replace the clutch shell. If the primary chain sprocket is worn, also check the primary chain and the compensating sprocket as described in this chapter.

5. Inspect the clutch hub for the following conditions:

a. The clutch plate teeth slide in the clutch hub splines (A, **Figure 68**). Inspect the splines for rough spots, grooves or other damage. Repair minor damage with a file or oil stone. If the damage is severe, replace the clutch hub.

b. Inspect the bolt towers (B, **Figure 68**) for thread damage or cracks at the base of the tower. Repair any thread damage with correct size of metric tap. If a tower is cracked or damaged, replace the clutch hub.

c. The friction disc tangs slide in slots on the clutch shell (C, **Figure 68**). Inspect the slots for cracks or galling. Repair minor damage with a file. If the damage is severe, replace the clutch shell.

6. Inspect the clutch hub inner splines (**Figure 69**). Check for galling, severe wear or other damage. Repair minor damage with a fine cut file. If damage is severe, replace the clutch hub.

7. If the clutch hub, the clutch shell or the bearing are damaged, replace them as described in this section.

Disassembly/Assembly

Do not separate the clutch shell and hub unless the bearing or either part must be replaced. The bearing is damaged when the shell and hub are separated. Removal and installation of the bearing requires the use of a hydraulic press.

1. Remove the friction discs and plain plates as described in *Clutch Assembly* (this chapter).

2. Remove the primary drive assembly as described in this chapter. Remove the clutch shell assembly from the primary drive chain.

3. Place the clutch hub on the bench with the starter gear side facing up.

4. Remove the small snap ring (**Figure 70**) from the clutch hub groove.

5. Support the clutch shell on the press bed with the starter gear side *facing up*.

6. Place a suitable size arbor or socket on the clutch hub surface, and press the clutch hub from the bearing (**Figure 71**).

7. Remove the clutch shell from the press bed.

8. Remove the large snap ring (**Figure 72**) from the clutch shell groove.

> *CAUTION*
> *Press the bearing out from the primary chain sprocket side of the clutch shell. The bearing bore has a shoulder on the starter ring gear side.*

9. Support the clutch shell in the press with the primary chain sprocket side *facing up*.

10. Place a suitable size arbor or socket on the bearing inner race, and press the bearing out of the clutch shell (**Figure 73**).

11. Thoroughly clean the clutch hub and shell in solvent. Dry them with compressed air.

12. Inspect the bearing bore in the clutch shell for damage or burrs. Clean off any burrs that would interfere with new bearing installation.

65 **CLUTCH ASSEMBLY (ALL MODELS EXCEPT SCREAMIN' EAGLE AND CVO)**

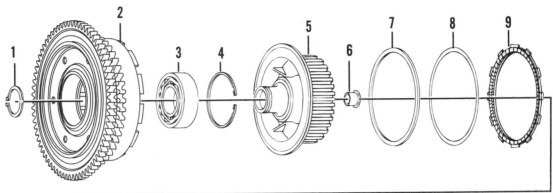

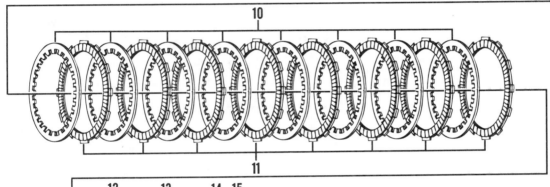

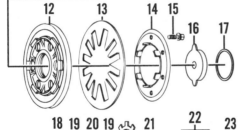

1. Snap ring	13. Diaphragm spring
2. Clutch shell and sprocket	14. Diaphragm spring retainer
3. Bearing	15. Bolt
4. Snap ring	16. Release plate
5. Clutch hub	17. Snap ring
6. Clutch nut	18. Snap ring
7. Damper spring seat	19. Thrust washer
8. Damper spring	20. Radial bearing
9. Friction disc B	21. Oil slinger
10. Plain plates	22. Pushrod (right side)
11. Friction disc A	23. Adjust screw
12. Pressure plate	24. Locknut

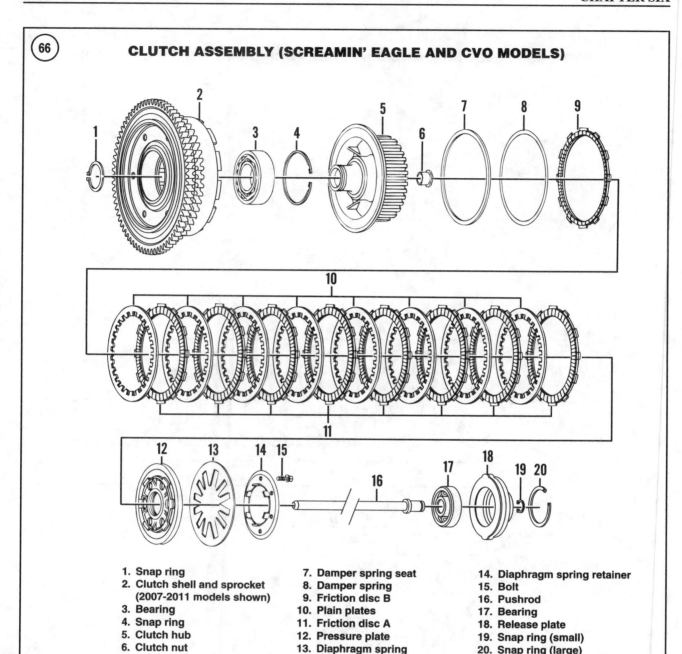

66

CLUTCH ASSEMBLY (SCREAMIN' EAGLE AND CVO MODELS)

1. Snap ring
2. Clutch shell and sprocket
   (2007-2011 models shown)
3. Bearing
4. Snap ring
5. Clutch hub
6. Clutch nut
7. Damper spring seat
8. Damper spring
9. Friction disc B
10. Plain plates
11. Friction disc A
12. Pressure plate
13. Diaphragm spring
14. Diaphragm spring retainer
15. Bolt
16. Pushrod
17. Bearing
18. Release plate
19. Snap ring (small)
20. Snap ring (large)

67

68

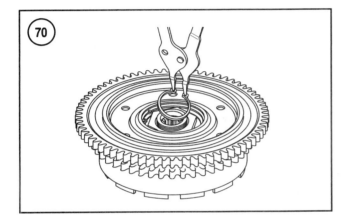

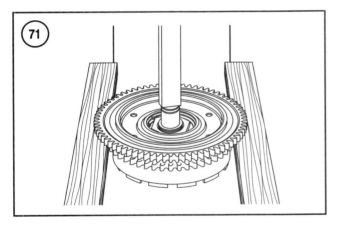

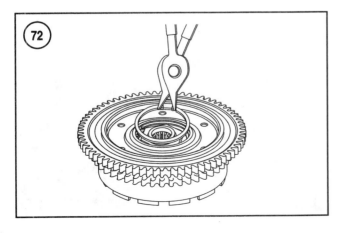

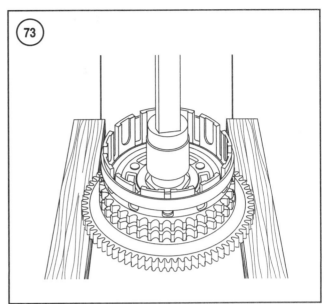

13. Support the clutch shell in the press with the starter gear side *facing up*.

14. Apply chaincase lubricant to the bearing bore in the clutch shell and to the outer surface of the bearing.

15. Align the bearing with the clutch shell bore.

16. Place a suitable size arbor on the bearing outer race, and slowly press the bearing into the clutch shell until it bottoms on the lower shoulder. Press only on the outer bearing race. Applying force to the bearing's inner race will damage the bearing. Refer to *Bearings* in Chapter One for additional information.

17. Position a *new*, large snap ring with its flat side against the bearing, and install the snap ring into the clutch shell groove (**Figure 72**). Make sure the snap ring completely seats in the clutch shell groove.

18. Press the clutch hub into the clutch shell as follows:

CAUTION
Failure to support the inner bearing race properly will cause bearing and clutch shell damage.

  a. Place the clutch shell in a press so the starter gear side *faces down*. Support the inner bearing race with a sleeve that matches the bearing inner race.

  b. Align the clutch hub with the bearing, and slowly press the clutch hub into the bearing until the clutch hub shoulder seats against the bearing inner race.

  c. Turn the assembly over, and install a *new* small snap ring (**Figure 70**) into the clutch hub. Make sure the snap ring is completely seated in the clutch hub groove.

19. After completing assembly, hold the clutch shell (A, **Figure 74**) and rotate the clutch hub (B) by hand. The shell must turn smoothly with no roughness or binding. If the clutch shell binds or turns roughly, the bearing was installed incorrectly. Repeat procedure until this problem is corrected.

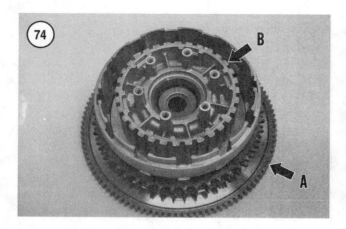

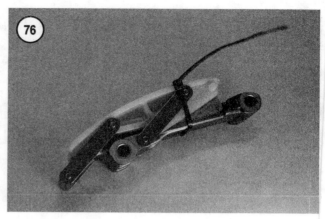

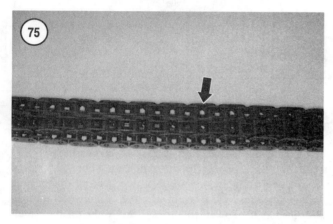

PRIMARY CHAIN
AND TENSIONER INSPECTION

1. Remove the primary chain as described in *Primary Drive Assembly* (this chapter).

2. Remove the compensating sprocket and the clutch shell from the primary chain.

3. Clean the primary chain in solvent and dry thoroughly.

4. Inspect the primary chain (**Figure 75**) for excessive link roller wear, cracked side plates or other damage. If the chain is worn or damaged, check both sprockets for wear and damage.

> *NOTE*
> *If the primary chain is near the end of its adjustment level or if no more adjustment is available, and the tensioner shoe is not worn or damaged; the primary chain is excessively worn. Service specifications for chain wear are not available.*

> *NOTE*
> *The tensioner assembly cannot be serviced. It must be replaced if any portion is worn or damaged.*

5. Inspect the chain tensioner shoe assembly (**Figure 76**) for cracks, severe wear or other damage. Replace the chain tensioner assembly if necessary.

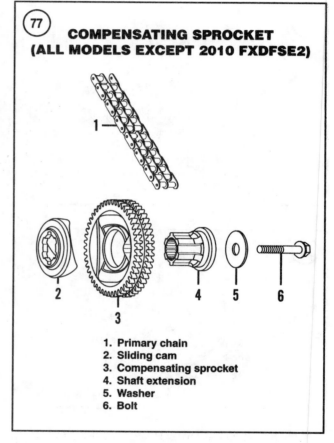

**COMPENSATING SPROCKET
(ALL MODELS EXCEPT 2010 FXDFSE2)**

1. Primary chain
2. Sliding cam
3. Compensating sprocket
4. Shaft extension
5. Washer
6. Bolt

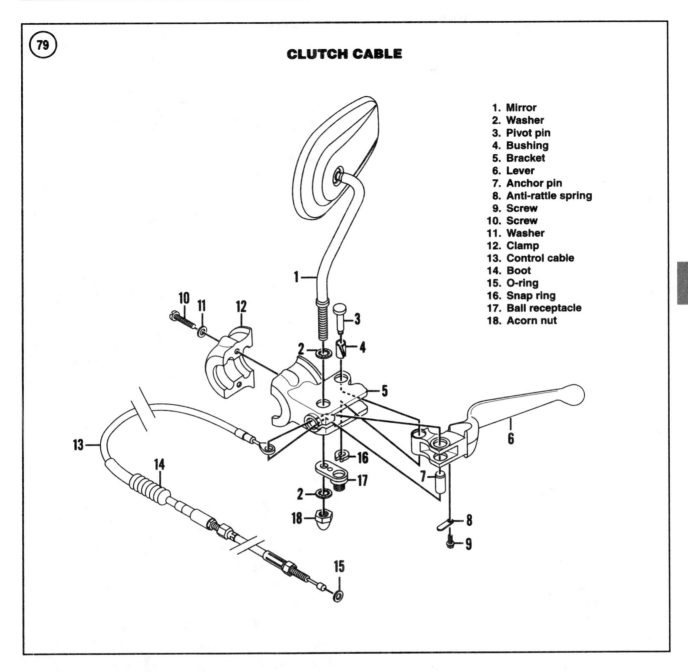

(79) **CLUTCH CABLE**

1. Mirror
2. Washer
3. Pivot pin
4. Bushing
5. Bracket
6. Lever
7. Anchor pin
8. Anti-rattle spring
9. Screw
10. Screw
11. Washer
12. Clamp
13. Control cable
14. Boot
15. O-ring
16. Snap ring
17. Ball receptacle
18. Acorn nut

COMPENSATING SPROCKET INSPECTION

Refer to **Figure 47** and **Figure 77**.

1. Remove the compensating sprocket assembly as described in *Primary Drive Assembly* (this chapter).

2. Clean all parts in solvent. Dry them with compressed air.

3. Check the ramps on the sliding cam (A, **Figure 78**) and compensating sprocket (B) for cracks, deep scoring or wear.

NOTE
If the compensating sprocket teeth are worn, also check the primary chain and the clutch shell gear teeth for wear.

4. Check the gear teeth (C, **Figure 78**) on the compensating sprocket for cracks or wear.

5. Check the compensating sprocket bore (D, **Figure 78**) for wear.

6. Check the sliding cam inner splines (E, **Figure 78**) for wear.

7. Check the shaft extension splines (F, **Figure 78**) for wear or galling.

8. Inspect the bolt threads for damage.

CLUTCH CABLE REPLACEMENT (ALL MODELS EXCEPT SCREAMIN' EAGLE AND CVO)

Refer to **Figure 79**.

1. Before removing the clutch cable, make a drawing of the cable's path from the handlebar, along the left frame down tube, under the engine mounting spacer and down to the clutch release cover. The new cable must follow the same path.

2. Perform the following at the clutch cable adjuster:
   a. Release the clutch cable from the clamp and slide the boot (**Figure 80**) away from the adjuster.
   b. Loosen the locknut (A, **Figure 81**), and turn the adjuster (B) to provide maximum slack.

3. Disconnect the clutch cable (**Figure 82**) from the clutch release mechanism and remove it from the release cover as described in this chapter.

4. Remove the acorn nut and lockwasher, or loosen the hex fitting (A, **Figure 83**) securing the ball retainer (B) and turn signal assembly and mirror. Remove the turn signal assembly and mirror from the bracket.

5. Remove the snap ring from the bottom of the clutch lever pivot pin.

6. Remove the pivot pin (C, **Figure 83**), and slide the clutch lever (D) from the bracket.

7. Remove the anchor pin (**Figure 84**), and disconnect the clutch cable from the lever.

8. Check the clutch lever components (**Figure 85**) for worn or damaged parts.

9. Make sure the anti-rattle spring screw (**Figure 86**) on the bottom of the clutch lever is tight.

10. Following the drawing made prior to removal, route the new clutch cable from the handlebar to the clutch release cover.

11. Fit the clutch cable end into the clutch lever. Secure it with the anchor pin (**Figure 84**).

12. Slide the clutch lever (D, **Figure 83**) into the bracket, and install the pivot pin (C).

13. Install the snap ring onto the bottom of the clutch lever pivot pin. Make sure it is seated correctly.

14. Install the turn signal assembly and mirror onto the bracket. Install the acorn nut and lockwasher, or tighten the hex fitting (A, **Figure 83**) securing the ball retainer (B) and turn signal assembly and mirror.

15. Reconnect the clutch cable (**Figure 82**) to the clutch release mechanism as described in this chapter.

16. Adjust the clutch as described in Chapter Three.

CLUTCH LEVER ASSEMBLY
(ALL MODELS EXCEPT
SCREAMIN' EAGLE AND CVO)

Removal

1. If necessary, disconnect the clutch cable from the lever assembly as described in *Clutch Cable Replacement* (this chapter).

2. Unscrew and remove the mirror (A, **Figure 87**).

3. Remove the screws securing the left handlebar switch assembly (B, **Figure 87**) together and separate the housing halves. Note how the ribs on the outside of the left handle-

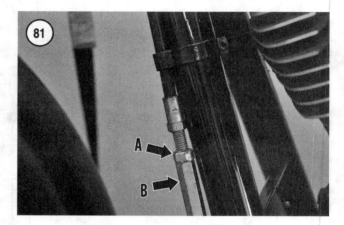

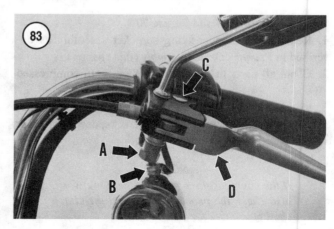

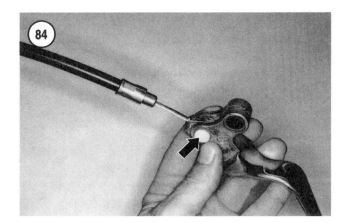

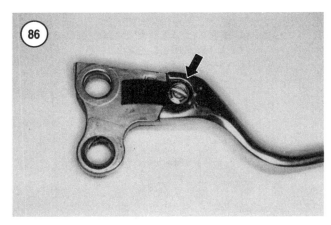

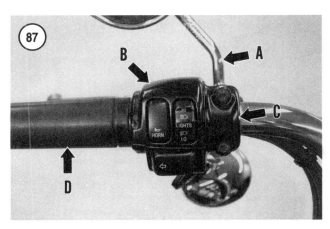

bar switch assembly engage the groove (**Figure 88**) in the handlebar grip. Remove the assembly from the handlebar.

4. Remove the clutch lever clamp (C, **Figure 87**) mounting bolts and washers and separate the clamp halves. Remove the assembly from the handlebar

5. If necessary, remove the handlebar grip (D, **Figure 87**) from the handlebar.

Installation

1. If removed, install a new handlebar grip (D, **Figure 87**) by performing the following:
   a. Clean all adhesive residue from the handlebar.
   b. Pour adhesive into the new grip and roll the grip to evenly spread the adhesive on the grip's inner surface.
   c. Roll the new grip onto the handlebar. Clean away any excess adhesive.

2. Fit the left handlebar switch assembly onto the handlebar so the switch ribs engage the groove (**Figure 88**) in the handlebar grip.

3. Install the left handlebar switch assembly (B, **Figure 87**) screws and finger-tighten.

4. Position the clutch lever assembly onto the handlebar so the groove in the clutch lever assembly engages the tab in the lower handlebar switch housing.

5. Fit the clutch lever clamp (C, **Figure 87**) into position and install the clutch lever clamp bolts.

6. Tighten the upper clutch lever clamp bolt first, and then the lower bolt. Tighten each bolt to 60-80 in.-lb. (6.8-9.0 N•m).

7. Starting with the bottom screw, tighten the left handlebar switch housing (B, **Figure 87**) screws to 35-45 in.-lb. (4.0-5.1 N•m).

8. Install the mirror (A, **Figure 87**), correctly adjust it, and tighten securely.

9. If removed, install the clutch cable as described in *Clutch Cable Replacement* (this chapter).

CLUTCH RELEASE COVER (ALL MODELS EXCEPT SCREAMIN' EAGLE AND CVO)

Removal

1. Remove the exhaust system as described in Chapter Four.
2. Drain the transmission oil as described in Chapter Three.

NOTE
If the cover is difficult to remove, apply the clutch lever after the mounting bolts have been removed. This usually breaks the cover loose.

3. Remove the clutch release cover mounting bolts (A, **Figure 89**) securing the cover.
4. Remove the cover and gasket from the transmission side door. Discard the cover gasket.
5. Do not lose the locating dowels (**Figure 90**) behind the cover.

Installation

1. If removed, install the locating dowels (**Figure 90**) into the transmission side door.
2. Install a *new* gasket.
3. Install the clutch release cover bolts (A, **Figure 89**). Using a crossing pattern, tighten the clutch release cover bolts to 84-108 in.-lb. (9.5-12.2 N•m).
4. If removed, tighten the clutch cable fitting (B, **Figure 89**) on 2006-2007 models to 36-60 in.-lb. (4.1-6.8 N•m). On 2008-2011 models, tighten the fitting to 90-120 in.-lb. (10.2-13.6 N•m).
5. Refill the transmission with oil as described in Chapter Three.
6. Install the exhaust system as described in a Chapter Four.
7. Adjust the clutch as described in Chapter Three.

Disassembly

Refer to **Figure 91**.
1. Remove the clutch release cover as described in this section.
2. Perform the following at the clutch cable adjuster:
   a. Release the clutch cable from the clamp and slide the boot (**Figure 80**) away from the adjuster.
   b. Loosen the locknut (A, **Figure 81**), and turn the adjuster (B) to provide maximum slack.

NOTE
*Before removing the snap ring, note the snap ring opening is centered on the cover slot (A, **Figure 92**). The snap ring must be reinstalled with its opening in the same position.*

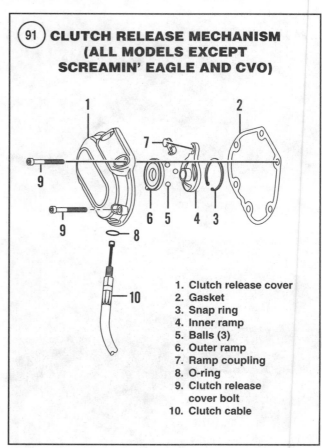

91) CLUTCH RELEASE MECHANISM (ALL MODELS EXCEPT SCREAMIN' EAGLE AND CVO)

1. Clutch release cover
2. Gasket
3. Snap ring
4. Inner ramp
5. Balls (3)
6. Outer ramp
7. Ramp coupling
8. O-ring
9. Clutch release cover bolt
10. Clutch cable

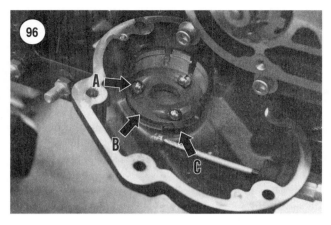

3. Remove the snap ring (B, **Figure 92**) from the groove in the side cover.

4. Disconnect the ramp coupling (A, **Figure 93**) from the inner ramp (B).

5. Disconnect the cable end (**Figure 94**) from the ramp coupling, and remove the coupling.

6. Lift the inner ramp (**Figure 95**) from the release cover.

7. Remove the three balls (A, **Figure 96**) from the outer ramp (B).

8. Remove the outer ramp (B, **Figure 96**).

9. If necessary, unscrew the clutch cable fitting (A, **Figure 97**), and remove the cable (B) from the clutch release cover.

Assembly

1. If removed, insert the cable (B, **Figure 97**) and install the clutch cable fitting (A) into the clutch release cover. Do not tighten the cable fitting at this time.

2. Install the outer ramp (B, **Figure 96**) into the cover so the ramp's tab (C) engages the slot in the bore. The ball sockets in the outer ramp must face up.

3. Seat a ball (A, **Figure 96**) into each socket in the outer ramp. Center a ball into each socket.

4. Align the inner ramp socket with the balls, and install the inner ramp (**Figure 95**) into the cover.

5. Connect the cable end (**Figure 94**) to the ramp coupling, and connect the ramp coupling (A, **Figure 93**) to the inner ramp (B).

6. Install the snap ring (B, **Figure 92**) into the clutch release cover groove. Position the snap ring so its opening is centered on the cover slot (A, **Figure 92**). Make sure the snap ring is completely seated in the groove.

Inspection

1. Clean the side cover and all components thoroughly in solvent, and then dry them with compressed air.
2. Check the release mechanism balls, inner ramp sockets and outer ramp sockets for cracks, deep scoring or excessive wear (**Figure 98**).
3. Check the clutch release cover for cracks or damage. Check the clutch cable threads and the coupling snap ring groove for damage. Check the ramp bore (C, **Figure 97**) in the release cover for excessive wear, or grooves that could catch and bind the ramps causing improper clutch adjustment.
4. Replace the clutch cable O-ring.
5. Replace all worn or damaged parts.

HYDRAULIC CLUTCH SERVICE (SCREAMIN' EAGLE AND CVO MODELS)

The hydraulic clutch release system transmits hydraulic pressure from the master cylinder to the clutch release mechanism in the clutch release cover. As the clutch components wear, the clutch release piston moves out. As this occurs, the fluid level in the master cylinder reservoir goes down. Occasionally adding fluid compensates for this drop.

The proper operation of this system depends on a supply of clean brake fluid (DOT 4). Always work in a clean environment when servicing the hydraulic clutch system. Even tiny particles of debris that enter the system can damage components and cause poor clutch performance.

Brake fluid is hygroscopic (easily absorbs moisture), and any moisture in the system reduces clutch performance. Purchase brake fluid in small containers and properly discard of any small quantities that remain. Small quantities of fluid quickly absorb moisture in the container. Use only fluid clearly marked DOT 4. Other types of brake fluid are not compatible with DOT 4. If possible, always use the same brand of brake fluid. Fluids from different manufacturers may not be compatible with one another. Do not reuse drained fluid. Properly discard all old brake fluid. Do not mix it with other fluids for recycling.

Perform clutch service procedures carefully. Do not use any sharp tools inside the master cylinder or release mechanism piston. Damage to these components could cause a loss in the system's ability to maintain hydraulic pressure. If there is any doubt about the ability to correctly and safely service the clutch system, have a professional technician perform the task.

When servicing the hydraulic clutch system, consider the following:
1. The hydraulic components rarely require disassembly. Make sure it is necessary.

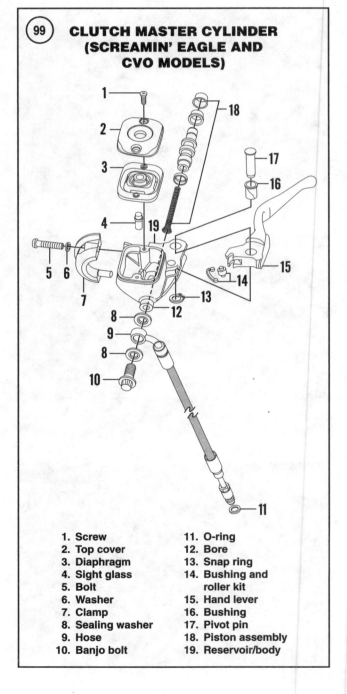

CLUTCH MASTER CYLINDER (SCREAMIN' EAGLE AND CVO MODELS)

1. Screw	11. O-ring
2. Top cover	12. Bore
3. Diaphragm	13. Snap ring
4. Sight glass	14. Bushing and roller kit
5. Bolt	15. Hand lever
6. Washer	16. Bushing
7. Clamp	17. Pivot pin
8. Sealing washer	18. Piston assembly
9. Hose	19. Reservoir/body
10. Banjo bolt	

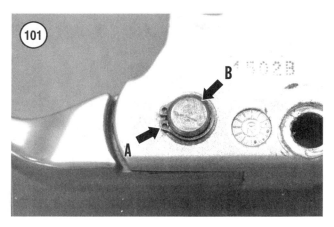

CAUTION
Wash brake fluid off any surface immediately, as it damages the finish. Use soapy water and rinse completely.

   b. Drain the clutch system as described in this chapter.

   c. Remove the banjo bolt securing the clutch hose to the master cylinder, along with the captive washers. Seal the clutch hose in a plastic bag so brake fluid cannot drip onto the motorcycle. Tie the loose end of the hose to the handlebar.

   d. Plug the bolt opening in the master cylinder to prevent drips when removing the master cylinder in the following steps.

4. Remove the clutch master cylinder clamp bolts, washers and the clamp. Then, lower the clutch master cylinder from the handlebar.

5A. If necessary, service the master cylinder as described in this section.

5B. If the master cylinder will not be serviced, suspend it from the motorcycle. With a bungee cord so the clutch hose is not strained. Keep the master cylinder upright.

6. Clean the handlebar, master cylinder and clamp mating surfaces.

7. Mount the master cylinder onto the handlebar and position it to rider's preference.

8. Install the master cylinder clamp, clamp bolts and washers.

9. Tighten the upper master cylinder clamp bolt first, and then the lower bolt. Tighten each clamp bolt to 60-80 in.-lb. (6.8-9.0 N•m).

NOTE
When the master cylinder clamp is correctly installed, the upper edge of the clamp touches the master cylinder, leaving a gap at the bottom.

10. If removed, secure the clutch hose to the master cylinder with the banjo bolt. Install a *new* sealing washer on each side of the clutch hose. Tighten the banjo bolt to the following:

   a. 2007-2008 models: 17-22 ft.-lb. (23.0-29.8 N•m).

   b. 2009-2011 models: 21-25 ft.-lb. (28.5-33.9 N•m).

11. Bleed the clutch system as described in this chapter.

12. Test ride the motorcycle carefully to ensure the clutch is operating correctly.

2. Keep the reservoir cover in place to prevent the entry of moisture and debris.

3. Clean parts with an aerosol brake parts cleaner or isopropyl alcohol. Never use petroleum-based solvents on internal clutch system components. They will cause seals to swell and distort.

4. Do not allow brake fluid to contact plastic, painted or plated parts. It quickly damages these surfaces.

5. Dispose of brake fluid properly.

6. If the hydraulic system, excluding the reservoir cover, has been opened, bleed the system to remove air from the system. Refer to *Clutch System Bleeding* in this chapter.

CLUTCH MASTER CYLINDER (SCREAMIN' EAGLE AND CVO MODELS)

Removal/Installation

   Refer to **Figure 99**.

1. Support the motorcycle on level ground using a swing arm stand.

2. Block the front wheel so the motorcycle cannot roll in either direction while on the swing arm stand.

3. If the master cylinder will be serviced, perform the following:

   a. Cover the fuel tank, front fairing and front fender with a heavy cloth or plastic tarp to protect them from accidental brake fluid spills.

Disassembly

1. Remove the master cylinder as described in this section.

2. If still in place, remove the master cylinder cover (**Figure 100**) and diaphragm. Pour out any remaining brake fluid and discard it.

3. Remove the snap ring (A, **Figure 101**) from hand lever pivot pin (B).

4. Apply slight hand pressure to the clutch lever and remove some of the spring pressure on the pivot pin.

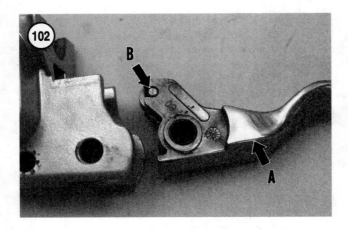

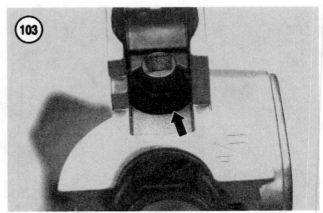

5. Withdraw the pivot pin from the master cylinder body, and remove the clutch lever (A, **Figure 102**). Watch for the bushing and roller kit (B, **Figure 102**) in the lever.

6. Remove the rubber boot (**Figure 103**) from the groove in the body at the end of the piston.

NOTE
If brake fluid is leaking from the piston bore, the piston cups are worn or damaged. Replace the piston assembly.

7. Remove the piston assembly and spring (A, **Figure 104**) from the master cylinder bore (B). Do not remove the primary and secondary cups from the piston.

Assembly

1. If the cover and diaphragm were disassembled, assemble them as follows:
    a. Insert the neck of the diaphragm into the cover. Press it until it seats correctly and the outer edges (**Figure 105**) align with the cover.
    b. Push the sight glass (**Figure 106**) straight down through the cover and the neck of the diaphragm until it snaps into place. The sight glass must lock these two part together to avoid a brake fluid leak.

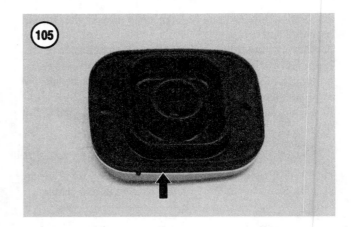

2. Soak the *new* cup, O-ring and piston assembly in new DOT 4 brake fluid for 15 minutes to make them pliable. Coat the inside of the cylinder bore with new brake fluid prior to the assembly of parts.

3. Install a bolt into the threaded banjo bolt hole and mount the master cylinder body in a vise (**Figure 107**),

4. If installing a new piston assembly, assemble it as described in this section.

5A. If reinstalling the existing piston assembly, lubricate the piston (A, **Figure 108**), primary cup (B), secondary cup (C) and cylinder bore with DOT 4 brake fluid.

5B. If installing a new piston assembly, coat the outside diameters of the piston primary and secondary cups and the cylinder bore using the lubricant provided with the H-D service parts kit.

6. Install the spring with the retainer end facing out, into the piston assembly (**Figure 109**).

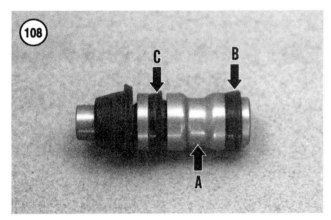

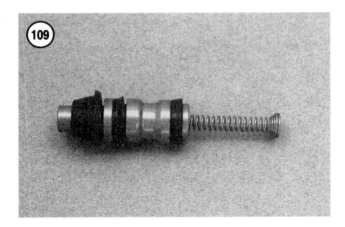

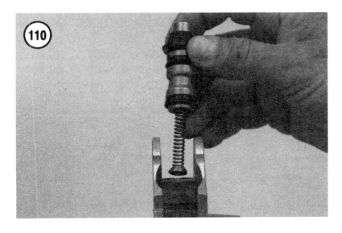

CAUTION
Do not allow the piston cups to tear or turn inside out when installing the piston into the master cylinder bore. Both cups are larger that the bore.

7. Insert the spring and piston assembly (**Figure 110**) into the master cylinder bore (B, **Figure 104**). Push in on the end of the piston until the entire assembly sits in the bore and completely compress the spring.

CAUTION
The rubber boot must completely seat in the master cylinder groove. Slowly push and release the piston a few times to make sure it moves smoothly and that the rubber boot does not pop out.

8. Hold the piston in place, and carefully install the rubber boot (**Figure 103**) into the groove in the master cylinder body. Make sure the entire perimeter of the boot is correctly seated in the groove.

9. If removed, install the bushing and roller kit (B, **Figure 102**) into the end of the hand lever. Position the bushing so it sits flush with both sides of the lever. When installed correctly it will snap into place (**Figure 111**).

10. Lubricate the pivot pin (B, **Figure 101**) with silicone brake grease.

11. Install the hand lever (A, **Figure 102**) onto the master cylinder body, and install the pivot pin (B, **Figure 101**) part way in from the top.

12. Slightly apply the hand lever to compress the spring, and push the piston in all the way.

13. Install a *new* snap ring (A, **Figure 101**) onto the pivot pin. Make sure it is correctly seated in the groove.

14. Check that the hand lever moves freely. If there is any binding or roughness, remove the pivot pin and hand lever, and inspect the parts.

15. Temporarily install the diaphragm and cover. Install the cover screws and finger-tighten them. Do not tighten the screws at this time, as brake fluid will be added later.

16. Install the master cylinder as described in this section.

Inspection

The manufacturer does not supply specifications for the clutch master cylinder. Replace visibly worn or damaged parts as described in this section.

1. Clean and dry the master cylinder assembly as follows:
   a. Handle the brake components carefully when servicing them.
   b. Use only DOT 4 brake fluid or denatured alcohol to wash rubber parts (rubber boot and piston assembly) in the clutch system. Never allow any petroleum-based cleaner to contact the rubber parts. These chemicals cause the rubber to swell, requiring their replacement.
   c. Clean the master cylinder piston rubber boot groove carefully. Use a small pick or brush to clean the groove. If a hard varnish residue has built up in the groove, soak the master cylinder in solvent to help soften the residue. Then, wash it in soapy water and rinse completely.
   d. Blow the master cylinder dry with compressed air.
   e. Place cleaned parts on a clean lint-free cloth until assembly.

> *CAUTION*
> *Do not get any oil or grease onto any of the master cylinder components. These chemicals cause the rubber parts in the brake system to swell, permanently damaging them.*

> *CAUTION*
> *Do not remove the primary and secondary cups from the piston assembly for cleaning or inspection purposes.*

2. Check the piston assembly for the following defects. If any of these parts are worn or damaged, replace the piston assembly.
   a. Check the piston (A, **Figure 112**) for scratches and/or corrosion.
   b. Worn, cracked, damaged or swollen primary (B, **Figure 112**) and secondary (C) cups.
   c. Worn or damaged rubber boot (D, **Figure 112**).
   d. Broken, distorted or collapsed piston return spring.
3. To assemble a *new* piston assembly, perform the following:
   a. If replacing the piston, install the *new* primary and secondary cups onto the piston. Use the original piston assembly as a reference when installing the new cups onto the piston.
   b. Lightly lubricate the inside of the primary cup (A, **Figure 113**) and fit it on the spring end of the piston so the closed end (smaller inside diameter) contacts evenly with the shoulder in the piston's primary cup groove.
   c. Lightly lubricate the inside of the secondary cup. Position the secondary cup with open flared end pointing toward the shoulder of the piston's secondary cup groove. Install the secondary cup (B, **Figure**

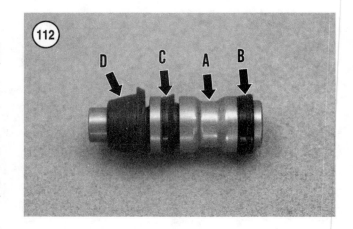

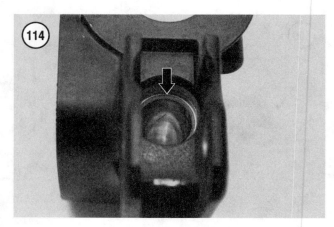

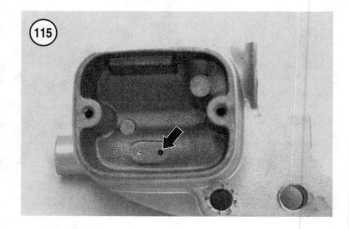

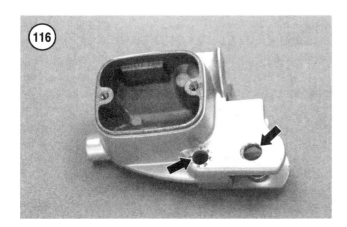

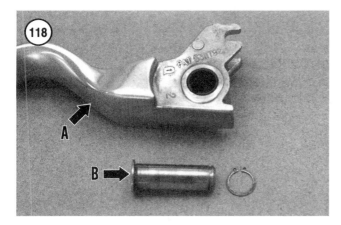

113) over the lip on the outboard end of the piston and into the groove.

d. Position the boot (C, **Figure 113**) with the large sealing end going on first and install it onto the piston.

4. Inspect the master cylinder bore (**Figure 114**). Replace the master cylinder if its bore is corroded, cracked or damaged in any way. Do not hone the master cylinder bore to remove scratches or other damage.

5. Make sure the fluid passageway (**Figure 115**) in the base of the body is clear. Clean out with compressed air is necessary.

6. Inspect the master cylinder body for cracks, damage and pivot pin and mirror hole elongation (**Figure 116**).

7. Check the holder, bolts and washers for damage.

8. Check the banjo bolt threads for damage.

9. Inspect the diaphragm (**Figure 117**) and cover for deterioration and other damage.

10. Check the hand lever assembly for the following:
   a. Damaged hand lever (A, **Figure 118**).
   b. Excessively worn or damaged pivot pin (B, **Figure 118**).
   c. Worn or damaged bushing (**Figure 119**).
   d. Inspect the bushing and roller kit (**Figure 120**) for wear or damage.

CLUTCH RELEASE COVER (SCREAMIN' EAGLE AND CVO MODELS)

Refer to **Figure 121**.

Removal

1. Support the motorcycle on level ground using a swing arm stand.

2. Block the front wheel so the motorcycle cannot roll in either direction while on the swing arm stand.

3. Remove the exhaust system as described in Chapter Four.

4. Drain the transmission oil as described in Chapter Three.

5. Cover the frame under the transmission case with a heavy cloth or plastic tarp to protect it from accidental brake fluid spills.

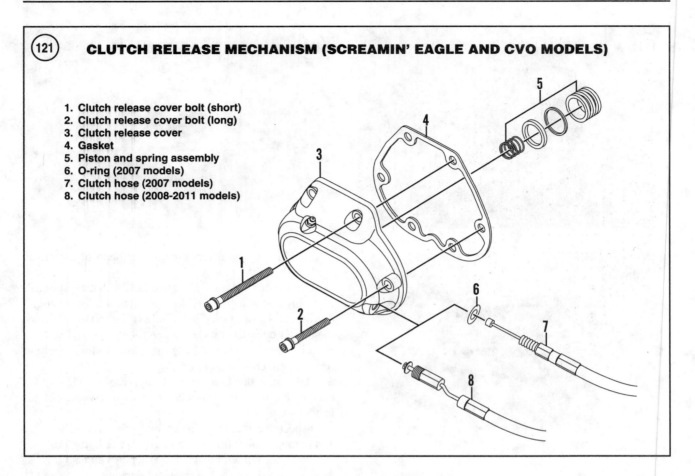

121   **CLUTCH RELEASE MECHANISM (SCREAMIN' EAGLE AND CVO MODELS)**

1. Clutch release cover bolt (short)
2. Clutch release cover bolt (long)
3. Clutch release cover
4. Gasket
5. Piston and spring assembly
6. O-ring (2007 models)
7. Clutch hose (2007 models)
8. Clutch hose (2008-2011 models)

6. Slightly loosen the clutch release cover bolts, and apply the clutch lever. This breaks the cover loose from the transmission case.

CAUTION
Wash brake fluid off any surface immediately, as it damages the finish. Use soapy water and rinse completely.

7. Drain the hydraulic fluid from the clutch system as described in this chapter.

8. Carefully loosen the flare nut securing the clutch hose to the cover. Do not scratch the chrome cover.

9. Disconnect the clutch hose from the cover, and place the end into a reclosable plastic bag. Remove the O-ring (**Figure 122**) from the end of the clutch hose. Discard the O-ring.

NOTE
Note that two different length cover bolts are used. The two short bolts are used at the top of the cover; long bolts are used at the four remaining locations.

10. Remove the clutch release cover bolts and remove the cover. Watch for the dowels (**Figure 123**) behind the cover.

11. Remove and discard the cover gasket.

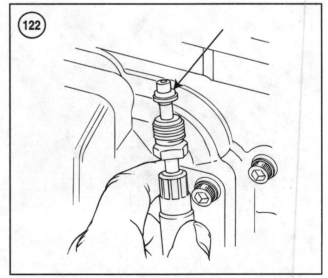

122

Installation

1. If removed, install the locating dowels (**Figure 123**).
2. Install a *new* gasket over the locating dowels.
3. Install the clutch release cover.
4. Install the two short bolts at the top of the clutch release cover and the long bolts at the four remaining locations. Using a crossing pattern, tighten the bolts to 80-132 in.-lb. (9.5-14.9 N•m).

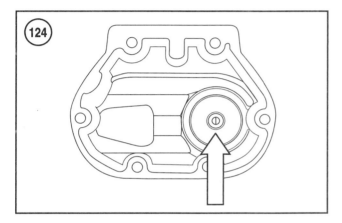

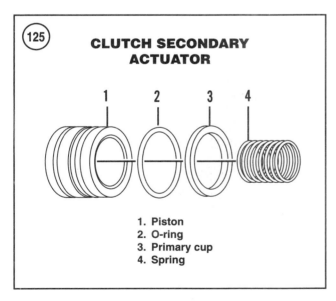

CLUTCH SECONDARY ACTUATOR

1. Piston
2. O-ring
3. Primary cup
4. Spring

5. Install a *new* O-ring (**Figure 122**) onto the end of the clutch hose.

6. Connect the clutch hose to the cover. Install the flare nut into the cover by hand until it bottoms. Do not cross thread the flare nut or scratch the cover. Tighten the clutch hose flare nut to the following:

    a. 2007 models: 80-115 (9-13 N•m).
    b. 2008-2011 models: 72-120 (8.1-13.6 N•m).

7. Refill the transmission oil as described in Chapter Three.

8. Install the exhaust system as described in Chapter Four.

9. Refill the clutch master cylinder and bleed the system as described in this chapter.

10. Start the engine, and slowly test ride the motorcycle to check for proper clutch operation.

CLUTCH SECONDARY ACTUATOR (SCREAMIN' EAGLE AND CVO MODELS)

Removal/Installation

1. Remove the clutch release cover as described in this chapter.

2. If removed, install the bleed valve and tighten as follows:

    a. 2007 models: 80-100 in-lb. (9.0-11.3 N•m).
    b. 2008-2011 models: 12-15 in.-lb. (1.4-1.7 N•m).

3. To remove the piston (**Figure 124**) from the clutch release cover, perform the following:

    a. Place a piece of soft wood on the work bench.
    b. Position the release cover with the piston side facing toward the work bench.
    c. Apply compressed air through the clutch hose port in the cover, and force the piston part way out of the cover receptacle.

4. Withdraw the piston assembly and spring from the cover receptacle.

5. If the primary cup was removed from the piston, install the cup so its raised leading-edge lip faces the spring end of the piston.

6. Apply DOT 4 brake fluid to the *new* primary cup, O-ring and piston. Also apply DOT 4 brake fluid to the cylinder in the cover.

7. Install the spring into the piston, and install the assembly into the cover cylinder. Guide the primary cup into the receptacle to prevent the lips from turning over.

8. Push the piston and spring in until they bottom. Press the piston into the bore and check that the spring pushes it back out part way. The piston must move freely within the bore.

9. Install the clutch release cover as described in this chapter.

Inspection

Replacement parts are not available for the piston assembly. If any part is worn or damaged, replace the piston and spring as an assembly. Refer to **Figure 125**.

1. Clean the cylinder bore and piston in DOT 4 brake fluid or isopropyl alcohol. Dry them with compressed air.

2. Inspect the spring for fractures or sagging.

3. Check the O-ring and primary cup for hardness or deterioration.

4. Check the piston and cylinder bore for scratches, scoring or other damage.

6

5. Check the piston O-ring groove and primary cup groove for damage.

6. Inspect the threaded flare nut hole in the cover. If it is worn or damaged, clean it out with a thread tap or replace the cover.

7. Inspect the threaded bleed valve hole in the cover. If it is worn or damaged, clean it out with a thread tap or replace the cover.

8. Inspect the bleed screw. Apply compressed air to the opening and make sure it is clear. Clean it out, if necessary, with brake fluid. Install the bleed screw and tighten to the specification in **Table 2**.

CLUTCH HYDRAULIC HOSE REPLACEMENT (SCREAMIN' EAGLE AND CVO MODELS)

1. Support the motorcycle on level ground using a swing arm stand.

2. Block the front wheel so the motorcycle cannot roll in either direction while on the swing arm stand.

3. Before removing the hose, make a drawing of its path from the handlebar to the clutch release cover. The new hose must be routed along the same path.

4. Remove the front cylinder exhaust pipe as described in Chapter Four.

5. Cover the frame under the transmission case with a heavy cloth or plastic tarp to protect it from accidental brake fluid spills.

> *CAUTION*
> *Wash brake fluid off any surface immediately, as it damages the finish. Use soapy water and rinse completely.*

6. Drain the fluid from the clutch system as described in this chapter.

7. Carefully loosen the flare nut securing the clutch hose to the clutch release cover. Do not scratch the chrome cover.

8. Disconnect the clutch hose from the cover, and seal its end in a plastic bag.

9. Remove the O-ring (**Figure 122**) from the end of the clutch hose, or if necessary, remove the O-ring from the threaded hose outlet in the cover.

10. Remove the banjo bolt and washers securing the clutch hose to the master cylinder. Seal the hose end in a plastic bag so brake fluid does not drip onto the motorcycle.

11. Plug the bolt opening in the master cylinder to prevent leaks and the entry of debris.

12. Release the hose from any hose clamps securing it to the frame. Note the location of each hose clamp, and remove the old hose.

13. Install the *new* clutch hose through the frame following the same path noted during removal. Secure it with the hose clamps noted during removal.

14. Secure the clutch hose to the master cylinder with the banjo bolt. Install a *new* sealing washer on each side of the clutch hose. Tighten the banjo bolt to the following:
   a. 2007-2008 models: 17-22 ft.-lb. (23-29.8 N•m).

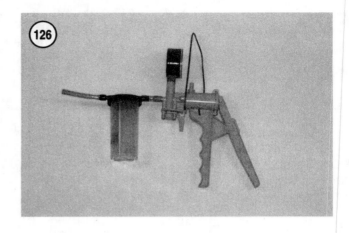

   b. 2009-2011 models: 21-25 ft.-lb. (28.5-33.9 N•m).

15. Install a *new* O-ring (**Figure 122**) onto the end of the clutch hose.

16. Connect the clutch hose (**Figure 121**) onto the cover. Install the flare nut into the cover by hand until it bottoms. Do not cross thread the flare nut or scratch the cover. Tighten the clutch hose flare nut to:
   a. 2007 models: 80-115 in.-lb. (9-13 N•m).
   b. 2008-2011 models: 72-120 in.-lb. (8.1-13.6 N•m).

17. Bleed the clutch as described in *Clutch System Bleeding* (this chapter).

18. Test ride the motorcycle to ensure the clutch is operating correctly.

CLUTCH SYSTEM FLUSHING (SCREAMIN' EAGLE AND CVO MODELS)

When flushing the clutch system, use DOT 4 brake fluid as a flushing fluid. Flushing consists of pulling *new* brake fluid through the clutch system until the new fluid appears at the release cover bleed valve without the presence of any air bubbles. To flush the clutch system, follow one of the bleeding procedures described in this chapter.

CLUTCH SYSTEM DRAINING (SCREAMIN' EAGLE AND CVO MODELS)

To drain the system, follow one of the bleeding procedures described in this chapter, but do not add fluid to the reservoir. Bleed the system until all fluid has been removed from the reservoir and hydraulic lines.

CLUTCH SYSTEM BLEEDING (SCREAMIN' EAGLE AND CVO MODELS)

Vacuum Bleeding

This procedure uses a hydraulic brake bleeding kit (Mityvac part No. MV8000), or an equivalent, that is available from automotive or motorcycle supply stores.

1. Remove the dust cap from the bleed valve on the clutch release cover.

2. Place a clean shop cloth over the exhaust pipe and frame to protect it from accidental brake fluid spills.

3. Assemble the vacuum bleeder tool (**Figure 126**) according to its manufacturer's instructions. Secure it to the bleed valve.

4. Clean the top of the master cylinder of all debris.

5. Turn the handlebars to level the clutch master cylinder and remove the screws, reservoir cover and diaphragm.

6. Fill the reservoir almost to the top with DOT 4 brake fluid and reinstall the diaphragm and cover. Leave the cover in place during this procedure to prevent the entry of dirt.

NOTE
Carefully monitor the fluid level in the reservoir. It will drop quite rapidly. Stop often and check the brake fluid level. Keep the level 10 mm (3/8 in.) from the top of the reservoir so air will not be drawn into the system. If this occurs, the bleeding procedure must be repeated.

7. Operate the vacuum pump several times to create a vacuum in the line, and open the bleed valve. Brake fluid will be quickly drawn from the system and into the pump's reservoir. Tighten the bleed valve well before the master cylinder runs empty. To prevent air from being drawn through the master cylinder, add fluid frequently to maintain its level at the top of the reservoir.

8. Continue the bleeding process until the fluid drawn from the bleed valve is bubble-free. If bubbles are withdrawn with the brake fluid, more air is trapped in the line. Repeat the bleeding procedure, making sure to refill the master cylinder to prevent air from being drawn into the system.

9. When the brake fluid is free of bubbles, tighten the bleed valve as follows:
   a. 2007 models: 80-100 in-lb. (9.0-11.3 N•m).
   b. 2008-2011 models: 12-15 in.-lb. (1.4-1.7 N•m).

10. Remove the vacuum bleeder tool. Reinstall the bleed valve dust cap.

11. If necessary, add fluid to correct the level in the master cylinder reservoir. When topping off the clutch master cylinder, turn the handlebar until the reservoir is level; add fluid to the full level mark in the reservoir.

12. Reinstall the reservoir diaphragm and cover. Install the reservoir cover screws, and tighten them to 6-8 in.-lb. (0.7-0.9 N•m).

13. Test the feel of the clutch lever. It must be firm and offer the same resistance each time it's operated. If it feels spongy, it is likely that there is still air in the system and it must be bleed again. After bleeding the system, check for leaks and tighten all fittings and connections as necessary.

WARNING
Do not ride the motorcycle until the clutch lever is operating correctly with full hydraulic advantage.

14. Test ride the motorcycle slowly at first to make sure that the clutch is operating properly.

Manual Bleeding

NOTE
Before bleeding the brake, check that all hoses and lines are tight.

1. Remove the dust cap from the bleed valve on the clutch release cover.

2. Place a clean shop cloth over the exhaust pipe and frame to protect it from accidental brake fluid spills.

3. Connect a length of clear tubing to the bleed valve on the release cover. Place the other end of the tube into a clean container. Fill the container with enough fresh DOT 4 brake fluid to keep the end of the tube submerged. The tube must be long enough so that a loop can be made higher than the bleeder valve to prevent air from being drawn into the release cylinder during bleeding.

4. Clean the top of the clutch master cylinder of all debris.

5. Remove the screws securing the master cylinder top cover and remove the cover and the diaphragm.

6. Fill the reservoir almost to the top with DOT 4 brake fluid and reinstall the diaphragm and cover. Leave the cover in place during this procedure to prevent the entry of dirt.

NOTE
During this procedure, it is important to check the fluid level in the master cylinder reservoir often. If the reservoir runs dry, more air will enter the system.

7. Slowly apply the clutch lever several times. Hold the lever in the applied position and open the bleed valve about 1/2 turn. Allow the lever to travel to its limit. When the limit is reached, tighten the bleed valve and release the clutch lever. As the brake fluid enters the system, the level will drop in the master cylinder reservoir. Maintain the level at the top of the reservoir to prevent air from being drawn into the system.

8. Continue the bleeding process until the fluid emerging from the hose is completely free of air bubbles. If the fluid is being replaced, continue until the fluid emerging from the hose is clean.

NOTE
If bleeding is difficult, allowing the fluid to stabilize for a few hours. Repeat the bleeding procedure when the tiny bubbles in the system settle out.

9. Hold the lever in the applied position and tighten the bleed valve as follows:
   a. 2007 models: 80-100 in-lb. (9.0-11.3 N•m).
   b. 2008-2011 models: 12-15 in.-lb. (1.4-1.7 N•m).

10. If necessary, add fluid to correct the level in the master cylinder reservoir. When topping off the front master cylinder, turn the handlebar until the reservoir is level. Then, add fluid to the full level mark in the reservoir.

11. Reinstall the reservoir diaphragm and cover. Install the reservoir cover screws, and tighten them to 6-8 in.-lb. (0.7-0.9 N•m).

12. Test the feel of the clutch lever. It must be firm and offer the same resistance each time it's operated. If it feels spongy, it is likely that there is still air in the system and it must bleed it again. After bleeding the system check for leaks and tighten all fittings and connections as necessary.

WARNING
Do not ride the motorcycle until the clutch is operating correctly with full hydraulic advantage.

13. Test ride the motorcycle slowly at first to make sure that the clutch is operating properly.

Table 1 CLUTCH SPECIFICATIONS AND SPROCKET SIZES

Item	Specification
Clutch type	Wet, multi plate disc
Clutch lever free play	1/16-1/8 in. (1.6-3.2 mm)
Clutch screw adjustment	loosen 1/2 to 1 full turn after lightly seating
Clutch friction plate thickness service limit	0.143 in. (3.63 mm)
Clutch plain plate warpage service limit	0.006 in. (0.15 mm)
Clutch pushrod and release plate movement (Screamin' Eagle and CVO models)	0.065 in. (0.165 mm) minimum
Clutch sprocket	46 teeth
Compensating sprocket	34 teeth
Rear wheel sprocket	
2006 models	70 teeth (domestic), 68 (HDI)
2007-2008 models	66 teeth (domestic), 64 (HDI)
2009-2011 models	66 teeth
Transmission sprocket	32 teeth

Table 2 CLUTCH AND PRIMARY CHAINCASE TORQUE SPECIFICATIONS

Item	ft.-lb.	in.-lb.	N•m
Clutch hub nut	70-80	–	94.9-108.5
Clutch inspection cover Torx screws	–	84-108	9.5-12.2
Clutch lever clamp bolts	–	60-80	6.8-9.0
Clutch master cylinder (Screamin' Eagle and CVO models)			
Banjo bolt			
2007-2008 models	17-22	–	23.0-29.8
2009-2011 models	21-25	–	28.5-33.9
Clamp bolt	–	60-80	6.8-9.0
Reservoir cover screw	–	6-8	0.7-0.9
Clutch release cover (all models except Screamin' Eagle and CVO)			
Bolts	–	84-108	9.5-12.2
Clutch cable fitting			
2006-2007 models	–	36-60	4.1-6.8
2008-2011 models	–	90-120	10.2-13.6
Clutch release cover (Screamin' Eagle and CVO models)			
Long and short bolts	–	84-132	9.5-14.9
Clutch hose flare nut			
2007 models	–	80-115	9.0-13.0
2008-2011 models	–	72-120	8.1-13.6
Bleed valve			
2007 models	–	80-100	9.0-11.3
2008-2011 models	–	12-15	1.4-1.7
(continued)			

Table 2 CLUTCH AND PRIMARY CHAINCASE TORQUE SPECIFICATIONS (continued)

Item	ft.-lb.	in.-lb.	N•m
Compensating sprocket bolt			
2006-2008 models	155-165	–	210.1-223.7
2009 models		Refer to text	
Diaphragm spring retainer bolts	–	90-110	10.2-12.4
Handlebar switch housing			
screws	–	35-45	4.0-5.1
Primary chain tensioner bolts	15-19	–	20.3-25.8
Primary chaincase cover bolts	–	108-120	12.2-13.6
Primary chaincase housing bolts			
2006 models	15-19	–	20.3-25.8
2007-2011 models	25-27	–	33.9-36.6
Primary chaincase sleeve and bolt			
(FXDWG and FXDF models)	15-19	–	20.3-25.8
Transmission			
Sprocket nut	35	–	47.5
Lockplate screw	–	84-108	9.5-12.2

6

CHAPTER SEVEN

TRANSMISSION

This chapter covers procedures for the transmission, shift linkage and oil pan. All models are equipped with a six-speed transmission, which is separate from the engine. The transmission shaft assemblies and the shift assemblies can be serviced with the transmission case mounted in the frame.

Tool requirements are described in the procedures. Refer to **Table 10** in Chapter One for tool part numbers discussed in this chapter.

Specifications are in **Tables 1-4** at the end of this chapter.

> *NOTE*
> *On models with the optional security system, disarm system before disconnecting the battery or pulling the Maxi-Fuse so the alarm will not sound. Refer to **Turn Signal** and **Security Modules** in Chapter Nine.*

SHIFT ASSEMBLY

The external shift linkage, internal shift cam and shift arm components are shown in **Figure 1** and **Figure 2**.

If a shift problem is encountered, refer to the troubleshooting procedures in Chapter Two and eliminate all clutch and shift mechanism possibilities *before* considering transmission repairs. On all models except Screamin' Eagle and CVO, improper clutch adjustment (Chapter Three) is often a cause of poor shifting.

Shift Linkage Adjustment

The shift linkage assembly connects the transmission shift rod lever to the foot-operated shift levers. The shift linkage does not require adjustment unless the shift linkage is replaced or the transmission gears do not engage properly.

1. Disconnect the negative battery cable as described in Chapter Nine.
2. Loosen the two shift linkage rod locknuts (A, **Figure 3**).
3. Remove the acorn nut (B, **Figure 3**) and washers securing the shift linkage rod to the inner shift lever.
4. Turn the shift linkage rod (C, **Figure 3**) as necessary to change the linkage adjustment.
5. Reconnect the shift linkage rod to the shift rod lever and tighten the locknuts to 80-120 in.-lb. (9-13.6 N•m).
6. Reinstall the washers and acorn nut securing the shift linkage rod to the inner shift lever. Tighten the acorn nut to 96-144 in.-lb. (10.8-16.3 N•m).
7. Recheck the shifting. Readjust if necessary.
8. If proper shifting cannot be obtained by performing this adjustment, check the shift linkage for any interference problems. Then, check the shift linkage assembly for worn or damaged parts.

EXTERNAL SHIFT MECHANISM

Removal/Installation

Refer to **Figure 1** or **Figure 2**.

① **SHIFTER ASSEMBLY (ALL MODELS EXCEPT SCREAMIN' EAGLE AND CVO)**

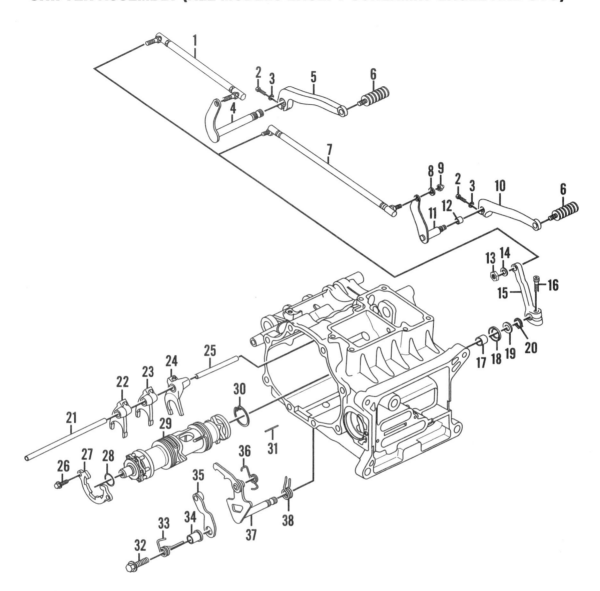

7

1. Shift rod (all models except FXDF, FXDWG)
2. Clamp bolt
3. Washer
4. Inner shift lever (all models except FXDF, FXDWG)
5. Outer shift lever (all models except FXDF, FXDWG)
6. Shift pad
7. Shift rod (FXDF, FXDWG models)
8. Washer
9. Acorn nut
10. Outer shift lever (FXDF, FXDWG models)

11. Inner shift lever (FXDF, FXDWG models)
12. Spacer
13. Nut
14. Washer
15. Shift shaft lever
16. Clamp bolt
17. Sleeve
18. Oil seal
19. Washer
20. Snap ring
21. Shift fork shaft (long)
22. 1st/2nd gear shift fork
23. 3rd/4th gear shift fork
24. 5th/6th gear shift fork

25. Shift fork shaft (short)
26. Bolt
27. Shift cam lockplate
28. Snap ring
29. Shift cam
30. Snap ring
31. Shift lever centering screw
32. Bolt
33. Spring
34. Sleeve
35. Detent lever
36. Return spring
37. Shift shaft/pawl assembly
38. Return spring

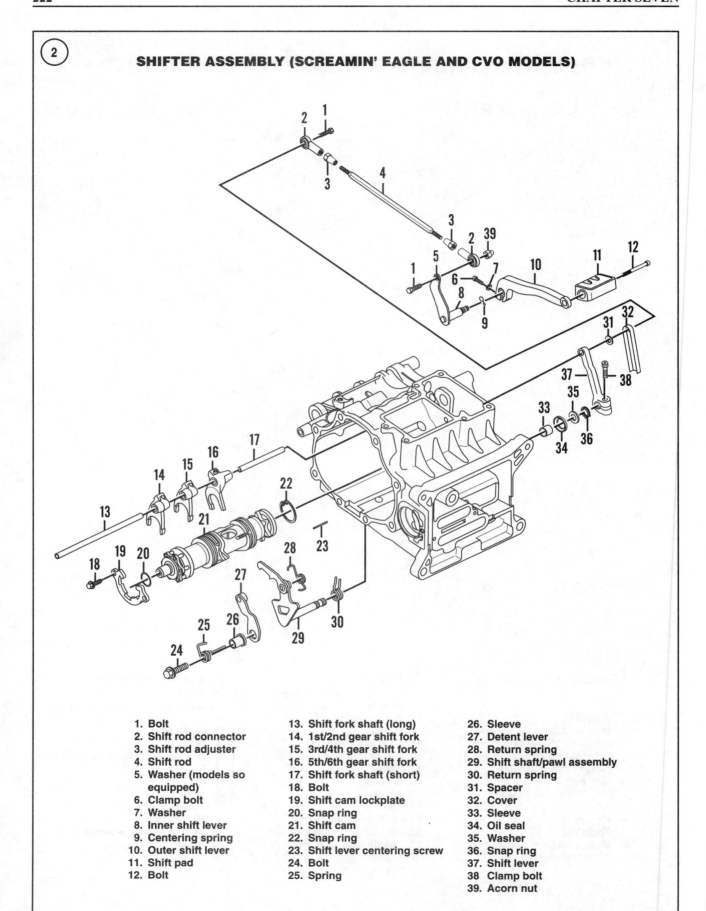

② SHIFTER ASSEMBLY (SCREAMIN' EAGLE AND CVO MODELS)

1. Bolt
2. Shift rod connector
3. Shift rod adjuster
4. Shift rod
5. Washer (models so equipped)
6. Clamp bolt
7. Washer
8. Inner shift lever
9. Centering spring
10. Outer shift lever
11. Shift pad
12. Bolt
13. Shift fork shaft (long)
14. 1st/2nd gear shift fork
15. 3rd/4th gear shift fork
16. 5th/6th gear shift fork
17. Shift fork shaft (short)
18. Bolt
19. Shift cam lockplate
20. Snap ring
21. Shift cam
22. Snap ring
23. Shift lever centering screw
24. Bolt
25. Spring
26. Sleeve
27. Detent lever
28. Return spring
29. Shift shaft/pawl assembly
30. Return spring
31. Spacer
32. Cover
33. Sleeve
34. Oil seal
35. Washer
36. Snap ring
37. Shift lever
38. Clamp bolt
39. Acorn nut

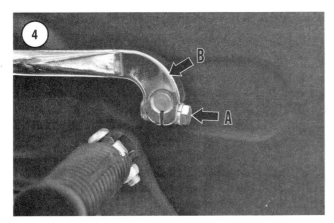

1. Disconnect the negative battery cable as described in Chapter Nine.

2. Make an alignment mark on the outer shift lever and the end of the inner shift lever shaft.

3. Remove the clamping bolt (A, **Figure 4**) and remove the outer shift lever (B) from the inner shift lever shaft.

4. Remove the acorn nut (A, **Figure 5**) and washers securing the shift linkage rod to the inner shift lever.

5. Remove the rod (B, **Figure 5**) from the inner shift lever.

6. Remove the nut and washer (A, **Figure 6**) securing the shift rod to the shift lever, and remove the shift rod (B).

7. Install by reversing the removal steps. Tighten the fasteners as follows:

    a. Acorn nut: 96-144 in.-lb/ (10.8-16.3 N•m).

    b. Nut: 80-120 in.lb. (9.0-13.6 N•m).

TRANSMISSION TOP COVER

The transmission top cover assembly can be serviced with the transmission installed in the frame.

Removal/Installation

1. Disarm the optional TSSM/HFSM security system and disconnect the negative battery cable as described in Chapter Nine.

2. Remove the exhaust system as described in Chapter Four.

3. Disconnect the vent hose (**Figure 7**) from the top cover fitting.

4. Remove the six bolts (A, **Figure 8**) securing the transmission cover to the transmission case. Remove the top cover (B, **Figure 8**) and the gasket.

5. Remove any gasket residue from the transmission cover and transmission case gasket surfaces.

6. Install a *new* gasket onto the transmission case.

7. Install the transmission top cover, the cover bolts and washers. Using a crossing pattern, tighten the bolts to 84-132 in.-lb. (9.5-14.9 N•m).

8. Reconnect the vent hose (**Figure 7**) to the cover fitting.

9. Install the exhaust system as described in Chapter Four.

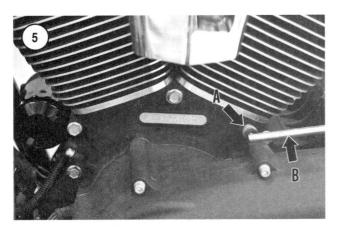

10. Connect the negative battery cable as described in Chapter Nine.

SHIFT ARM ASSEMBLY

Removal/Disassembly

Refer to **Figure 9**.

1. Remove the transmission side door assembly as described in this chapter.

2. Make an alignment mark on the shift pawl shaft (A, **Figure 10**) that relates to the split part (B) of the shift rod lever.

3. Remove the clamp bolt (C, **Figure 10**) and remove the rear shift rod lever (D) from the shift pawl shaft.

4. Remove the snap ring (A, **Figure 11**) and washer (B) from the shift lever shaft.

5. Withdraw the shift shaft, sleeve and return spring as an assembly (A, **Figure 12**) from the inside of the transmission case.

6. Remove the shift shaft oil seal from the transmission case. Discard the seal and snap ring (A, **Figure 11**).

Assembly

1. Check that the sleeve is still in place in the transmission case.

2. Slide the shift shaft spring over the shift shaft and against its body. Make sure the arms (A, **Figure 13**) of the spring straddle the tab on the shift shaft body.

3. If removed, install the shift pawl spring.

4. Install the shift shaft/pawl assembly (A, **Figure 12**) into the transmission case so the arms of the shift shaft spring straddle the centering screw (B) in the case.

5. Carefully install a new oil seal over the shift shaft and into the transmission case. Make sure the shift shaft splines do not damage the seal.

6. Install washer (B, **Figure 11**) and a new snap ring (A) onto the shaft. Make sure the snap ring is correctly seated in the shaft.

Installation

1. Install the shift pawl assembly into the transmission case.

2. Align the return spring with the centering screw in transmission case.

3. Refer to the alignment marks made during removal and install the shift rod lever onto the shift pawl shaft. Push it on until the bolt hole aligns with the shift rod lever groove.

4. Install the clamp bolt and tighten to 18-22 ft.-lb. (24-30 N•m).

5. Install the transmission side door assembly as described in this chapter.

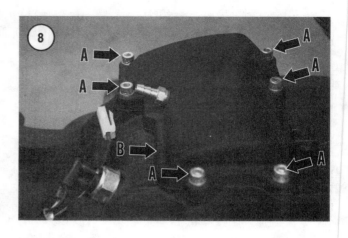

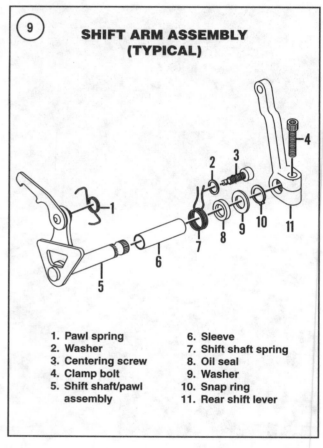

SHIFT ARM ASSEMBLY (TYPICAL)

1. Pawl spring
2. Washer
3. Centering screw
4. Clamp bolt
5. Shift shaft/pawl assembly
6. Sleeve
7. Shift shaft spring
8. Oil seal
9. Washer
10. Snap ring
11. Rear shift lever

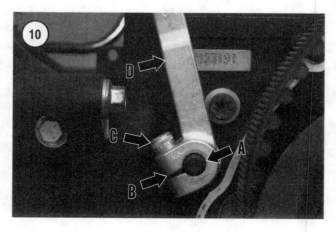

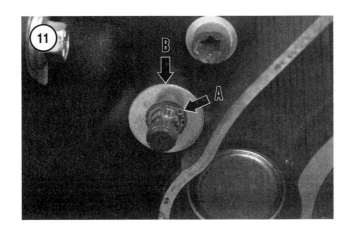

Inspection

Replace any part that is worn or damaged.

1. Check the shift pawl (B, **Figure 13**) for wear. Replace the shift shaft/pawl assembly if the pawl is damaged.

2. Check the shift shaft spring (A, **Figure 13**) and pawl spring (C) for fatigue or damage.

3. Check the shift shaft for wear or damage. Make sure the end splines (D, **Figure 13**) are in good condition.

4. Check the rear shift lever (D, **Figure 10**) for wear or damage. Make sure the internal splines are in good condition.

SHIFT FORKS AND SHIFT CAM

A 6-speed shift fork shaft remover (JIMS part No. 985), a twist-type screw extractor, or an equivalent tool, is needed for this procedure.

Refer to **Figure 1** or **Figure 2**.

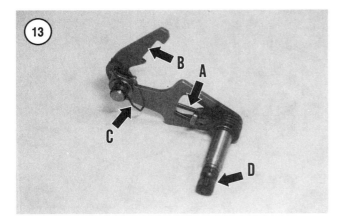

Removal

1. Remove the transmission side door assembly as described in this chapter.

2. If still installed, remove the clutch push rod from the mainshaft tunnel.

> *CAUTION*
> *Use a waterproof felt-tip pen or scribe, mark the installed position of each shift fork (U, M, or L, **Figure 14**) as it sits in the transmission. Each shift fork is unique and must be reinstalled in the groove of a particular dog ring. Also mark the top of the shift fork shafts (L or S, **Figure 14**) so they can be reinstalled with the original orientation.*

3. Carefully install the shift fork remover tool (A, **Figure 15**) and remove the short shift fork (B).

4. Remove the middle 3rd/4th gear shift fork (A, **Figure 16**) and the lower 1st/2nd shift fork (B).

5. Carefully install the shift fork remover tool (A, **Figure 17**), and remove the long shift fork (B).

6. Remove the upper 5th/6th gear shift fork (**Figure 18**).

7

7. Remove the bolts (**Figure 19**) securing the shift cam lock plate and remove the shift cam lock plate (**Figure 20**). Discard the bolts.

8. Use a flat-bladed screwdriver to gently push the detent arm (A, **Figure 21**) away from the shift cam.

9. Pull straight up and withdraw the shift cam (B, **Figure 21**) and bearing from the bore in transmission door.

10. If necessary, remove the detent arm assembly (A, **Figure 22**) by performing the following:

   a. Before removal, note how the lower arm of the detent spring engages the boss (B, **Figure 22**) in the side door. The assembly must be reinstalled so this arm engages the correct boss.

   b. Remove the detent arm bolt (C, **Figure 22**) and remove the detent arm (A). Note how the upper arm of the detent spring (D, **Figure 22**) passes through the hole in the detent arm.

   c. Remove the sleeve and the detent spring. Discard the bolt.

11. Inspect all parts as described in this section.

Installation

1. Coat all bearing and sliding surfaces with transmission oil.

2. If removed, install the detent arm assembly (A, **Figure 22**) by performing the following:

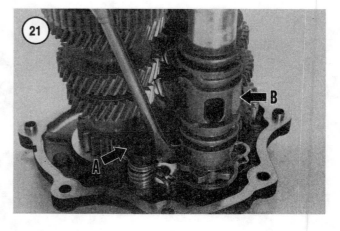

a. Assemble the detent arm with a *new* bolt (C, **Figure 22**). Make sure the detent spring's upper arm engages the hole in the detent arm. Install the sleeve into the detent spring.

b. Lower the assembly into the side door so the spring's lower arm engages the boss (B, **Figure 22**) noted during removal.

c. Install the detent arm bolt (C, **Figure 22**), and tighten it to 120-150 in.-lb. (13.6-17.0 N•m).

3. Move the detent arm out of the way, and hold it in this position.

4. Lower the shift cam (A, **Figure 23**) so its bearing engages the bore (B) in transmission side door. Carefully push straight down on the shift cam (B, **Figure 21**) until the bearing bottoms. Once the shift cam is correctly installed, release the detent arm onto the shift cam.

5. Install the shift cam lock plate (**Figure 20**), and then install *new* lock plate bolts. Tighten the shift cam lock plate bolts (**Figure 19**) to 57-63 in.-lb. (6.4-7.1 N•m).

6. Install the upper 5th/6th gear shift fork (**Figure 18**) into the slot of the dog ring atop mainshaft 5th gear.

7. Move the shift fork into alignment with the shift-fork-shaft receptacle in the side door. Position the long shift fork shaft (A, **Figure 24**) with the marked end facing up, and install it through the shift fork (B) and into the shaft receptacle in the side door (**Figure 25**). Tap the shaft in until it bottoms in the receptacle.

8. Install the lower 1st/2nd shift fork (B, **Figure 16**) into slot of the dog ring between countershaft 1st and 2nd gear.

9. Install the middle 3rd/4th shift fork (A, **Figure 16**) into slot of the dog ring between countershaft 3rd and 4th gear.

10. Move the shift forks so they align with the shift-fork-shaft boss in the side door. Position the short shift fork shaft (A, **Figure 26**) with the marked end facing up, and install it through both shift forks (B) and into the shaft receptacle (C) in the side door. Tap the shaft in until it bottoms in the receptacle.

11. The clutch pushrod will be installed in the mainshaft channel once the transmission side door assembly is installed in the transmission case.

7

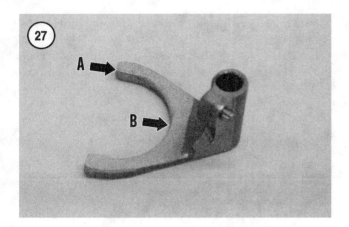

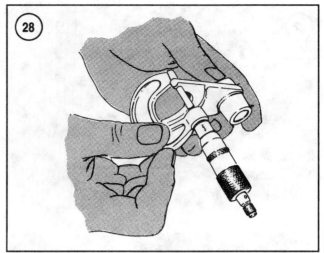

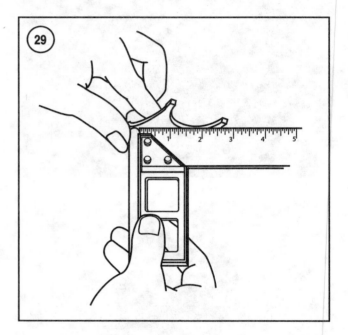

Inspection

Replace any part that is worn, damaged or out of specification.

1. Inspect each shift fork (A, **Figure 27**) for excessive wear or damage. Replace worn or damaged shift forks as required.

2. Measure the thickness of each shift fork finger (**Figure 28**) where it contacts the dog ring groove. Replace the shift fork if any finger is worn to the service limit (**Table 2**).

3. Inspect the shift forks for any arc-shaped wear or burn marks (B, **Figure 27**).

4. Place each shift fork along the side of a square (**Figure 29**) and check for bending.

5. Roll each shift fork shaft on a flat surface and check for bending.

6. Install each shift fork onto its shaft and slide it back and forth (**Figure 30**). Each shift fork must slide smoothly with no binding or tight spots.

7. Check the ramp (A, **Figure 31**) and the pins (B) on the shift cam for wear or damage.

8. Inspect the shift cam grooves (C, **Figure 31**) for wear or roughness.

9. Check that the bearing (D, **Figure 31**) is tight on the end of shift cam. Turn the bearing by hand. It must rotate freely with no binding. The bearing cannot be replaced separately.

10. Make sure the roller (A, **Figure 32**) on the detent arm turns freely.

11. Inspect the sleeve (B, **Figure 32**) for wear or roughness.

12. Inspect the detent spring (C, **Figure 32**) for cracks or other signs of fatigue.

TRANSMISSION SIDE DOOR ASSEMBLY

The transmission side door assembly includes the side door, mainshaft, countershaft, shift forks and shift cam. The transmission side door assembly can be serviced with the transmission case installed in the frame.

Tools

The following tools, or their equivalents, are used during side door assembly removal/installation or disassembly/assembly:

1. A mainshaft bearing race puller and installation tool (JIMS part No. 34902-84 or H-D part No. HD-34902-C).

2. A 6-speed main drive gear installer (JIMS part No. 981).

3. A 6-speed transmission side door puller (JIMS part No. 984).

4. A 6-speed mainshaft pulley nut socket (JIMS part No. 989).

Removal

Refer to **Figure 33**.

1. Remove the exhaust system as described in Chapter Four.

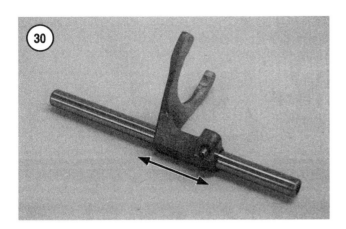

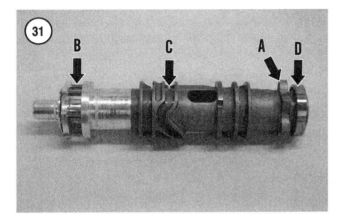

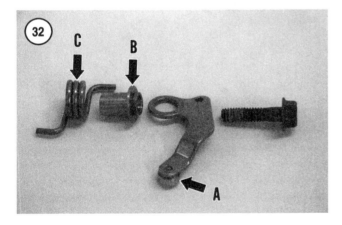

8. Remove the bearing inner race (B, **Figure 37**) from the mainshaft as follows:

   a. Attach the mainshaft bearing race puller and installation tool (A, **Figure 38**) against the inner bearing race (B) following the tool manufacturer's instructions.

   b. Tighten the puller bolt and withdraw the inner race (B, **Figure 38**) from the mainshaft.

   c. Remove the tool and the inner race.

9. Remove the transmission top cover as described in this chapter.

10. Lift the shift pawl from the shift cam pins, and set it onto the top cover gasket flange (**Figure 39**).

11. If the transmission gear assemblies will be removed from the side door, perform the following:

   a. Turn the transmission by hand and shift the transmission into 6th gear to keep the gears from rotating.

   b. Loosen, but do not remove, the countershaft (A, **Figure 40**) and mainshaft (B) locknuts.

12. If the main drive gear is going to be removed, remove the transmission drive sprocket as described in this chapter.

NOTE
*There are two different lengths of side door bolts. The two longer (C, **Figure 40**) bolts are located in the bottom two holes of the side door.*

13. Using a crossing pattern, evenly loosen the side door bolts (C and D, **Figure 40**), and remove them.

CAUTION
When removing the transmission side door, do not tap against the mainshaft from the opposite side. This will damage the side door bearings.

14A. Install the 6-speed transmission door remover (**Figure 41**) onto the side door following the tool manufacturer's instructions. Tighten the outside screws one-half turn at a time, alternating from side-to-side until the side door releases from the transmission case. Remove the tool.

14B. If the door remover is not available, use a soft-face mallet, and carefully tap against the transmission side door to loosen its seal against the transmission case. If necessary, insert a large, flat-bladed screw driver into the pry points (**Figure 42**) and work the door (**Figure 43**) loose.

15. Slowly withdraw the transmission side door and the transmission assemblies (**Figure 44**) from the transmission case, and remove it. Do not loose the dowels behind the side door.

16. Remove and discard the transmission side door gasket.

17. If necessary, service the side door and transmission assembly as described in *Transmission Shafts* (this chapter).

2. Drain the transmission oil and the primary chaincase oil as described in Chapter Three.

3. Remove the transmission filler plug/dipstick (**Figure 34**). If left in place it will interfere with the removal of the transmission side door assembly.

4. Remove the primary chaincase housing and the clutch release cover as described in Chapter Six.

5. On all models except Screamin' Eagles and CVO, remove the oil slinger (**Figure 35**) from the mainshaft.

6. Withdraw the clutch pushrod (**Figure 36**).

7. Tape the clutch splines (A, **Figure 37**) on the mainshaft so they will not damage the needle bearings in the main drive gear.

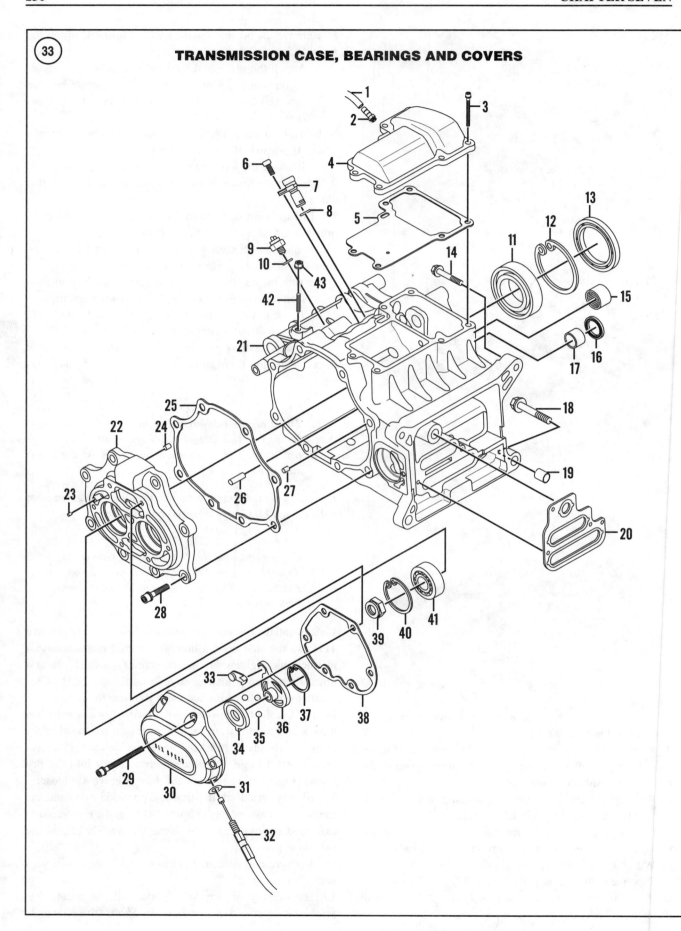

33

TRANSMISSION CASE, BEARINGS AND COVERS

1. Breather hose
2. Fitting
3. Bolt
4. Top cover
5. Gasket
6. Bolt
7. Vehicle speed sensor (VSS)
8. O-ring
9. Neutral indicator switch
10. O-ring
11. Oil seal (mainshaft)
12. Snap ring
13. Oil seal
14. Bolt (short)
15. Needle bearing
16. Oil seal
17. Sleeve
18. Bolt (long)
19. Dowel pin
20. Gasket
21. Transmission case
22. Side door
23. Locating pin
24. Locating pin
25. Gasket
26. Locating pin
26. Bushing
27. Locating dowel
28. Bolt
29. Bolt
30. Clutch release cover
31. O-ring
32. Clutch cable or hydraulic hose
33. Coupling*
34. Outer ramp*
35. Ball (3)*
36. Inner ramp*
37. Snap ring*
38. Gasket
39. Locknut (transmission shafts)
40. Snap ring
41. Bearing
42. Ground stud
43. Flange nut

*Items 33-37 not included on Screamin'
Eagle or CVO model.

7

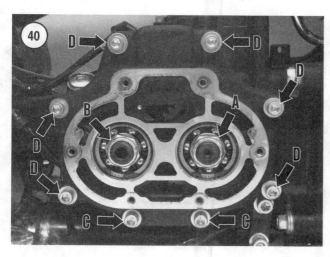

Installation

1. If the main drive gear was removed, install it as described in this chapter.

2. Remove all residue from gasket mating surfaces of the side door and transmission case.

3. If removed, install the dowels. Then, install a *new* side-door gasket onto the transmission case.

4. Wrap the clutch splines on the mainshaft (A, **Figure 37**) with tape to protect the main drive gear needle bearings and oil seal during installation.

5. Apply clean transmission oil to the following:

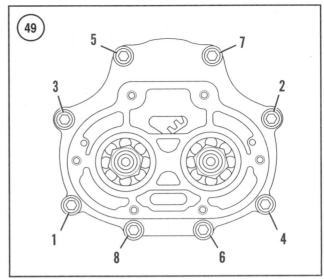

a. Main drive gear small oil seal (A, **Figure 45**), outer needle bearing (B) and inner needle bearing (A, **Figure 46**).

b. Countershaft needle bearings (B, **Figure 46**).

c. The journals on the mainshaft (A, **Figure 47**), countershaft (B), and shift cam (C).

d. The end of the long shift fork shaft (D, **Figure 47**).

6. Slowly and carefully slide the side door assembly into the transmission case (**Figure 44**) so the mainshaft passes through the main drive gear needle bearings (A, **Figure 46**), the countershaft seats in its needle bearing (B, **Figure 46**), the shift cam seats in its transmission case receptacle (A, **Figure 48**) and the long shift fork shaft sits in its receptacle (B, **Figure 48**). Check all of these items if the side door does not seat directly against the transmission case.

NOTE
*There are two different length side door bolts. The two longer bolts (C, **Figure 40**) are located in the bottom two holes of the side door.*

7. Install the two longer side door bolts and captive washers and finger-tighten the bolts. Install the remaining six shorter bolts (D, **Figure 40**), and finger-tighten them. Following the sequence shown in **Figure 49**, evenly tighten the transmission side door bolts to 13-18 ft.-lb. (17.6-24.4 N•m).

8. If the main drive gear was removed, install the transmission drive sprocket as described in this chapter.

9. If the transmission gear assemblies were removed from the side door, perform the following:

a. Turn the transmission by hand and shift the transmission into 6th gear to keep the gears from turning.

b. Tighten the countershaft (A, **Figure 40**) and mainshaft (B) locknuts to 45-55 ft.-lb. (61.074.6 N•m) on 2006-2008 models, or 55-65 ft.-lb. (74.6-88.1 N•m) on 2009-2011 models.

10. Install the clutch pushrod (**Figure 36**) into the mainshaft.

11. On all models except Screamin' Eagle and CVO, install the oil slinger assembly (**Figure 35**) into the mainshaft.

12. Move the shift pawl forward and lower the free end down onto engagement with the shift cam pins.

13. Install the transmission top cover as described in this chapter.

14. Install the mainshaft bearing inner race (A, **Figure 37**) onto the mainshaft by performing the following:

   a. Assemble the same tool set used for bearing inner race removal with the proper attachment recommended by the tool manufacturer.

   b. Apply clean oil to the mainshaft shaft bearing surface, shaft threads and to the inner surface of the inner race.

   c. Position the bearing inner race with the chamfered end goes on first. Slide the bearing inner race onto the mainshaft until it stops prior to being pressed on.

   d. Install the extension shaft (A, **Figure 50**) onto the mainshaft.

   e. Place the pusher tube (B, **Figure 50**) over the extension shaft, along with the two flat (C) washers and nut (D).

CAUTION
Install the inner bearing race to the dimension listed. Doing so aligns the race with the bearing outer race installed in the primary chaincase. Installing the wrong race or installing it incorrectly will damage the bearing and race assembly.

   f. Hold the extension shaft (A, **Figure 50**) and tighten the nut (D) to press the bearing inner race onto the mainshaft. Install the race so that its inside edge is 0.100-0.125 in. (2.540-3.180 mm) away from the main drive gear.

   g. Remove the tools.

15. Install the primary chaincase housing, primary drive and clutch release cover as described in Chapter Six.

16. Install the drain plugs, and add oil to the transmission and to the primary chaincase as described in Chapter Three.

17. Install the transmission filler plug/dipstick (**Figure 34**).

18. Install the exhaust system as described in Chapter Four.

19. Test-ride the motorcycle slowly and check for proper transmission operation.

TRANSMISSION SHAFTS

The snap rings are very difficult to loosen and remove. Heavy-duty retaining ring pliers (H-D part No. J-5586), or an equivalent, are recommended for this procedure.

Refer to **Figure 51**.

CAUTION
*The needle bearings on the mainshaft and countershaft are split bearings (**Figure 52**) and must be opened during removal. Since*

this weakens the plastic cage, discard all removed needle bearings. They must be replaced during assembly.

Mainshaft Disassembly

First, second, third and forth gears are an integral part of the mainshaft assembly and cannot be replaced separately. If any one of these is damaged, the mainshaft must be replaced.

1. Remove the transmission side door assembly, the shift forks and the shift cam as described in this chapter.

2. If still in place, remove the dowels (A, **Figure 53**) from the inboard side of the side door.

3. Remove the locknut (A, **Figure 54**) from the right end of the mainshaft. If the countershaft will also be serviced, remove the locknut from the countershaft (B, **Figure 54**).

4. Remove the snap ring (**Figure 55**) from the left end of the mainshaft.

5. Slide the dog ring (A, **Figure 56**) and its guide hub (B) off the mainshaft.

6. Remove fifth gear (A, **Figure 57**).

7. Remove the fifth-gear needle bearing (**Figure 58**).

8. Place the transmission assembly on the hydraulic press with the side door (A, **Figure 59**) facing up. Make sure the side door lies flat on the press bed.

CAUTION
Do not apply pressure on the bearing inner race as the bearing and/or side door will be damaged.

9. Place an appropriate size mandrel or socket (B, **Figure 59**) onto the end of the mainshaft.

10. Hold the lower end of the mainshaft assembly, and slowly press the assembly out of the side door bearing. Carefully guide the mainshaft gears past the countershaft gears.

11. If the countershaft also requires service, remove it as described in *Countershaft Disassembly* (this section).

NOTE
The side door bearing should be replaced whenever the shaft(s) is removed.

51

TRANSMISSION

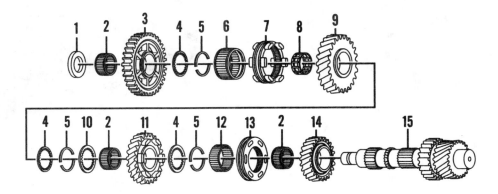

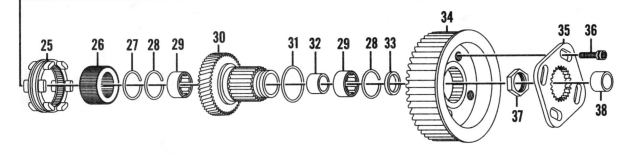

7

1. Spacer
2. Needle bearing
3. Countershaft first gear
4. Lock ring
5. Securing segment
6. Dog-ring guide hub
7. Dog ring
8. Needle bearing
9. Countershaft second gear
10. Splined washer
11. Countershaft third gear
12. Dog-ring guide hub
13. Dog ring, slotted
14. Countershaft fourth gear
15. Countershaft
16. Snap ring (all models except Screamin' Eagle and CVO)
17. Thrust bearing race (all models except Screamin' Eagle and CVO)
18. Thrust bearing (all models except Screamin' Eagle and CVO)

19. Thrust bearing race (all models except Screamin' Eagle and CVO)
20. Oil slinger (all models except Screamin' Eagle and CVO)
21. Locknut
22. Mainshaft
23. Needle bearing (split bearing)
24. Mainshaft fifth gear
25. Dog ring
26. Dog-ring guide hub
27. Snap ring
28. Snap ring
29. Needle bearing
30. Main drive gear
31. O-ring
32. Spacer
33. Oil seal
34. Transmission drive sprocket
35. Lockplate
36. Lockplate bolt
37. Sprocket nut
38. Mainshaft bearing inner race

12. Replace the side door bearing as described in this chapter.

13. Inspect all parts (**Figure 60**) as described in this section.

Mainshaft Assembly

> *CAUTION*
> *Install a **new** snap ring to ensure proper gear alignment and engagement. Never re-install a snap ring that has been removed since it has become distorted and weakened and may fail. Make sure the **new** snap ring is correctly seated in its respective shaft groove.*

1. If the countershaft was serviced, install it into the side door as described in *Countershaft Assembly* (this section).

2. Apply a light coat of clean transmission oil to the side door bearing inner race and to the mainshaft bearing surface.

3. Place the mainshaft on the press plate so it is supported by fourth gear.

4. Place the side door and countershaft assembly next to the mainshaft, and align both transmission shaft assemblies (A, **Figure 61**).

5. Position the countershaft so it clears the press bed. Have an assistant secure both shaft assemblies in this position.

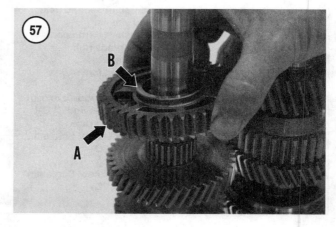

CAUTION
*Failure to keep the dog ring (A, **Figure 62**) engaged with countershaft third gear (B) will push the shafts out of alignment and cause damage to the bearings and gears on both shafts. Do **not** press the side door onto the mainshaft while this dog ring engages countershaft fourth gear.*

6. Have the assistant lift the countershaft dog ring (A, **Figure 62**) up so it is fully engaged with countershaft third gear (B) during the following steps.

7. Place a properly-sized mandrel or socket onto the side door bearing inner race (B, **Figure 61**). The outer diameter of the mandrel or socket must rest only on the inner race of the side door bearing.

8. Slowly press the side door bearing onto the mainshaft until the bearing inner race contacts mainshaft first gear. The gear must contact the bearing inner race to ensure correct alignment between both shaft assemblies.

9. Release ram pressure, and remove the side door assembly from the press bed.

10. Slowly rotate both shaft assemblies within the side door (**Figure 63**) to ensure the gears are aligned correctly. Do not spin too hard as the locknuts are not in place.

11. Install a *new* needle bearing (**Figure 58**) onto the mainshaft. Make sure it is seated correctly on the shaft.

12. Position mainshaft fifth gear (A, **Figure 57**) with the dog ring engagement slots (B) going on last. Then, install fifth gear.

13. Position the guide hub (**Figure 64**) with the counterbored end going on first and facing fifth gear. Install the guide hub with the flat side facing out.

14. Install the dog ring (A, **Figure 56**) onto fifth gear and make sure it is correctly seated.

15. Install a *new* snap ring (**Figure 55**). Make sure it is seated correctly in the mainshaft groove.

16. Refer to B, **Figure 53** to ensure the correct placement of the gears. Also check that the gears mesh properly with an adjoining gear where applicable. This is the last opportunity to check the shaft assemblies before they are installed into the transmission case. Make sure they are correctly assembled.

> *CAUTION*
> *The transmission shafts must be installed in the transmission case when the shaft locknuts are tightened so the case bosses can keep the shafts properly aligned. The side door bearings can be damaged if the locknuts are tightened while the assembly is on the bench.*

17. If removed, install the dowels (A, **Figure 53**) onto the inboard side of the side door.

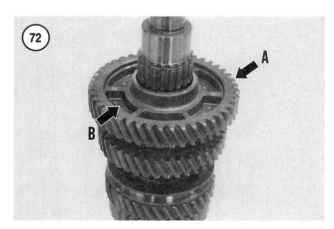

18. Use the dog rings to lock the two shafts together, and temporarily install the side door and transmission assembly into the transmission case.

19. Install a *new* locknut onto the mainshaft (A, **Figure 65**) and the countershaft (B).

20. Tighten each locknut (**Figure 66**) to the following specification:
    a. 2006-2008 models: 45-55 ft.-lb. (61.0-74.6 N•m).
    b. 2009-2011 models: 55-65 ft.-lb. (74.6-88.2 N•m).

21. Remove the side door assembly, and install the shift forks and the shift cam as described in this chapter.

22. Install the transmission side door assembly as described in this chapter.

Countershaft Disassembly

Fifth and sixth gears are an integral part of the countershaft assembly and cannot be replaced separately. If either of these gears is damaged, the countershaft must be replaced.

1. Remove the transmission side door assembly, shift forks and shift cam as described in this chapter.

2. Press the mainshaft from the side door as described in *Mainshaft Disassembly* (this section).

3. Remove the locknut (B, **Figure 54**) from the right side of the countershaft.

4. Place the transmission assembly in the hydraulic press with the side door (A, **Figure 67**) facing up. Make sure the side door lies flat on the press bed.

CAUTION
Do not apply pressure to the bearing inner race as the bearing and/or side door will be damaged.

5. Place an appropriate size mandrel or socket (B, **Figure 67**) onto the end of the countershaft.

6. Secure the lower end of the countershaft assembly, and slowly press the assembly out of the side door bearing.

7. Remove the side door and countershaft assembly from the press bed.

8. Remove the spacer (A, **Figure 68**) and first gear (B) from the side door end of the countershaft.

9. Remove the needle bearing (A, **Figure 69**), the lock ring (B), and the dog ring (C).

10. Remove both securing segments (**Figure 70**) from with the guide hub counter bore.

11. Remove the guide hub (A, **Figure 71**).

12. Remove second gear (A, **Figure 72**) and its needle bearing (**Figure 73**) from the shaft.

13. Remove the lock ring (**Figure 74**), both securing segments (**Figure 75**), and the splined washer (**Figure 76**) from the countershaft

14. Remove third gear (A, **Figure 77**) and its needle bearing (**Figure 78**) from the countershaft.

15. Remove the lock ring (**Figure 79**).

16. Remove both securing segments (**Figure 80**) and the slotted dog ring (**Figure 81**) from the shaft.

17. Remove the guide hub (A, **Figure 82**) and fourth gear (B).

18. Remove fourth gear needle bearing (**Figure 83**).

19. Replace the side door bearings as described in this chapter.

20. Inspect all parts (**Figure 84**) as described in this section.

Countershaft Assembly

CAUTION
When installing lock rings next to securing segments, make sure the shouldered side of the lock ring faces and surrounds the securing segments. The parts are properly installed when the securing segments are nested within the lock ring (Figure 85).

1. Apply a light coat of clean transmission oil to all sliding surfaces and needle bearings.

2. Install a *new* needle bearing (**Figure 83**). Make sure it is seated correctly on the shaft.

3. Position countershaft fourth gear with the shift dogs (C, **Figure 82**) facing up, and then install fourth gear (B).

4. Install the guide hub (A, **Figure 82**) and the slotted dog ring (**Figure 81**).

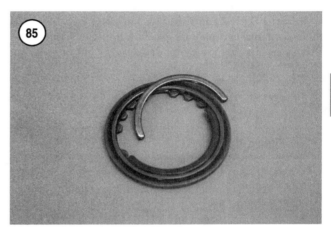

7

5. Install both securing segments (**Figure 80**) so their straight sides faces the guide hub. Each segment must be completely seated in the shaft groove.

6. Install the lock ring (**Figure 79**) so its shouldered side faces and surrounds the securing segments.

7. Install a *new* needle bearing (**Figure 78**). Make sure it is seated correctly on the shaft.

8. Position countershaft third gear so the shouldered side (B, **Figure 77**) faces out, and install third gear (A).

9. Install the splined washer (**Figure 76**).

10. Seat both securing segments (**Figure 75**) in the shaft groove so their straight sides face the splined washer.

11. Install the lock ring (**Figure 74**) so it's shouldered side faces and surrounds the securing segments.

12. Install a *new* needle bearing (**Figure 73**). Make sure it is seated correctly on the shaft.

13. Position second gear so the dog ring engagement slots (B, **Figure 72**) face out and then install second gear (A).

14. Position the guide hub with the recessed side facing out (B, **Figure 71**) and install the guide hub (A).

15. Seat both securing segments (**Figure 70**) in the guide hub so their straight sides face the hub.

16. Install the dog ring (**Figure 86**) onto the guide hub (B).

17. Install the lock ring (B, **Figure 69**) so its shouldered side faces and surrounds the securing segments.

18. Install a *new* needle bearing (A, **Figure 69**). Make sure it is seated correctly on the shaft.

19. Position countershaft first gear so its engagement slots face the dog ring and install countershaft first gear (B, **Figure 68**).

20. Install the spacer (A, **Figure 68**).

21. Refer to **Figure 87** to ensure all gears are in the correct location.

Transmission Inspection

Maintain the alignment of the transmission components when cleaning and inspecting the individual parts in the following section. To prevent mixing parts, work on only one shaft at a time.

Refer to **Table 2** and **Table 3** when inspecting the service clearance and end play of the indicated gears and shafts. Replace parts that are worn, damaged or out of specification.

1. Clean and dry the shaft assemblies.

2. Inspect the mainshaft (**Figure 88**) and countershaft (**Figure 89**) for:

   a. Worn or damages splines (A, **Figure 88** and B, **Figure 89**).

   b. Excessively worn or damaged bearing surfaces (A, **Figure 89**).

   c. Cracked or rounded-off securing segment grooves (C, **Figure 89**).

   d. Worn or damaged threads (B, **Figure 88**).

3. Check each gear for excessive wear, burrs, pitting, or chipped or missing teeth (A, **Figure 90**).

4. Check the gear bore bushing surface (B, **Figure 90**) for wear, cracks or other damage.

5. To check gears for wear, install them on their correct shaft and in the original operating position. If necessary, use the old snap rings to secure them in place. Then, spin the gear by hand. The gear should turn smoothly. A rough turning gear indicates heat damage: check for a dark, bluish color or galling on the operating surfaces. Rocking indicates excessive wear, either to the gear or shaft or both.

6. Check for excessive wear or damage on the inner splines (A, **Figure 91**) of the dog rings and on the inner (B) and outer (C) splines of the guide hubs.

7. To check the dog rings and guide hubs, install them onto their correct shaft and in their original operating position. They should slide back and fourth without any binding or excessive play.

8. Check the shift fork groove (A, **Figure 92**) on each dog ring for wear or damage.

9. Check the dogs on the gears (**Figure 93**) and dog rings (D, **Figure 91**) for excessive wear, rounding, cracks or other damage. When wear is noticeable, make sure it is consistent on each gear dog. If one dog is worn more than the others, the others will be overstressed during operation and will eventually crack and fail. Check engaging gears as described in this section.

10. Check each engagement slot in the gears (C, **Figure 90**) and slotted dog ring (B, **Figure 92**) for cracks, round-

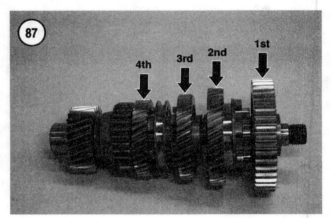

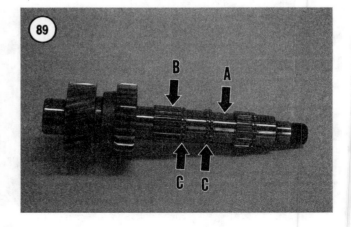

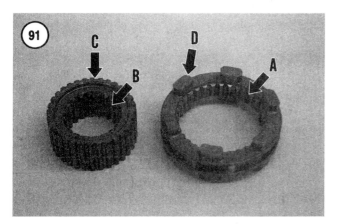

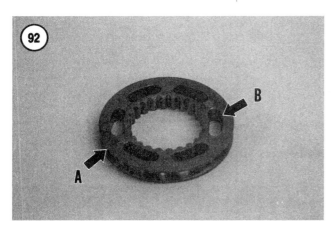

ing and other damage. Check engaging gears as described in this section.

> *NOTE*
> *If there is excessive or uneven wear to the gear engagement dogs, check the shift forks carefully for bending and other damage. Refer to* **Shift Assembly** *in this chapter.*

> *NOTE*
> *Replace defective gears along with their mating gears, though they may not show as much wear or damage.*

11. Check engaging gears by installing the two gears on their respective shaft and in their original operating position. Mesh the gears together. Twist one gear against the other, and then check the dog engagement. Then, reverse the thrust load to check in the other operating position. Make sure the engagement in both directions is positive and without any slippage. Check that there is equal engagement across all of the engagement dogs.

12. Replace all of the snap rings during re-assembly. In addition, check the splined washers for any burn marks, scoring or cracks. Replace as necessary.

13. Check the spacers for wear or damage.

SIDE DOOR BEARINGS

Replacement

The side door bearings (**Figure 94**) are pressed into place and secured with a snap ring. They can be removed and installed using a transmission door bearing remover and installer set (JIMS part No. 1078), or an equivalent. If this tool set (**Figure 95**) is not available, a press is required.

Replace the side door bearings whenever the shafts have been removed.

1. Clean the side door and bearings in solvent, and dry them with compressed air.

2. Remove each snap ring (**Figure 96**) from the outer surface of the side door.

3A. If the remover/installer set is used, follow the tool manufacturer's instructions and remove the bearings.

3B. If a press is used, perform the following:

    a. Support the side door (A, **Figure 97**) on the press bed with its inner surface facing up.

    b. Use a driver or socket (B, **Figure 97**) that matches the diameter of the bearing inner race, and press the bearing out of the side-door bore.

    c. Repeat process to remove the opposite bearing.

4. Clean the side door again in solvent and dry thoroughly.

5. Inspect the bearing bores in the side cover for cracks or other damage. Replace the side door if damaged.

> *NOTE*
> *Both side door bearings have the same part number.*

94

TRANSMISSION CASE, BEARINGS AND COVERS

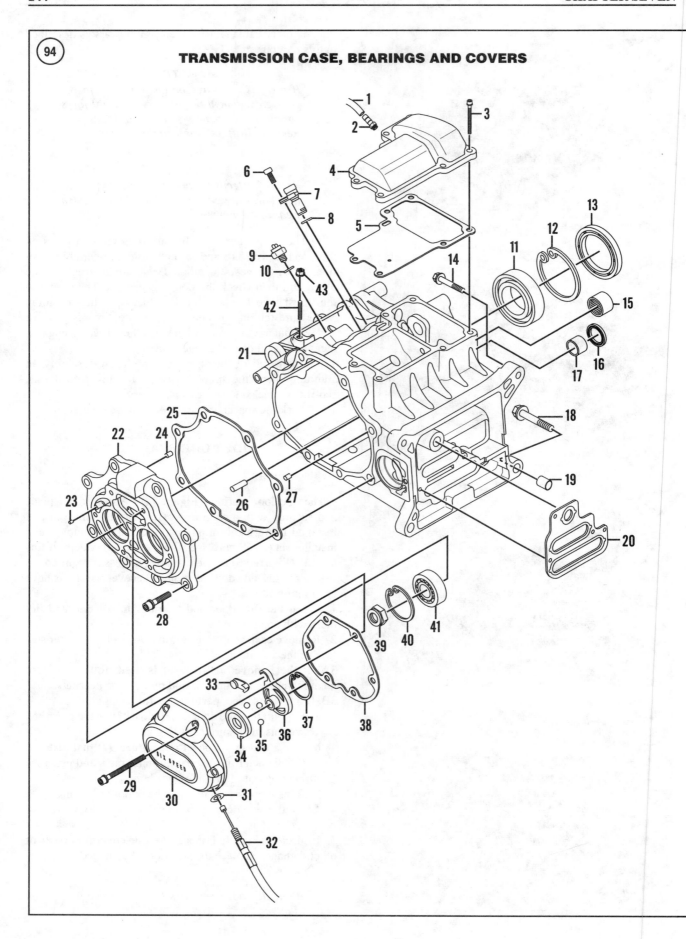

1. Breather hose
2. Fitting
3. Bolt
4. Top cover
5. Gasket
6. Bolt
7. Vehicle speed sensor (VSS)
8. O-ring
9. Neutral indicator switch
10. O-ring
11. Oil seal (mainshaft)
12. Snap ring
13. Oil seal
14. Bolt (short)
15. Needle bearing
16. Oil seal
17. Sleeve
18. Bolt (long)
19. Dowel pin
20. Gasket
21. Transmission case
22. Side door
23. Locating pin
24. Locating pin
25. Gasket
26. Locating pin
27. Locating dowel
28. Bolt
29. Bolt
30. Clutch release cover
31. O-ring
32. Clutch cable or hydraulic hose
33. Coupling*
34. Outer ramp*
35. Ball (3)*
36. Inner ramp*
37. Snap ring*
38. Gasket
39. Locknut (transmission shafts)
40. Snap ring
41. Bearing
42. Ground stud
43. Flange nut

*Items 33-37 not included on Screamin'
Eagle or CVO model.

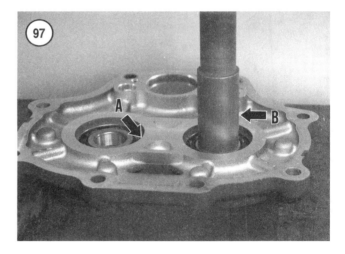

6A. If the remover/installer set is used, follow the tool manufacturer's instructions and install the bearings.

6B. If a press is used, perform the following:

    a. Support the side door in a press with its outer surface facing up (A, **Figure 98**).

    b. Center the bearing in the bore so the side with the marks faces up.

    c. Using a driver (B, **Figure 98**) that presses against the bearing outer race, press the bearing into the bore until it bottoms.

    d. Repeat process to install the opposite bearing.

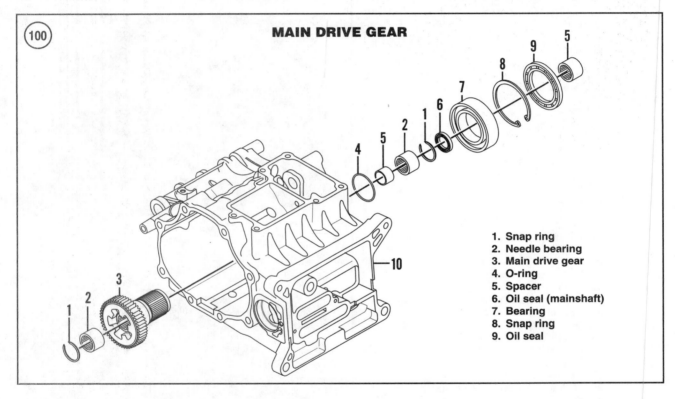

MAIN DRIVE GEAR

1. Snap ring
2. Needle bearing
3. Main drive gear
4. O-ring
5. Spacer
6. Oil seal (mainshaft)
7. Bearing
8. Snap ring
9. Oil seal

7. Install a *new* snap ring so the side with the sharp edge faces the bearing outer race. Make sure the snap ring (**Figure 99**) is correctly seated in the side door groove.

MAIN DRIVE GEAR

The main drive gear assembly (**Figure 100**) is pressed into the transmission case. Whenever the main drive gear is removed, the main drive bearing is damaged and must be replaced at the same time.

Tools

If the transmission case has been removed, a press can be used. If the transmission case is installed in the frame, the following tools are required to remove and install the main drive gear and the main drive bearing.

1. A main drive gear/bearing remover and installer (H-D part No. HD-35316-C).
2. A main drive gear large oil seal installer (JIMS part No. 972 or HD-47856).
3. A 6-speed main drive gear installer (JIMS part No. 981).

Removal

1. Remove the transmission side door assembly and the transmission drive sprocket as described in this chapter.
2. Remove main-drive-gear large oil seal (A, **Figure 101**).
3. Remove the snap ring from the main drive bearing behind the large seal.

NOTE
If the main drive gear will not release from the bearing due to corrosion, remove the tools and heat the bearing with a heat gun.

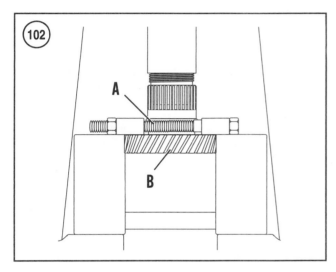

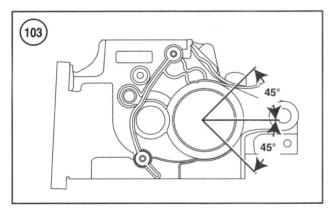

4. Assemble the remover/installer tool set onto the main drive gear following the tool manufacturer's instructions. Tighten the puller nut slowly to pull the main drive gear from the main drive bearing in the transmission case.

5. Remove the main drive bearing from the transmission case as described in this section.

NOTE
The main drive bearing inner race may remain on the main drive gear. If the main drive gear will be reinstalled, the inner race must be removed.

6. Remove the bearing inner race from the main drive gear by performing the following:
   a. Install a wedge attachment (H-D part No HD-95637-46B), a bearing puller (A, **Figure 102**) or their equivalent, beneath the inner race.
   b. Support the tool in a hydraulic press, and press the main drive gear (B, **Figure 102**) from the inner face.
   c. Be prepared to catch the main drive gear as it is released from the bearing.

Installation

1. Install a new main drive bearing as described in this section.
2. Install a *new* snap ring so its flat side faces the bearing.
3. Position the snap ring with the open end facing the rear of the transmission and within a 45° angle to horizontal (**Figure 103**). Make sure it is fully seated in the snap ring groove.
4. Lubricate a new O-ring with engine oil, and install it into the groove on the main drive gear.
5. Apply transmission oil to the main drive bearing inner race and to the outer surface of the main drive gear. Also apply oil to the nut and threaded shaft of the installer tool.
6. Insert the main drive gear into the main drive gear bearing as far as it will go. Hold it in place and assemble the remover/installer tool onto the main drive gear and transmission case following the manufacturer's instructions.
7. Slowly tighten the puller nut to pull the main drive gear into the bearing in the transmission case. Continue until the gear bottoms in the bearing inner race.
8. Disassemble and remove the installation tool.
9A. If a main-drive-gear large oil seal installer (H-D part No. HD-47856) is available, install the large oil seal (A, **Figure 102**) per the tool manufacturer's instructions.
9B. If the remover/installer tool is not available, perform the following:
   a. Lubricate the lips of a new main-drive-gear large oil seal with clean transmission oil.
   b. Position the seal in the bearing bore so its closed side faces out.
   c. Using a mandrel that matches the diameter of the seal, drive the seal into the bore until the seal (A, **Figure 101**) is flush with the outer edge of the transmission case.
10. Install the transmission side door assembly and the transmission drive sprocket as described in this chapter.

NOTE
If a new small oil seal was not installed into the main drive gear during needle bearing installation or if the small oil seal is damaged, it can be replaced now. A main drive gear seal installer tool (JIMS part No. 972 or H-D part No. HD-47933), or its equivalent, is needed for this procedure.

11. If necessary, install the small oil seal (B, **Figure 101**) by performing the following:
   a. Install the tool's protector sleeve over the mainshaft.

b. Lubricate the sleeve and the small oil seal with clean transmission oil.

c. Fit the oil seal over the protector sleeve so the seal's closed side faces out.

d. Slide the seal driver onto the protector, and manually press the seal into the main drive gear. The seal is properly seated when the tool bottoms against the main drive gear.

Inspection

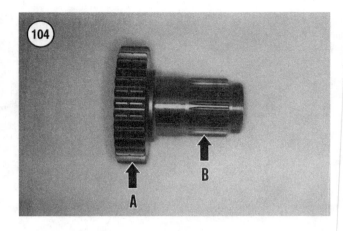

NOTE
Do not let solvent enter the inside of the main drive gear. The solvent will wash contaminants behind the needles in the bearings. If this occurs, the needle bearing must be replaced.

1. Clean the main drive gear in solvent, and dry with compressed air, if available.

2. Check each gear tooth (A, **Figure 104**) for excessive wear, burrs, galling and pitting. Check also for broken or missing teeth.

3. Check the gear splines (B, **Figure 104**) for excessive wear, galling or other damage.

4. Inspect the two main drive gear needle bearings (**Figure 105** and **Figure 106**) for excessive wear or damage. Insert the mainshaft into the main drive gear to check bearing wear. If necessary, replace the bearings as described in this section.

Needle Bearing Replacement

Both main drive gear needle bearings must be installed to a correct depth within the main drive gear. The correct depth is obtained with a main drive gear bearing and seal installation tool (JIMS part No. 986 or H-D part No HD-47932), or an equivalent. This tool (**Figure 107**) is also used to install the small oil seal.

If the tool is not available, measure the depth of both bearings before removing them.

Replace both main drive gear needle bearings as a set.

CAUTION
Never reuse a main drive gear needle bearing, as it was distorted during removal.

1. Remove the main drive gear as described in this section.

2. Remove O-ring from the clutch side of the main drive gear. Discard the O-ring.

3. Remove the small oil seal (**Figure 108**) from the clutch side of the main drive gear.

4. Remove the retaining ring (**Figure 109**) from each end of the main drive gear bore. Discard the rings.

5. If the installer tool is not available, measure and record the depth of both bearings.

6. Use a blind bearing puller, or an equivalent, to remove the needle bearings and spacer.

7. Clean the main drive gear and its bearing bore in solvent. Dry it thoroughly.

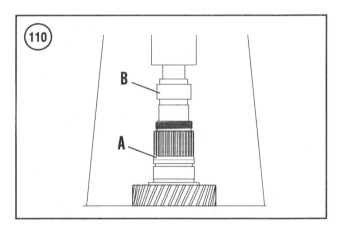

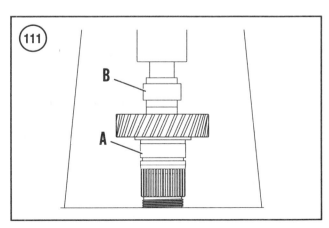

8. Apply transmission oil to the bearing bore in the main drive gear and to the outer surface of both bearings.

NOTE
Install each needle bearing with the mark facing out.

9. Set the main drive gear in the press so its clutch side faces up (A, **Figure 110**). Center the main drive gear bore under the press ram.

10. Set a *new* needle bearing into the clutch side of the drive gear bore. Insert the 0.400-in. (10.16 mm) step of the seal installation tool (B, **Figure 110**) into the bearing.

11. Press the bearing into the bore until the installation tool lightly contacts the main drive gear.

12. Raise the press ram. Install a new retaining ring so the ring's flat side faces the bearing.

13. Insert a *new* small oil seal into the drive gear bore. The side with the mark must face out.

14. Insert the 0.090-in. (2.29 mm) end of the seal installation tool into the oil seal, and press the seal into the bore until the installation tool lightly contact the main drive gear.

15. Turn the main drive gear over so its transmission side faces up (A, **Figure 111**), install the spacer, and center the bore under the press ram.

16. Start a *new* needle bearing into the bore.

17. Insert the 0.188-in. (4.78 mm) step of the installation tool (B, **Figure 111**) into the needle bearing, and press the bearing into the bore until the tool lightly contacts the main drive gear.

18. Install a *new* retaining ring into the main drive gear. Make sure the ring is completely seated in its groove.

19. Install the *new* small oil seal (**Figure 108**) into the clutch side of the main drive gear.

20. Install the *new* O-ring into the clutch side of the main drive gear.

21. Install the main drive gear as described in this section.

Main Drive Bearing Replacement

The main drive bearing (**Figure 100**) is pressed into the transmission case. Whenever the main drive gear is removed, the main drive bearing is damaged and must be replaced.

Tools

The following tools, or their equivalents, are used to remove and install the main drive bearing if the transmission case is installed in the frame:

1. A main drive gear/bearing remover and installer (H-D part No. HD-35316-C).

2. A 6-speed main drive gear bearing installer (JIMS part No. 987).

Procedure

If the transmission has been removed, use a press to remove the main drive gear bearing.

7

CAUTION
Failure to use the correct tools to install the bearing will cause premature failure of the bearing and related parts.

1. Remove the main drive gear from the transmission case as described in this section.
2. Assemble the installer tool set onto the main drive bearing following the tool manufacturer's instructions. Tighten the bolt and nut slowly to pull the main drive gear bearing from the transmission case.
3. Clean the bearing bore and dry with compressed air. Check the bore for nicks or burrs. Check the snap ring groove for damage.

NOTE
Install the bearing into the transmission case with the mark facing out.

4. Apply transmission oil to the bearing bore in the transmission case and to the outer surface of the bearing. Also apply oil to the nut and threaded shaft of the installer tool.
5. Install the bearing onto the installation tool and assemble the installation tool following the tool manufacturer's instructions.
6. Slowly tighten the puller nut to pull the bearing into the transmission case. Continue until the bearing bottoms in the case.
7. Disassemble and remove the installation tool.

TRANSMISSION DRIVE SPROCKET

Removal/Installation

A sprocket locker tool (JIMS part No.: 2260 or H-D part No. HD-46282) and a mainshaft pulley nut socket (JIMS part No. 989 or H-D part No. HD-47910), or their equivalents, are used to remove the transmission drive sprocket.

NOTE
It is not necessary to remove the mainshaft bearing inner race when removing the transmission drive sprocket.

1. Remove the primary chaincase housing as described in Chapter Six.
2. If necessary, remove the belt guard and debris deflector (Chapter Twelve).
3. Perform the following to create sufficient slack in the drive belt.
  a. On Screamin' Eagle and CVO models so equipped, loosen the set screw and remove the trim cap from the rear axle nut.
  b. Remove the e-clip (A, **Figure 112**) and loosen the rear axle nut (B).
  c. Support the motorcycle with the rear wheel off the ground.
  d. Turn each axle adjuster (C, **Figure 112**) in equal amounts to allow slack in the drive belt.

  e. Push the rear wheel forward to provide sufficient slack in the drive belt.
4. Remove the two Allen bolts (A, **Figure 113**) and the lock plate (B).
5. Install a sprocket locker tool (A, **Figure 114**) onto the transmission drive sprocket, following the tool manufacturer's instructions.
6. Install the inner collar (B, **Figure 114**) onto the mainshaft.
7. Install the pulley nut socket (**Figure 115**), and loosen the pulley nut.
8. Remove the tools and the sprocket nut (C, **Figure 114**) from the mainshaft.

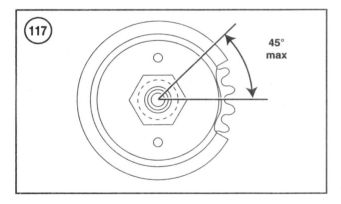

12. Install the inner collar (B, **Figure 114**) and pulley nut socket (**Figure 115**).

13. Loosen the nut, and retighten it to 35 ft.-lb. (47.5 N•m).

14. Scribe a horizontal line onto the sprocket nut and onto the sprocket as shown in **Figure 117**.

> *CAUTION*
> *Do not tighten the nut past an additional 45°*
> *to align the lockplate bolt holes. The nut will*
> *be damaged.*

15. Tighten the nut an additional 35-40° until the lockplate holes align with the holes on the drive sprocket.

16. Remove the tools.

> *CAUTION*
> *Once the nut has been re-tightened to 35 ft-*
> *lb. (47.5 N•m), the final tightening of the nut*
> *must not exceed 45°, which is 1/8th of a turn.*
> *If further tightening is needed, watch the*
> *scribe lines so total nut movement does not*
> *exceed 45° (Figure 117).*

17. Install the lockplate (B, **Figure 113**) over the nut, aligning two of the opposite holes with the threaded holes in the sprocket nut. Remove and refit the lockplate until two opposite holes align. If hole alignment cannot be achieved; tighten the nut as needed. However, the total movement of the nut must not exceed maximum of 45°.

> *NOTE*
> *New lockplate bolts have threadlock pre-ap-*
> *plied to the threads and can be reused up to*
> *three times. They must be replaced after the*
> *fourth use.*

> *NOTE*
> *Apply Loctite High Strength Threadlocker*
> *271 (red), or an equivalent threadlock, if re-*
> *using the old bolts. Do not apply threadlock*
> *when using new bolts.*

18. Install and tighten the lockplate bolts (A, **Figure 113**) to 84-108 in.-lb. (9.5-12.2 N•m).

TRANSMISSION CASE

Only remove the transmission case (**Figure 118**) if it requires replacement or when performing extensive frame repair or replacing the frame. All internal components can be removed with the case in the frame.

Removal/Installation

1. Disconnect the negative battery cable as described in Chapter Nine.

2. Drain the transmission oil and engine oil as described in Chapter Three.

3. Remove the exhaust system as described in Chapter Four.

9. Carefully slide the transmission drive sprocket (**Figure 116**) from the mainshaft so the bearing inner race (D, **Figure 114**) will not be damaged.

10. Fit the drive belt onto the pulley, and slide the transmission drive pulley onto the mainshaft.

11. Finger-tighten the pulley nut onto the main drive gear.

   a. If installing a *new* sprocket nut, apply a very light coat of clean engine oil onto the inboard side of the new nut. Do not allow any oil to contact the patch of threadlock on the sprocket nut.

   b. If reinstalling the old nut, apply Loctite High Strength Threadlocker 271 (red) to the nut threads. Also apply a very light coat of clean engine oil onto the inboard face of the locknut and to the surface of the sprocket where the nut makes contact.

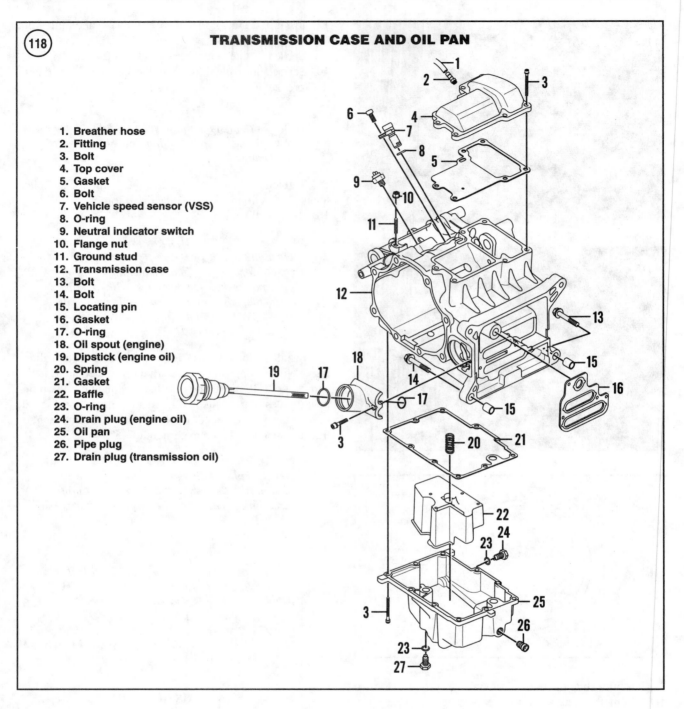

(118)   **TRANSMISSION CASE AND OIL PAN**

1. Breather hose
2. Fitting
3. Bolt
4. Top cover
5. Gasket
6. Bolt
7. Vehicle speed sensor (VSS)
8. O-ring
9. Neutral indicator switch
10. Flange nut
11. Ground stud
12. Transmission case
13. Bolt
14. Bolt
15. Locating pin
16. Gasket
17. O-ring
18. Oil spout (engine)
19. Dipstick (engine oil)
20. Spring
21. Gasket
22. Baffle
23. O-ring
24. Drain plug (engine oil)
25. Oil pan
26. Pipe plug
27. Drain plug (transmission oil)

4. Remove the starter motor as described in Chapter Nine.

5. Disconnect the connector (A, **Figure 119**) from the vehicle speed sensor (VSS) on top of the transmission case under the starter motor.

6. Remove the neutral switch (B, **Figure 119**) as described in Chapter Nine.

7. Remove the flange nut from the ground post on the top of the transmission case.

8. Disconnect the ground cable from the post on top of the transmission case.

9. Remove the primary chaincase cover as described in Chapter Six.

10. Remove the clutch assembly as described in Chapter Six.

11. Remove the transmission side cover (this chapter) and clutch release mechanism (Chapter Six).

12. Remove the primary chaincase housing as described in Chapter Six.

13. Remove the transmission drive sprocket as described in this chapter.

14. Remove the side door and transmission shaft assemblies as described in this chapter, if necessary.

15. Make an alignment mark on the shift rod lever and the end of the shift shaft.

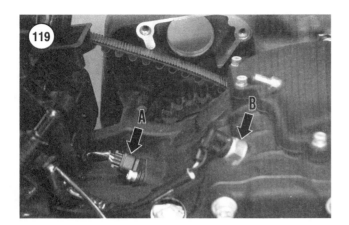

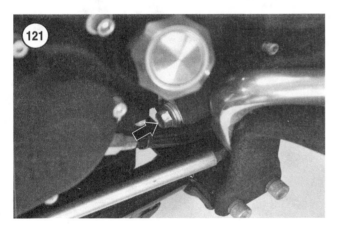

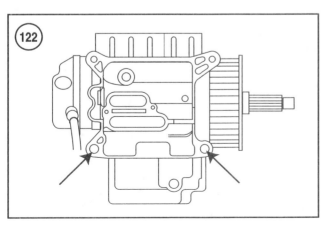

16. Remove the external shift linkage from the transmission as described in this chapter.

17. Remove the rear wheel as described in Chapter Ten.

18. Place a jack under the lower frame cross member to support the motorcycle.

19. Remove the swing arm as described in Chapter Twelve.

20. Remove the short, upper (**Figure 120**) and the long, lower (**Figure 121**) bolts and washers on each side securing the engine to the transmission.

21. Move the transmission case to the rear to clear the two lower locating dowels, and rest it on the frame cross member.

22. Move the transmission toward the left side and remove the transmission case from the frame.

23. Remove the gasket and discard it.

24. Install the transmission case by reversing the removal steps, while noting the following:

   a. Thoroughly clean all oil deposits from the pockets on the crankcase mounting flange.

   b. Make sure the two locating dowels (**Figure 122**) are in place on the engine or transmission case.

   c. Install a *new* gasket between the transmission and engine.

   d. Install the shorter (1/2-in.) transmission mounting bolts at the upper locations and the longer (9/16-in.) transmission mounting bolts at the lower locations.

   e. Using a crossing pattern, tighten the transmission bolts evenly to an initial torque of 15 ft.-lb. (20.3 N•m). Then, tighten the bolts to a final torque of 30-35 ft.-lb. (40.6-47.5 N•m).

   f. Following the torque sequence shown in **Figure 123**, tighten the oil pan bolts to 84-108 in.-lb. (9.5-12.2 N•m).

   g. Refill all lubricants as described in Chapter Three.

   h. Adjust drive belt tension as described in Chapter Three.

OIL PAN

The oil pan mounts onto the bottom of the transmission case (**Figure 118**). It can be removed with the transmission mounted in the frame.

Removal

1. Drain the transmission oil as described in Chapter Three.

2. Remove the engine oil dipstick (**Figure 124**).

3. Raise the front or rear of the motorcycle sufficiently to allow the oil pan to be lowered from the transmission case. Secure the motorcycle on level ground in this position.

4. Remove the ten bolts securing the oil pan to the transmission case.

5. Lower the oil pan, and then remove it and the gasket from the transmission case.

6. Remove the gasket and discard it.

7. Remove the spring and baffle assembly from the oil pan.

Installation

1. Thoroughly clean the gasket surface of the oil pan, and dry.
2. Apply several drops of Hylomar gasket sealer to the gasket surface of the oil pan.
3. Install a *new* oil tank gasket on the oil pan.
4. Install the baffle and the spring into the oil pan.
5. Install the oil pan onto the bottom of the transmission case.
6. Holding the oil pan in place, install the ten bolts. Using a crossing pattern, finger-tighten the bolts 2 full turns.
7. Check that the oil pan is still positioned correctly. Following the torque sequence shown in **Figure 123**, tighten the bolts to 84-108 in.-lb. (9.5-12.2 N•m).
8. If necessary, replace the engine oil filter as described in Chapter Three.
9. Refill the transmission oil as described in Chapter Three.
10. Start the engine and check for leaks.

Inspection

1. Separate the baffle from the oil pan. Clean the oil pan, baffle and spring in solvent and dry thoroughly.
2. Remove all old gasket residue from the oil pan and transmission case gasket surfaces.
3. Inspect the oil pan for cracks or damage. Replace if necessary.
4. Check the baffle spring for weakness or damage and replace if necessary.

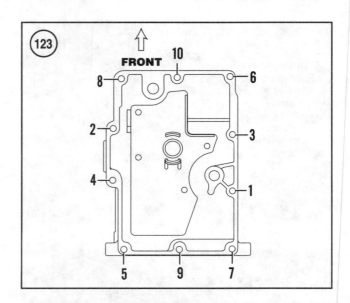

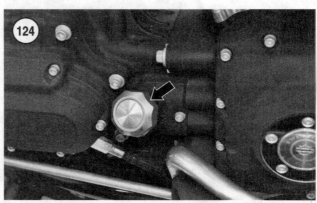

Table 1 TRANSMISSION GENERAL SPECIFICATIONS

Transmission type	6-speed, constant mesh
Gear ratios	
First	3.34
Second	2.31
Third	1.72
Fourth	1.39
Fifth	1.18
Sixth	1.00
Transmission fluid capacity (approximate)	32 oz. (946.4 ml)

Table 2 TRANSMISSION SERVICE SPECIFICATIONS

Item	In.	mm
Countershaft		
Runout	0.000-0.003	0.00-0.08
Endplay	None	None
First gear		
Clearance	0.0004-0.0015	0.010-0.038
End play	0.002-0.0023	0.05-0.058
Second gear		
Clearance	0.0001-0.0012	0.003-0.031
End play	0.002-0.040	0.05-1.02
	(continued)	

Table 2 TRANSMISSION SERVICE SPECIFICATIONS (continued)

Item	In.	mm
Countershaft (continued)		
Third gear		
Clearance	0.0004-0.0015	0.010-0.038
End play	0.002-0.042	0.05-1.07
Fourth gear		
Clearance	0.0004-0.0015	0.010-0.038
End play	0.001-0.028	0.03-0.71
Mainshaft		
Runout	0.00-0.003	0.00-0.08
Endplay	None	None
Fifth gear		
Clearance	0.0004-0.0015	0.010-0.038
End play	0.002-0.026	0.05-0.66
Main drive gear (sixth)		
Bearing fit in transmission case	0.0003-0.0017	0.0076-0.043
Fit in bearing (press-fit)	None	None
Fit on mainshaft	0.0009-0.0022	0.023-0.056
End play	None	None
Shift dog service limit		
First	0.015-0.112	0.381-2.845
Second	0.021-0.136	0.533-3.454
Third	0.014-0.118	0.356-2.997
Fourth	0.033-0.115	0.838-2.921
Fifth	0.016-0.115	0.406-2.921
Sixth	0.026-0.123	0.660-3.124
Shift forks		
Shift fork-to-cam groove end play	0.004-0.012	0.102-0.305
Shift fork-to-gear groove end play	0.004-0.013	0.102-0.330
Shift fork service limit		
First and second gear shift fork	0.258	6.55
Third and fourth gear shift fork	0.198	5.03
Fifth and sixth gear shift fork	0.258	6.55

Table 3 SIDE DOOR BEARINGS SPECIFICATIONS

Item	Specification
Fit in side door	0.001-0.0014 (0.025-0.036)
Fit on countershaft and mainshaft	
Tight fit	0.0007 (0.018)
Loose fit	0.001 (0.025)

Table 4 TRANSMISSION TORQUE SPECIFICATIONS

Item	ft.-lb.	in.-lb.	N•m
Mainshaft/countershaft locknuts			
(at side door)			
2006-2008	45-55	–	61.0-74.6
2009-2011	55-65	–	74.6-88.1
Oil pan bolts	–	84-108	9.5-12.2
Shift cam detent arm bolt	–	120-150	13.6-17.0
Shift cam lock plate bolt	–	57-63	6.4-7.1
Shift linkage rod			
Acorn nut	–	96-144	10.8-16.3
Nut	–	80-120	9.0-13.6
Shift arm clamp bolt	18-22	–	24.4-29.8
Top cover bolts	–	84-132	9.5-14.9
Transmission side door bolts	13-18	–	17.6-24.4
Transmission drain plug	14-21	–	19.0-28.5
Transmission mounting bolt			
Initial torque	15	–	20.3
Final torque	30-35	–	40.6-47.5
Transmission drive sprocket			
Mounting nut		Refer to text	
Lockplate bolts	–	84-108	9.5-12.2

7

CHAPTER EIGHT

FUEL SYSTEM

This chapter includes procedures for the fuel injection and emission control systems. Refer to Chapter One for safety precautions. Refer to Chapter Three for maintenance procedures.

Refer **Table 1** and **Table 2** at the end of the chapter for fuel system specifications.

NOTE
*On models with the optional security system, disarm system before disconnecting the battery or pulling the Maxi-Fuse so the alarm will not sound. Refer to **Turn Signal and Security Modules** in Chapter Nine.*

AIR FILTER BACKPLATE (ALL 2006-2007 MODELS, 2007-2008 FXDSE AND 2009 FXDFSE CVO HDI MODELS)

Routine air filter maintenance is described in Chapter 3. Refer to **Figure 1** and **Figure 2**.

Removal

1A. On Screamin' Eagle and CVO Models, perform the following:
   a. Remove the screws and the trim panel from the cover.
   b. Remove the air filter cover Allen screw. Then, remove the cover.
1B. On all other models, remove the air filter cover Allen screw (A, **Figure 3**). Then, remove the cover (B).

2. Remove the Torx (T27) screws and bracket (A, **Figure 4**) from the air filter element (B).
3. Gently pull the air filter element away from the backplate and disconnect the two breather hoses (A, **Figure 5**) from the breather hollow bolts on the backplate. Remove the air filter element (B, **Figure 5**).
4. Remove the outboard gasket (**Figure 6**) from the inboard side of the element. Discard the gasket.
5. Use a deep socket and remove the breather hollow bolts (**Figure 7**) securing the backplate to the cylinder heads.
6. Pull the backplate away from the cylinder heads. Disconnect the 2-pin intake air temperature (IAT) connector (**Figure 8**) from the inboard side of the backplate.
7. Remove the backplate and inner gasket.
8. Remove and discard the outer gasket from the backplate.
9. Inspect the components as described in this chapter.

Installation

1. Apply a small amount of gasket sealer to a *new* backplate gasket. Correctly align all holes and fit it onto the induction module (**Figure 9**).
2. Move the backplate part way into position, and reconnect the 2-pin intake air temperature (IAT) connector (**Figure 8**) onto the inboard side of the backplate.
3. Position the backplate against the induction module. Reposition the gasket as necessary to align the bolt holes with those of the induction module.
4. Install the breather hollow bolts (**Figure 7**), and secure the backplate to the cylinder heads. Tighten the breather bolts to 22-24 ft.-lb. (29.8-32.6 N•m).

AIR FILTER (2006-2007 MODELS EXCEPT SCREAMIN' EAGLE AND CVO)

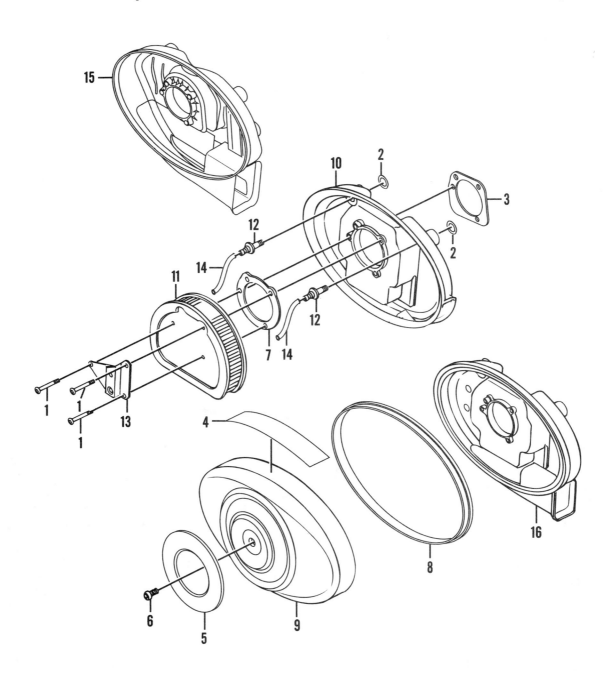

1. Torx screw
2. O-ring
3. Inboard gasket
4. Label
5. Trim
6. Screw
7. Outboard gasket
8. Seal ring
9. Cover
10. Backplate (Domestic)
11. Filter element
12. Breather hollow bolt
13. Mounting bracket
14. Breather hose
15. Backplate (HDI-Japan)
16. Backplate (HDI-UK and Australia)

8

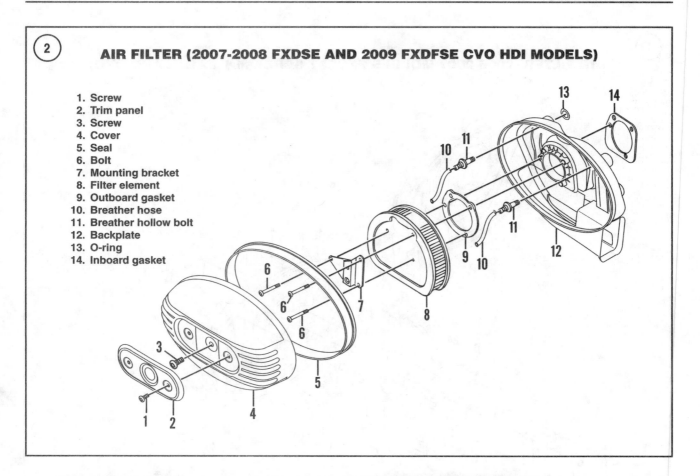

② AIR FILTER (2007-2008 FXDSE AND 2009 FXDFSE CVO HDI MODELS)

1. Screw
2. Trim panel
3. Screw
4. Cover
5. Seal
6. Bolt
7. Mounting bracket
8. Filter element
9. Outboard gasket
10. Breather hose
11. Breather hollow bolt
12. Backplate
13. O-ring
14. Inboard gasket

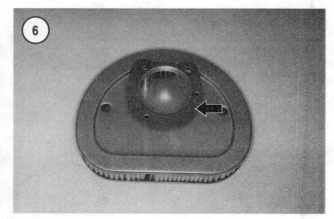

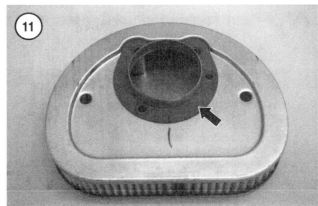

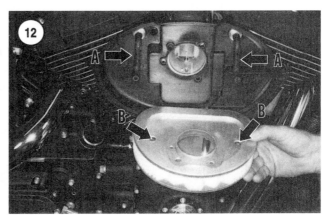

5. Install the breather hoses (**Figure 10**) onto the breather bolt fittings.

6. Apply a small amount of gasket sealer to a *new* air filter gasket (**Figure 11**). Fit the gasket onto air filter element.

7. Position the element with the flat side facing down and insert the breather hoses (A, **Figure 12**) into the backside of the element (B).

8. Move the element (B, **Figure 4**) into position and install the mounting bracket (A). Install the Torx screws through the mounting bracket and element. Align bracket and element with the screw holes and tighten the mounting bracket Torx screws to 40-60 in.-lb. (4.5-6.8 N•m).

9. Install the air filter cover (B, **Figure 3**) and the cover screw (A). Apply Loctite Threadlocker 243 (blue), or an equivalent threadlock, to the screw threads, and tighten the cover screw to 36-60 in.-lb. (4.1-6.8 N•m).

10. Install the trim plate on models so equipped. Tighten the trim plate screw(s) to 27-36 in.-lb. (3.0-3.6 N•m).

11. Apply a drop of Loctite Threadlocker 243 (blue), or an equivalent threadlock, to the cover screw prior to installation.

12. On Screamin' Eagle and CVO models, perform the following:

    a. Install the air filter cover and Allen screw. Tighten the cover screw to 36-60 in.-lb. (4.1-6.8 N•m).

    b. Install the trim plate onto the cover and tighten the screws to 27-36in.-lb. (3.0-3.6 N•m).

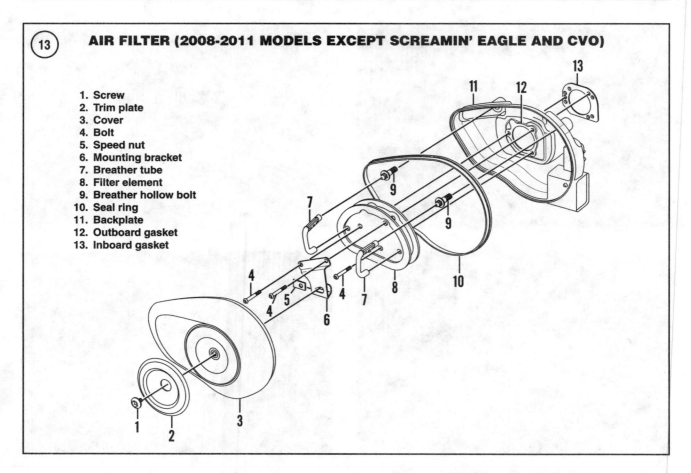

AIR FILTER (2008-2011 MODELS EXCEPT SCREAMIN' EAGLE AND CVO)

1. Screw
2. Trim plate
3. Cover
4. Bolt
5. Speed nut
6. Mounting bracket
7. Breather tube
8. Filter element
9. Breather hollow bolt
10. Seal ring
11. Backplate
12. Outboard gasket
13. Inboard gasket

AIR FILTER BACKPLATE (2008-2011 MODELS EXCEPT SCREAMIN' EAGLE AND CVO)

Routine air filter maintenance is described in Chapter Three.

Refer to **Figure 13**.

Removal

1. Remove the Allen screw (A, **Figure 14**) and remove the cover (B).

2. Gently disconnect the breather hoses (**Figure 15**) from the air filter element.

3. Slide the speed nut (**Figure 16**) to the left to access the bolt behind it.

4. Remove the Torx (T27) screws (A, **Figure 17**) and bracket (B) from the air filter element.

5. Remove the air filter element (C, **Figure 17**) from the backplate.

6. Remove the outboard gasket (**Figure 18**) from the inboard side of the element. Discard the gasket.

7. Use a deep socket and remove the breather hollow bolts (A, **Figure 19**) securing the backplate (B) to the cylinder heads.

8. Pull the backplate away from the cylinder heads. Disconnect the 2-pin intake air temperature (IAT) electrical connector (**Figure 20**) from the inboard side of the backplate.

9. Remove the inboard gasket from the backplate or induction module. Discard the gasket.

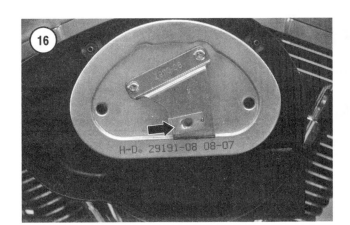

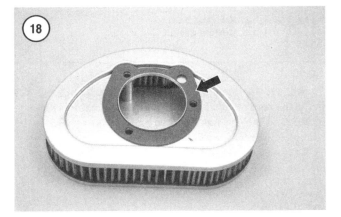

10. Inspect the components as described in this chapter.

Installation

1. Apply a small amount of gasket sealer to a *new* inboard backplate gasket. Correctly align all holes and fit it onto the induction module (**Figure 21**).

2. Move the backplate part way into position, and reconnect the 2-pin intake air temperature (IAT) connector (**Figure 20**) onto the inboard side of the backplate.

3. Install the breather hollow bolts (A, **Figure 19**) and secure the backplate to the cylinder heads. Tighten the breather hollow bolts to 22-24 ft.-lb. (29.8-32.6 N•m).

4. Position the element (C, **Figure 17**) with the flat side facing down and into position on the back plate.

5. Install the mounting bracket (B, **Figure 17**) and install the Torx screws (A) through the mounting bracket and element. Align the bracket and element with the screw holes and tighten the Torx (T27) screws to 40-60 in.-lb. (4.5-6.8 N•m).

6. Slide the speed nut (**Figure 16**) to the right.

7. Install both breather hoses. Insert one end into the element (A, **Figure 22**) and attach the other end (B) to the backplate.

8. Ensure that the cover seal ring (**Figure 23**) is in place.

9. Apply a drop of Loctite 243 (blue), or an equivalent, threadlock to the cover screw prior to installation.

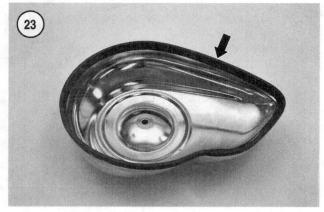

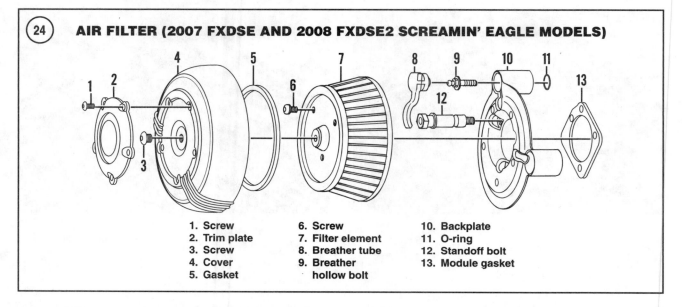

24 **AIR FILTER (2007 FXDSE AND 2008 FXDSE2 SCREAMIN' EAGLE MODELS)**

1. Screw	6. Screw	10. Backplate
2. Trim plate	7. Filter element	11. O-ring
3. Screw	8. Breather tube	12. Standoff bolt
4. Cover	9. Breather	13. Module gasket
5. Gasket	hollow bolt	

10. Install the air filter cover (B, **Figure 14**) and the cover screw (A). Tighten the Allen screw to 36-60 in.-lb. (4.1-6.8 N•m).

AIR FILTER BACKPLATE (2007 FXDSE AND 2008 FXDSE2 SCREAMIN' EAGLE MODELS)

Routine air filter maintenance is described in Chapter Three.

Refer to **Figure 24**.

Removal

1. Remove the trim plate screws and trim plate. Remove the air filter cover Allen screw. Then, remove the cover.
2. Remove the screws (A, **Figure 25**) from the air filter element (B).
3. Gently pull the air filter element away from the backplate and remove it.
4. Carefully pull the breather tubes (A, **Figure 26**) from the backplate and remove them.

5. Remove the standoff bolts (B, **Figure 26**). Then, remove the backplate (C, **Figure 26**) and inboard gasket.
6. Remove the O-rings from the breather bolt bosses in the backplate. Discard the O-rings.
7. Remove and discard the module gasket.
8. Inspect the components as described in this chapter.

Installation

1. Install a *new* module gasket.
2. Install *new* O-rings into the inboard side of the breather bolt bosses in the backplate.
3. Position the backplate (C, **Figure 26**) against the module gasket. Reposition the gasket as necessary to align the bolt holes with the induction module.
4. Install the standoff bolts (B, **Figure 26**), and tighten to 55-60 in.-lb. (6.3-6.7 N•m).
5. Install the breather tubes (A, **Figure 26**) onto the backplate. Push them until they are seated securely.
6. Install the element (B, **Figure 25**) onto the backplate and align the screw holes.
7. Install screws (A, **Figure 25**) through the air filter element, and tighten to 40-60 in.-lb. (4.5-6.8 N•m).

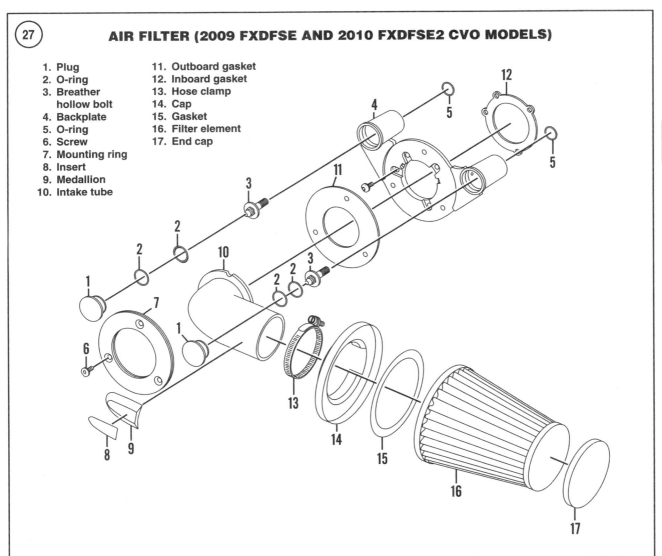

AIR FILTER (2009 FXDFSE AND 2010 FXDFSE2 CVO MODELS)

1. Plug
2. O-ring
3. Breather hollow bolt
4. Backplate
5. O-ring
6. Screw
7. Mounting ring
8. Insert
9. Medallion
10. Intake tube
11. Outboard gasket
12. Inboard gasket
13. Hose clamp
14. Cap
15. Gasket
16. Filter element
17. End cap

8. Apply a drop of Loctite 243 (blue), or an equivalent, threadlock to the cover screw prior to installation.

9. Install the air filter cover and Allen screw. Tighten the cover screw to 60-90 in.-lb. (6.8-10.2 N•m).

10. Install the trim plate and Allen screws. Tighten the trim screws securely.

AIR FILTER BACKPLATE (2009-2010 FXDFSE2 CVO MODELS)

Routine air filter maintenance is described in Chapter Three.

Refer to **Figure 27**.

Removal

1. Loosen the hose clamp and slide the air filter element assembly off the intake tube.
2. Remove the intake tube screws, and remove the mounting ring, intake tube and gasket from the backplate.
3. Remove the plugs and O-rings from the backplate.
4. Remove the three screws securing the backplate to the induction module.
5. Remove the breather hollow bolts securing the backplate to the cylinder heads.
6. Pull the backplate away from the cylinder heads, and remove the backplate and inboard gasket. Discard the gasket.
7. Remove the O-rings from the rear of the backplate.
8. Inspect the components as described in this chapter.

Installation

1. Install *new* O-rings onto the rear of the backplate.
2. Apply a small amount of gasket sealer to a *new* inboard backplate gasket. Fit the gasket onto the rear of the backplate.
3. Position the backplate against the induction module. Reposition the gasket as necessary to align its bolts holes with those of the induction module.
4. Install the three screws securing the backplate to the induction module and tighten to 55-60 in.-lb. (6.2-6.8 N•m).
5. Install the breather hollow bolts and tighten to 22-24 ft.-lb. (29.8-32.6 N•m).
6. Coat four *new* O-rings with Vaseline. Install two new O-rings onto each plug.
7. Install the plugs into the backplate and press in until they bottom.
8. Install the mounting ring onto the intake tube.
9. Apply a small amount of gasket sealer to the *new* outboard gasket and install it onto the rear of the mounting ring. Reposition the gasket as necessary to align its bolts holes with those of the mounting ring.
10. Apply a drop of Loctite 243 (blue), or an equivalent, threadlock to the mounting ring screws prior to installation.
11. Install the intake tube assembly onto the back plate and install the three screws. Tighten the screws 55-60 in.-lb. (6.2-6.8 N•m).
12. Install the air filter element onto the intake tube, and rotate it the seam faces toward the engine.
13. Position the hose clamp with the screw at the bottom and just forward of the intake tube. Tighten the screw to 45-55 in.-lb. (5.1-6.2 N•m).

BACKPLATE INSPECTION (ALL MODELS)

1. Inspect the backplate for damage. Refer to **Figure 28** and **Figure 29**.
2. Make sure the breather hollow bolts (A, **Figure 30**) and breather hoses (B) are clear. Clean out if necessary.
3. On HDI models, make sure the trap door (**Figure 31**) swings freely.

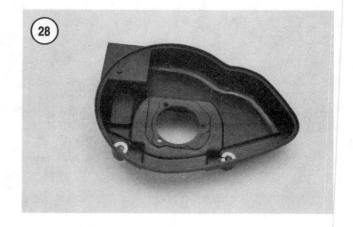

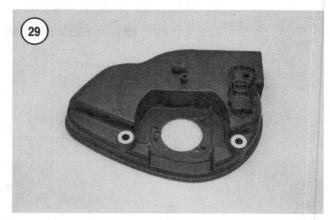

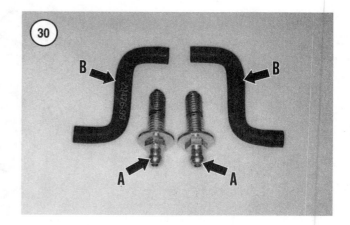

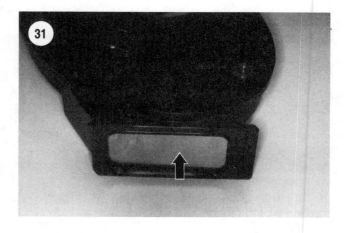

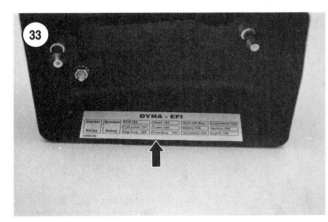

DEPRESSURIZING THE FUEL SYSTEM

The fuel system is under pressure at all times, even when the engine is not operating. The system must be depressurized prior to loosening fittings or disconnecting any fuel lines within the fuel injection system. Gasoline will spray out unless the system is depressurized.

1. Pull straight out on the electrical caddy cover (**Figure 32**) and remove it.

NOTE
*Refer to **Figure 33** for fuse and relay description and location.*

2. Pull straight out and remove the fuel pump fuse (**Figure 34**) from the fuse block.
3. Start the engine. Let it idle until it runs out of gasoline.
4. After the engine has stopped, operate the starter for three seconds to eliminate any residual gasoline in the fuel lines.
5. After the fuel system has been completely depressurized, install the fuel pump fuse (**Figure 34**).
6. Push the electrical caddy cover (**Figure 32**) straight on. Push on it until it bottoms.

FUEL TANK

WARNING
Some fuel may spill from the fuel tank hose during this procedure. Because gasoline is extremely flammable and explosive, perform this procedure away from all open flames, including appliance pilot lights and sparks. Do not smoke or allow anyone to smoke in the work area, as an explosion and fire may occur. Always work in a well-ventilated area. Wipe up any spills immediately.

WARNING
Make sure to route the fuel tank vapor hoses so that they cannot contact any hot engine or exhaust component. These hoses contain flammable vapors. If a hose melts from contacting a hot part, leaking vapors may ignite, causing a fire.

Draining

1. Depressurize the fuel system as described in this chapter.
2. Make a drain hose from 5/16 inch (7.9 mm) I.D. hose and plug one end of it. Make it long enough to go from the fuel tank crossover hose fitting to a gas can.
3. Place a shop cloth directly under one the crossover fittings.
4. Secure a clamping tool (A, **Figure 35**) on the fuel line to cut off fuel flow.

8

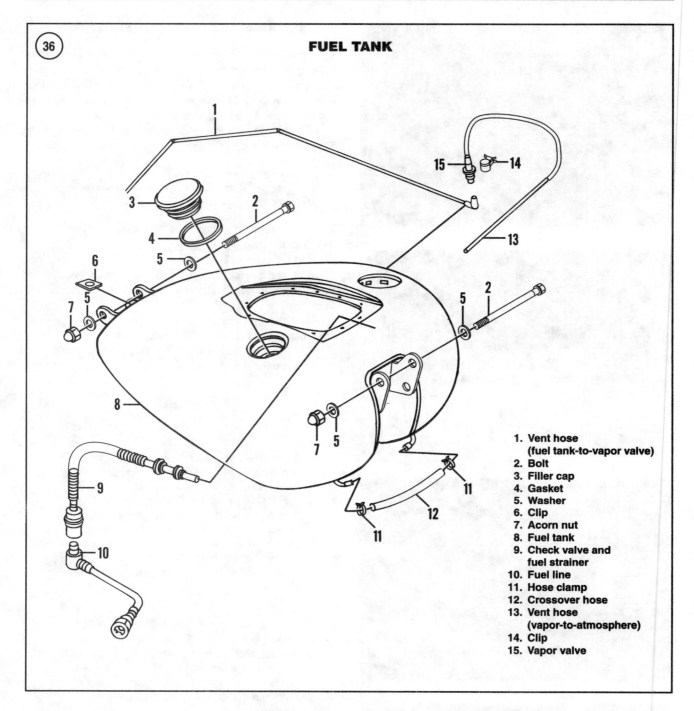

36 **FUEL TANK**

1. Vent hose
   (fuel tank-to-vapor valve)
2. Bolt
3. Filler cap
4. Gasket
5. Washer
6. Clip
7. Acorn nut
8. Fuel tank
9. Check valve and
   fuel strainer
10. Fuel line
11. Hose clamp
12. Crossover hose
13. Vent hose
   (vapor-to-atmosphere)
14. Clip
15. Vapor valve

5. Carefully cut and remove the hose clamp (B, **Figure 35**).

6. Disconnect the crossover hose from one of the fittings on the fuel tank. Immediately connect the drain hose to the fuel tank fitting.

7. Remove the fuel filler cap.

8. Place the plugged end of the drain hose into the gas can and remove the plug. Drain the fuel from that side of the fuel tank.

9. Disconnect the drain hose and reinstall the plug into one end of it.

10. Repeat the procedure to drain for the other side of the fuel tank.

11. Plug the fuel tank crossover fittings to prevent any residual fuel from draining.

Removal/Installation

The crossover fuel hose is secured to the fuel tank with non-reusable clamps. If the same type of clamps are going to be reinstalled, purchase *new* ones before servicing the fuel tank.

Refer to **Figure 36**.

1. Depressurize the fuel system as described in this chapter.

2. Disconnect the negative battery cable as described in Chapter Nine.

3. Remove the seat as described in Chapter Fourteen.

4. Remove the fuel tank console as described in this chapter.

5. Drain the fuel tank as described in this section.

6. Disconnect the vent hose from the fuel tank.

7. Place a shop cloth directly under one of the cross over fittings.

8. Secure a clamping tool (A, **Figure 35**) on the fuel line to cut off fuel flow.

9. Carefully cut and remove the hose clamp (B, **Figure 35**).

10. Disconnect the crossover hose from one of the fittings on the fuel tank.

11. Plug the tank opening and the crossover hose.

12. On models so equipped, disconnect the fuel gauge connector (**Figure 37**) at the bottom left side of the fuel tank.

13. Disconnect the fuel pump connector (A, **Figure 38**) at the fuel pump top plate.

14. Disconnect the vapor vent hose (B, **Figure 38**) from the fitting on the fuel pump top plate.

> *WARNING*
> *A small amount of fuel will drain out of the fuel tank when the fuel line is disconnected from the base of the tank. Place several shop cloths under the fuel line fittings to catch any spilled fuel prior to disconnecting them. Dispose of any fuel-soaked shop cloths in a safe manner.*

> *CAUTION*
> *Do not twist the plastic fuel line fitting as it may crack and cause a fuel leak.*

15. On the left side, pull up the chrome sleeve on the fuel line quick-connect fitting (A, **Figure 39**) and disconnect the fuel supply line (B) from the fuel tank.

16. At the front of the fuel tank, loosen and remove the acorn nut and washer on the left side. Withdraw the bolt and washer (**Figure 40**) from the right side securing the fuel tank to the frame.

17. At the rear of the fuel tank, remove the acorn nut and washer on the left side. Withdraw the bolt and washer (A, **Figure 41**) from the right side securing the fuel tank to the frame.

18. Lift up, pull toward the rear and remove the fuel tank (B, **Figure 41**).

19. Drain any remaining fuel left in the tank into a gas can.

> *WARNING*
> *Store the fuel tank in a safe place well away from open flames or where it could be damaged.*

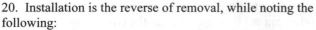

20. Installation is the reverse of removal, while noting the following:

a. Tighten the acorn nuts to 10-18 ft.-lb. (13.6-24.4 N•m) on 2006-2007 models or 15-20 ft.-lb. (20.3-27.1 N•m) on 2008-2011 models.

b. Install a new hose clamp (**Figure 42**) and secure with a pincer tool (JIMS part No. 1171), or an equivalent.

c. Reconnect the fuel line quick-connect fitting (A, **Figure 39**) onto the fuel tank until it clicks into the locked position. Pull down on the fuel line to make sure it is secured to the fitting.

d. Refill the tank and check for leaks.

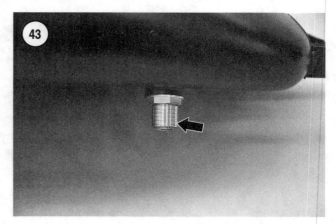

Inspection

1. Inspect the fuel tank quick-connect fitting (**Figure 43**) for leaks. Replace the fitting as necessary.

2. Inspect the fuel crossover hose (A, **Figure 44**) for cracks or deterioration and replace as necessary.

3. On models so equipped, inspect the fuel gauge harness and connector (B, **Figure 44**) for damage.

4. Check the front (**Figure 45**) and rear mounting tabs (**Figure 46**) for cracks or fractures.

5. Remove the filler cap and inspect the tank for rust or contamination. If there is a rust buildup inside the tank, clean and flush the tank.

6. Inspect the fuel tank for leaks.

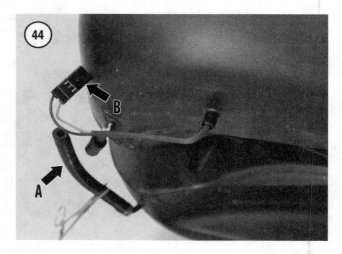

FUEL SUPPLY CHECK VALVE

Removal/Installation

The check valve is mounted in the quick-connect fitting. The valve keeps fuel from draining from the tank when the external line is disconnected.

Refer to **Figure 47**.

1. Remove the fuel tank as described in this chapter.

2. Remove the fuel pump/level sender assembly (this chapter).

3. Place several towels or a blanket on the work bench to protect the fuel tank finish.

4. Turn the fuel tank upside down on the towels or blanket.

5. Install a 7/8 in. deep socket over the quick-connect fitting (**Figure 43**) and onto its hex head.

6. Remove the fitting, and then carefully remove the check valve and fuel line from the fuel tank.

7. Remove and discard the fitting O-ring.

8. Lubricate a *new* O-ring with a light coat of clean engine oil, and install the O-ring onto the fitting.

9. Insert the fuel line into the fuel tank opening. Install the quick-connect fitting into the tank by hand and finger-tighten until it is snug. Tighten the quick-connect fitting to 18 ft.-lb. (24.4 N•m).

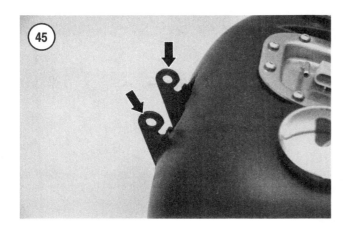

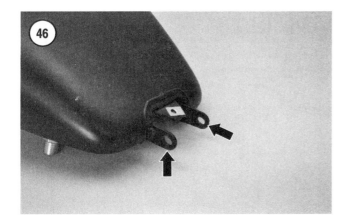

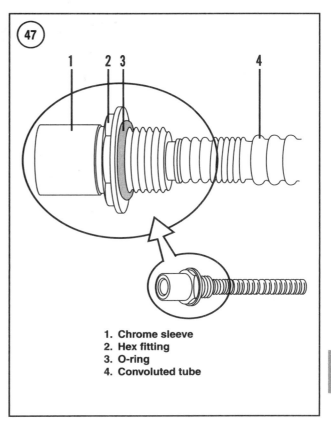

1. Chrome sleeve
2. Hex fitting
3. O-ring
4. Convoluted tube

10. Install fuel pump/level sender assembly as described in this chapter.

11. Install the fuel tank as described in this chapter.

TOP PLATE

Refer to **Figure 48**.

Removal

1. Depressurize the fuel system as described in this chapter.

2. Remove the seat (Chapter Fourteen), and disconnect the negative battery cable (Chapter Nine).

3. Drain the fuel tank as described in this chapter.

4. Remove the fuel tank console as described in this chapter.

5. Depress the tab and disconnect the fuel pump connector (A, **Figure 38**) on the top of the fuel pump top plate.

6. Disconnect the vapor vent hose (B, **Figure 38**) from the fitting on the fuel pump top plate.

NOTE
The following steps are shown with the fuel tank removed from the frame for photo clarity. This procedure can be performed with the fuel tank in installed on the frame.

7. Using a crossing pattern, loosen and remove the top plate screws. Discard the screws as they cannot be reused.

8. On all models except FXD and 2007-2008 FXDSE, rotate the top plate (**Figure 49**) toward the right side until the vent tube clears the fuel tank opening.

9. Partially remove the top plate and depress the tab and disconnect the fuel pump/sender connector (**Figure 50**) from the bottom of the top plate.

10. Remove the top plate from the fuel tank and discard the gasket.

Installation

1. Move the electrical harness (**Figure 51**) back into place within the fuel tank cavity. Make sure it does not get pinched while installing the top plate.

2. Apply several small dots of gasket sealer to the *new* gasket, and install the gasket (**Figure 52**) onto the top plate.

3. On all models except FXD and 2007-2008 FXDSE, tilt the top plate toward the right side so the vent tube (A, **Figure 53**) will clear the fuel tank opening.

4. Connect the fuel pump/sender connector (B, **Figure 53**) to the terminal on the bottom side of the top plate. Push the connector on until it locks into place (**Figure 50**).

5. Correctly position the top plate (**Figure 49**) on the fuel tank and install *new* screws. Following the torque sequence indicated in **Figure 54** or **Figure 55**, tighten the screws to 20 in.-lb. (2.3 N•m).

6. Connect the vapor vent hose (B, **Figure 38**) onto the fuel pump top plate fitting.

7. Connect the fuel pump electrical connector to the fitting (A, **Figure 38**) on the top side of the fuel pump top plate.

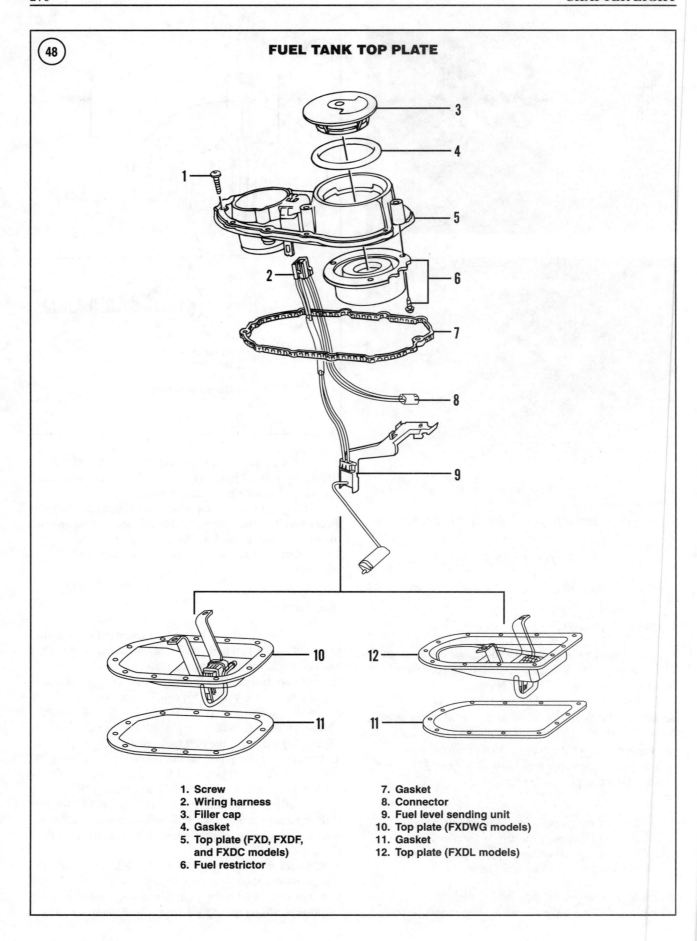

FUEL TANK TOP PLATE

1. Screw
2. Wiring harness
3. Filler cap
4. Gasket
5. Top plate (FXD, FXDF, and FXDC models)
6. Fuel restrictor
7. Gasket
8. Connector
9. Fuel level sending unit
10. Top plate (FXDWG models)
11. Gasket
12. Top plate (FXDL models)

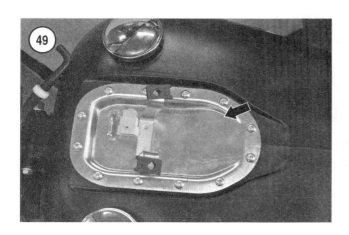

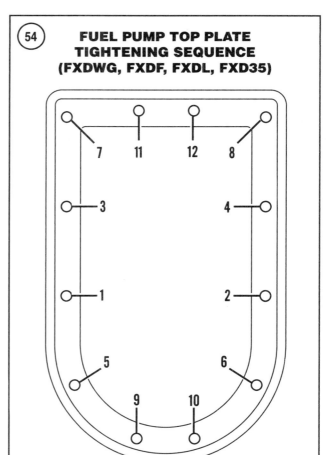

FUEL PUMP TOP PLATE TIGHTENING SEQUENCE (FXDWG, FXDF, FXDL, FXD35)

8. Install the fuel tank console as described in this chapter.

9. Install the seat as described in Chapter Fourteen.

10. Connect the negative battery cable as described in Chapter Nine.

Inspection

1. Check the mounting flange (A, **Figure 56**) for bending and distortion. Straighten if necessary to ensure a good leak free seal against the fuel tank.

2. Check that the vent tube opening (B, **Figure 56**) is clear. Apply low air pressure to clean it out if necessary.

3. Inspect the fuel pump/sender terminals (C, **Figure 56**) for bending and corrosion. Straighten or clean if necessary.

4. Inspect the mounting bracket for bending and distortion; straighten if necessary. Make sure both speed nuts (D, **Figure 56**) are in place.

FUEL LEVEL SENDING UNIT

Refer to **Figure 57**.

Removal/Installation

1. Remove the top plate as described in this chapter.
2. Carefully cut the tie (A, **Figure 58**) securing the electrical harnesses together.
3. Disconnect the sending unit connector (B, **Figure 58**) from the fuel pump harness.
4. Lift up on tab (A, **Figure 59**), move the unit (B) toward the rear and release it from the top of the fuel pump assembly.
5. Slowly lift up and rotate the assembly (**Figure 60**) toward the right side. Remove the assembly, being careful to not bend the float arm.
6. Inspect the unit (**Figure 61**) for deterioration or damage; replace if necessary.
7. Install by reversing the removal steps. Push the unit forward (**Figure 62**) until it locks into place (**Figure 63**).

FUEL PUMP ASSEMBLY

Refer to **Figure 57**.

Removal

1. Remove the top plate as described in this chapter.
2. Remove the fuel level sending unit as described in this chapter.
3. Depress the upper and lower tabs (A, **Figure 64**) and disconnect the fuel line (B) from the fuel pump assembly (C).
4. Lift up on the fuel pump assembly tab (**Figure 65**). Push the fuel pump toward the front of the fuel tank and disengage it form the fuel tank.
5. Slowly rotate the fuel pump assembly (**Figure 66**) *clockwise* and up and withdraw it from the left side of the fuel tank.

Installation

1. Carefully insert the fuel pump assembly (**Figure 66**) into the left side of the fuel tank.

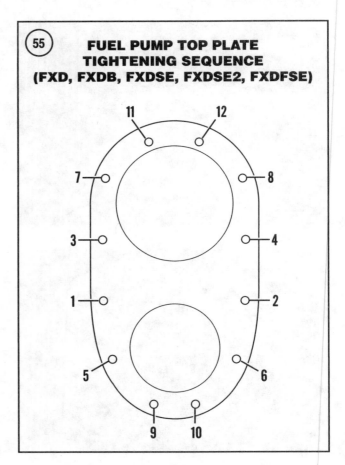

55 **FUEL PUMP TOP PLATE TIGHTENING SEQUENCE (FXD, FXDB, FXDSE, FXDSE2, FXDFSE)**

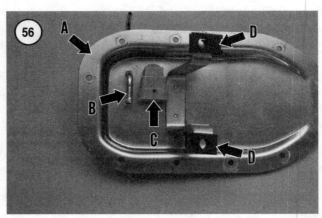

56

2. Slowly rotate the fuel pump assembly *counterclockwise* and downward into position within the fuel tank. Exercise caution so the float arm is not damaged.

3. Move fuel pump into position and secure the end cap onto the mounting tabs. Gently move the fuel pump toward the rear to make sure it is engaged correctly.

4. Install the fuel level sending unit as described in this chapter.

5. Install the top plate as described in this chapter.

FUEL FILTER

Refer to **Figure 57**.

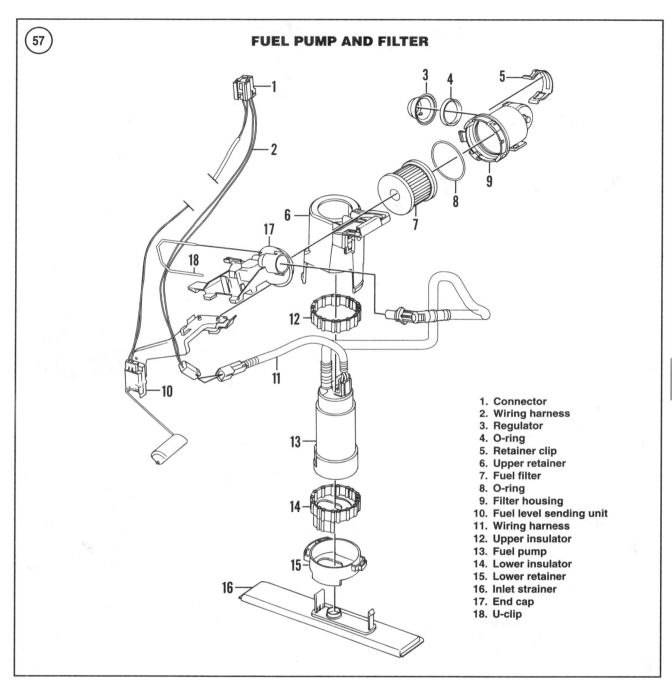

57

FUEL PUMP AND FILTER

1. Connector
2. Wiring harness
3. Regulator
4. O-ring
5. Retainer clip
6. Upper retainer
7. Fuel filter
8. O-ring
9. Filter housing
10. Fuel level sending unit
11. Wiring harness
12. Upper insulator
13. Fuel pump
14. Lower insulator
15. Lower retainer
16. Inlet strainer
17. End cap
18. U-clip

8

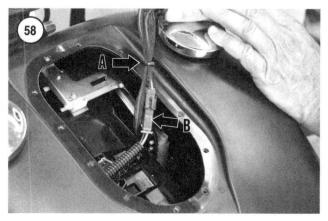

58

59

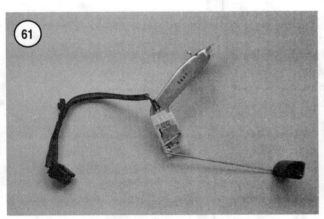

Removal/Installation

1. Remove the fuel pump assembly as described in this chapter.

2. Depress the fuel filter retainer clip tab (**Figure 67**) and withdraw the U-shaped clip (**Figure 68**).

3. Separate the end cap (A, **Figure 69**) from the fuel pump body (B, **Figure 69**) and separate them (**Figure 70**).

4. Disconnect the electrical connector (C, **Figure 69**) and release it from the clip (D), if necessary.

5. Withdraw the fuel filter (**Figure 71**) from filter housing, and discard it.

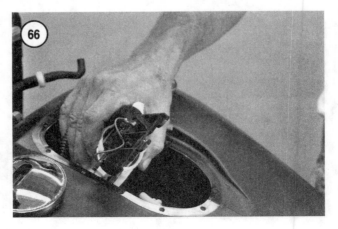

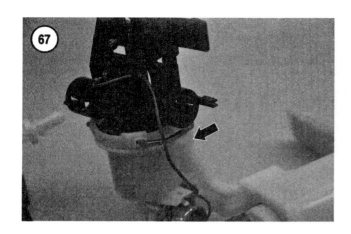

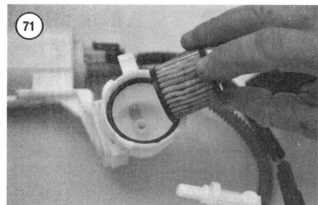

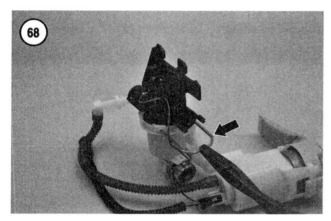

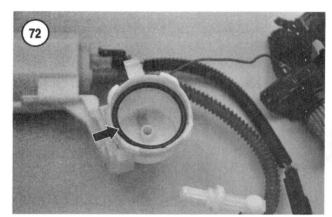

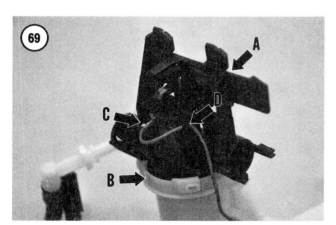

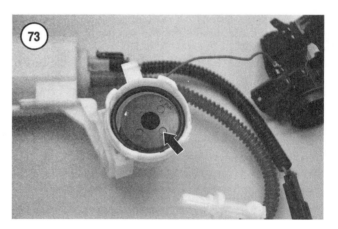

6. Remove the O-ring (**Figure 72**) from the end cap, and discard it.

7. Install a *new* O-ring (**Figure 72**) onto the end cap.

8. Install a *new* fuel filter (**Figure 73**) into filter housing.

9. Install the end cap (A, **Figure 69**) onto the fuel pump body (B). Make sure it is seated correctly into the locating tab (**Figure 74**).

10. Connect the purple wire electrical connector (C, **Figure 69**) and hook it onto the clip (D), if disconnected.

11. Install the U-shaped clip (**Figure 68**), and push it in until it locks into place by the fuel retainer clip tab (**Figure 67**). Pull up on the end cap to ensure it is locked in place.

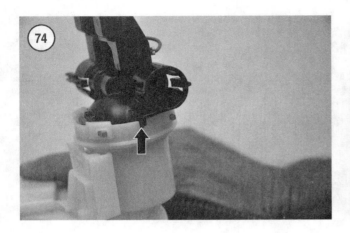

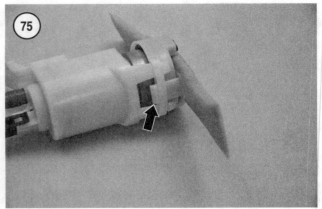

12. Install the fuel pump assembly as described in this chapter.

INLET STRAINER

Refer to **Figure 57**.

Removal/Installation

1. Remove the fuel pump assembly as described in this chapter.
2. Carefully depress the locking tab (**Figure 75**) on each side of the lower retainer.
3. Remove the inlet strainer (**Figure 76**) from the lower retainer.
4. Inspect the inlet strainer for contamination and damage; replace as necessary.
5. Align the inlet strainer with the fuel pump inlet fitting and install the strainer onto the fuel pump.
6. Push the inlet strainer on until the locking tabs (**Figure 75**) on each side of the lower retainer are correctly engaged. Pull gently on the inlet strainer to ensure it is locked into place.
7. Install the fuel pump assembly as described in this chapter.

FUEL PUMP

Refer to **Figure 57**.

Removal/Installation

1. Remove the fuel pump assembly as described in this chapter.
2. Remove the inlet strainer as described in this chapter.
3. Carefully release the three locking tabs (**Figure 77** and **Figure 78**) on each side of the lower retainer. Remove the lower retainer.
4. Disconnect the connector (A, **Figure 79**) from the fuel pump.
5. Withdraw the fuel pump (A, **Figure 80**) from the upper retainer (B, **Figure 79**).

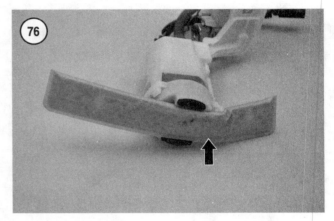

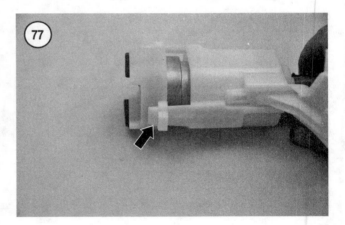

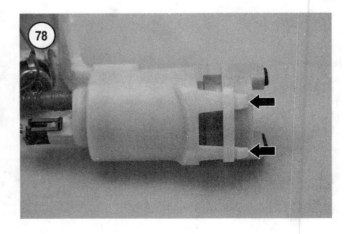

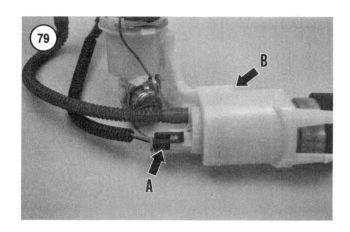

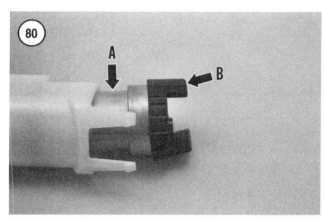

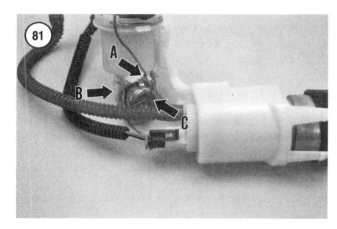

6. If removed, install the insulators (B, **Figure 80**) into upper and lower retainers.

7. Install the fuel pump (A, **Figure 80**) into the upper retainer (B, **Figure 79**).

8. Install the lower retainer onto the upper retainer. Push it on until the three tabs (**Figure 77** and **Figure 78**) seat correctly.

9. Connect the connector (A, **Figure 79**) onto the fuel pump.

10. Install the inlet strainer as described in this chapter.

11. Install the fuel pump assembly as described in this chapter.

FUEL PRESSURE REGULATOR

Refer to **Figure 57**.

Removal/Installation

1. Remove the fuel pump assembly as described in this chapter.

2. Disconnect the wire terminal (A, **Figure 81**) from end of the regulator.

3. Remove the retainer clip (B, **Figure 81**) and remove the regulator (C) from the filter housing.

4. Remove the O-ring and discard it.

5. Install a *new* O-ring onto the regulator.

6. Install the regulator (C, **Figure 81**) into the filter housing. Then, install the retainer clip (B, **Figure 81**). Make sure the clip is seated correctly.

7. Connect the wire terminal (A, **Figure 81**) onto end of the regulator.

8. Install the fuel pump assembly as described in this chapter.

FUEL PRESSURE TEST

> *WARNING*
> *This procedure is performed adjacent to a hot exhaust system while handling fuel-related test equipment. Have an approved fire extinguished rated for gasoline fires (Class B) available.*

1. The following tools, or their equivalents, are required for this test:

    a. Fuel pressure gauge (H-D part No. HD-41182).

    b. Two fuel pressure gauge adapters (H-D part No. HD-44061).

2. Depressurize the fuel system as described in this chapter.

3. Lift the chrome sleeve (A, **Figure 82**) on the quick-connect fitting, and disconnect the fuel line (B) from the fuel tank.

4. Install the pressure gauge adapters as follows:

    a. Pull in the knurled sleeve on the female end of the first fuel pressure gauge adapter.

8

b. Insert male end of second adapter into the first adapter, and push down on knurled sleeve until locked. Gently tug on the adapters to make sure they are locked in place and will not come loose.

c. Pull in the knurled sleeve on the second fuel pressure gauge adapter. Insert the male end of fuel supply line (A, **Figure 83**) into the second adapter, and then pull down on the knurled sleeve until locked. Gently tug on the fuel supply fitting to make sure it is locked in place and will not come loose.

d. Pull up on the fuel tank quick-connect chrome sleeve (B, **Figure 83**), insert the male end of the first fuel pressure gauge adapter. Pull down on the chrome sleeve until locked. Gently tug on the adapter to make sure it is locked in place and will not come loose.

5. Make sure the fuel valve and the air bleed petcock on the fuel pressure gauge are in the *closed* position.

6. Remove the protective cap from the Schrader valve on the fuel pressure gauge adapter closest to the fuel tank. Connect the fuel pressure gauge (C, **Figure 83**) to the Schrader valve. Gently tug on the fuel pressure gauge to make sure it is locked in place and will not come loose.

7. Install the fuel pump fuse.

WARNING
The exhaust system warms up rapidly, so take preventive measures if necessary.

8. Start the engine to pressurize the fuel system. Allow the engine to idle.

9. Slowly open the fuel valve (D, **Figure 83**) and allow fuel to flow to the pressure gauge.

10. Position the clear air bleed tube into a suitable container. Open and close the air bleed petcock to purge the air from the fuel gauge and hose. Repeat several times until only bubble-free fuel flows from the bleed tube into the container. Close the petcock.

11. Increase engine above idle and then decrease engine speed several times. Note the gauge readings. The fuel pressure should remain constant at the fuel pressure specified in **Table 1** for all engine speeds. Repeat several times.

12. Turn the engine off.

13. Open the air bleed petcock to relieve all fuel pressure and purge fuel from the pressure gauge.

14. Place a shop cloth beneath the Schrader valve to catch any remaining fuel, and disconnect the fuel pressure gauge from the Schrader valve. Dispose of the shop cloth in a suitable manner.

15. Install the protective cap onto the Schrader valve, and tighten it securely.

16. Disconnect the fuel pressure adapters from the fuel supply line and from the quick-connect fitting on the tank.

17. Pull up the chrome sleeve of quick-connect fitting, and insert fuel supply line onto fitting. Gently pull down in the fuel supply line to make sure it is locked in place and will not come loose.

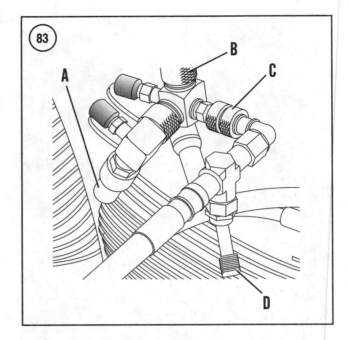

FUEL TANK CONSOLE

FXD and FXDSE Models
Removal/Installation

Refer to **Figure 84**.

1. Disconnect the negative battery cable as described in Chapter Nine.

2. Remove the seat as described in Chapter Fourteen.

3. Remove the screw at the rear of the fuel tank console.

4. Remove the four screws adjacent to the fuel gauge.

5. Remove the screws securing the trim ring to the trim ring mounting boss. Note the location of the different length screws to ensure correct placement during installation.

6. Carefully lift the console up off the fuel tank.

7. Remove the trim ring mounting boss from the fuel tank.

8. If necessary, remove the fuel gauge from the top plate as described in Chapter Nine.

9. Install the trim ring mounting boss onto the fuel tank.

10. If disconnected, connect the fuel gauge connector.

11. Align the fuel gauge tabs and insert the fuel gauge into the top plate.

12. Install the trim ring mounting boss over the fuel gauge.

13. Carefully install the console onto the fuel tank. Align the screw holes with the fuel tank and mounting boss.

14. Install the screw at the rear of the fuel tank console and tighten to 18-24 in.-lb. (2.0-2.7 N•m).

15. Install the four front screws adjacent to the fuel gauge and tighten to 18-27 in.-lb. (2.0-3.0 N•m).

16. Install the trim ring and align the screw holes. Install the screws securing the trim ring to the trim ring mounting boss in the locations noted during removal. Tighten the trim ring screws as follows:

a. Short screws: 18-22 in.-lb. (2.0-2.5 N•m).

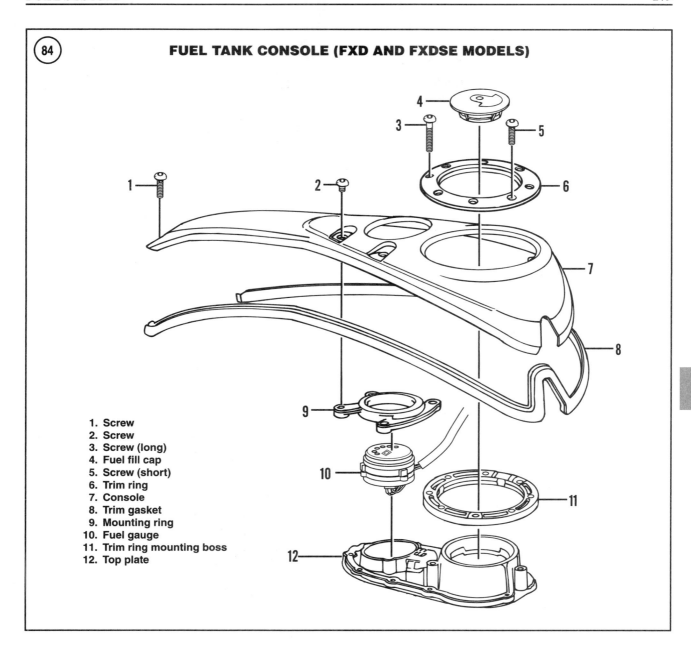

FUEL TANK CONSOLE (FXD AND FXDSE MODELS)

84

1. Screw
2. Screw
3. Screw (long)
4. Fuel fill cap
5. Screw (short)
6. Trim ring
7. Console
8. Trim gasket
9. Mounting ring
10. Fuel gauge
11. Trim ring mounting boss
12. Top plate

8

b. Long screws: 12-15 in.-lb. (1.4-1.7 N•m).

17. Connect the negative battery cable as described in Chapter Nine.

FXDL Models
Removal/Installation

Refer to **Figure 85**.

1. Disconnect the negative battery cable as described in Chapter Nine.

2. Remove the seat as described in Chapter Fourteen.

3. Remove the screw at the rear of the fuel tank console.

4. Remove the two screws adjacent to the tachometer.

5. Partially lift the fuel tank console up off the fuel tank. Turn it upside down and lay it on several towels.

6. Disconnect the 12-pin tachometer and 12-pin speedometer connectors from the meters.

7. Disconnect the 3-pin ignition switch connector.

8. Remove the fuel tank console.

9. Install by reversing the removal steps. Tighten the fuel tank console screws to 18-24 in.-lb. (2.0-2.7 N•m).

FXDC, FXD35, FXDWG, FXDF, FXDB
and FXDSE2 Models
Removal/Installation

Refer to **Figures 86-88**.

1. Disconnect the negative battery cable as described in Chapter Nine.

2. Remove the seat as described in Chapter Fourteen.

3. Remove the screw (**Figure 89**) at the rear of the leather trim panel or fuel tank console.

4. Remove the two screws (A, **Figure 90**) adjacent to the speedometer.

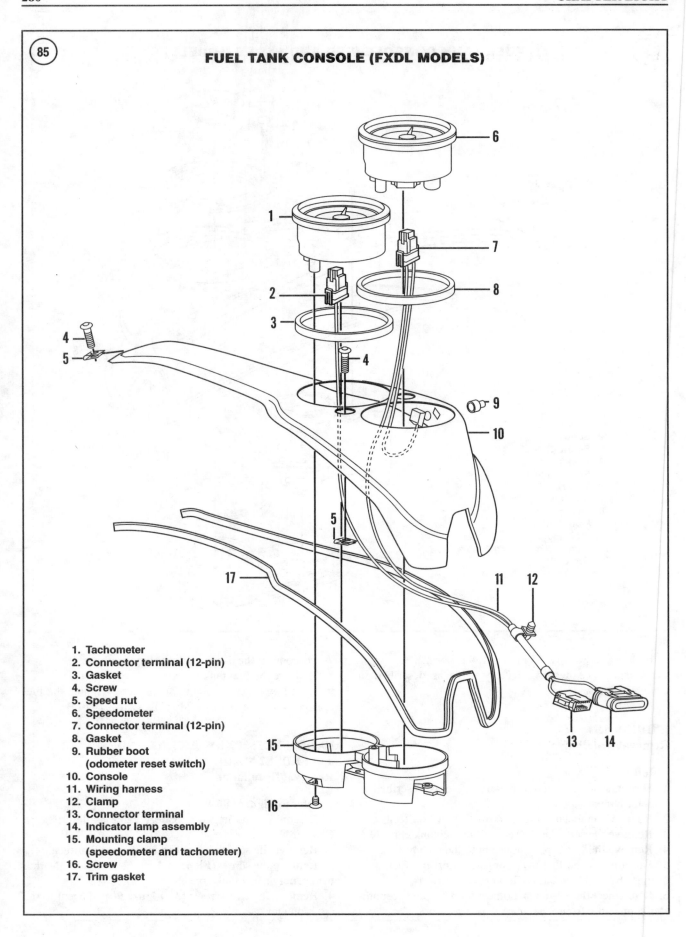

FUEL TANK CONSOLE (FXDL MODELS)

85

1. Tachometer
2. Connector terminal (12-pin)
3. Gasket
4. Screw
5. Speed nut
6. Speedometer
7. Connector terminal (12-pin)
8. Gasket
9. Rubber boot
   (odometer reset switch)
10. Console
11. Wiring harness
12. Clamp
13. Connector terminal
14. Indicator lamp assembly
15. Mounting clamp
    (speedometer and tachometer)
16. Screw
17. Trim gasket

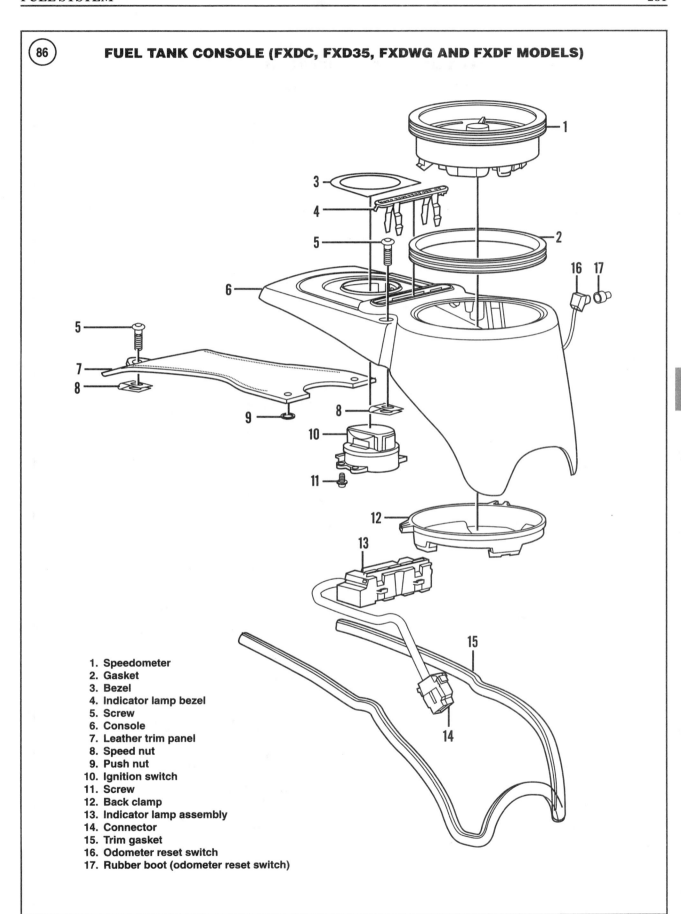

86

FUEL TANK CONSOLE (FXDC, FXD35, FXDWG AND FXDF MODELS)

1. Speedometer
2. Gasket
3. Bezel
4. Indicator lamp bezel
5. Screw
6. Console
7. Leather trim panel
8. Speed nut
9. Push nut
10. Ignition switch
11. Screw
12. Back clamp
13. Indicator lamp assembly
14. Connector
15. Trim gasket
16. Odometer reset switch
17. Rubber boot (odometer reset switch)

8

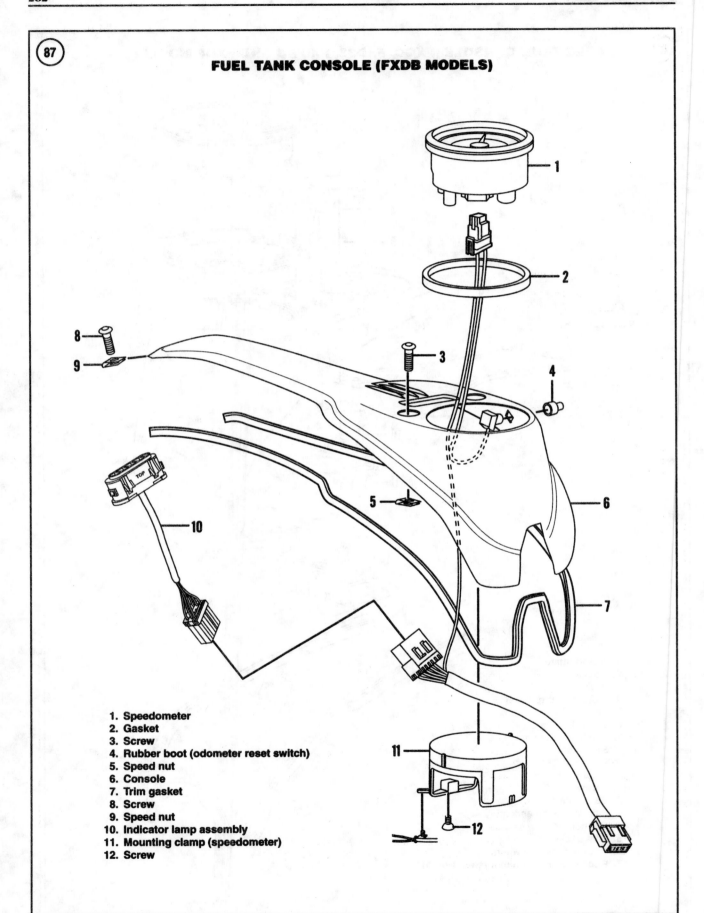

87

FUEL TANK CONSOLE (FXDB MODELS)

1. Speedometer
2. Gasket
3. Screw
4. Rubber boot (odometer reset switch)
5. Speed nut
6. Console
7. Trim gasket
8. Screw
9. Speed nut
10. Indicator lamp assembly
11. Mounting clamp (speedometer)
12. Screw

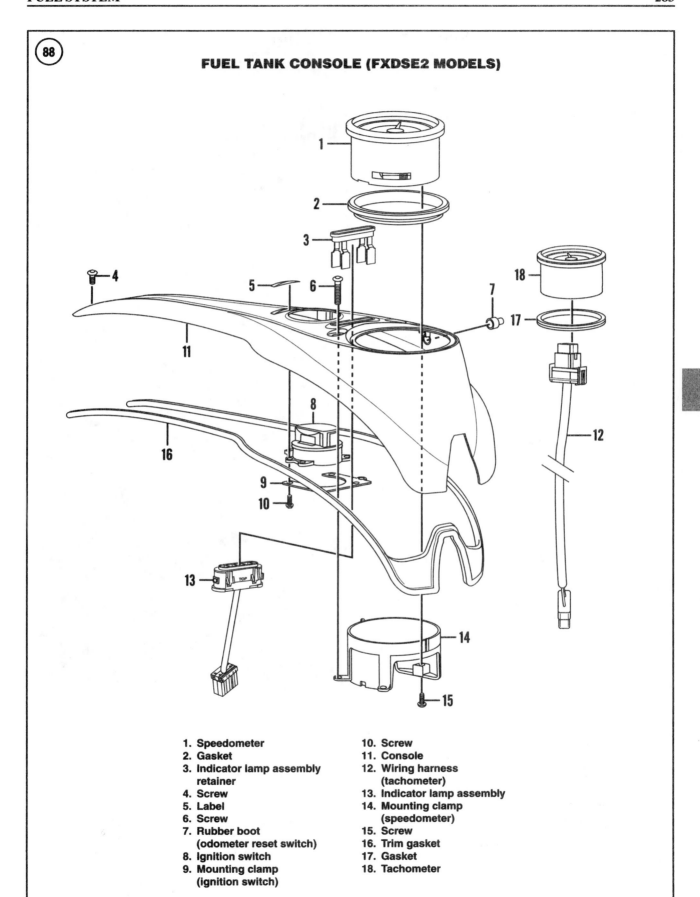

88

FUEL TANK CONSOLE (FXDSE2 MODELS)

8

1. Speedometer
2. Gasket
3. Indicator lamp assembly retainer
4. Screw
5. Label
6. Screw
7. Rubber boot (odometer reset switch)
8. Ignition switch
9. Mounting clamp (ignition switch)
10. Screw
11. Console
12. Wiring harness (tachometer)
13. Indicator lamp assembly
14. Mounting clamp (speedometer)
15. Screw
16. Trim gasket
17. Gasket
18. Tachometer

5. Unscrew the rubber boot (B, **Figure 90**) from the odometer reset switch. Carefully push the reset switch into the console.

6. Partially lift the fuel tank console up off the fuel tank. Turn it upside down and lay it on several towels.

7. Disconnect the 12-pin speedometer connector (A, **Figure 91**) from the speedometer.

8. Disconnect the 8-pin connector (B, **Figure 91**) from the indicator lamp assembly.

9. Remove the fuel tank console.

10. Install by reversing the removal steps. Tighten the fuel tank console screws to 18-24 in.-lb. (2.0-2.7 N•m).

FXDFSE2 Models
Removal/Installation

Refer to **Figure 92**.

1. Disconnect the negative battery cable as described in Chapter Nine.

2. Remove the seat as described in Chapter Fourteen.

3. Remove the screw at the rear of the fuel tank console.

4. Remove the two screws adjacent to the speedometer.

5. Partially lift the fuel tank console up off the fuel tank. Turn it upside down and lay it on several towels.

6. Disconnect the 12-pin speedometer connector from the speedometer.

7. Disconnect the 8-pin connector from the indicator lamp assembly.

8. Disconnect the 3-pin ignition switch connector.

9. Remove the fuel tank console.

10. Install by reversing the removal steps. Tighten the fuel tank console screws to 18-24 in.-lb. (2.0-2.7 N•m).

ELECTRONIC FUEL INJECTION (EFI)

This section describes the components and the operation of the electronic, sequential-port fuel injection (EFI) system. Fuel injection eliminates an inefficient cold start enrichment device, yet it provides accurate idle-speed control. It also improves torque characteristics while increasing fuel economy and reducing exhaust emissions. The fuel injection system constantly adjusts the air/fuel ratio and ignition timing to match the load conditions. Engine performance can be modified by simply changing the operating parameters of the electronic control module (ECM).

Complete service of the system requires a H-D digital technician, a breakout box and a number of other special tools. However, basic troubleshooting diagnosis is no different on a fuel-injected motorcycle than on a carbureted one. If the check engine light comes on or if there is a drivability problem, troubleshoot the system as described in Electronic Diagnostic System (Chapter Two). Make sure all related electrical connections are clean and secure. A high or erratic idle speed may indicate a vacuum leak. If the basic tests fail to reveal the cause of a problem, refer service to a dealership. Incorrectly-performed diagnostic

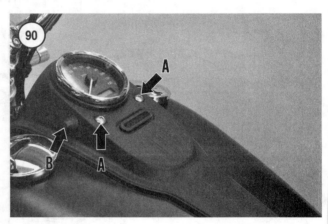

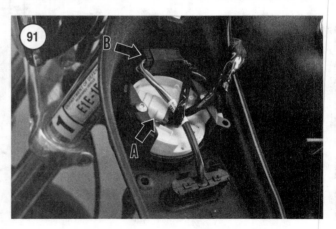

procedures can result in damage to the fuel injection system.

Electronic Control Module (ECM) and Sensors

The electronic control module, or ECM (**Figure 93**), is mounted within the electrical caddy on the right side behind the cover (**Figure 94**). It determines the optimum fuel injection and ignition timing based on input from six or seven sensors. Do not tamper with the ECM; it is sealed to prevent moisture contamination. **Figure 95** shows some of the engine-mounted sensors. Additional sensors (**Figure 96**), their locations and functions are as follows:

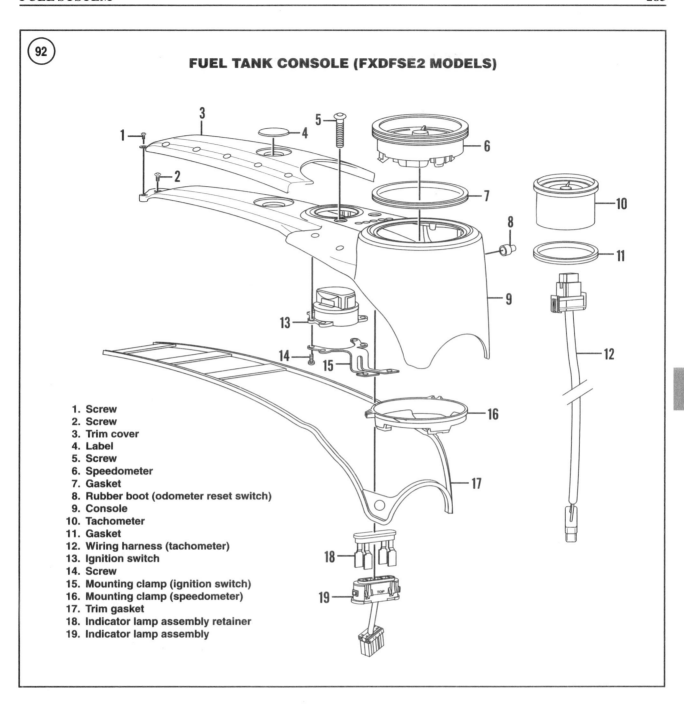

FUEL TANK CONSOLE (FXDFSE2 MODELS)

1. Screw
2. Screw
3. Trim cover
4. Label
5. Screw
6. Speedometer
7. Gasket
8. Rubber boot (odometer reset switch)
9. Console
10. Tachometer
11. Gasket
12. Wiring harness (tachometer)
13. Ignition switch
14. Screw
15. Mounting clamp (ignition switch)
16. Mounting clamp (speedometer)
17. Trim gasket
18. Indicator lamp assembly retainer
19. Indicator lamp assembly

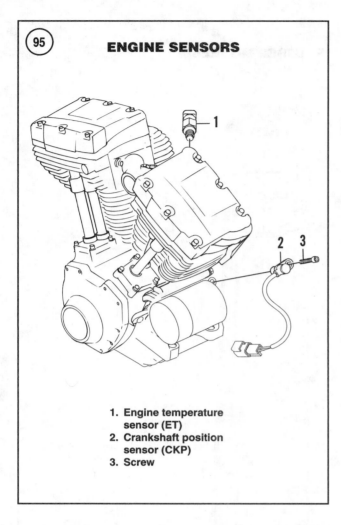

95 **ENGINE SENSORS**

1. Engine temperature sensor (ET)
2. Crankshaft position sensor (CKP)
3. Screw

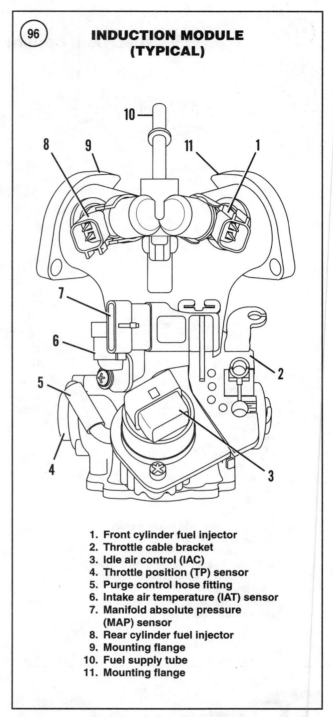

96 **INDUCTION MODULE (TYPICAL)**

1. Front cylinder fuel injector
2. Throttle cable bracket
3. Idle air control (IAC)
4. Throttle position (TP) sensor
5. Purge control hose fitting
6. Intake air temperature (IAT) sensor
7. Manifold absolute pressure (MAP) sensor
8. Rear cylinder fuel injector
9. Mounting flange
10. Fuel supply tube
11. Mounting flange

1. The throttle position (TP) sensor, located on the front of the induction module and attached directly to the throttle shaft, indicates throttle angle. The ECM indicates the air volume entering the engine based on the throttle angle.

2. The intake air temperature (IAT) sensor is located inside the induction module (rear cylinder's intake runner). The ECM determines the air density and adjusts the injector opening time based on input from this sensor.

3. The manifold absolute pressure (MAP) sensor is located on top of the induction module. The MAP monitors intake manifold pressure (vacuum) and sends this information to the ECM.

4. Idle air control (IAC) is located on top of the induction module. The ECM controls the engine speed by moving the IAC to open or close the passage around the throttle plate.

5. The crankshaft position (CKP) sensor, located on the forward position of the left crankcase, is an inductive-type sensor. The ECM determines the engine speed by how fast the machined teeth on the flywheel pass by the sensor.

6. The engine temperature (ET) sensor is located on the left side of the front cylinder head. The ECM adjusts the injector opening time based on input from this sensor.

7. Vehicle speed sensor (VSS) is located on top of the transmission just behind the top cover. The VSS monitors gear tooth movement on top gear and sends data to the ECM.

8. Oxygen sensors (O2) are located on the front and rear exhaust header. The O2 sensors monitor the oxygen content of the exhaust system, and adjust the air/fuel mixture to maintain the desired 14.7:1 air/fuel mixture.

9. Active intake solenoid (HDI models only) is located in the air filter backplate. The solenoid opens a valve in the backplate to allow additional air to enter the air/fuel mixture at speeds greater than 43 mph (70 kph) with the throttle opening greater than 50%.

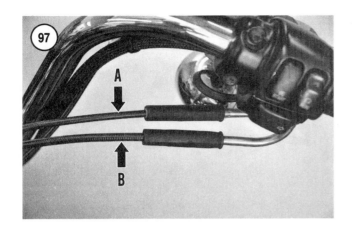

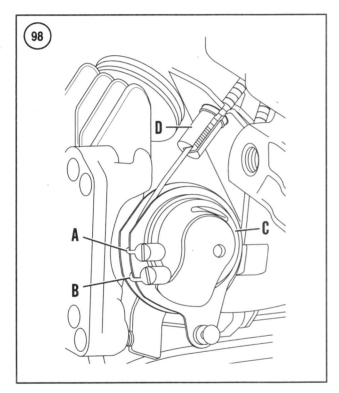

is pressurized at 58 psi (400 kPa) and is controlled by the pressure regulator.

A check valve is located on both the supply and return lines where they attach to the fuel tank.

Fuel injectors

The solenoid-actuated, constant-stroke, pintle-type fuel injectors consist of a solenoid plunger, needle valve and housing. The fuel injector's opening is fixed and fuel pressure is constant. The fuel injectors are part of the fuel rail assembly.

The ECM controls the time the injectors open and close.

Induction module

The induction module consists of two fuel injectors, a throttle position sensor (TPS), an intake air temperature (IAT) sensor, a manifold absolute pressure (MAP) sensor, an idle air control (IAC), a fuel rail, a fuel supply tube and a purge tube fitting (California models).

THROTTLE AND IDLE CABLES

WARNING
Do not ride the motorcycle until the throttle control cables are properly adjusted. Improper cable routing and adjustment can cause the throttle to stick open. This could cause loss of control. Recheck the adjustment before riding the bike.

There are two different throttle cables. At the throttle grip, the front cable is the throttle control cable (A, **Figure 97**) and the rear cable is the idle control cable (B). At the induction control module, the idle control cable (A, **Figure 98**) is located at the top of the throttle wheel and the throttle control cable (B) is located at the bottom.

Refer to **Figure 99**.

Removal

1. Remove the fuel tank as described in this chapter.
2. Remove the air filter and backplate as described in this chapter.
3. Make a drawing or take a picture of the control cable routing from the induction module through the frame to the right side handlebar. Note any clamps or ties securing the cables.
4. Roll the boots (**Figure 100**) off the cable adjusters.
5. At the handlebar, loosen both control cable adjuster locknuts (A, **Figure 101**), and turn the cable adjusters (B) *clockwise* as far as possible to increase cable slack.
6. Use needlenose pliers, and disconnect the throttle control cable (B, **Figure 98**) and the idle control cable (A) from the throttle wheel (C) at the induction module.

Fuel Supply System

Fuel pump and filters

The fuel pump and filter assembly is located inside the fuel tank. This assembly is part of the removable top plate that is attached to the top of the fuel tank. The top plate allows for easy removal and installation of the attached components without having to work within the fuel tank cavity. To provide maximum filtration prior to the fuel reaching the fuel injectors, there is an inlet screen on the fuel pump and then a secondary fuel filter canister located downstream from the fuel pump.

Fuel lines

One fuel line, equipped with a quick-connect fitting, is located at the base of the fuel tank. The supply fuel line

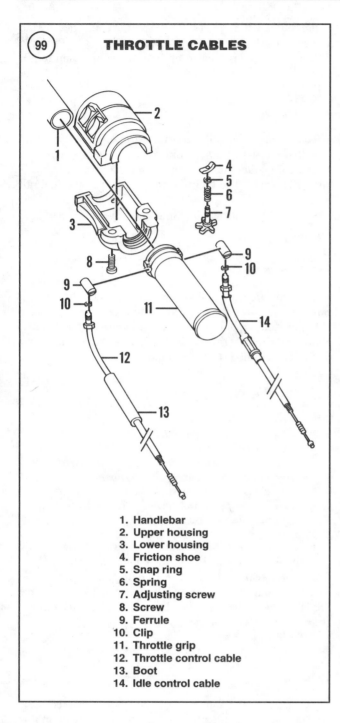

99 **THROTTLE CABLES**

1. Handlebar
2. Upper housing
3. Lower housing
4. Friction shoe
5. Snap ring
6. Spring
7. Adjusting screw
8. Screw
9. Ferrule
10. Clip
11. Throttle grip
12. Throttle control cable
13. Boot
14. Idle control cable

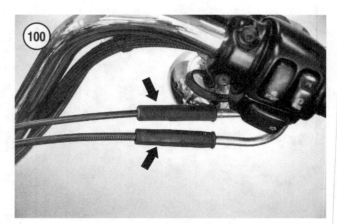

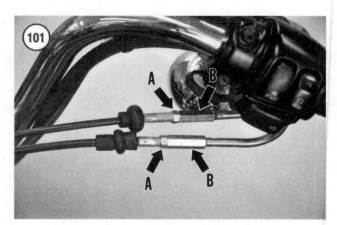

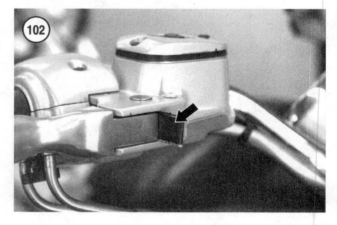

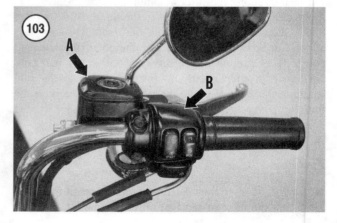

7. Release the cables from the integral cable guides (D, **Figure 98**) on the induction module.

> *CAUTION*
> *Failure to install the spacer will result in damage to the rubber boot and plunger on the front brake switch.*

8. Insert a 5/32 in. (4 mm) thick spacer (**Figure 102**) between the brake lever and lever bracket. Make sure the spacer stays in place during the following steps.

9. Remove the front brake master cylinder (A, **Figure 103**) as described in Chapter Thirteen.

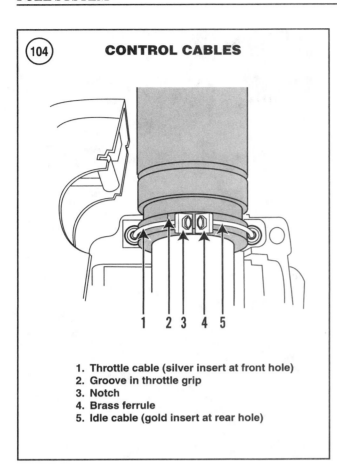

CONTROL CABLES

1. Throttle cable (silver insert at front hole)
2. Groove in throttle grip
3. Notch
4. Brass ferrule
5. Idle cable (gold insert at rear hole)

10. Remove the upper and lower Torx (T25) screws securing the right handlebar switch assembly (B, **Figure 103**) together.

11. Separate the switch halves and note the location of both idle and throttle control cables within the throttle grip (**Figure 104**).

NOTE
The friction shoe is a loose fit and may fall out or move if the switch lower housing is turned upside down or is shaken.

12. Remove the friction shoe (**Figure 105**) from the end of the friction adjusting screw.

13. Remove the brass ferrules from the notches on the inboard side of the throttle grip (**Figure 106**). Remove the ferrules from the cable end fittings.

NOTE
Use a rocking motion while pulling on the control cable housings. If necessary, place a drop of engine oil on the housings retaining rings to ease removal.

14. Remove the throttle grip from the handlebar.

15. Pull the crimped inserts at the end of the throttle and idle control cable housings from the switch lower housing.

16. Remove the clip securing the throttle and idle control cables to the handlebar.

17. Remove all clips and ties securing the throttle and idle control cables onto the right side of the frame.

18. Remove the cables from the frame.

19. Clean the throttle grip assembly and dry thoroughly. Check the throttle slots for cracks or other damage. Replace the throttle if necessary.

20. The friction adjust screw is secured to the lower switch housing with a snap ring. If necessary, remove the friction spring, snap ring, spring and friction adjust screw. Check these parts for wear or damage. Replace damaged parts and reverse the removal steps to install. Make sure the snap ring seats in the friction screw groove completely.

21. Clean the throttle area on the handlebar with solvent.

Installation

1. Apply a light coat of graphite to the surfaces inside the housing and to the handlebar.

2. Push the larger diameter silver insert on the throttle cable into the larger hole in front of the tension adjusting screw in the switch lower housing. Push it in until it snaps into place.

3. Push the smaller diameter gold insert on the throttle cable into the smaller hole in the rear of the tension adjusting screw in the switch lower housing. Push it in until it snaps into place.

4. Install the friction shoe (**Figure 107**) into the lower housing. Match the curvature on the friction shoe with the handlebar.

8

5. Install the throttle grip onto the handlebar. Push it on until it stops, and pull it back about 1/8 in. (3.2 mm). Rotate it until the ferrule notches are at the top.

6. Hold the lower switch housing below the throttle grip. Install the brass ferrules onto the cables so the end fittings seat in the ferrule recess. Seat ferrules in their respective notches on the throttle control grip. Check that the cables are captured in the molded grooves in the grip (**Figure 104**).

7. Assemble the upper and lower switch housings (B, **Figure 103**) and the throttle grip. Install the switch housing screws and finger-tighten the screws.

8. If not in place, insert the 5/32 in. (4 mm) thick spacer (**Figure 102**) between the brake lever and lever bracket. Make sure the spacer stays in place during the installation procedure.

9. Install the front brake master cylinder (A, **Figure 103**) as described in Chapter Thirteen.

10. Starting with the bottom screw, tighten the switch housing screws to 35-45 in.-lb. (4.0-5.1 N•m).

11. Remove the cardboard insert from the front master cylinder.

12. Operate the throttle and make sure both cables move in and out properly.

13. Route the cables from the handlebar to the induction module along the path noted during removal. Secure the cables with any clamps or tie-wraps.

14. At the induction module, perform the following:

   a. Install the idle cable (A, **Figure 98**) ball end over the top of the throttle barrel (C) and install the cable ball end into the upper hole in the throttle barrel. Make sure it is properly seated.

   b. Install the throttle control cable (B, **Figure 98**) ball end under the bottom of the throttle barrel (C) install the cable ball ends into the lower hole in the throttle barrel. Make sure it is properly seated.

   c. Install the cables into the integral cable guides in the induction module.

15. At the throttle grip, tighten the cables to keep the ball ends from being disconnected from throttle barrel.

16. Operate the throttle a few times, making sure the throttle barrel operates smoothly with no binding. Also check that both cable ends are seated squarely in their cable bracket guides and in the throttle barrel.

17. Adjust the throttle and idle control cables as described in Chapter Three.

18. Install the backplate and air filter as described in this chapter.

19. Install the fuel tank as described in this chapter.

20. Start the engine and allow it to idle in NEUTRAL. Then, turn the handlebar from side to side. Do not operate the throttle. If the engine speed increases when turning the handlebar assembly, the throttle cables are routed incorrectly or damaged. Recheck cable routing and adjustment.

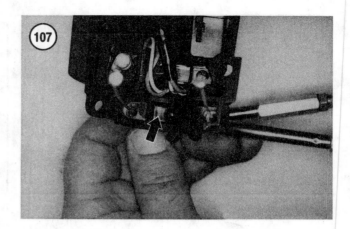

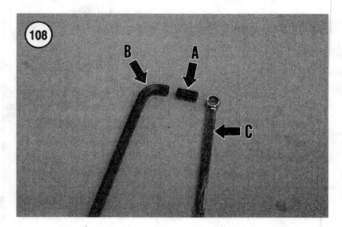

INDUCTION MODULE

Tools

Allen bolts are used to mount the induction module in place. An intake manifold wrench (K&L part No. 35-3975 or H-D part No. HD-47250), or an equivalent, greatly assists induction module removal and installation.

If this tool is not available, fashion a tool by performing the following:

1. Cut a 9/16 in. (14 mm) long stub (A, **Figure 108**) from a 1/4-in. Allen wrench.

2. Use the shortened wrench (B, **Figure 108**) when leverage is needed to break loose or tighten an Allen bolt.

3. Use the stub (A, **Figure 108**) and a 1/4-in. wrench (C) to remove or install an Allen bolt.

Removal

Refer to **Figures 109-111**.

1. Remove the fuel tank as described in this chapter.

2. Remove the air filter and backplate as describe in this chapter.

3. Remove the horn assembly as described in Chapter Nine.

4. On California models, remove the purge hose from the fitting on top of the induction module (A, **Figure 112**).

5. Disconnect the throttle (A, **Figure 113**) and idle control (B) cables from the throttle wheel as described in this chapter.

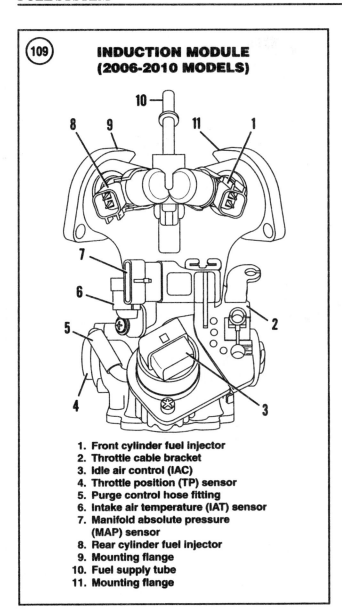

INDUCTION MODULE (2006-2010 MODELS)

1. Front cylinder fuel injector
2. Throttle cable bracket
3. Idle air control (IAC)
4. Throttle position (TP) sensor
5. Purge control hose fitting
6. Intake air temperature (IAT) sensor
7. Manifold absolute pressure (MAP) sensor
8. Rear cylinder fuel injector
9. Mounting flange
10. Fuel supply tube
11. Mounting flange

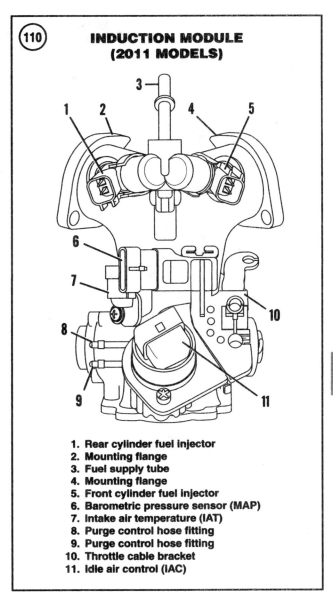

INDUCTION MODULE (2011 MODELS)

1. Rear cylinder fuel injector
2. Mounting flange
3. Fuel supply tube
4. Mounting flange
5. Front cylinder fuel injector
6. Barometric pressure sensor (MAP)
7. Intake air temperature (IAT)
8. Purge control hose fitting
9. Purge control hose fitting
10. Throttle cable bracket
11. Idle air control (IAC)

6. Carefully use a rocking motion and disconnect the connector from each fuel injector (**Figure 114**).

7. Disconnect the connector from the following:

   a. IAC (B, **Figure 112**).

   b. MAP sensor (C, **Figure 112**).

   c. TP sensor (**Figure 115**).

   d. IAT sensor (**Figure 116**).

8. Pull back the boot, and disconnect the connector from engine temperature sensor (A, **Figure 117**).

9. Press the button (A, **Figure 118**) on the fuel line (B), and disconnect the fuel supply line from the induction module supply tube.

10. Working on the left side of the motorcycle, loosen the lower flange bolts (B, **Figure 117**) that secure the induction module flange to the front and rear cylinder heads. Leave these bolts in place in the heads.

11. Working on the right side of the motorcycle, use the Allen wrench stub (A, **Figure 109**) and 1/4 inch wrench (C) to loosen and remove the upper flange bolts (**Figure 119**).

NOTE
Each flange rotates on its induction module port.

12. Slide the induction module flanges off the lower flange bolts, and partially remove the induction module (A, **Figure 120**) from the right side.

13. Remove the mounting flanges (A, **Figure 121**), and discard the seals (B). Mark each flange so it can be reinstalled on the correct port.

14. Inspect the induction module and fuel hose as described in this section.

Installation

1. Refer to the marks made during removal, and install the flanges onto the correct sides of the induction module (**Figure 122**). Make sure the seal counter bore of each flange faces outward, away from the induction module.

8

INDUCTION MODULE (2006-2011 MODELS)

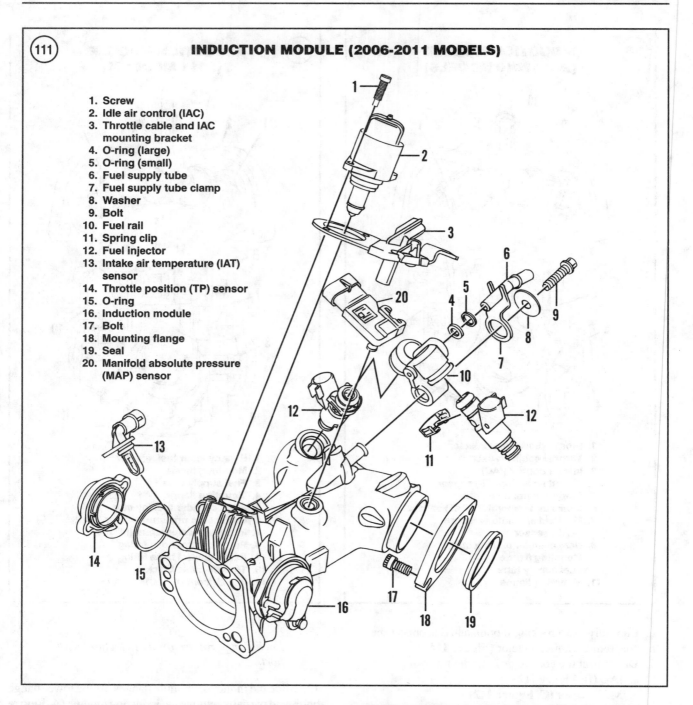

1. Screw
2. Idle air control (IAC)
3. Throttle cable and IAC mounting bracket
4. O-ring (large)
5. O-ring (small)
6. Fuel supply tube
7. Fuel supply tube clamp
8. Washer
9. Bolt
10. Fuel rail
11. Spring clip
12. Fuel injector
13. Intake air temperature (IAT) sensor
14. Throttle position (TP) sensor
15. O-ring
16. Induction module
17. Bolt
18. Mounting flange
19. Seal
20. Manifold absolute pressure (MAP) sensor

2. Install a *new* O-ring seal (B, **Figure 121**) into each flange so the beveled side faces into the flange.

3. On the right side, carefully position the induction module (A, **Figure 120**) between the cylinder head ports. Slide the flanges into place onto the lower flange bolts (B, **Figure 120**).

4. Align the mounting flanges with the cylinder head ports. Install the two upper flange bolts (**Figure 119**) and finger-tighten.

5. To ensure correct alignment of the induction module to the cylinder heads, perform the following:

   a. Fit the air filter backplate into place against the cylinder heads. Install the breather hollow bolts (A, **Figure 123**) and finger-tighten.

8

b. Install the air filter bracket Torx (T27) screws (B, **Figure 123**) to secure the backplate to the induction module, and finger-tighten the screws.

6. Working on the right side of the motorcycle, tighten the two upper flange bolts (**Figure 119**) until snug. Do not tighten to the final torque specification at this time. Use the same tool set up used to loosen the Allen bolts.

7. Working on the left side of the motorcycle, tighten the two lower flange bolts (B, **Figure 120**) to 96-144 in.-lb. (11-16-3 N•m).

8. Remove the filter bracket screws and breather hollow bolts. Then, remove the backplate.

9. Working on the right side of the motorcycle, tighten the two upper flange induction module bolts (**Figure 119**) to 96-144 in.-lb. (10.8-16.3 N•m).

10. Connect the fuel supply line (B, **Figure 118**) onto the induction module supply tube. Pull on the fuel line gently to ensure it is attached correctly and the button is locked onto the supply tube.

11. Carefully attach the connector onto each fuel injector (**Figure 114**). Push the connector on until it latches in place.

12. Connect the connector onto the following:
   a. IAT sensor (**Figure 116**).
   b. TP sensor (**Figure 115**).
   c. MAP sensor (C, **Figure 112**).
   d. IAC (B, **Figure 112**).

13. Connect the throttle (A, **Figure 113**) and idle control (B) cables onto the throttle wheel as described in this chapter. Adjust the cables as described in Chapter Three.

14. On California models, install the purge hose (A, **Figure 112**) onto the fitting on top of the induction module.

15. Connect the engine temperature sensor connector to the sensor (A, **Figure 117**), and roll the boot over the sensor.

16. Install the backplate and air filter as described in this chapter.

17. Install the fuel tank as described in this chapter.

18. Turn the ignition switch to IGN., and then back off to reset the idle air control to its park position.

Inspection

1. Check the induction module for wear, deterioration or other damage.

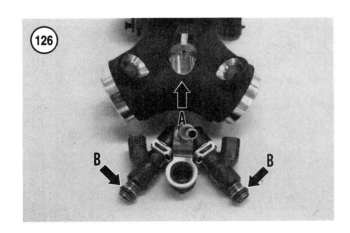

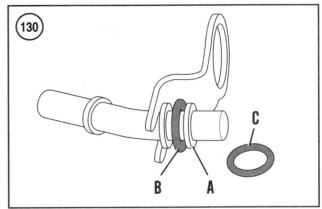

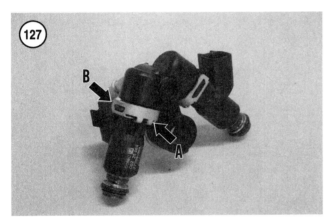

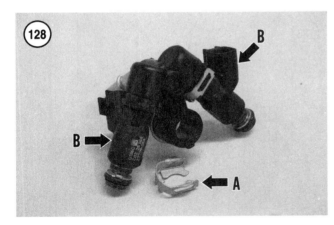

2. Inspect each flange (A, **Figure 124**) and its port (B) on the induction module.

FUEL INJECTORS

Removal

1. Remove the induction module as described in this chapter.
2. Remove the fuel supply tube bolt (A, **Figure 125**) and washer.
3. Gently rock the fuel injector and fuel rail assembly (B, **Figure 125**) back and forth while pulling up, and remove the assembly from the induction module (A, **Figure 126**). Account for the bottom O-ring (B, **Figure 126**) on each fuel injector.
4. Rotate the fuel injector 90° so the closed end of the spring clip (A, **Figure 127**) is accessible. Note that the arms of the spring clip straddle the tab (B, **Figure 127**) on the injector.
5. Remove the spring clip (A, **Figure 128**), and pull the fuel injector (B) from the fuel rail. If necessary, gently rock the injector back and forth to remove it.
6. Remove and discard the fuel injector's top (A, **Figure 129**) and bottom (B) O-rings.
7. Repeat procedure to remove the remaining fuel injector.
8. If necessary, remove the fuel supply tube (C, **Figure 129**) from the fuel rail (D).
9. Remove the sealing washer (A, **Figure 130**) and O-ring (B) from the fuel supply tube. Discard the washer and O-ring.
10. Remove the second O-ring (C, **Figure 130**) from the fuel rail bore. Discard the O-ring.

Installation

1. Apply a light coat of clean engine oil onto all *new* O-rings.
2. Install a *new* O-ring (B, **Figure 130**) onto the fuel supply neck until it contacts the collar, and install the sealing washer (A). Install the second O-ring (C, **Figure 130**) into the fuel rail bore.
3. Install a *new* O-ring with the thicker base and smaller ID onto the fuel rail end (A, **Figure 129**) of each fuel in-

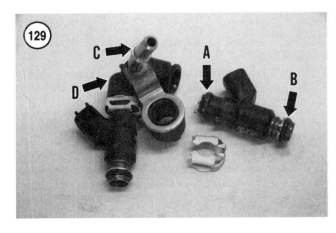

jector. Install the remaining *new* O-ring onto the induction module end (B, **Figure 129**) of each fuel injector.

4. Push the connector side of each fuel injector (B, **Figure 128**) into the fuel rail until it bottoms.

5. Position the spring clip concave side (A, **Figure 128**) toward the fuel rail, and press the spring clip into the slot in the fuel injector. When properly installed, the spring clip engages the lip on each side of the fuel injector and the fingers on the back of the clip straddle the tab (B, **Figure 127**) on the fuel injector.

6. Rotate the fuel injectors so the closed side of the spring clip faces the fuel rail.

7. Position the fuel rail assembly onto the induction module so each injector is started into its port (A, **Figure 131**).

8. Carefully install the fuel injectors into the induction module ports until the fuel rail tab (B, **Figure 131**) engages the slot (**Figure 132**) at the top of the induction module.

9. Install the fuel supply tube bolt (A, **Figure 125**) and washer. Tighten the fuel supply tube bolt to 90-110 in.-lb. (10.2-12.4 N•m).

10. Install the induction module assembly as described in this chapter.

Inspection

1. Inspect the fuel injectors for damage. Check for corrosion on the connector pins; clean if necessary.

2. Inspect the fuel rail and fuel supply tube for damage.

3. Inspect the injector ports (**Figure 133**) in the induction module.

4. Replace any worn or damaged part.

INTAKE AIR TEMPERATURE (IAT) SENSOR

Removal/installation

Refer to **Figure 134**.

1. Disconnect the negative battery cable as described in Chapter Nine.

2. Remove the air filter and backplate as described in this chapter.

3. On California models, remove the purge hose from the fitting on top of the induction module (A, **Figure 135**).

4. Disconnect the IAC connector (B, **Figure 135**) and the MAP sensor connector (C).

5. Disconnect the 2-pin connector (A, **Figure 136**) from the IAT sensor.

6. Remove the IAT sensor screw (B, **Figure 136**) and captive washer and remove the sensor (C) from the induction module and throttle shaft.

7. Remove and discard the IAT sensor O-ring.

8. Apply a light coat of clean engine oil onto the *new* O-ring.

9. Install a *new* O-ring onto the sensor.

10. Install the IAT sensor (C, **Figure 136**) into the induction module and push it in until it bottoms. Turn the sensor

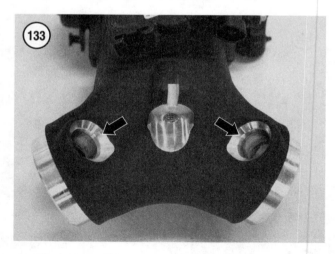

until the connector (A, **Figure 136**) faces the left side of the motorcycle

11. Install a *new* screw (B, **Figure 136**) and captive washer securing the sensor. Tighten the IAT sensor screw to 15-20 in.-lb. (1.7-2.3 N•m).

12. Reconnect the 2-pin connector onto the IAT sensor (A, **Figure 136**).

13. Reconnect the IAC connector (B, **Figure 135**) and the MAP sensor connector (C, **Figure 135**). On California models, reconnect the purge hose (A, **Figure 135**) to its fitting.

14. Install the backplate and air filter as described in this chapter.

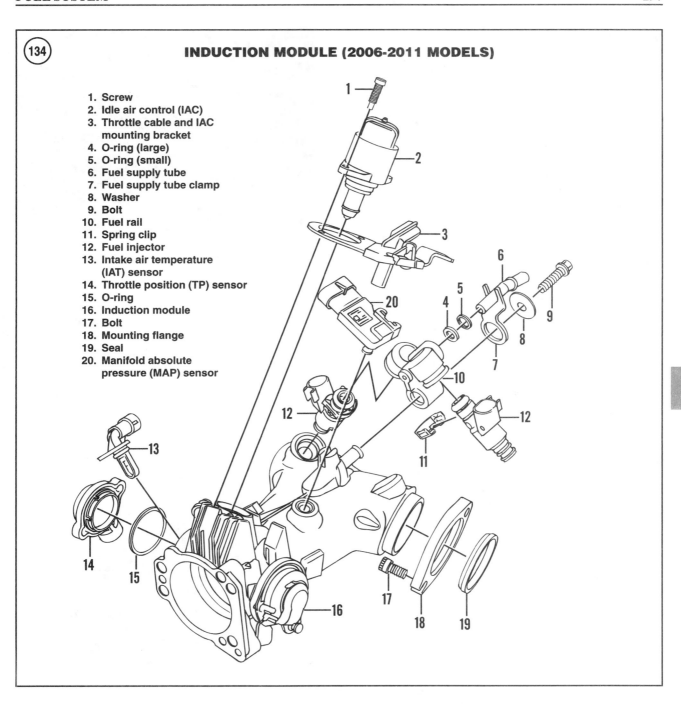

INDUCTION MODULE (2006-2011 MODELS)

1. Screw
2. Idle air control (IAC)
3. Throttle cable and IAC mounting bracket
4. O-ring (large)
5. O-ring (small)
6. Fuel supply tube
7. Fuel supply tube clamp
8. Washer
9. Bolt
10. Fuel rail
11. Spring clip
12. Fuel injector
13. Intake air temperature (IAT) sensor
14. Throttle position (TP) sensor
15. O-ring
16. Induction module
17. Bolt
18. Mounting flange
19. Seal
20. Manifold absolute pressure (MAP) sensor

15. Connect the negative battery cable as described in Chapter Nine.

THROTTLE POSITION (TP) SENSOR

Removal/installation

1. Disconnect the negative battery cable as described in Chapter Nine.
2. Remove the air filter and backplate (this chapter).
3. Disconnect the 3-pin connector (A, **Figure 137**) from the TP sensor.
4. Remove the TP sensor screws and captive washers (B, **Figure 137**) and remove the sensor (C) from the induction module. Discard the screws and washers.
5. Remove the O-ring from the sensor.
6. Apply a light coat of clean engine oil onto a *new* O-ring. Install the *new* O-ring onto the sensor.
7. Slide the TP sensor onto the throttle shaft so the sensor's flat side (A, **Figure 138**) engages the shaft, and the indexing pin (B) engages the hole on the induction module.
8. Install *new* screws (B, **Figure 137**) and captive washers securing the sensor (C). Tighten the TP sensor screws to 15-20 in.-lb. (1.7-2.3 N•m).
9. Operate the throttle several times to open and close the throttle plates. Make sure the sensor operates smoothly.
10. Connect the 3-pin connector (A, **Figure 137**) onto the TP sensor.
11. Install the backplate and air filter and as described in this chapter.
12. Connect the negative battery cable as described in Chapter Nine.

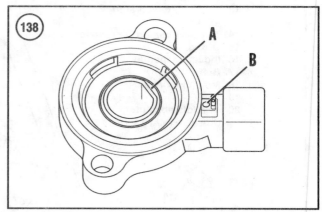

IDLE AIR CONTROL (IAC)

Removal/installation

1. Remove the induction module as described in this chapter.
2. Remove the throttle cable bracket screws (A, **Figure 139**), and lift the throttle cable bracket (B) from the IAC. Discard the screws.
3. Gently rock the IAC (A, **Figure 140**) back and forth and pull it from the induction module.
4. Remove the O-ring (**Figure 141**) from the induction module bore. Discard the O-ring
5. Apply a light coat of clean engine oil onto a *new* O-ring, and install it into the induction module bore.
6. Position the IAC so its connector faces the left side of the induction module. Press the IAC (A, **Figure 140**) into the induction module bore until the IAC bottoms.
7. Set the throttle cable bracket (B, **Figure 139**) over the IAC so the bracket's indexing pin aligns with the indexing hole (C, **Figure 139**) in the induction module.
8. Install new throttle cable bracket screws (A, **Figure 139**). Make sure the screws pass through the holes on the IAC and into the threads in the induction module.

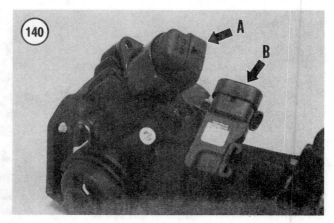

9. Tighten the throttle cable bracket screws to 20-35 in.-lb. (2.3-4.0 N•m).

10. Install the induction module as described in this chapter.

MANIFOLD ABSOLUTE PRESSURE (MAP) SENSOR

Removal/installation

The MAP sensor (**Figure 142**) is located on top of the induction module.

CAUTION
Do not try to remove the MAP sensor with the induction module installed on the engine as the sensor will be damaged.

1. Remove the induction module as described in this chapter.

2. Remove the throttle cable bracket screws (A, **Figure 139**), and lift the throttle cable bracket (B) from the IAC. Discard the screws.

3. Gently rock the MAP sensor (B, **Figure 140**) back and forth while pulling up and remove it from the induction module.

4. Inspect the sensor seal for tears or deterioration; replace if necessary.

5. Position the sensor with the connector facing opposite the throttle wheel. Install the MAP sensor and push it in until it bottoms.

6. Set the throttle cable bracket (B, **Figure 139**) over the IAC so the bracket's indexing pin aligns with the indexing hole (C, **Figure 139**) in the induction module.

7. Install new throttle cable bracket screws (A, **Figure 139**). Make sure the screws pass through the holes on the IAC and turn into the threads in the induction module.

8. Tighten the throttle cable bracket screws to 20-35 in.-lb. (2.3-4.0 N•m).

9. Install the induction module as described in this chapter.

ENGINE TEMPERATURE (ET) SENSOR

Removal/installation

1. Disconnect the negative battery cable as described in Chapter Nine.

2. Remove the horn assembly as described in Chapter Nine.

3. Working at the front cylinder head, pull the rubber boot away from the ET sensor.

4. Disconnect the 2-pin connector (A, **Figure 143**) from the ET sensor (B).

5. Use a deep-well socket to loosen the sensor (B, **Figure 143**). After the sensor is loosened, remove the sensor by hand.

6. Install the ET sensor (B, **Figure 143**) into the front cylinder by hand. Do not cross thread it.

7. Tighten the ET sensor to 10-15 ft.-lb. (13.6-20.3 N•m).

8. Connect the 2-pin connector (A, **Figure 143**) onto the ET sensor (B).

9. Roll the rubber boot onto the ET sensor connector.

10. Install the horn assembly as described in Chapter Nine.

11. Connect the negative battery cable as described in Chapter Nine.

OXYGEN (O2) SENSOR

Removal/installation

An oxygen sensor mounts to the inboard side of the front and rear exhaust pipe. An oxygen sensor socket (JIMS part

8

No. 969 or H-D part No. HD-48262), or its equivalent, must be used to remove and install the sensor. Other sockets will damage the sensor.

1. Disconnect the negative battery cable as described in Chapter Nine.

2. Remove the seat as described in Chapter Fourteen.

3. On California models, remove the charcoal canister as described in this chapter.

4. Disconnect the front oxygen sensor as follows:
   a. Follow the front oxygen sensor wiring harness to the front electrical caddy.
   b. Depress the tabs and open the front electrical caddy cover (**Figure 144**).
   c. Release the connector from the electrical caddy directly below the voltage regulator.
   d. Disconnect the 2-pin front oxygen sensor connector (**Figure 145**).
   e. Note the path of the sensor wiring harness though the frame as it must be routed in the same path during installation.

5. Disconnect the rear oxygen sensor as follows:
   a. Follow the rear oxygen sensor wiring harness to the connector under the seat.
   b. In the frame opening under the seat area, disconnect the 2-pin rear oxygen sensor connector (**Figure 146**).
   c. Note the path of the sensor wiring harness though the frame as it must be routed in the same path during installation.

6. Note the location of any cable ties or clamps securing the wiring to the frame, and release the wiring from the cable ties or clamps.

NOTE
***Figure 147** is shown with the exhaust system removed for clarity.*

7. Install the sensor removal tool (**Figure 147**) onto the sensor without damaging the electrical cables.

8. Loosen the sensor. After the sensor is loosened, remove the sensor by hand.

NOTE
Do not reinstall a sensor that has been dropped or struck by other components as it may be damaged internally, and will not function correctly.

9. Apply a light coat of Loctite Anti-Seize, or an equivalent, to the threads prior to installation.

10. Carefully install the sensor into the exhaust pipe by hand. Do not cross thread it.

11. Install the sensor removal tool (**Figure 147**) onto the sensor without damaging the electrical cables.

12. Tighten the oxygen sensor to 29-44 ft.-lb. (39.3-59.7 N•m).

13. Route the wiring along the path noted during removal.

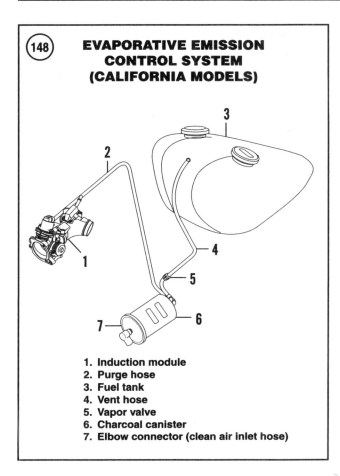

148

EVAPORATIVE EMISSION CONTROL SYSTEM (CALIFORNIA MODELS)

1. Induction module
2. Purge hose
3. Fuel tank
4. Vent hose
5. Vapor valve
6. Charcoal canister
7. Elbow connector (clean air inlet hose)

14. Connect the oxygen sensor connector. Secure the wiring to the frame using cable ties or clamps at the locations noted during removal.

15. Install the seat as described in Chapter Fourteen.

16. On California models, install the charcoal canister as described in this chapter.

17. Connect the negative battery cable as described in Chapter Nine.

EVAPORATIVE EMISSION CONTROL SYSTEM (ALL CALIFORNIA MODELS)

The evaporative emission control system prevents gasoline vapor from escaping into the atmosphere.

When the engine is not running, the system directs the fuel vapor from the fuel tank through the vapor valve and into the charcoal canister.

When the engine is running, these vapors are drawn through a purge hose and into the induction module, where they burn in the combustion chambers. The vapor valve also prevents gasoline vapor from escaping from the charcoal canister if the motorcycle falls onto its side.

Models other than California are equipped with a vapor valve, or vapor vent tube, but no charcoal canister or purge control valve. The lower end of the vent tube is routed to the atmosphere.

Inspection

Refer to the following illustrations for components and the hose routing. Before removing the hoses from any of the parts, mark the hose and the fitting with a piece of masking tape to identify where the hose goes.

1. Check all emission control lines and hoses to make sure they are correctly routed and connected.

WARNING
Make sure the fuel tank vapor hoses are routed so they cannot contact any hot engine or exhaust component. These hoses contain flammable vapor. If a hose melts from contacting a hot part, leaking vapor may ignite, causing severe bike damage and rider injury.

2. Make sure there are no kinks in the lines or hoses. Also inspect the hose and lines for excessive wear or burning on lines that are routed near engine hot spots.

3. Check the physical condition of all lines and hoses in the system. Check for cuts, tears, cracking or loose connections. These lines and hoses are subjected to various temperature and operating conditions and eventually become brittle and crack. Replace damaged lines and hoses.

4. Check all components in the emission control system for damage, such as broken fittings or broken nipples on the component.

Charcoal Canister Removal/Installation

Refer to **Figure 148**.

1. Disconnect the negative battery cable as described in Chapter Nine.

2. On Screamin' Eagle models, remove the front spoiler as described in Chapter Fourteen.

3. Disconnect the clean air hose from the left side of the charcoal canister.

4. Lift the tang on the canister bracket with a screwdriver and slide the canister to the side and off the mounting bracket.

5. Label the hose and fitting locations prior to disconnecting them from the right side of the canister.

6. Disconnect the purge hose from the top fitting and remove the vent hose from the lower fitting on the canister.

7. Remove the charcoal canister from the right side of the frame.

8. Install the charcoal canister by reversing the removal steps while noting the following:
  a. Slide the canister into the bracket mounting grooves until it clicks.
  b. Attach the hoses to the correct fittings as noted during removal.

Vapor Valve Removal/Installation

1. Label the hose and fitting locations prior to disconnecting them from the vapor valve.

8

2. Disconnect the hoses from the vapor valve.

3. Remove the vapor valve from the clip on the frame.

4. Install the vapor valve with the longer end facing up, and install it onto the frame clip.

5. Connect the hoses onto the vapor valve. Push them on until they are completely seated.

Vapor Vent Tube Removal/Installation

1. Remove the Maxi-Fuse as described in Chapter Nine.

2. Remove the seat as described in Chapter Fourteen.

3. Remove the fuel tank console as described in this chapter.

4. Disconnect the vapor vent tube from the fitting on the fuel tank top plate.

5. Follow the vapor vent tube down the frame to the charcoal canister.

6. Disconnect the tube from the lower fitting on the charcoal canister.

7. Install the vapor vent tube by reversing the removal steps. Make sure the tube is not pinched or kinked and that there is no contact with the exhaust system.

Purge Tube Removal/Installation

1. Remove the fuel tank as described in this chapter.

2. Disconnect the purge tube from the induction module fitting.

3. Follow the purge tube down the frame to the charcoal canister.

4. Disconnect the purge tube from the upper fitting on the charcoal canister.

5. Install the purge tube by reversing the removal steps. Make sure the tube is not pinched or kinked and that there is no contact with the exhaust system.

Clean Air Tube Removal/Installation

1. Remove the fuel tank as described in this chapter.

2. Disconnect the clean air tube from the fitting on the left side of the charcoal canister.

3. Follow the clean air tube toward the rear of the frame area.

4. Install the clean air tube by reversing the removal steps. Make sure the tube is not pinched or kinked and that there is no contact with the exhaust system.

Table 1 FUEL SYSTEM SPECIFICATIONS

Item	Specification
Idle speed	950-1050 rpm
Fuel tank capacity (total)	
2006 models	
FXD, FXDC	4.8 gal (18.17 L)
FXDL, FXDB	4.7 gal (17.79 L)
FXDWG, FXD35	5.1 gal (19.31 L)
2007 models	
FXD	4.8 gal (18.17 L)
FXDL, FXDB	4.7 gal (17.79 L)
FXDWG, FXDC	5.1 gal (19.31 L)
FXDSE	5.0 gal (18.93 L)
2008-2011 models	
FXD, FXDL, FXDB	4.8 gal (18.17 L)
FXDWG, FXDC, FXDF	5.1 gal (19.31 L)
FXDSE2, FXDFSE	5.0 gal (18.93 L)
Fuel pressure	55-62 psi (379-427 kPa)

Table 2 FUEL SYSTEM TORQUE SPECIFICATIONS

Item	ft.-lb.	in.-lb.	N•m
Air filter (2007 FXDSE and 2008 FXDSE2 models)			
Breather hollow bolts	22-24	–	29.8-32.5
Standoff bolts	–	55-60	6.2-6.8
Element screw	–	40-60	4.5-6.8
Cover screw	–	60-90	6.8-10.2
Air filter (2009-2010 FXDFSE2 CVO models)			
Backplate screws	–	55-60	6.2-6.8
Breather hollow bolts	22-24	–	29.8-32.5
Hose clamp screw	–	45-55	5.1-6.2
Intake tube assembly screws	–	55-60	6.2-6.8
Cover screw	–	60-90	6.8-10.2
Air filter (all other models)			
Breather bolts			
2006 models	–	120-144	13.6-16.3
2007-2011 models	22-24	–	29.8-32.5
Cover screw	–	36-60	4.1-6.8
Mounting bracket Torx screws	–	40-60	4.5-6.8
Trim plate screws	–	27-36	3.0-3.6
Engine temperature (ET) sensor	–	120-180	13.6-20.3
Fuel pump/level sender top plate screw	–	20	2.3
Fuel supply			
Check valve fitting	18	–	24.4
Supply tube bolt	–	90-110	10.2-12.4
Fuel tank console (all models except FXD and FXDSE)			
mounting screws	–	18-24	2.0-2.7
Fuel tank console (FXD and FXDSE models)			
Mounting screws			
Front	–	18-27	2.0-3.0
Rear	–	18-24	2.0-2.7
Trim ring screws	–	18-27	2.0-3.0
Short	–	18-22	2.0-2.5
Long	–	12-15	1.4-1.7
Fuel tank front and rear mounting bolt acorn nut			
2006-2007 models	10-18	–	13.6-24.4
2008-on models	15-20	–	20.3-27.1
Induction module	–	96-144	10.8-16.3
Idle air control sensor (IAC)			
Throttle cable bracket screws	–	20-35	2.3-4.0
Intake air temperature (IAT) sensor	–	15-20	1.7-2.3
Oxygen sensor	29-44	–	39.3-59.7
Manifold absolute pressure sensor			
Throttle cable bracket screws	–	20-35	2.3-4.0
Throttle position (TP) sensor screws	–	15-20	1.7-2.3

8

CHAPTER NINE

ELECTRICAL SYSTEM

This chapter contains service and test procedures for electrical system components. Refer to Chapter Three for spark plug service procedures.

Specifications are in **Tables 1-5** at the end of the chapter. Wiring diagrams are located ont the CD inserted into the back cover of this manual.

> *NOTE*
> *On models with the optional security siren, disarm the security system (TSSM/HFSM) before disconnecting the battery or before pulling the Maxi-Fuse so the siren will not sound. Refer to **Turn Signal and Security Modules** in this chapter.*

ELECTRICAL COMPONENT REPLACEMENT

Most motorcycle dealerships and part suppliers will not accept the return of any electrical part. If the exact cause of an electrical system malfunction cannot be determined, have a dealership retest the specific system to verify test results. If a new electrical component is installed and the system still does not work, the unit, in most cases, cannot be returned for a refund.

Consider any test results carefully before replacing a component that tests only slight out of specification, especially when testing for resistance. A number of variables affect test results dramatically. These include the test meter's internal circuitry, ambient air temperature, and the condition under which the machine has been operated. All instructions and specifications have been checked for accuracy. However, successful test results depend largely upon individual accuracy.

FUSES

All models are equipped with a series of fuses to protect the electrical system. The number of fuses varies depending on the model. The fuse specifications are in **Table 3**.

The fuse panel is located on the left side and is part of the electrical caddy. If there is an electrical failure, first check for a blown fuse. A blown fuse has a break in the element.

Whenever a fuse blows, find the reason for the failure before replacing the fuse. Usually, the trouble is a short circuit in the wiring. This may be caused by worn-through insulation or a disconnected wire shorted to ground. Check the circuit that the fuse protects.

Spare fuses are also included in the fuse block. When a spare fuse is used, replace it as soon as possible.

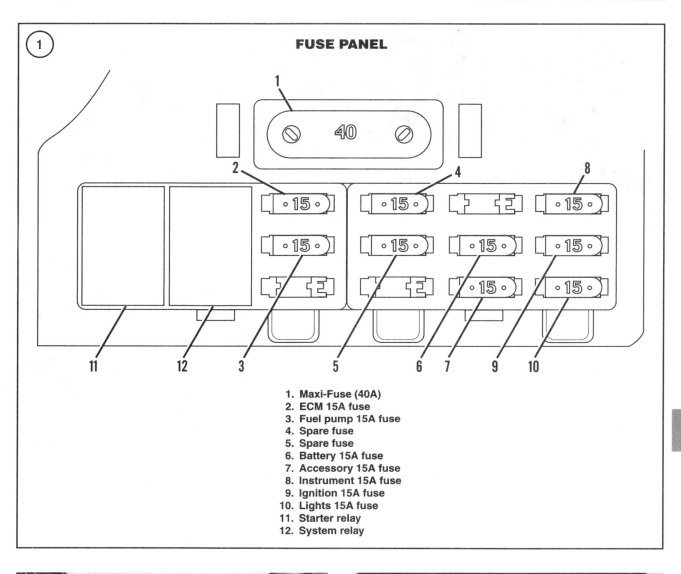

FUSE PANEL

1. Maxi-Fuse (40A)
2. ECM 15A fuse
3. Fuel pump 15A fuse
4. Spare fuse
5. Spare fuse
6. Battery 15A fuse
7. Accessory 15A fuse
8. Instrument 15A fuse
9. Ignition 15A fuse
10. Lights 15A fuse
11. Starter relay
12. System relay

9

Removal/Installation

Refer to **Figure 1**.

1. Disconnect the negative battery cable as described in this chapter.

2. Grasp the electrical caddy cover (**Figure 2**) on both sides, pull straight out and remove the cover. Fuse description and location is printed on the fuse block cover (**Figure 3**).

3. Locate the blown fuse (A, **Figure 4**, typical) and install a new one of the *same* ampere rating.

4. Install the caddy cover (**Figure 2**) and push it on until it bottoms.

5. Connect the negative battery cable as described in this chapter.

MAXI-FUSE

Removal/Installation

The 40-amp Maxi-Fuse functions as the main electrical system fuse.

1. Disconnect the negative battery cable as described in this chapter.

2. Grasp the electrical caddy cover (**Figure 2**) on both sides, pull straight out and remove the cover. Fuse description and location is printed on the fuse block cover (**Figure 3**).

3. Locate the Maxi-Fuse (B, **Figure 4**), remove it and install a *new* Maxi-Fuse with the *same* amperage.

4. Install the caddy cover and push it on until it bottoms.

5. Connect the negative battery cable as described in this chapter.

GROUND WIRES AND STUDS

Removal/Installation

1. Remove the battery and battery tray as described in this chapter.

2. Identify each wire and the stud where it is attached.

3. Remove the nuts, and then remove the wires from the studs on the frame.

4. Install the wires onto their correct studs and tighten the nuts securely.

5. Install the battery tray and battery as described in this chapter.

BATTERY

A sealed, maintenance-free battery is installed on all models. The battery electrolyte level cannot be serviced. When replacing the battery, use a sealed type. Do not install a non-sealed battery as the electrolyte will leak out. Never attempt to remove the sealing caps from the top of the battery. The battery does not require periodic electrolyte inspection or refilling.

On all models in this manual, the negative side is the ground. Disconnect the negative battery cable (ground) first, and then the positive cable. This minimizes the chance of a tool shorting to ground when disconnecting the battery positive cable.

Refer to Chapter Two for charging system troubleshooting procedures.

Cover Removal/Installation

1. Remove the lower screw (**Figure 5**) securing the battery cover.

2. Pull out on the bottom of the battery cover, lift up and release it from the two index tabs (**Figure 6**) at the top.

3. Remove the battery cover (**Figure 7**).

4. Correctly install the battery cover onto the two index tabs (**Figure 6**) at the top and push the cover back into place until it bottoms.

5. Install the lower screw (**Figure 5**) and tighten securely.

Negative Cable Removal

Some of the component replacement procedures and some of the test procedures in this chapter require disconnecting the negative battery cable first as a safety precaution.

1. Turn the ignition switch off.

2. Remove the battery cover as described in this section.

3. Unhook and remove the strap (A, **Figure 8**) securing the battery (B) to the box.

4. Remove the terminal bolt (A, **Figure 9**) securing the negative cable to the battery. Move the cable away from the battery to avoid making accidental contact with the battery post.

5. Connect the negative cable onto the battery, reinstall the terminal bolt and tighten to 60-96 in.-lb. (6.8-10.8 N•m).

6. Install the battery cover as described in this section.

Cable Service

To ensure good electrical contact between the battery and the electrical cables, the cables must be clean and free of corrosion.

1. If the electrical cable terminals are badly corroded, disconnect them from the motorcycle's electrical system.

2. Thoroughly clean each connector with a wire brush and a baking soda solution. Rinse thoroughly with clean water and wipe dry with a clean cloth.

3. After cleaning, apply a thin layer of dielectric grease to the battery terminals before reattaching the cables.

4. Reconnect the electrical cables to the motorcycle's electrical system if they were disconnected.

5. After connecting the electrical cables, apply a light coat of dielectric grease to the connectors to retard corrosion.

Removal/Installation

Refer to **Figure 10**.

1. Turn the ignition switch off.

2. Remove the battery cover as described in this section.

3. Unhook and remove the strap (A, **Figure 8**) securing the battery (B) to the box.

4. Remove the bolt (A, **Figure 9**) securing the negative cable to the battery.

5. Remove the bolt (B, **Figure 9**) securing the positive cable to the battery.

6. Carefully pull the battery (C, **Figure 9**) out of the battery tray.

7. Inspect the battery tray for corrosion or damage. Replace if necessary.

8. Position the battery with the terminals facing outward and slide the battery into the battery tray.

9. Secure the battery (B, **Figure 8**) with the strap (A); ensure the strap is secure.

10. Connect the positive cable (B, **Figure 9**) onto the battery. Tighten the terminal bolt to 60-96 in.-lb. (6.8-10.8 N•m).

11. Connect the negative cable (A, **Figure 9**) onto the battery. Tighten the terminal bolt to 60-96 in.-lb. (6.8-10.8 N•m).

12. After connecting the electrical cables, apply a light coating of dielectric grease to the electrical terminals of the battery to retard corrosion.

13. Install the battery cover as described in this section.

Inspection

The battery electrolyte level cannot be serviced in a maintenance-free battery. *Never* attempt to remove the sealing bar cap from the top of the battery. The battery does not require periodic electrolyte inspection or water refilling. Refer to the label (A, **Figure 11**) on top of the battery.

Even though the battery is sealed, protect eyes, skin and clothing. The corrosive electrolyte may have spilled out and can cause severe chemical skin burns and permanent injury. The battery case may be cracked and leaking electrolyte.

WARNING
Electrolyte is extremely harmful. Always wear safety glasses while working with a battery. If electrolyte gets into the eyes, call a

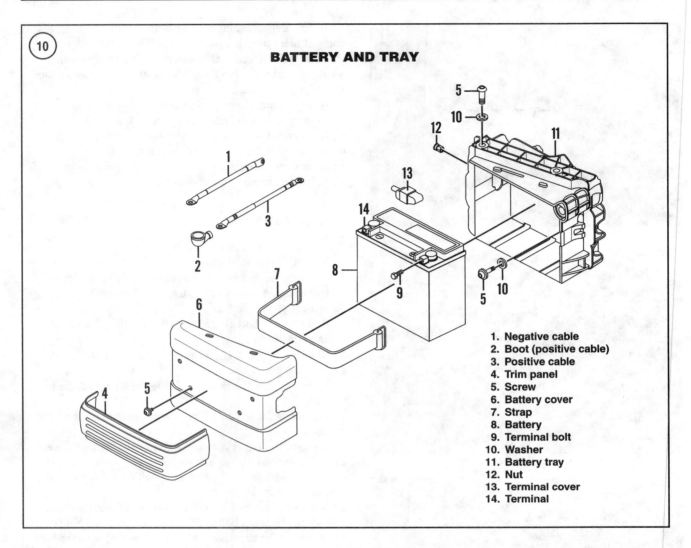

BATTERY AND TRAY

1. Negative cable
2. Boot (positive cable)
3. Positive cable
4. Trim panel
5. Screw
6. Battery cover
7. Strap
8. Battery
9. Terminal bolt
10. Washer
11. Battery tray
12. Nut
13. Terminal cover
14. Terminal

physician immediately. Force the eyes open, and flood them with cool, clean water for approximately 15 minutes. If electrolyte is spilled or splashed on clothing or skin, immediately neutralize it with a baking soda and water solution, and flush with an abundance of clean water.

1. Remove the battery as described in this section. Do not clean the battery while it is mounted in the frame.

2. Set the battery on a stack of newspapers or shop cloths to protect the surface of the workbench.

3. Check the entire battery case for cracks or other damage. If the battery case is warped, discolored or has a raised top, the battery has been overcharged and overheated.

4. Check the battery terminal bolts (B, **Figure 11**), spacers and nuts for corrosion or damage. Clean parts thoroughly with a baking soda and water solution. Replace corroded or damaged parts.

5. If the top of the battery is corroded, clean it with a stiff bristle brush using the baking soda and water solution.

6. Check the battery cable ends for corrosion and damage. If corrosion is minor, clean the battery cable ends with

a stiff wire brush and a baking soda and water solution. Replace worn or damaged cables.

7. Perform the open circuit voltage test (this section).

8. Inspect the battery case for contamination or damage. Clean it with a baking soda and water solution.

9. Install the battery as described in this section.

Open Circuit Voltage Test

1. Remove the battery as described in this section.

2. Connect a digital voltmeter between the battery negative and positive terminals. Note the following:

   a. If the battery voltage is 12.7 volts, or greater at 68° F (20° C), the battery is fully charged. At 12.6 volts, it is 75% charged.

   b. If the battery voltage is 12.0 to 12.5 volts at 68° F (20° C), or lower, the battery is undercharged and requires charging.

3. If the battery is undercharged, recharge it as described in this section. Then, test the charging system as described in Chapter Two.

4. Install the battery as described in this section.

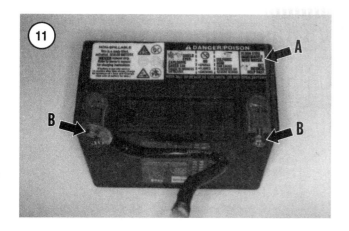

Load Test

A load test checks the battery's performance under full current load and is the best indication of battery condition. A battery load tester is required for this procedure. When using a load tester, follow the tester manufacturer's instructions

1. Remove the battery from the motorcycle as described in this section.

NOTE
Let the battery stand for at least one hour after charging before performing this test.

2. The battery must be fully charged before beginning this test. If necessary, charge the battery as described in this section.

WARNING
The battery load tester must be turned off prior to connecting or disconnecting the test cables to the battery. Otherwise, a spark could cause the battery to explode.

CAUTION
To prevent battery damage during load testing, do not load test a discharged battery and do not load test the battery for more than 20 seconds. Performing a load test on a discharged battery can cause permanent battery damage.

3. Load test the battery as follows:
   a. Connect the load tester cables to the battery following its manufacturer's instructions.
   b. Load the battery at 50% of the cold cranking amperage (CCA) or 135 amperes.
   c. After 15 seconds, the voltage reading with the load still applied must be 9.6 volts or higher at 70° F (21° C). Now quickly remove the load and turn the tester off.

4. If the voltage reading is 9.6 volts or higher, the battery output capacity is good. If the reading is below 9.6 volts, the battery is defective.

5. With the tester off, disconnect the cables from the battery.
6. Install the battery as described in this section.

Charging

WARNING
During charging, highly-explosive hydrogen gas is released from the battery. Only charge the battery in a well-ventilated area away from open flames, including pilot lights on appliances. Do not allow smoking in the area. Never check the charge of the battery by arcing across the terminals; the resulting spark can ignite the hydrogen gas.

CAUTION
Always disconnect the battery cables from the battery before charging. If the cables are left connected during the charging procedure, the charger may damage the diodes within the voltage regulator/rectifier.

Refer to *Battery Initialization* in this section if the battery is new.

To recharge a maintenance-free battery, a digital voltmeter and a charger with an adjustable amperage output are required. If this equipment is not available, have the battery charged by a shop with the proper equipment. Excessive voltage and amperage from an unregulated charger can damage the battery and shorten service life.

The battery should only self-discharge approximately one percent of its given capacity each day. If a battery not in use, without any loads connected, loses its charge within a week after charging, the battery is defective.

If the motorcycle is not used for long periods of time, an automatic battery charger with variable voltage and amperage outputs is recommended for optimum battery service life.

1. Remove the battery from the motorcycle as described in this section.
2. Set the battery on a stack of newspapers or shop cloths to protect the surface of the workbench.
3. Make sure the battery charger is turned off prior to attaching the charger leads to the battery.
4. Connect the positive charger lead to the positive battery terminal and the negative charger lead to the negative battery terminal.
5. Set the charger at 12 volts. If the output of the charger is variable, select the low setting.
6. The charging time depends on the discharged condition of the battery. Refer to **Table 2** for the suggested charging time. Normally, a battery should be charged at 1/10th its given capacity.

CAUTION
If the battery emits an excessive amount of gas during the charging cycle, decrease the charge rate. If the battery becomes hotter

9

etc.

than 110° F (43° C) during the charging cycle, turn the charger off and allow the battery to cool. Then continue with a reduced charging rate and continue to monitor the battery temperature.

7. Turn the charger on.

8. After the battery has been charged for the predetermined time, turn the charger off, disconnect the leads and measure the battery voltage. Refer to the following:

   a. If the battery voltage is 12.7 volts or greater at 68° F (20° C), the battery is fully charged

   b. If the battery voltage is 12.5 volts or lower at 68° F (20° C), the battery is undercharged and requires additional charging time.

9. If the battery remains stable for one hour, the battery is charged.

10. Install the battery into the motorcycle as described in this section.

Initialization

> *NOTE*
> ***Recycle the old battery***. *When a new battery is purchased, turn in the old one for recycling. Most motorcycle dealerships will accept the old battery in trade for a new one. Never place an old battery in the household trash.*

A new battery must be *fully* charged to a specific gravity of 1.260-1.280 before installation. To bring the battery to a full charge, give it an initial charge. Using a new battery without an initial charge will cause permanent battery damage. The battery will never be able to hold more than an 80% charge. Charging a new battery after it has been used will not bring its charge to 100%. When purchasing a new battery, verify its charge status.

BATTERY TRAY

Removal/Installation

Refer to **Figure 12**.

1. Remove the battery from the motorcycle as described in this chapter.

2. Release the battery cables from the recess in the upper corners of the battery tray.

3. Remove the top two screws (**Figure 13**) and washers securing the battery tray to the frame.

4. Remove the screw (A, **Figure 14**) and washer at the back of the battery tray.

5. Guide the battery cables (B, **Figure 14**) out the openings in the rear section of the battery try. Carefully pull the battery tray out of the frame and remove it.

6. Install by reversing the removal steps. Tighten the battery tray screws to 96-120 ft.-lb. (10.9-13.6 N•m).

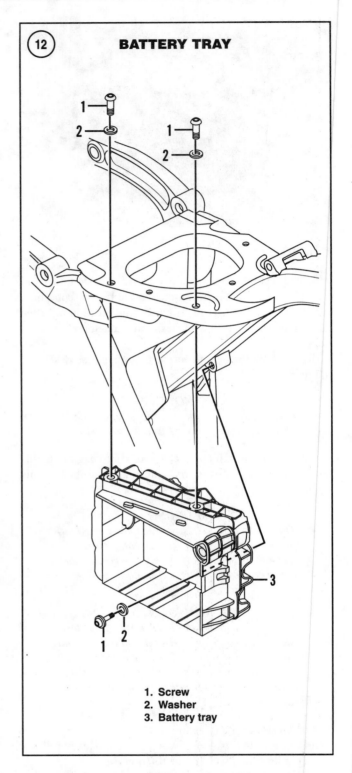

BATTERY TRAY

1. Screw
2. Washer
3. Battery tray

CHARGING SYSTEM

Refer to **Figure 15**.

The charging system consists of the battery, alternator and a voltage regulator/rectifier. Alternating current generated by the alternator is rectified to direct current. The voltage regulator maintains the voltage to the battery and additional electrical loads, such as the lights and ignition system, at a constant voltage regardless of variations in en-

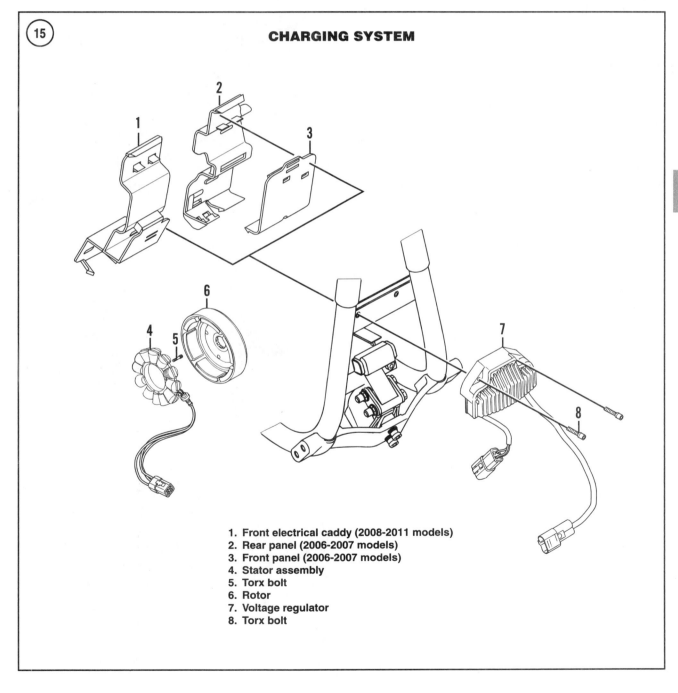

CHARGING SYSTEM

1. Front electrical caddy (2008-2011 models)
2. Rear panel (2006-2007 models)
3. Front panel (2006-2007 models)
4. Stator assembly
5. Torx bolt
6. Rotor
7. Voltage regulator
8. Torx bolt

9

gine speed and load. A malfunction in the charging system generally causes the battery to remain undercharged.

Service Precautions

To prevent damage to the alternator and the regulator/rectifier when testing and repairing the charging system, note the following precautions:

1. Always disarm the optional TSM/TSSM/HFSM security system before disconnecting the battery or maxi-fuse so the siren will not sound.

2. Always disconnect the negative battery cable, as described in this chapter, before removing a component from the charging system.

3. To charge the battery, remove the battery from the motorcycle and recharge it as described in this chapter.

Inspection

A malfunction in the charging system generally causes the battery to remain undercharged. Perform the following visual inspections to determine the cause of the problem. If the visual inspection proves satisfactory, test the charging system as described in Chapter Two.

1. Make sure the battery cables are properly connected to the battery terminals and that the negative cable is properly connected to the frame ground.

2. Inspect the terminals for loose or corroded connections. Tighten or clean them as required.

3. Inspect the battery case. Look for bulges or cracks in the case, leaking electrolyte or corrosion buildup.

4. Carefully check all connections at the alternator to make sure they are clean and tight.

5. Check the circuit wiring for corroded or loose connections. Clean, tighten or connect wiring as required.

6. Check the charging system wiring for signs of chafing, deterioration or other damage.

ALTERNATOR

Rotor Removal/Installation

Refer to **Figure 15**.

1. Disconnect the negative battery cable as described in this chapter.

2. Remove the primary chaincase cover and inner housing as described in Chapter Six.

3. Remove the primary chain, clutch assembly, chain tensioner assembly and compensating sprocket components as described in Chapter Six.

4. If still in place, remove the shaft extension and washer from the crankshaft.

5. Install a large bearing puller (**Figure 16**) or a strap-type flywheel holder (**Figure 17**) onto the rotor.

6. Pull on the bearing puller or flywheel holder and remove the rotor from the crankshaft.

7. Separate the tool from the rotor.

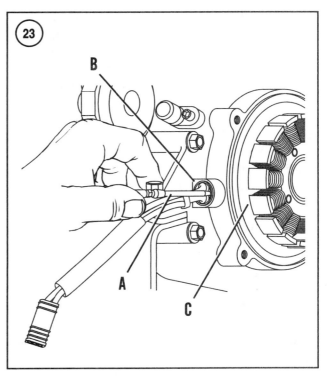

9

ping fingers between the rotor and the sharp edge of the crankcase (Figure 19).

10. Install by reversing the removal steps.

Stator Removal

NOTE
Some of the photographs in this procedure are shown with the engine removed to better illustrate the steps.

1. Remove the rotor as described in this section.
2. Depress the tabs and open the front electrical caddy cover (**Figure 20**).
3. Release the latch and disconnect the round 3-pin connector (**Figure 21**) from the left side base of the voltage regulator.

NOTE
Spray electrical contact cleaner or glass cleaner around the wiring harness grommet to help ease it out of the crankcase boss receptacle.

4. Move the stator grommet (A, **Figure 22**) aside, and spray a lubricant into the grommet. Repeat on the other side of the grommet.
5. Remove the four Torx (T27) screws (B, **Figure 22**) securing the stator assembly to the crankcase and discard the screws.
6. Insert a small awl (A, **Figure 23**), or screwdriver, carefully lift the capped rib (B) on the grommet away from the crankcase opening (C). Insert it into the between the

8. Inspect the rotor magnets (A, **Figure 18**) for small bolts, washers or other metal debris that may have been picked up by the magnets. These small metal particles can cause severe damage to the alternator stator assembly.
9. Check the inner splines (B, **Figure 18**) for wear or damage. Replace the rotor if necessary.

WARNING
*Do **not** try to install the rotor without the special tool used during removal. The magnets will quickly pull the rotor into place, trap-*

grommet and the crankcase. Tilt the awl slightly and squirt isopropyl alcohol or glass cleaner into the opening. Repeat this at one or two additional locations around the opening.

7. Push on the capped rib (B, **Figure 23**) from the outside of the opening. Place needlenose pliers on the cable stop, and withdraw the grommet through the crankcase bore. Rock the grommet back and forth to ease removal if necessary. Be careful not to damage the grommet ribs if the stator is going to be reused.

8. Withdraw the stator wiring harness from the frame and remove the stator assembly.

Stator Installation

1. Thoroughly clean the grommet with isopropyl alcohol so the ribs are free of oil residue and debris.

2. Apply a light coat of glass cleaner to the wiring harness grommet to help ease it into the crankcase boss receptacle.

3. Insert the electrical harness and grommet into the crankcase boss receptacle and carefully pull it through until the grommet is correctly seated.

> *CAUTION*
> *New Torx screws must be installed. The threadlock originally applied to the Torx screws is sufficient for one time use only. If a used Torx screw is installed it can work loose and cause engine damage.*

4. Move the stator into position on the crankcase and install four *new* Torx (T27) screws (B, **Figure 22**). Tighten the stator screws to 55-75 in.-lb. (6.2-8.5 N•m).

5. Insert the electrical harness through the frame and forward along the outboard side of the voltage regulator.

6. Connect the round 3-pin electrical connector (**Figure 21**) to the left side base of the voltage regulator. Push it in until it bottoms. Snap the latch into place.

7. Close the front electrical caddy cover (**Figure 20**) and snap the tabs into place.

8. Install the rotor as described in this section.

Inspection

1. Inspect the stator mounting surface on the crankcase for any oil residue that may have been left by a damaged oil seal. Clean off if necessary.

2. Inspect the stator wires (A, **Figure 24**) for fraying or damage.

3. Inspect the rubber grommet (B, **Figure 24**) for deterioration or hardness.

4. Check the stator connector pins for corrosion, looseness or damage.

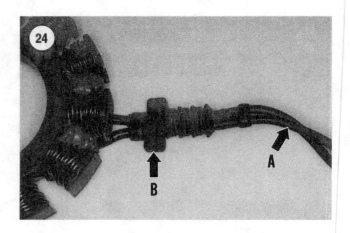

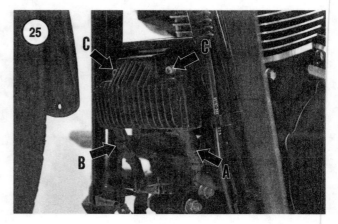

VOLTAGE REGULATOR

Removal/Installation

1. Disconnect the negative battery cable as described in this chapter.

2A. On 2006-2007 models, perform the following:
   a. Remove the two mounting bolts and partially remove the voltage regulator from the frame.
   b. Depress the tabs on the upper front portion of the front electrical caddy cover. Remove the cover.
   c. Release the latch and disconnect the round 3-pin stator connector from the left side base of the voltage regulator and the 2-pin connector from the right side.
   d. Remove the voltage regulator from the frame.

2B. On 2008-2011 models, perform the following:
   a. Depress the tabs and open the front electrical caddy cover (**Figure 20**).
   b. Release the latch and disconnect the round 3-pin stator connector (A, **Figure 25**) from the left side base of the voltage regulator and the 2-pin connector (B) from the right side.
   c. Remove the two mounting bolts (C, **Figure 25**) and remove the voltage regulator from the frame.

3. Install by reversing the removal steps while noting the following:

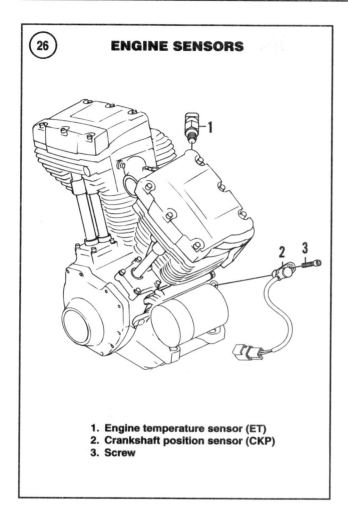

ENGINE SENSORS

1. Engine temperature sensor (ET)
2. Crankshaft position sensor (CKP)
3. Screw

sensor, intake air temperature (IAT) sensor, idle air control (IAC), engine temperature (ET) sensor and vehicle speed sensor (VSS). Refer to **Figure 26** for sensor locations on the engine. The remaining sensors are located on the induction module.

The ECM is located on the electrical caddy. The ECM determines the spark advance for correct ignition timing based on signals from the IAT, ET, TP and oxygen sensors. The ignition system fires the spark plugs near top dead center for starting, and then varies the spark advance from 0° to 50° depending on engine speed, crankshaft position, and intake manifold pressure. It also regulates the low-voltage circuits between the battery and the ignition coil. The ECM is not repairable and must be replaced if defective.

The crankshaft position (CKP) sensor is located in the front left side of the crankcase. The CKP sensor takes its readings off the 30 teeth on the left side flywheel. There is a gap in the rotor the distance of two teeth. This gap creates a reference point to determine engine speed so the ECM can determine ignition timing. The gap can also be used as a reference point to establish TDC.

The MAP sensor is located on top of the induction module. This sensor monitors the intake manifold vacuum and sends this information to the electronic control module. The electronic control module adjusts the ignition timing advance curve for maximum performance.

The bank angle sensor is an integral part of the turn signal/turn signal security module (TSM/TSSM/HFSM). The sensor consists of a small magnetic disc that rides within a V-shaped channel. If the motorcycle is tilted at a 45° angle for more than one second, the ignition system shuts off. Once the sensor is activated, the motorcycle must be uprighted and the ignition turned off, and then back to IGN. before the engine can be restarted.

The basic components of the ignition systems are shown in **Figure 27**. When servicing the ignition system, refer to the wiring diagrams located on the CD inserted into the back cover of this manual. Refer to Chapter Two for troubleshooting procedures.

a. Install both connectors onto the voltage regulator. Push them on until they bottom. Snap the latches into place.
b. Install the voltage regulator bolts (C, **Figure 25**) and tighten to 60-80 in.-lb. (6.8-9.0 N•m).

Inspection

1. Remove the voltage regulator as described in this section.
2. Thoroughly clean both electrical terminals at the base of the voltage regulator and both wiring harness connectors with contact cleaner.
3. Inspect all terminals for corrosion, bending and damage. Repair as necessary.
4. Make sure the wiring harness connectors lock into place on the voltage regulator to achieve a water tight seal.
5. Check the voltage regulator housing for damage and replace as necessary.

IGNITION SYSTEM

The ignition system consists of an ignition coil, two spark plugs, electronic control module (ECM), crankshaft position (CKP) sensor, manifold absolute pressure (MAP)

IGNITION COIL

Removal/Installation

1. Disconnect the negative battery cable as described in this chapter.
2. Remove the fuel tank as described in Chapter Eight.

NOTE
Label all wiring connectors prior to disconnecting them in the following steps.

3. Disconnect the secondary cables (A, **Figure 28**) from both spark plugs.
4. Carefully remove the secondary leads from the clip (B, **Figure 28**) on the engine mounting bracket.
5A. On FXDL and FXDWG models, perform the following:

⟨27⟩   **IGNITION SYSTEM**

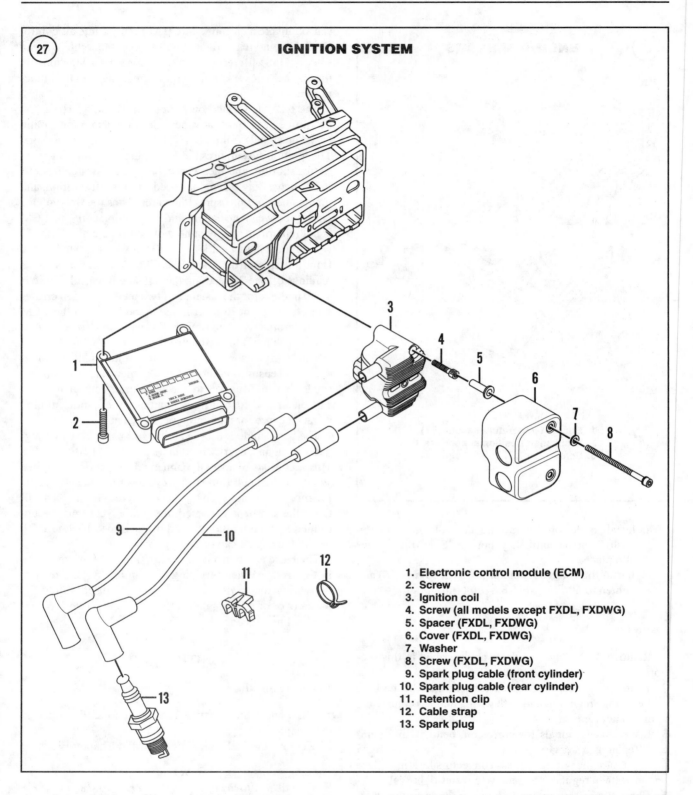

1. Electronic control module (ECM)
2. Screw
3. Ignition coil
4. Screw (all models except FXDL, FXDWG)
5. Spacer (FXDL, FXDWG)
6. Cover (FXDL, FXDWG)
7. Washer
8. Screw (FXDL, FXDWG)
9. Spark plug cable (front cylinder)
10. Spark plug cable (rear cylinder)
11. Retention clip
12. Cable strap
13. Spark plug

a. Remove the two long screws, washers and the cover from the electrical caddy.

b. Remove the ignition coil and secondary cables from the side electrical caddy.

c. Disconnect the 4-pin connector from the backside of the ignition coil.

d. Do not lose the two screw spacers within the cover.

5B. On all other models, perform the following:

a. Remove the two screws (A, **Figure 29**) securing the ignition coil to the electrical caddy.

b. Remove the ignition coil (B, **Figure 29**) and secondary cables from the side electrical caddy.

c. Disconnect the 4-pin connector from the backside of the ignition coil.

6. Install the ignition coil by reversing the removal steps. Tighten the screws securely to 50 in.-lb. (5.6 N•m).

Performance Test

1. Disconnect the plug wire and remove one of the spark plugs as described in Chapter Three.

> *NOTE*
> *A spark tester (**Figure 30**) is a useful tool for testing the ignition system spark output. This tool (Motion Pro part No. 08-0122) is inserted in the spark plug cap and its base is grounded against the cylinder head. The tool's air gap is adjustable, and it allows the visual inspection of the spark while testing the intensity of the spark.*

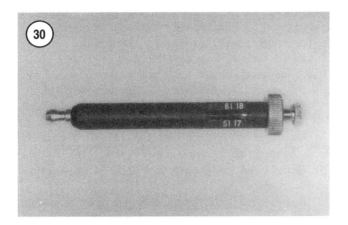

2. Insert a clean shop cloth into the spark plug hole in the cylinder head to lessen the chance of gasoline vapors being emitted from the hole.

> *WARNING*
> *Mount the spark plug, or tester, away from the spark plug hole in the cylinder so that the spark or tester cannot ignite the gasoline vapors in the cylinder. If the engine is flooded, do not perform this test. The firing of the spark plug can ignite fuel that is ejected through the spark plug hole.*

> *NOTE*
> *If not using a spark tester, always use a new spark plug for this test.*

3. Insert a new spark plug (**Figure 31**), or the spark tester (**Figure 32**), into one of the plug caps and touch the spark plug base against the cylinder head to ground it. Position the spark plug so the electrode is visible.

> *WARNING*
> *If necessary, hold onto the spark plug wire with a pair of insulated pliers. Do **not** hold the spark plug, wire or connector or a serious electrical shock may result.*

4. Crank the engine over with the starter. A fat, blue spark should be evident across the spark plug electrode, or spark

tester. If there is strong sunlight on the plug, or tester, shade it so the spark is more visible.

5. If a fat blue spark occurs, the ignition coil is good. If not, perform the ignition coil resistance test (this section).

6. Repeat test for the other cylinder.

Resistance Test

1. Remove the ignition coil as described in this section.
2. Disconnect the secondary wires from the ignition coil.
3. Use an ohmmeter and measure the primary coil resistance between terminals (**Figure 33**) as follows:
    a. Front coil: Terminal A and D.
    b. Rear coil: Terminal A and C.
4. Set the ohmmeter to the highest scale. Measure the resistance between the secondary ignition terminals.
5. Compare the measured resistance value to the specification in **Table 1**. If the resistance values are less than specified, there is most likely a short in the coil windings. Replace the coil.
6. If the resistance values are more than specified, this may indicate corrosion or oxidation of the coil's terminals. Thoroughly clean the terminals, and spray with an aerosol electrical contact cleaner. Repeat the test and if the resistance value is still high, replace the coil (this section).
7. If the coil resistance does not meet (or come close to) either of these specifications, the coil must be replaced. If the coil exhibits visible damage, it should be replaced as described in this section.
8. Install the ignition coil as described in this section.

ELECTRONIC CONTROL MODULE (ECM)

Removal/Installation

1. Disconnect the negative battery cable as described in this chapter.
2. Remove the electrical caddy as described in this chapter.
3. Remove the two screws securing the ECM and ground wire to the electrical caddy.
4. Install the ECM by reversing the removal steps. Tighten the screws securely.

SIDE ELECTRICAL CADDY

Removal/Installation

Refer to **Figure 34**.

1. Disconnect the negative battery cable as described in this chapter.
2. Remove the seat as described in Chapter Fourteen.
3. Pull straight out and remove the cover (**Figure 35**) from the electrical caddy.
4. Remove the fuse and relay panels as follows:
    a. Insert a small screwdriver into the slot under each panel (A, **Figure 36**).

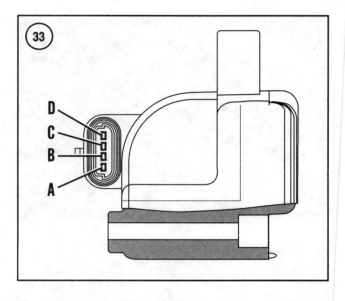

b. Disengage the panels from the electrical caddy.
5. Remove the Maxi-Fuse as follows:
    a. Insert a small screwdriver into the slots under the Maxi-Fuse (B, **Figure 36**).
    b. Depress the tabs of the Maxi-Fuse connector and disengage it from the electrical panel.
6. Depress the tab on the electrical caddy and release the TSSM/HFSM. Pull the TSSM/HFSM module (C, **Figure 36**) part way out of the electrical caddy, and disconnect the connector from it.
7. Slide the data link connector (D, **Figure 36**) forward and disengage it from the electrical caddy.
8. Disconnect the ECM connector as follows:
    a. Push the connector onto the ECM.
    b. Depress the thumb lever against the connector until the latch is released from the catch on the ECM.
    c. Carefully pull the connector straight out and disconnect it from the ECM.
9. Disconnect the ignition coil connector (E, **Figure 36**) from the electrical caddy.
10. Remove the ignition coil (F, **Figure 36**) as described in this chapter,
11. Remove the long front caddy mounting screw and washer located under the data link connector.
12. Remove the two upper screws (G, **Figure 36**) and washers securing the electrical caddy to the top of the frame.
13. Remove the wiring harness from the backside of the electrical caddy.
14. Remove the screws and ground wire securing the ECM to the caddy, and then remove the ECM from the electrical caddy from the frame.
15. Install by reversing the removal steps, noting the following:
    a. Tighten two upper caddy screws to 90-110 in.-lb. (10.2-12.4 N•m).
    b. Tighten lower long caddy screw to 40-60 in.-lb. (4.5-6.8 N•m).

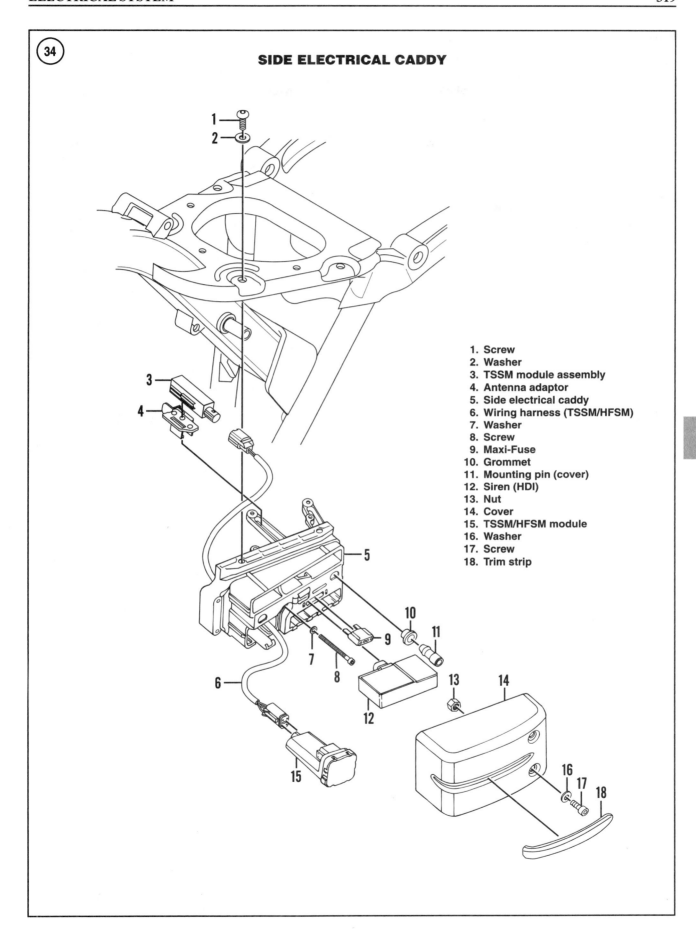

SIDE ELECTRICAL CADDY

1. Screw
2. Washer
3. TSSM module assembly
4. Antenna adaptor
5. Side electrical caddy
6. Wiring harness (TSSM/HFSM)
7. Washer
8. Screw
9. Maxi-Fuse
10. Grommet
11. Mounting pin (cover)
12. Siren (HDI)
13. Nut
14. Cover
15. TSSM/HFSM module
16. Washer
17. Screw
18. Trim strip

9

CRANKSHAFT POSITION (CKP) SENSOR

Removal/Installation (2006-2007 Models)

NOTE
Always disarm the optional security system (TSM/TSSM/HFSM) before disconnecting the battery or before pulling the Maxi-Fuse so the siren will not sound.

1. Disconnect the negative battery cable as described in this chapter.
2. Remove the two mounting bolts and partially remove the voltage regulator from the frame.
3. Depress the tabs on the upper front portion of the front electrical caddy cover. Remove the cover.
4. Remove the CKP sensor connector from the clip on the electrical caddy.
5. Disconnect the CKP connector from the main harness.
6. Remove the secondary locks and disconnect the appropriate terminals from within the socket housing as described in this chapter. Note the wire color locations within the connector as they must be installed in the correct location.
7. On the front, left side of the motorcycle, remove the Allen screw and withdraw the CKP sensor and O-ring from the crankcase. Discard the O-ring.
8. Note the path of the harness through the frame, and carefully pull the wiring harness out of the frame.
9. Install by reversing the removal steps. Note the following:
   a. Apply clean engine oil to a *new* O-ring and install it on the CKP sensor.
   b. Install the CKP sensor and tighten the Allen screw to 90-120 in.-lb. (10.2-13.6 N•m).

Removal/Installation (2008-2011 Models)

1. Disconnect the battery negative cable as described in this chapter.
2. Depress the tabs on the upper front portion of the front electrical caddy cover, and open the cover.

3. Remove the CKP sensor connector from the clip on the electrical caddy.
4. Disconnect the CKP connector from the main harness (**Figure 37**).
5. On the front left side of the motorcycle, remove the Allen screw (A, **Figure 38**) and withdraw the CKP sensor (B) and O-ring from the crankcase. Discard the O-ring.
6. Note the path of the harness through the frame, and carefully pull the wiring harness out of the frame.
7. Install by reversing the removal steps. Note the following:
   a. Apply clean engine oil to a *new* O-ring and install it on the CKP sensor (**Figure 39**).
   b. Install the CKP sensor and tighten the Allen screw to 90-120 in.-lb. (10.2-13.6 N•m).

ENGINE TEMPERATURE (ET) SENSOR

Removal/Installation

1. Disconnect the negative battery cable as described in this chapter.
2. Remove the horn assembly as described in this chapter.
3. Working at the front cylinder head, pull the rubber boot away from the ET sensor.
4. Disconnect the 2-pin connector (A, **Figure 39**) from the ET sensor.

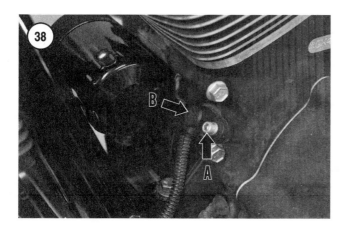

5. Use a deep-well socket to loosen the sensor (B, **Figure 39**). After the sensor is loosened, remove the sensor by hand.

6. Install the ET sensor (B, **Figure 39**) into the front cylinder by hand. Do not cross thread it.

7. Tighten the ET sensor to 10-15 ft.-lb. (13.6-20.3 N•m).

8. Connect the 2-pin connector (A, **Figure 39**) to the ET sensor.

9. Roll the rubber boot down onto the ET sensor connector.

10. Install the horn assembly as described in this chapter.

11. Connect the negative battery cable as described in this chapter.

BANK ANGLE (BAS) SENSOR

The bank angle sensor is an integral part of the Turn Signal Security Module.

VEHICLE SPEED (VSS) SENSOR

Removal/Installation

1. Disconnect the negative battery cable as described in this chapter.

NOTE
Figure 40 is shown with the swing arm removed for photo clarity.

2. Remove the starter (A, **Figure 40**) as described in this chapter.

3. Disconnect the 3-pin VSS connector (B, **Figure 40**) on the top of the transmission case.

4. Remove the Allen screw securing the VSS to the top right side of the transmission housing and withdraw the sensor from the transmission case.

5. Install by reversing the removal steps. Note the following:
   a. Apply clean engine oil to a *new* O-ring and install it on the VSS sensor.
   b. Install the sensor and tighten the Allen screw to 84-108 in.-lb. (9.5-12.2 N•m).

STARTING SYSTEM

When servicing the starting system, refer to the wiring diagrams located on the CD inserted into in the back cover of this manual.

CAUTION
Do not operate the starter for more than five seconds at a time. Let it cool for approximately 10 seconds before operating it again.

Troubleshooting

Refer to Chapter Two.

STARTER

Refer to **Figure 41** and **Figure 42**.

Removal (All Years)

1. Remove the seat as described in Chapter Fourteen.

2. Remove the exhaust system as described in Chapter Four.

3. Remove the battery and battery tray as described in this chapter.

4. Remove the cover screw (A, **Figure 43**) and chrome cover, on models so equipped.

5. Slide back the rubber boot (B, **Figure 43**), remove the terminal nut (A, **Figure 44**) from the starter battery-termi-

9

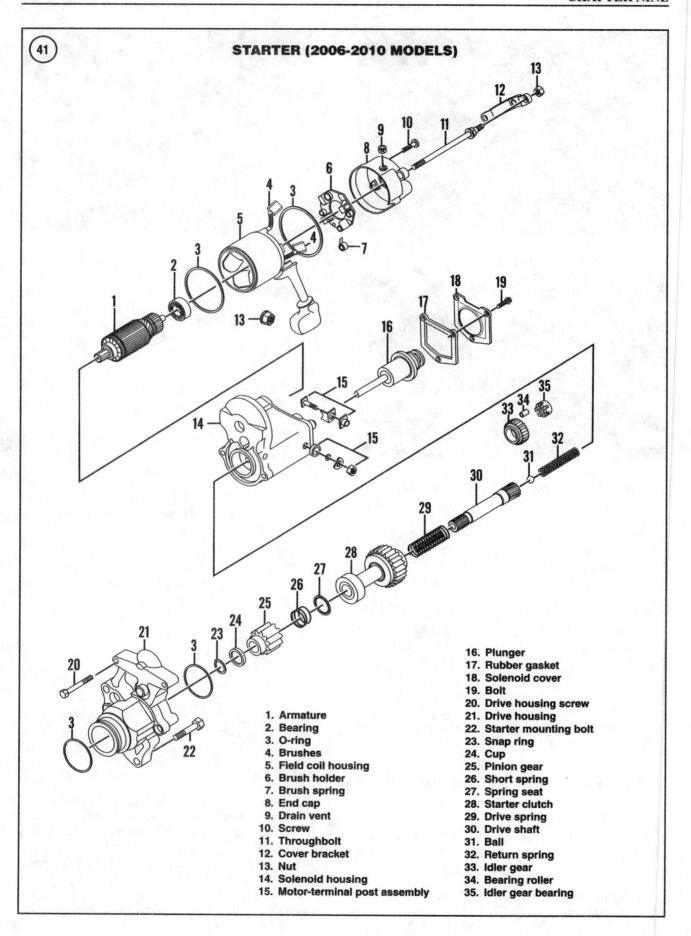

STARTER (2006-2010 MODELS)

1. Armature
2. Bearing
3. O-ring
4. Brushes
5. Field coil housing
6. Brush holder
7. Brush spring
8. End cap
9. Drain vent
10. Screw
11. Throughbolt
12. Cover bracket
13. Nut
14. Solenoid housing
15. Motor-terminal post assembly
16. Plunger
17. Rubber gasket
18. Solenoid cover
19. Bolt
20. Drive housing screw
21. Drive housing
22. Starter mounting bolt
23. Snap ring
24. Cup
25. Pinion gear
26. Short spring
27. Spring seat
28. Starter clutch
29. Drive spring
30. Drive shaft
31. Ball
32. Return spring
33. Idler gear
34. Bearing roller
35. Idler gear bearing

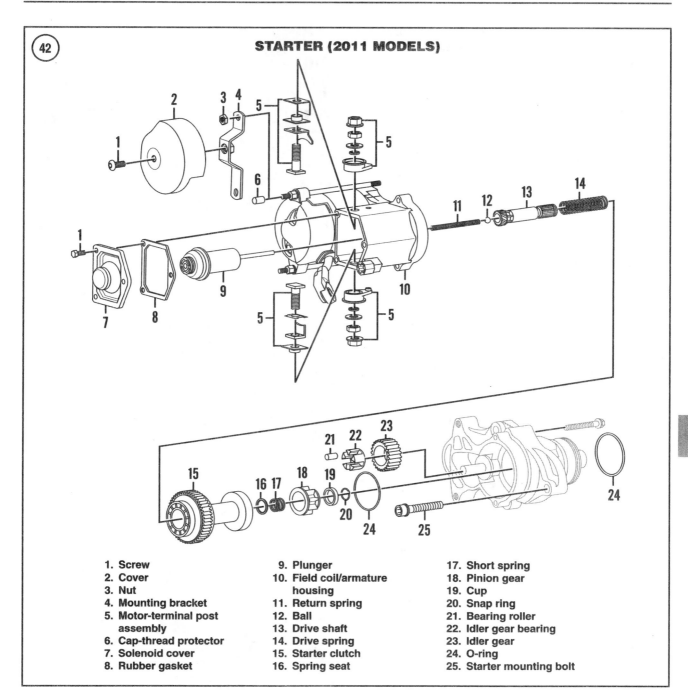

STARTER (2011 MODELS)

1. Screw
2. Cover
3. Nut
4. Mounting bracket
5. Motor-terminal post assembly
6. Cap-thread protector
7. Solenoid cover
8. Rubber gasket
9. Plunger
10. Field coil/armature housing
11. Return spring
12. Ball
13. Drive shaft
14. Drive spring
15. Starter clutch
16. Spring seat
17. Short spring
18. Pinion gear
19. Cup
20. Snap ring
21. Bearing roller
22. Idler gear bearing
23. Idler gear
24. O-ring
25. Starter mounting bolt

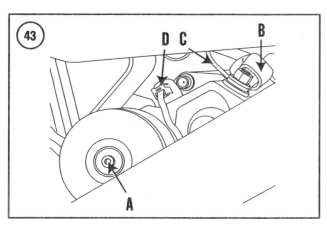

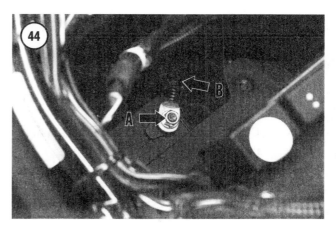

nal post, and disconnect the positive battery cable (B) from the post.

6. Remove the ring terminal (C, **Figure 42**) from the battery-terminal post, on models so equipped.

7. Disconnect the solenoid connector (A, **Figure 45**) from the starter.

8. Remove the starter mounting bolts (B, **Figure 45**) and washers.

9. From the right side of the motorcycle, pull the starter straight out of the crankcase and remove it. Do not lose the two dowels (**Figure 46**).

10. If necessary, service the motor, drive housing or solenoid housing as described in this chapter.

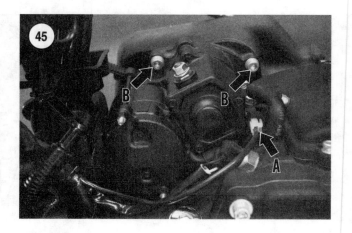

Installation (All Years)

1. Press the dowels (**Figure 46**) into the crankcase, if removed.

2. Install the starter, and push it in until it bottoms.

3. Apply Loctite Threadlocker 243 (blue), or an equivalent threadlock, to the bolt threads. Install the starter mounting bolts (B, **Figure 45**) and washers. Tighten the bolts to the following:

   a. 2006-2007 models: 13-20 ft.-lb. (17.6-27.1 N•m).

   b. 2008-2011 models: 25-27 ft.-lb. (33.9-36.6 N•m).

4. Connect the solenoid connector (A, **Figure 45**) to the starter.

5. Fit the ring terminal (C, **Figure 43**) onto the starter battery-terminal post, on models so equipped.

6. Connect the positive battery cable (B, **Figure 44**) onto the starter battery-terminal post, and install the terminal nut (A). Tighten the terminal nut to 65-85 in.-lb. (7.3-9.6 N•m), and slide the rubber boot (B, **Figure 43**) into position. Where equipped, install the chrome cover onto the end of the starter. Tighten the cover bolt (A, **Figure 43**) securely.

7. Install the exhaust system as described in Chapter Four.

8. Install the battery tray and battery as described in this chapter.

9. Install the seat as described in Chapter Fourteen.

Disassembly (2006-2010 Models)

NOTE
*If just the solenoid assembly requires service, refer to **Solenoid Housing Disassembly/ Inspection/Assembly** in this section.*

1. Clean all grease, dirt and carbon from the exterior of the starter assembly.

2. Where equipped, remove the nuts from the through-bolts, and remove the cover bracket

3. Pull the field coil boot (A, **Figure 47**) from the motor-terminal post on the solenoid housing.

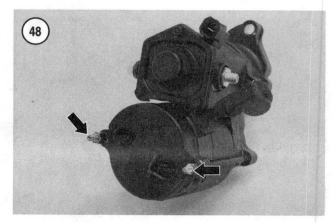

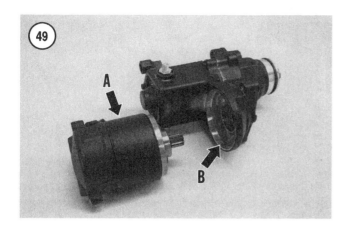

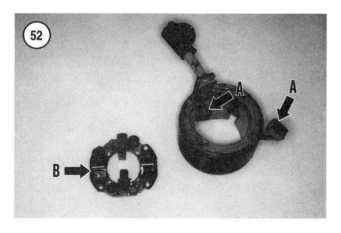

4. Loosen and remove the nut (B, **Figure 47**) from the motor-terminal post. Then, disconnect the field coil wire from the post.

5. Remove the throughbolts (**Figure 48**), and pull the motor (A, **Figure 49**) from the solenoid housing.

6. Remove the end cap screws (A, **Figure 50**), washers and O-rings, and remove the end cap (B) from the field coil assembly.

7. Pull the brush holder (A, **Figure 51**) away from the commutator, and remove the armature (B) from the field coil housing (C)

8. Remove the two field coil brushes (A, **Figure 52**) from the brush holder (B).

CAUTION
Be extremely careful when selecting a solvent to clean the electrical components. Do not immerse any of the wire windings in solvent, because the insulation may be damaged. Wipe the windings with a cloth lightly moistened with solvent, and allow the solution to dry thoroughly.

9. Clean all grease, dirt and carbon from the armature, field coil assembly and end cover.

10. To service the drive housing assembly, refer to *Drive Housing Disassembly/Inspection/Assembly* (this section).

11. To service the solenoid housing, refer to *Solenoid Housing Disassembly/Inspection/Assembly* (this section).

9

Disassembly (2011 Models)

NOTE
Do not remove the armature and brush plate from the housing as replacement parts are not available for these components.

1. Clean all grease, dirt and carbon from the exterior of the starter assembly.

2. Where equipped, remove the nuts from the through bolts, and remove the cover bracket

3. Pull the field coil boot (A, **Figure 47**) from the motor-terminal post on the solenoid housing.

4. Loosen and remove the nut (B, **Figure 47**) from the motor-terminal post, and disconnect the field coil wire from the post.

5. Remove the throughbolts (**Figure 48**), and pull the motor (A, **Figure 49**) from the solenoid housing.

6. To service the drive housing assembly, refer to *Drive Housing Disassembly/Inspection/Assembly* in this chapter.

7. To service the solenoid housing, refer to *Solenoid Housing Disassembly/Inspection/Assembly* in this chapter.

Inspection (2006-2010 Models)

1. Measure the length of each brush with a caliper (**Figure 53**).

a. Measure the field coil brushes (A, **Figure 54**) and the brush holder brushes (**Figure 55**).

NOTE
*The field coil brushes (A, **Figure 54**) are soldered into position. To replace them, unsolder the brushes by heating their joints with a soldering gun, and pull them out with a pair of pliers. Position the new brushes and solder them in place with rosin-core solder. Do not use acid-core solder.*

b. If the brush length is less than the specification in **Table 1**, replace all of the brushes as a set.

2. Inspect the commutator (A, **Figure 56**) on the armature. The mica should be below the surface of the copper commutator segments (**Figure 57**). If the commutator bars are worn to the same level as the mica insulation, have the commutator serviced by a dealership or electrical repair shop.

3. Inspect the commutator copper segments for discoloration. If the commutator segments are rough, discolored or worn, have the commutator serviced by a dealership or electrical repair shop.

4. Measure the outer diameter of the commutator with a caliper (**Figure 58**). Replace the armature if the commutator outside diameter is less than the specification in **Table 1**.

5. Use an ohmmeter to perform the following tests.

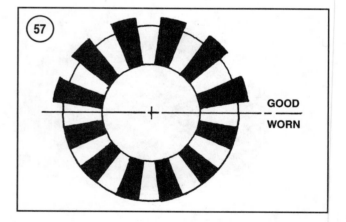

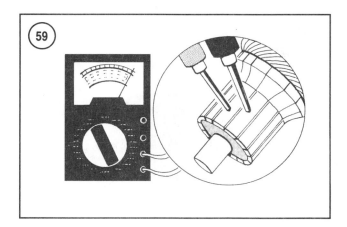

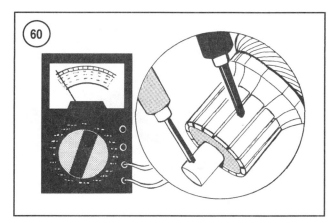

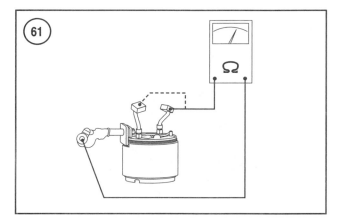

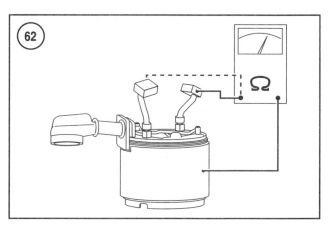

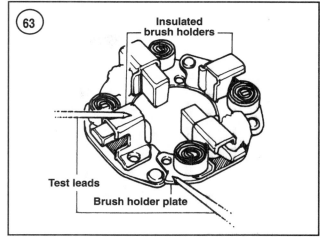

a. Check for continuity between the commutator bars (**Figure 59**). There should be continuity between pairs of bars.

b. Check for continuity between any commutator bar and the shaft (**Figure 60**). There should be no continuity.

c. If the unit fails either test, replace the armature.

6. Use an ohmmeter to perform the following tests.

a. Check for continuity between the field coil wire and each field coil brush (**Figure 61**). There should be continuity.

b. Check for continuity between the field coil housing and each field coil brush (**Figure 62**). There should be no continuity.

c. If the unit fails either test, replace the field coil assembly.

7. Use an ohmmeter to check for continuity between the brush holder plate and each positive (insulated) brush holder (**Figure 63**). There should be no continuity. If the unit fails this test, replace the brush holder plate.

8. Inspect the armature bearings as follows:

a. Check the bearings (B, **Figure 56**) on the armature shaft. Replace worn or damaged bearings.

b. Check the bearing bores in the end cover and solenoid housing (B, **Figure 49**). Replace the cover or housing if the bore is worn or cracked.

Inspection (2011 Models)

NOTE
There are no inspection procedures or specification available from the manufacturer for the 2011 models. Refer to the NOTE in the inspection procedure for 2006-2010 models.

Assembly (2006-2010 Models)

1. If necessary, assemble the drive housing as described in this section.

2. If necessary, assemble the solenoid housing as described in this section.

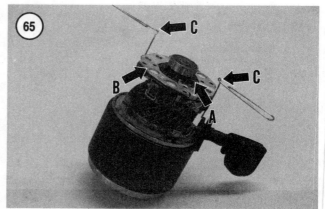

3. Lubricate the armature bearings (B, **Figure 56**) with high-temperature grease.

4. Install a *new* O-ring (B, **Figure 54**) onto each end of the field coil housing.

5. At the brush holder (A, **Figure 64**), pull each spring back from its brush, and insert a paper clip between the spring and brush holder to keep spring pressure off the brush.

6. Install the each field coil brush (B, **Figure 64**) into it brush holder. Pull the spring back from the brush, and clip the spring over the edge of the holder.

7. Install armature into the housing so the commutator goes through the brush holder (**Figure 65**).

8. Pull the paper clips (A, **Figure 65**) and release the field coil brush springs from the holder. Make sure each brush presses against the commutator.

9. Install the end cap (A, **Figure 66**) onto the field coil housing so the cap's cutout engages the grommet (B) on the field coil wire.

10. Thread the end cap screws (A, **Figure 50**) into the brush holder. Keep the housing horizontal so the armature will not fall out of the housing.

11. Align the motor (A, **Figure 49**) with the solenoid housing (B) and assemble both housings.

12. Install the throughbolts (**Figure 48**) and tighten to 39-64 in.-lb. (4.4-7.3 N•m).

13. Connect the field coil wire to the motor-terminal post on the solenoid housing, and install the nut (B, **Figure 46**). Tighten the field coil terminal post nut to 70-90 in.-lb. (7.9-10.2 N•m).

14. Install the boot (A, **Figure 47**) over the motor-terminal post.

Assembly (2011 Models)

1. If necessary, assemble the drive housing as described in this chapter.

2. If necessary, assemble the solenoid housing as described in this chapter.

3. Align the motor (A, **Figure 50**) with the solenoid housing (B) and assemble both housings.

4. Install the through bolts (**Figure 48**) and tighten to 39-64 in.-lb. (4.4-7.3 N•m).

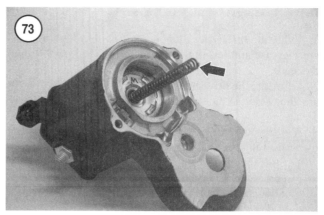

5. Connect the field coil wire to the motor-terminal post on the solenoid housing, and turn on the nut (B, **Figure 46**). Tighten the motor-terminal nut to 70-90 in.-lb. (7.9-10.2 N•m).

6. Install the boot (A, **Figure 47**) over the motor-terminal post.

Drive Housing Disassembly/Inspection (All Years)

1. Remove the motor as described in this section.
2. Remove the two drive housing Phillips screws (**Figure 67**).
3. Tap the drive housing, and remove it from the solenoid housing.
4. Remove the idler gear (**Figure 68**) from the bearing cage, and remove the bearing cage (**Figure 69**). Watch for the five rollers in the cage.
5. Push on the drive shaft, and remove the starter clutch assembly (A, **Figure 70**) from the housing.
6. If necessary, disassemble the starter clutch assembly by performing the following:

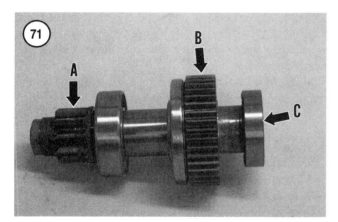

   a. Compress the assembly's internal springs, and remove the snap ring from the end of the drive shaft.
   b. Remove the cup and pinion gear (A, **Figure 71**).
   c. Remove the short spring and spring seat.
   d. Press the splined end of the drive shaft, and remove it from the starter clutch.
   e. Remove the return spring (A, **Figure 72**) from the drive shaft (B) or from the solenoid plunger shaft (**Figure 73**) in the solenoid housing.
   f. Remove the steel ball from the drive shaft bore.
   g. Remove the drive spring (C, **Figure 72**) from the drive shaft.

7. Inspect the idler-gear bearing and cage assembly (A, **Figure 74**) for worn or damaged parts.
8. Inspect the springs for kinks or fatigue.
9. Check the idler gear (B, **Figure 74**), pinion gear (A, **Figure 71**) and starter clutch gear (B) for worn or damage teeth.
10. Inspect the drive shaft (B, **Figure 72**) for worn or damaged splines or gear teeth.
11. Inspect the drive housing outer O-ring (B, **Figure 70**) and the O-ring in the housing bore. Replace as needed.

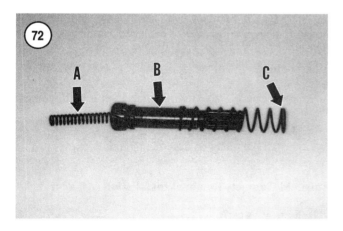

Drive Housing Assembly (All Years)

1. Lubricate the starter plunger shaft with a high-temperature grease and install the return spring (**Figure 73**) onto the shaft.

2. Lubricate the drive housing outer O-ring (B, **Figure 70**) and the O-ring in the housing bore with a high-temperature grease.

3. If disassembled, assemble the starter clutch assembly by performing the following:

   a. Slide the drive spring (C, **Figure 72**) onto the splined end of the drive shaft (B).

   b. Slide the splined end of the drive shaft into the gear end of the starter clutch bore (C, **Figure 71**).

   c. Select a deep socket that matches the outside diameter of the drive shaft. Insert the socket into the starter clutch bore, and stand the socket upright on the bench.

   d. Press the starter clutch down so the socket presses the drive shaft into the starter clutch bore until the splined end of the shaft emerges from the starter clutch bearing.

   e. Install the spring seat, short spring, pinion gear and cup onto the splined end of the drive shaft. The collar on the pinion gear and the concave side of the cup must face up away from the starter clutch.

   f. Continue to compress the assembly, and install a new snap ring onto the drive shaft. Make sure the ring is completely seated in the shaft groove. Release the tension on the starter clutch and check the snap ring. It must be completely seated within the concave part of the cup.

   g. Remove the socket from the starter clutch bore.

4. Lubricate the starter clutch bearing with a high-temperature grease, and install the starter clutch (A, **Figure 70**) into the drive housing. Make sure the clutch bearing is seated in the bearing bore.

5. Lubricate the idle-gear bearing rollers and bearing cage with a high-temperature grease. Install the rollers (A, **Figure 74**) into the cage, and install the bearing cage (**Figure 69**) onto the shaft in the drive housing.

6. Lubricate the idler gear (**Figure 68**) with a high-temperature grease, and install it over the bearing cage.

7. Insert the ball (**Figure 75**) into the starter clutch, and seat the ball in the drive shaft bore.

8. Fit the drive housing onto the solenoid housing so the return spring (**Figure 73**) slides into the drive shaft bore within the starter clutch.

9. Install the two drive housing Phillips screws (**Figure 67**) and tighten securely.

10. Install the motor as described in this section.

Solenoid Housing
Disassembly/Inspection/Assembly (All Years)

Refer to **Figure 76**.

1. Remove the motor as described in this section.

2. Remove the two drive housing Phillips screws (**Figure 67**).

3. Tap the drive housing, and remove it from the solenoid housing. If the return spring (**Figure 73**) remains with the solenoid plunger, watch for the ball (**Figure 75**) in the starter clutch bore.

4. Remove the solenoid cover bolts (A, **Figure 77**), and remove the solenoid cover (B) and gasket.

5. Remove the plunger assembly (**Figure 78**) from the solenoid housing.

6. Inspect the rubber cap (A, **Figure 79**) for hardness or deterioration, replace if necessary.

7. Inspect the plunger (B, **Figure 79**) and shaft (C) for wear or damage, replace if necessary.

8. Inspect the solenoid housing (**Figure 80**) for wear, cracks or other damage.

9. Inspect each terminal post assembly on the solenoid housing. If any part is worn or damaged, install a new solenoid repair kit. Individual terminal parts are not available.

10. Assemble the solenoid housing by reversing the removal steps:

   a. Lubricate the solenoid plunger with a high-temperature grease.

   b. Install a new gasket.

   c. Install the motor as described in this section.

Solenoid Contacts Removal/Installation (All Years)

Refer to **Figure 76**.

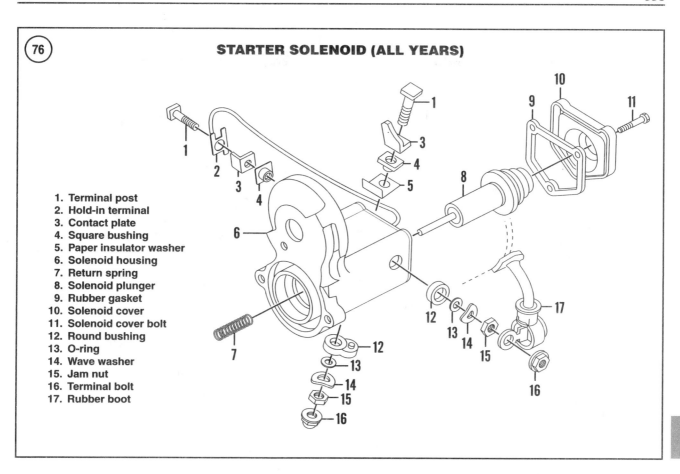

STARTER SOLENOID (ALL YEARS)

1. Terminal post
2. Hold-in terminal
3. Contact plate
4. Square bushing
5. Paper insulator washer
6. Solenoid housing
7. Return spring
8. Solenoid plunger
9. Rubber gasket
10. Solenoid cover
11. Solenoid cover bolt
12. Round bushing
13. O-ring
14. Wave washer
15. Jam nut
16. Terminal bolt
17. Rubber boot

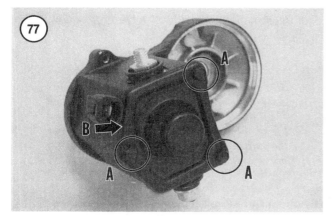

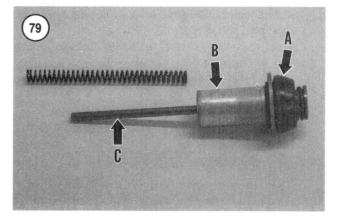

NOTE
A solenoid contact repair kit is available from the manufacturer.

1. Purchase a solenoid contact repair kit prior to starting this procedure.
2. Perform *Solenoid Housing Disassembly* as described in this section.
3. Disassemble the field coil short post (A, **Figure 81**) as follows:
   a. Remove the hex nut, if still in place.
   b. Remove the jam nut, wave washer, round bushing and O-ring from the post.
   c. On the inside, remove the post bolt, field coil hold-in terminal, contact plate and square bushing.
4. Disassemble the battery long post (B, **Figure 81**) as follows:
   a. Remove the hex nut, if still in place.
   b. Remove the jam nut, wave washer, round bushing and O-ring from the post.
   c. On the inside, remove the post bolt, contact plate, square bushing and paper insulator washer.
5. Assemble the field coil short post (A, **Figure 81**) as follows:
   a. Working inside the housing, insert the square bushing into the hole in the housing.
   b. Align the inboard foot against the solenoid winding, align the contact plate hole with the square bushing
   c. Move the hold-in terminal into position and insert the short post bolt through the hold-in terminal, contact plate, square bushing and solenoid housing. Hold the short post bolt in place.
   d. From the outside, install the round bushing, O-ring and wave washer onto the post bolt.
   e. Install the jam nut, but do not tighten it at this time.
6. Assemble the battery long post (B, **Figure 81**) as follows:
   a. Working inside the housing, align the paper insulator washer with the hole in the housing.
   b. Insert the square bushing sleeve into the paper insulator.
   c. Align the inboard foot against the solenoid winding, align the contact plate hole with the square bushing.
   d. Insert the long post bolt through the contact plate, square bushing and solenoid housing. Hold the long post bolt in place.
   e. From the outside, install the round bushing, O-ring and wave washer onto the post bolt. Check that the round bushing index pin indexes the blind hole in the solenoid housing.
   f. Install the jam nut, but do not tighten it at this time.
7. Perform *Solenoid Housing Assembly* as described in this section.
8. Alternately tighten the solenoid contacts jam nuts to 65-80 in.-lb. (7.3-9.0 N•m). Ensure that the contact plates are still correctly aligned with the plunger. If not, loosen the jam nut(s), reposition the contact plates and tighten the jam nuts to specification.

LIGHTING SYSTEM

The lighting system consists of a headlight, passing lamps, tail/brake light combination and turn signals.

Always use the correct bulb. The use of a larger wattage bulb will give a dim light and a smaller wattage bulb will burn out prematurely. Refer to **Table 4** for bulb specifications.

HEADLIGHT

WARNING
If the headlight has just burned out or just been turned off it will be hot. To avoid burned fingers, allow the bulb to cool prior to removal.

CAUTION
All models are equipped with a quartz-halogen bulb. Do not touch the bulb glass. Traces of oil on the bulb will drastically reduce the life of the bulb. Clean all traces of oil from the bulb glass with a cloth moistened in alcohol or lacquer thinner.

Headlight Bulb Replacement (All Models Except FXDF, FXDFSE and FXDFSE2)

Refer to **Figure 82**.
1. Place a shop cloth or towel on the front fender to protect the finish.
2. Remove the screw (A, **Figure 83**) at the base of the trim ring and remove the trim ring (**Figure 84**) from the headlight lens assembly.
3. Pull the lens assembly (A, **Figure 85**) out of the housing.
4. Pull straight out and disconnect the connector (B, **Figure 85**) from the bulb and remove the headlight assembly.
5. Remove the rubber boot (**Figure 86**) from the back of the headlight lens. Check the rubber boot for tears or deterioration; replace if necessary.

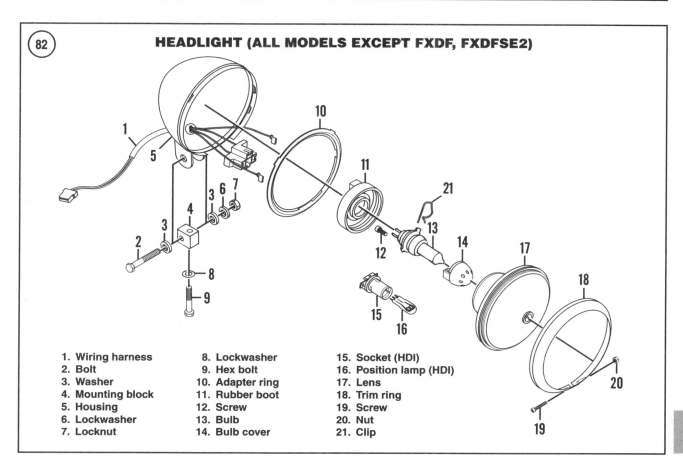

HEADLIGHT (ALL MODELS EXCEPT FXDF, FXDFSE2)

1. Wiring harness
2. Bolt
3. Washer
4. Mounting block
5. Housing
6. Lockwasher
7. Locknut
8. Lockwasher
9. Hex bolt
10. Adapter ring
11. Rubber boot
12. Screw
13. Bulb
14. Bulb cover
15. Socket (HDI)
16. Position lamp (HDI)
17. Lens
18. Trim ring
19. Screw
20. Nut
21. Clip

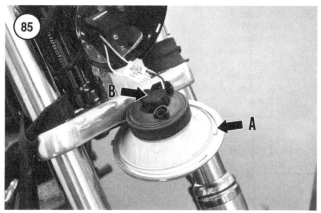

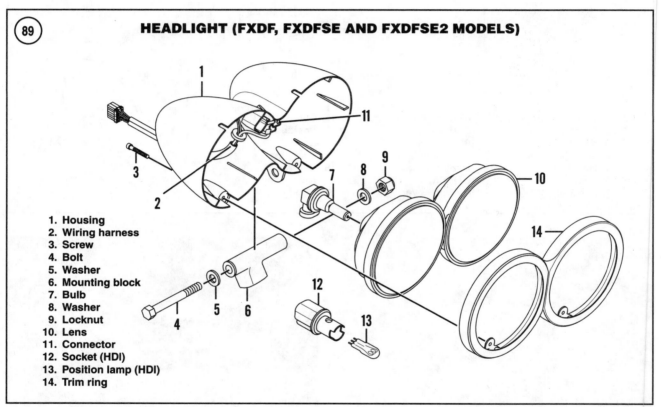

HEADLIGHT (FXDF, FXDFSE AND FXDFSE2 MODELS)

1. Housing
2. Wiring harness
3. Screw
4. Bolt
5. Washer
6. Mounting block
7. Bulb
8. Washer
9. Locknut
10. Lens
11. Connector
12. Socket (HDI)
13. Position lamp (HDI)
14. Trim ring

6. Unhook the light bulb retaining clip (A, **Figure 87**) and pivot it out of the way.

7. Remove and discard the blown bulb (B, **Figure 87**).

8. Align the tangs on the new bulb with the notches (**Figure 88**) in the headlight lens and install the bulb (B, **Figure 87**).

9. Securely hook the retaining clip (A, **Figure 87**) onto the bulb.

10. Install the rubber boot (**Figure 86**) and make sure it is correctly seated against the bulb and the retainer.

11. Correctly align the connector (B, **Figure 85**) terminals with the bulb and connect it. Push it straight on until it bottoms in the bulb and the rubber cover.

12. Check headlight operation.

13. Insert the lens (A, **Figure 85**) into the headlight housing and seat it correctly.

14. Align the slots and tabs in the headlight housing, adapter ring and trim ring.

15. Install the trim ring (**Figure 84**) and screw. Tighten the screw (A, **Figure 83**) securely.

16. Check headlight adjustment as described in this chapter.

**Headlight Bulb Replacement
(FXDF, FXDFSE and FXDFSE2 Models)**

Refer to **Figure 89**.

1. Place a shop cloth or towel on the front fender to protect the finish.

2. Support the lens and trim ring assembly, and remove the two screws at the rear of the housing.

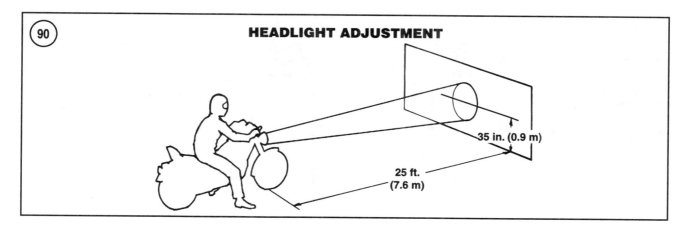

HEADLIGHT ADJUSTMENT

35 in. (0.9 m)

25 ft. (7.6 m)

3. Carefully pull straight out and remove the lens and trim ring assembly from the housing.

4. Raise the latch lock and depress the latch securing the connector to the backside of the bulb socket. Remove the connector from the bulb assembly.

5. Grasp the bulb socket and turn it counterclockwise. Withdraw it from the headlight lens assembly.

6. Repeat the process to remove the remaining bulb, if necessary.

CAUTION
Position the lens assembly with the vents (yellow dots) facing up, if both bulbs were removed. Failure to do so will result in excessive heat within the lens assembly.

7. Align the tangs on the new bulb with the notches in the headlight lens and install the bulb. Turn it *clockwise* until it is locked in place.

8. Attach the connector to the backside of the bulb socket. Push it on until the latch locks it into place.

9. Move the headlight lens and trim ring into place in the housing. Install the two screws and tighten securely.

Headlight Adjustment

1. Park the motorcycle on a level surface approximately 25 ft. (7.6 m) from a wall (**Figure 90**). The area should have a minimum ambient light level.

2. Check tire inflation pressure; if necessary readjust to the correct pressure if necessary as described in Chapter Three.

3. Have a helper the approximate weight of the principal rider sit on the seat.

4. Draw a horizontal line on the wall that is the same height above floor as the center of the headlight or approximately 35 in. (0.9 m).

5. Position the front wheel so it is pointing straight ahead.

6. Aim the headlight at the wall and turn on the headlight. Switch the headlight to the high beam.

7. Turn the ignition switch to IGN.

8. Check the headlight beam alignment. The broad, flat pattern of light (main beam of light) must be centered on the horizontal line (equal area of light above and below line).

9. Check the headlight beam lateral alignment. With the headlight beam pointed straight ahead (centered), there must be an equal area of light to the left and right of center.

10. If the beam pattern is incorrect, adjust it as follows.

   a. For vertical adjustment; loosen the bolt (**Figure 91**) and nut at the base of the headlight assembly. Move the headlight assembly to achieve correct alignment. Tighten the bolt and nut to 25-30 ft.-lb. (33.9-40.7 N•m).

   b. For horizontal vertical adjustment; loosen the bolt (B, **Figure 83**) securing the mounting block to the lower fork bridge. Move the headlight assembly to achieve correct alignment. Tighten the bolt to 25-30 ft.-lb. (33.9-40.7 N•m).

TURN SIGNALS

Bulb Replacement

1. Locate a notch in the lens (A, **Figure 92**) and insert a coin into it. Carefully twist the coin until the lens (B, **Figure 92**) comes off the housing.

2. Push in on the bulb (**Figure 93**), rotate it counterclockwise 1/4 turn and remove it from the socket.

3. Inspect the socket contacts and clean if necessary with a small wire brush and contact cleaner.

4. Install a *new* bulb, push in on it and rotate clockwise 1/4 turn until locked into place.

5. Push the lens into the housing until it snaps into place.

9

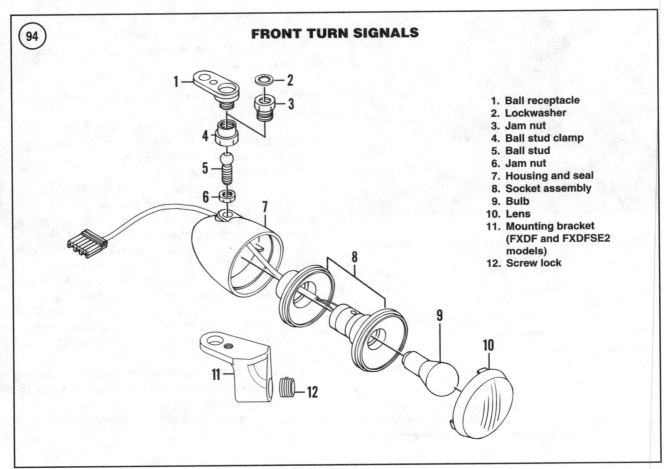

FRONT TURN SIGNALS

1. Ball receptacle
2. Lockwasher
3. Jam nut
4. Ball stud clamp
5. Ball stud
6. Jam nut
7. Housing and seal
8. Socket assembly
9. Bulb
10. Lens
11. Mounting bracket (FXDF and FXDFSE2 models)
12. Screw lock

Front Turn Signal Removal/Installation

Refer to **Figure 94**.

NOTE
The front turn signal wiring is routed within the within the handlebar tubing on FXDWG, FXDF, FXDSE2, FXDFSE and FXDFSE2 models. On all other models, the wiring is routed through the lower handlebar switch housing.

1. Support the motorcycle with the front wheel off the ground. Refer to *Motorcycle Stands* (Chapter Ten).

2. Disconnect the negative battery cable as described in this chapter.

3. Remove the seat as described in Chapter Fourteen.

4. Remove the fuel tank as described in Chapter Eight.

5. Unsnap and remove the harness shield (A, **Figure 95**) to gain access to the connectors within the frame backbone. Remove the plug (B, **Figure 95**) on each side of the frame.

6. Follow the wiring harness (A, **Figure 96**) down the handlebar and into the frame plug (B).

7. Carefully pull the wiring harness down from within the frame backbone.

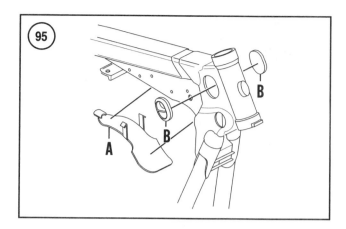

8. Label and identify the connectors and their wire colors to assist in reconnecting. Refer to the wiring diagrams located on the CD inserted into the back cover of the manual.

9. Disconnect the front turn signal electrical connectors (**Figure 97**) from the main harness.

10. Remove the wire leads from the turn signal connector socket terminals as described in this chapter. Remove the connector.

11A. On FXDWG, FXDF, FXDSE2, FXDFSE and FXDFSE2, remove the handlebar as described in Chapter Eleven in order to remove the wiring harness from within the handlebar.

11B. On all other models, attach a length of heavy-duty fish wire to each set of the disconnected terminals. Wrap the connectors and wire with electrical tape to assist in withdrawing the connectors and wiring from the frame backbone.

12. Remove the right side turn signal housing as follows:
   a. Loosen the ball clamp stud until the turn signal assembly is free from the retainer.
   b. Loosen the jam nut and remove the ball stud and ball stud clamp from the housing. Remove the housing.

13. Remove the left side turn signal housing as follows:
   a. Loosen the ball stud clamp (A, **Figure 98**) until the turn signal assembly is free from the ball receptacle.
   b. Loosen the jam nut and remove the ball stud and ball stud clamp from the housing. Remove the housing (B, **Figure 98**).

14. Secure the loose end of the mechanic wire to the frame to avoid pulling the wire completely out of the frame backbone or handlebar.

NOTE
Before removing the wiring harness from the frame, make a drawing of the harness routing from the handlebar and through the frame. This information will prove helpful when reinstalling the harness and connecting the cables.

15. Remove the wiring harness from the frame.

16. To install a *new* assembly, perform the following:
   a. Lay the old assembly next to the new one and cut the new wires to the exact same length as the old one.
   b. Install a *new* terminal onto each wire.

17. Install the ball stud, ball stud clamp and jam nut in the *new* housing.

18. On the right side, move the housing into position, and loosely install the ball stud clamp to the ball retainer, and tighten the jam nut.

19. On the left side, move the housing into position, and loosely install the ball stud clamp to the ball receptacle, and tighten the jam nut.

20. Carefully pull the fish wire and harness back through the frame backbone or handlebar.

21. Correctly route the wiring harness through the frame.

22. Connect the wire leads onto the turn signal connector socket terminals as described in this chapter.

23. Connect the front turn signal connectors to the main harness.

9

24. Insert the rear of the harness shield (A, **Figure 99**) into the frame backbone, and snap it into place (B). Snap the plugs into each side.

25. Install the fuel tank as described in Chapter Eight.

26. Install the seat as described in Chapter Fourteen.

27. Connect the negative battery cable as described in this chapter.

28. Correctly position the housing straight ahead and tighten the ball stud clamp securely.

29. Lay a blanket over the fuel tank. Slowly move the handlebar from full right to full left to ensure the turn signal housing does not contact the fuel tank. Loosen the fastener and reposition the housing away from the fuel tank, making sure the lens is still positioned correctly.

30. Turn the ignition switch to IGN and check for proper turn signal operation.

Rear Turn Signal Removal/Installation

Refer to **Figure 100**.

1. Support the motorcycle on a swing arm stand.

2. Disconnect the negative battery cable as described in this chapter.

3. Remove the seat as described in Chapter Fourteen.

4. Remove the tail/brake light lens as described in this chapter.

5. Using a small screwdriver, depress the locking tabs and disconnect the 2-pin rear turn signal connectors (**Figure 101**) from the tail/brake light printed circuit board.

6. Cut and remove the cable straps securing the turn signal conduit to the frame.

7. Label and identify the connectors and their wire colors to assist in reconnecting. Refer to the wiring diagrams located on the CD inserted into the back cover of the manual.

8. Remove the wire leads from the turn signal connector socket terminals as described in this chapter. Remove the connector.

9. Attach a length of thin fish wire to each set of the two disconnected terminals. Wrap the connectors and wire with electrical tape to assist in withdrawing the connectors and wiring from the wiring conduit.

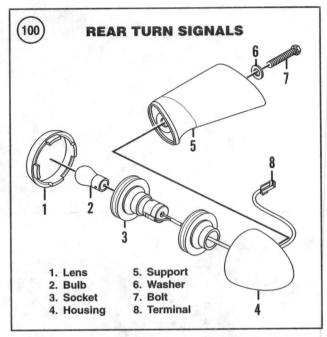

REAR TURN SIGNALS

1. Lens
2. Bulb
3. Socket
4. Housing
5. Support
6. Washer
7. Bolt
8. Terminal

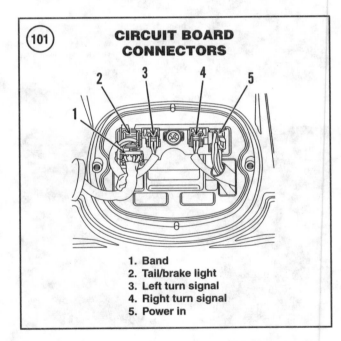

CIRCUIT BOARD CONNECTORS

1. Band
2. Tail/brake light
3. Left turn signal
4. Right turn signal
5. Power in

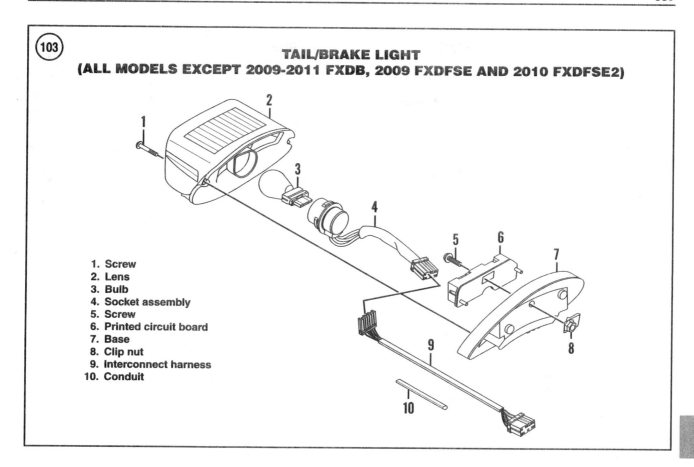

(103)

TAIL/BRAKE LIGHT
(ALL MODELS EXCEPT 2009-2011 FXDB, 2009 FXDFSE AND 2010 FXDFSE2)

1. Screw
2. Lens
3. Bulb
4. Socket assembly
5. Screw
6. Printed circuit board
7. Base
8. Clip nut
9. Interconnect harness
10. Conduit

10. Secure the loose end of the fish wire to the frame to avoid pulling the wire completely out of the conduit or handlebar.

11. Hold onto the housing (A, **Figure 102**). Working under the rear fender, remove the bolt and washer securing the rear turn signal housing support to the rear fender support (B, **Figure 102**).

12. Move the support and housing away from the rear fender support.

13. Carefully pull on the housing and support, withdrawing the wiring, connector terminals and fish wire through the taillight printed circuit board opening, and out of the rear frame support and conduit.

NOTE
Before removing the wiring harness from the frame, make a drawing of the harness routing from the taillight and through the frame. This information will prove helpful when reinstalling the harness and connecting the cables.

14. Remove the wiring harness from the frame.

15. To install a *new* assembly, perform the following:
   a. Lay the old assembly next to the new one and cut the new wires to exactly the same length as the old one.
   b. Install a *new* terminal onto each wire.

16. Move the housing and support part way into position.

17. Carefully pull the fish wire and harness back through the frame support, conduit and tail/brake light printed circuit board opening.

18. Connect the wire leads onto the turn signal connector socket terminals as described in this chapter.

19. Connect the rear turn signal connectors to the main harness.

20. Hold the housing (A, **Figure 102**) into position. Working under the rear fender, install the bolt and washer securing the rear turn signal housing support to the rear fender support (B, **Figure 102**).

21. Correctly position the housing so it is pointed directly to the rear. Tighten the rear turn signal housing support bolt to 12-16 ft.-lb. (16.3-21.7 N•m).

22. Connect the 2-pin rear turn signal connectors (**Figure 101**) onto the tail/brake light printed circuit board. Push them on until the lock into place.

23. Install the tail/brake light lens as described in this chapter.

24. Install the seat as described in Chapter Fourteen.

25. Connect the negative battery cable as described in this chapter.

26. Turn the ignition switch to IGN and check for proper turn signal operation.

TAIL/BRAKE LIGHT

**Tail/Brake Light Bulb Replacement
(All Models Except 2009-2011 FXDB, 2009 FXDFSE and 2010 FXDFSE2)**

Refer to **Figure 103**.

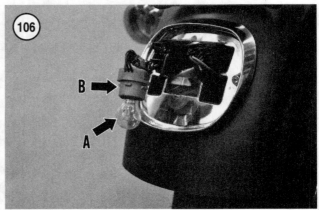

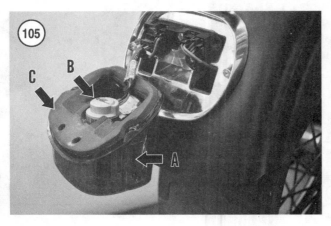

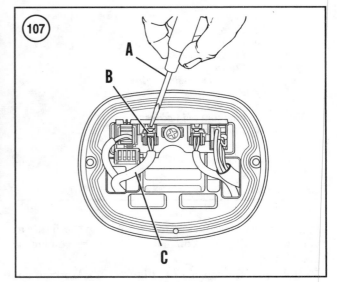

NOTE
The 2009-2010 FXDB, 2009 FXDFSE and 2010 FXDFSE2 models are equipped with non-replaceable LED bulb assembly. The entire assembly must be replaced if either section of the light is inoperative.

1. Remove the screw (A, **Figure 104**) on each side securing the lens (B).

2. Pull the lens (A, **Figure 105**) off the base.

3. Rotate the bulb/socket assembly (B, **Figure 105**) 1/4 turn *counterclockwise* and pull it from the backside of the lens.

4. Gently pull the bulb (A, **Figure 106**) straight out of the socket assembly (B).

5. Apply a *light* coat of dielectric grease to the base of the new bulb.

6. Install a *new* bulb into the socket.

7. Rotate the bulb/socket assembly (B, **Figure 105**) 1/4 turn *clockwise* and push it back into the backside of the lens.

8. Inspect the lens gasket (C, **Figure 105**) for deterioration or damage; replace if necessary.

9. Make sure the gasket is in place on the lens.

10. Install the lens (B, **Figure 104**) and screws (A). Tighten the screws securely, but do not overtighten them as the lens may crack.

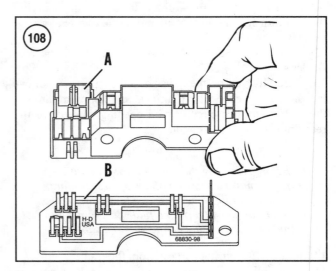

Tail/Brake Light Circuit Board/Chrome Base Removal/Installation (All Models Except 2009-2011 FXDB, 2009 FXDFSE and 2010 FXDFSE2)

Refer to **Figure 103**.

1. Remove the screw (A, **Figure 104**) on each side securing the lens (B).

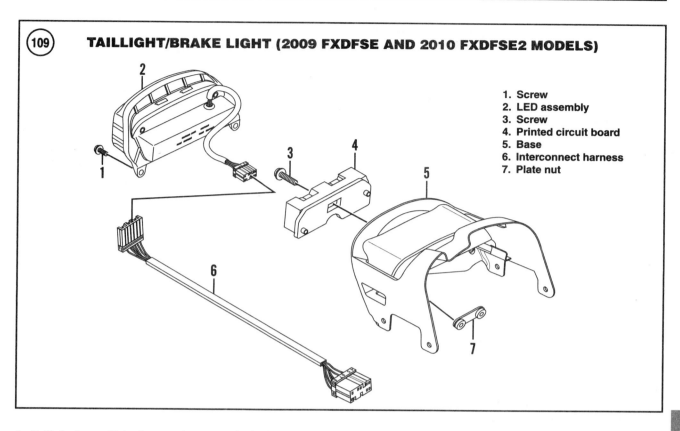

TAILLIGHT/BRAKE LIGHT (2009 FXDFSE AND 2010 FXDFSE2 MODELS)

1. Screw
2. LED assembly
3. Screw
4. Printed circuit board
5. Base
6. Interconnect harness
7. Plate nut

2. Pull the lens off the base and remove the bulb.

3. Disconnect the 4-pin socket assembly connector (**Figure 101**).

4. Use a pick or small, flat-bladed screwdriver (A, **Figure 107**) and depress the release button (B) on both 2-pin connectors. Disconnect the connectors (**Figure 101**) from the circuit board.

5. Disconnect the power-in connector (**Figure 101**) by using the same tool and technique.

6. On all models except FXDWG and FXDF, remove the screw and captive washer securing the center of the circuit board and base to the rear fender.

7. Remove the circuit board from the base. Separate the pin housing (A, **Figure 108**) from the circuit board (B), if necessary.

8. Remove the two screws and nuts securing the base to the rear fender.

9. Using both thumbs, push the chrome base upward to free it from the rear fender, and remove it from the rear fender.

10. Carefully feed the wiring harnesses (C, **Figure 107**) and terminal connectors out through the openings in the chrome base.

11. Install by reversing the removal steps. Note the following:

   a. Install the center scew and captive washer. Then, tighten the center screw to 40-48 in.-lb. (4.5-5.4 N•m).

   b. Tighten the base screws securely.

   c. Tighten the lens screws securely, but do not overtighten as the lens may crack.

Tail/Brake Light LED Replacement
(2009 FXDFSE and 2010 FXDFSE2 Models)

Refer to **Figure 109**.

1. Remove the screw on each side securing the lens and LED assembly to the mounting bracket.

2. Remove the LED assembly from the base.

3. Separate the lens from the LED assembly.

4. Disconnect the 4-pin LED assembly connector from the circuit board.

5. Remove the mounting screw and circuit board from the base, if necessary.

6. Install the circuit board to the base and tighten the circuit board screw to 40-48 in.-lb. (4.5-5.4 N•m), if removed.

7. Connect the *new* 4-pin LED assembly connector to the circuit board.

8. Install the LED assembly into position and insert its mounting tabs into the base notches.

9. Secure the LED assembly and install the cover onto it. Install the two lens mounting screws and tighten to 30-36 in.-lb. (3.4-4.1 N•m).

Tail/Brake Light Base Replacement
(2009 FXDFSE and 2010 FXDFSE2 Models)

Refer to **Figure 109**.

1. Remove the LED assembly from the mounting bracket as described in this section.

2. Remove the rear fender as described in Chapter Fourteen.

9

3. Remove the two bolts, washers, locknuts and mounting brackets on each side securing the base to the rear fender.

4. Remove the mounting screw and circuit board from the base, if still in place.

5. Install the circuit board to the base and tighten the screw to 40-48 in.-lb. (4.5-5.4 N•m), if removed.

6. Install the base onto the rear fender.

7. Install the two bolts, washers, locknuts and mounting brackets securing the base on each side. Tighten the locknuts to 60-72 in.-lb. (6.8-8.1 N•m).

8. Install the rear fender as described in Chapter Fourteen.

9. Install the LED assembly onto the mounting bracket as described in this chapter.

Tail/Brake Light Removal/Installation (2009 FXDB Models)

Refer to **Figure 110**.

1. Remove the plug from the assembly under the rear fender.

2. Remove the three screws securing the assembly to the rear fender.

3. Lift the tail/brake light assembly off the rear fender and disconnect the 3-pin connector from the assembly.

4. Carefully withdraw the two remaining electrical connectors from within the assembly.

5. Remove the tail/brake light assembly from the rear fender.

6. Move the tail/brake light assembly into position and attach the 3-pin connector.

7. Carefully insert the two remaining connectors into the assembly.

8. Install the assembly onto the rear fender, making sure the wires are not pinched between the assembly and the rear fender.

9. Install the screws and tighten to 84-108 in.-lb. (9.5-12.2 N•m).

10. Install the plug onto the assembly and make sure it snaps into place.

FUEL TANK CONSOLE MOUNTED INSTRUMENTS

1. Remove the fuel tank console as described in Chapter Eight.

2. Place the fuel tank console upside down on several towels to protect the finish.

3. Disconnect the connector(s) (A, **Figure 111**, typical).

4. Remove the screws (B, **Figure 111**) securing the mounting clamp (C) to the backside of the fuel tank console.

5. Remove the speedometer and/or tachometer (FXDL, FXDB models) and gasket from the console.

6. Install by reversing the removal steps. Tighten the mounting clamp screws to 18-24 in.-lb. (2.0-2.7 N•m).

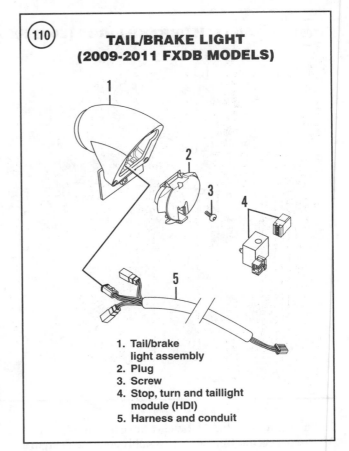

110

TAIL/BRAKE LIGHT (2009-2011 FXDB MODELS)

1. Tail/brake light assembly
2. Plug
3. Screw
4. Stop, turn and taillight module (HDI)
5. Harness and conduit

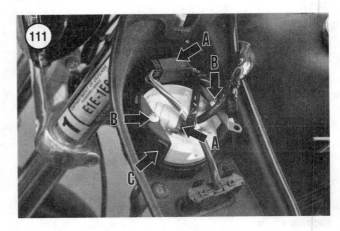

111

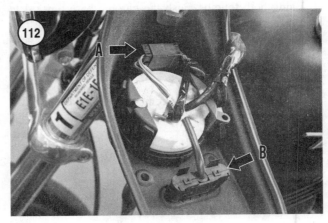

112

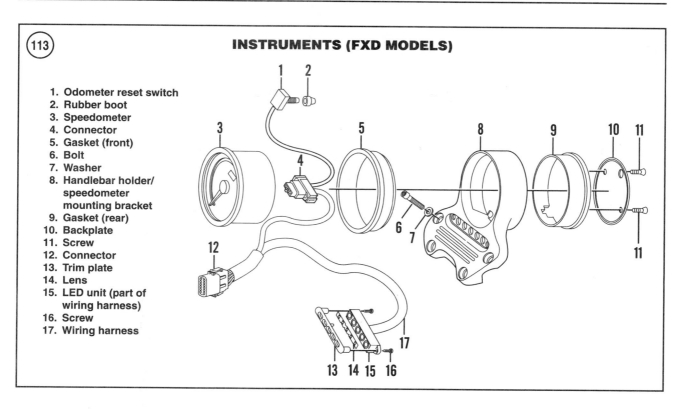

INSTRUMENTS (FXD MODELS)

1. Odometer reset switch
2. Rubber boot
3. Speedometer
4. Connector
5. Gasket (front)
6. Bolt
7. Washer
8. Handlebar holder/
   speedometer
   mounting bracket
9. Gasket (rear)
10. Backplate
11. Screw
12. Connector
13. Trim plate
14. Lens
15. LED unit (part of
    wiring harness)
16. Screw
17. Wiring harness

INDICATOR LAMPS

The indicator lamp assembly consists of LED's. If any portion of the assembly is faulty, the entire assembly must be replaced.

Removal/Installation (All Models Except FXD, FXDL and FXDB)

1. Remove the fuel tank console as described in Chapter Eight.
2. Place the fuel tank console upside down on several towels to protect the finish.
3. Disconnect the connector (A, **Figure 112**).
4. Squeeze the retainer clips together to release the indicator lamp assembly (B, **Figure 112**).
5. Note the orientation of the indicator lamp assembly and remove it from the backside of the console.
6. Install by reversing the removal steps.

Removal/Installation (FXD Models)

NOTE
The indicator lamp assembly is wired into the speedometer harness and cannot be replaced separately.

1. Remove the two screws securing the indicator lamp assembly to the backside of the speedometer mounting bracket on the handlebar.
2. Carefully pull the indicator lamp assembly from the backside of the speedometer mounting bracket.

3. Install the indicator lamp assembly into the backside of the speedometer mounting bracket.
4. Install the two screws and tighten securely.

Removal/Installation (FXDL and FXDB Models)

NOTE
The indicator lamp assembly is wired into the speedometer and tachometer harness and cannot be replaced separately.

1. Remove the screw securing the riser cover, and remove the cover and cover retainer.
2. Squeeze the retainer clips together to release the indicator lamp assembly from the handlebar clamp.
3. Install the indicator lamp assembly into the handlebar cover.
4. Engage the retainer clips onto the tabs of the indicator lamp assembly.
5. Install the riser cover, retainer and screw. Tighten the riser cover screw to 50-60 in.-lb. (5.6-6.8 N•m).

HANDLEBAR MOUNTED INSTRUMENTS

NOTE
Speedometers and/or tachometers not included in this section are housed in the fuel tank console and are covered in Chapter Eight.

Removal/Installation (FXD Models)

Refer to **Figure 113**.

9

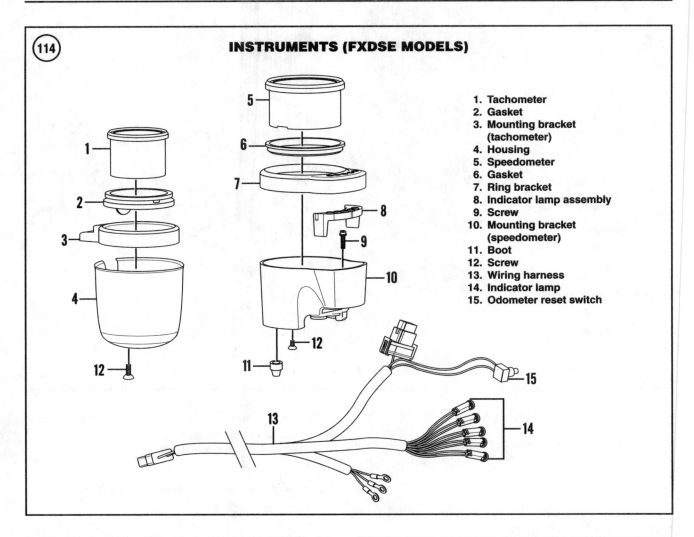

INSTRUMENTS (FXDSE MODELS)

1. Tachometer
2. Gasket
3. Mounting bracket (tachometer)
4. Housing
5. Speedometer
6. Gasket
7. Ring bracket
8. Indicator lamp assembly
9. Screw
10. Mounting bracket (speedometer)
11. Boot
12. Screw
13. Wiring harness
14. Indicator lamp
15. Odometer reset switch

1. Disconnect the negative battery cable as described in this chapter.

2. Remove the two screws on the backplate and remove it. Remove the rear gasket if necessary.

3. Depress the tab and disconnect the 12-pin connector from the backside of the speedometer.

4. Carefully push on the backside of the speedometer and remove it from the handlebar holder/speedometer mounting bracket.

5. Remove the front gasket from the speedometer, if necessary.

NOTE
If necessary, apply alcohol or glass cleaner to the gasket surfaces to ease installation of the meter.

6. Carefully press the speedometer into the handlebar holder/speedometer mounting bracket. Press it in until it bottoms in the bracket. Correctly position the speedometer within the bracket.

7. Connect the 12-pin connector onto the backside of the speedometer. Push it in until it locks into place.

8. Route the wiring harness thought the slot in the back of the mounting bracket.

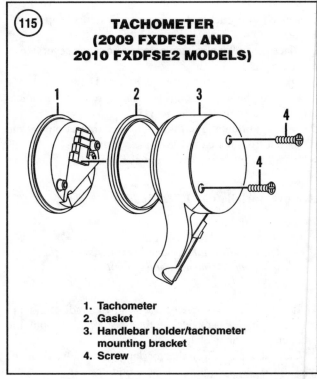

TACHOMETER (2009 FXDFSE AND 2010 FXDFSE2 MODELS)

1. Tachometer
2. Gasket
3. Handlebar holder/tachometer mounting bracket
4. Screw

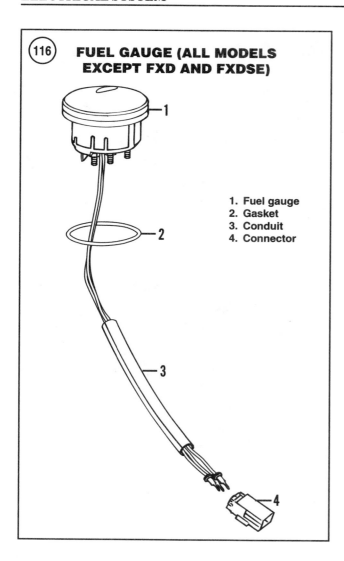

FUEL GAUGE (ALL MODELS EXCEPT FXD AND FXDSE)

1. Fuel gauge
2. Gasket
3. Conduit
4. Connector

10. Remove the speedometer mounting bracket and tachometer mounting bracket from the handlebar.

11. Install the speedometer and tachometer mounting brackets onto the handlebar. Tighten the mounting bracket screws to 12-15 ft.-lb. (16.3-20.3 N•m).

12. Guide the 12-pin connector harness into the speedometer mounting bracket.

13. Install the gasket onto the speedometer, if removed.

14. Install the speedometer and gasket into the speedometer ring bracket.

15. Connect the 12-pin connector onto the speedometer. Push it on until it locks into place.

16. Install the speedometer assembly into the mounting bracket. Tighten the assembly screws to 18-26 in.-lb. (2.0-2.9 N•m).

17. Install the tachometer and gasket into the tachometer mounting bracket.

18. Connect the 3-pin connector onto the tachometer.

19. Install the tachometer housing and tighten the assembly screws to 20-30 in.-lb. (2.3-3.4 N•m).

Removal/Installation (2009 FXDFSE and 2010 FXDFSE2 Models)

Refer to **Figure 115**.

1. Disconnect the negative battery cable as described in this chapter.

2. Remove the two screws from the backside of the tachometer mounting bracket.

3. Gently withdraw the mounting ring bracket from the tachometer mounting bracket.

4. Disconnect the 6-pin connector from the tachometer.

5. Remove the tachometer.

6. Install the gasket onto the tachometer, if removed.

7. Install the tachometer and gasket into the tachometer mounting bracket.

8. Connect the 6-pin connector onto the tachometer.

9. Install the tachometer mounting screws and tighten the screws to 18-26 in.-lb. (2.0-2.9 N•m).

10. Connect the negative battery cable as described in this chapter.

FUEL GAUGE

Removal/Installation (All Models Except FXD and FXDSE)

Refer to **Figure 116**.

1. Disconnect the negative battery cable as described in this chapter.

2. Remove fuel tank as described in Chapter Eight.

3. Label and identify the connectors and their wire colors to assist in reconnecting. Refer to the wiring diagrams located on the CD inserted into the back cover of the manual.

4. Remove the wire leads from the fuel gauge connector socket terminals (A, **Figure 117**) as described in this chapter. Remove the connector.

9. Install the rear gasket, if removed.

10. Install the backplate and tighten the two screws securely.

Removal/Installation (FXDSE Models)

Refer to **Figure 114**.

1. Remove the seat as described in Chapter Fourteen.

2. Disconnect the negative battery cable as described in this chapter.

3. Remove the two screws from the backside of the speedometer mounting bracket.

4. Gently withdraw the mounting ring bracket from the speedometer mounting bracket.

5. Disconnect the 12-pin connector from the speedometer.

6. Remove the speedometer.

7. Remove the screw securing the tachometer housing to the tachometer, and remove the housing.

8. Disconnect the 3-pin connector from the tachometer and remove the tachometer.

9. Remove the two mounting screws within the speedometer mounting bracket.

CAUTION
Do not twist the fuel gauge and wiring harness during removal from fuel tank.

5. Pull straight up on gauge (**Figure 118**) and withdraw it and the gasket from the fuel tank. Pull the wiring harness (B, **Figure 117**) from the fuel tank and tube within the fuel tank. Discard the gasket.

6. Install a *new* gasket onto the fuel gauge.

7. Carefully insert the wiring harness into the fuel tank tube, and slowly push it in until the fuel gauge is close to the fuel tank.

8. Slightly rock the fuel gauge back and forth while pushing it into the fuel tank. Push the fuel gauge in until it bottoms.

9. Connect the wire leads to the fuel gauge connector socket terminals as described in this chapter.

10. Install fuel tank as described in Chapter Eight.

11. Connect the negative battery cable as described in this chapter.

Removal/Installation
(FXD and FXDSE Models)

Refer to **Figure 119**.

NOTE
Always disarm the optional security system (TSM/TSSM/HFSM) before disconnecting the battery or before pulling the maxi-fuse so the siren will not sound.

1. Disconnect the negative battery cable as described in Chapter Nine.

2. Remove the seat as described in Chapter Fourteen.

3. Remove the screw at the rear of the fuel tank console.

4. Remove the four mounting ring screws adjacent to the fuel gauge.

5. Remove the screws securing the trim ring to the trim ring mounting boss. Note the location of the different length screws to ensure correct placement during installation.

6. Carefully lift the console up off the fuel tank.

7. Remove the trim ring mounting boss from the fuel tank.

8. Loosen fuel tank mounting bolts and nuts as described in Chapter Eight.

9. Move the fuel tank toward the rear to gain access to the fuel gauge connector.

10. Remove any cable ties securing the wiring harness to the frame.

11. Disconnect the 4-pin fuel gauge connector from the harness on the left side of the tank.

12. Note the routing of the wiring harness within the top plate. Remove the fuel gauge, gasket and wiring harness from the top plate.

13. Align the fuel gauge tabs and insert the fuel gauge and gasket into the top plate.

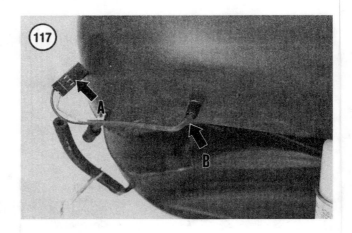

14. Correctly route the electrical harness along the left side of the fuel fill cap.

15. Connect the 4-pin fuel gauge connector to the harness.

16. Secure the wiring harness to the frame with new cable ties.

17. Move the fuel tank back into position. Install the fuel tank mounting bolts and nuts as described in Chapter Eight.

18. Install the trim ring mounting boss onto the fuel tank.

19. Install the console onto the fuel tank.

20. Install the trim ring mounting boss over the fuel gauge.

21. Carefully install the console onto the fuel tank. Align the screw holes with the fuel tank and mounting boss.

22. Install the screw at the rear of the fuel tank console and tighten to 18-24 in.-lb. (2.0-2.7 N•m).

23. Install the four mounting ring screws adjacent to the fuel gauge and tighten to 18-27 in.-lb. (2.0-3.0 N•m).

24. Install the trim ring and align the screw holes. Install the screws securing the trim ring to the trim ring mounting boss in the locations noted during removal. Tighten the trim ring screws to 18-22 in.-lb. (2.0-2.5 N•m).

25. Connect the negative battery cable as described in Chapter Nine.

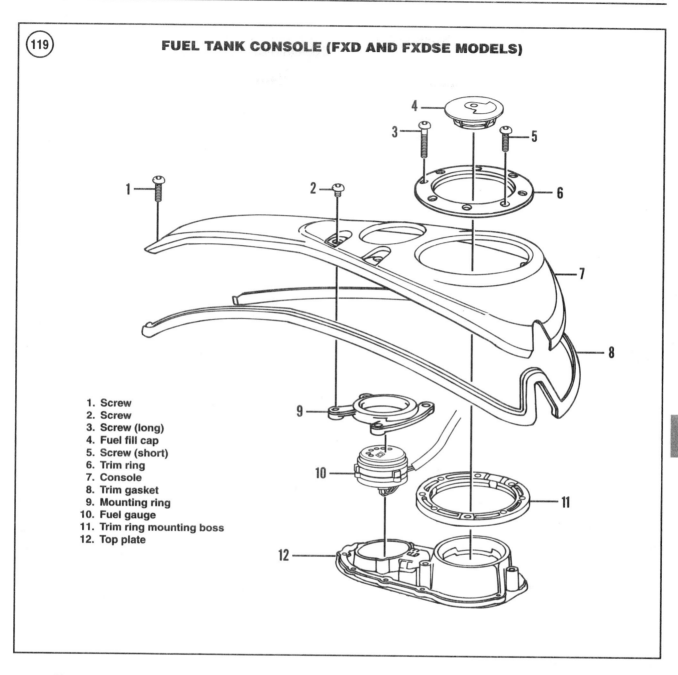

FUEL TANK CONSOLE (FXD AND FXDSE MODELS)

119

1. Screw
2. Screw
3. Screw (long)
4. Fuel fill cap
5. Screw (short)
6. Trim ring
7. Console
8. Trim gasket
9. Mounting ring
10. Fuel gauge
11. Trim ring mounting boss
12. Top plate

9

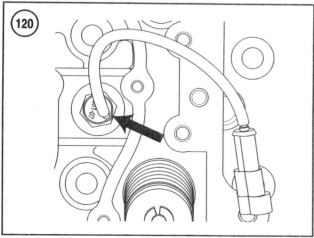

120

AUTOMATIC COMPRESSION RELEASE (ACR) SOLENOID (SCREAMIN' EAGLE AND CVO MODELS)

Removal/Installation

1. Remove the rocker arm support plate as described in Chapter Four.

2. Use an ACR solenoid socket (H-D part No. HD-48498 or JIMS part No. 969), or its equivalent, and remove the ACR solenoid (**Figure 120**) from the cylinder head.

3. Installation is the reverse of removal. Note the following:

    a. Apply three dots of Loctite 246 (blue) Threadlocker, or an equivalent threadlock, to the lower third of the threads on the ACR solenoid (**Figure 121**).

Equally space the dots around the outer circumference of the threads.

   b. Tighten the ACR solenoid to 11-15 ft.-lb. (14.9-20.3 N•m).

SWITCHES

Testing

Test switches for continuity by using an ohmmeter (see Chapter One) or a self-powered test light at the switch connector while moving the switch to its various operating positions. Compare the results with the switch operating schematic included in the wiring diagrams located on the CD inserted into the back cover of the manual.

For example, **Figure 122** shows the continuity diagram for a typical ignition switch. The horizontal lines on the diagram indicate which terminals should show continuity when the switch is in a given position. When the switch is turned to IGN, there should be continuity between the red/black, red and red/gray terminals. An ohmmeter connected between these three terminals should indicate little or no resistance, or a test light should light. When the starter switched off, there should be no continuity between the same terminals.

Replace a switch or button if it does not perform properly.

When testing the switches, note the following:

1. Check the battery as described in this chapter. Charge or replace the battery if necessary.
2. Disconnect the negative battery cable as described in this chapter.
3. Detach all connectors located between the switch and the electrical circuit.

> *CAUTION*
> *Do not attempt to start the engine with the battery disconnected.*

4. When separating a connector, pull the connector housings not the wires.
5. After locating a defective circuit, check the connectors to make sure are clean and properly mated. Check all wires going into a connector housing to make sure each wire is positioned properly and the wire end is not loose.
6. To reconnect a connector, push the housings together until they click or snap into place.

Handlebar Switches

Left handlebar switch description

The left-side handlebar switch housing (**Figure 123**) contains the following switches:

1. Headlight HI-LO beam.
2. Horn.
3. Left turn signal.
4. Clutch interlock.

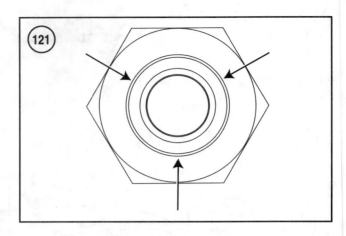

Right handlebar switch description

The right-side handlebar switch housing (**Figure 124**) contains the following switches:

1. Engine stop/run.
2. Starter.
3. Right turn signal.
4. Front brake light.

Handlebar switch replacement

Refer to **Figure 125** for the left-side switch assemblies or **Figure 126** for the right-side switch assemblies.

1. Remove the screws securing the left-side switch housing (**Figure 127**) or the right-side switch housing (**Figure 128**) to the handlebar.
2. Carefully separate the switch housing to access the defective switch (left housing: **Figure 129**; right housing: **Figure 130**). Note how the wires are routed within the housing.

> *NOTE*
> *To service the front brake light switch, refer to **Front Brake Light Switch Replacement** in this chapter.*

3A. On models without splices, remove the screw and bracket.
3B. On models with splices, remove the cable strap.
4. Pull the switch(s) out of the housing.
5. Cut the switch wire(s) from the defective switch(s).
6. Slip a piece of heat shrink tubing over each wire that was cut.
7. Solder the wire end(s) to the new switch. Then, shrink the tubing over the wire(s).
8. Install the switch by reversing the removal steps. Note the following:

   a. Position the handlebar switch so the notch (A, **Figure 131**) in the front brake master cylinder or the notch in the clutch lever assembly aligns with the locating tab (B) on the lower portion of the handlebar switch.

   b. When tightening the handlebar switch housing screws, check the wiring harness routing position to make sure it is not pinched between the housing and

(122)

IGNITION SWITCH (TYPICAL)

Position \ Switch	Red/black	Red	Red/gray
Off		●	
Accessory		●———	———●
Ignition	●———	———●———	———●

(123)

LEFT SIDE HANDLEBAR SWITCH

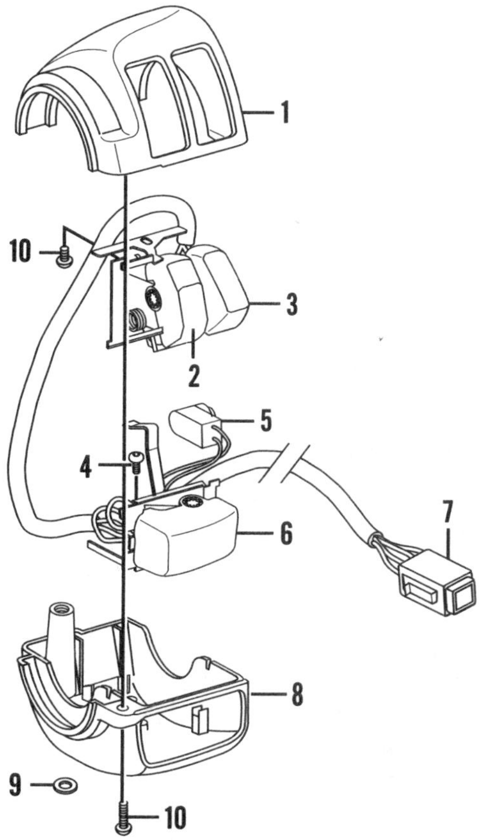

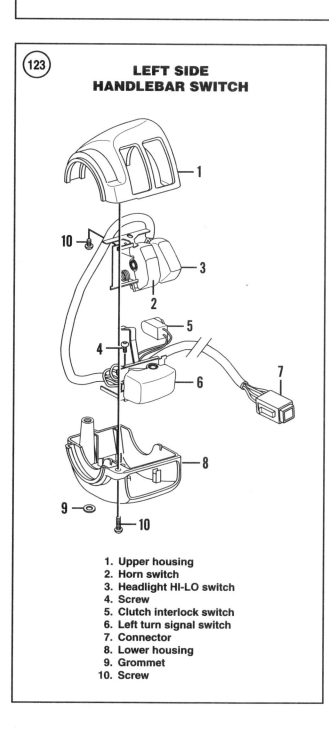

1. Upper housing
2. Horn switch
3. Headlight HI-LO switch
4. Screw
5. Clutch interlock switch
6. Left turn signal switch
7. Connector
8. Lower housing
9. Grommet
10. Screw

(124)

RIGHT SIDE HANDLEBAR SWITCH

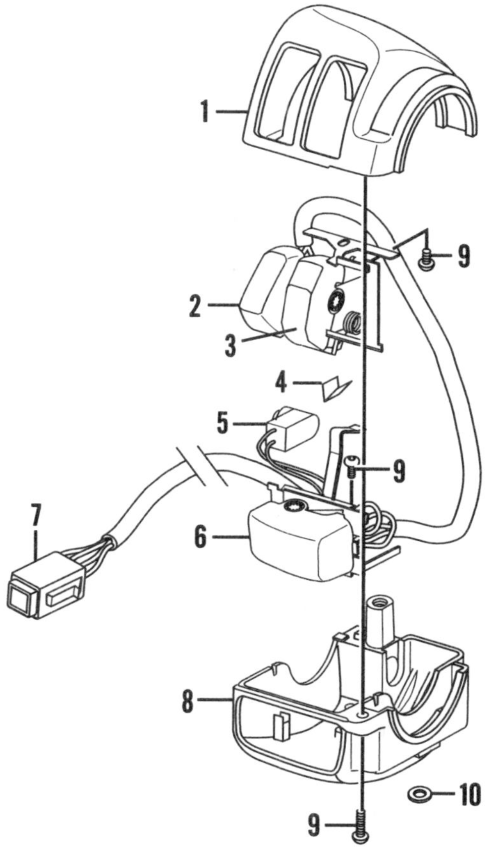

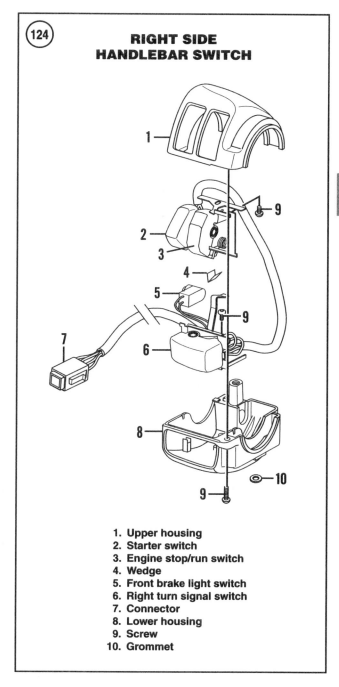

1. Upper housing
2. Starter switch
3. Engine stop/run switch
4. Wedge
5. Front brake light switch
6. Right turn signal switch
7. Connector
8. Lower housing
9. Screw
10. Grommet

9

LEFT-SIDE HANDLEBAR SWITCH

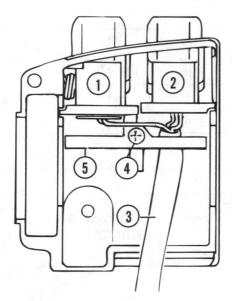

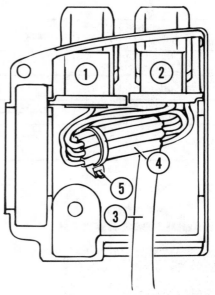

Upper housing without splices

1. Horn switch
2. Headlight high/low beam switch
3. Conduit
4. Phillips screw and washer
5. Bracket

Upper housing with splices

1. Horn switch
2. Headlight high/low beam switch
3. Conduit
4. Splices
5. Cable strap

RIGHT-SIDE HANDLEBAR SWITCH

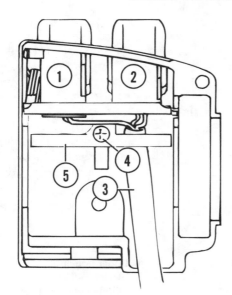

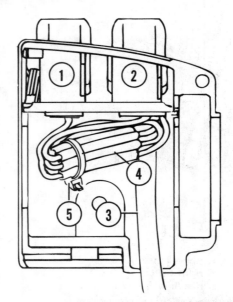

Upper housing without splices

1. Start switch
2. Stop switch
3. Conduit
4. Phillips screw and washer
5. Bracket

Upper housing with splices

1. Start switch
2. Stop switch
3. Conduit
4. Splices
5. Cable strap

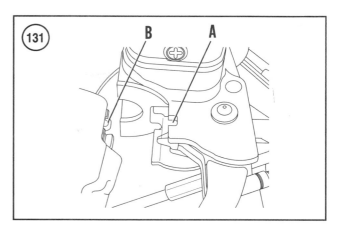

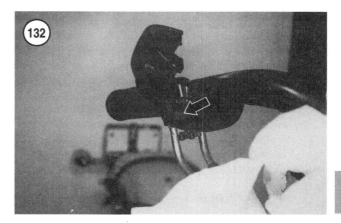

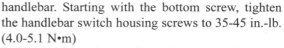

9

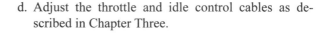

handlebar. Starting with the bottom screw, tighten the handlebar switch housing screws to 35-45 in.-lb. (4.0-5.1 N•m)

c. When replacing the handlebar, install the right handlebar switch, front brake master cylinder and throttle as described in *Throttle and Idle Cables* (Chapter Eight). Install the left handlebar switch, clutch lever, and left hand grip as described in *Clutch Lever Assembly* (Chapter Six).

> *WARNING*
> *Do not ride the motorcycle until the throttle cables are properly adjusted. Make sure the cables do not catch or pull when the handlebar is turned. Improper cable routing and adjustment can cause the throttle to stick open. This could cause loss of control.*

d. Adjust the throttle and idle control cables as described in Chapter Three.

Front Brake Light Switch Replacement

The front brake light switch (**Figure 132**) is mounted in the right-side switch lower housing.

1. Separate the right-side switch housing as described in this section.

2. If still in place, remove the wedge between the switch and the switch housing.

3. While depressing the switch plunger, slowly rotate the switch upward while rocking it slightly, and then remove it from the switch housing.

4. Cut the switch wires from the defective switch.

5. Slip a piece of heat shrink tubing over each wire that was cut.

6. Solder the wire ends to the new switch. Then, shrink the tubing over the wires.

7. Install the switch by reversing the removal steps. Note the following:

   a. When clamping the switch housing onto the handlebar, check the wiring harness routing position to make sure it is not pinched between the housing and handlebar.

   b. To install the right-side switch housing, refer to *Throttle and Idle Cables* (Chapter Eight).

> *WARNING*
> *Do not ride the motorcycle until the throttle and idle cables are properly adjusted. Likewise, the cables must not catch or pull when the handlebars are turned. Improper cable routing and adjustment can cause the throttle to stick open. This could cause loss of control. Recheck the work before riding the motorcycle.*

   c. Adjust the throttle and idle cables as described in Chapter Three.

Clutch Interlock Switch Replacement

The clutch interlock switch (A, **Figure 133**) is mounted in the left-side switch lower housing.

1. Separate the left-side switch housing as described in this section.

2. Cut the switch wires (B, **Figure 133**) from the defective switch.

3. Slip a piece of heat shrink tubing over each wire that was cut.

4. Solder the wire ends to the new switch. Then shrink the tubing over the wires.

5. Install the switch by reversing the removal steps. Note the following:

   a. When clamping the switch housing onto the handlebar, check the wiring harness routing position to make sure it is not pinched between the housing and handlebar.

   b. Tighten the switch housing screws to 35-45 in.-lb. (4.0-5.1 N•m).

Ignition Switch/Fork Lock Removal/Installation (FXD, FXDL, FXDB and FXDSE Models)

1. Disconnect the negative battery cable as described in this chapter.

2. Remove the seat as described in Chapter Fourteen.

3. Remove the fuel tank as described in Chapter Eight.

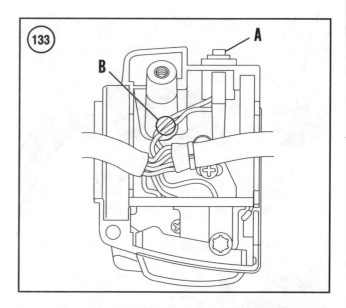

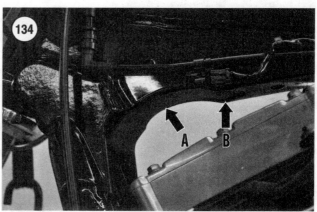

4. Unsnap and remove the harness shield (A, **Figure 134**) to gain access to the connectors within the frame backbone.

5. Carefully pull the connectors down from within the frame backbone. Do not disconnect any connectors.

6. Place the ignition switch/fork lock wrench (H-D part No. HD-47853), or an equivalent, onto the face nut.

7. Turn the wrench *clockwise* and loosen the face nut.

8. Turn the face nut *clockwise* and remove from the ignition switch/fork lock.

9. Rotate the ignition switch/fork lock *clockwise* until the fork lock boss to clears the fork lock cavity in the frame.

10. Remove the ignition switch/fork lock from the frame.

11. Disconnect the 3-pin connector (**Figure 135**) from the ignition switch/fork lock.

12. Connect the 3-pin connector (**Figure 135**) onto the ignition switch/fork lock.

13. Apply a drop of Loctite 246 (blue) Threadlocker, or an equivalent threadlock, to the face nut prior to installation.

14. Position the ignition switch/fork lock with the lock boss facing forward, and insert it into the frame receptacle.

15. Align the flats on the ignition switch/fork lock with the slots in the frame and hold it in this position.

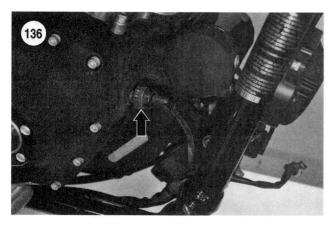

16. Install the face nut onto the ignition switch/fork lock and turn it *counterclockwise* and tighten slightly.

17. Rotate the ignition switch/fork lock until the lock boss engages the fork lock boss cavity.

18. Hold the ignition switch/fork lock as far forward as possible in the frame and tighten the face nut securely.

19. Install the ignition switch/fork lock wrench (H-D part No. HD-47853), or an equivalent, onto the face nut.

20. Turn the wrench *counterclockwise* and tighten the face nut securely.

21. Carefully push all harness connectors back into the frame backbone.

22. Insert the rear (B, **Figure 134**) of the harness shield into the frame back backbone first, and snap it into place.

23. Install the fuel tank as described in Chapter Eight.

24. Install the seat as described in Chapter Fourteen.

25. Connect the negative battery cable as described in this chapter.

Ignition Switch Removal/Installation (FXDWG, FXDC, FXD35, FXDF, FXDSE2, FXDFSE Models)

1. Disconnect the negative battery cable as described in this chapter.

2. Remove the seat as described in Chapter Fourteen.

3. Lay several towels or a blanket on the frame and rear fender.

4. Remove the fasteners securing the fuel tank console.

5. Turn the fuel tank console over onto towels and disconnect the 3-pin connector from the ignition switch.

6. Release the wiring harness from the clip.

7. Remove the four screws securing the ignition switch to the bottom surface of the fuel tank console. Remove the bracket, on models so equipped.

8. Remove the ignition switch.

9. Install by reversing the removal steps while noting the following:

   a. Install the new ignition switch with the connector terminal facing toward the rear of the fuel console.

   b. Tighten the four ignition switch mounting screws to 18-24 in.-lb. (2.0-2.7 N•m).

Oil Pressure Switch/Sender

Operation

The oil pressure switch, or sender, is located on the front right side of the crankcase.

A pressure-actuated, diaphragm-type oil pressure switch, or sender, is used. When the oil pressure is low or when oil is not circulating through a running engine, spring tension inside the switch, or sender, holds the switch contacts closed. This completes the signal light circuit and causes the oil pressure indicator lamp to light.

The oil pressure signal light should turn on when any of the following occurs:

> *NOTE*
> *The oil pressure indicator light may not come on when the ignition switch is turned off and then back on immediately. This is due to the oil pressure retained in the oil filter housing. The following steps test the electrical part of the oil pressure switch. If the oil pressure switch, indicator lamp and related wiring are in good condition, inspect the lubrication system as described in Chapter Two.*

1. The ignition switch is turned on prior to starting the engine.

2. The engine idle is below idle speed of 950-1050 rpm.

3. The engine is operating with low oil pressure.

4. Oil is not circulating through the running engine.

Testing/replacement

1. Slide the rubber boot off the connector.

2. Pull straight out and disconnect the connector from the switch (**Figure 136**).

3. Turn the ignition switch to IGN.

4. Ground the switch wire to the engine.

5. The oil pressure indicator lamp on the instrument panel must light.

6. If the indicator lamp does not light, check for a defective indicator lamp and inspect all wiring between the switch and the indicator lamp assembly.

7A. If the oil pressure warning light operates properly, attach the connector to the switch. Make sure the connection is tight and free from oil. Slide the rubber boot back into position.

7B. If the warning light remains on when the engine is running, shut the engine off. Check the engine lubrication system as described in Chapter Two.

8. To replace the switch, perform the following:
   a. Use a 15/16 in. open-end crowfoot wrench and unscrew the switch from the engine.

NOTE
New switch threads have a sealant pre-applied to the threads. Do not apply any additional sealant to the threads.

   b. If the original switch is being reinstalled, apply Loctite pipe sealant with Teflon 565, or an equivalent, to the switch threads prior to installation.
   c. Install the oil pressure switch and tighten to 96-144 in.-lb. (10.8-16.3 N•m).
   d. Test the new switch as described in this section.

Neutral Indicator Switch Testing/Replacement

The neutral indicator switch is located on the left, rear side of the transmission case. The neutral indicator light on the instrument panel must light when the ignition is turned to IGN and the transmission is in neutral.

1. Shift the transmission into neutral.
2. Cover the transmission top cover to protect the finish.
3. Disconnect the connector from the neutral indicator switch (**Figure 137**).
4. Turn the ignition switch to IGN.

NOTE
The neutral switch connector can be attached to either stud on the switch as it is not polarity sensitive.

5. Ground either neutral indicator switch stud to the transmission case.
6. If the neutral indicator lamp lights, the neutral switch is defective. Replace the neutral indicator switch and retest.
7. If the neutral indicator lamp does not light, check for a defective indicator lamp, faulty wiring or a loose or corroded connection.
8. If the neutral switch operates correctly, attach the connector to the neutral switch. Make sure the connection is tight and free from oil.
9. To replace the old switch, perform the following:
   a. Shift the transmission into neutral.
   b. Unscrew and remove the old switch and O-ring from the transmission top cover.
   c. Apply clean transmission oil to the *new* O-ring seal.
   d. Install the neutral switch and tighten to 10-15 in.-lb. (14-20 N•m).

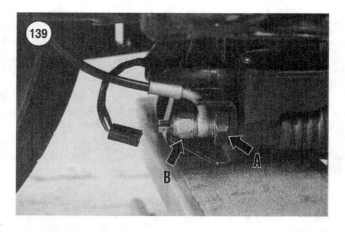

Rear Brake Light Switch Testing/Replacement

A hydraulic, normally-open rear brake light switch is used on all models. The rear brake light is attached to the rear brake caliper brake hose assembly. When the rear brake pedal is applied, hydraulic pressure closes the switch contacts, providing a ground path so the rear brake lamp comes on. If the rear brake lamp does not come on, perform the following.

NOTE
Removal of the exhaust system is not necessary, but it does provide additional space to work for this procedure.

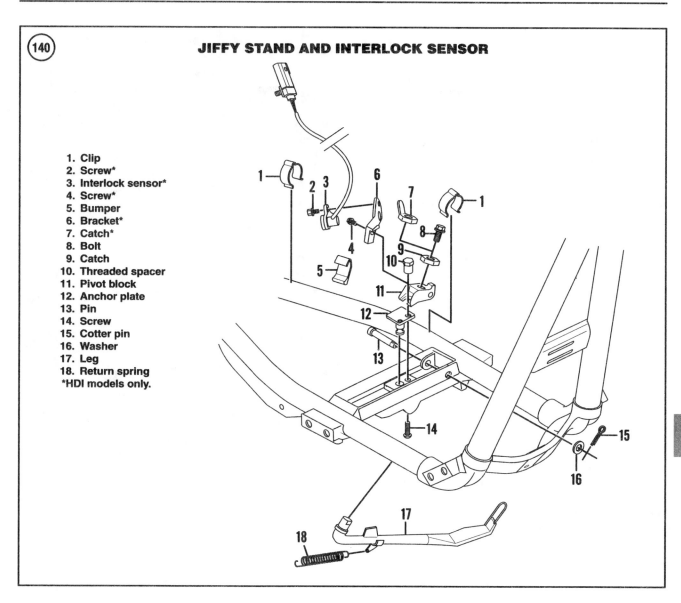

JIFFY STAND AND INTERLOCK SENSOR

1. Clip
2. Screw*
3. Interlock sensor*
4. Screw*
5. Bumper
6. Bracket*
7. Catch*
8. Bolt
9. Catch
10. Threaded spacer
11. Pivot block
12. Anchor plate
13. Pin
14. Screw
15. Cotter pin
16. Washer
17. Leg
18. Return spring
*HDI models only.

1. Remove the exhaust system as described in Chapter Four, if necessary.

2. Turn the ignition switch off.

3. Disconnect the electrical connector (**Figure 138**) from the rear brake light switch.

4. Connect an ohmmeter between the switch terminals and check the following:

   a. Apply the rear brake pedal. There should be continuity.

   b. Release the rear brake pedal. There should be no continuity.

   c. If the switch fails either of these tests, replace the switch as described in this section.

5. Place a drip pan under the switch to catch brake fluid that drains out when the switch is removed.

6. Secure the master cylinder jam nut (A, **Figure 139**) with a suitable size wrench to prevent it from rotating.

7. Unscrew the switch (B, **Figure 139**) from the end of the master cylinder.

8. Apply Loctite pipe sealant with Teflon 565, or an equivalent, to the switch threads prior to installation. Do not allow sealant to make contact with the end of the switch as this will contaminate the brake fluid.

9. Secure the master cylinder jam nut (A, **Figure 139**) with a suitable size wrench to prevent it from rotating.

10. Install the *new* switch (B, **Figure 139**) and tighten it to 12-15 ft.-lb. (16.3-20.3 N•m).

11. Reconnect the rear brake light switch connector.

12. Bleed the rear brake as described in Chapter Thirteen.

13. Check the rear brake light with the ignition switch turned to IGN and the rear brake applied.

14. If necessary, install the exhaust system as described in Chapter Four.

JIFFY STAND INTERLOCK SENSOR (HDI)

Replacement

Refer to **Figure 140**.

1. Remove the seat as described in Chapter Fourteen.

2. Disconnect the negative battery cable as described in this chapter.

3. Note the routing of the wiring harness through the frame.

4. Disconnect the 3-pin interlock sensor connector from the main harness, located under the seat.

5. Remove the small clip securing the wiring harness to the left side frame rail.

6. Remove the large clip securing the wiring harness and vent line to the rear vertical frame rails.

7. Remove the screw securing the interlock sensor to the bracket and remove it.

8. Remove the screw and bracket from the pivot block, if necessary.

9. Install by reversing the removal steps. Note the following:

   a. The sensor harness must be routed on the inside of the left side lower frame rail and under the engine mount.

   b. Correctly route the harness in both small and large clips on the frame.

   c. Tighten the interlock sensor and bracket screws to 96-144 in.-lb. (10.8-16.3 N•m).

HORN

Testing

1. Remove the seat as described in Chapter Fourteen.

2. Remove the acorn nut and washer (**Figure 141**) securing the horn assembly to the frame's rubber mount stud.

3. Turn the horn assembly around.

4. Disconnect the yellow/black connector (**Figure 142**) from the backside of the horn.

5. Connect a voltmeter as follows:

   a. Positive test lead to the yellow/black connector.

   b. Negative test lead to ground.

6. Turn the ignition switch on.

7. Depress the horn button. If battery voltage is present the horn is faulty or is not grounded properly. If there is no battery voltage, either the horn switch or the horn wiring is faulty.

8. Replace the horn or horn switch as necessary.

Replacement

Refer to **Figure 143**.

1. Remove the seat as described in Chapter Fourteen.

2. Disconnect the negative battery cable as described in this chapter.

3. Remove the acorn nut and washer (**Figure 141**) securing the horn assembly to the frame's rubber mount stud.

4. Turn the horn assembly around.

5. Disconnect the yellow/black and black connectors (**Figure 142**) from the backside of the horn.

6. Remove the screw (A, **Figure 144**) securing the wiring J-clamp.

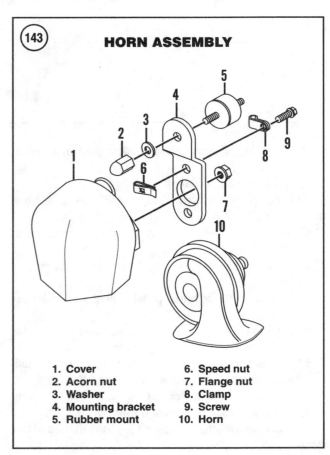

HORN ASSEMBLY

1. Cover
2. Acorn nut
3. Washer
4. Mounting bracket
5. Rubber mount
6. Speed nut
7. Flange nut
8. Clamp
9. Screw
10. Horn

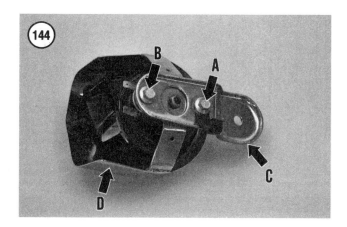

b. Install the washer and acorn nut (**Figure 141**) securing the horn assembly to the frame's rubber mount stud. Tighten the acorn nut to 10-15 ft.-lb. (13.6-20.3 N•m).

c. Check that the horn operates correctly.

TURN SIGNAL SECURITY MODULES (TSM, TSSM AND HFSM)

NOTE
The security system is activated, and the optional siren sounds whenever the ignition circuit is tampered with, if the vehicle is moved, or whenever the battery or ground connection is broken. Always disarm the security system before servicing the motorcycle, before disconnecting the negative battery cable or before pulling the maxi-fuse.

This section describes the service procedures for the turn signal module, turn signal and security module, and the hands-free security module. The turn signal module (TSM) is an electronic microprocessor that controls the turn signals and four-way hazard flasher. The turn signal module receives information from the speedometer and turn signal switches. The bank angle sensor (BAS) is integrated into the module and provides motorcycle movement signals to the ECM.

The turn signal and security module (TSSM) performs the same function as the TSM. The TSSM, however, also provides additional security and immobilization functions. When activated, the security system alternately flashes the left and right turn signals and sounds an optional siren, on models so equipped.

The hands-free security module (HFSM) performs the same functions as a TSSM, and it includes a key fob for convenient arming and disarming of the security system. Whenever the TSM/TSSM/HFSM is replaced, the new device must be reprogrammed using the H-D digital technician. Take the motorcycle to a dealership or other qualified shop for reprogramming.

Removal/Installation

NOTE
*The turn signals cannot operate when the ignition switch is turned to **ACC**. They only operate when the ignition switch is turned to **IGN**.*

1. Remove the electrical caddy cover as described in this chapter.
2. Disconnect the negative battery cable as described in this chapter.
3. Depress the lower tab (**Figure 147**) and pull the TSM/TSM/TSSM/HFSM module (A, **Figure 148**) part way out of the electrical caddy.

7. Remove the remaining screw (B, **Figure 144**) from the backside of the horn mounting bracket. Remove the mounting bracket (C, **Figure 141**) from the cover.

8. Remove the nut (A, **Figure 145**) and remove the horn (B) from the cover.

9. Unscrew and remove the rubber mount (**Figure 146**) from the engine mount bracket.

10. Install by reversing the removal steps. Note the following:

a. Install the flange nut securing the cover to the horn. Tighten the flange nut to 10-15 ft.-lb. (13.6-20.3 N•m).

4. Disconnect the 12-pin connector (B, **Figure 148**) from the module and remove the module.

5. On models with HFSM, also disconnect the 4-pin antenna connector (C, **Figure 148**) from the module and remove the module.

6. Install the module by reversing the removal steps. Note the following:

    a. Make sure the connector(s) is/are free of moisture.

    b. Make sure the turn signal and flasher systems work properly.

Turn Signal Operation

Automatic cancellation

NOTE
The turn signal security module will not cancel the signal before the turn is actually completed.

1. When the turn signal button is depressed, and then released, the system begins a 20 count. As long as the motorcycle is moving above 7 MPH (11 KPH), the turn signals will always cancel after 20 bulb flashes, providing the system does not receive any additional input.

2. If the motorcycle's speed drops to 7 MPH (11 KPH) or less, including stopping, the turn signals will continue to flash. Flash counting will continue when the motorcycle reaches 8 MPH (13 KPH) and will automatically cancel when the count total equals 20 bulb flashes.

3. The turn signals will cancel within two seconds after the turn of 45° or more is completed.

Manual cancellation

1. After the turn signal button is depressed, and then released, the system begins a 20 count. To cancel the turn signal from flashing, depress the turn signal button a second time.

2. If the turn direction is to be changed, depress the opposite turn signal button. The primary signal is cancelled and the opposite turn signal will flash.

Four-way flashing

1. Turn the ignition switch to IGN. On models so equipped, disarm the security system. Press the right and left turn signal buttons at the same time. All four turn signals will flash.

2. On models with the security system, the system can be armed so all four signals flash for up to two hours. Turn the ignition key off and arm the security system. Press both the right and left turn signal buttons at the same time.

3. To cancel four-way flashing, disarm the security system on models so equipped, and press both the right and left turn signal buttons at the same time.

Bank Angle Sensor

The bank angle sensor is an integral part of the TSM/TSM/TSSM/HFSM unit. The angle sensor automatically shuts off the engine if the motorcycle tilts more than 45° for longer than one second. The shutoff occurs even at a very slow speed.

To restart the motorcycle, return the motorcycle to vertical. Turn the ignition key from OFF to IGN, and then restart the engine.

Security System Operation

NOTE
Always disarm the optional TSM/TSSM/HFSM before disconnecting the battery or the siren will sound. If the TSSM is in auto-alarming mode, disarm the system with two clicks of the key fob, and disconnect the battery or remove the TSSM fuse before the 30-second arming period expires.

If a theft attempt is detected when the TSM/TSSM/HFSM is armed, the system immobilizes the starting and ignition systems. It also alternately flashes the right and left turn signals and sounds the siren, if so equipped. The following conditions activate the armed security system.

1. If the system detects tampering with the ignition system or detects vehicle movement, it issues the first warning: the turn signals flash three times and the optional siren chirps once. If the motorcycle is not returned to its original position within four seconds, the system issues a second warning. If the tampering continues, the system goes into full alarm: the turn signals alternately flash and the optional siren sounds for 30 seconds. If the motorcycle is not returned to its original position after a ten second pause, the system repeats full alarm. It repeats this cycle (30-seconds on/10-seconds off) for ten times or for a total of five minutes.

2. If the system detects a battery or ground disconnect, the optional siren sounds but the turn signals do not flash.

RELAYS

Starter and System Relay Replacement

1. Remove the electrical caddy cover as described in this chapter.

2. Disconnect the negative battery cable as described in this chapter.

3. Firmly grasp both side of the starter relay (A, **Figure 149**), or system relay (B) and pull straight out of the fuse panel. Remove the relay(s).

4. Install the *new* relay(s) into the fuse panel. Press in until the relay bottoms in the panel.

5. Connect the negative battery cable as described in this chapter.

6. Install the electrical caddy cover as described in this chapter.

ELECTRICAL CONNECTOR SERVICE

A variety of electrical connectors are used throughout the electrical system. These connectors are designed for a superior seal to prevent dirt and moisture from entering the connector and damaging a pin connector.

The following procedures describe the disassembly of the connectors so individual wires can be replaced.

NOTE
On models with an optional security system, disarm the system before disconnecting the negative battery cable or pulling the Maxi-Fuse so the siren will not sound.

Deutsch Connectors

Socket terminal removal/installation

This procedure shows how to remove and install the electrical terminals in the socket housing. It is shown performed on a 12-pin Deutsch connector, but it also applies to 2-, 3-, 4- and 6-pin Deutsch connectors. Refer to **Figure 150** and **Figure 151**.

1. Disconnect the negative battery cable (2006 models) or pull the Maxi-Fuse (2007-2011 models) as described in this chapter.

2. Separate the connector housings.

3. Remove the secondary locking wedge as follows:
   a. Locate the secondary locking wedge (**Figure 150** or **Figure 151**).
   b. Insert a wide-bladed screwdriver between the socket housing and the secondary locking wedge. Turn the screwdriver 90° to force the secondary locking wedge up (**Figure 152**).
   c. Remove the secondary locking wedge.

4. Lightly press the terminal latches inside the socket housing and remove the socket terminal through the holes in the rear wire seal.

5. Repeat the process for each remaining socket terminal.

6. If necessary, remove the wire seal.

7. Install the wire seal into the socket housing if it was removed.

8. Hold onto the socket housing and insert each socket terminal through the hole in the wire seal so it enters the correct chamber hole. Continue until the socket terminal locks into place. Then, lightly tug on the wire to make sure it is locked into place.

9. Set the internal seal onto the socket housing if it was removed.

NOTE
*With the exception of the 3-pin Deutsch connector, all of the secondary locking wedges are symmetrical. When assembling the 3-pin socket housing, install the housing so the arrow on the secondary locking wedge points toward the external latch as shown in **Figure 153**.*

NOTE
If the secondary locking wedge does not slide into position easily, one or more of the socket terminals are not installed correctly. Correct the problem at this time.

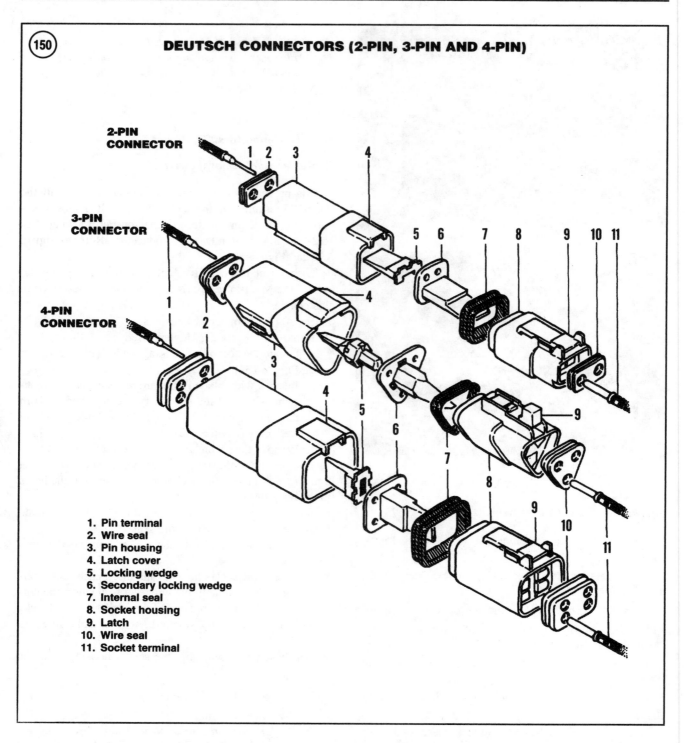

DEUTSCH CONNECTORS (2-PIN, 3-PIN AND 4-PIN)

2-PIN CONNECTOR

3-PIN CONNECTOR

4-PIN CONNECTOR

1. Pin terminal
2. Wire seal
3. Pin housing
4. Latch cover
5. Locking wedge
6. Secondary locking wedge
7. Internal seal
8. Socket housing
9. Latch
10. Wire seal
11. Socket terminal

10. Install the secondary locking wedge into the socket housing as shown in **Figure 150** or **Figure 151**. Press the secondary locking wedge down until it locks into place.

Pin terminal removal/installation: *2-, 3-, 4-, 6- and 12- pin*

This procedure shows how to remove and install the electrical terminals at the pin housing. It is shown performed on a 12-pin Deutsch connector, but it also applies to all Deutsch connectors (2-, 3-, 4- and 6-pin). Refer to **Figure 150** or **Figure 151**.

1. Disconnect the negative battery cable as described in this chapter.
2. Separate the connector housings.
3. Use needlenose pliers to remove the locking wedge.
4. Lightly press the terminal latches inside the pin housing, and remove the pin terminal(s) through the holes in the rear wire seal.
5. Repeat the process for each remaining pin terminal.
6. If necessary, remove the wire seal.

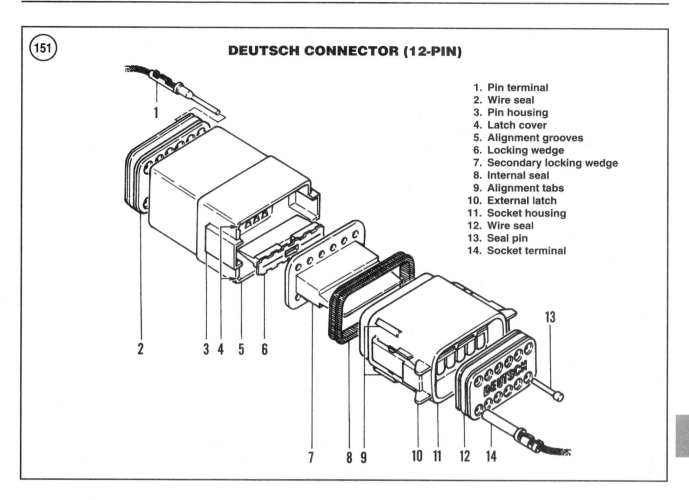

DEUTSCH CONNECTOR (12-PIN)

1. Pin terminal
2. Wire seal
3. Pin housing
4. Latch cover
5. Alignment grooves
6. Locking wedge
7. Secondary locking wedge
8. Internal seal
9. Alignment tabs
10. External latch
11. Socket housing
12. Wire seal
13. Seal pin
14. Socket terminal

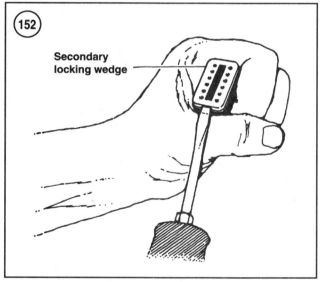

Secondary locking wedge

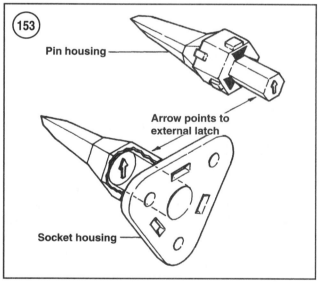

Pin housing

Arrow points to external latch

Socket housing

7. Install the wire seal into the pin housing if it was removed.

8. Hold onto the pin housing and insert the pin terminals through the holes in the wire seal so they enter their correct chamber holes. Continue until the pin terminal locks into place. Lightly tug on the wire to make sure the pin is locked into place.

9. Set the internal seal onto the socket housing if it was removed.

NOTE
With the exception of the 3-pin Deutsch connector, all of the locking wedges are symmetrical. When assembling the 3-pin connector, install the pin housing so the arrow on the

locking wedge is pointing toward the external latch as shown in **Figure 153**.

NOTE
If the locking wedge does not slide into position easily, one or more of the pin terminals are not installed correctly. Correct the problem at this time.

10. Install the locking wedge into the pin housing as shown in **Figure 150** or **Figure 11**. Press the locking wedge down until it locks into place. When properly installed, the wedge fits into the pin housing center groove.

Single-pin connector removal/installation

1. Disconnect the negative battery cable as described in this chapter.
2. Separate the connector housings.
3. Pull the wire seal from back of the housing, and slide it down voltage regulator cable.
4. Insert the terminal tool pick (Deutsch part No. 114008) into the cable until the tapered end of the tool (A, **Figure 154**) is in the wire end of the housing (B).
5. Push tool pick into wire end of housing until it bottoms.
6. Gently tug on housing, and pull the wire (C, **Figure 154**) from the terminal.
7. Remove tool from electrical cable.
8. Insert the wire into the terminal until it *clicks* and is locked into place. Pull on the wire slightly to ensure it is locked into place.

Packard Connectors

Wire form-type removal/installation

This procedure shows how to remove and install the electrical terminals in the pull-to-seat wire form-type connector shown in **Figure 155**.
1. Disconnect the negative battery cable as described in this chapter.
2. Depress the wire form and separate the connector.
3. Hold the connector so the wire form is facing down.
4. Look into the mating end of the connector, and locate the plastic rib that separates the wire terminals. The terminal is on each side of the rib with the tang at the rear.
5. Use the thin, flat blade of an X-Acto knife, or an equivalent, to depress the tang. Tilt the blade at an angle and place the tip at the inboard edge of the terminal. Push down slightly until the spring tension is relieved and a click is heard. Repeat this step several times. The click represents the tang returning to the locked position as it slips from the point of the knife blade. Continue to push down until the clicking stops indicating the tang has been depressed.
6. Remove the knife blade, push the wire end of the lead and remove the lead from the connector. If additional slack

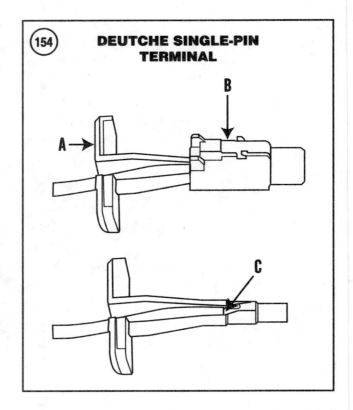

154 **DEUTCHE SINGLE-PIN TERMINAL**

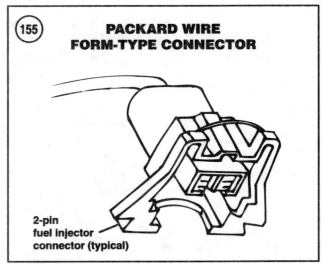

155 **PACKARD WIRE FORM-TYPE CONNECTOR**

2-pin fuel injector connector (typical)

is necessary, pull back on the harness conduit and remove the wire seal at the back of the connector.
7. To install the terminal and wire back into the connector, use the thin, flat blade of an X-Acto knife, or an equivalent, to carefully bend the tang away from the terminal.
8. Carefully pull the lead and terminal into the connector until a click is heard indicating the terminal is seated correctly within the connector. Gently push and pull on the lead to ensure the terminal is securely seated.
9. If necessary, install the wire seal and push the harness conduit back into position on the backside of the connector.
10. Push the socket halves together until the latch(es) are locked together.

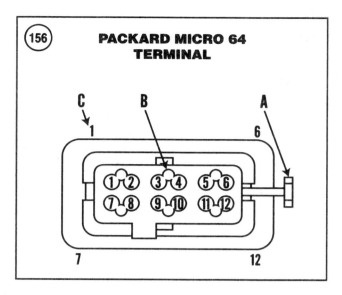

PACKARD MICRO 64 TERMINAL

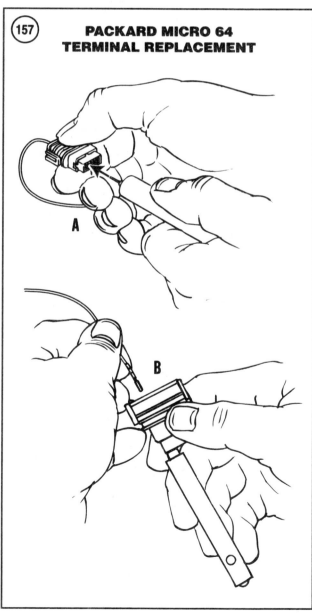

PACKARD MICRO 64 TERMINAL REPLACEMENT

Micro 64 removal/installation

This procedure shows how to remove and install the electrical terminals in the socket housing.

1. Disconnect the negative battery cable as described in this chapter.
2. Bend back the external latches slightly and separate the connector.
3. Locate the head of the secondary lock (A, **Figure 156**).
4. Insert the tip of a narrow, flat-bladed screwdriver between the center ear of the lock and the housing. Pry out the lock, and remove it.

NOTE
Connector terminals are numbered 1-6 in one row and 7-12 in the remaining row. The numbers 1, 6, 7 and 12 are stamped on the connector to identify the row numbers.

5. Locate the pin hole (B, **Figure 156**) between terminals on the mating end of the connector. Refer to C, **Figure 156** for terminal number locations.
6. Push the adjacent terminal all the way into the connector housing. Insert the Packard Terminal Remover (H-D part No. HD-45928) into the hole, and press the remover (A, **Figure 157**) in until it bottoms.
7. With the tool in place, gently pull on the wires and pull one or both terminals from wire end of connector (B, **Figure 157**). Remove the tool.
8. To install the terminal, insert wire and terminal into the correct location on the wire end of the connector. Push on the terminal until it bottoms. Slightly pull on the wire and wiggle it a little to ensure it is locked into place.
9. The special tool releases two terminals at the same time. Repeat removal and installation process for the adjacent terminal even if it was not removed.
10. Position the head of the secondary lock (A, **Figure 156**) facing the mating end of the connector. Press in on the secondary lock until it is flush with the connector housing.
11. Push the connector halves together until the latches lock together.

100W ECM connector removal/installation

1. Disconnect the negative battery cable as described in this chapter.
2. Disconnect the connector housing from the ECM (this chapter).
3. Press the latch (A, **Figure 158**) on each end of the connector, and remove the secondary lock (B).
4. Clip the cable tie (C, **Figure 158**), and release the strain relief collar (D) from the conduit (E).
5. Insert the thin, flat blade of an X-Acto knife, or an equivalent, into the housing seam, and pry the housing halves apart until the pins (A, **Figure 159**) release. Pivot the housing halves from one another.
6. Push the relevant wire, and remove the socket (B, **Figure 159**) from the housing.

9

7. Insert the new wire into the relevant chamber of the housing, and carefully pull the wire until the socket is seated in the housing chamber.

8. Carefully close the housing halves together so no wires are pinched. Press the halves together until the pins (A, **Figure 159**) lock.

9. Install a new cable tie (C, **Figure 158**) so the tie seats in the groove of the strain relief collar (D). Make sure the collar secures the conduit (E, **Figure 158**) in place.

10. Install the secondary lock (B, **Figure 158**) over the terminals, and lock it in place.

150 Metri-pack connector, removal/installation

This procedure shows how to remove and install the electrical terminals from the Packard 150 Metri-pack connectors shown in **Figure 160**. Two types of 150 metri-pack connectors are used: pull-to-seat connectors (**Figure 161**) and push-to-seat connectors (**Figure 162**).

1. Disconnect the negative battery cable as described in this chapter.

2. Bend back the external latch(es) slightly and separate the connector.

3. On push-to-seat connectors, remove the wire lock (A, **Figure 162**) from the connector housing.

4. Look into the mating end of the connector on the external latch side, and locate the locking tang (A, **Figure 161**) in the middle chamber. On locking-ear connectors, the tang is on the side opposite the ear.

5A. On pull-to-seat connectors insert the point of a one-inch safety pin (B, **Figure 161**) about 1/8 in. into the middle chamber. Pivot the end of the safety pin up toward the terminal body until a click is heard.

5B. On push-to-seat connectors, insert the safety pin (B, **Figure 162**) into the small opening in the housing until a click is heard.

6. Repeat this process several times. The click is the tang returning to the locked position as it slips from the point of the safety pin. Continue to pick at the tang until the clicking stops and the safety pin seems to slide in at a slightly greater depth indicating the tang has been depressed. Remove the safety pin.

7A. On pull-to-seat connectors, push the wire end of the lead and remove the terminal and wire (C, **Figure 161**) from the connector. If additional slack is necessary, pull back on the harness conduit, and remove the wire seal at the back of the connector.

7B. On push-to-seat connectors, pull the wire, and remove the terminal (C, **Figure 162**) from the housing.

8. To install the terminal and wire back into the connector, use the thin, flat blade of an X-Acto knife, or an equivalent, to carefully bend the tang (D, **Figure 161** or D, **Figure 162**) away from the terminal.

9. Carefully pull or push the lead and terminal into the connector until a click is heard indicating the terminal is seated correctly within the connector. Push or pull the lead gently to ensure the terminal is correctly seated.

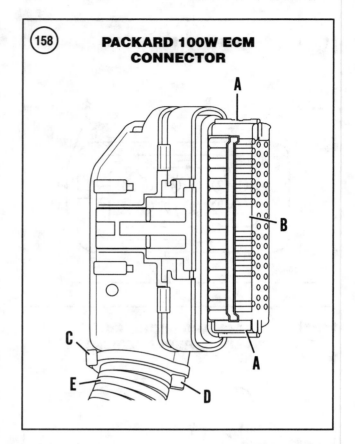

(158) PACKARD 100W ECM CONNECTOR

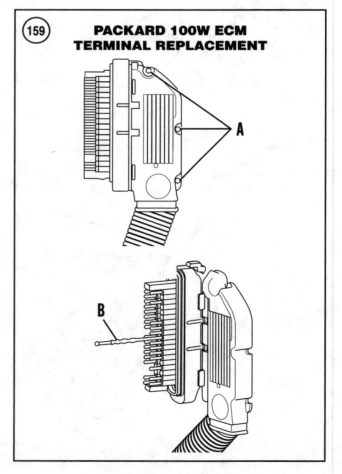

(159) PACKARD 100W ECM TERMINAL REPLACEMENT

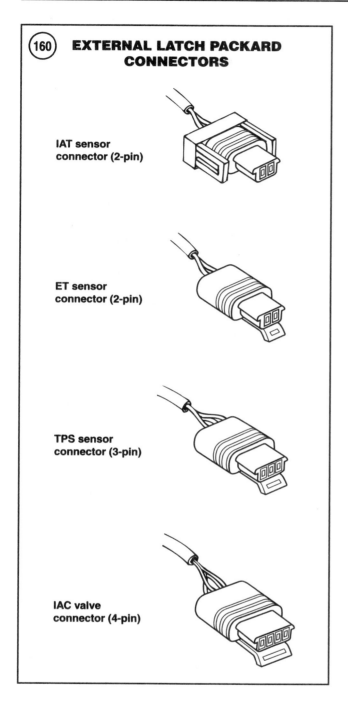

160 EXTERNAL LATCH PACKARD CONNECTORS

IAT sensor connector (2-pin)

ET sensor connector (2-pin)

TPS sensor connector (3-pin)

IAC valve connector (4-pin)

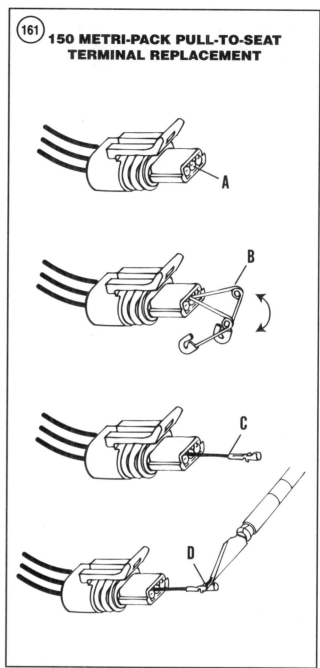

161 150 METRI-PACK PULL-TO-SEAT TERMINAL REPLACEMENT

9

10. If necessary, install the wire seal and push the harness conduit back into position on the backside of the connector.
11. Push the socket halves together until the latch(es) are locked together.

280 Metri-pack connector removal/installation

1. Release the lock, and pull the connector halves apart.
2. Pry the rubber seal from the end of the connector housing, and slide the seal down the wires (A, **Figure 163**).
3. At the wire end of the housing, insert a safety pin (B, **Figure 163**) between the top of the terminal and in the chamber wall. Push the safety pin into the chamber until

the terminal is seen moving slightly, which indicates the tang has been depressed.
4. Remove the safety pin. Push the wire into the housing until the terminal (C, **Figure 163**) emerges from the chamber, and remove the terminal and its wire.
5. To install the terminal and wire back into the connector, use the thin, flat blade of an X-Acto knife, or an equivalent, to carefully bend the tang (D, **Figure 163**) away from the terminal.
6. Carefully pull the wire (E, **Figure 163**) into the housing until a click is heard indicating the terminal is correctly seated within the chamber.
7. Seat the rubber seal into the end of the housing.

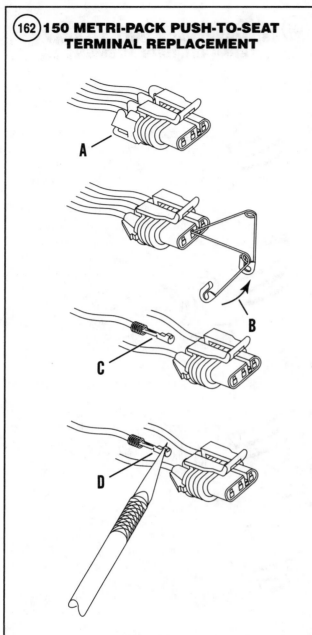

162 **150 METRI-PACK PUSH-TO-SEAT TERMINAL REPLACEMENT**

163 **280 METRI-PACK TERMINAL REPLACEMENT**

480 Metri-pack connector removal/installation

1. Use a small-bladed screwdriver to press the button on the lock (A, **Figure 164**), and separate the connector halves.

2. Slightly pry the latch and release one side of the secondary lock (B, **Figure 164**). Repeat on the other side of the housing, and open the secondary lock (C, **Figure 164**).

3. Examine the mating end of the housing chamber(s). Note that the tang on each terminal sits against the side of the chamber with a square-shaped opening. Insert a large pin into the chamber so the pin (D, **Figure 164**) sits between the tang and the chamber wall.

4. Press the pin toward the terminal to compress the tang.

5. Remove the pin, and pull the wire until the terminal emerges from the housing.

6. Use the thin, flat blade of an X-Acto knife, or an equivalent, to bend the tang away from the terminal.

7. Insert the terminal into the chamber until it clicks into place. Make sure the tang faces the chamber side with the square-shaped opening.

8. Latch the secondary lock on both sides of the housing.

9. Connect both halves of the connector and make sure they are securely fastened together.

630 Metri-pack connector removal/installation

1. Disconnect the negative battery cable as described in this chapter.

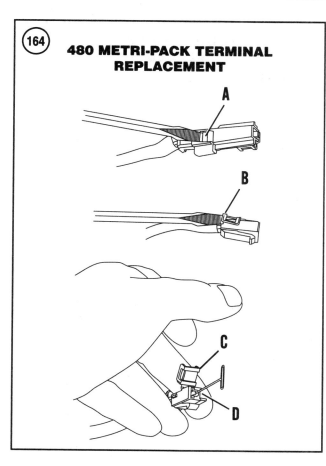

164

480 METRI-PACK TERMINAL REPLACEMENT

A

B

C

D

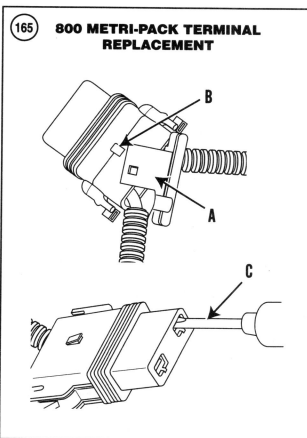

165

800 METRI-PACK TERMINAL REPLACEMENT

B

A

C

2. Bend back the external latch slightly and separate the socket halves.

3. Bend back the latch slightly and free one side of the secondary lock. Repeat for the latch on the remaining side.

4. Rotate the secondary lock outward on the hinge to expose the terminals in the chambers of the housing connector. The terminal is locked in place by the rib in the chamber wall.

5. At the mating end of the connector, insert a pin or a small pick tool (Snap-on part No. TT600-3), or an equivalent, into the small opening on the chamber wall until it bottoms.

6. Pivot the end of the pin or pick toward the terminal and depress the locking tang.

7. Remove the pin or pick, and gently pull the wiring to withdraw the terminal from the wire end of the connector. Repeat this step if the terminal is still locked in place.

8. Latch the secondary locks on both sides of the housing.

9. Connect both halves of the connector and make sure they are securely fastened.

800 Metri-pack connectors removal/installation

1. Disconnect the negative battery cable as described in this chapter.

2. Gently pull the socket housing and disengage the slots on the secondary lock (A, **Figure 165**) from the tabs (B) on the socket housing. Remove the secondary lock from the cable.

3. Carefully insert the blade of a small screwdriver (C, **Figure 165**) into the opening until it stops. Pivot the screwdriver toward the terminal body and hold it in this position.

4. Carefully pull the wire and withdraw the socket from the wire cable end of the housing.

5. Repeat this process to remove the remaining socket terminal, if necessary.

6. Use a flat-bladed screwdriver and carefully bend the tang away from terminal body.

7. Insert socket and wire lead into wire end of socket housing until it clicks into place. Gently pull on the wire to ensure the terminal is correctly seated.

8. Push rubber seal back into place on the wire end of socket terminal, if necessary.

9. Repeat this process to install the remaining socket terminal, if necessary.

10. Install the secondary lock (A, **Figure 165**) onto the cable and then push it onto the wire end of the socket housing until the slots engage the tabs (B) on the sides of the socket housing.

AMP Single Connectors

Socket removal/installation

1. Grasp the lead on the wire end of the socket housing (A, **Figure 166**) and push the terminal forward toward the mating end of the connector until it bottoms. This disengages the locking tang from the connector groove.

9

2. Install the barrel (B, **Figure 166**) of the socket terminal tool (H-D part No. HD-39621-27) over the socket housing.

3. Lightly rotate the tool, and push it in until it bottoms (C, **Figure 166**) in the socket housing allowing the plunger (D) to back out of the handle.

4. Secure the socket housing and keep the tool firmly depressed into the socket housing (E, **Figure 166**).

5. Depress the plunger (F, **Figure 166**) and the terminal (G) will eject out of the wire end of the connector (H).

6. Insert the wire and terminal into the flat lip side of the socket housing.

7. Push the lead into the socket housing until it a *click* is heard. Gently pull on the lead to ensure the terminal is correctly seated.

Pin terminal removal/installation

1. Grasp the wire on the end of the pin housing. Push the terminal forward toward the mating end of the connector until it stops and unlocks the tang from the groove in the connector.

2. Install the barrel (A, **Figure 167**) of the pin terminal tool (H-D part No. HD-39621-28) over the pin (B).

3. Lightly rotate the tool and push it in until it bottoms (C, **Figure 167**) in the pin housing allowing the plunger (D) to back out of the handle.

4. Secure the pin housing and keep the tool firmly depressed.

5. Depress the plunger (E, **Figure 167**) and eject the pin (F) out of the wire end of the connector.

6. Insert the pin into the pin housing until a *click* is heard. Gently pull on the lead to ensure the pin is correctly seated.

AMP Multilock Connectors

2-, 3-, 4-, 6- and 10-pin connector terminal removal/installation

Refer to **Figure 168**.

1. Disconnect the negative battery terminal as described in this chapter.

2. Press the release button on the socket side of the housing, and pull the connector apart.

3. Slightly bend the latch back and free one side of the secondary lock. Repeat this step for the other side of the secondary lock.

4. Open the secondary lock (A, **Figure 169**) around the hinge to access the terminals within the connector.

> *NOTE*
> *Do not pull too hard on the wire until the tang is released or the terminal will be difficult to remove.*

5. Insert a pin or a pick tool (B, **Figure 169**) into the flat edge of the terminal cavity until it stops. Pivot the pick tool away (C) from the terminal and gently pull on the wire to

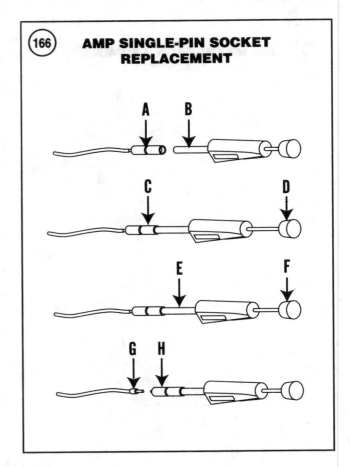

166 **AMP SINGLE-PIN SOCKET REPLACEMENT**

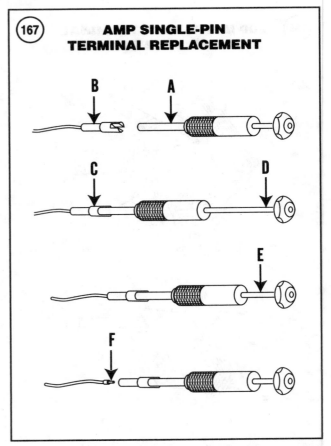

167 **AMP SINGLE-PIN TERMINAL REPLACEMENT**

AMP MULTILOCK CONNECTORS

3-PIN CONNECTOR

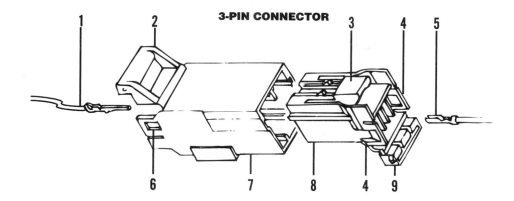

6-PIN CONNECTOR

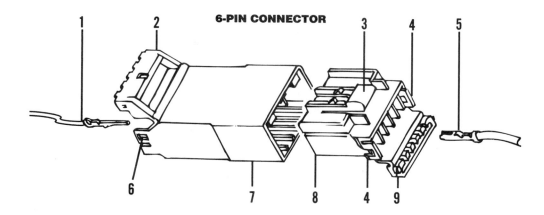

10-PIN CONNECTOR

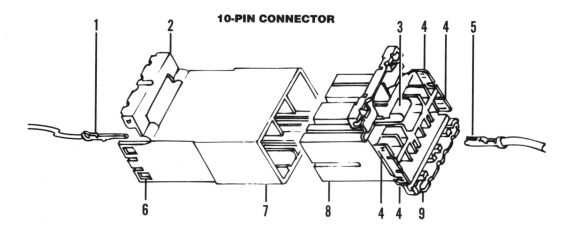

1. Pin terminal
2. Secondary lock
3. Button
4. Latch
5. Socket terminal
6. Latch
7. Pin housing
8. Socket housing
9. Secondary lock

pull the terminal (D) from the terminal chamber. Note the wire location number (**Figure 170**) on the connector.

> *NOTE*
> *The release button used to separate the connectors is at the top of the connector.*

6. A tang in each chamber engages the terminal slot to lock the terminal into position. The tangs (**Figure 169**) are located as follows:

    a. Pin-housing side: the tangs are located at the bottom of each chamber. The pin terminal slot, on the side opposite the crimp, must face downward.

    b. Socket-housing side: the tangs are located at the top of each chamber. The socket terminal slot, on the same side as the crimp, must face upward.

7. On the secondary-lock side of the connector, push the wire and terminal into the correct location until it snaps into place. Gently pull on the lead to ensure the terminal is correctly seated.

8. Rotate the hinged secondary lock down and inward until the tabs are fully engaged with the latches on both sides of the connector. Pull upward to make sure the tabs are locked in place.

9. Insert the socket housing into the pin housing and push it in firmly until it locks into place.

3-, 6- and 10-terminal connector removal/installation

1. Disconnect the negative battery cable as described in this chapter.

2. Slide the connector attachment clip T-stud to the large end of the opening.

3. Press the release button on the socket side of the housing, and pull the connector apart.

4. Slightly bend the latch (1, **Figure 171**) back and free one side of the secondary lock (2). Repeat this step for the other side.

5. Look into the terminal side of the connector that is opposite the secondary lock, and note the location of each terminal and cavity.

6. Insert a pin or a pick tool into the terminal cavity until it stops.

> *NOTE*
> *Use the release button to determine the up or down side of the connector. The release button is on the top of the connector.*

7. Press the tang in the housing to release a terminal. A "click" is heard when the tang is released.

    a. Press down on the tang (7, **Figure 171**) to release a pin.

    b. Lift up on the tang (8, **Figure 171**) to release a socket.

> *NOTE*
> *Do not pull too hard on the wire. If the tang is bent outward, the terminal will be difficult to*

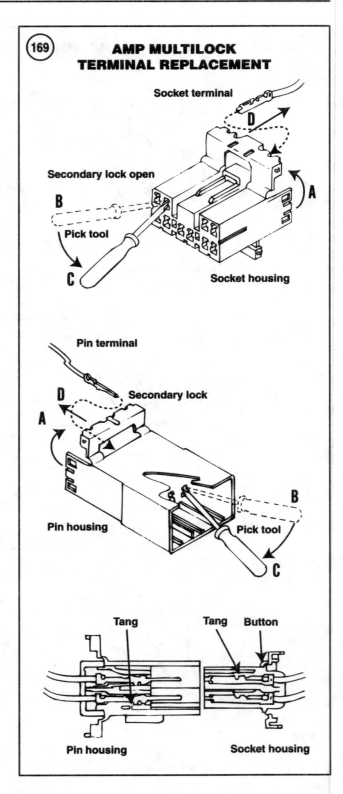

169 **AMP MULTILOCK TERMINAL REPLACEMENT**

Socket terminal

Secondary lock open

Pick tool

Socket housing

Pin terminal

Secondary lock

Pin housing

Pick tool

Tang   Tang   Button

Pin housing   Socket housing

remove. If necessary, repeat the process and release the tang.

8. Gently pull the wire and terminal (5 and 6, **Figure 171**) from the terminal chamber. Note the wire location number on the connector (**Figure 170**).

9. Hold a terminal so its catch faces the tang in the chamber.

AMP MULTILOCK TERMINAL IDENTIFICATION

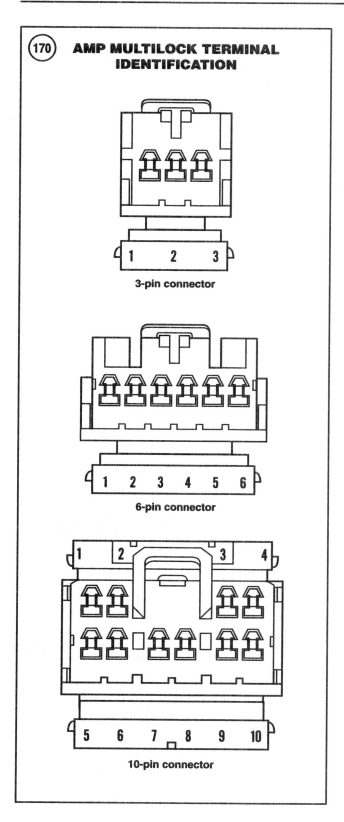

3-pin connector

6-pin connector

10-pin connector

AMP MULTILOCK TERMINAL REPLACEMENT

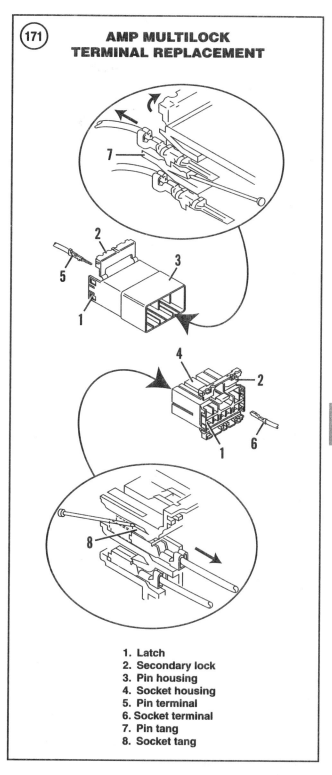

1. Latch
2. Secondary lock
3. Pin housing
4. Socket housing
5. Pin terminal
6. Socket terminal
7. Pin tang
8. Socket tang

a. On the pin housing (3, **Figure 171**), the tangs sit at the bottom of the housing (7). Install a pin so its catch faces down.

b. On the socket housing (4, **Figure 171**), the tangs sit on the top of the housing. Install a socket so its catch faces up (8).

10. Insert the terminal into the secondary lock side of the housing, and push the wire and terminal into the correct location until it snaps into place. Gently pull on the lead to ensure the terminal is correctly seated.

11. Rotate the hinged secondary lock (2, **Figure 171**) inward until the tabs fully engage the latches (1, **Figure 171**) on both sides of the connector. Pull upward to make sure the tabs are locked in place.

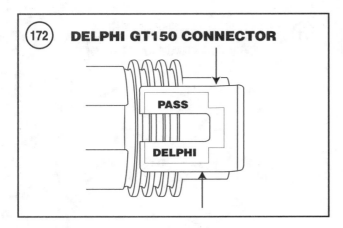

172 **DELPHI GT150 CONNECTOR**

PASS

DELPHI

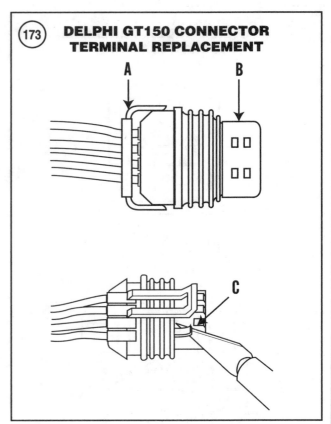

173 **DELPHI GT150 CONNECTOR TERMINAL REPLACEMENT**

12. Insert the socket housing into the pin housing, and push it in until it locks into place.

Delphi GT150 Connector Removal/Installation

This procedure shows how to remove and install the electrical terminals in the socket housing,

1. Disconnect the negative battery cable as described in this chapter.

2. Bend back the external latch(es) (**Figure 172**) and remove them from the socket halves.

3. Free one side of the wire lock (A, **Figure 173**) from the ear on the wire end of the socket housing. Release the wire lock on the other side.

4. Release the wires from the channels in the wire lock, and remove them from the socket housing.

5. Remove the terminal lock (B, **Figure 173**) from the socket housing.

6. Use the thin, unsharpened end of an X-Acto knife blade, or an equivalent, and gently pry the tang (C, **Figure 173**) outward away from the terminal.

7. Carefully pull the wire to back the terminal out of the connector, and remove it. Do not pull the wire until the terminal is released or it will be difficult to remove it.

8. Gently push the tang on the socket housing inward toward the chamber.

9. Position the terminal so its open side faces the tang, insert the terminal into the wire end of the housing, and seat the terminal in its chamber. Gently pull the wire to ensure the terminal is correctly seated.

10. Install the terminal lock (B, **Figure 173**) onto the socket housing.

11. Install the wire lock onto each side of the socket housing. Make sure they are correctly seated.

12. Push the connector halves together until the external latches engage (**Figure 172**).

Delphi GT280 ECM Connector

Removal/installation

1. Disconnect the negative battery cable as described in this chapter.

174

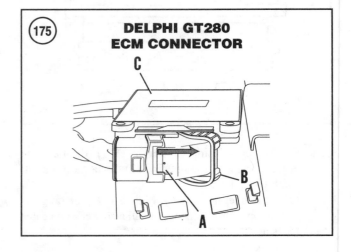

175 **DELPHI GT280 ECM CONNECTOR**

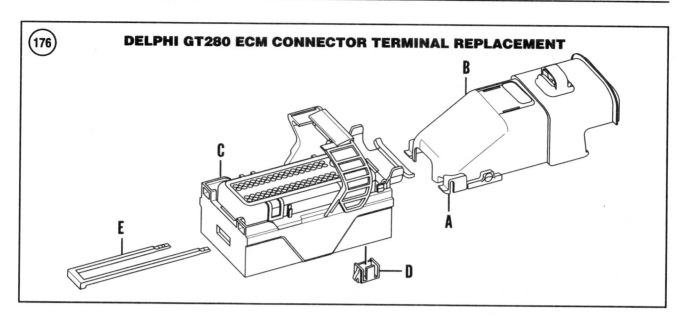

DELPHI GT280 ECM CONNECTOR TERMINAL REPLACEMENT

(176)

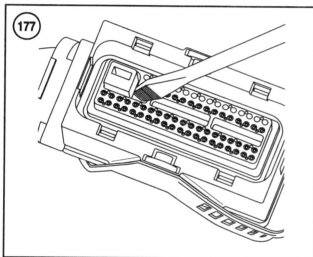

(177)

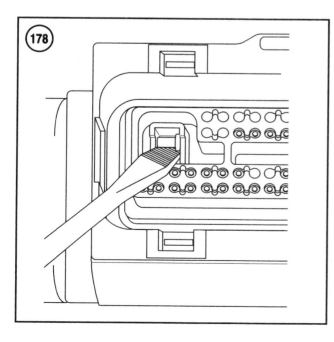

(178)

9

NOTE
The ECM is shown removed from the electrical caddy for clarity.

2. Remove the seat as described in Chapter Fourteen.
3. Pull straight out and remove the cover (**Figure 174**) from the side electrical caddy.
4. Remove the strap. Press on the latch (A, **Figure 175**), and rotate the lock lever (B) to the released position.
5. Disconnect the connector from the ECM (C, **Figure 175**).
6. Cut the cable strap and release the harness from the strain relief collar on the connector housing.
7. Release the latch (A, **Figure 176**) on each side and release the cover (B) from the housing (C). Remove the cover.
8. Install the cover (**Figure 174**) onto the side electrical caddy. Press it on unit it snaps into place.
9. Install the seat as described in Chapter Fourteen.
10. Connect the negative battery cable as described in this chapter.

Connector terminals removal/installation

This procedure shows how to remove and install the electrical terminals in the socket housing.
1. To remove the terminals within the connector, refer to *Micro 64 removal/installation* (this section).
2. To remove the ground terminal, perform the following:
   a. Remove the ground secondary lock (D, **Figure 176**), and the secondary lock (E) from the terminal housing (C).
   b. Use a thin-bladed screwdriver (**Figure 177**), and gently pry the ground terminal retainer from the terminal housing (C, **Figure 176**).
   c. Use a thin-bladed screwdriver, release the latch (**Figure 178**) and pull the ground wire, wire seal and terminal from the cover side of the housing.

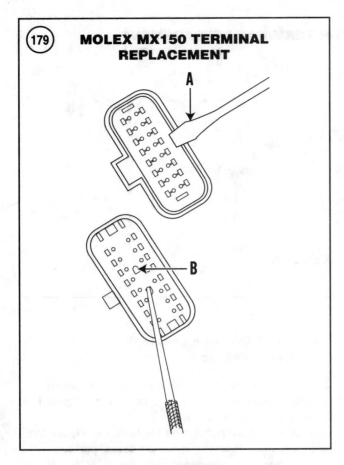

⑰⁷⁹ **MOLEX MX150 TERMINAL REPLACEMENT**

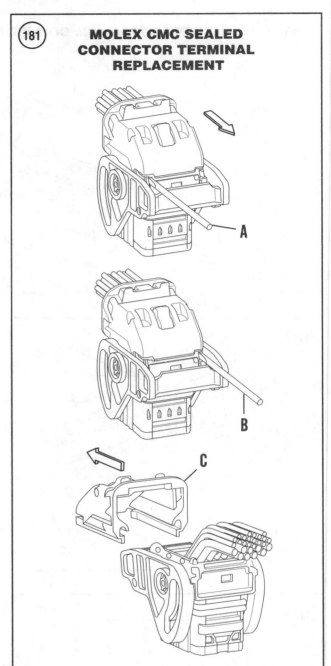

⑱¹ **MOLEX CMC SEALED CONNECTOR TERMINAL REPLACEMENT**

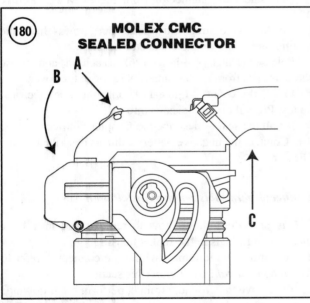

⑱⁰ **MOLEX CMC SEALED CONNECTOR**

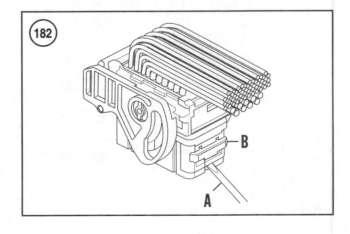

⑱²

d. Push the terminal into place from the cover side of the terminal housing (C, **Figure 176**) until the cover latch (A) engages. Gently pull on the wire to ensure the terminal is correctly seated.

e. Correctly position the secondary lock (one short leg and one long leg), and install it (E, **Figure 176**) into the terminal housing. Push it in until it bottoms, and install the ground secondary lock (D, **Figure 176**).

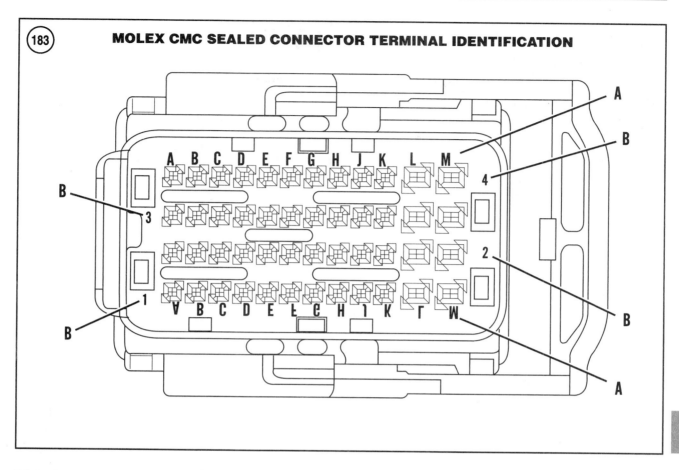

MOLEX CMC SEALED CONNECTOR TERMINAL IDENTIFICATION

Molex MX150 Connector Removal/Installation

This procedure describes the removal and installation of electrical terminals in the socket and pin housings.

1. Disconnect the battery negative cable as described in this chapter.

2. Pull the secondary lock approximately 3/16 in (4.8 mm) away from the terminals until it stops by performing the following. Do not remove the secondary lock.

   a. On the socket housing, insert a flat-bladed screwdriver into the pry slot (A, **Figure 179**) and pry the secondary lock from the terminals.

   b. On the pin housing, use a hooked pick or needle nose pliers and loosen the secondary lock (B, **Figure 179**).

3. Insert the Molex Electrical Connector Terminal Remover (H-D part No. HD-48114) into the correct terminal pin hole until the tool bottoms.

4. Gently pull on the wire lead and remove it from the housing cavity.

5. Insert the wire into the correct terminal chamber.

6. Orient the terminal so the tang opposite the crimp engages the slot in the terminal cavity. Push the terminal into the cavity until it bottoms. Gently pull on the wire lead to ensure the terminal is correctly seated.

7. Push the secondary lock into the socket housing, and lock the terminals into the housing.

8. Install the socket housing into the terminal.

Molex CMC Sealed Connector Terminals Removal/Installation

This procedure shows how to remove and install the electrical terminals in the socket housing.

1. Disconnect the negative battery cable as described in this chapter.

2. Press the catch (A, **Figure 180**), rotate the lever arm (B) down, and lift the connector (C) from the component.

3. Use a thin-bladed screwdriver (A, **Figure 181**), and insert it into the connector.

4. Maintain pressure on the cap and insert the second thin-bladed screwdriver (B, **Figure 181**) into the connector.

5. Slide off the cap (C, **Figure 181**).

6. Use a thin-bladed screwdriver (A, **Figure 182**), and insert it into the secondary lock in the connector.

7. Completely withdraw the secondary lock (B, **Figure 182**) from the connector.

8. Locate the wire terminal using the alpha-numeric coordinates (**Figure 183**).

9. Insert the pins of the CMC extractor tool (A, **Figure 184**) into the access slots (B) of the terminal cavity, and extract the connector lead and terminal (C).

10. Insert the terminal and connector lead into the correct access slot until it locks into place. Gently pull on the connector lead to ensure the terminal is correctly seated.

11. Slide the cap (C, **Figure 181**) over the connector lead bundle. Push it on until it locks into place.

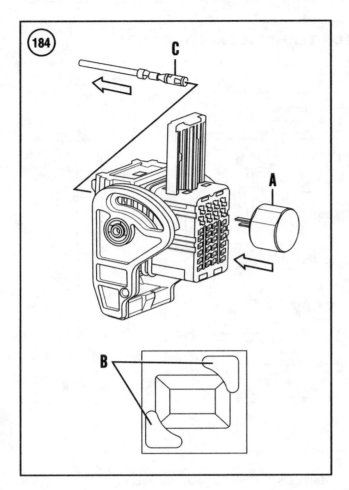

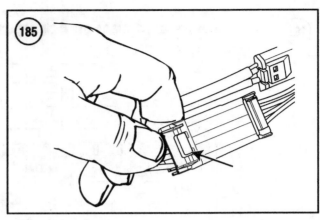

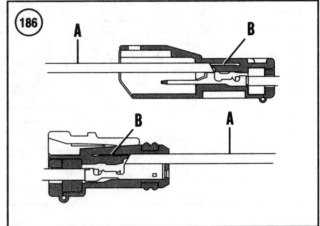

12. Attach the connector onto the component. Press on the front guard and to release the catch (A, **Figure 181**), and rotate the lever arm (B) up into position.

13. Connect the negative battery cable as described in this chapter.

JAE MX19 Sealed Connector Terminals
Removal/Installation

This procedure shows how to remove and install the electrical terminals in the socket housing.

1. Disconnect the negative battery cable as described in this chapter.

2. Press the release button (**Figure 185**) on each side of the connector, and separate the connector.

3. File a 45° angle on the front edge of the terminal extractor (H-D part No. H-D B-50085).

4. Insert the extractor (A, **Figure 186**) into the terminal opening above the terminal, and press the plastic molding (B) up and out of the way.

5. Pull the connector lead and terminal out of the back of the housing.

6. Insert the terminal and connector lead into the housing until it clicks into place. Gently pull on the connector lead to ensure the terminal is correctly seated.

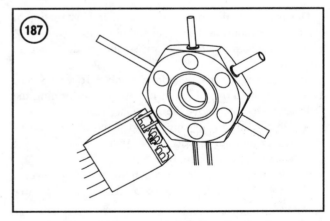

7. Attach the connector halves together and ensure they are locked together.

8. Connect the negative battery cable as described in this chapter.

Autofuse Connectors

The Autofuse connector terminals are located in the ignition switch and on some fuse blocks. Use a terminal pick (JIMS part No. 1764 or Snap-on part No. GA500A) for this procedure.

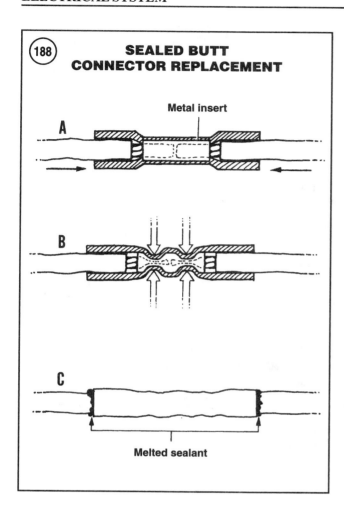

188

SEALED BUTT CONNECTOR REPLACEMENT

A

Metal insert

B

C

Melted sealant

1. Insert the smallest pair of the terminal picks (**Figure 187**) into the mating chamber on the end of the socket housing. Simultaneously depress the tangs on each side of the terminal housing.

2. Gently pull the wire and remove the terminal from the socket housing.

3. Crimp *new* terminals onto the end of the wires, if necessary.

4. Use the thin, unsharpened end of an X-Acto knife blade, or an equivalent, and gently pry the tang outward away from the terminal body.

5. Position the open side of the terminal with the rib facing down.

6. Insert the terminal into the wire side of the chamber and carefully push it until it locks in place.

Sealed Butt Connectors

Replacing some switches requires sealed butt connectors to connect the switch wiring to the existing wiring. Stagger the position of the connectors so they are not side-by-side.

1. Insert the stripped wire into the connector (A, **Figure 188**).

2. Crimp the connector/wire ends (B, **Figure 188**).

3. Heat the connector (C, **Figure 188**) and allow it to cool.

WIRING DIAGRAMS

Color wiring diagrams for all models are located on the CD inserted into the back cover of the manual.

9

Table 1 ELECTRICAL SYSTEM SPECIFICATIONS

Item	Specification
ACR solenoid compression test	
ACR-connector connected	130-170 psi (896-1172 kPa)
ACR-connector disconnected	200-220 psi (1379-1517 kPa)
Alternator	
AC voltage output	
2006 models	16-20 VAC per 1000 rpm
2007-on models	16-23 VAC per 1000 rpm
Stator coil resistance	
2006 models	0.1-0.3 ohm
2007-on models	0.1-0.2 ohm
Voltage regulator	
Voltage output @ 3600 rpm	14.3-14.7 @ 75 ° F (24 ° C)
Amps @ 3600 rpm	
2006 models	34-36 amps
2007-on models	35-50 amps
Battery capacity	12 volts, 28 amp hour
Ignition coil resistance	
Primary resistance	0.5-0.7 ohm (2006-2009 models)
	0.3-0.5 (2010-2011 models)
Secondary resistance	5500-7500 ohms (2006-2009 models)
	3500-4500 ohms (2010-2011 models)
	(continued)

Table 1 ELECTRICAL SYSTEM SPECIFICATIONS (continued)

Item	Specification
Spark plug wire resistance	
Front cylinder	
2006-2009 models	4750-11,230
2010-2011 models	5475-14,941
Rear cylinder	
2006-2009 models	1812-4375
2010-2011 models	1813-5003
Spark plug	
Size	12 mm
Gap	0.038-0.043 in. (0.97-1.09 mm)
Type	H-D No. 6R12
Starter	
Minimum free speed	3000 rpm @ 11.5 volts
Maximum free current	90 amp @ 11.5 volts
Cranking current	200 amp maximum @ 68° F (20° C)
Brush length (minimum)	0.433 in. (11.0 mm)
Commutator	
Diameter (minimum)	1.14 in. (28.981 mm)
Mica depth (minimum)	0.008 (0.203 mm)

Table 2 BATTERY CHARGING RATES/TIMES (APPROXIMATE)

Voltage	% of charge	3 amp charger	6 amp charger	10 amp charger	20 amp charger
12.8	100%	–	–	–	–
12.6	75%	1.75 hours	50 minutes	30 minutes	15 minutes
12.3	50%	3.5 hours	1.75 hours	1 hour	30 minutes
12.0	25%	5 hours	2.5 hours	1.5 hours	45 minutes
11.8	0%	6 hours and 40 minutes	3 hours and 20 minutes	2 hours	1 hour

Table 3 FUSE SPECIFICATIONS (AMPERES)

Item	Specification
Maxi-fuse	40
Accessory	15
Active exhaust/intake (HDI)	15
Battery	15
Brakes	15
ECM power	15
Engine control (HDI)	15
Fuel pump	15
Headlamp	15
Ignition	15
Instruments	15
Lighting	15
Parts and accessories	15
Security fuse (EFI models)	15

Table 4 BULB SPECIFICATIONS

Item	Current draw amperage	Quantity
Headlamp (high beam/low beam)		
All models except FXDF	5.0/4.85	1
FXDF models	5.0/4.85	2
	(continued)	

Table 4 BULB SPECIFICATIONS (continued)

Item	Current draw amperage	Quantity
Position lamp (HDI)	0.32	1
Tail/stop lamp		
All models except FXDB	0.59/2.10	1
FXDB models	LED[1]	1
Front turn signal/running lamps	2.25/0.59	2
Front turn signal (HDI)	1.75	2
Rear turn signal	2.25	2
Rear turn signal (HDI)	1.75	2
Indicator lamps	LED[1]	1
Fuel level gauge	LED[2]	–

1. LED unit must be replaced as an assembly.
2. LED built into fuel gauge.

Table 5 ELECTRICAL SYSTEM TORQUE SPECIFICATIONS

Item	ft.-lb.	in.-lb.	N•m
Active exhaust module screw	–	30-60	3.4-5.8
Alternator stator Torx screws	–	55-75	6.2-8.5
Automatic compression release (ACR) solenoid (Screamin' Eagle models)	11-15	–	14.9-20.3
Battery			
Terminal bolts	–	60-96	6.8-10.9
Tray screws	–	96-120	10.8-13.6
Electrical caddy			
Top screws	–	90-110	10.2-12.4
Front screws	–	40-60	4.5-6.8
Fuel gauge (FXD and FXDSE models)			
Tank console rear screw	–	18-24	2.0-2.7
Trim ring screws (adjacent to fuel gauge)	–	18-27	2.0-3.0
Trim ring mounting boss short/long screws	–	18-22	2.0-2.5
Fuel tank speedometer clamp screw	–	18-24	2.0-2.7
Headlight horizontal and vertical adjust nut	25-30	–	33.9-40.7
Handlebar switch housing screws	–	35-45	4.0-5.1
Horn			
Mounting nut	10-15	–	13.6-20.3
Stud mounting flange nut	10-15	–	13.6-20.3
Ignition coil screws	–	50	5.6
Ignition switch screws	–	18-24	2.0-2.7
Indicator lamp riser cover screw (FXDL and FXDB models)	–	50-60	5.6-6.8
Instrument console screws	–	18-24	2.0-2.7
Instruments (2007 FXDSE models)			
Speedometer			
Bracket screw	12-15	–	16.3-20.3
Assembly screws	–	18-26	2.0-2.9
Tachometer			
Assembly screws	–	20-30	2.3-3.4
Mounting screws	–	18-26	2.0-2.9
Jiffy stand sensor screw (HDI)	–	96-144	10.8-16.3
Neutral indicator switch	–	120-180	13.6-20.3
Oil pressure switch	–	96-144	10.8-16.2
Rear brake light switch	12-15	–	16.3-20.3
Rear turn signal support bolt	–	30-50	3.4-5.6

(continued)

Table 5 ELECTRICAL SYSTEM TORQUE SPECIFICATIONS (continued)

Item	ft.-lb.	in.-lb.	N•m
Sensors			
Manifold absolute pressure			
(MAP) Torx screw	–	20-35	2.3-4.0
Crankshaft position			
(CKP) Allen screw	–	90-120	10.2-13.6
Engine temperature (ET)	–	120-180	13.6-20.3
Vehicle speed (VSS) Allen screw	–	84-108	9.5-12.2
Solenoid contacts jam nuts	–	65-80	7.3-9.0
Starter			
Field coil terminal post nut	–	70-90	7.9-10.2
Mounting bolts			
2006-2007 models	13-20	–	17.6-27.1
2008-2011 models	25-27	–	33.9-36.6
Positive terminal nut	–	65-85	7.3-9.6
Through bolt	–	39-65	4.4-7.3
Stator screw	–	55-75	6.2-8.5
Tail/brake light assembly			
2009-2011 FXDB models			
Mounting screw	–	84-108	9.5-12.2
FXDFSE and FXDFSE2 models			
Base locknut	–	60-72	6.8-8.1
Circuit board screw	–	40-48	4.5-5.4
Lens screw	–	30-36	3.4-4.1
All other models			
Base mounting screws and nut	–	40-48	4.5-5.4
Lens screw	–	20-24	2.3-2.7
Turn signals			
Front turn signal acorn nut	–	120-168	13.6-19.0
Rear turn signal screws	–	96-120	10.8-13.6
Rear turn signal housing			
support bolt	12-16	–	16.3-21.7
Voltage regulator bolts	–	60-80	6.8-9.0

CHAPTER TEN

WHEELS, HUBS AND TIRES

This chapter includes procedures for the front and rear wheels, the hubs and tire service. For routine maintenance, refer to Chapter Three.

Refer to **Tables 1-4** at the end of this chapter for specifications.

MOTORCYCLE STANDS

Many procedures in this chapter require that the front or rear wheel be lifted off the ground. A quality motorcycle front end stand (**Figure 1**) or suitable size jack is required. Before purchasing or using a stand, check the manufacturer's instructions to make sure the stand will work with the specific model being worked on. If any adjustments or accessories are required to use the stand with the motorcycle, perform the necessary adjustments or install the correct parts before lifting the motorcycle. When using the stand, have an assistant standing by to help. Some means to tie down one end of the motorcycle may also be required. After lifting it on a stand, make sure the motorcycle is properly supported before walking away from it.

If a motorcycle stand is not available, use a scissor jack that fits onto the frame tubes.

BRAKE ROTOR PROTECTION

Avoid contacting the brake rotor when removing, handling and installing a wheel. A rotor can withstand tremendous rotational loads, but it can be damaged when subjected to side impact loads.

Never set a wheel down on the brake rotor. It may be bent or scratched. When a wheel must be placed on its side, support the wheel on wooden blocks. Position the blocks along the outer circumference of the wheel so the rotor lies between the blocks and does not rest on them.

If the rotor is knocked out of true by a side impact, a pulsation will be felt during braking. Damaged rotors must be replaced.

FRONT WHEEL
(ALL MODELS EXCEPT 2007 FXDSE, 2008 FXDSE2, 2009 FXDFSE AND 2010 FXDFSE2)

Removal

1. Support the motorcycle with the front wheel off the ground as described in this chapter.
2. On the right side, insert a drift (A, **Figure 2**) or screwdriver through the front axle hole (B) to prevent it from rotating.
3. Loosen the axle nut (A, **Figure 3**) on the left side.
4. Remove the axle nut (A, **Figure 3**), and flat washer (B).
5. On the right side, loosen the bolts on the fork slider cap (A, **Figure 4**).

NOTE
Place a spacer between the brake pads in place of the disc. Then, if the brake lever is inadvertently applied, the pistons will not be forced out of the calipers. If this occurs, disassembly of the caliper is required to reseat the pistons.

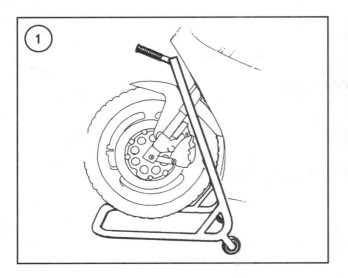

6. Remove the caliper mounting bolts (A, **Figure 5**) and remove the caliper (B) as described in Chapter Thirteen. Remove remaining caliper on models so equipped.

7. Prior to removing the front axle, note and mark the location of the short, right-side spacer (**Figure 6**) and long, left-side spacer (**Figure 7**). The spacers are not interchangeable and must be reinstalled on the correct side during installation.

8. Using a drift or screwdriver, withdraw the front axle (B, **Figure 4**) from the fork sliders and front wheel on the right side. Remove the tool from the axle.

9. Pull the wheel away from the fork sliders and remove it.

10. Remove the short, right-side spacer and the long, left-side spacer from the wheel.

> *CAUTION*
> *Do not set the wheel down on the brake disc*
> *surface, as it may be damaged.*

11. Inspect the front wheel as described in this chapter.

Installation

1. Clean the axle in solvent and dry thoroughly. Make sure the axle bearing surfaces on both fork sliders and on the axle are free of burrs and nicks.

2. Apply an antiseize lubricant to the axle shaft prior to installation.

3. If the fork slider cap was removed, position the cap with the cast-in spacer toward the rear of the vehicle and install it. Do not tighten the screws.

4. If the bearings were replaced, confirm front axle spacer alignment as described in this chapter.

5. Install the short, right-side spacer and the long, left-side spacer onto the correct side of the wheel.

6. Install the wheel between the fork tubes.

7. Check that the axle spacers are still located correctly.

8. Install the axle from the right side. Push the front axle through the right fork leg, right spacer (**Figure 6**), through the hub, the left spacer (**Figure 7**), and left fork leg.

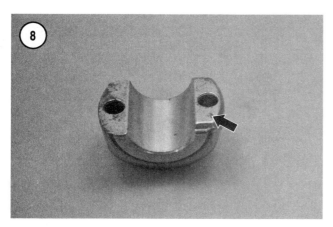

9. Install the flat washer (B, **Figure 3**) and axle nut (A). Finger-tighten the nut. Check that axle spacer(s) are installed correctly.

10. Correctly position the slider cap with the raised pad (**Figure 8**) toward the rear of the motorcycle. Install the slider cap (**Figure 9**) and bolts. Finger-tighten the bolts.

11. Insert a drift (A, **Figure 2**) or screwdriver into the hole (B) in the end of the front axle to keep it from rotating.

12. Tighten the front axle nut (A, **Figure 3**) as follows:
    a. 2006-2007 models: 50-55 ft.-lb. (67.8-74.6 N•m).
    b. 2008-2011 models: 60-65 ft.-lb. (81.3-88.1 N•m).

13. Tighten the slider cap (A, **Figure 4**) rear bolt to 10-14 ft.-lb. (13.6-19.0 N•m), and then tighten the front bolt to 10-14 ft.-lb. (13.6-19.0 N•m).

14. Remove the drift or screwdriver from the front axle hole.

15. Remove the spacer block from between the brake pads.

16. Install the front brake caliper(s) as described in Chapter Thirteen.

17. With the front wheel off the ground, rotate it several times and apply the front brake to seat the brake pads against the discs.

18. Remove the stand and lower the front wheel onto the ground.

FRONT WHEEL (2007 FXDSE, 2008 FXDSE2, 2009 FXDFSE AND 2010 FXDFSE2 MODELS)

Removal

1. Support the motorcycle with the front wheel off the ground as described in this chapter.

2. Unscrew and remove the front axle cover on the right side.

> *NOTE*
> *Do not loosen lower set screw on the underside of the left fork.*

3. On the underside of the right fork leg, remove the lower set screws securing the front axle.

> *NOTE*
> *Place a spacer between the brake pads in place of the disc. Then, if the brake lever is inadvertently applied, the pistons will not be forced out of the calipers. If this occurs, disassemble the caliper to reseat the pistons.*

4. Remove the brake caliper(s) as described in Chapter Thirteen.

5. Prior to removing the front axle, note and mark the location of the short, right-side spacer and long, left-side spacer. The spacers are not interchangeable and must be reinstalled on the correct side during installation.

6. Unscrew the front axle from the left fork slider.

7. Pull the wheel away from the fork sliders and remove it.

10

8. Remove the short, right-side spacer and the long, left-side spacer from the wheel.

CAUTION
Do not set the wheel down on the brake disc surface, as it may be damaged.

9. Inspect the front wheel as described in this chapter.

Installation

1. Clean the axle in solvent and dry thoroughly. Make sure the axle bearing surfaces on both fork sliders and the axle are free of burrs and nicks.

2. Apply an antiseize lubricant to the axle shaft prior to installation.

3. If the bearings were replaced, confirm front axle spacer alignment as described in this chapter.

4. Install the short, right-side spacer and the long, left-side spacer onto the correct side of the wheel.

5. Install the wheel between the fork tubes.

6. Check that axle spacers are still located correctly.

7. Install the axle from the right side. Push the front axle through the right fork leg and right spacer, and then on through the hub and left spacer.

8A. On 2007 FXDSE and 2008 FXDSE2 models, install the axle into the left fork leg and tighten to 65-70 ft.-lb. (88.1-94.9 N•m).

8B. On 2009 FXDFSE and 2010 FXDFSE2 models, install the front axle into the left fork leg and tighten to 62-67 ft.-lb. (84-91 N•m).

9. Apply Loctite 243 (blue), or an equivalent threadlock, to the lower set screws securing the front axle. Install the set screws on the underside of the right fork leg and tighten the set screws to 11-15 ft.-lb. (14.9-20.4 N•m).

10. Remove the spacer from between the brake pads.

11. Install the front brake calipers as described in Chapter Thirteen.

12. With the front wheel off the ground, rotate it several times and apply the front brake to seat the brake pads against the discs.

13. Install the front axle cover and tighten securely.

14. Remove the stand and lower the front wheel onto the ground.

REAR WHEEL

Removal

1. Remove both saddlebags, on models so equipped.

2. Remove the rear cylinder muffler as described in Chapter Four.

3. Support the motorcycle with the rear wheel off the ground as described in this chapter.

4A. On 2007-2008 FXDSE models, remove the set screw securing the rear axle cover, and remove the cover from the axle on both sides.

4B. On 2009 FXDFSE and 2010 FXDFSE2 models, remove the two screws securing the rear axle cover. Remove the cover from the mounting bracket on the swing arm.

5. Remove the rear belt guard bolt, washer and nut (A, **Figure 10**), and the front screw and washer (B). Then, remove the belt guard (C, **Figure 10**) from the swing arm. Do not lose the spacer within the rubber grommets.

6. Remove the three mounting screws (A, **Figure 11**), and then remove the debris deflector (B) from the swing arm.

7. Remove the large E-clip (A, **Figure 12**) from the rear axle nut and axle.

8. Loosen and remove the axle nut (B, **Figure 12**) and washer.

9. Loosen the rear axle adjuster (C, **Figure 12**) evenly on each side to allow drive belt slack.

10. Very carefully pry the rear brake pads away from the brake disc.

NOTE
Place a spacer between the brake pads in place of the disc. Then, if the brake pedal is inadvertently depressed, the pistons will not be forced out of the caliper. If this occurs, disassembly of the caliper is required to reseat the pistons.

11. On 2008-2011 models, remove the two Torx bolts (A, **Figure 13**), and then remove the rear caliper assembly (B) from the caliper mounting bracket (Chapter Thirteen). Tie the caliper (A, **Figure 14**) securely to the frame with a bungee cord or wire.

NOTE
The rear wheel is heavy and can be difficult to remove. Check the tire-to-ground clearance before removing the rear axle. If necessary, have an assistant help place wooden blocks under the wheel.

12. Using a soft-faced mallet, gently tap the rear axle toward the right side.

13. From the right side, withdraw the rear axle (B, **Figure 14**) while holding onto the rear wheel. Lower the wheel to the ground (**Figure 15**).

14. Disengage the drive belt from the driven sprocket and remove the rear wheel.

NOTE
Mark the wheel bearing spacers with an R (right side) and L (left side). The spacers are unique and must be reinstalled onto the correct side of the wheel during installation.

15. Remove the right side (A, **Figure 16**) and left side (**Figure 17**) spacers from the wheel hub.

CAUTION
Do not set the wheel down on the brake disc surface, as it may be damaged.

10

16A. On 2006-2007 models, remove the rear brake caliper from the swing arm and tie it securely to the frame with a bungee cord or wire.

16B. On 2008-2011 models, remove the rear caliper mounting bracket (B, **Figure 16**) from the swing arm weldment.

17. Inspect the rear wheel as described in this chapter.

Installation

> *CAUTION*
> *The rear wheel bearing spacers must be installed onto the correct side of the rear wheel. If installed incorrectly, the wheel will be offset to the wrong side within the swing arm. This will result in the drive belt being out of alignment with the driven sprocket resulting in rapid drive belt wear.*

1. Clean the axle in solvent and dry thoroughly. Make sure the bearing surfaces on the axle are free from burrs and nicks.

2. Apply an antiseize lubricant to the axle shaft prior to installation.

3. On 2008-2011 models, install the rear caliper mounting bracket (B, **Figure 16**) onto the swing arm weldment.

4. Position the rear wheel between the swing arm sides and place the drive belt on the sprocket.

5. Install the right side (A, **Figure 16**) and left side (**Figure 17**) spacers onto the wheel hub.

6. Remove the spacer block from between the brake pads.

7. On 2006-2007 models, move the rear brake caliper into position on the swing arm.

> *CAUTION*
> *On 2006-2007 models, when installing the rear wheel, insert the brake disc carefully between the brake pads in the caliper assembly. Do not force the brake disc as it can damage the leading edge of both brake pads.*

8. Lift the rear wheel and install the rear axle (**Figure 14**) from the right side. Install the axle through the swing arm, the rear brake caliper mounting bracket and the other side of the swing arm.

9. After the rear axle is installed, check to make sure the axle spacers are still in place on the right side (A, **Figure 16**) and left side (**Figure 17**) of the rear wheel.

10. On 2008-2011 models, install the rear caliper assembly onto the caliper mounting bracket as described in Chapter Thirteen.

11. Install the rear axle washer (A, **Figure 18**) and nut (B).

12. Check drive belt tension and alignment as described in Chapter Three.

13. Tighten the rear axle nut as follows:
   a. On 2006 models: 60-65 ft.-lb. (81.3-88.1 N•m).
   b. On 2007 models: 92-98 ft.-lb. (124.7-132.9 N•m).

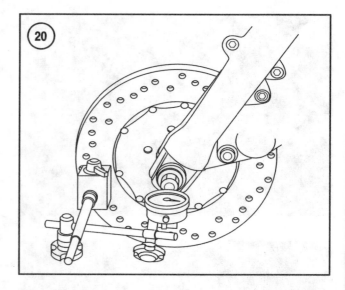

   c. On 2008-2011 models: 95-105 ft.-lb. (128.8-142.4 N•m).

14. Install a *new* E-clip (**Figure 19**) and make sure it is correctly seated in the axle groove.

15. Rotate the wheel several times to make sure it rotates freely. Then, apply the rear brake pedal several times to seat the pads against the disc.

16. Install the debris deflector (B, **Figure 11**) onto the swing arm. Tighten the three screws (A, **Figure 11**) to 40-60 in.-lb. (4.5-6.8 N•m).

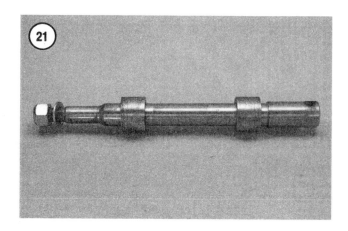

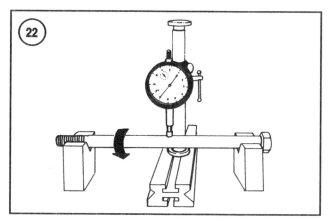

17. Install the belt guard onto the swing arm as follows:
   a. Install the grommets and spacers onto the rear mounting bracket, if removed.
   b. Install the rear bolt, washer and nut (A, **Figure 10**) and tighten to 10-15 ft.-lb. (13.6-20.3 N•m).
   c. Install the front screw and washer (B, **Figure 10**) and tighten to 10-15 ft.-lb. (13.6-20.3 N•m).

18A. On 2007 FXDSE and 2008 FXDSE2 models, install rear axle cover on both sides. Tighten the set screw to 60-84 in.-lb. (6.8-9.5 N•m).

18B. On 2009 FXDFSE and 2010 FXDFSE2 models, install the rear axle cover onto the mounting bracket. Tighten the screws to 20-30 in.-lb. (2.3-3.4 N•m).

19. Install the rear cylinder muffler as described in Chapter Four.

20. Remove the jack and lower the rear wheel to the ground.

21. On models so equipped, install the saddlebags.

WHEEL INSPECTION

Replace any worn or damaged parts as described in this section.

1. Inspect the bearing end play as follows:
   a. Support the motorcycle with the front or rear wheel off the ground as described in this chapter.
   b. Turn the wheel through several revolutions and check for noise from the bearing area.
   c. Mount a magnetic-base dial indicator onto the brake disc and position the indicator pointer on the end of the axle (**Figure 20**).
   d. Slowly move the wheel from side-to-side and check for bearing end play.
   e. The bearings are okay if the radial end play is less than the service limit of 0.002 in. (0.051 mm).
   f. Replace the bearings as a set if the end play is greater than the service limit.

2. Turn each bearing inner race by hand. The bearing must turn smoothly.

3. If one bearing is damaged, replace both bearings as a set as described in *Front and Rear Hubs* (this chapter).

4. Clean the axle and axle spacers (**Figure 21**, typical) in solvent to remove all grease and dirt. Make sure the axle contact surfaces are clean and free of dirt and old grease.

5. Check the axle runout with a set of V-blocks and dial indicator (**Figure 22**). If the axle is bent, replace it. The manufacturer does not provide a service limit for the axle.

6. Check the spacers for wear, burrs and damage. Replace as necessary.

7. Check the brake disc bolts (**Figure 23** and **Figure 24**) for tightness. To service the brake disc, refer to Chapter Thirteen.

8. Check wheel runout as described in this chapter.

9. Check the final drive sprocket bolts (**Figure 25**) for tightness as described in this chapter.

10

FRONT AND REAR HUBS

Sealed ball bearings are installed on each side of the hub. Do not remove the bearing assemblies unless they require replacement.

Preliminary Inspection

Inspect each wheel bearing prior to removing it from the wheel hub.

> *CAUTION*
> *Do not remove the wheel bearings for inspection purposes as they will be damaged during the removal process. Remove wheel bearings only if they are to be replaced.*

1. Remove the front or rear wheel as described in this chapter. Remove the axle spacers, if still in place.
2. Turn each bearing by hand. The bearings must turn smoothly with no roughness.
3. Inspect the play of the inner race of each wheel bearing. Check for excessive axial play and radial play (**Figure 26**). Replace the bearing if it has an excess amount of free play.

Disassembly

This procedure applies to both the front and rear wheel and hub assemblies. Where differences occur between them, they are identified. Refer to **Figures 27-32** for the front wheel or to **Figures 33-38** for the rear wheel.
1A. Remove the front wheel as described in this chapter.
1B. Remove the rear wheel as described in this chapter.
2. If still in place, remove the axle spacer from each side of the hub.
3. If necessary, remove the bolts securing the brake disc and remove the disc.
4. Before proceeding further, inspect the wheel bearings (**Figure 39**) as described in this chapter. If they must be replaced perform the procedure as described in this section.
5A. If the special tools are not used, perform the following:

   a. To remove the right- and left-hand bearings and spacer collar, insert a soft aluminum or brass drift into one side of the hub.
   b. Push the spacer collar over to one side and place the drift on the inner race of the lower bearing.
   c. Tap the bearing out of the hub with a hammer, working around the perimeter of the inner race (**Figure 40**). Remove the bearing and distance collar.
   d. Repeat the process to remove the bearing on the other side.

> *WARNING*
> *Wear safety glasses while using the wheel bearing remover set.*

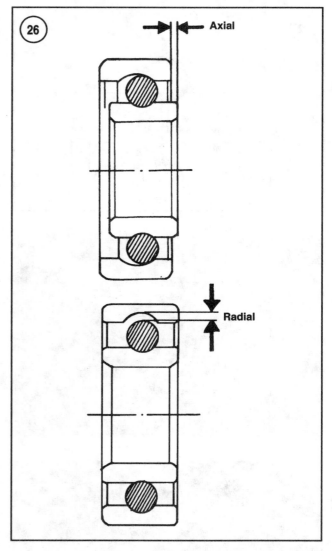

5B. Remove the bearings with an expanding-collet bearing removal tool (Motion Pro part No. 08-0410), or an equivalent, by performing the following:

   a. Select the correct size of remover head tool and insert it into the bearing.
   b. Turn the wheel over and insert the remover shaft into the backside of the adapter. Tap the wedge and force

FRONT LACED WHEEL

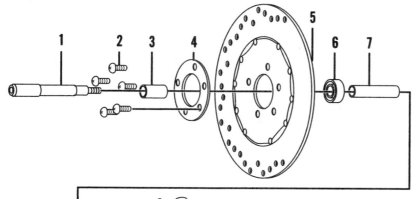
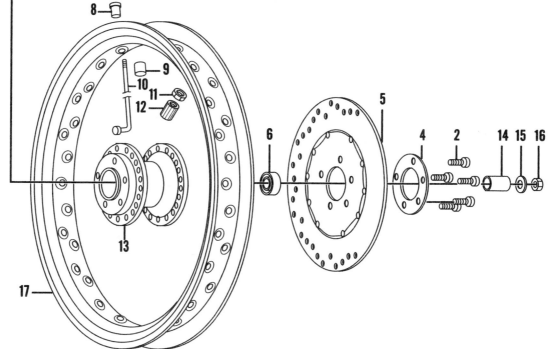

10

1. Front axle
2. Bolt
3. Axle spacer (right side)
4. Hub cap
5. Brake disc
6. Bearing
7. Spacer sleeve
8. Spoke nipple
9. Balance weight
10. Spoke
11. Nut
12. Valve stem cap
13. Wheel hub
14. Axle spacer (left side)
15. Washer
16. Axle nut
17. Rim

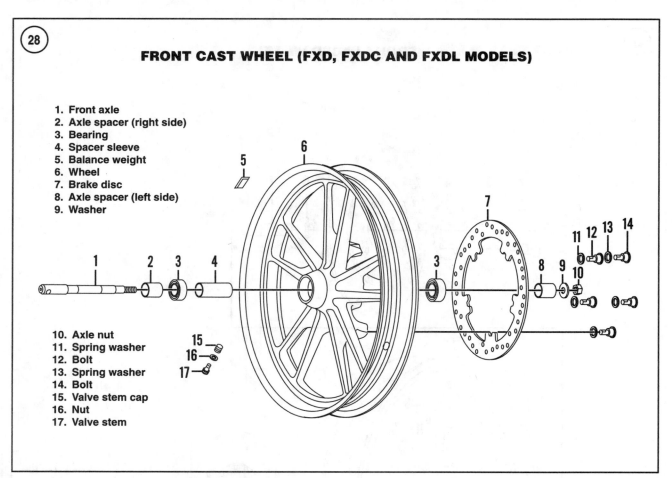

FRONT CAST WHEEL (FXD, FXDC AND FXDL MODELS)

1. Front axle
2. Axle spacer (right side)
3. Bearing
4. Spacer sleeve
5. Balance weight
6. Wheel
7. Brake disc
8. Axle spacer (left side)
9. Washer

10. Axle nut
11. Spring washer
12. Bolt
13. Spring washer
14. Bolt
15. Valve stem cap
16. Nut
17. Valve stem

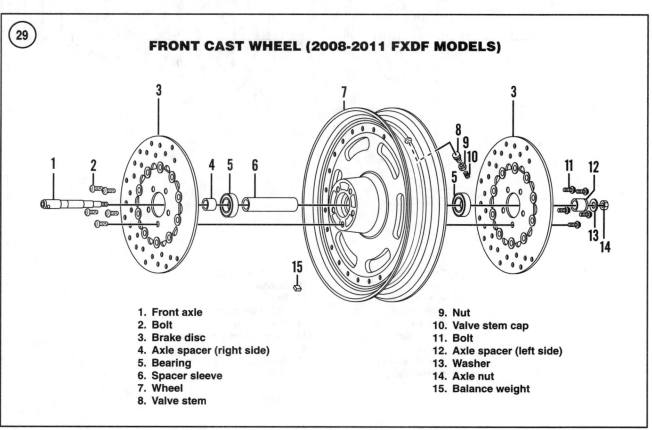

FRONT CAST WHEEL (2008-2011 FXDF MODELS)

1. Front axle
2. Bolt
3. Brake disc
4. Axle spacer (right side)
5. Bearing
6. Spacer sleeve
7. Wheel
8. Valve stem

9. Nut
10. Valve stem cap
11. Bolt
12. Axle spacer (left side)
13. Washer
14. Axle nut
15. Balance weight

FRONT CAST WHEEL (2009 FXDFSE AND 2010 FXDFSE2 MODELS)

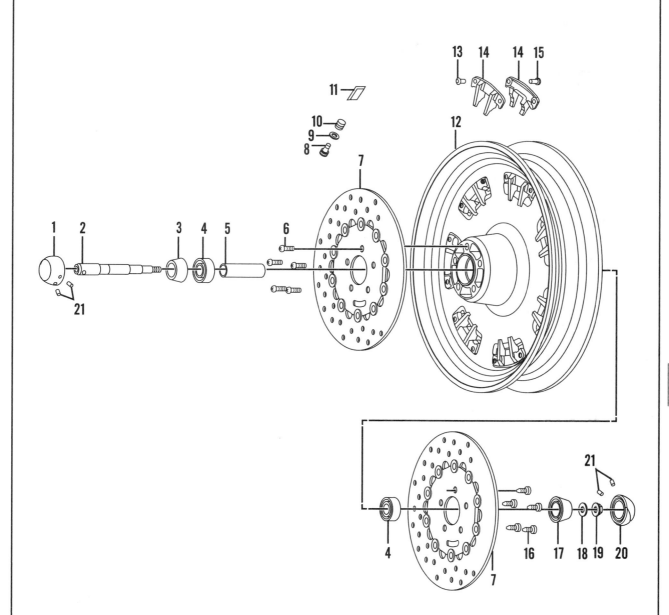

1. Axle cover
2. Front axle
3. Axle spacer (right side)
4. Bearing
5. Spacer sleeve
6. Bolt
7. Brake disc
8. Valve stem
9. Nut
10. Valve stem cap
11. Balance weight
12. Wheel
13. Screw
14. Trim strips
15. Nut
16. Bolt
17. Axle spacer (left side)
18. Washer
19. Axle nut
20. Axle cover
21. Set screw

31

FRONT CAST WHEEL (2007 FXDSE MODELS)

1. Axle cover
2. Front axle
3. Axle spacer (right side)
4. Bearing
5. Spacer sleeve
6. Screw
7. Hub cap

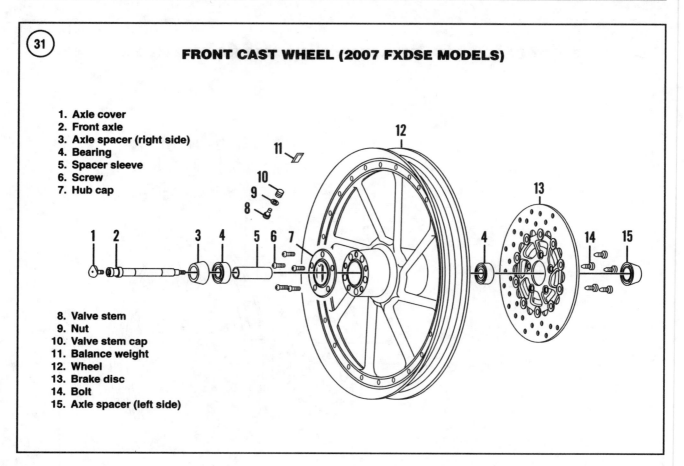

8. Valve stem
9. Nut
10. Valve stem cap
11. Balance weight
12. Wheel
13. Brake disc
14. Bolt
15. Axle spacer (left side)

32

FRONT CAST WHEEL (2008 FXDSE2 MODELS)

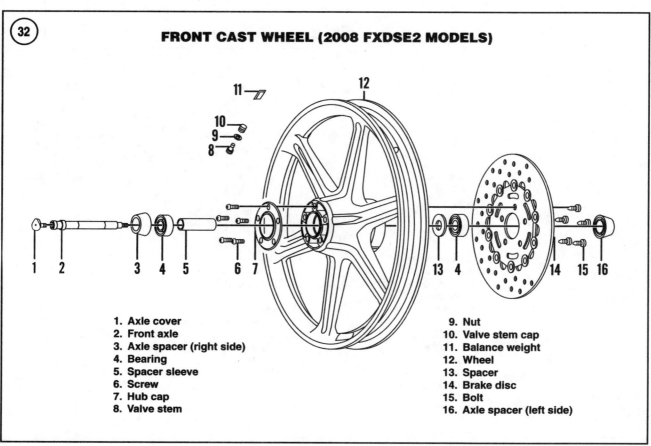

1. Axle cover
2. Front axle
3. Axle spacer (right side)
4. Bearing
5. Spacer sleeve
6. Screw
7. Hub cap
8. Valve stem

9. Nut
10. Valve stem cap
11. Balance weight
12. Wheel
13. Spacer
14. Brake disc
15. Bolt
16. Axle spacer (left side)

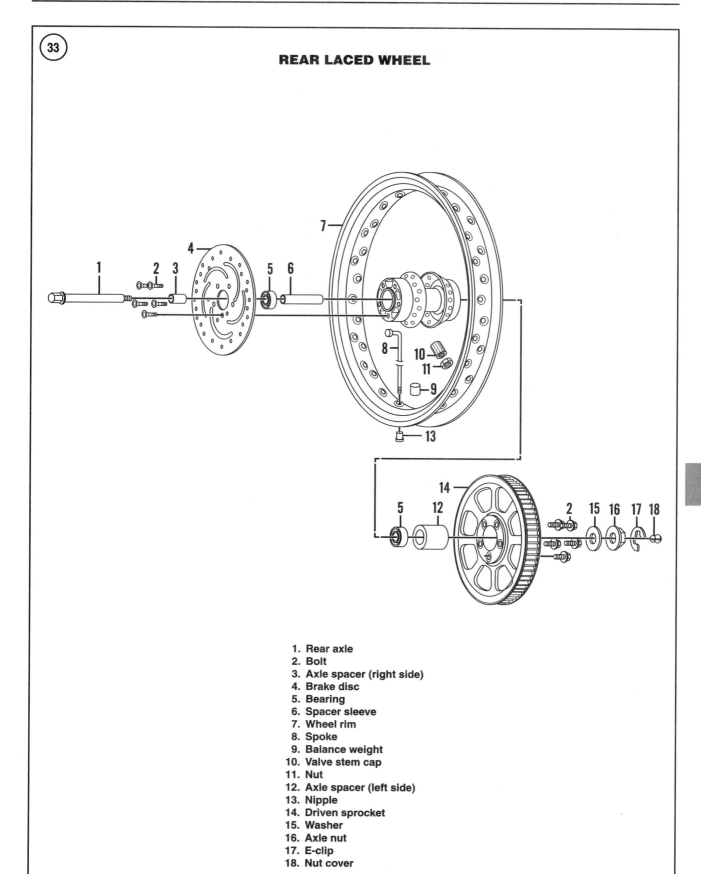

REAR LACED WHEEL

10

1. Rear axle
2. Bolt
3. Axle spacer (right side)
4. Brake disc
5. Bearing
6. Spacer sleeve
7. Wheel rim
8. Spoke
9. Balance weight
10. Valve stem cap
11. Nut
12. Axle spacer (left side)
13. Nipple
14. Driven sprocket
15. Washer
16. Axle nut
17. E-clip
18. Nut cover

34

REAR CAST WHEEL (FXD, FXDC AND FXDL MODELS)

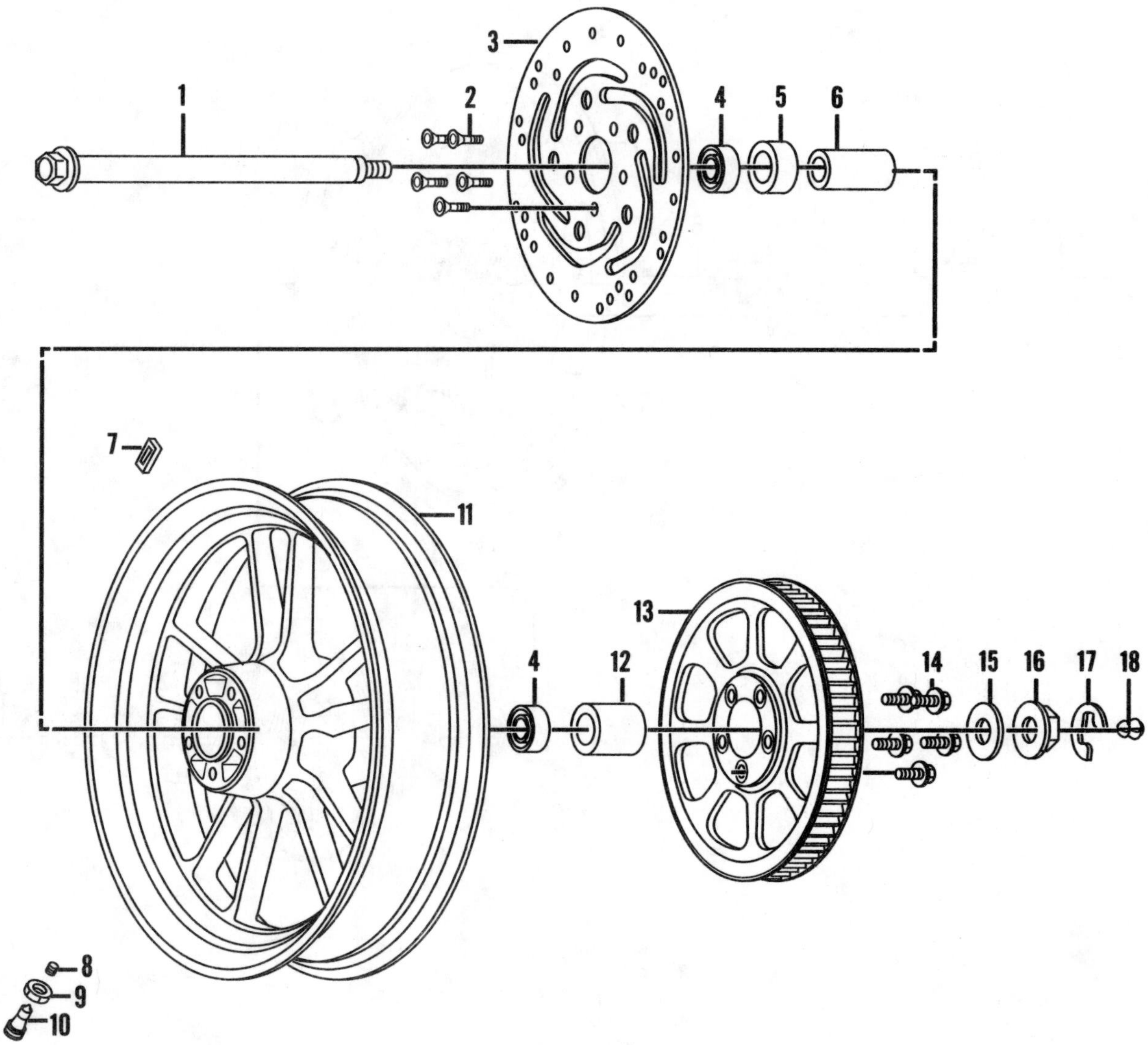

1. Rear axle
2. Bolt
3. Brake disc
4. Bearing
5. Axle spacer (right side)
6. Spacer sleeve
7. Balance weight
8. Valve stem cap
9. Nut
10. Valve stem
11. Wheel
12. Axle spacer (left side)
13. Driven sprocket
14. Bolt
15. Washer
16. Axle nut
17. E-clip
18. Nut cover

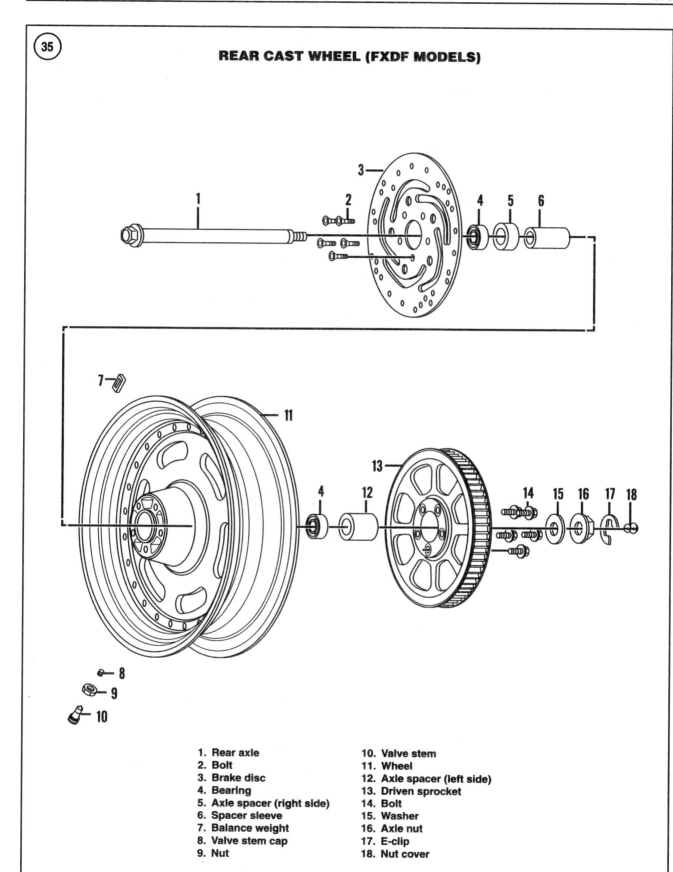

REAR CAST WHEEL (FXDF MODELS)

1. Rear axle
2. Bolt
3. Brake disc
4. Bearing
5. Axle spacer (right side)
6. Spacer sleeve
7. Balance weight
8. Valve stem cap
9. Nut
10. Valve stem
11. Wheel
12. Axle spacer (left side)
13. Driven sprocket
14. Bolt
15. Washer
16. Axle nut
17. E-clip
18. Nut cover

10

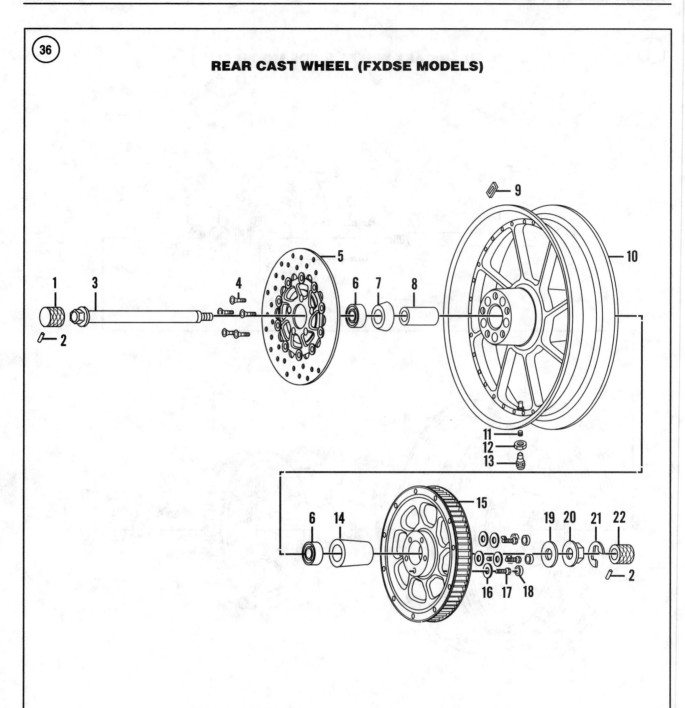

36

REAR CAST WHEEL (FXDSE MODELS)

1. Axle cover (right side)
2. Set screw
3. Rear axle
4. Bolt
5. Brake disc
6. Bearing
7. Axle spacer (right side)
8. Spacer sleeve
9. Balance weight
10. Wheel
11. Valve stem cap
12. Nut
13. Valve stem
14. Axle spacer (left side)
15. Driven sprocket
16. Washer
17. Bolt
18. Bolt cover
19. Washer
20. Axle nut
21. E-clip
22. Axle cover (left side)

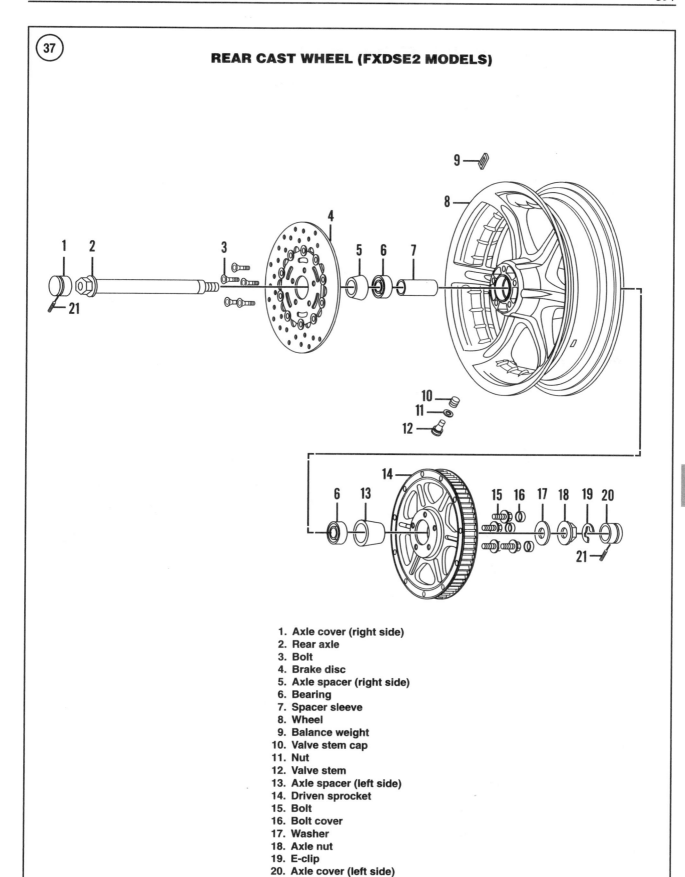

REAR CAST WHEEL (FXDSE2 MODELS)

1. Axle cover (right side)
2. Rear axle
3. Bolt
4. Brake disc
5. Axle spacer (right side)
6. Bearing
7. Spacer sleeve
8. Wheel
9. Balance weight
10. Valve stem cap
11. Nut
12. Valve stem
13. Axle spacer (left side)
14. Driven sprocket
15. Bolt
16. Bolt cover
17. Washer
18. Axle nut
19. E-clip
20. Axle cover (left side)
21. Set screw

10

38

REAR CAST WHEEL (2009 FXDFSE AND 2010 FXDFSE2 MODELS)

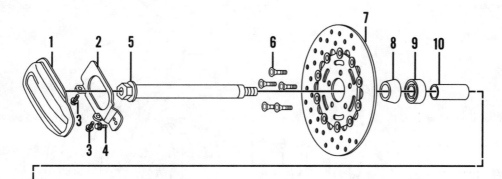

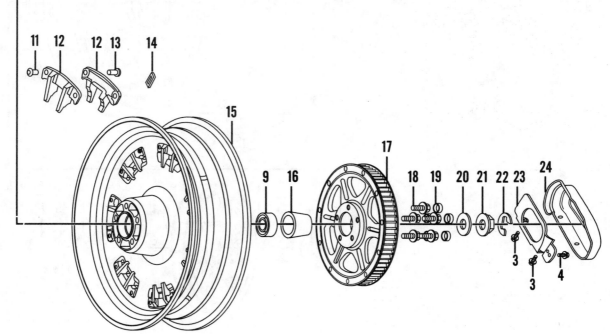

1. Axle cover (right side)
2. Cover bracket
3. Screw
4. Screw
5. Rear axle
6. Bolt
7. Brake disc
8. Axle spacer (right side)
9. Bearing
10. Spacer sleeve
11. Screw
12. Trim strips
13. Nut
14. Balance weight
15. Wheel
16. Axle spacer (left side)
17. Driven sprocket
18. Bolt
19. Bolt cover
20. Washer
21. Axle nut
22. E-clip
23. Cover bracket
24. Axle cover (left side)
25. Valve stem cap
26. Nut
27. Valve stem

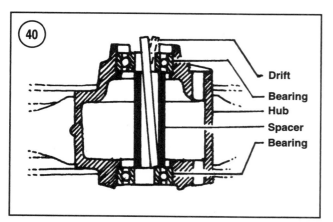

Drift
Bearing
Hub
Spacer
Bearing

it into the slit in the adapter (**Figure 41**). This will force the adapter against the bearing inner race.

c. Tap on the end of the wedge bar with a hammer and drive the bearing (**Figure 42**) out of the hub. Remove the bearing and the distance collar.

d. Repeat the process to remove the bearing on the other side.

6. Clean the inside and the outside of the hub with solvent. Dry with compressed air.

Assembly

CAUTION
The removal process will generally damage the bearings. Replace the wheel bearings in pairs along with the one located within the driven sprocket drum. ***Never*** *reinstall them after they are removed always install* ***new*** *bearings.*

1. Blow any debris out of the hub prior to installing the new bearings.

2. Apply a light coat of wheel bearing grease to the bearing seating areas of the hub. This will make bearing installation easier.

CAUTION
Install non-sealed bearings with the single sealed side facing outward. Tap the bearings squarely into place and tap on the outer race only. Do not tap on the inner race or the bearing might be damaged. Be sure that the bearings are completely seated.

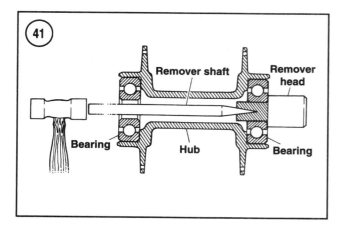

Remover shaft
Remover head
Bearing
Hub
Bearing

3. Select a driver, or socket (**Figure 43**) with an outside diameter slightly smaller than the bearing's outside diameter.

4. Tap the right side bearing squarely into place and tap on the outer race only. Tap the bearing into the hub bore until it bottoms. Be sure that the bearing is completely seated (**Figure 39**).

5. Turn the wheel over (right side up) on the workbench and install the spacer collar.

10

6. Use the same tool set-up and drive in the left side bearing.

7. If the brake disc was removed, install it as described in Chapter Thirteen.

8A. Install the front wheel as described in this chapter.

8B. Install the rear wheel as described in this chapter.

DRIVEN SPROCKET

Inspection

Inspect the sprocket teeth (**Figure 44**). If the teeth are visibly worn, replace the drive belt along with both drive and driven sprockets.

Removal/Installation

Refer to **Figure 45**.

1. Remove the rear wheel as described in this chapter.

2. Remove the bolts (**Figure 46**) and washers (models so equipped) securing the driven sprocket to the hub and remove the sprocket.

3. Position the sprocket onto the rear hub.

4. Apply a few drops of Loctite 243 (blue) threadlock, or an equivalent, onto the mounting bolts.

5. Install the bolts (**Figure 46**) and washers (on models so equipped) securing the sprocket.

6. Tighten the driven sprocket bolts to the following:

  a. On 2006-2007 models: 55-60 ft.-lb. (74.6-81.3 N•m).

  b. On 2008-2011 models: 55-65 ft.-lb. (74.6-88.1 N•m).

DRIVE SPROCKET

The drive sprocket is covered in Chapter Seven under *Transmission Drive Sprocket*.

DRIVE BELT

CAUTION
When handling a new or used drive belt, never wrap the belt in a loop that is smaller than 5 in. (130 mm) in diameter, or bend it sharply in any direction. This will weaken or break the belt fibers and cause premature belt failure.

Removal/Installation

NOTE
If the existing drive belt is going to be reinstalled, it must be installed so it travels in the same direction. Before removing the belt, draw an arrow facing forward on the top surface of the belt.

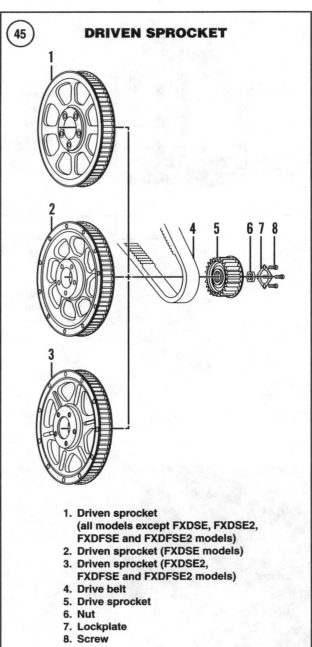

DRIVEN SPROCKET

1. Driven sprocket
   (all models except FXDSE, FXDSE2, FXDFSE and FXDFSE2 models)
2. Driven sprocket (FXDSE models)
3. Driven sprocket (FXDSE2, FXDFSE and FXDFSE2 models)
4. Drive belt
5. Drive sprocket
6. Nut
7. Lockplate
8. Screw

1. Remove the rear wheel as described in this chapter.
2. Remove the swing arm as described in Chapter Twelve.
3. Remove the primary chaincase housing as described in Chapter Six.
4. Remove the drive belt (A, **Figure 47**) from the drive sprocket (B).
5. Installation is the reverse of removal. Adjust the drive belt tension as described in Chapter Three.

Inspection

Do not allow, or apply, any type of lubricant to the drive belt. Inspect the drive sprocket for signs of oil residue on each side (A, **Figure 48**) of the area (B) where the drive belt (C) has been riding.

If there is oil present on the drive sprocket, the transmission mainshaft oil seal in the transmission housing is damaged. Replace the seal as described in Chapter Six.

Inspect the drive belt and teeth (**Figure 49**) for severe wear, damage or oil contamination.

Refer to **Figure 50** for various types of drive belt wear or damage. Replace the drive belt if worn or damaged.

LACED WHEEL SERVICE

The laced or wire wheel assembly consists of a rim, spokes, nipples and hub (containing the wheel bearings, distance collars and seals).

Loose or improperly tightened spokes can cause hub damage. Periodically inspect the wheel assembly for loose, broken or missing spokes, rim damage and runout. Service wheel bearings as described in this chapter.

Component Condition

Wheels are subjected to a significant amount of punishment. Inspect the wheels regularly for lateral (side-to-side) and radial (up and down) runout, and for visible damage. When a wheel has a noticeable wobble, it is out of true. Loose spokes usually cause this, but it can be caused by impact damage.

Truing a wheel corrects the radial and lateral runout to bring the wheel back into specification. The condition of the individual wheel components will affect the ability to successfully true the wheel. Note the following:
1. Spoke condition—Do not attempt to true a wheel with bent or damaged spokes. Doing so places an excessive amount of tension on the spoke and rim. The spoke may break and/or pull through the hole in the rim. Inspect spokes carefully and replace any that are damaged.
2. Nipple condition—When truing a wheel, the nipple should turn freely on the spoke. It is common for the spoke threads to become corroded and make turning the nipple difficult. Spray a penetrating liquid onto the nipple and allow sufficient time for it to penetrate. Use a spoke wrench and work the nipple in both directions and apply additional

10

penetrating liquid. If the spoke wrench rounds off the nipple, remove the tire from the rim and cut the spoke(s) out of the wheel.

3. Rim condition—Minor rim damage can be corrected by truing; however, trying to correct excessive runout caused by impact damage will damage the hub and rim due to over-tightened spokes. Inspect the rims for cracks, flat spots or dents. Check the spoke holes for cracks or enlargement.

Wheel Truing Preliminaries

Before checking runout and truing the wheel, note the following:

1. Make sure the wheel bearings are in good condition.
2. A small amount of runout is acceptable, do not attempt to true the wheel to a perfect zero reading. Refer to **Table 1** for runout specifications.
3. Perform a quick runout check with the wheel on the motorcycle by placing a pointer against the fork or swing arm and slowly rotating the wheel (**Figure 51**).
4. Perform major wheel truing with the tire removed and the wheel mounted in a wheel truing stand.
5. Use a spoke nipple wrench of the correct size. Using the wrong type of tool or one that is the incorrect size will round off the spoke nipples, making adjustment difficult. Quality wrenches grip the nipple on four corners to prevent damage. Tighten spokes to a minimum of 55 in.-lb. (6.2 N•m).

Wheel Truing Procedure

1. Set the wheel in a truing stand.
2A. Use a dial indicator, and check rim runout as follows:
   a. Measure the radial runout with a dial indicator positioned as shown in **Figure 52**. If radial runout exceeds the service limit specified in **Table 2**, replace the rim.
   b. Measure the lateral runout with a dial indicator positioned as shown in **Figure 52**. If lateral runout exceeds the service limit specified in **Table 2**, replace the rim.
2B. If a dial indicator is not available, check rim runout as follows:
   a. Position a pointer facing toward the rim as shown in **Figure 53**. Spin the wheel slowly and check the lateral runout.
   b. Adjust the position of the pointer and check the radial runout.

> *NOTE*
> *The number of spokes to loosen and tighten will depend on the amount of runout. As a minimum, always adjust two or three spokes in the vicinity of the rim runout. If runout affects a greater area along the rim, adjust a greater number of spokes.*

3. If lateral runout is out of specification, the rim needs to be moved relative to the centerline of the wheel (**Figure**

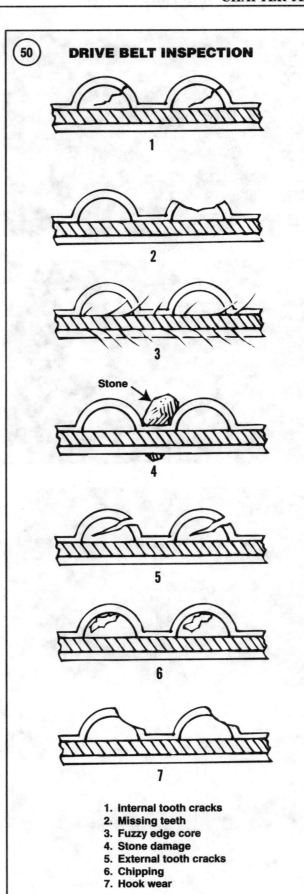

50 DRIVE BELT INSPECTION

1. **Internal tooth cracks**
2. **Missing teeth**
3. **Fuzzy edge core**
4. **Stone damage**
5. **External tooth cracks**
6. **Chipping**
7. **Hook wear**

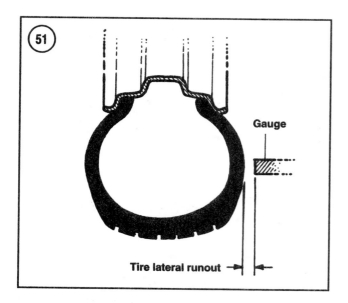

Tire lateral runout

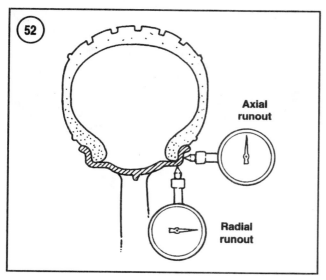

Axial runout

Radial runout

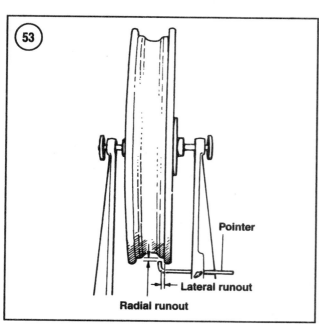

Pointer

Lateral runout

Radial runout

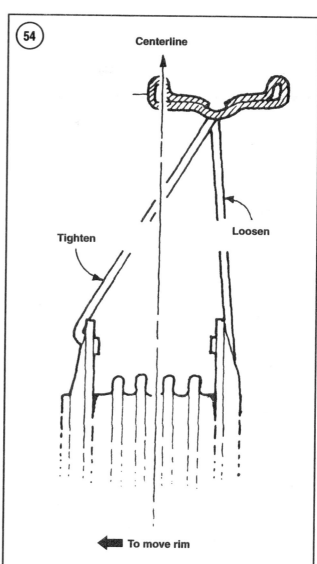

Centerline

Tighten

Loosen

To move rim

54). To move the rim to the left, for example, tighten the spoke(s) on the left of the rim and loosen the opposite spoke(s) on the right.

4. If radial runout is excessive, the hub is not centered within the rim. The rim needs to move relative the centerline of the hub (**Figure 55**). Draw the high point of the rim toward the centerline of the hub by tightening the spokes in the area of the high point and by loosening spokes on the low side. Tighten and loosen the spokes in equal amounts to prevent distortion.

5. Rotate the wheel and check runout. Continue adjusting the spokes until runout is within the specification listed in **Table 1**. Be patient and thorough, adjusting the position of the rim a little at a time.

6. After truing the wheel, seat each spoke in the hub by tapping it with a flat nose punch and hammer. Then, recheck the wheel runout. Readjust if necessary.

7. Check the ends of the spokes on the tube side of the rim. Grind off any spoke that protrudes from the nipple so it will not puncture the tube.

10

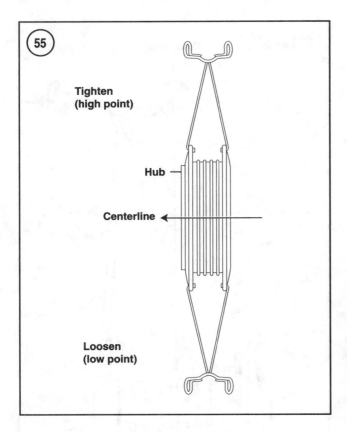

Tighten
(high point)

Hub

Centerline

Loosen
(low point)

WHEEL BALANCE

An unbalanced wheel is unsafe. Depending on the degree of unbalance and the speed of the motorcycle, a rider may experience anything from a mild vibration to a violent shimmy that may result in loss of control.

Before balancing a wheel, thoroughly clean the wheel assembly. Make sure the wheel bearings are in good condition and properly lubricated. The wheel must rotate freely. Also make sure the balance mark on the tire aligns with the valve stem. If not, break the tire loose from the rim and align it before balancing the wheel. Refer to *Tire Changing* in this chapter.

NOTE
Balance the wheels with the brake disc and/ or driven sprocket assembly attached. These components rotate with the wheel and affect the balance.

1. Remove the wheel as described in this chapter.
2. Make sure the valve stem and the valve cap are tight.
3. Mount the wheel on a stand such as the one shown in **Figure 56** so it can rotate freely.
4. Check the wheel runout as described in this chapter. Do not try to balance a wheel with excessive runout.
5. Remove any balance weights mounted on the wheel.
6. Give the wheel a spin and let it coast to a stop. Mark the tire at the highest point (12 o'clock). This is the wheel's lightest point.
7. Spin the wheel several more times. If the wheel keeps coming to rest at the same point, it is out of balance. If the

wheel stops at different points each time, the wheel is balanced.

NOTE
Adhesive test weights are available from motorcycle dealerships. These are adhesive-backed weights that can be cut to the desired length and attached directly to the rim.

8. Loosely attach a balance weight (or temporarily tape a test weight) at the upper or light side (12 o'clock) of the wheel.
9. Rotate the wheel 1/4 turn (3 o'clock). Release the wheel and observe the following:

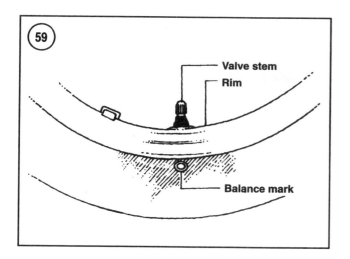

Valve stem

Rim

Balance mark

a. If the wheel does not rotate (if it stays at the 3 o'clock position), the correct balance weight was installed. The wheel is balanced.

b. If the wheel rotates and the weighted portion goes up, replace the weight with the next heavier size.

c. If the wheel rotates and the weighted portion goes down, replace the weight with the next lighter size.

d. Repeat this process until the wheel remains at rest after being rotated 1/4 turn. Rotate the wheel another 1/4 turn, another 1/4 turn, and another to see if the wheel is correctly balanced.

10. Remove the test weight and permanently install the correct weight as follows:

    a. On laced wheels, firmly crimp the balance weight (**Figure 57**) onto the spoke(s) with a pair of pliers.

    b. On cast or alloy wheels, crimp the balance weight (**Figure 58**) onto the rim.

TIRE CHANGING (LACED WHEELS)

The laced or wire wheels can easily be damaged during tire removal. Special care must be taken with tire irons to avoid scratches and gouges to the outer rim surface. Insert rim protectors or scraps of leather between the tire iron and the rim.

Removal

CAUTION
Support the wheel on two blocks of wood so the brake disc does not contact the floor.

1. Remove the wheel as described in this chapter.
2. If the tire will be reinstalled, place a balance mark on the tire opposite the valve stem location (**Figure 59**) so the tire can be reinstalled in the same position for easier balancing.
3. Remove the valve core to deflate the tire.
4. Press the entire bead on both sides of the tire away from the rim and into the center of the rim.
5. Lubricate both beads with soapy water.

NOTE
Use rim protectors between the tire irons and the rim to protect the rim from damage. Also, use only quality tire irons without sharp edges. If necessary, file the ends of the tire irons to remove rough edges.

6. Insert the tire iron under the upper bead next to the valve stem (**Figure 60**). Press the lower bead into the center of the rim and pry the upper bead over the rim with the tire iron.
7. Insert a second tire iron next to the first to hold the bead over the rim (**Figure 61**). Work around the tire, prying the bead over the rim with the first tool. Be careful not to pinch the inner tube with the tire irons.
8. When the upper bead is off the rim, remove the nut from the valve stem. Remove the valve from the hole in the rim and remove the tube from the tire (**Figure 62**).
9. Stand the wheel upright. Force the second bead into the center of the rim. Insert the tire iron between the second bead and the side of the rim that the first bead was pried over. Pry the second bead off the rim (**Figure 63**), working around the wheel with two tire irons as described in this section.
10. Inspect the rim as described in this chapter.

10

Installation

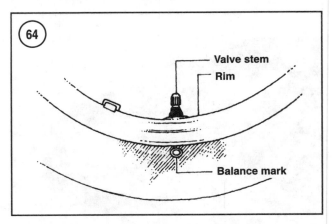

NOTE
Before installing the tire, place it in the sun or in a hot, closed car. The heat will soften the rubber and ease installation.

1. Install a *new* rubber rim band. Align the hole in the band with the valve hole in the rim.
2. Liberally sprinkle the inside of the tire with talcum powder to reduce chafing between the tire and tube.
3. Most tires have directional arrows on the sidewall. Install the tire so the arrow points in the direction of forward rotation.
4. If the tire was removed, lubricate the lower bead of the tire with soapy water and place the tire against the rim. Align the valve stem balance mark (**Figure 64**) with the valve stem hole in the rim.
5. Using your hand, push as much of the lower bead past the upper rim surface as possible. Work around the tire in both directions (**Figure 65**).
6. Install the valve core into the valve stem in the inner tube.
7. Put the tube into the tire and insert the valve stem through the hole in the rim. Inflate the tube just enough to round it out. Too much air will make tire installation difficult; too little air increases the chance of pinching the tube with the tire irons.
8. Lubricate the upper tire bead and rim with soapy water.
9. Press the upper bead into the rim opposite the valve stem. Pry the bead into the rim on both sides of this initial point with your hands and work around the rim to the valve stem. If the tire pulls up on one side, either use a tire iron or a knee to hold the tire in place. The last few inches are usually the toughest and also the place where most tubes are pinched. If possible, continue to push the tire into the rim with your hands. Re-lubricate the bead if necessary. If the tire bead pulls out from under the rim, use both of your knees to hold the tire in place. If necessary, use a tire iron (**Figure 66**) and rim protector for the last few inches.

CAUTION
*Make sure the valve stem is not cocked in the rim (**Figure 67**).*

10. Wiggle the valve stem to make sure the tube is not trapped under the bead. Set the valve squarely in its hole.

WARNING
*Seat the tire on the rim by inflating the tire to approximately 10% above the recommended inflation pressure listed in **Table 3**. Do not exceed 10%. Never stand directly over a tire*

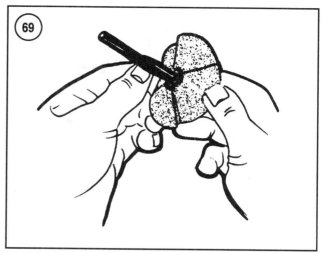

12. Bleed the tire pressure down to the recommended pressure listed in **Table 3**. Install the valve stem nut, and tighten it against the rim. Then, install the valve stem cap.

13. Balance the wheel as described in this chapter.

Inspection

1. Remove and inspect the rubber rim band. Replace the band if it is deteriorated or broken.

2. Clean the inner and outer rim surfaces of all dirt, rust, corrosion and rubber residue.

3. Inspect the valve stem hole in the rim. Remove any dirt or corrosion from the hole.

4. Inspect the rim profiles for any cracks or other damage.

5. If the tube will be reused, reinstall the valve core, inflate the tube and check it for any leaks.

6. While the tube is inflated, clean it with water.

7. When reusing the tire, carefully check it inside and outside for damage. Replace the tire if there is any damage.

8. Make sure the spoke ends do not protrude from the nipples into the center of the rim.

10

TIRE CHANGING (ALLOY WHEELS)

WARNING
Do not install an inner tube inside a tubeless tire. The tube will cause an abnormal heat buildup in the tire.

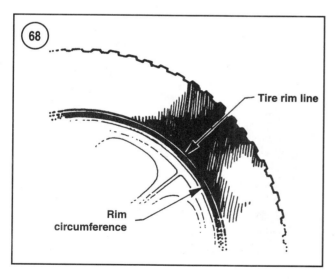

Tubeless tires have the word TUBELESS molded in the tire sidewall and the rims have TUBELESS ALLOY on them.

If the tire is punctured, remove it from the rim to inspect the inside of the tire and apply a combination plug/patch (**Figure 69**) from inside the tire. A plug applied from the outside of the tire should only be used as a temporary roadside repair.

Follow the repair kit manufacturer's instructions as to applicable repairs and any speed limitations. Replace a patched or plugged tire as soon as possible.

while inflating it. The tire could burst and cause severe injury.

11. Check the bead on both sides of the tire for an even fit around the rim, and then re-lubricate both sides of the tire. Inflate the tube to seat the tire on the rim. Check to see that both beads are fully seated and the tire rim lines (**Figure 68**) are the same distance from the rim all the way around the tire. If the beads will not seat, release the air from the tire. Lubricate the rim and beads with soapy water, and re-inflate the tube.

Removal

The wheels can easily be damaged during tire removal. Special care must be taken with tire irons to avoid scratching and gouging the outer rim surface. Protect the rim by using rim protectors or scraps of leather between the tire iron and the rim. The stock alloy wheels are designed for use with tubeless tires.

When removing a tubeless tire, be careful not to damage the tire beads, the inner liner of the tire or the wheel rim flange. Use tire levers or flat-handled tire irons with rounded ends.

> *NOTE*
> *While removing a tire, support the wheel on two blocks of wood so the brake disc does not contact the floor.*

1. Place a balance mark opposite the valve stem (**Figure 64**) on the tire sidewall so the tire can be reinstalled in the same position for easier balancing.
2. Remove the valve core to deflate the tire.

> *CAUTION*
> *Removal of tubeless tires from their rims can be very difficult because of the exceptionally tight bead/rim sealing surface. Breaking the bead seal may require the use of a bead breaker (**Figure 70**). Do not scratch the inside of the rim or damage the tire bead.*

3. Press the entire bead on both sides of the tire into the center of the rim.
4. Lubricate the beads with soapy water.

> *NOTE*
> *Use rim protectors or insert scraps of leather between the tire irons and the rim to protect the rim from damage.*

5. Insert the tire iron under the bead next to the valve stem (**Figure 71**). Force the bead on the opposite side of the tire into the center of the rim and pry the bead over the rim with the tire iron.
6. Insert a second tire iron next to the first to hold the bead over the rim (**Figure 72**). Then, work around the tire with the first tool prying the bead over the rim.
7. Set the wheel on its edge. Insert a tire tool between the second bead and the same side of the rim that the first bead was pried over (**Figure 73**). Force the bead on the opposite side from the tool into the center of the rim. Pry the second bead off the rim, working around the wheel with two tire irons as described in this section.
8. Inspect the valve stem seal. Because rubber deteriorates with age, it is advisable to replace the valve stem when replacing a tire.

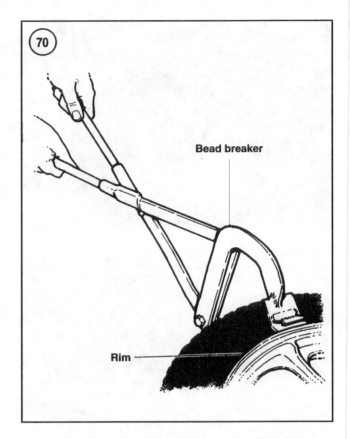

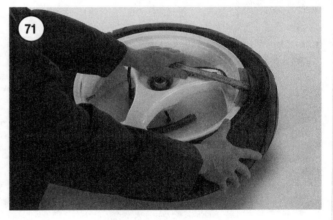

Installation

1. Carefully inspect the tire for any damage, especially inside.

2. A new tire may have balancing rubbers inside. These are not patches and should not be disturbed.

3. Manufacturers place a colored spot near the bead, indicating a lighter point on the tire. Install the tires so this balance mark (either the manufacturer's or the one made during removal) sits opposite the valve stem (**Figure 64**).

4. Most tires have directional arrows on the sidewall that indicate the direction of rotation. Install the tire so the arrow points in the direction of forward rotation.

5. Lubricate both beads of the tire with soapy water.

6. Place the backside of the tire into the center of the rim. The lower bead should go into the center of the rim and the upper bead outside. Work around the tire in both directions (**Figure 74**).

7. Starting at the side opposite the valve stem, press the upper bead into the rim (**Figure 75**). Pry the bead into the rim on both sides of the initial point with a tire tool, working around the rim to the valve (**Figure 76**).

8. Check the bead on both sides of the tire for an even fit around the rim.

> *WARNING*
> *Never exceed 40 psi (279 kPa) inflation pressure as the tire could burst causing severe injury. Never stand directly over the tire while inflating it.*

9. Place an inflatable band around the circumference of the tire. Slowly inflate the band until the tire beads are pressed against the rim. Inflate the tire enough to seat it against the rim. Deflate and remove the band.

10. After inflating the tire, check to see that the beads are fully seated and the tire rim lines are the same distance from the rim all the way around the tire (**Figure 68**). If the beards will not seat, deflate the tire, re-lubricate the rim and beads with soapy water and re-inflate the tire.

11. Inflate the tire to the required pressure. Refer to tire inflation pressure specifications listed in **Table 3**. Screw on the valve stem cap.

12. Balance the wheel assembly as described in this chapter.

TIRE REPAIRS

> *WARNING*
> *Do not install an inner tube inside a tubeless tire. The tube will cause an abnormal heat buildup in the tire.*

Tubeless tires have the word TUBELESS molded into the sidewall and the rims have SUITABLE FOR TUBELESS TIRES or equivalent stamped or cast on them.

If the tire is punctured, it must be removed from the rim to inspect the inside of the tire and to apply a combination

10

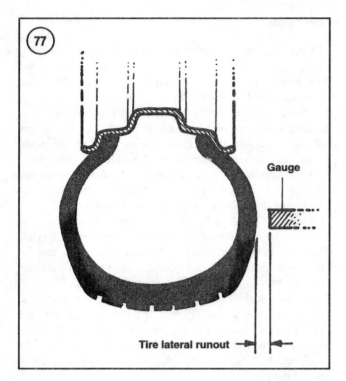

Tire lateral runout

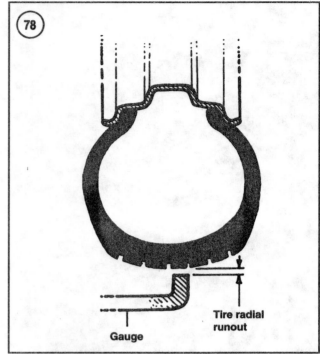

Tire radial runout

Gauge

plug/patch (**Figure 69**) from inside the tire. Never attempt to repair a tubeless motorcycle tire using a plug or cord patch applied from outside the tire.

After repairing a tubeless tire, do not exceed 50 mph (80 km/h) for the first 24 hours.

As soon as possible, replace the patched tire with a new one.

Repair

Do not rely on a plug or cord patch applied from outside the tire. Use a combination plug/patch (**Figure 69**) applied from inside the tire.

1. Remove the tire from the wheel rim as described in this chapter.

2. Inspect the rim inner flange. Smooth any scratches on the sealing surface with emery cloth. If a scratch is deeper than 0.020 in. (0.5 mm), the wheel should be replaced.

3. Inspect the tire inside and out. Replace a tire if any of the following is found:

    a. A puncture larger than 1/8 in. (3 mm) diameter.

    b. A punctured or damaged side wall.

    c. More than 2 punctures in the tire.

4. Apply the plug/patch following the patch kit manufacturer's instructions.

5. As soon as possible, replace the patched tire with a new one.

TIRE RUNOUT

Check the tires for excessive lateral and radial runout after a wheel has been mounted or if the motorcycle devel-

ops a wobble that cannot be traced to another component. Mount the wheels on their axles when making the following checks.

1. *Lateral runout*—Check the tire for excessive side-to-side play as follows:

    a. Position a fixed pointer next to the tire sidewall as shown in **Figure 77**. Position the pointer tip so it is not directly in line with the molded tire logo or any other raised surface.

    b. Rotate the tire and measure lateral runout.

    c. The lateral runout should not exceed 0.080 in. (2.03 mm). If runout is excessive, remove the tire from the wheel and recheck the wheel's lateral runout as described in this chapter. If the runout is excessive, the wheel must be trued (laced wheels) or replaced (alloy wheels). If wheel runout is correct, the tire runout is excessive and the tire must be replaced.

2. *Radial runout*—Check the tire for excessive up-and-down play as follows:

    a. Position a fixed pointer at the center bottom of the tire tread as shown in **Figure 78**.

    b. Rotate the tire and measure the amount of radial runout.

    c. The radial runout should not exceed 0.090 in. (2.29 mm). If runout is excessive, remove the tire from the wheel and recheck the wheel's radial runout as described in this chapter. If the runout is excessive, true (laced wheel) or replace the wheel. If wheel runout is correct, the tire runout is excessive and the tire must be replaced.

Table 1 LACED WHEEL OFFSET

Model/Wheel size	Offset in. (mm)
2006-2007 models	
Steel laced	
17 in.	0.620-0.640 (15.75-16.26)
19 in.	1.140-1.160 (28.96-29.46)
21 in.	1.530-1.550 (38.86-39.37)
Chrome aluminum profile laced	
17 in.	0.390-0.410 (9.91-10.41)
19 in.	0.890-0.910 (22.61-23.11)
21 in.	1.560-1.580 (39.62-40.13)
2008-2011 models	
Steel laced	
17 in.	0.615-0.645 (15.62-16.38)
19 in.	1.135-1.165 (28.83-29.59)
21 in.	1.525-1.555 (38.74-39.50)
Chrome aluminum profile laced	
17 in.	0.385-0.415 (9.78-10.54)
19 in.	0.885-0.915 (22.48-23.24)
21 in.	1.555-1.585 (39.50-40.26)

Table 2 WHEEL, TIRE AND HUB SPECIFICATIONS

Item	In.	mm
Bearing end play	0.002	0.051
Laced and cast wheels (front and rear)		
Lateral runout		
2006-2007 models	0.40	10.16
2008-2011 models	0.30	7.62
Radial runout	0.30	7.62

10

Table 3 TIRE INFLATION PRESSURE (COLD)*

	PSI	kPa
Front wheel (all models except FXDF)		
Rider only	30	207
Rider and one passenger	30	207
Front wheel (FXDF models)		
Rider only	36	248
Rider and one passenger	36	248
Rear wheel		
Rider only	36	248
Rider and passenger	40	276

*Tire pressure for OE equipment tires. Aftermarket tires may require different inflation pressure.

Table 4 WHEEL TORQUE SPECIFICATIONS

Item	ft.-lb.	in.-lb.	N•m
Brake disc bolts			
Front wheel	16-24	–	21.7-32.5
Rear wheel	30-45	–	40.7-61.0
	(continued)		

Table 4 WHEEL TORQUE SPECIFICATIONS (continued)

Item	ft.-lb.	in.-lb.	N•m
Drive belt			
Debris deflector mounting screws	–	40-60	4.5-6.8
Guard fasteners	10-15	–	13.6-20.3
Driven sprocket bolts			
2006-2007 models	55-60	–	74.6-81.3
2008-2011 models	55-65	–	74.6-88.1
Front axle nut (except FXDSE,			
FXDSE2, FXDFSE and FXDFSE2 models)			
2006-2007 models	50-55	–	67.8-74.6
2008-2011 models	60-65	–	81.3-88.1
Front axle			
FXDSE and FXDSE2 models	65-70	–	88.1-94.9
FXDFSE and FXDFSE2 models	62-67	–	84.0-90.8
Right-side lower set screws			
(FXDSE and FXDSE2 models)	11-15	–	14.9-20.4
Front axle cover set screw			
(FXDFSE and FXDFSE2 models)	–	10-12	1.1-1.4
Front fork slider cap bolts	10-14	–	13.6-19.0
Rear axle cover set screw			
FXDSE and FXDSE2 models	–	60-84	6.8-9.5
FXDFSE and FXDFSE2 models	–	20-30	2.3-3.4
Rear axle nut			
2006 models	60-65	–	81.3-88.1
2007 models	92-98	–	124.7-132.9
2008-2011 models	95-105	–	128.8-142.4
Shock absorber			
All models except FXDSE and FXDSE2			
Lower bolt	30-40	–	40.7-54.2
Upper acorn nut	30-40	–	40.7-54.2
FXDSE and FXDSE2 models			
Lower bolt	30-40	–	40.7-54.2
Upper bolt	75-85	–	101.7-115.2
Mounting stud nut	70-85	–	101.7-115.2
Spoke nipples (all models)–minimum	–	55	6.2

CHAPTER ELEVEN

FRONT SUSPENSION AND STEERING

This chapter covers the handlebar, steering head and front fork assemblies.

Refer to **Table 1** and **Table 2** at the end of this chapter for specifications.

HANDLEBAR (FXD, FXDC, FXDL, AND FXDB MODELS)

Removal/Installation

Refer to **Figure 1** and **Figure 2**.

1. Disconnect the negative battery cable as described in Chapter Nine.

2. Support the motorcycle with the front wheel off the ground. Refer to *Motorcycle Stands* in Chapter Ten.

NOTE
Cover the fuel tank to protect it from accidental scratches or dents when removing the handlebar.

NOTE
Before removing the handlebar, make a drawing of the clutch and throttle cable routing from the handlebar and through the frame.

3. On the right side of the handlebar, perform the following:
   a. Unscrew and remove the mirror (A, **Figure 3**).

   b. Remove the screws securing the brake master cylinder (B, **Figure 3**). Do not disconnect the hydraulic brake line.

   c. Secure the brake master cylinder to the frame with a bungee cord or wire. Make sure the reservoir remains upright.

   d. Remove the screws securing the right side switch assembly (C, **Figure 3**) together and separate the housing halves. Remove the assembly from the handlebar.

   e. Slide the throttle housing assembly (D, **Figure 3**) off the handlebar.

4. On the left side of the handlebar, perform the following:
   a. Unscrew and remove the mirror (A, **Figure 4**).

   b. Remove the screws securing the left side switch assembly (B, **Figure 4**) together and separate the housing halves. Remove the assembly from the handlebar.

   c. Remove the clutch lever clamp (C, **Figure 4**) mounting bolts and washers and separate the clamp halves. Remove the assembly from the handlebar.

5. Disconnect or remove any wiring harness clamps at the handlebar.

6A. On FXD and FXDC models, perform the following:
   a. Remove the two screws securing the speedometer bracket and cover, and then remove both components.

   b. On FXD models, remove the bolts securing the upper clamp and speedometer assembly. Secure the

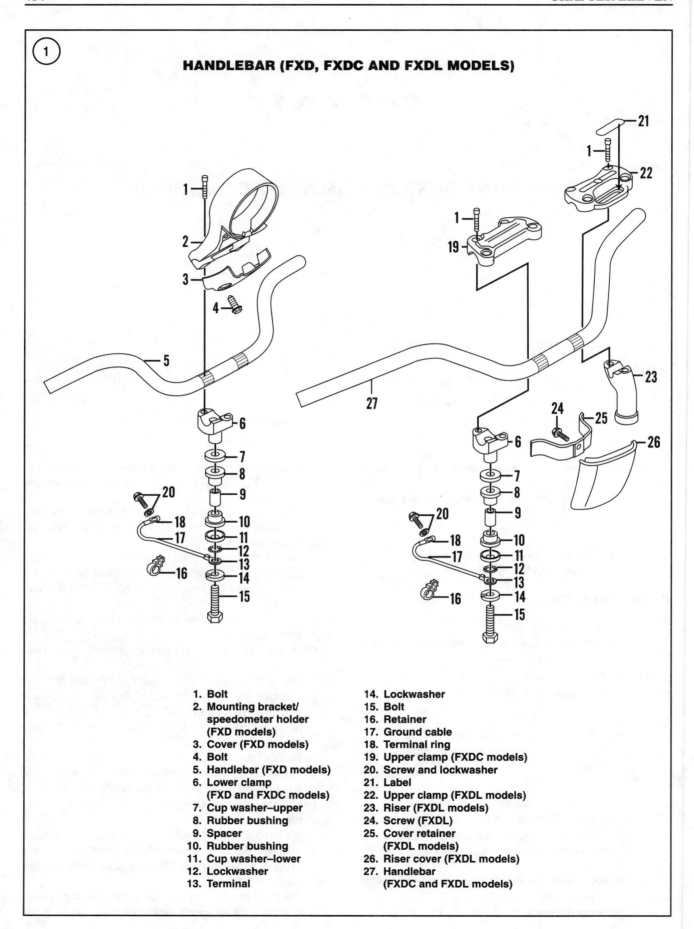

HANDLEBAR (FXD, FXDC AND FXDL MODELS)

1. Bolt
2. Mounting bracket/
   speedometer holder
   (FXD models)
3. Cover (FXD models)
4. Bolt
5. Handlebar (FXD models)
6. Lower clamp
   (FXD and FXDC models)
7. Cup washer–upper
8. Rubber bushing
9. Spacer
10. Rubber bushing
11. Cup washer–lower
12. Lockwasher
13. Terminal
14. Lockwasher
15. Bolt
16. Retainer
17. Ground cable
18. Terminal ring
19. Upper clamp (FXDC models)
20. Screw and lockwasher
21. Label
22. Upper clamp (FXDL models)
23. Riser (FXDL models)
24. Screw (FXDL)
25. Cover retainer
    (FXDL models)
26. Riser cover (FXDL models)
27. Handlebar
    (FXDC and FXDL models)

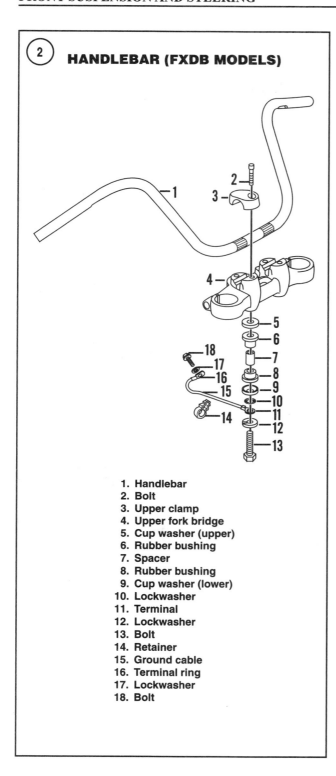

② HANDLEBAR (FXDB MODELS)

1. Handlebar
2. Bolt
3. Upper clamp
4. Upper fork bridge
5. Cup washer (upper)
6. Rubber bushing
7. Spacer
8. Rubber bushing
9. Cup washer (lower)
10. Lockwasher
11. Terminal
12. Lockwasher
13. Bolt
14. Retainer
15. Ground cable
16. Terminal ring
17. Lockwasher
18. Bolt

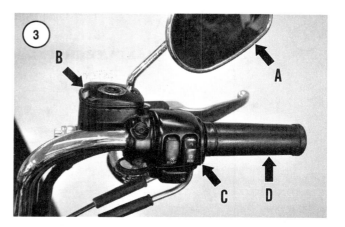

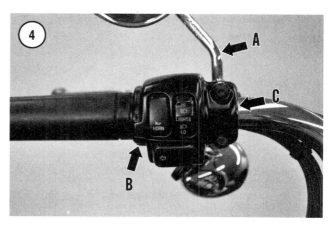

11

speedometer and wiring harness to the upper fork bridge or frame.

   c. On FXDC models, hold onto the handlebar, and remove the bolts securing the upper clamp.

   d. Remove the upper clamp and the handlebar from the lower clamps.

6B. On FXDB models, perform the following:

   a. Hold onto the handlebar and remove the bolts (**Figure 5**) securing the upper clamps.

   b. Remove the upper clamps and the handlebar from the lower clamps.

6C. On FXDL models, perform the following:

   a. Remove the screw securing the riser cover, and then remove the cover and cover retainer.

   b. Hold onto the handlebar and remove the bolts securing the upper clamp.

   c. Remove the upper clamp and handlebar.

7. Install the handlebar by reversing the removal steps. Note the following:

   a. After installing the handlebar, reposition the handlebar while sitting on the motorcycle.

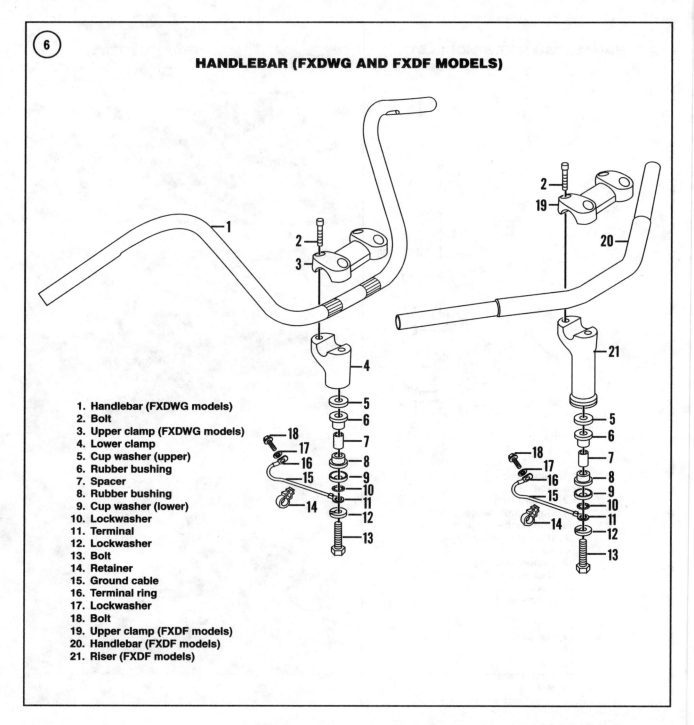

⑥

HANDLEBAR (FXDWG AND FXDF MODELS)

1. Handlebar (FXDWG models)
2. Bolt
3. Upper clamp (FXDWG models)
4. Lower clamp
5. Cup washer (upper)
6. Rubber bushing
7. Spacer
8. Rubber bushing
9. Cup washer (lower)
10. Lockwasher
11. Terminal
12. Lockwasher
13. Bolt
14. Retainer
15. Ground cable
16. Terminal ring
17. Lockwasher
18. Bolt
19. Upper clamp (FXDF models)
20. Handlebar (FXDF models)
21. Riser (FXDF models)

b. Tighten the front handlebar clamp bolts first, and then the rear. Tighten the bolts to 12-16 ft.-lb. (16.3-21.7 N•m). There should be a slight gab between the clamps at the front after tightening the bolts.

c. On FXDL models, install the riser cover and retainer and tighten the screw to 50-60 in.-lb. (5.6-6.8 N•m).

d. Adjust both mirrors.

e. Adjust the throttle and idle cables as described in Chapter Three.

f. Install the front brake master cylinder as described in Chapter Thirteen.

HANDLEBAR (FXDWG, FXDF, 2008 FXDSE2, 2009 FXDFSE AND 2010 FXDFSE2 MODELS)

Removal/Installation

Refer to **Figure 6** and **Figure 7**.

1. Disconnect the negative battery cable as described in Chapter Nine.

2. Support the motorcycle with the front wheel off the ground. Refer to *Motorcycle Stands* in Chapter Ten.

3. Remove the fuel tank as described in Chapter Eight.

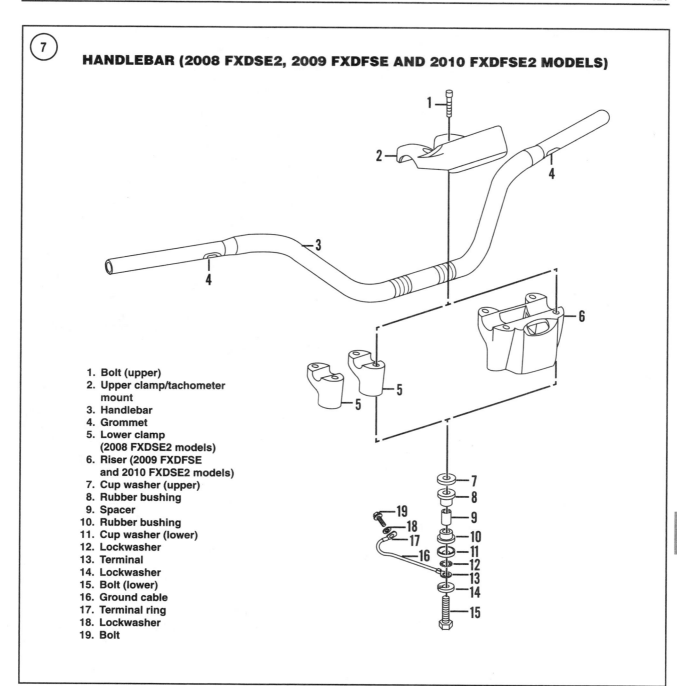

⑦ HANDLEBAR (2008 FXDSE2, 2009 FXDFSE AND 2010 FXDFSE2 MODELS)

1. Bolt (upper)
2. Upper clamp/tachometer mount
3. Handlebar
4. Grommet
5. Lower clamp (2008 FXDSE2 models)
6. Riser (2009 FXDFSE and 2010 FXDSE2 models)
7. Cup washer (upper)
8. Rubber bushing
9. Spacer
10. Rubber bushing
11. Cup washer (lower)
12. Lockwasher
13. Terminal
14. Lockwasher
15. Bolt (lower)
16. Ground cable
17. Terminal ring
18. Lockwasher
19. Bolt

11

4. Unsnap and remove the harness shield (A, **Figure 8**) to gain access to the connectors within the frame backbone.

5. Follow the wiring harness (A, **Figure 9**) down the handlebar and through the frame plug (B).

6. Carefully pull the wiring harness (**Figure 10**) down from within the frame backbone to gain access to the connectors.

7. Label and identify the connectors and their wire colors to assist in reconnecting. Refer to the wiring diagrams located on the CD inserted into the back cover of the manual.

8. Disconnect the following connectors:

   a. Right-side handlebar switch connector.

b. Left-side handlebar switch connector.

c. Front turn signal connectors.

9. Attach a length of heavy string to the disconnected terminals for each side. Wrap the connectors and string with electrical tape to assist in withdrawing the terminal connectors and wiring. Attach the loose end of the string to the frame.

10. Carefully withdraw each wiring harness and the string from the plug (B, **Figure 9**) on each side of the frame.

11. On 2009 FXDFSE and 2010 FXDFSE2 models, pull the harness and string up through the center opening in the riser.

12. Disconnect the string from each wiring harness. Leave the string in place within the frame to assist in pulling each harness back through the frame plug areas.

NOTE
Before removing the handlebar, make a drawing of the clutch and throttle cable routing from the handlebar and through the frame.

13. On the right side of the handlebar, perform the following:

a. Unscrew and remove the mirror (A, **Figure 3**).

b. Remove the screws securing the brake master cylinder (B, **Figure 3**). Do not disconnect the hydraulic brake line.

c. Secure the brake master cylinder to the frame with a bungee cord or wire. Make sure the reservoir remains upright.

d. Remove the screws securing the right side switch assembly (C, **Figure 3**) together and separate the housing halves.

e. Slide the throttle housing assembly (D, **Figure 3**) off the handlebar.

14. On the left side of the handlebar, perform the following:

a. Unscrew and remove the mirror (A, **Figure 4**).

b. Remove the screws securing the left side switch assembly (B, **Figure 4**) together and separate the housing halves.

c. On Screamin' Eagle and CVO models, remove the clutch master cylinder as described in Chapter Six. Secure the master cylinder to the frame with a bungee cord or wire. Make sure the reservoir remains upright.

d. On models other than Screamin' Eagle and CVO, remove the clutch lever clamp (C, **Figure 4**) mounting bolts and washers, and then separate the clamp halves. Remove the assembly from the handlebar.

15A. On FXDWG and FXDF models, perform the following:

a. Hold onto the handlebar and remove the bolts securing the upper clamp.

b. Remove the upper clamp and handlebar.

15B. On 2008 FXDSE2, 2009 FXDFSE and 2010 FXDFSE2 models, perform the following:

a. Remove the tachometer as described in Chapter Nine.

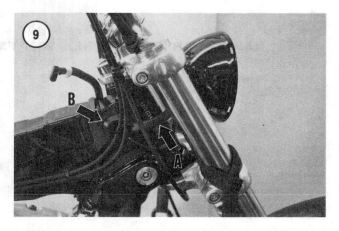

b. Hold onto the handlebar and remove the bolts securing the upper clamp/tachometer mount.

c. Remove the upper clamp/tachometer mount.

d. On FXDFSE models, carefully pull the wiring harness and string up and out of the opening in the center of the riser.

e. Disconnect the string from the wiring harness. Leave the string attached to the frame.

f. Remove the handlebar.

16. On 2008 FXDSE2, 2009 FXDFSE and 2010 FXDFSE2 models, take handlebar assembly to a workbench for further disassembly, if necessary.

17. Install the handlebar by reversing the removal steps. Note the following:

a. After installing the handlebar, reposition the handlebar while sitting on the motorcycle.

b. Tighten the front handlebar clamp bolts first, and then the rear bolts. Tighten the bolts to 12-16 ft.-lb. (16.3-21.7 N•m). There should be an even gap between the clamps after tightening the bolts.

c. Adjust both mirrors.

d. Adjust the throttle and idle cables as described in Chapter Three.

e. Insert the rear (B, **Figure 8**) of the harness shield (A) into the frame back backbone, and snap it into place.

f. Install the front brake master cylinder as described in Chapter Thirteen.

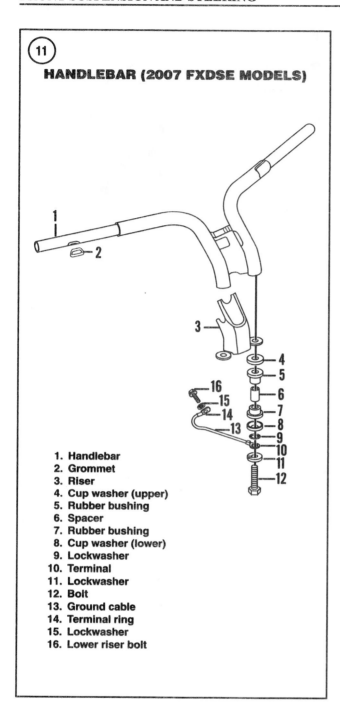

(11)

HANDLEBAR (2007 FXDSE MODELS)

1. Handlebar
2. Grommet
3. Riser
4. Cup washer (upper)
5. Rubber bushing
6. Spacer
7. Rubber bushing
8. Cup washer (lower)
9. Lockwasher
10. Terminal
11. Lockwasher
12. Bolt
13. Ground cable
14. Terminal ring
15. Lockwasher
16. Lower riser bolt

g. On Screamin' Eagle and CVO models, install the clutch master cylinder as described in Chapter Six.

HANDLEBAR (2007 FXDSE MODELS)

Removal/Installation

Refer to **Figure 11**.

1. Disconnect the negative battery cable as described in Chapter Nine.
2. Support the motorcycle with the front wheel off the ground. Refer to *Motorcycle Stands* in Chapter Ten.
3. Remove the fuel tank as described in Chapter Eight.

4. Unsnap and remove the harness shield (A, **Figure 8**) to gain access to the connectors within the frame backbone.
5. Follow the wiring harness (A, **Figure 9**) down the handlebar and through the frame plug (B).
6. Carefully pull the wiring harness (**Figure 10**) down from within the frame backbone to gain access to the connectors.
7. Label and identify the connectors and their wire colors to assist in reconnecting.
8. Disconnect the following numbered connectors:
   a. Right-side handlebar switch connector.
   b. Left-side handlebar switch connector.
   c. Front turn signal multi-lock connectors.
9. Attach a length of heavy string to the disconnected terminals for each side. Wrap the connectors and string with electrical tape to assist in withdrawing the terminal connectors and wiring. Attach the loose end of the string to the frame.
10. Carefully withdraw each wiring harness and the string from the frame plug area (B, **Figure 9**) on each side.
11. Disconnect the string from each wiring harness. Leave the string in place within the frame to assist in pulling each harness back through the frame plug areas.

NOTE
Before removing the handlebar, make a drawing of the throttle cable routing from the handlebar and through the frame.

12. On the right side of the handlebar, perform the following:
   a. Unscrew and remove the mirror (A, **Figure 3**).
   b. Remove the screws securing the brake master cylinder (B, **Figure 3**). Do not disconnect the hydraulic brake line.
   c. Secure the brake master cylinder to the frame with a bungee cord or wire. Make sure the reservoir remains upright.
   d. Remove the screws securing the right side switch assembly (C, **Figure 3**) together and separate the housing halves.
   e. Slide the throttle housing assembly (D, **Figure 3**) off the handlebar.
13. On the left side of the handlebar, perform the following:
   a. Unscrew and remove the mirror (A, **Figure 4**).
   b. Remove the screws securing the left side switch assembly (B, **Figure 4**) together and separate the housing halves.
   c. Remove the clutch master cylinder as described in Chapter Six. Secure the master cylinder to the frame with a bungee cord or wire. Make sure the reservoir remains upright.
14. Remove the speedometer and tachometer assembly as described in Chapter Nine.
15. Have an assistant hold onto the handlebar.
16. Loosen both handlebar riser mounting bolts located under the upper fork bridge.

11

17. Remove the two mounting bolts, lockwashers, cup washers, ground cable, bushings and spacers from the handlebar.

18. Remove the handlebar and riser from the upper fork bridge.

19. Take handlebar assembly to the workbench for further disassembly, if necessary.

20. Install the handlebar by reversing the removal steps. Note the following:

   a. Install the riser onto the handlebar, and install the assembly onto the upper fork bridge.

   b. Refer to **Figure 11** for the correct component location on the mounting bolt. Do not forget the ground strap on the left side bolt.

   c. Install the mounting bolts with the related components in place through the upper fork bridge, and tighten securely.

   d. After installing the handlebar, reposition the handlebar while sitting on the motorcycle.

   e. Apply Loctite 271 (red) threadlock, or an equivalent, to the bolt threads.

   f. Tighten the lower riser bolts to 35-40 ft.-lb. (47.5-54.2 N•m).

   g. Adjust both mirrors.

   h. Adjust the throttle and idle cables as described in Chapter Three.

   i. Insert the rear (B, **Figure 8**) of the harness shield (A) into the frame back backbone, and snap it into place.

   j. Install the front brake master cylinder as described in Chapter Thirteen.

   k. Install the clutch master cylinder as described in Chapter Six.

HANDLEBAR WIRING (2007 FXDSE, 2008 FXDSE2, 2009 FXDFSE AND 2010 FXDFSE2 MODELS)

The right and left hand handlebar switch wiring harnesses are routed within the handlebar. Extra care must be taken during the removal and installation to avoid scraping off the wiring insulation. This procedure is only necessary if the handlebar and/or switches are going to be replaced.

Removal

The wiring harnesses for the right and left hand handlebar switches are routed within the handlebar. Extra care must be taken during the removal and installation to avoid scraping off the wiring insulation.

1. Remove the handlebar assembly as described in this chapter.

2. Remove the wire leads from the connector sockets as described in Chapter Nine. Remove the connectors.

3. Remove the screws and separate the right and/or left side handlebar switch assemblies.

4. Attach a 3 ft. (91.4 cm) length of fish wire to the end of each wiring harness assembly.

5. Bundle one of the combined wiring harness/fish wire assemblies together and wrap with several layers of electrical tape to prevent damage to the terminal connectors as the wiring is pulled out through the handlebar. Do not make the bundle too fat, which would make it difficult to withdraw the wiring harness through the handle bar center opening.

6. Apply liquid glass cleaner to each bundle to ease the removal of the wiring assemblies from the handlebar.

CAUTION
The electrical wire(s) must be replaced if any insulation is scraped off during removal and installation.

NOTE
Do not completely pull the loose end of the fish wire out of the handlebar as it will be used to pull the new wiring harness back through the handlebar.

7. From the switch end of the harness, slowly and carefully pull one of the combined wiring harness/fish wire assemblies out from the handlebar. Guide the harness as it passes through the handlebar center opening and out the oval hole near the end of the handlebar. Avoid scraping off any insulation.

8. Remove the electrical tape and untie the fish wire from the wiring harness. Leave the fish wire in place within the handlebar as it will be used during installation.

9. Repeat for the remaining wiring harness, if necessary.

10. Repair or replace any defective switch or wiring sockets as necessary as described in Chapter Nine.

Installation

1. Make sure the rubber grommets are in place in the oval hole near each end of the handlebar.

2. Tie the end of the fish wire to one end of the wiring harness the same way it was secured during removal.

3. Apply liquid glass cleaner to the bundle of wiring to ease the installation of the wiring harness into the handlebar.

CAUTION
If there is any resistance in pulling the wiring harness assembly back into the handlebar, stop and solve the problem immediately. Do not damage any portion of the assembly.

4. Slowly pull the combined fish wire/wiring harness assembly into the oval hole near the switch end of the handlebar.

5. Continue to carefully pull the wiring harness until it is pulled through the center opening in the handlebar. Remove the electrical tape and fish wire from the wiring harness.

6. Connect the wire leads to the connector sockets as described in Chapter Nine.

7. Repeat for the remaining wiring harness assembly, if necessary.

8. Install the right and left side handlebar switch assemblies as described in Chapter Nine.

9. Install the handlebar assembly as described in this chapter.

HANDLEBAR INSPECTION

1. Check the knurled rings on the handlebar for galling and bits of aluminum. Clean the knurled section with a wire brush.

2. Check the handlebar for cracks, bends or other damage. Replace the handlebar if necessary. Do not attempt to repair it.

3. Thoroughly clean the clamp halves of all residue.

LOWER CLAMP RUBBER BUSHING REPLACEMENT

Removal

1. Turn the front fork completely to the right and loosen the bolt securing the left side lower clamp, or riser.

2. Turn the front fork completely to the left and loosen the bolt securing the right side lower clamp, or riser.

3. Remove the handlebar assembly as described in this chapter.

4. Secure the lower clamp to prevent rotation and loosen the bolts.

5A. On the right side, remove the bolt, lockwasher, ground strap, lockwasher from the lower surface of the upper fork bridge.

5B. On the left side, remove the bolt, and lockwasher from the lower surface of the upper fork bridge.

6. Withdraw the lower cup washer and rubber bushing from the lower surface of the upper fork bridge.

7. Remove the upper cup washer, rubber bushing and spacer from upper surface of the upper fork bridge.

8. Repeat the process for the remaining bolt assembly.

Installation

1. Install *new* rubber bushings onto the upper and lower surface of the upper fork bridge. Push them in until they are seated.

2. Install the spacer into the rubber bushings until they are flush with both rubber bushings.

3. Position the cup washer with the concave side going on last and install onto the rubber bushing. Push them in until they are seated.

4A. On the right side, install the lockwasher, ground strap, and lockwasher onto the bolt.

4B. On the left side, install the lockwasher onto the bolt.

5. Apply Loctite 271 (red) threadlock, or an equivalent, to the bolt threads.

6. Correctly position the lower clamp, or riser, onto the upper fork bridge.

7. Insert the bolt up through the upper fork bridge and thread it into lower clamp, or riser.

8. Repeat for the remaining clamp assembly.

9. Temporarily install the handlebar onto the lower clamps to align them correctly.

10. Secure the lower clamp to prevent rotation and tighten the bolts.

11. Turn the front fork completely to the right and tighten the left side lower clamp bolt to 30-40 ft.-lb. (41-54 N•m).

12. Turn the front fork completely to the left and tighten the right side lower clamp bolt to 30-40 ft.-lb. (41-54 N•m).

13. Install the handlebar as described in this chapter.

FRONT FORK (ALL MODELS EXCEPT 2007 FXDSE AND 2008 FXDSE2)

Before assuming that a fork is malfunctioning internally, drain the front fork oil and refill with the proper type and quantity fork oil as described in Chapter Three. If there is still a problem, such as poor damping, a tendency to bottom or top out or oil seal leaks, follow the service procedures in this section.

To simplify fork service and to prevent the mixing of parts, remove, service and install the fork legs individually.

Removal (Not For Service)

1. Support the motorcycle with the front wheel off the ground. Refer to *Motorcycle Stands* in Chapter Ten.

2. Remove the front wheel as described in Chapter Ten.

3. Remove the front fender as described in Chapter Fourteen.

4. If both fork legs are going to be removed, mark them with an R (right side) and L (left side) so they will be reinstalled on the correct side.

5. Loosen the upper (A, **Figure 12**) and lower (B) fork bracket pinch bolts.

6. Carefully slide the fork leg out of the upper and lower fork brackets. It may be necessary to rotate the fork leg slightly while pulling it down and out. Wrap the assembly in a bath towel or blanket to protect the surface from damage.

7. Repeat the procedure to remove the remaining fork leg, if necessary.

Installation (Not Serviced)

1. Install a fork leg through the lower fork bracket and through the top fork bracket.

2. Push it up until the fork leg protrudes 0.45-0.50 in. (11.4-12.7 mm) above the top surface of the upper fork bracket (**Figure 13**).

3. Tighten the upper and lower pinch bolts to 18-20 ft.-lb. (24.4-27.1 N•m).

4. Install the front fender as described in Chapter Fourteen.

5. Install the front wheel as described in Chapter Ten.

6. Apply the front brake and pump the front forks several times to seat the forks and front wheel.

Removal (For Service)

1. Support the motorcycle with the front wheel off the ground. Refer to *Motorcycle Stands* in Chapter Ten.

2. Remove the front wheel as described in Chapter Ten.

3. Remove the front fender as described in Chapter Fourteen.

4. If both fork legs are going to be removed, mark them with an R (right side) and L (left side) so they will be reinstalled on the correct side.

5. Loosen the upper (A, **Figure 12**) fork bracket pinch bolt.

6. Loosen, but *do not* remove, the fork cap bolt (**Figure 14**).

7. Loosen the lower (B, **Figure 12**) bracket pinch bolt.

8. Slide the fork leg part way down and retighten the lower bracket pinch bolt.

9. Place a drain pan under the fork slider to catch the fork oil.

10. Use a 12-mm Allen wrench and impact driver and loosen the damper rod Allen bolt at the base of the slider.

11. Remove the Allen bolt and drain the fork oil. Pump the slider several times to expel most of the fork oil. Reinstall the Allen bolt to keep residual oil in the fork.

12. Insert a small, flat-tipped screwdriver under the dust seal cover and carefully pry it off the slider. Move it up onto the fork tube.

> *NOTE*
> *It may be necessary to slightly heat the area on the slider around the oil seal prior to removal. Use a rag soaked in hot water; do not apply a flame directly to the fork slider.*

13. Move the dust seal off the slider and move it up the fork tube.

14. Remove the retaining ring from the fork slider.

15. Lower the fork slider on the fork tube.

16. There is an interference fit between the bushing in the fork slider and the bushing on the fork tube. In order to remove the fork tube from the slider, pull hard on the fork tube using quick in-and-out strokes (**Figure 15**). This will withdraw the bushing and the oil seal from the slider.

17. Remove the slider from the fork tube. If still in place, remove the oil lock piece from the damper rod.

18. Loosen the lower pinch bolt, and slide the fork tube out of the lower fork bracket.

19. Remove the fork leg and take it to the workbench for service.

20. Repeat the procedure to remove the remaining fork.

21. Disassemble the fork leg as described in this section.

Installation (Serviced)

1. Assemble the fork leg as described in this section.

2. Install a fork leg through the lower fork bracket and through the top fork bracket.

3. Push the fork leg up until it protrudes 0.450-0.500 in. (11.4-12.7 mm) above the top surface of the upper fork bracket (**Figure 13**).

4. Tighten the upper (A, **Figure 12**) and lower (B) pinch bolts to 18-20 ft.-lb. (24.4-27.1 N•m).

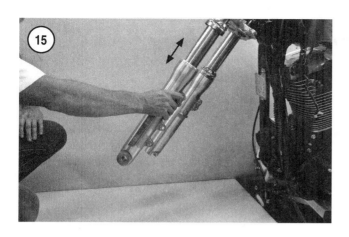

5. Tighten the 12-mm Allen bolt to 106-159 in.-lb. (11.9-18.0 N•m).

6. Install the front fender as described in Chapter Fourteen.

7. Install the front wheel as described in Chapter Ten.

8. Apply the front brake and pump the front forks several times to seat the forks and front wheel.

Disassembly

Refer to **Figure 16**.

1. Clamp the front fork slider's axle boss in a vise with soft jaws. Do not clamp the slider in a vise at any point above the fork axle boss.

WARNING
Be careful when removing the top cap, or top plug, as the spring is under pressure. Protect your eyes and face accordingly.

2. With the fork leg held vertical, remove the fork top cap from the fork tube.

3. Remove the spring from the fork tube.

4. Remove the fork leg from the vise and pour the oil into a drain pan. Pump the fork several times by hand to expel most of the remaining oil.

5. If still in place, insert a small, flat-tipped screwdriver under the dust cover and carefully pry the dust cover out of the slider and remove it.

6. Remove the dust seal (**Figure 17**).

7. Pry the retaining ring (**Figure 18**) out of the groove in the slider and remove it.

8. Remove the Allen bolt (**Figure 19**) and washer at the bottom of the slider.

9. Withdraw the fork tube from the slider.

NOTE
Do not remove the fork tube bushing unless it is going to be replaced. Inspect it as described in this chapter.

10. Remove the oil lock piece (A, **Figure 20**) from the damper rod (B).

11. Remove the damper rod and rebound spring (**Figure 21**) from the fork tube.

Assembly

1. Coat all parts with Harley-Davidson Type E, or an equivalent, fork oil before assembly.

2. Install the rebound spring (**Figure 21**) onto the damper rod and slide the damper rod into the fork tube until it extends out the end of the fork tube.

3. Install the oil lock piece (A, **Figure 20**) onto the end of the damper rod (B).

4. Temporarily install the fork spring (A, **Figure 22**) into the fork tube so that the tapered side of the spring faces down toward the damper rod.

5. Install the fork top cap (B, **Figure 22**), screw it into place to hold the damper rod in place.

6. Push the fork slider and damper rod through the opening in the bottom of the fork tube.

7. Make sure the oil lock piece is mounted on the end of the damper rod. Install the fork tube into the slider (**Figure 23**) until it bottoms. Insert a Phillips screwdriver through the opening in the base of the slider and guide the oil lock piece into position in the slider. Remove the screwdriver.

8. Install a *new* washer onto the damper rod Allen bolt.

9. Apply Loctite 243 (blue) threadlock, or an equivalent, to the damper rod Allen bolt threads prior to installation. Insert the Allen bolt (**Figure 19**) through the lower end of the slider and thread it into the damper rod. Tighten the bolt securely, but do not tighten to specification at this time. Final torque will be applied after the fork is installed.

NOTE
To protect the oil and dust seal lips, place a thin plastic bag on top of the fork tube. Before installing the seals in the following steps, lightly coat the bag and the seal lips with fork oil.

10. Slide the fork slider bushing (A, **Figure 24**), oil seal spacer (B) and oil seal (C [with the letters facing up]) down into the fork tube receptacle.

NOTE
A 39-mm fork seal driver (Jims part No. 2046), or an equivalent, is required to install the fork tube bushing and seal into the fork tube. Another method is to use a piece of pipe or metal collar with correct dimensions to slide over the fork tube and seat against the seal. When selecting or fabricating a driver tool, it must have sufficient weight to drive the bushing and oil seal into the fork tube.

11. Slide the fork seal driver down the fork tube and seat it against the seal (**Figure 25**).

12. Operate the driver and drive the fork slider bushing and new seal into the fork tube. Continue until the retain-

11

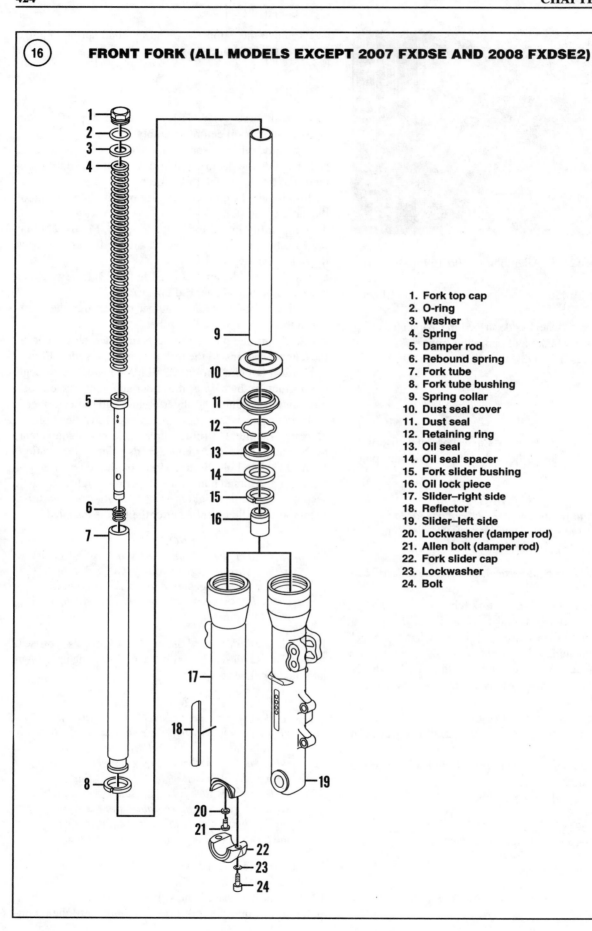

16 **FRONT FORK (ALL MODELS EXCEPT 2007 FXDSE AND 2008 FXDSE2)**

1. Fork top cap
2. O-ring
3. Washer
4. Spring
5. Damper rod
6. Rebound spring
7. Fork tube
8. Fork tube bushing
9. Spring collar
10. Dust seal cover
11. Dust seal
12. Retaining ring
13. Oil seal
14. Oil seal spacer
15. Fork slider bushing
16. Oil lock piece
17. Slider–right side
18. Reflector
19. Slider–left side
20. Lockwasher (damper rod)
21. Allen bolt (damper rod)
22. Fork slider cap
23. Lockwasher
24. Bolt

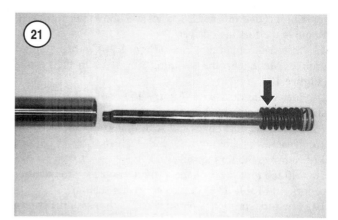

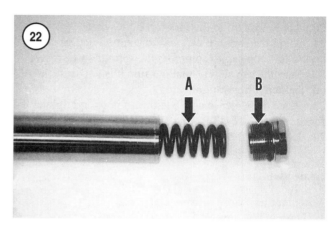

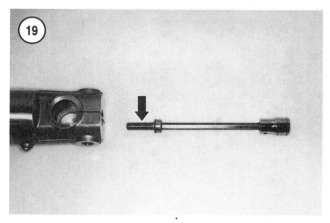

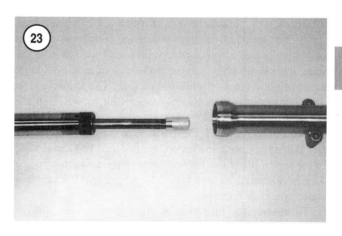

11

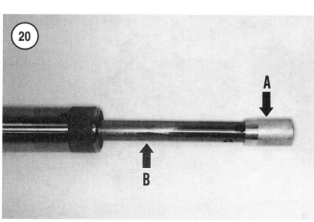

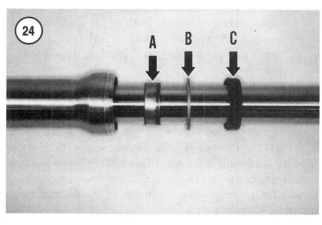

ing ring groove in the tube is visible above the fork seal. Remove the fork seal driver.

13. Install the retaining ring (**Figure 26**) into the slider groove. Make sure the retaining ring seats in the groove (**Figure 18**).

14. Install the dust seal (**Figure 17**) and seat it into the slider. Then, install the dust seal cover.

15. Install the dust cover and seat it into the slider.

16. Unscrew and remove the fork top cap.

17. Remove the fork spring.

18. Fill the fork leg with the correct viscosity and quantity of fork oil (**Table 1**) as described in this section.

19. The fork spring is tapered at one end. Install the spring (A, **Figure 22**) with the tapered end facing down toward the damper rod.

20. Apply fork oil to the fork top cap O-ring.

21. Align the fork top cap with the spring and push down on the fork top cap to compress the spring.

22. Start the cap slowly, making sure it is not cross threaded. Tighten it finger-tight.

23. Place the slider in a vise with soft jaws and tighten the fork top cap to 16-43 ft.-lb. (21.7-58.3 N•m).

24. Install the fork leg as described in this section.

Inspection

Replace any worn or damaged parts.

1. Thoroughly clean all parts in solvent and dry them. Check the fork tube for signs of wear or scratches.

2. Check the fork tube (A, **Figure 27**) for bending, nicks, rust or other damage. Place the fork tube on a set of V-blocks and check runout with a dial indicator. If the special tools are not available, roll the fork tube on a large piece of plate glass or other flat surface. The manufacturer does not provide service specifications for runout. Replace the fork tube if it is not straight.

3. Check the slider (B, **Figure 27**) for dents or other exterior damage. Check the retaining ring groove (**Figure 28**) in the top of the slider for cracks or other damage.

4. Check the slider and fork tube bushings for excessive wear, cracks or damage.

5. To remove the fork tube bushing, perform the following:

   a. Expand the bushing slit (**Figure 29**) with a screwdriver, and then slide the bushing off the fork tube.

   b. Coat the new bushing with clean fork oil.

   c. Install the new bushing by expanding the slit with a screwdriver.

   d. Seat the new bushing into the fork tube groove.

6. Check the damper rod piston rings (**Figure 30**) for excessive wear, cracks or other damage. If necessary, replace both rings as a set.

7. Check the damper rod for straightness with a set of V-blocks and a dial indicator (**Figure 31**) or by rolling it on a piece of plate glass. The manufacturer does not provide a service limit specification for runout. If the damper rod is not straight, replace it.

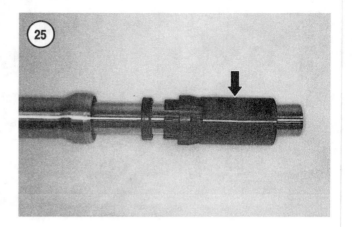

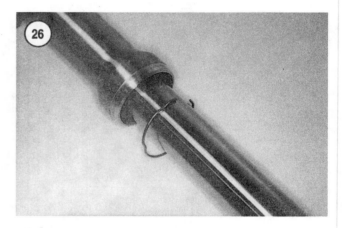

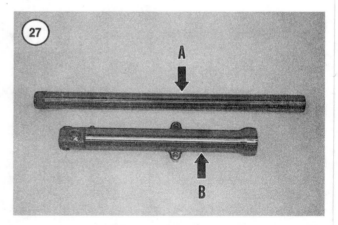

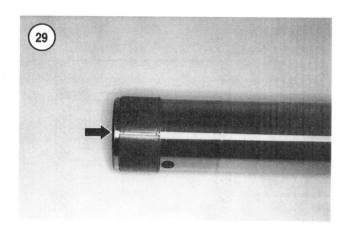

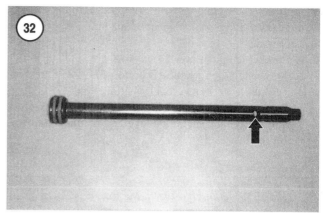

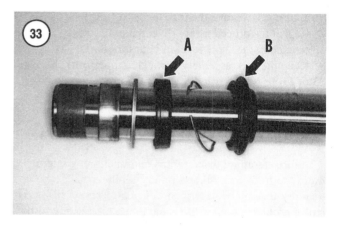

10. Check the damper rod rebound spring and the fork spring for wear or damage. The manufacturer does not provide a service limit specification for spring free length.

11. Replace the oil seals (A, **Figure 33**) whenever they are removed. Always replace both oil seals as a set.

12. Inspect the dust seals (B, **Figure 33**) or dust covers, for cracks, deterioration or other damage. A damaged dust seal, or dust cover, will allow dirt to pass through and damage the oil seal.

13. Replace the fork top cap O-ring if leaking or if wear or damage is apparent.

Front Fork Oil Change and Adjustment

This section describes steps on filling the fork with oil, setting the oil level and completing fork assembly.

1. Perform Steps 1-17 of *Front Fork Assembly* (this section).

2. Secure the fork leg upright in a vise with soft jaws and fully compress the fork leg.

3. Fill the fork assembly with approximately 11 oz. (325 ml) of Harley-Davidson Type E fork oil, or an equivalent.

4. Hold the slider with one hand and slowly move the fork tube up and down. Repeat until the fork tube moves smoothly with the same amount of tension throughout the compression and rebound travel strokes. Stop when the fork tube has bottomed.

8. Make sure the oil passage holes in the damper rod (**Figure 32**) are open. If clogged, flush with solvent and dry with compressed air.

9. Check the threads in the bottom of the damper rod for stripping, cross-threading or sealer residue. Use a tap to true up the threads and to remove threadlock residue.

11

5. Set the fork leg in a vertical position for approximately 5 minutes to allow any suspended air bubbles to surface and dissipate.

6. Set the oil level (**Figure 34**) as follows:

   a. Make sure the fork tube is bottomed against the slider and placed in a vertical position.

   b. Use a fork level gauge (**Figure 35**), or vernier caliper **Figure 36**, and set the oil level to the specification in **Table 3**.

NOTE
If no oil is drawn out when setting the oil level, not enough oil is in the fork tube. Add more oil and reset the level.

   c. If used, remove the fork oil level gauge.

7. Repeat the procedure for the remaining fork leg. Set the oil to exactly the same level in both fork legs.

8. Keep the fork assembly vertical and perform Steps 19-23 of *Front Fork Assembly* (this section).

FRONT FORK
(2007 FXDSE AND 2008 FXDSE2 MODELS)

Before assuming that a fork is malfunctioning internally, drain the front fork oil and refill with the proper type and quantity fork oil as described in Chapter Three. If there is still a problem, such as poor damping, a tendency to bottom or top out or leakage around the oil seals, follow the service procedures in this section.

To simplify fork service and to prevent the mixing of parts, remove, and service and install the fork legs individually.

Fork Bracket Pinch Bolts Service

Every time the fork bracket pinch bolts are loosened for fork removal, they must be completely removed and cleaned of all existing threadlock residue. Complete retention of these bolts is necessary to properly secure the fork assemblies.

1. Remove all eight bolts from the fork bracket.
2. Use a wire brush and thoroughly clean off all old threadlock residue from the bolt threads.
3. Clean in solvent and dry with compressed air.
4. If necessary, clean the threads with a thread die.
5. Replace the bolts if it is not possible to remove the threadlock residue.

Removal

1. Support the motorcycle with the front wheel off the ground. Refer to *Motorcycle Stands* in Chapter Nine.
2. Remove the front wheel as described in Chapter Ten.
3. Remove the front fender as described in Chapter Fourteen.

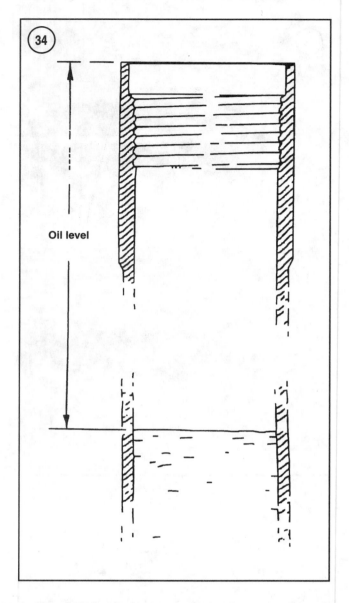

4. If both fork tube legs are going to be removed, mark them with an R (right side) and L (left side) so the assemblies will be reinstalled on the correct side.
5. If the fork is going to be serviced, use an Allen wrench and impact driver and loosen the cartridge Allen bolt at the base of the slider.
6. Loosen the upper fork bracket pinch bolts.
7. Loosen and remove the fork cap from the tube.
8. Loosen the lower fork bracket pinch bolts.
9. Carefully slide the fork leg out of the upper and lower fork brackets. It may be necessary to rotate the fork tube slightly while pulling it down and out.
10. Keep fork leg vertical to void the loss of fork oil. Thread the cap back into place and tighten securely.
11. Wrap the fork leg in a bath towel or blanket to protect the surface from damage.
12. Repeat procedure to remove the remaining fork assembly.
13. Remove all eight pinch bolts from the fork bracket and service them as described in this section.

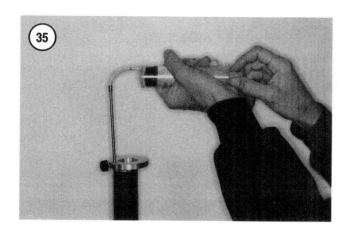

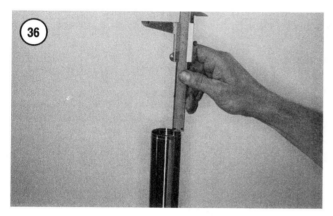

Installation

1. Service the fork bridge bolts as described in this section.

2. Carefully spread the upper and lower brackets with a wedge to gain clearance for the fork legs.

3. Install a fork leg through the lower fork bracket and into the top fork bracket until it bottoms in the bore. Install the fork top cap and tighten securely.

4. Secure the fork assembly and install the pinch bolts. Tighten the pinch bolts sufficiently to hold the fork assembly in place. Do not tighten the bolts to the final torque specification at this time.

5. Install the front fender as described in Chapter Fourteen.

6. Install the front wheel as described in Chapter Ten.

7. Apply the front brake and pump the front forks several times to seat the forks and front wheel.

8. Remove all eight pinch bolts.

9. Apply Loctite 243 (blue) threadlock, or an equivalent, to the pinch bolts.

10. Tighten the upper, and then the lower pinch bolts to 18-20 ft.-lb. (24.4-27.1 N•m).

Disassembly

Refer to **Figure 37**.

1. Clamp the fork tube (A, **Figure 38**) in a fork tube holder (H-D part No. 41177), or equivalent. Do not overtighten the clamp (B, **Figure 38**) as the tube will be distorted.

2. Unscrew and remove the fork top cap from the fork tube.

3. Loosen the locknut on top of the fork cartridge.

4. Push down on the fork spring and release the end plate from the fop of the spring. Remove the fork spring from the fork tube.

5. Remove the fork tube from the holder and pour the oil into a drain pan. Pump the fork several times by hand to expel most of the remaining oil.

6. If the Allen bolt was not loosened prior to removal, use an Allen wrench and impact driver and loosen the cartridge Allen bolt at the base of the slider. Remove the Allen bolt and washer.

7. Withdraw the cartridge and preload spacer from the assembly.

8. Insert a small, flat-tipped screwdriver under the dust cover and carefully pry the dust cover off the fork tube.

9. Remove the dust seal and slide the dust seal and cover off the slider.

10. Pry the retaining ring out of the internal groove in the fork tube and remove it.

NOTE
It may be necessary to slightly heat the area on the slider around the oil seal prior to removal. Use a rag soaked in hot water; do not apply a flame directly to the fork slider.

11. There is an interference fit between the bushing in the fork slider and the bushing on the fork tube. In order to remove the fork tube from the slider, pull hard on the fork slider using quick in-and-out strokes. This will withdraw the bushing and the oil seal from the fork tube.

12. Remove the slider from the fork tube.

13. Remove the oil seal and spacer from the slider.

NOTE
Do not remove the slider bushing unless it is going to be replaced.

14. Inspect all parts as described in this section.

Assembly

1. Coat all parts with Harley-Davidson Type E, or an equivalent, fork oil before assembly.

NOTE
To protect the oil and dust seal lips, place a thin plastic bag on top of the fork tube. Before installing the seals in the following steps, lightly coat the bag and the seal lips with fork oil.

2. Slide the dust seal cover, dust seal, retaining ring onto the slider.

3. Position the oil seal with the marks going on first and slide the *new* oil seal onto the slider.

4. Slide the fork tube bushing onto the slider.

5. Remove the plastic bag.

11

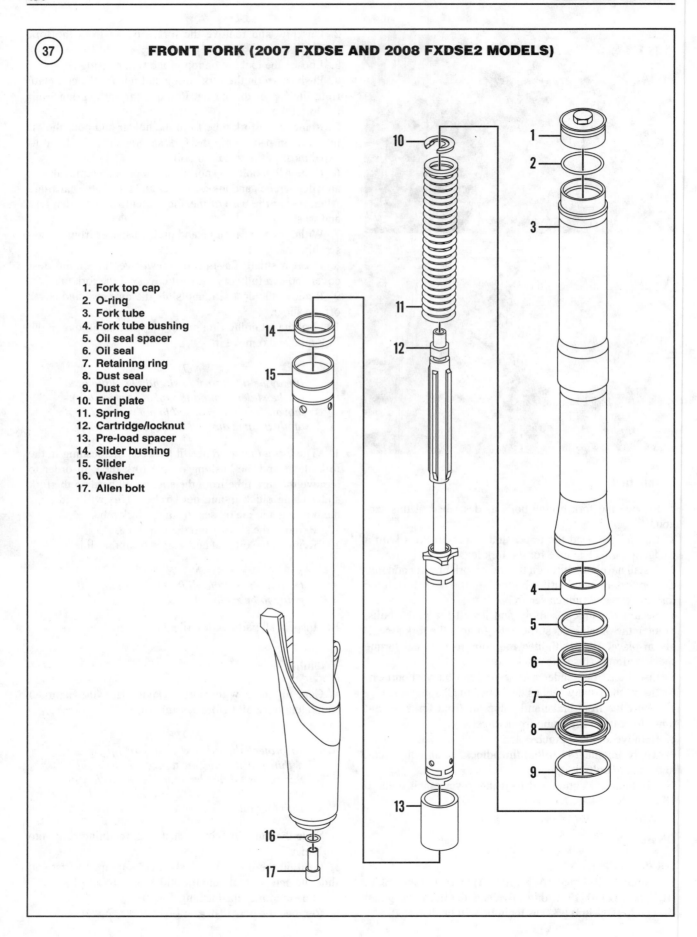

FRONT FORK (2007 FXDSE AND 2008 FXDSE2 MODELS)

1. Fork top cap
2. O-ring
3. Fork tube
4. Fork tube bushing
5. Oil seal spacer
6. Oil seal
7. Retaining ring
8. Dust seal
9. Dust cover
10. End plate
11. Spring
12. Cartridge/locknut
13. Pre-load spacer
14. Slider bushing
15. Slider
16. Washer
17. Allen bolt

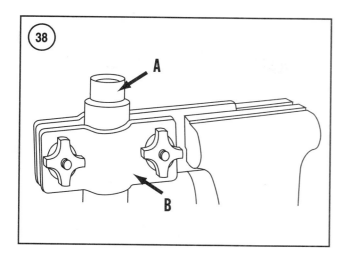

6. Install the slider into the fork tube. Move the fork tube bushing, spacer and oil seal against the fork tube.

NOTE
A fork seal driver (Jims part No. 2046), or an equivalent, is required to install the fork tube bushing and seal into the fork tube. Another method is to use a piece of pipe or metal collar with correct dimensions to slide over the fork tube and seat against the seal. When selecting or fabricating a driver tool, it must have sufficient weight to drive the bushing and oil seal into the fork tube.

7. Slide the fork seal driver down the fork tube and seat it against the oil seal.

8. Operate the driver and drive the fork tube bushing and new seal into the fork tube. Continue until the retaining ring groove in the tube is visible above the fork seal. Remove the fork seal driver.

9. Install the retaining ring into the fork tube groove. Make sure the retaining ring seats in the groove.

10. Install the dust seal and seat it into the slider, and then install the dust seal cover and seat it into the slider.

11. Install the cartridge into the fork tube bore. Insert a Phillips screwdriver through the opening in the base of the slider and guide the cartridge into position in the slider. Remove the screwdriver.

12. Install the Allen bolt and washer into the base of the slider.

13. Apply Loctite 243 (blue) threadlock, or an equivalent, to the damper rod Allen bolt threads prior to installation. Insert the Allen bolt through the lower end of the slider and thread it into the damper rod. Tighten the Allen bolt to 12-18 ft.-lb. (16.3-24.4 N•m).

14. Clamp the fork tube (A, **Figure 38**) in a fork tube holder (H-D part No. 41177), or an equivalent. Do not overtighten the clamp (B, **Figure 38**) as the tube will be distorted.

15. Install the preload spacer onto the cartridge.

16. Fill the fork assembly with 17.75 oz. (525 ml) of Harley-Davidson Type E fork oil, or an equivalent.

17. Pump the cartridge 10 times to remove air bubbles. Repeat the movement of the cartridge until it moves with the same amount of tension throughout the compression and rebound travel strokes.

18. Set the fork assembly in a vertical position for approximately 5 minutes to allow any suspended air bubbles to surface and dissipate.

19. Set the oil level (**Figure 34**) as follows:
    a. Make sure the fork tube is bottomed against the slider and placed in a vertical position.
    b. Use a fork level gauge (**Figure 35**), or a caliper (**Figure 36**), and set the oil level to the specification in **Table 3**.

NOTE
If no oil is drawn out when setting the oil level, not enough oil is in the fork tube. Add more oil and reset the level.

    c. If used, remove the fork oil level gauge.

20. Install the locknut and tighten until it bottoms on the cartridge.

21. Install the fork spring into the fork tube onto the preload spacer.

22. Press down on the spring and insert the end plate under the locknut and onto the top of the spring. Make sure the end plate is correctly seated on the spring and into the cartridge groove.

23. Thread the fork top cap onto the end of the cartridge until it bottoms. Secure the fork top cap and securely tighten the cartridge locknut up against it.

24. Pull up on the fork tube and thread the fork top cap onto the fork tube until it has bottomed.

25. Install the fork leg as described in this chapter.

Inspection

Replace any worn or damaged parts.

1. Thoroughly clean all parts in solvent and dry them. Check the fork tube for signs of wear or scratches.

2. Check the fork tube for bending, nicks, rust or other damage. Place the fork tube on a set of V-blocks and check runout with a dial indicator. If the special tools are not available, roll the fork tube on a large piece of plate glass or other flat surface. The manufacturer does not provide service specifications for runout.

3. Check the slider for dents or other exterior damage. Check the retaining ring groove in the top of the slider for cracks or other damage.

4. Check the slider and fork tube bushings for excessive wear, cracks or damage.

5. To remove the fork slider bushing, perform the following:
    a. Expand the bushing slit with a screwdriver and then slide the bushing off the fork tube.
    b. Coat the new bushing with new fork oil.
    c. Install the new bushing by expanding the slit with a screwdriver.
    d. Seat the new bushing into the fork tube groove.

11

6. Make sure the oil passage holes in the cartridge are open. If clogged, flush with solvent and dry with compressed air.

7. Check the threads in the bottom of the cartridge for stripping, cross-threading or sealer residue. Use a tap to true up the threads and to remove sealer deposits.

8. Replace the oil seals whenever they are removed. Always replace both oil seals as a set.

9. Inspect the dust seals for cracks, deterioration or other damage. A damaged dust seal, or dust cover, will allow dirt to pass through and damage the oil seal.

10. Replace the fork top cap O-ring if leaking or if wear or damage is apparent.

STEERING HEAD AND STEM

Removal

Refer to **Figure 39** and **Figure 40**.

1. Remove the headlight assembly as described in Chapter Nine.

2. Support the motorcycle with the front wheel off the ground. Refer to *Motorcycle Stands* in Chapter Ten.

3. Remove the front wheel as described in Chapter Ten.

4. Remove the front fender as described in Chapter Fourteen.

5. Remove both front fork legs as described in this chapter.

6. Remove the handlebar (A, **Figure 41**) as described in this chapter.

7. On dual disc models, remove the bolt securing the front brake hose assembly to the bottom of the lower fork bracket. Do not disconnect any brake hose connections.

8A. On all models except 2007 FXDSE and 2008 FXDSE2, remove the cap (B, **Figure 41**).

8B. On 2007 FXDSE and 2008 FXDSE2 models, perform the following:

   a. Loosen the set screw and remove the cap.

   b. Bend down the tab(s) on the lockwasher under the steering stem nut.

9. Loosen and remove the steering stem nut (A, **Figure 42**) and washer (B).

10. Remove the upper fork bridge (**Figure 43**) and rest it on a shop rag on the frame.

NOTE
Hold or secure the steering stem as it may fall after removing the bearing adjuster.

11. Remove the bearing adjuster (**Figure 44**) and dust shield.

12. Use a rubber mallet and tap the steering stem/lower fork bridge to free it from the upper bearing cone.

13. Slide the steering stem/lower fork bridge (**Figure 45**) out of the steering head.

14. Remove the upper bearing from the steering head.

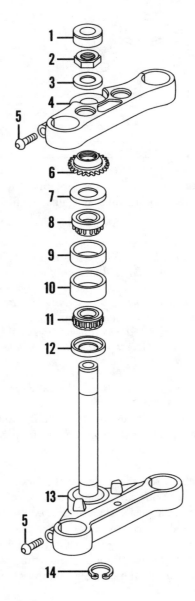

(39)

STEERING STEM (ALL MODELS EXCEPT 2007 FXDSE AND 2008 FXDSE2)

1. Cap
2. Nut
3. Washer
4. Upper fork bridge
5. Pinch bolt
6. Bearing adjuster
7. Upper dust seal
8. Upper bearing
9. Upper bearing outer race
10. Lower bearing outer race
11. Lower bearing
12. Lower dust seal
13. Steering stem/lower fork bridge
14. Snap ring

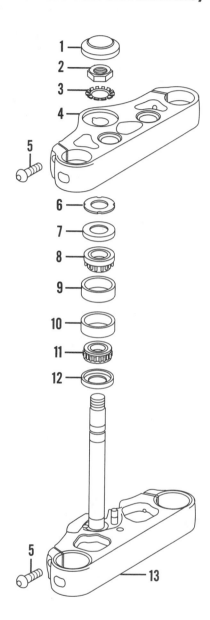

40

STEERING STEM (2007 FXDSE AND 2008 FXDSE2 MODELS)

1. Cap
2. Nut
3. Lockplate
4. Upper fork bridge
5. Pinch bolt
6. Bearing adjuster
7. Upper dust seal
8. Upper bearing
9. Upper bearing outer race
10. Lower bearing outer race
11. Lower bearing
12. Lower dust seal
13. Steering stem/lower fork bridge

41

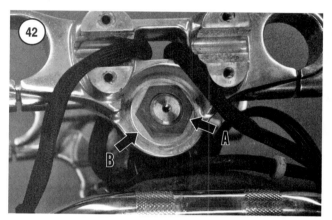

42

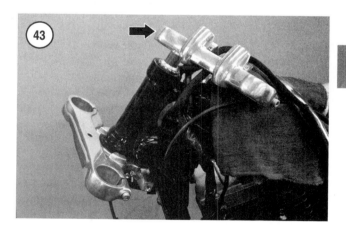

43

44

11

15. Remove the lower bearing (**Figure 46**) and dust shield from the lower fork bracket as described in this chapter, if necessary.

16. Inspect the steering stem and bearing assembly as described in this section.

Installation

1. Make sure to seat both steering head bearing races in place in the steering head.

2. Wipe the bearing races with a clean, lint-free cloth. Then, lubricate each race with bearing grease.

3. Pack the upper and lower bearings with a quality bearing grease.

4. If removed, install a *new* lower dust shield (**Figure 47**) on the steering stem and press it down until seated.

5. If removed, install the lower bearing (**Figure 48**) onto the steering stem. Press the bearing into place with both thumbs until it bottoms against the dust seal.

> *NOTE*
> *Before installing the steering stem, make sure the steering stem threads are clean.*

6. Insert the steering stem (**Figure 45**) into the frame steering head and hold it firmly in place.

7. Install the upper bearing (**Figure 49**) and seat it into to the upper race.

8. Install the upper dust shield (**Figure 50**) and seat it in the upper race.

> *WARNING*
> *The bearing adjuster must be installed as shown in **Figure 51** so the upper fork bridge will seat correctly. If installed upside down the upper fork bridge will be unstable and will move from side-to-side, resulting in unstable steering control.*

9. Position the bearing adjuster with the toothed adjuster side facing down (**Figure 51**) and the tapered cone side facing up. Install the bearing adjuster (**Figure 44**), and tighten to remove all bearing play within the steering head.

10. Install the upper fork bridge (**Figure 43**) over the steering stem.

> *WARNING*
> *On all models except 2007 FXDSE and 2008 FXDSE2, the special washer under the nut is made from hardened steel. Do not substitute with a common washer of lesser material as it could allow the nut to loosen, resulting in unstable steering control.*

11A. On all models except 2007 FXDSE and 2008 FXDSE2, install the special washer (B, **Figure 42**).

11B. On 2007 FXDSE and 2008 FXDSE2 models, install a new lockplate.

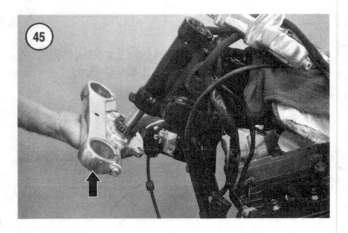

> *WARNING*
> *On all models except 2007 FXDSE and 2008 FXDSE2, the original nut had a blue lubricant applied to the threads, and the new replacement nuts do not.*

12. On all models except 2007 FXDSE and 2008 FXDSE2, apply a light coat of anti-seize lubricant to the nut threads

13. Install the steering stem nut (A, **Figure 42**). Finger-tighten the nut at this time.

14. Install the front fork legs as described in this chapter.

> *CAUTION*
> *Do not overtighten the steering stem nut or damage will occur to the bearings and races. Final adjustment of the fork stem will take place after the front wheel is installed.*

15. Tighten the steering stem nut until there is no noticeable free play between the bearings and races. The fork stem must turn freely from side-to-side.

16. On 2007 FXDSE and 2008 FXDSE2 models, bend up the tab(s) on the lockwasher against the steering stem nut.

17. Do not install the cap (B, **Figure 41**) until the steering play is adjusted (this chapter) on models so equipped.

18. On dual-disc models, move the front brake hose assembly onto the bottom of the lower fork bracket. Install the bolt and tighten securely.

19. Install the handlebar (A, **Figure 41**) as described in this chapter.

20. Install the front fender as described in Chapter Fourteen.

21. Install the front wheel as described in Chapter Ten.

22. Install the headlight assembly as described in Chapter Nine.

23. Adjust the steering play as described in this chapter.

24. Adjust the headlight as described in Chapter Nine.

Inspection

The bearing outer races are pressed into the steering head. Do not remove them unless they are going to be replaced as described in this chapter.

1. Wipe the bearing races with a solvent-soaked rag and then dry with compressed air or a lint-free cloth. Check the races in the steering head (**Figure 52** and **Figure 53**) for pitting, scratches, galling or excessive wear. If any of these conditions exist, replace the races as described in this chapter. If the races are okay, wipe each race with grease.

2. Clean the bearings in solvent to remove all of the old grease. Blow the bearing dry with compressed air, making sure not to allow the air jet to spin the bearing. Do not remove the lower bearing from the fork stem unless it is to be replaced. Clean the bearing while installed in the steering stem.

3. After the bearings are dry, hold the inner race with one hand and turn the outer race with the other hand. Turn the bearing slowly, the bearing must turn smoothly with no

roughness. Visually check the bearing (**Figure 54**) for pitting, scratches or visible damage. If the bearings are worn, check the dust covers for wear or damage or for improper bearing lubrication. Replace the bearing if necessary. If a bearing is going to be reused, pack it with grease and wrap it with wax paper or some other type of lint-free material until it is reinstalled. Do not store the bearings for any length of time without lubricating them to prevent rust.

4. Check the steering stem (**Figure 55** and **Figure 56**) for cracks or damage.

5. Check the threads (**Figure 57**) at the top of the stem for damage. Check the steering stem nut for damage. Install it onto the steering stem and make sure the nut turns easily with no roughness.

6. Ensure that the snap ring (**Figure 58**) is secure on the steering stem, on models so equipped. Replace if necessary.

7. Replace all worn or damaged parts. Replace bearing races as described in this chapter.

8. If necessary, replace the lower steering stem bearing and the dust shield as described in this chapter.

9. Check for broken welds on the frame around the steering head. If any are found, have them repaired by a competent frame shop or welding service familiar with motorcycle frame repair.

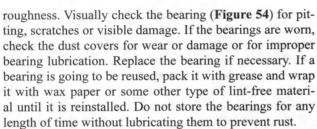

STEERING HEAD BEARING RACE REPLACEMENT

The upper and lower bearing outer races are pressed into the frame. Do not remove the bearing races unless replacement is necessary. If removed, replace both the outer race along with the bearing at the same time. Never reinstall an outer race that has been removed as it is no longer true and will damage the bearing if reused.

1. Remove the steering stem as described in this chapter.

2. To remove a race (**Figure 52** and **Figure 53**), insert an aluminum or brass drift (**Figure 59**) into the steering head and carefully tap the race out from the inside. Tap all around the race so that neither the race nor the steering head is bent.

3. Clean the steering head with solvent and dry thoroughly.

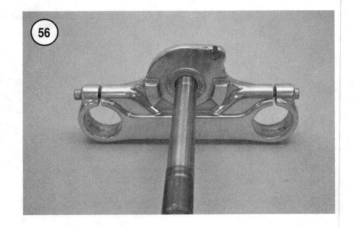

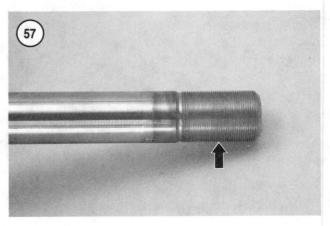

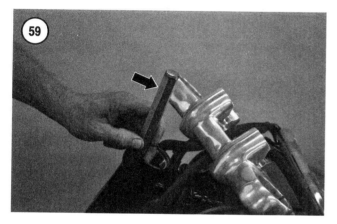

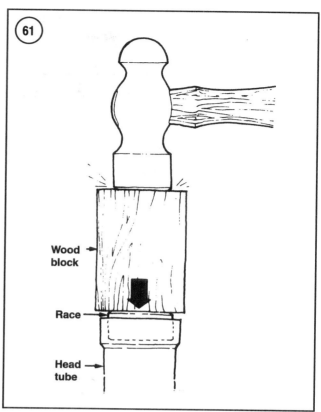

4A. Install the bearing races with a steering head bearing race installer (JIMS part No. 1725), or an equivalent, by following the tool (**Figure 60**) manufacturer's instructions.

4B. If the special tools are not available, install the bearing races as follows:

    a. Place the new bearing races in the freezer for about one hour. This will slightly reduce the outer diameter.

    b. Clean the race thoroughly before installing it.

    c. Position the bearing with the bevel side facing out.

    d. Align the *new* outer race with the frame steering head and tap it slowly and squarely in place (**Figure 61**). Make sure not to contact the bearing race surfaces.

Drive the race into the steering head until it bottoms out on the bore shoulder.

    e. Repeat the process and install the lower race into the steering head.

5. Apply bearing grease to the face of each race.

FORK STEM LOWER BEARING REPLACEMENT

NOTE
*This procedure is only necessary if the lower bearing (**Figure 62**) was not easily removed as described in **Steering Head and Stem Removal** (this chapter).*

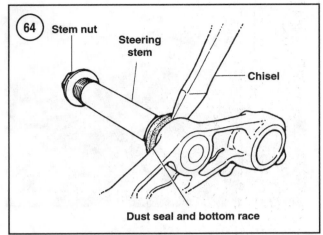

Stem nut / Steering stem / Chisel / Dust seal and bottom race

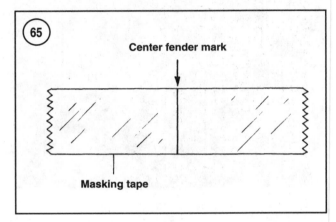

Center fender mark / Masking tape

Do not remove the steering stem lower bearing and lower seal unless it is going to be replaced. The lower bearing can be difficult to remove. If the lower bearing cannot be removed as described in this procedure, take the steering stem to a dealership and have them remove it and reinstall a new part.

Never reinstall a lower bearing that has been removed as it is no longer true and will damage the rest of the bearing assembly if reused.

1A. Remove the lower bearing with a fork stem bearing remover (JIMS part No. 1414), or an equivalent, by following the tool manufacturer's instructions.

1B. If the special tools (**Figure 63**) are not available, remove the bearing as follows:

   a. Install the steering stem nut onto the top of the steering stem to protect the threads.

   b. Loosen the lower bearing from the shoulder at the base of the steering stem with a screwdriver or chisel as shown in **Figure 64**. Withdraw the lower bearing and grease seal from the steering stem.

2. Clean the steering stem with solvent and dry thoroughly.

3. Position the *new* lower dust seal with the flange side facing up, and install it onto the steering stem.

4. Slide the *new* lower bearing onto the steering stem until it stops on the raised shoulder.

5. Align the lower bearing with the machined shoulder on the steering stem. Press the bearing down with both thumbs until it bottoms on the dust seal.

STEERING PLAY INSPECTION AND ADJUSTMENT

If any accessories have been installed on the handlebars, they must be removed at this time as they could affect this adjustment

Checking Swing Pattern

1. Use a centrally-located floor jack under the frame. Support the motorcycle on level ground with the front

wheel off the ground. Block the rear wheel to the motorcycle will not roll backwards.

2. Remove the windshield (if installed) and all other accessories added to the handlebar and front forks.

3. Apply a strip of masking tape across the front end of the front fender. Draw a vertical line across the tape at the center of the fender (**Figure 65**). Then, draw two lines on each side of the centerline 1 in. (25.4 mm) apart from each other.

4. Turn the handlebar to that the front wheel faces straight ahead.

5. Install a pointer on a stationary stand and center the pointer so that its tip points to the center of the fender (tape mark) when the wheel is facing straight ahead.

NOTE
If the clutch cable is routed so that it pulls the handlebar one way or the other, disconnect it.

6. Lightly tap the front fender toward the right side until the front end starts to turn by itself. Mark this point on the tape.

7. Repeat the process for the left side.

8. Measure the distance between the two marks on the tape. For proper bearing adjustment, the distance should be 2.0-4.0 in. (50.8-101.6 mm). If the distance is incorrect, adjust the steering play as described in this section.

9. Adjust the steering play as follows:
   a. Remove the cap (**Figure 66**).

   b. Loosen the steering stem nut (**Figure 67**).
   c. Loosen the lower fork bridge pinch bolts (**Figure 68**) on each side.
   d. Tighten or loosen the steering stem nut (**Figure 67**) until the measurement is correct.

NOTE
***Figure 69** is shown with the upper fork bridge removed for clarity.*

   e. If the distance is greater than 4.0 in. (101.6 mm), turn the steering stem adjust nut (**Figure 69**) *counterclockwise* to loosen.
   f. If the distance is less than 2.0 in. (50.8 mm), turn the steering stem adjust nut (**Figure 69**) *clockwise* to tighten.

10. Remove the steering stem nut (**Figure 67**).

11. On all models except 2007 FXDSE and 2008 FXDSE2, apply a light coat of anti-seize lubricant to the nut threads.

12. Tighten the steering stem nut to the following:
   a. On all models except 2007 FXDSE and 2008 FXDSE2: 70-80 ft.-lb. (95-108.5 N•m).
   b. On 2007 FXDSE and 2008 FXDSE2 models: 35-40 ft.-lb. (47.5-54.2 N•m).

13. Tighten the lower fork bridge pinch bolts to 18-20 ft.-lb. (24.4-27.1 N•m).

14. Repeat this procedure to ensure the adjustment is correct.

15. Lower the motorcycle to the ground.

16. Connect and adjust the clutch cable (Chapter Three), if removed.

17. Install all other accessories removed from the handlebar and front forks. Install the windshield, if removed.

18. Test ride the motorcycle.

11

Tables 1-2 are on the following pages.

Table 1 FORK OIL CAPACITY AND OIL LEVEL SPECIFICATIONS

Model	Capacity - each fork leg U.S. oz. (cc) approximate	Oil level height* in. (mm)
All models (except 2007 FXDSE, 2008 FXDSE2 and FXDWG)	26.6 (787)	4.3 (109)
FXDWG models	29.6 (875)	4.4 (112)
2007 FXDSE and 2008 FXDSE2 models	17.75 (525)	2.75 (70 mm)

*Measured from the top of the fork tube with the fork spring removed and the fork leg fully compressed.

Table 2 FRONT SUSPENSION TORQUE SPECIFICATIONS

Item	ft.-lb.	in.-lb.	N•m
Front axle nut (except Screamin' Eagle models)			
2006-2007 models	50-55	–	67.8-74.6
2008-2011 models	60-65	–	81.3-88.1
Front axle (Screamin' Eagle models)			
Axle nut (2007 FXDSE and 2008 FXDSE2 models)	65-70	–	88.1-94.9
Front axle (2009 FXDFSE and 2010 FXDSE2 models)	62-67	–	84.0-90.8
Front axle cover set screw			
(2009 FXDFSE and 2010 FXDFSE2 models)	–	10-12	1.1-1.4
Front axle set screws	11-15	–	14.9-20.4
Front fender nuts or screws	15-21	–	20.3-28.5
Front fork (all models except 2007 FXDSE and 2008 FXDSE2)			
Top cap	16-43	–	21.7-58.3
Allen bolt	–	106-159	11.9-18.0
Front fork (2007 FXDSE and 2008 FXDSE2 models)	refer to text for correct procedure		
Fork bridge pinch bolt	18-20	–	24.4-27.1
Handlebar (all models except FXDSE, FXDSE2, FXDFSE and FXDSE2)			
Clamp bolts	12-16	–	16.3-24.4
Lower clamp rubber bushing bolt	30-40	–	40.7-54.2
Riser cover screw (FXDL models)	–	50-60	5.7-6.8
Handlebar (2007 FXDSE models)			
Lower riser bolts	35-40	–	47.5-54.2
Handlebar (2008 FXDSE2, 2009 FXDFSE and 2010 FXDFSE2 models)			
Clamp bolts	12-16	–	16.3-21.7
Lower clamp rubber bushing bolt	30-40	–	40.7-54.2
Steering stem nut			
2007 FXDSE and 2008 FXDSE2 models	35-40	–	47.5-54.2
All models except 2007 FXDSE and 2008 FXDSE2	70-80	–	95.0-108.5

CHAPTER TWELVE

REAR SUSPENSION

This chapter describes repair and replacement procedures for the rear suspension components. Refer to **Table 1** at the end of this chapter for specifications.

SHOCK ABSORBERS

The shock absorbers are spring-controlled and hydraulically-damped. Spring preload is adjustable on all models. Refer to *Shock Absorber Adjustment* in this chapter.

Removal/Installation
(All Models Except FXDSE)

Refer to **Figure 1** and **Figure 2**.

When servicing the rear shocks, remove one shock at a time. If it is necessary to remove both shocks, support the motorcycle with the rear wheel off the ground.

1. Remove the saddlebag, on models so equipped.

2. Support the motorcycle with the rear wheel off the ground as described in Chapter Ten.

3. Place wooden blocks under the rear wheel to place the rear wheel in a neutral position with no strain on the shock absorber mounting hardware.

4A. On the right side, remove the lower Torx bolt (**Figure 3**) securing the shock absorber to the swing arm shock mount.

4B. On the left side, secure the nut (A, **Figure 4**) on the inner surface of the swing arm. Loosen and remove the lower

Torx bolt (B, **Figure 4**) and nut (A) securing the shock absorber to the swing arm shock mount.

5. Remove the upper acorn nut (**Figure 5**) and washer (A, **Figure 6**) securing the shock absorber to the frame shock stud.

6. Remove the cover (B, **Figure 6**) and washer (A, **Figure 7**).

7. Pull the shock absorber straight off the mounting stud and remove the shock absorber.

8. Check the mounting stud (B, **Figure 7**) for looseness. Tighten the stud nut to 70-85 ft.-lb. (94.9-115.2 N•m).

9. Repeat the procedure to remove the other shock absorber if necessary.

10. Inspect the shock absorber as described in this section.

11. Install the shock absorber straight onto the mounting stud and push it on until it bottoms.

12. Install the washer (A, **Figure 7**) onto the stud.

13. Apply a few drops of Loctite 243 (blue) threadlock, or an equivalent, to the shock stud and lower bolt threads.

14. Align the top chrome cover bolt hole with the shock body bolt hole, and install the cover (B, **Figure 6**), on models so equipped.

15. Install the washer (A, **Figure 6**) and upper acorn nut onto the stud. Finger-tighten the nut at this time.

16A. On the right side, install the lower Torx bolt (**Figure 3**) and finger-tighten.

16B. On the left side, install the lower Torx bolt (B, **Figure 4**) and the nut (A) on the inner surface of the swing arm, and fingertighten.

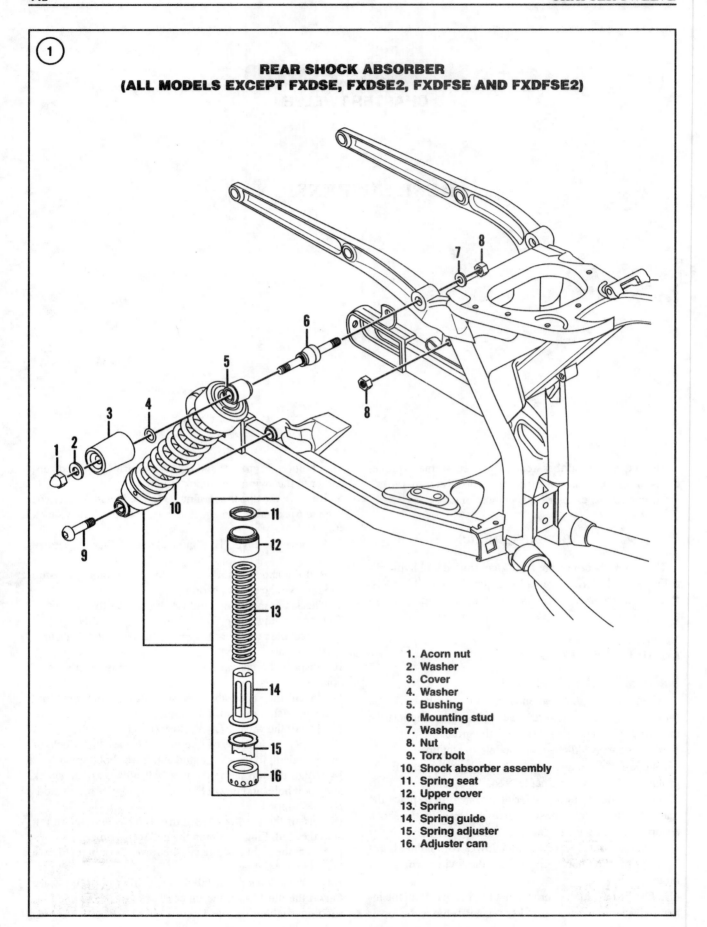

**① REAR SHOCK ABSORBER
(ALL MODELS EXCEPT FXDSE, FXDSE2, FXDFSE AND FXDFSE2)**

1. Acorn nut
2. Washer
3. Cover
4. Washer
5. Bushing
6. Mounting stud
7. Washer
8. Nut
9. Torx bolt
10. Shock absorber assembly
11. Spring seat
12. Upper cover
13. Spring
14. Spring guide
15. Spring adjuster
16. Adjuster cam

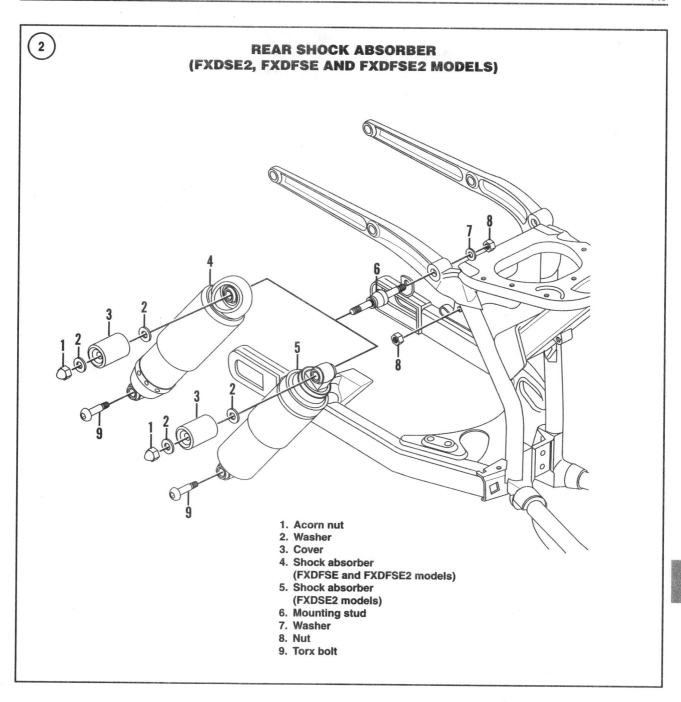

**REAR SHOCK ABSORBER
(FXDSE2, FXDFSE AND FXDFSE2 MODELS)**

1. Acorn nut
2. Washer
3. Cover
4. Shock absorber
   (FXDFSE and FXDFSE2 models)
5. Shock absorber
   (FXDSE2 models)
6. Mounting stud
7. Washer
8. Nut
9. Torx bolt

12

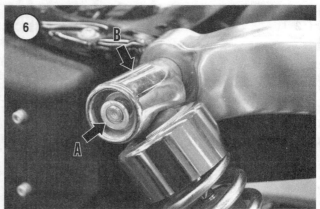

CAUTION
Do not scratch or damage the cover while tightening the acorn nut, since it may rotate while tightening the bolt.

17. Tighten the bolts and nuts to 30-40 ft.-lb. (40.7-54.2 N•m).
18. Adjust the shock absorbers as described in this chapter.
19. Lower the motorcycle and test ride it slowly at first to make sure the rear suspension is working properly.

Removal/Installation (FXDSE Models)

Refer to **Figure 8**.
When servicing the rear shocks, remove one shock at a time. If it is necessary to remove both shocks, support the bike with the rear wheel off the ground.
1. Remove the saddlebag, on models so equipped.
2. Support the motorcycle with the rear wheel off the ground as described in Chapter Ten.
3. Place wooden blocks under the rear wheel to place the rear wheel in a neutral position with no strain on the shock absorber mounting hardware.
4A. On the right side, remove the lower Torx bolt securing the shock absorber to the frame shock mount.
4B. On the left side, secure the nut on the inner surface of the swing arm. Remove the lower Torx bolt and nut securing the shock absorber to the frame shock mount.
5. Remove the upper bolt and washer securing the shock absorber to the frame. Catch the spacer located between the shock and the frame.
6. Repeat the procedure to remove the other shock absorber if necessary.
7. Inspect the shock absorber as described in this chapter.
8. Apply a few drops of Loctite 243 (blue) threadlock, or an equivalent, to the bolt threads.
9. Insert the washer and cover onto the upper bolt. Insert bolt through the upper mount and install spacer onto the bolt.
10. Install the shock onto the frame and install the upper bolt into the frame. Finger-tighten the upper bolt at this time.
11. Install the lower bolt securing the shock to the swing arm.

CAUTION
Do not scratch or damage the cover while tightening the upper bolt, since it will rotate while tightening the bolt.

12. Tighten the upper bolt to 75-85 ft.-lb. (101.7-115.2 N•m).
13. Tighten the lower Torx bolt and nut to 30-40 ft.-lb. (40.7-54.2 N•m).
14. Adjust the shock absorbers as described in this chapter.
15. Lower the motorcycle and test ride it to make the rear suspension is working properly.

Inspection
(All Models Except FXDSE, FXDFSE and FXDFSE2)

Refer to **Figure 1**.
1. Remove the shock absorber as described in this section.
2. Inspect the upper (**Figure 9**) and lower (**Figure 10**) shock bushings for wear and deterioration. Replace worn or damaged bushings.
3. Inspect the shock absorber. If the damper housing (A, **Figure 11**) is leaking, bent, or in any way damaged, replace the shock absorber.
4. Inspect the shock spring (B, **Figure 11**), spring retainer, cover and cam for cracks or damage. If necessary, replace the shock spring as described in this section.

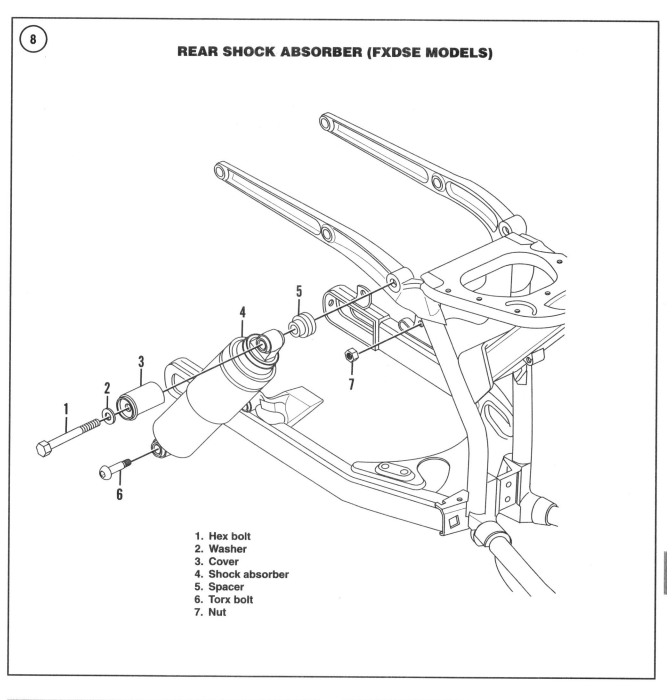

REAR SHOCK ABSORBER (FXDSE MODELS)

8

1. Hex bolt
2. Washer
3. Cover
4. Shock absorber
5. Spacer
6. Torx bolt
7. Nut

9

10

12

Inspection
(FXDSE, FXDSE2, FXDFSE and FXDFSE2 Models)

There are no replacement parts for shocks on these models except for the mounting bolts and nuts. If any other part is damaged, replace the shock assembly.

1. Remove the shock absorber as described in this section.

2. Inspect the upper and lower shock bushings for wear and deterioration. These bushings are not replaceable; if they are damaged, replace the shock absorber.

3. Inspect the shock absorber. If the damper housing is leaking, bent, or in any way damaged, replace the shock absorber.

4. Rotate the preload adjuster through all of its settings. Make sure the adjuster rotates freely and make sure it engages the detent at stop of the settings.

Shock Bushing Inspection and Replacement
(All Models Except FXDSE, FXDSE2, FXDFSE and FXDFSE2 Models)

Replace both bushings at the same time.

1. Remove the shock absorber as described in this section.

> *CAUTION*
> *When supporting the shock absorbers in a press, position the press blocks or other equipment so that they do not dent or otherwise damage the damper body.*

2. Support the shock absorber in a press and press out the bushing.

3. Repeat for the bushing on the other end.

4. Clean the shock eyelets of all rust and rubber residue. Check the eyelets for cracks, burrs, dents and other problems. Replace the shock absorber if damaged.

> *NOTE*
> *The upper and lower shock bushings are identical.*

5. Align the new bushing with the shock eyelet and start it into place. Then, support the shock absorber in a press and press the bushing into place, centering it in the shock eyelet.

6. Repeat for the bushing on the other end.

Spring Removal/Installation (All Models Except FXDSE, FXDSE2, FXDFSE and FXDFSE2)

A spring compressor (**Figure 12**), or an equivalent, is required to remove and install the shock spring. Refer to **Figure 1**.

1. Remove the shock absorber as described in this section.

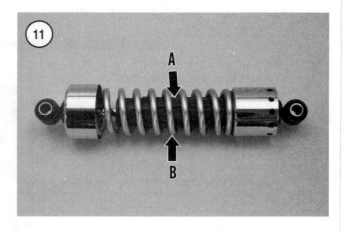

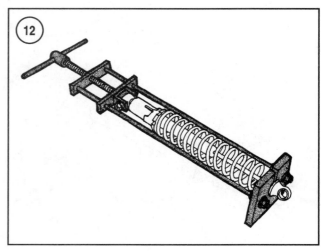

2. Rotate the spring adjuster cam to the lowest setting to reduce the amount of spring pressure present on the shock absorber.

3. Mount the shock absorber in a spring compressor tool (**Figure 12**).

> *WARNING*
> *Do not attempt to remove the spring from the shock absorber without some type of spring compressor tool. Because the spring is under considerable pressure, using makeshift tools or incorrect procedures may allow the spring retainer to fly off, causing personal injury.*

4. Compress the spring and remove the spring seat. Then, release spring tension and remove the shock absorber from the tool. Complete disassembly by removing the parts in the order shown in **Figure 1**.

5. The manufacturer does not provide the stock spring's free length specification. If the spring has sagged, remove the other shock spring and compare the length of both springs. Replace both springs if one is shorter than the other.

6. Inspect the spring adjuster for cracks, excessive wear or other damage.

7. Assemble by reversing the disassembly steps. Note the following:

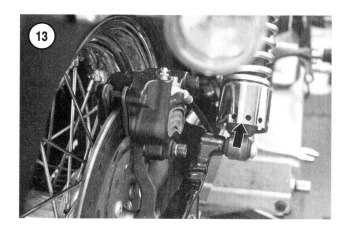

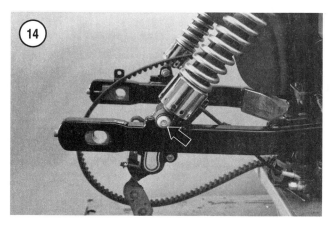

a. Make sure the spring seat is seated correctly in the upper cover before releasing the pressure from the spring compressor tool.

b. Adjust the spring pre-load as described in this chapter.

SHOCK ABSORBER ADJUSTMENT

Spring Preload Adjustment (All Models Except FXDFSE and FXDFSE2)

The ride height (height of a motorcycle at rest with no rider or passenger) can be adjusted with the cam preload adjuster at the base of each shock spring. Turning the cam adjuster to the five different steps moves the cam ramps up or down, either compressing or extending the spring. Increasing the cam angle increases the spring load and raises the ride height. Spring preload also controls how far the shock absorber compresses under the weight of the bike and rider.

Select the position that best suits the vehicle load requirements. The cam positions range from 1 (for a rider with no luggage) to 5 (for the maximum allowable GVWR loads listed in the owner's manual). The standard factory setting is the 3rd cam step position.

Rotate the cam (**Figure 13**) with a spanner wrench to compress the spring (heavy loads) or extend the spring

(light loads). Set the cam on both shock absorbers to the same preload position.

Spring Preload Adjustment (FXDFSE and FXDFSE2 Models)

The ride height (height of a motorcycle at rest with no rider or passenger) can be adjusted with the cam preload adjuster at the top cover of the each shock absorber. Turning the adjuster to the five different steps moves the cam ramps up or down, either compressing or extending the spring. Increasing the cam angle increases the spring load and raises the ride height. Spring preload also controls how far the shock absorber compresses under the weight of the bike and rider.

Select the position that best suits the vehicle load requirements. The cam positions range from 1 (for a rider with no luggage) to 5 (for the maximum allowable GVWR loads in the owner's manual). The standard factory setting is the 3rd cam step position.

Rotate the top cover by hand to compress the spring (heavy loads) or extend the spring (light loads). Set the cam on both shock absorbers to the same preload position to avoid potentially dangerous handling problems.

SWING ARM

Rear Swing Arm Bearing Check

The swing arm bearing on the left side will wear in time and require replacement. A worn or damaged bearing can produce erratic and dangerous handling. Common symptoms are wheel hop, pulling to one side during acceleration and pulling to the other side during braking.

1. Remove the rear wheel as described in Chapter Ten.
2. Remove the lower bolt (**Figure 14**) and nut securing both shock absorbers to the swing arm. Move them up away from the swing arm.
3. Make sure the swing arm pivot shaft flange nut is tight.
4. Have an assistant hold the motorcycle securely.
5. Grasp the back of the swing arm and try to move it from side to side. Any play between the swing arm and the frame, or swing arm and transmission, may suggest a worn or damaged bearing. If there is any play, remove the swing arm and inspect the bearing assembly.
6. Install all components removed.

Removal

Refer to **Figure 15**.
1. Remove the saddlebags, on models so equipped.
2. Remove the exhaust system as described in Chapter Four.
3. Remove the rear bolt (A, **Figure 16**), washer and nut, and the front screw (B) and washer. Then, remove the drive belt guard (C, **Figure 16**) from the swing arm. Do not lose the spacer within the rubber grommets.

12

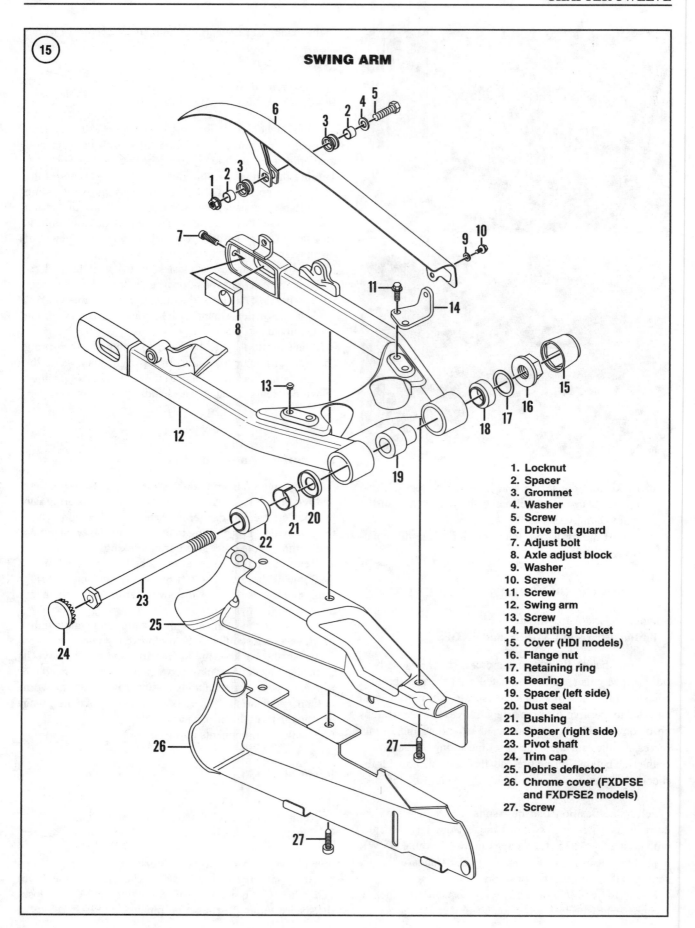

SWING ARM

1. Locknut
2. Spacer
3. Grommet
4. Washer
5. Screw
6. Drive belt guard
7. Adjust bolt
8. Axle adjust block
9. Washer
10. Screw
11. Screw
12. Swing arm
13. Screw
14. Mounting bracket
15. Cover (HDI models)
16. Flange nut
17. Retaining ring
18. Bearing
19. Spacer (left side)
20. Dust seal
21. Bushing
22. Spacer (right side)
23. Pivot shaft
24. Trim cap
25. Debris deflector
26. Chrome cover (FXDFSE and FXDFSE2 models)
27. Screw

4. Remove the three mounting screws (A, **Figure 17**) and remove the debris deflector (B) from the swing arm.

5. Remove the rear wheel as described in Chapter Ten.

6. Remove the shock absorber lower mounting bolt on both sides. Move the shock absorber up and out of the way. Secure the shocks to the frame.

7. Remove the cover from the pivot shaft nut (HDI models only).

8. Remove the pivot shaft trim cap (**Figure 18**) on the right side.

9. Secure the pivot shaft (**Figure 19**) and loosen the pivot shaft nut (**Figure 20**) with a Crescent wrench (**Figure 21**). Do not remove the nut at this time.

10. Place wooden blocks or a floor jack under the transmission and engine assembly to support it after the swing arm pivot shaft is removed.

11. Remove the bolt (**Figure 22**), star washer and clamp securing the brake line to the swing arm. Move the brake line out of the way.

12. Support the swing arm on a box.

13. Unscrew and remove the pivot shaft nut (**Figure 20**).

14. Use a suitable size drift and tap on the pivot shaft from the left side. Drive the pivot shaft (**Figure 19**) out through the right side.

15. Slowly pull back and withdraw the swing arm from the transmission case and frame swing arm brackets.

16. Inspect the swing arm as described in this section.

12

Installation

1. Install the large plastic clip (**Figure 23**) securing the electrical harnesses to the frame, if removed.

2. Install the right side (**Figure 24**) and left side (**Figure 25**) spacers into the swing arm pivot bores, if removed.

3. Position the drive belt on the inboard side of the swing arm and position the swing arm onto the pivot area of the transmission case and support it in this position. If necessary, use a soft-faced mallet and tap the swing arm into position.

4. Coat the pivot shaft with Loctite antiseize lubricant, or an appropriate type of grease. Do not get any grease on the exposed threads.

5. Insert the pivot shaft (**Figure 19**) in from the right side. Slowly press the push shaft through the frame swing arm brackets and transmission case. Push the pivot shaft in until it bottoms. If necessary, wiggle the swing arm slightly to create clearance for the pivot shaft.

6. Apply a few drops of Loctite 243 (blue) threadlock, or an equivalent, to the pivot shaft threads.

7. Install the pivot shaft nut (**Figure 20**) and finger-tighten.

8. Secure the nut (**Figure 26**) to prevent it from rotating, and tighten the pivot shaft (**Figure 19**) to 71-75 ft.-lb. (96.3-101.7 N•m).

9. Slowly raise and lower the swing arm to ensure ease of movement. If binding occurs, repeat the procedure and correct the problem.

10. Install the pivot shaft trim cap (**Figure 18**), and the pivot shaft nut cover (HDI models).

11. Move the shock absorbers into position and install the lower mounting bolt/nut. Tighten the lower mounting bolt/nut to 30-40 ft.-lb. (40.7-54.2 N•m).

12. Install the rear wheel as described in Chapter Ten.

13. Install the debris deflector (B, **Figure 17**) onto the swing arm. Install the three screws (A, **Figure 17**) and tighten to 40-60 in.-lb. (4.5-6.8 N•m).

14. Install the drive belt guard onto the swing arm as follows:

   a. Install the grommets and spacers onto the rear mounting bracket, if removed.

   b. Install the rear bolt, washer and nut (A, **Figure 16**) and tighten to 10-15 ft.-lb. (13.6-20.3 N•m).

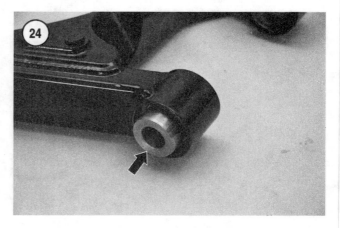

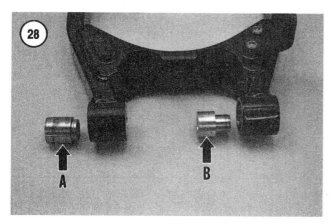

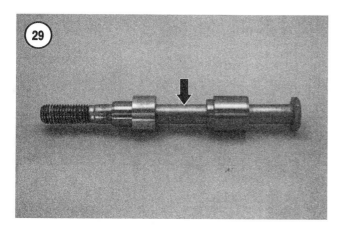

c. Install the front screw and washer (B, **Figure 16**) and tighten to 10-15 ft.-lb. (13.6-20.3 N•m).

15. Install the exhaust system as described in Chapter Four.

16. Install the saddlebags, on models so equipped.

Inspection

1. Clean the exterior of the swing arm in solvent and thoroughly dry with compressed air.

2. Inspect the welded sections on the swing arm (**Figure 27**) for cracks or fractures.

3. Remove the right side (A, **Figure 28**) and left side (B) spacers from the swing arm pivot areas.

4. Inspect the pivot shaft (**Figure 29**) for surface cracks, deep scoring, wear or heat distortion. Replace if necessary.

5. Turn the left-side bearing (**Figure 30**) with a finger. The bearing should turn smoothly with no signs of roughness or damage. This bearing is sealed for lifetime lubrication and requires no routine service. If necessary, replace the bearing as described in this section.

6. Inspect the right side bushing for wear or distortion. If necessary, replace the bushing as described in this section.

7. Inspect the spacers (**Figure 31**) for wear or distortion; replace them as a pair, if necessary.

Left Side Bearing Replacement

Remove and install the bearing only if the bearing must be replaced. Never reinstall a bearing that has been removed.

A hydraulic press is required for bearing replacement.

1. Push the left side spacer (**Figure 32**) out toward the inboard side of the pivot bore. Tap it out with a drift, if necessary.

2. Remove the snap ring (**Figure 33**) from pivot bore.

3. Push the right side spacer (**Figure 34**) out toward the outboard side of the pivot bore. Tap it out with a drift, if necessary.

12

4. Place the swing arm on the press bed with the left side facing down. Place a wooden block on the press bed to protect the swing arm finish.

5. Place a socket with an inner diameter larger than the bearing on the press bed under the left side pivot point.

6. Place a long socket extension with another socket that matches the outer diameter of the bearing down through the right side of the pivot point and place it on the left side bearing.

7. Make sure the swing arm pivot areas are square with the press bed.

8. Hold the swing arm vertical and square. Then, slowly apply ram pressure on the long extension and drive the bearing assembly out of the left side pivot bore.

9. Release ram pressure and remove the tools from the swing arm.

10. Clean the swing arm bearing bore with solvent and dry with compressed air.

11. Place the swing arm on the press bed with the left side facing up. Place a wooden block on the press bed to protect the swing arm finish.

12. Center the *new* bearing into the pivot bore.

13. Place a socket that matches the outer diameter of the bearing.

14. Center the assembly under the press and apply ram pressure. Press the bearing into the pivot bore until it bottoms against the pivot bore inner shoulder (**Figure 35**).

15. Remove the tools from the swing arm.

16. Install a *new* snap ring (**Figure 33**) into the groove in the pivot bore. Make sure the snap ring (**Figure 36**) is seated correctly.

17. Apply a light coat of wheel bearing grease to the outer surface of the left side spacer (**Figure 32**). Install spacer from the inboard side of the pivot bore, and tap it into place, if necessary.

18. Apply a light coat of wheel bearing grease to the outer surface of the right side spacer. Position the spacer with the chamfered end facing in. Install the right side spacer (**Figure 34**) from the outboard side of the pivot bore. Tap it into place with a drift, if necessary.

Right Side Bushing and Dust Seal Replacement

Remove and install the bushing only if the bushing must be replaced. Never reinstall a bushing that has been removed. A hydraulic press is required for bushing and dust seal replacement.

1. Push the left side spacer (**Figure 32**) out toward the inboard side of the pivot bore. Tap it out with a drift, if necessary.

2. Push the right side spacer (**Figure 34**) out toward the outboard side of the pivot bore. Tap it out with a drift, if necessary.

3. Place the swing arm on the press bed with the inside surface facing down. Place a wooden block on the press bed to protect the swing arm finish.

4. Place a socket that matches the outer diameter of the bushing over the pivot bore.

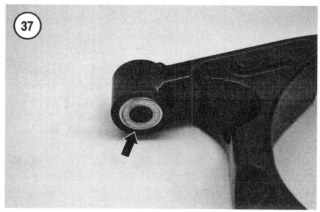

5. Make sure the swing arm pivot areas are square with the press bed.

6. Hold the swing arm vertical and square, slowly apply ram pressure and drive the dust seal and bushing out of the right side pivot bore.

7. Release ram pressure and remove the tools from the swing arm.

8. Clean the swing arm bearing bore with solvent and dry with compressed air.

9. Place the swing arm on the press bed with the outer surface facing down. Place a wooden block on the press bed to protect the swing arm finish.

10. Center the *new* dust seal and bushing onto the pivot bore.

11. Center the assembly under the press and apply ram pressure. Press the dust seal and bushing into the pivot bore until the dust shield is flush to within 0.060 in. (1.50 mm) above the pivot bore (**Figure 37**).

12. Remove the tools from the swing arm.

13. Apply a light coat of wheel bearing grease to the outer surface of the left side spacer (**Figure 32**). Install in from the inboard side of the pivot bore, and tap it into place, if necessary.

14. Apply a light coat of wheel bearing grease to the outer surface of the right side spacer. Position the spacer with the chamfered end facing in. Install the right side spacer (**Figure 34**) in from the outboard side of the pivot bore. Tap it into place with a drift, if necessary.

Table 1 REAR SUSPENSION TORQUE SPECIFICATIONS

Item	ft.-lb.	in.-lb.	N•m
Debris deflector screw	–	40-60	4.5-6.8
Drive belt guard bolt and nut	10-15	–	13.6-20.3
Shock absorber			
All models except FXDSE and FXDSE2			
Lower Torx bolt and nut	30-40	–	40.7-54.2
Mounting stud nut	70-85	–	94.9-115.2
Upper acorn nut	30-40	–	40.7-54.2
FXDSE and FXDSE2 models			
Lower Torx bolt and nut	30-40	–	40.7-54.2
Upper bolt	75-85	–	101.7-115.2
Swing arm pivot shaft nut	71-75	–	96.3-101.7

12

CHAPTER THIRTEEN

BRAKES

This chapter covers repair and replacement procedures for all brake system components.

Refer to **Table 1** and **Table 2** at the end of this chapter for specifications.

BRAKE SERVICE

WARNING
*When working on the brake system, do **not** inhale brake dust. It may contain asbestos, which is a known carcinogen. Do **not** use compressed air to blow off brake dust. Use an aerosol brake parts cleaner. Wear a face-mask and wash thoroughly after completing the work.*

The disc brake system transmits hydraulic pressure from the master cylinders to the brake calipers. This pressure is transmitted from the caliper(s) to the brake pads, which grip both sides of the brake disc(s) and slow the motorcycle. As the pads wear, the pistons move out of the caliper bores to automatically compensate for wear. As this occurs, the fluid level in the master cylinder reservoir goes down. Compensate for this change by occasionally adding fluid.

The proper operation of this system depends on a supply of clean brake fluid (DOT 4) and a clean work environment when any service is being performed. Any particle of debris that enters the system can damage the components and cause poor brake performance.

Brake fluid is hygroscopic (easily absorbs moisture), and moisture in the system reduces brake performance. Purchase brake fluid in small containers and properly discard any small quantities that remain. Small quantities of fluid will quickly absorb the moisture in the container. Only use fluid clearly marked DOT 4. If possible, use the same brand of fluid. One manufacturer's brake fluid may not be compatible with another's. Do not replace the fluid with a silicone-based fluid (DOT 5). It is not possible to remove all of the old fluid. Other types are not compatible with DOT 4. Do not reuse drained fluid. Do not combine brake fluid with fluids for recycling.

When adding fluid, punch a small hole into the edge of the fluid container's seal to help control the fluid flow. This is especially important to prevent spills while adding fluid to the small reservoirs.

Perform service procedures carefully. Do not use sharp tools inside the master cylinders or calipers or on the pistons. Damage to these components could cause a loss in the system's ability to maintain hydraulic pressure. If there is any doubt about the ability to correctly and safely service the brake system, have a professional technician perform the task.

Consider the following when servicing the brake system:

1. The hydraulic components rarely require disassembly. Make sure disassembly is necessary.

2. Keep the reservoir covers in place to prevent the entry of moisture and debris.

3. Clean parts with an aerosol brake parts cleaner, DOT 4 brake fluid or isopropyl alcohol. Never use petroleum-based solvents on internal brake system components. They will cause seals to swell and distort.

4. Brake fluid mars most surfaces on a motorcycle. To prevent brake fluid damage, note the following:

   a. Anticipate which parts are likely to leak or drip brake fluid. Cover the areas beneath these parts with a large

tarp or piece of plastic. Even a few drops of brake fluid can damage painted, plated or plastic surfaces.

   b. Keep a bucket of soap and water close to the motorcycle while working on the brake system. If brake fluid spills on any surface, immediately wash the area with soap and water then rinse it thoroughly.

5. Dispose of brake fluid properly.

6. If the hydraulic system, not including the reservoir cover, has been opened, bleed the system to remove air from the system. Refer to *Brake Bleeding* (this chapter).

7. The manufacturer does not provide service limit specifications for the caliper and master cylinder assemblies. Use good judgment when inspecting these components or consult a professional technician for advice.

FRONT BRAKE PAD REPLACEMENT

CAUTION
Check the pads more frequently when the lining approaches the pad metal backing plate. If pad wear is uneven for some reason, the backing plate may contact with the disc and cause damage.

There is no recommended mileage interval for changing the friction pads in the disc brakes. Pad wear depends on riding habits and conditions. Frequently check the brake pads for wear. Inspect the pads more frequently as the wear

indicator reaches the edge of the brake disc. After removal, measure the thickness of each brake pad with a caliper or ruler. Compare measurements to the specifications in **Table 1**.

Always replace both pads in the caliper at the same time to maintain even brake pressure on the disc. Do not disconnect the hydraulic brake hose from the brake caliper for brake pad replacement. Only disconnect the hose if the caliper assembly is going to be serviced.

2006-2007 Models

1. Refer to *Brake Service* in this chapter.

2. Support the motorcycle on level ground using a swing arm stand.

3. Block the front wheel so the motorcycle will not roll in either direction while on the swing arm stand.

4. Cover the fuel tank to protect it from any accidental brake fluid spills.

5. To prevent the brake lever from being applied, place a spacer or wood block between the brake lever and the throttle grip and secure it in place. If the brake lever is inadvertently squeezed, this will prevent the pistons from being partially forced out of the cylinders.

6. To prevent the reservoir from overflowing while repositioning the pistons in the caliper, perform the following:

   a. Move the front wheel so the front master cylinder is level.

   b. Clean the top of the master cylinder of all dirt and debris.

   c. Remove the screws (A, **Figure 1**) securing the cover (B) and remove the cover and diaphragm.

   d. Use a shop syringe and remove about 50% of the brake fluid from the reservoir. This will prevent the master cylinder from overflowing when the pistons are compressed for reinstallation. Do *not* drain more than 50% of the brake fluid or air will enter the system. Discard the brake fluid properly.

7. Loosen the pad pin bolts (**Figure 2**).

CAUTION
When pushing against the disc, support the disc adjacent to the caliper to prevent damage to the disc.

8. Hold the caliper body from the outside and push it toward the brake disc. This will push the outer pistons into the caliper bores to make room for the new brake pads. Constantly check the reservoir to ensure brake fluid does not overflow. Remove fluid, if necessary, before it overflows. Install the diaphragm and cover. Finger-tighten the cover screws.

9. Remove the caliper mounting bolts (**Figure 3**) and remove the caliper from the fork.

10. Remove the pad pin bolts (**Figure 2**).

11. Remove the inboard and outboard brake pads from the caliper.

13

12. Check the brake pads for wear or damage. Measure the thickness of the brake pad friction material. Replace the brake pads if they are worn to the service limit in **Table 1**.

13. Carefully remove any rust or corrosion from the disc.

14. Thoroughly clean the pad pin bolts of any corrosion or debris.

15. Check the friction surface of the new pads for any debris or manufacturing residue. If necessary, clean off with an aerosol brake parts cleaner.

> *NOTE*
> *When purchasing new pads, check with the dealership to ensure the friction compound of the new pad is compatible with the disc material. Remove any roughness from the backs of the new pads with a fine-cut file, and then thoroughly clean off.*

> *NOTE*
> *The pads are not symmetrical. The pad with one tab (A, **Figure 4**) must be installed on the inboard of the left side caliper, and on the outboard side of the right side caliper. The pad with two tabs (B, **Figure 4**) must be installed on the outboard side of the left caliper and on the inboard side of the right side caliper.*

16. Install the outboard pad (**Figure 5**). Hold it in place and install the anti-rattle spring and install both pad pin bolts (**Figure 6**) through the caliper and outboard brake pad.

17. Install the inboard pad (**Figure 7**) into the caliper. Hold the pad in place against the anti-rattle spring and push both pad pin bolts through the inboard brake pad and into the caliper. Finger-tighten the pad pin bolts.

18. Separate the brake pads (**Figure 8**) to allow room for the brake disc.

19. Carefully install the caliper onto the brake disc and install the mounting bolts (**Figure 3**). Tighten the bolts to 28-38 ft.-lb. (38.0-51.5 N•m).

20. Tighten the pad pins (**Figure 2**) to 180-200 in.-lb. (20.3-22.6 N•m).

21. Remove the spacer from the front brake lever.

22. Ensure there is sufficient brake fluid in the master cylinder reservoir. Top off if necessary with DOT 4 brake fluid.

23. Pump the front brake lever to reposition the brake pads against the brake disc.

24. Refill the master cylinder reservoir, if necessary, to maintain the correct fluid level of 1/8-1/4 in. (3.2-6.4 mm) from the top surface of the master cylinder body. Install the diaphragm and the top cover. Tighten the cover screws to 6-8 in.-lb. (0.7-0.9 N•m).

> *WARNING*
> *Do not ride the motorcycle until the front brakes operate correctly with full hydraulic advantage. If necessary, bleed the brake as described in this chapter.*

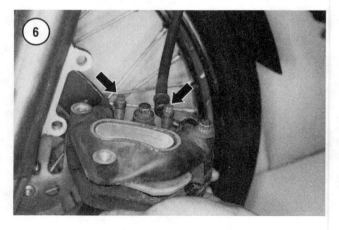

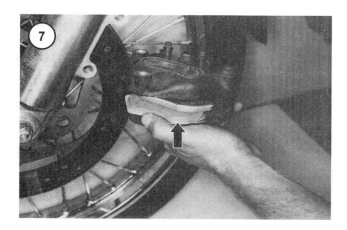

CAUTION
The break-in period for new brake pads is the first 100 miles (160 kilometer) of use. During the break-in period, avoid hard braking. Moderately apply the brakes for the first 100 miles (160 kilometers) of operation.

25. Test ride the motorcycle slowly at first to verify proper brake function.

2008-2011 Models

1. Read the information in *Brake Service* (this chapter).
2. Support the motorcycle on level ground using a swing arm stand.
3. Block the front wheel so the motorcycle will not roll in either direction while on the swing arm stand.
4. Cover the fuel tank to protect it from any accidental brake fluid spills.
5. To prevent the brake lever from being applied, place a spacer or wood block between the brake lever and the throttle grip and secure it in place. If the brake lever is inadvertently squeezed, this will prevent the pistons from being partially forced out of the cylinders.
6. To prevent the reservoir from overflowing while repositioning the pistons in the caliper, perform the following:
   a. Clean the top of the master cylinder of all debris.
   b. Remove the screws (A, **Figure 9**) securing the cover (B), and remove the cover and diaphragm.
   c. Use a shop syringe and remove about 50% of the brake fluid from the reservoir to prevent overflow. Do *not* drain more than 50% of the brake fluid or air will enter the system. Discard the brake fluid properly.
7. Loosen the pad pin (A, **Figure 10**) in the caliper, but do not remove it at this time.

CAUTION
When pushing against the disc in the following step, support the disc adjacent to the caliper to prevent damage to the disc.

8. Hold the caliper body from the outside and push it toward the brake disc. This will push the outer pistons into the caliper bores to make room for the new brake pads. Constantly check the reservoir to ensure brake fluid does not overflow. Remove fluid, if necessary, before it overflows. Install the diaphragm and cover. Finger-tighten the screws.

NOTE
There are two different length mounting bolts. The upper bolt is longer and the lower bolt is shorter.

9. Remove the long upper bolt (B, **Figure 10**) and the short lower bolt (C) securing the caliper to the fork slider and remove the caliper (D).
10. Remove the pad pin bolt (**Figure 11**) and discard it.

13

CAUTION
*Do not pry or pull the brake pads **away** from the pistons as the internal piston pad springs will be distorted and must be replaced.*

NOTE
*If the existing brake pads are going to be reinstalled; mark them with **IN** and **OUT** as shown in **Figure 12** so they will be reinstalled in the same locations.*

11. Slide the brake pad straight down and release tabs from each pad spring. If necessary, use a flat blade screwdriver and carefully pry the brake pad straight out of the caliper body. Remove the inboard and outboard brake pads from the caliper.

12. Inspect the pad pin bolt for wear. Measure the bolt in the wear area and measure the non-wear area. Replace the bolt if worn more than 0.015 in. (0.38 mm).

13. Carefully remove any rust or corrosion from the disc.

14. Check the friction surface (A, **Figure 13**) of the new pads for debris or manufacturing residue. If necessary, clean them off with an aerosol brake parts cleaner.

NOTE
When purchasing new pads, check with the dealership to ensure the friction compound of the new pad is compatible with the disc material. Remove roughness from the backs of the new pads with a fine-cut file and thoroughly clean them off.

15. The brake pad directional tab (B, **Figure 13**) must face *down* when the caliper is installed on the fork.

16. Slide the outboard brake pad (**Figure 14**) into the caliper and hook it onto the pad springs within the piston (**Figure 15**).The pad is installed correctly when the pad is flush with the inner surface of the caliper (**Figure 16**). If there is a gap; remove the pad and reposition it correctly.

17. Install the inboard brake pad (**Figure 17**) into the caliper and hook it onto the pad springs within the piston (**Figure 15**). The pad will be flush with the inner surface of the caliper (**Figure 18**) when the pad is installed correctly. If there is a gap; remove the pad and reposition it correctly.

18. Align the pad pin holes in the brake pads and caliper and install a *new* pad pin bolt (**Figure 11**). Finger-tighten the pad pin bolt at this time.

19. Reinstall the caliper onto the fork slider.

20. Install the long upper bolt (B, **Figure 10**) and the short lower bolt (C) securing the caliper.

21. Tighten the lower bolt first, and then the upper bolt. Tighten the caliper mounting bolts to 28-38 ft.-lb. (38.0-51.5 N•m).

22. Tighten the pad pin bolt to 15-16 ft-lb. (20.3-21.7 N•m).

23. Remove the spacer from the front brake lever.

24. Ensure there is sufficient brake fluid in the master cylinder reservoir. Top it off if with DOT 4 brake fluid if nec-

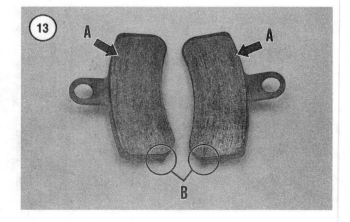

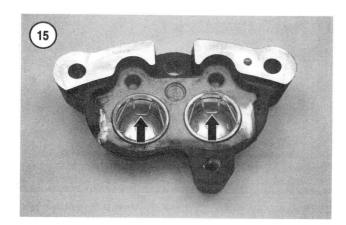

essary. Temporarily install the cover and finger-tighten the screws.

25. Pump the front brake lever to reposition the brake pads against the brake disc.

26. Refill the master cylinder reservoir, if necessary, to maintain the correct fluid level of 1/8-1/4 in. (3.2-6.4 mm) from the top surface of the master cylinder body. Install the diaphragm and the top cover. Tighten the cover screws to 6-8 in.-lb. (0.7-0.9 N•m).

WARNING
Do not ride the motorcycle until the front brakes operate correctly with full hydraulic advantage. If necessary, bleed the brake as described in this chapter.

CAUTION
The break-in period for new brake pads is the first 100 miles (160 kilometer) of use. During the break-in period, avoid hard braking. Moderately apply the brakes for the first 100 miles (160 kilometers) of operation.

27. Test ride the motorcycle slowly at first to verify proper brake function.

FRONT BRAKE CALIPER
(2006-2007 MODELS)

Refer to *Brake Service* (this chapter).

Removal/Installation

WARNING
Do not ride the motorcycle until the front brake is operating correctly with full hydraulic advantage. If necessary, bleed the brakes as described in this chapter.

1. Support the motorcycle on level ground using a swing arm stand.

2. Block the front wheel so the motorcycle will not roll in either direction.

3. If the caliper assembly is going to be disassembled for service, perform the following:

   a. Loosen the two caliper body assembly bolts (A, **Figure 19**).

   b. Remove the caliper mounting bolts (**Figure 20**), and then remove the caliper from the brake disc and front fork.

NOTE
Compressed air may not be necessary for piston removal during caliper disassembly if they can be removed hydraulically as described in this section.

   c. Remove the brake pads as described in this chapter.

13

d. Insert a piece of wood in place of the brake pads.

e. Slowly apply the brake lever to push the pistons part way out of the caliper assembly for ease of removal during caliper service.

f. Remove the piece of wood.

4. Remove the banjo bolt (B, **Figure 19**) and sealing washers attaching the brake hose to the caliper assembly.

5. Place the loose end of the brake hose in a reclosable plastic bag to prevent the entry of debris and to prevent residual brake fluid from leaking out.

6. Remove the caliper mounting bolts (**Figure 20**), and remove the caliper from the brake disc and front fork.

7. If necessary, disassemble and service the caliper assembly as described in this chapter. If the front caliper is not going to be serviced, place it in a reclosable plastic bag to keep it clean.

8. Install by reversing the removal steps. Note the following:

a. Install the caliper assembly onto the disc, being careful not to damage the leading edge of the brake pads.

b. Install the caliper mounting bolts (**Figure 20**) securing the brake caliper assembly to the front fork and tighten to 28-38 ft.-lb. (38.0-51.5 N•m).

c. Apply clean DOT 4 brake fluid to the rubber portions of the *new* sealing washers prior to installation.

d. Install *new* sealing washers against each side of the hose fitting.

e. Install the banjo bolt (B, **Figure 19**). Tighten the banjo bolt to 17-22 ft.-lb. (23.1-29.8 N•m).

f. Bleed the brakes as described in this chapter.

Disassembly

Refer to **Figure 21**.

1. Remove the brake pads as described in this chapter, if still in place.

2. Remove the caliper as described in this section, if still in place.

NOTE
If the pistons were partially forced out of the caliper body during removal the application of compressed air may not be necessary. If the pistons or caliper bores are corroded or very dirty, a small amount of compressed air may be necessary to completely remove the pistons from the body bores.

3. Place a piece of soft wood or a folded shop cloth over the end of the pistons and the caliper body. Turn the assembly over and place it on the workbench with the pistons facing down.

WARNING
Compressed air will force the pistons out of the caliper bodies under considerable force.

Do not block the piston with hands as injury will occur.

NOTE
The brake caliper was assembled at the factory with Versilube silicone grease (G.E. part No. GE322L). Removal of the pistons from the piston bores is very difficult as this lubricant creates a very tight bond between the piston and the bore. It may be necessary to use padded pliers to assist in withdrawing the piston from the bore after it has been loosened with compressed air. Do not damage the piston walls during removal.

4. Apply air pressure in short bursts to the hydraulic fluid passageway to force out the pistons. Repeat this for the other caliper body half. Use a service station air hose if compressed air is not available.

5. Remove the two caliper body assembly bolts (**Figure 22**) loosened during the removal procedure.

6. Separate the caliper body halves. Remove the crossover O-ring seals (**Figure 23**) and discard them. *New* O-ring seals must be installed every time the caliper is disassembled.

7. Remove both pistons. Due to the tight fit of the piston in the bore, the use of padded pliers may be necessary.

8. Remove the anti-rattle spring from the outboard caliper body.

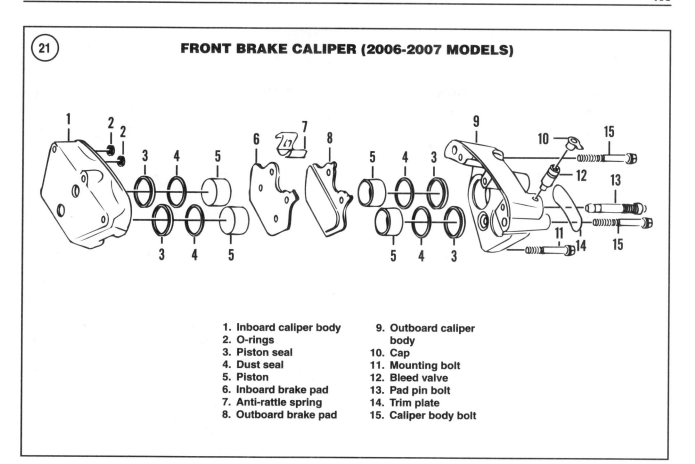

FRONT BRAKE CALIPER (2006-2007 MODELS)

21

1. Inboard caliper body
2. O-rings
3. Piston seal
4. Dust seal
5. Piston
6. Inboard brake pad
7. Anti-rattle spring
8. Outboard brake pad
9. Outboard caliper body
10. Cap
11. Mounting bolt
12. Bleed valve
13. Pad pin bolt
14. Trim plate
15. Caliper body bolt

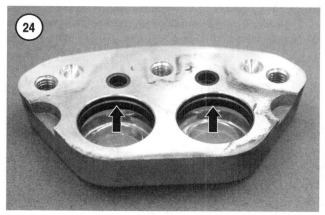

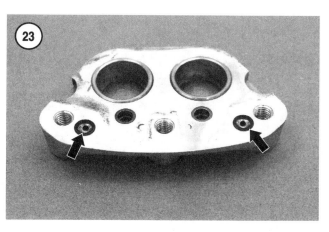

CAUTION
Do not use a sharp tool to remove the dust and piston seals from the caliper cylinders. Do not damage the cylinder surface.

9. Use a piece of wood or a plastic scraper to carefully push the dust seal and the piston seal (**Figure 24**) in toward the caliper cylinder and out of their grooves. Remove the dust and piston seals from all four cylinders.

10. If necessary, unscrew and remove the bleed valve (**Figure 25**).

11. Inspect the caliper assembly as described in this section.

13

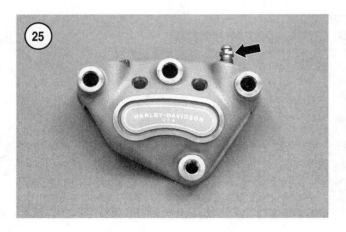

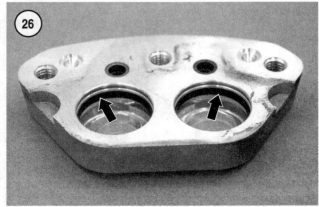

Assembly

> *CAUTION*
> *Do not use DOT 4 brake fluid for lubrication. If used, it will result in increased brake lever travel.*

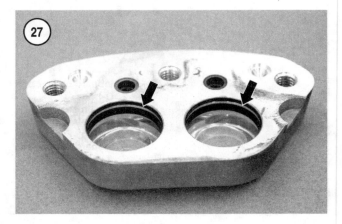

> *NOTE*
> *Never reuse old dust seals or piston seals. Very minor damage or age deterioration can make the seals ineffective.*

1. Apply a light coat of Versilube silicone grease (G.E. part No. GE322L), disc brake caliper lube (Permatex part No. 20356), or an equivalent, to the following parts:
   a. Inside diameter surfaces of both piston and dust seals.
   b. Caliper bores.
   c. Outside surfaces of pistons.
   d. Closed end of pistons.
2. All remaining surfaces must remain dry.
3. Carefully install *new* piston seals (**Figure 26**) into the lower grooves . Ensure the seals are properly seated in their respective grooves in all four cylinders.
4. Carefully install *new* dust seals (**Figure 27**) into the upper grooves. Ensure all seals are properly seated in their respective grooves (**Figure 24**) in all four cylinders.
5. Position the pistons with the open end facing out (**Figure 28**) and install the pistons into the caliper cylinders (**Figure 29**). Push the pistons in until they all bottom (**Figure 30**).
6. Repeat procedure to install the pistons into the other caliper body half. Ensure all pistons are installed correctly.
7. Install the anti-rattle spring into the outboard caliper body. Ensure the locating foot is located as shown in **Figure 31**. The upper edge of the spring (**Figure 32**) must be flush with the caliper mating surface or the caliper bodies cannot be assembled correctly.
8. Install *new* O-rings (**Figure 23**) into the interconnecting parts of the inboard caliper body.
9. Install the outboard caliper body onto the inboard body. Ensure the O-ring seals are still in place during the assembly of the caliper bodies.

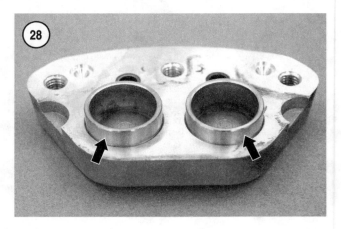

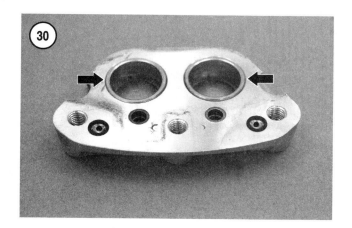

10. Install the two caliper body assembly bolts (**Figure 22**), and tighten securely. They will be tightened to the final specification after installation of the caliper.

11. If the bleed valve was removed, install it and tighten to 80-100 in.-lb. (9.0-11.3 N•m).

12. Install the brake pads as described in this chapter.

13. Install the caliper as described in this section.

14. Tighten the two caliper body assembly bolts (**Figure 22**) to 28-38 ft.-lb (38.0-51.5 N•m).

15. Bleed the brakes as described in this chapter.

13

Inspection

1. Clean both caliper body halves and pistons in clean DOT 4 brake fluid, or denatured alcohol and thoroughly dry them with compressed air.

2. Ensure the fluid passageways (**Figure 33**) in the piston bores are clear. Apply compressed air to the openings to ensure they are clear. Clean them out, if necessary, with clean brake fluid.

3. Ensure all fluid passageways (**Figure 34**) in both caliper bodies are clear. Apply compressed air to the openings to ensure they are clear. Clean them out, if necessary, with fresh brake fluid.

4. Inspect the piston and dust seal grooves (**Figure 35**) in both caliper bodies for damage. If they are damaged or corroded, replace the caliper assembly.

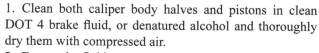

5. Inspect the threaded banjo bolt hole (**Figure 36**) in the outboard caliper body. If it is worn or damaged, clean it out with a thread tap or replace the caliper assembly.

6. Inspect the banjo bolt passage (**Figure 37**). Apply compressed air to the opening and ensure it is clear. Clean it out, if necessary, with clean brake fluid.

7. Inspect the threaded bleed valve hole in the caliper body. If it is worn or damaged, clean it out with a thread tap or replace the caliper assembly.

8. Inspect the bleed valve. Apply compressed air to the opening and ensure it is clear. Clean it out, if necessary, with clean brake fluid. Install the bleed valve and tighten it to 80-100 in.-lb. (9.0-11.3 N•m).

9. Inspect both caliper bodies (**Figure 38**) for damage. Check the inboard caliper mounting bolt hole threads (**Figure 39**) for wear or damage. Clean the threads with an appropriately sized tap or replace the caliper assembly.

10. Inspect the cylinder walls and pistons (**Figure 40**) for scratches, scoring or other damage.

11. Check the anti-rattle spring (**Figure 41**) for cracks or damage.

FRONT BRAKE CALIPER (2008-2011 MODELS)

Refer to *Brake Service* in this chapter.

Removal/Installation

1. Support the motorcycle on level ground using a swing arm stand.

2. Block the front wheel so the motorcycle will not roll in either direction.

3. If the caliper assembly is going to be disassembled for service, perform the following:

    a. Loosen the caliper body assembly bolt (A, **Figure 42**).

    b. Loosen the pad pin (A, **Figure 43**).

    c. Remove the long upper bolt (B, **Figure 43**) and the short lower bolt (C) securing the caliper to the fork slider and remove the caliper (D, **Figure 43**).

> *NOTE*
> *Compressed air may not be necessary for piston removal during caliper disassembly if they can be removed hydraulically as described in this section.*

    d. Remove the brake pads as described in this chapter.

    e. Insert a piece of wood in place of the brake pads.

    f. Slowly apply the brake lever to push the pistons part way out of the caliper assembly for ease of removal during caliper service.

    g. Remove the piece of wood.

4. Remove the banjo bolt (B, **Figure 42**) and sealing washers attaching the brake hose to the caliper assembly.

5. Place the loose end of the brake hose in a reclosable plastic bag to prevent the entry of debris and to prevent residual brake fluid from leaking out.

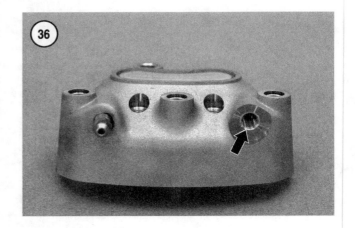

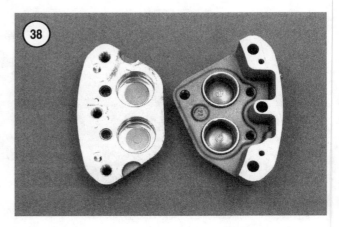

NOTE
There are two different length mounting bolts. The upper bolt is longer and the lower bolt is shorter.

6. If necessary, disassemble and service the caliper assembly as described in this section. If the front caliper is not going to be serviced, place it in a reclosable plastic bag to keep it clean.

7. Install by reversing the removal steps. Note the following:

   a. Install the caliper assembly onto the disc, being careful not to damage the leading edge of the brake pads.

   b. Install the long bolt (B, **Figure 43**) into the upper hole, and the short bolt (C) in the lower hole.

   c. Tighten the lower bolt first, and then the upper bolt. Tighten the bolts to 28-38 ft.-lb. (38.0-51.5 N•m).

   d. Tighten the caliper body assembly bolt (A, **Figure 42**) to 28-38 ft.-lb. (38.0-51.5 N•m).

   e. Apply clean DOT 4 brake fluid to the rubber portions of *new* sealing washers prior to installation.

   f. Install *new* sealing washers against the side of each hose fitting.

   g. Install the banjo bolt (B, **Figure 42**). Tighten the banjo bolt to 21-25 ft.-lb. (28.5-33.9 N•m).

   h. Bleed the brakes as described in this chapter.

Disassembly

Refer to **Figure 44**.

NOTE
The brake caliper was assembled at the factory with Versilube silicone grease (G.E. part No. GE322L). Removal of the pistons from the piston bores is very difficult as this lubricant creates a very tight bond between the piston and the bore. It may be necessary to use padded pliers to assist in withdrawing the piston from the bore after it has been loosened with compressed air. Do not damage the piston walls during removal

1. Remove the caliper as described in this chapter, if still in place.

NOTE
If the pistons were partially forced out of the caliper body during removal, the application of compressed air may not be necessary. If the pistons or caliper bores are corroded or very dirty, a small amount of compressed air may be necessary to completely remove the pistons from the body bores.

2. Place a piece of soft wood or a folded shop cloth between the pistons in the caliper body.

13

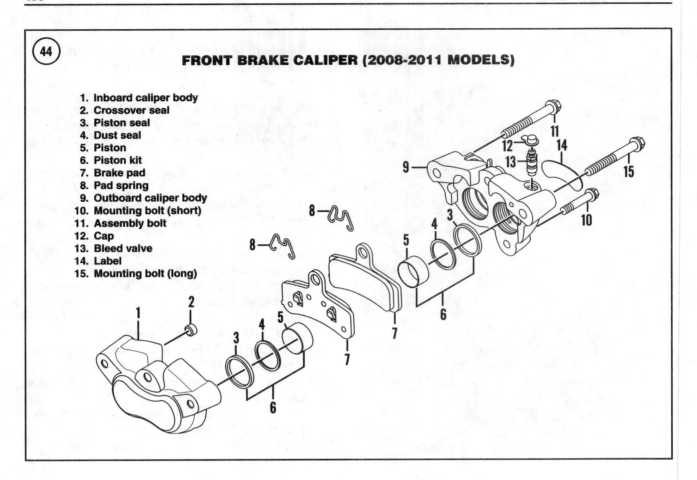

FRONT BRAKE CALIPER (2008-2011 MODELS)

44

1. Inboard caliper body
2. Crossover seal
3. Piston seal
4. Dust seal
5. Piston
6. Piston kit
7. Brake pad
8. Pad spring
9. Outboard caliper body
10. Mounting bolt (short)
11. Assembly bolt
12. Cap
13. Bleed valve
14. Label
15. Mounting bolt (long)

WARNING
Compressed air will force the pistons out of the caliper bodies under considerable force. Do no block the piston by hand as injury will occur.

3. Apply air pressure in short bursts to the hydraulic fluid passageway to force out the pistons. Repeat this for the other caliper body half. Use a service station air hose if compressed air is not available.

4. Remove the caliper body assembly bolt (**Figure 45**) loosened during the removal procedure.

5. Separate the caliper body halves. Remove the crossover seal (**Figure 46**) and discard it. A *new* crossover seal must be installed every time the caliper is disassembled.

6. Use a flat-bladed screwdriver (**Figure 47**) and carefully pry the brake pad toward the lower side (**Figure 48**) of the caliper body and release the pad from the pad springs (A, **Figure 49**) within the pistons.

7. Repeat process to remove the remaining brake pad.

8. Remove both pistons (B, **Figure 49**). Due to the tight fit of the piston in the bore, the use of padded pliers may be necessary.

CAUTION
Do not use a sharp tool to remove the dust and piston seals from the caliper cylinders. Do not damage the cylinder surface.

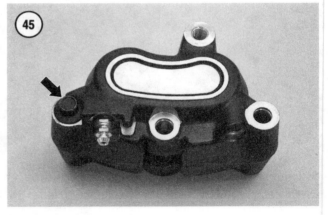

45

46

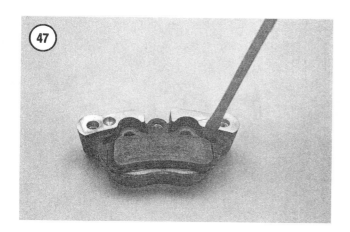

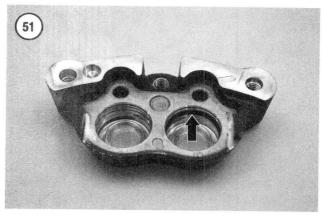

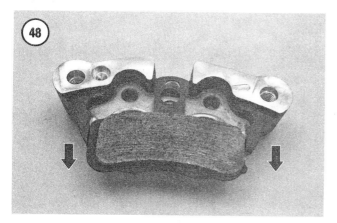

9. Use a piece of wood or a plastic scraper to carefully push the dust seal (A, **Figure 50**) and the piston seal (B) in toward the caliper cylinder and out of their grooves. Remove the dust and piston seals from both caliper bodies.

10. Unscrew and remove the bleed valve, if necessary.

11. Inspect the caliper assembly as described in this section.

Assembly

> *CAUTION*
> *Do not use DOT 4 brake fluid for lubrication. If used, it will result in increased brake lever travel.*

> *NOTE*
> *Never reuse old dust seals or piston seals. Very minor damage or age deterioration can make the seals ineffective.*

1. Apply a light coat of Versilube silicone grease (G.E. part No. GE322L), disc brake caliper lube (Permatex part No. 20356), or an equivalent, to the following parts:
   a. Inside diameter surfaces of both piston and dust seals.
   b. Caliper bores.
   c. Outside surfaces of pistons.
   d. Closed end of pistons.

2. All remaining surfaces must remain dry.

3. Install the seals into the *inboard* caliper body piston bores as follows:
   a. Carefully install a *new* piston seal (**Figure 51**) into the lower groove.
   b. Carefully install a *new* dust seal (**Figure 52**) into the upper groove.
   c. Repeat procedure to install the seals in the remaining piston bore.
   d. Ensure the four seals are properly seated in their respective grooves.

4. Repeat procedure to install the seals in the *outboard* caliper body.

5. Position the piston with the open end facing out and install the piston (**Figure 53**) into the piston bore. Push it down until completely seated (A, **Figure 54**).

13

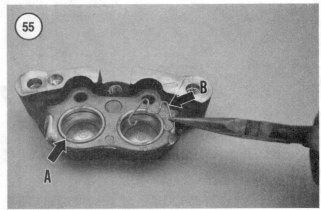

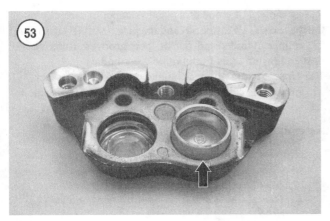

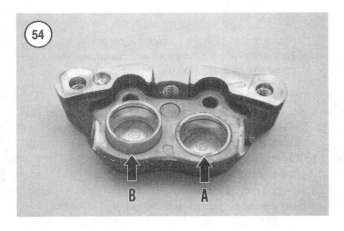

6. Position the remaining piston with the open end facing out and install the piston into the piston bore (B, **Figure 54**). Push it down until completely seated (A, **Figure 55**).

7. Install the pad springs into each caliper body as follows:

    a. Position the pad spring as shown in B, **Figure 55**.

    b. Insert one end of the pad spring into the piston groove, and push the other end into the groove (**Figure 56**).

    c. Insert the remaining pad spring and ensure that the springs are correctly seated in the piston grooves (**Figure 57**).

    d. Correctly position the springs (A, **Figure 58**) so the brake pad clips (B) can properly engage them.

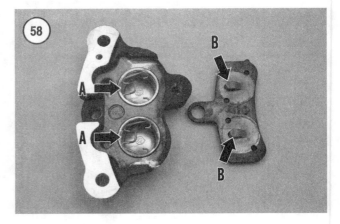

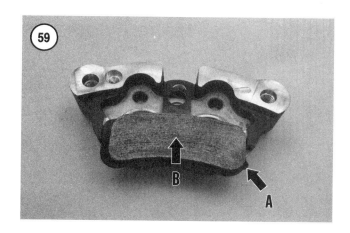

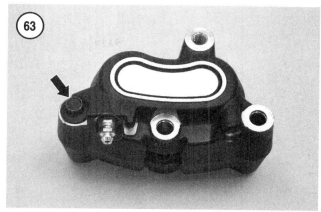

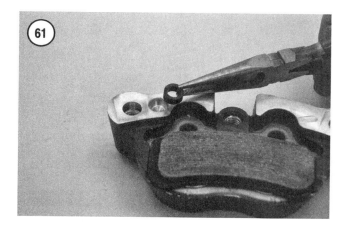

8. Correctly position the brake pad so the directional tab (A, **Figure 59**) faces down with the caliper in installed. Some brake noise may occur if the directional tab is facing up.

9. Push the brake pad (B, **Figure 59**) forward into place until it is locked into place on the pad springs. Ensure that the directional tab is facing down (**Figure 60**); reposition if necessary.

10. Repeat process to install the brake pad on the remaining caliper body.

11. Install a *new* crossover seal (**Figure 61**) and make sure it is correctly seated (**Figure 62**) in the inboard caliper body receptacle.

12. Assemble the two caliper bodies, install the assembly bolt (**Figure 63**) and tighten the bolt securely. It will be tightened to final specification after the caliper is installed on the fork slider.

13. Install the bleed valve (**Figure 64**) and tighten it to 80-100 in.-lb. (9.0-11.3 N•m), if removed.

Inspection

1. Clean both caliper body halves and pistons (**Figure 65**) in clean DOT 4 brake fluid, or denatured alcohol and thoroughly dry them with compressed air.

2. Ensure the fluid passageways (**Figure 66**) in the piston bores are clear. Apply compressed air to the openings to

13

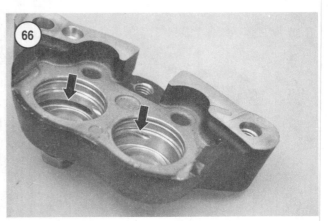

ensure they are clear. Clean them out, if necessary, with fresh brake fluid.

3. Inspect the piston and dust seal grooves (**Figure 67**) in both caliper bodies for damage. If they are damaged or corroded, replace the caliper assembly.

4. Inspect the threaded banjo bolt hole in the outboard caliper body. If it is worn or damaged, clean it out with a thread tap or replace the caliper assembly.

5. Inspect the banjo bolt passage. Apply compressed air to the opening and ensure it is clear. Clean it out, if necessary, with clean brake fluid.

6. Inspect the threaded bleed valve hole in the caliper body. If it is worn or damaged, clean it out with a thread tap or replace the caliper assembly.

7. Inspect the bleed valve. Apply compressed air to the opening (A, **Figure 68**) and ensure it is clear. Clean it out, if necessary, with clean brake fluid. Install a *new* O-ring (B, **Figure 68**) on bleed valve. Then, install the valve and tighten it to 80-100 in.-lb. (9.0-11.3 N•m).

8. Inspect both caliper bodies (**Figure 69**) for damage.

9. Check the inboard caliper assembly bolt hole threads (**Figure 70**) for wear or damage. Clean the threads with an appropriately sized tap or replace the caliper assembly.

10. Inspect the cylinder walls and pistons (**Figure 71**) for scratches, scoring or other damage.

11. Check the pad springs (**Figure 72**) for cracks or damage.

12. Inspect the spring pad tabs (**Figure 73**) for damage; replace the brake pads as necessary.

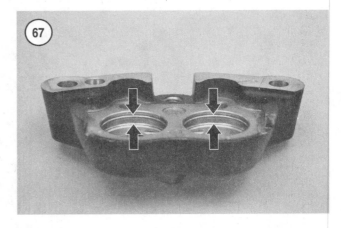

FRONT MASTER CYLINDER

Refer to *Brake Service* in this chapter.

Removal

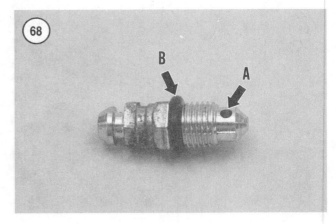

> *CAUTION*
> *Cover the fuel tank and front fender with a heavy cloth or plastic tarp to protect them from accidental brake fluid spills. Wash brake fluid off painted, plated, or plastic surfaces immediately as it will destroy most surfaces*

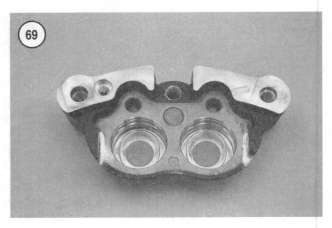

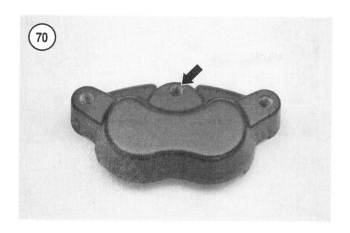

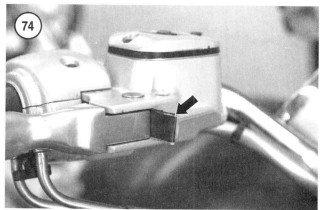

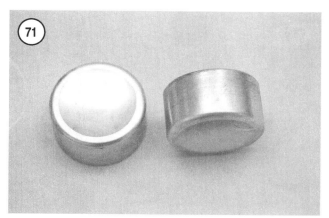

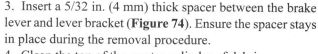

it contacts. Use soapy water and rinse completely.

1. Support the motorcycle on level ground using a swing arm stand.

2. Block the front wheel so the motorcycle will not roll in either direction while the rear wheel is off ground.

CAUTION
Failure to install the spacer will result in damage to the rubber boot and plunger on the front brake switch within the right side switch assembly.

3. Insert a 5/32 in. (4 mm) thick spacer between the brake lever and lever bracket (**Figure 74**). Ensure the spacer stays in place during the removal procedure.

4. Clean the top of the master cylinder of debris.

5. Remove the screws securing the cover, and then remove the cover (**Figure 75**) and diaphragm.

6. Use a shop syringe to draw all of the brake fluid out of the master cylinder reservoir. Temporarily reinstall the diaphragm and the cover. Finger-tighten the screws.

7. Remove the mirror from the master cylinder.

8. Remove the right handlebar switch assembly from the master cylinder as described in Chapter Nine.

9. Remove the banjo bolt (**Figure 76**) and sealing washers securing the brake hose to the master cylinder.

13

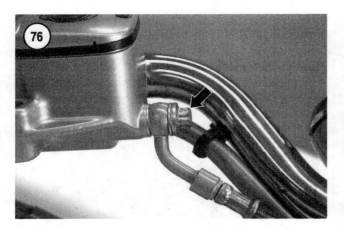

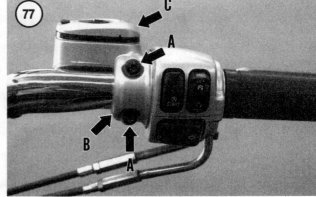

10. Place the loose end of the brake hose in a reclosable plastic bag to prevent the entry of moisture and debris. Tie the loose end of the hose to the handlebar.

11. Remove the Torx bolts (A, **Figure 77**) and washers securing the clamp and master cylinder to the handlebar.

12. Remove the clamp (B, **Figure 77**) and the master cylinder assembly (C) from the handlebar.

13. Drain any residual brake fluid from the master cylinder and dispose of it properly.

14. If the master cylinder assembly is not going to be serviced, reinstall the clamp, Torx bolts and washers on the master cylinder. Place the assembly in a reclosable plastic bag to protect it.

Installation

1. Insert a 5/32 in. (4 mm) thick spacer between the brake lever and lever bracket (**Figure 74**). Ensure the spacer stays in place during the installation procedure.

2. Position the front master cylinder onto the handlebar. Align the master cylinder notch (**Figure 78**) with the locating tab on the lower portion of the right handlebar switch assembly.

CAUTION
Do not damage the front brake light switch and rubber boot when installing the master cylinder.

3. Push the master cylinder all the way onto the handlebar. Hold it in this position and install the upper portion of the switch. Install the switch assembly screws and tighten the screws to 35-45 in.-lb. (4.0-5.1 N•m) starting with the bottom screw.

4. Position the master cylinder clamp and install the Torx bolts and washers. Tighten the upper, and then the lower mounting bolt as follows:
    a. On 2006-2007 models: 70-80 in.-lb. (7.9-9.0 N•m).
    b. On 2008-2011 models: 60-80 in.-lb. (6.8-9.0 N•m).

5. Apply clean DOT 4 brake fluid to the rubber portions of the *new* sealing washers prior to installation, and then install *new* sealing washers against each side of the hose fitting.

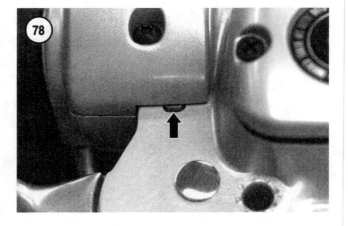

6. Install the banjo bolt (**Figure 76**) securing the brake hose to the master cylinder with new sealing washers. Tighten the banjo bolt as follows:
    a. On 2006-2007 models: 17-22 ft.-lb. (23.1-29.8 N•m).
    b. On 2008-2011 models: 21-25 ft.-lb. (28.5-33.9 N•m).

7. Remove the spacer (**Figure 74**) from the brake lever.

8. Temporarily install the diaphragm and top cover (**Figure 75**) onto the reservoir, if not in place. Finger-tighten the cover screws at this time.

9. Install the mirror onto the master cylinder and adjust to rider preference.

10. Install the right handlebar switch assembly onto the master cylinder as described in Chapter Nine.

11. Refill the master cylinder reservoir and bleed the brake system as described in this chapter.

12. Install the diaphragm and reservoir cover. Then, install the cover screws and tighten to 6-8 in.-lb. (0.7-0.9 N•m).

Disassembly

Refer to **Figure 79**.

NOTE
Store the master cylinder components in a divided container, like as egg carton, to help maintain their correct alignment positions.

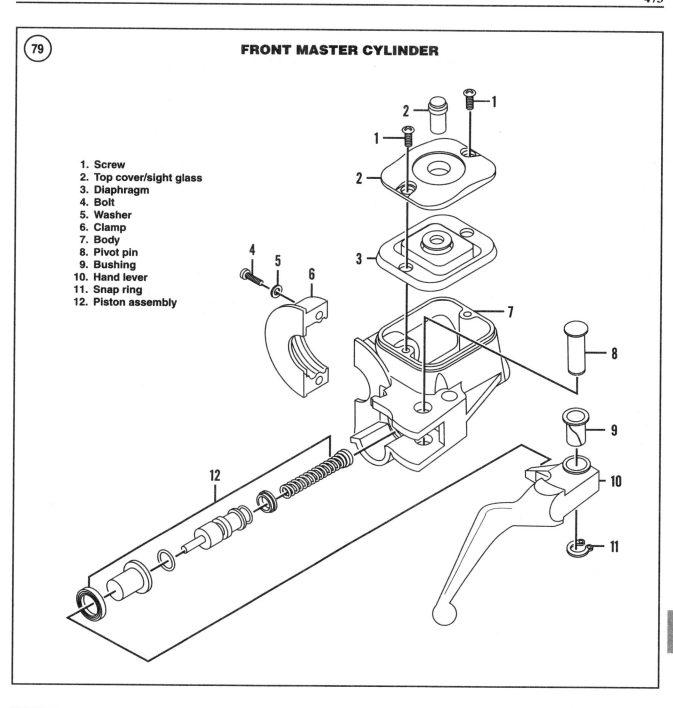

FRONT MASTER CYLINDER

1. Screw
2. Top cover/sight glass
3. Diaphragm
4. Bolt
5. Washer
6. Clamp
7. Body
8. Pivot pin
9. Bushing
10. Hand lever
11. Snap ring
12. Piston assembly

13

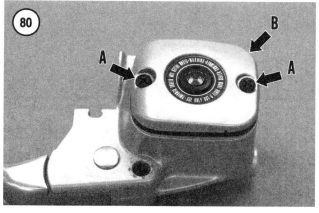

1. If still in place, remove the screws (A, **Figure 80**) securing the top cover (B). Remove the top cover and the diaphragm from the master cylinder.

2. Remove the snap ring (A, **Figure 81**) and the pivot pin securing the hand lever to the master cylinder. Remove the hand lever (B, **Figure 81**).

3. Remove the retainer (A, **Figure 82**) and the rubber boot (B) from the area where the hand lever actuates the piston assembly.

4. Remove the piston assembly (**Figure 83**) and the spring.

5. Inspect all parts as described in this section.

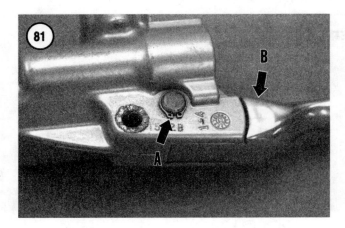

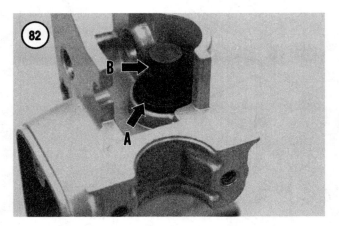

Assembly

> **CAUTION**
> *The cover and diaphragm must be assembled as described. If the sight glass is not installed correctly through the cover and diaphragm neck, brake fluid will leak past these components.*

> **NOTE**
> *When installing a new piston assembly, apply the lubricant, provided with the Harley-Davidson service parts kit. Coat all existing parts with a light coat of Versilube silicone grease (G.E. part No. GE322L), disc brake caliper lube (Permatex part No. 20356), or an equivalent, prior to installation.*

1. If the cover and the diaphragm were disassembled, assemble them as follows:

    a. Insert the neck of the diaphragm into the cover. Press it in until it seats correctly and the outer edges are aligned with the cover (**Figure 84**).

    b. Push the sight glass (**Figure 85**) straight down through the cover and the neck of the diaphragm until it snaps into place. The sight glass must lock these two parts together (**Figure 86**) to avoid a brake fluid leak.

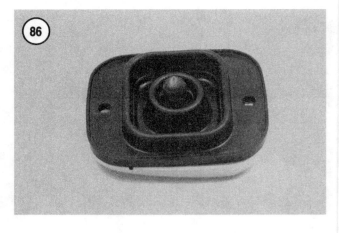

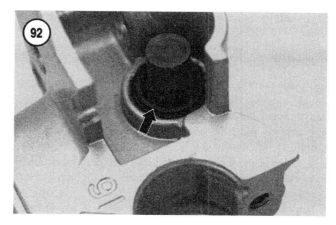

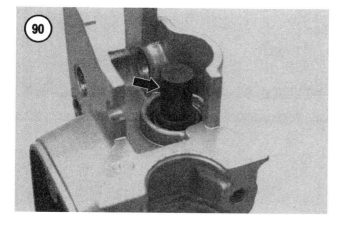

2. Coat the inside of the master cylinder bore with the provided lubricant.

3. Install a bolt into the threaded banjo bolt hole and mount the master cylinder in a vise (**Figure 87**).

4. Install the spring into piston assembly (**Figure 88**) with retainer end facing away from the piston.

CAUTION
When installing the piston assembly, do not allow the cup to turn inside out as it will be damaged and allow brake fluid leaks within the cylinder bore.

5. Install the spring and piston assembly into the cylinder. Push it in until it bottoms in the cylinder (**Figure 83**).

6. Install the rubber boot (**Figure 89**) onto the piston assembly.

7. Push down on the piston and rubber boot until the rubber boot seats (**Figure 90**).

8. Position the retainer with the large side (**Figure 91**) going on first and install the retainer onto the rubber boot. Ensure the retainer is correctly seated in the body (**Figure 92**).

9. Ensure the bushing (**Figure 93**) is in place in the hand lever pivot area.

10. Install the hand lever (B, **Figure 81**) into the master cylinder. Install the pivot pin and secure it with the snap ring (A, **Figure 81**). Ensure the snap ring is correctly seated in the pivot pin groove.

11. Slowly apply the lever to ensure it pivots freely.

13

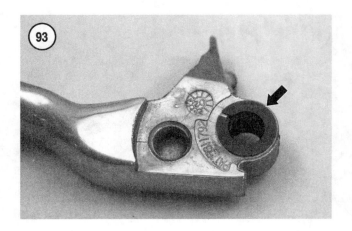

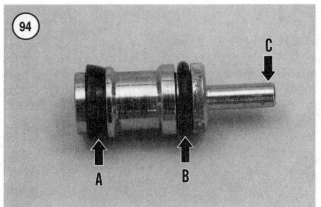

12. Install the master cylinder as described in this section.

Inspection

Replace worn or damaged parts as described in this section. The manufacturer recommends installing a new service kit every time the master cylinder is re-assembled.

1. Clean all parts in denatured alcohol or clean DOT 4 brake fluid. Inspect the body cylinder bore surface for signs of wear and damage. If it is less than perfect, replace the master cylinder assembly. The body cannot be replaced separately.

2. Inspect the piston cup (A, **Figure 94**), and the O-ring (B) for wear, and damage.

3. Ensure the fluid passage (**Figure 95**) in the bottom of the master cylinder body is clear. Clean it out if necessary.

4. Inspect the piston contact surface (**Figure 96**) for signs of wear and damage.

5. Check the end of the piston (C, **Figure 94**) for wear caused by the hand lever.

6. Check the hand lever pivot lugs (A, **Figure 97**) in the master cylinder body for cracks or elongation.

7. Inspect the mirror threaded hole (B, **Figure 97**) in the master cylinder body. If it is worn or damaged, clean it out with a thread tap or replace the master cylinder assembly.

8. Inspect the hand lever pivot hole and bushing (A, **Figure 98**) and the pivot pin (B) for wear, cracks or elongation.

9. Inspect the rubber boot and retainer (**Figure 99**) for deterioration, wear or damage.

10. Inspect the threaded banjo bolt hole (C, **Figure 97**). If it is worn or damaged, clean it out with a thread tap or replace the master cylinder assembly.

11. Check the top cover and diaphragm (**Figure 100**) for deterioration, damage or deterioration.

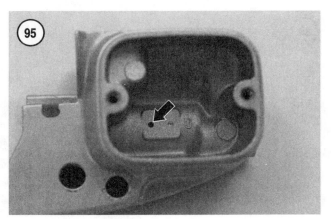

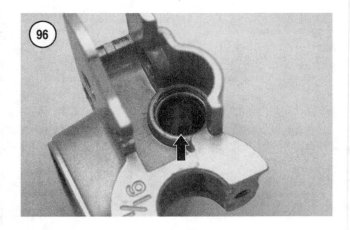

REAR BRAKE PAD REPLACEMENT

There is no recommended mileage interval for changing the friction pads. Pad wear depends on riding habits and conditions. Frequently check the pads for wear. Increase the inspection interval when the wear indicator reaches the edge of the brake disc. After removal, measure the thick-

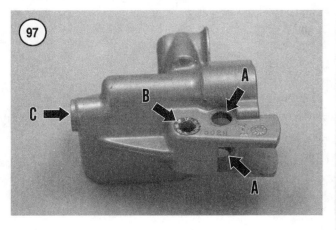

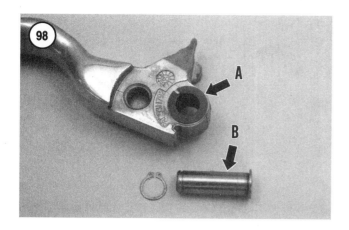

ness of each brake pad with a caliper or ruler, and compare measurements to the dimensions in **Table 1**.

Always replace both pads in a caliper at the same time to maintain even brake pressure on the disc. Do not disconnect the hydraulic brake hose from the brake caliper for brake pad replacement. Only disconnect the hose if the caliper assembly must be removed for service.

Refer to *Brake Service* in this chapter.

> *CAUTION*
> *Check the pads more frequently when the lining approaches the pad metal backing plate. If pad wear happens to be uneven for some reason the backing plate may come in contact with the disc and cause damage.*

2006-2007 Models

1. Support the motorcycle on level ground using a swing arm stand.
2. Block the front wheel so the motorcycle will not roll in either direction while the rear wheel is off ground.
3. Remove the right side saddlebag, on models so equipped.

> *NOTE*
> *Exhaust system removal is not necessary, but it does provide additional work area to access the rear master cylinder.*

4. Remove the exhaust system as described in Chapter Four.
5. Clean the rear master cylinder cover of all debris.
6. Tie the end of the brake pedal to the frame. If the brake pedal is inadvertently applied, this will prevent the piston from being forced out of the cylinder.
7. Remove the screws securing the reservoir cover, and then remove the cover and diaphragm.
8. Use a shop syringe to remove about 50% of the brake fluid from the reservoir. This will prevent the master cylinder from overflowing when the pistons are compressed for reinstallation. Do *not* drain more than 50% of the brake fluid or air will enter the system. Discard the brake fluid.
9. Loosen the pad pin bolts (**Figure 101**).

> *CAUTION*
> *Do not allow the master cylinder to overflow when pushing the pistons back into their bores. Wash brake fluid off any painted, plated or plastic surfaces or plastic parts immediately, as it will destroy most surfaces it contacts. Use soapy water and rinse completely.*

> *CAUTION*
> *The brake disc is thin and easily damaged. When pushing against the disc, support the disc adjacent to the caliper to prevent damage.*

10. Hold the caliper body from the outside and push it toward the brake disc. This will push the outer pistons into

13

the caliper bores to make room for the new brake pads. Constantly check the reservoir to ensure brake fluid does not overflow. Remove fluid prior to it overflowing, if necessary. Install the diaphragm and cover. Finger-tighten the screws.

11. Remove the pad pin bolts (**Figure 101**).

12. Remove the inboard and outboard brake pads from the caliper.

13. Check the brake pads for wear or damage. Measure the thickness of the brake pad friction material. Replace the brake pads if they are worn to the service limit in **Table 1**.

14. Carefully remove any rust or corrosion from the disc.

15. Thoroughly clean the pad pins of any corrosion or debris.

16. Check the friction surface of the new pads for any debris or manufacturing residue. If necessary, clean off with an aerosol brake parts cleaner.

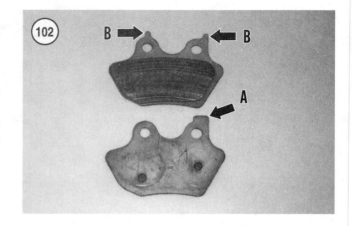

> *NOTE*
> *When purchasing new pads, check with the dealer to ensure the friction compound of the new pad is compatible with the disc material. Remove any roughness from the backs of the new pads with a fine-cut file, and then thoroughly clean them off.*

> *NOTE*
> *The pads are not symmetrical. The pad with one tab (A, **Figure 102**) must be installed on the outboard side. The pad with two tabs (B, **Figure 102**) must be installed on the inboard side of the caliper.*

17. Install the outboard pad (**Figure 103**) into the caliper.

18. Hold the pad in place and install the pad pin bolts (**Figure 104**) part way in to hold the outboard pad in place.

19. Install the inboard pad (**Figure 105**) into the caliper.

20. Push the pad pin bolts until they click into place. Do not tighten at this time.

21. Ensure there is sufficient brake fluid in the master cylinder reservoir. Top it off with DOT 4 brake fluid, if necessary.

22. Untie the brake pedal from the frame and pump the rear brake pedal to reposition the brake pads against the brake disc.

23. Tighten the pad pin bolts to 15-16 ft.-lb. (20.3-21.7 N•m).

24. Refill the master cylinder reservoir, if necessary, to maintain the correct fluid level as indicated on the side of the reservoir (Chapter Three). Install the diaphragm and the top cover. Finger-tighten the cover screw sand tighten to 6-8 in.-lb. (0.7-0.9 N•m).

25. Install the right side saddlebag as described in Chapter Seventeen, if so equipped.

26. Install the exhaust system as described in Chapter Four, if removed.

> *CAUTION*
> *The break-in period for new brake pads is the first 100 miles (160 kilometer) of use. During the break-in period, avoid hard braking.*

Moderately apply the brakes for the first 100 miles (160 kilometers) of operation.

2008-2011 Models

1. Support the motorcycle on level ground using a swing arm stand.
2. Block the front wheel so the motorcycle will not roll in either direction while the rear wheel is off ground.
3. Remove the right side saddlebag, on models so equipped.

NOTE
Exhaust system removal is not necessary, but it does provide additional work area to access the rear master cylinder.

4. Remove the exhaust system as described in Chapter Four.
5. Tie the end of the brake pedal to the frame. If the brake pedal is inadvertently applied, this will prevent the piston from being forced out of the cylinder.
6. Clean the rear master cylinder cover of all debris.

NOTE
***Figure 106** is shown with the exhaust system and mounting bracket removed for photo clarity.*

7. Remove the screws (A, **Figure 106**) securing the cover, and then remove the cover (B) and diaphragm.
8. Use a shop syringe to remove about 50% of the brake fluid from the reservoir. This will prevent the master cylinder from overflowing when the pistons are compressed for reinstallation. Do *not* drain more than 50% of the brake fluid or air will enter the system. Discard the brake fluid.
9. Loosen, but do not remove the pad pin bolt (**Figure 107**).
10. Insert a stiff plastic or wooden wedge into the caliper between the outboard brake pad and carefully push the brake pad partway back into to caliper bores. This will make room for the new thicker brake pads. Constantly check the reservoir to ensure brake fluid does not overflow. Remove fluid, if necessary, before it overflows. Install the diaphragm and cover. Finger-tighten the cover screws.
11. Withdraw the pad pin bolt and remove the outboard brake pad (**Figure 108**) and the inboard pad (**Figure 109**).
12. Inspect the pad pin bolt for wear. Measure the bolt in the wear area and measure the non-wear area. Replace the bolt if worn more than 0.015 in. (0.38 mm).
13. Check the brake pads for wear or damage. Measure the thickness of the brake pad friction material. Replace the brake pads if they are worn to the service limit in **Table 1**.
14. Remove any rust or corrosion from the disc.
15. Check the friction surface of the new pads for debris or manufacturing residue. If necessary, clean them off with an aerosol brake parts cleaner.
16. Ensure the spring pad is still located properly within the caliper body. If the spring has come off, remove the caliper and reseat the spring.

13

17. Position the inboard brake pad with the curved portion facing up. Insert the inboard pad into the caliper (**Figure 110**) and hook the tab onto the slot (**Figure 111**) in the caliper housing.

18. Position the outboard brake pad with the curved portion facing up. Insert the outboard pad into the caliper (**Figure 112**), and hook the tab onto the slot in the caliper housing.

19. Hold the pads in place and insert the pad pin bolt (A, **Figure 113**) through both pads (B) and install it into the caliper body. Tighten the pad pin bolt to 80-120 in.-lb. (9.0-13.6 N•m).

20. Untie the brake pedal from the frame and pump the rear brake pedal to reposition the brake pads against the brake disc. Continue to pump the brake pedal as many times as it takes to refill the cylinders in the caliper and correctly position the brake pads against the disc.

21. Refill the master cylinder reservoir, if necessary, to maintain the correct fluid level as indicated on the side of the reservoir. Install the diaphragm and the top cover. Tighten the cover screws to 6-8 in.-lb. (0.7-0.9 N•m).

22. Install the right side saddlebag, models so equipped.

23. Install the exhaust system as described in Chapter Four, if removed.

CAUTION
The break-in period for new brake pads is the first 100 miles (160 kilometer) of use. During the break-in period, avoid hard braking. Moderately apply the brakes for the first 100 miles (160 kilometers) of operation.

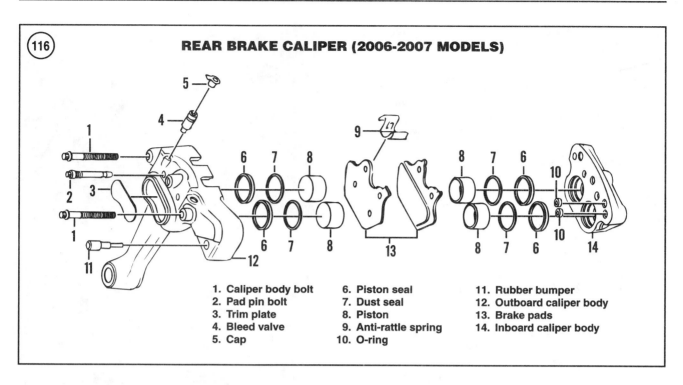

REAR BRAKE CALIPER (2006-2007 MODELS)

1. Caliper body bolt
2. Pad pin bolt
3. Trim plate
4. Bleed valve
5. Cap
6. Piston seal
7. Dust seal
8. Piston
9. Anti-rattle spring
10. O-ring
11. Rubber bumper
12. Outboard caliper body
13. Brake pads
14. Inboard caliper body

REAR BRAKE CALIPER (2006-2007 MODELS)

Removal/Installation

Refer to *Brake Service* in this chapter.

1. Support the motorcycle on level ground using a swing arm stand.

2. Block the front wheel so the motorcycle will not roll in either direction while the rear wheel is off ground.

3. Remove the right side saddlebag, on models so equipped.

4. Tie the end of the brake pedal to the frame. If the brake pedal is inadvertently applied, this will prevent the piston from being forced out of the cylinder.

5. If the caliper assembly is going to be disassembled for service, perform the following:

NOTE
Compressed air may not be necessary for piston removal during caliper disassembly if they can be removed hydraulically as described in this section.

  a. Remove the brake pads as described in this chapter.

CAUTION
Do not allow the pistons to travel out far enough to come in contact with the brake disc. If this happens the pistons may scratch or gouge the disc during caliper removal.

  b. Slowly apply the brake lever to push the pistons part way out of caliper assembly for ease of removal during caliper service.

  c. Loosen the three body mounting bolts (A, **Figure 114**).

  d. Loosen the brake hose banjo bolt (B, **Figure 114**).

6. Remove the banjo bolt and sealing washers attaching the brake hose to the caliper assembly.

7. Place the loose end of the brake hose in a reclosable plastic bag to prevent the entry of debris and prevent any residual brake fluid from leaking out.

8. Refer to Chapter Ten and follow the rear wheel removal procedure until the rear axle is removed sufficiently to allow removal of the rear caliper assembly (**Figure 115**). After removal of the caliper assembly, push the rear axle back into place and install the nut on the other side.

9. If necessary, disassemble and service the caliper assembly as described in this section.

10. If the rear caliper is not going to be serviced, place it in a reclosable plastic bag to keep it clean.

11. Install by reversing the removal steps. Note the following:

  a. Carefully install the caliper assembly onto the disc, being careful not to damage the leading edge of the brake pads.

  b. Refer to Chapter Ten and complete the installation of the rear axle.

  c. Apply clean DOT 4 brake fluid to the rubber portions of the *new* sealing washers prior to installation.

  d. Install *new* sealing washers against the side of each hose fitting.

  e. Install the banjo bolt (B, **Figure 114**). Tighten the banjo bolt to 17-22 ft.-lb. (23.1-29.8 N•m).

  f. If disassembled, tighten the three caliper mounting bolts (A, **Figure 114**) to 28-38 ft.-lb. (38-51.5 N•m).

  g. Bleed the brake as described in this chapter.

Disassembly

Refer to **Figure 116**.

13

1. Remove brake pads as described in this chapter.
2. Remove the caliper as described in this section.

> *NOTE*
> *If the pistons were partially forced out of the caliper body during removal, the application of compressed air may not be necessary. If the pistons or caliper bores are corroded or very dirty, a small amount of compressed air may be necessary to completely remove the pistons from the body bores.*

3. Place a piece of soft wood or folded shop cloth between the pistons within the caliper body.

> *WARNING*
> *Compressed air will force the pistons out of the caliper bodies under considerable force. Do not block the piston by hand, as injury will result.*

4. Apply air pressure in short bursts to the hydraulic fluid passageway and force out the pistons. Use a service station air hose if compressed air is not available.
5. Remove the three caliper body bolts (**Figure 117**) loosened during the removal procedure.
6. Separate the caliper body halves. Remove the O-ring seals (**Figure 118**) from the inboard caliper half and discard them. New O-ring seals must be installed every time the caliper is disassembled.

> *CAUTION*
> *Do not use a sharp tool to remove the dust and piston seals from the caliper cylinders. Do not damage the cylinder surface.*

7. Use a piece of wood or plastic scraper and carefully push the dust seal (A, **Figure 119**) and the piston seal (B) in toward the caliper cylinder and out of their grooves. Remove the dust and piston seals.
8. If necessary, unscrew and remove the bleed valve (**Figure 120**).
9. Inspect the caliper assembly as described in this section.

Assembly

> *CAUTION*
> *Do not use DOT 4 brake fluid for lubrication. If used, it will result in increased brake lever travel.*

> *NOTE*
> *Never reuse old dust seals or piston seals. Very minor damage or age deterioration can make the seals ineffective.*

1. Apply a light coat of Versilube silicone grease (G.E. part No. GE322L), disc brake caliper lube (Permatex part No. 20356), or an equivalent, to the following parts:

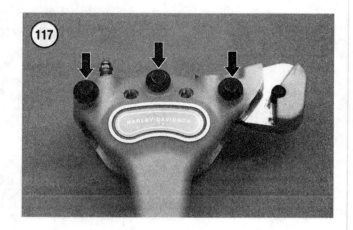

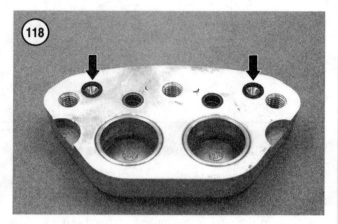

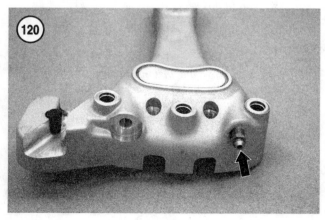

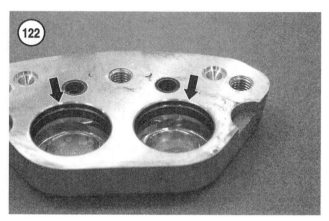

a. Inside diameter surfaces of both piston and dust seals.
b. Caliper bores.
c. Outside surfaces of pistons.
d. Closed end of pistons.

2. All remaining surfaces must remain dry.

3. Carefully install the *new* piston seals (**Figure 121**) into the lower grooves. Ensure the seals are properly seated in their respective grooves.

4. Carefully install the *new* dust seals (**Figure 122**) into the upper grooves. Ensure all seals are properly seated in their respective grooves.

5. Repeat the procedure to install new seals in the other caliper body.

6. Position the pistons with the open end facing out and install the pistons into the caliper cylinders (**Figure 123**). Push the pistons in until they bottom (**Figure 124**).

7. Repeat procedure to install pistons into the other caliper body. Ensure all pistons are installed correctly.

8. Install the anti-rattle spring into the outboard caliper body. Ensure the positioning foot is located as shown in **Figure 125**. The upper edge of the spring (**Figure 126**) must be flush with the caliper mating surface or the caliper cannot be assembled correctly.

9. Install *new* O-rings (**Figure 118**) into the inboard caliper body.

10. Install the outboard caliper half onto the inboard half. Ensure the O-rings are still in place and assemble the caliper.

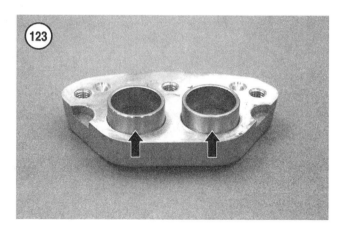

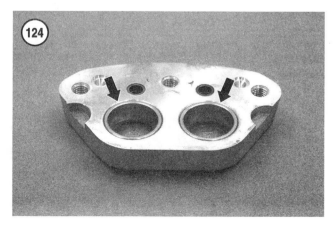

13

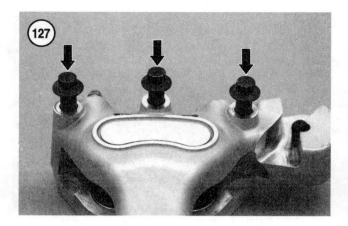

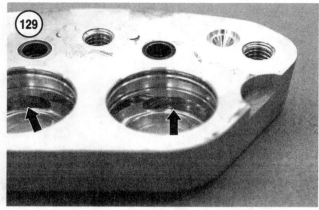

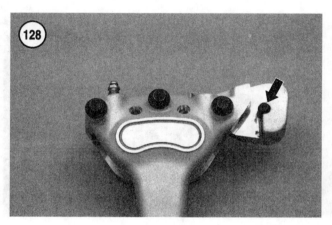

11. Install the three caliper body bolts (**Figure 127**) and tighten securely. They will be tightened to specification after the caliper is installed on the swing arm.

12. Install a *new* rubber bumper (**Figure 128**) if it was removed.

13. Install the bleed valve assembly (**Figure 120**) if it was removed. Tighten the bleed valve to 80-100 in.-lb. (9.0-11.3 N•m).

14. Install the caliper as described in this section.

15. Install the rear brake pads as described in this chapter.

16. Tighten the three caliper body mounting bolts to 28-38 ft.-lb. (38.0-51.5 N•m).

17. Bleed the brake as described in this chapter.

Inspection

1. Clean both caliper body halves and pistons in clean DOT 4 brake fluid or isopropyl alcohol and dry with compressed air.

2. Ensure the fluid passageways (**Figure 129**) in the piston bores are clear. Apply compressed air to the openings to ensure they are clear. Clean out if necessary with clean brake fluid.

3. Make sure the fluid passageways (**Figure 130**) in both caliper bodies are clear. Apply compressed air to the openings to make sure they are clear. Clean them out, if necessary, with clean brake fluid.

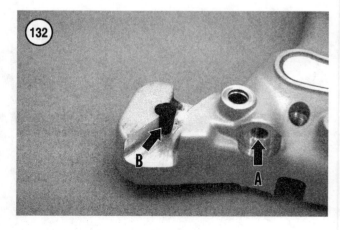

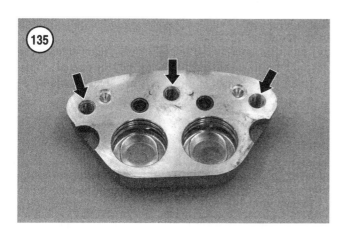

4. Inspect the piston and dust seal grooves (**Figure 131**) in both caliper halves for damage. If they are damaged or corroded, replace the caliper assembly.

5. Inspect the threaded banjo bolt hole (A, **Figure 132**) in the outboard caliper body. If it is worn or damaged, clean out with a thread tap or replace the caliper assembly.

6. Inspect the banjo bolt passage (**Figure 133**). Apply compressed air to the opening and ensure it is clear. Clean it out with fresh brake fluid. Install the banjo bolt and tighten to 17-22 ft.-lb. (23.1-29.8 N•m).

7. Inspect the threaded bleed valve hole in the outboard caliper body. If it is worn or damaged, clean out with a thread tap or replace the caliper assembly.

8. Inspect the bleed valve. Apply compressed air to the opening and ensure it is clear. Clean out if necessary with new brake fluid. Install the bleed valve and tighten to 80-100 in.-lb. (9.0-11.3 N•m).

9. Inspect both caliper bodies (**Figure 134**) for damage. Check the inboard caliper mounting bolt hole threads (**Figure 135**) for wear or damage. Clean up with an appropriate size tap or replace the caliper assembly.

10. Inspect the cylinder walls and pistons (**Figure 136**) for scratches, scoring or other damage.

11. Check the anti-rattle spring (**Figure 137**) for wear or damage.

12. Check the rubber bumper (**Figure 128**) for damage or deterioration; replace as necessary.

REAR BRAKE CALIPER (2008-2011 MODELS)

Removal/Installation

Read *Brake Service* in this chapter.

1. Support the motorcycle on level ground using a swing arm stand.

2. Block the front wheel so the motorcycle will not roll in either direction while the rear wheel is off ground.

3. Remove the right side saddlebag, on models so equipped.

4. Tie the end of the brake pedal to the frame. If the brake pedal is inadvertently applied, this will prevent the piston from being forced out of the cylinder.

5. If the caliper assembly is going to be disassembled for service, perform the following:

NOTE
Compressed air may not be necessary for piston removal during caliper disassembly if the pistons can be removed hydraulically as described in this section.

a. Remove the brake pads as described in this chapter.

CAUTION
Do not allow the pistons to travel out far enough to come in contact with the brake disc. If this happens the pistons may scratch or gouge the disc during caliper removal.

b. Slowly apply the brake lever to push the pistons part way out of caliper assembly for ease of removal during caliper service.

6. Remove the banjo bolt (A, **Figure 138**) and copper sealing washes attaching the brake hose to the caliper assembly.

7. Place the loose end of the brake hose in a reclosable plastic bag to prevent the entry of debris and to prevent residual brake fluid from leading out.

8. Remove the Torx (T40) slider pin (B, **Figure 138**) and Torx (T40) mounting bolt (C) securing the caliper to the mounting bracket.

9. Slide the rear brake caliper (D, **Figure 138**) toward the rear and off the brake disc and mounting bracket.

10. Place the rear caliper in a reclosable plastic bag to keep it clean.

11. Ensure the torque clip (**Figure 139**) is in place on the caliper mount.

12. Ensure the phenolic insulators are in place in the pistons.

13. Install the caliper assembly onto the disc, being careful not to damage the leading edge of the brake pads.

14. Slide the rear brake caliper onto the mounting bracket.

15. Tighten the Torx mounting bolt to 10-14 ft.-lb. (13.6-19.0 N•m).

16. Tighten the Torx slider pin to 10-14 ft.-lb. (13.6-19.0 N•m).

17. Apply clean DOT 4 brake fluid to *new* copper sealing washers prior to installation.

18. Install *new* sealing washers against the side of each hose fitting.

19. Install the banjo bolt and tighten to 21-25 ft.-lb. (28.5-33.9 N•m).

20. Install the brake pads as described in this chapter.

21. Bleed the brakes as described in this chapter, if necessary.

Disassembly

Refer to **Figure 140**.

NOTE
The brake caliper was assembled at the factory with Versilube silicone grease (G.E. part No. GE233L). Removal of the pistons from the piston bores is very difficult as this lubricant creates a very tight bond between the piston and the bore. It may be necessary to use padded pliers to assist in withdrawing the piston from the bore after it has been loosened with compressed. Do not damage the piston walls during removal.

1. Remove the rear brake pads as described in this chapter.

2. Remove the caliper as described in this section.

3. Remove the phenolic insulators from the pistons.

4. Pull the anti-rattle spring (**Figure 141**) straight up and off the caliper body.

NOTE
If the pistons were partially forced out of the caliper body during removal, the use of compressed air may not be necessary. If the pistons or caliper bores are corroded or very dirty, a small amount of compressed air may be necessary to completely remove the pistons from the caliper body bores.

5. Place a piece of soft wood or folded shop cloth over the end of the pistons and the caliper body. Turn this assembly over with the pistons facing down over a workbench top. Tighten the bleed valve (A, **Figure 142**).

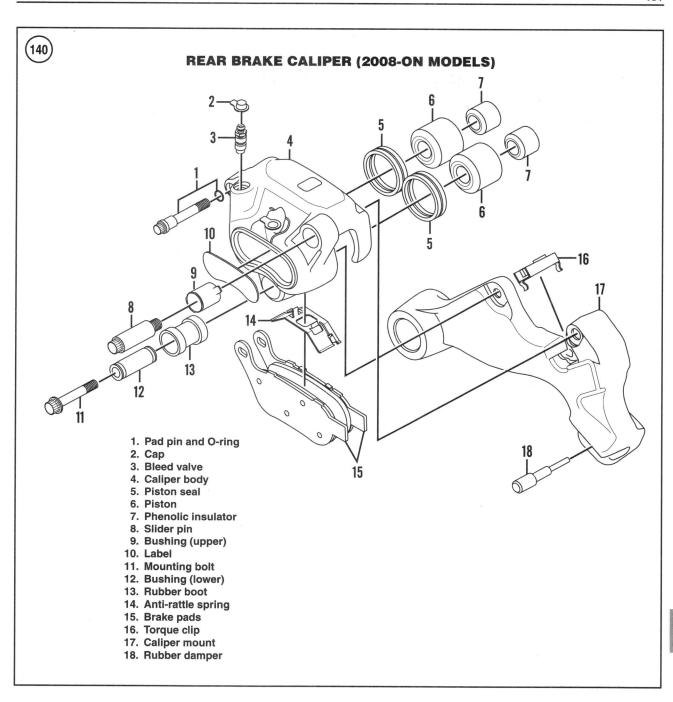

(140)

REAR BRAKE CALIPER (2008-ON MODELS)

1. Pad pin and O-ring
2. Cap
3. Bleed valve
4. Caliper body
5. Piston seal
6. Piston
7. Phenolic insulator
8. Slider pin
9. Bushing (upper)
10. Label
11. Mounting bolt
12. Bushing (lower)
13. Rubber boot
14. Anti-rattle spring
15. Brake pads
16. Torque clip
17. Caliper mount
18. Rubber damper

13

(141)

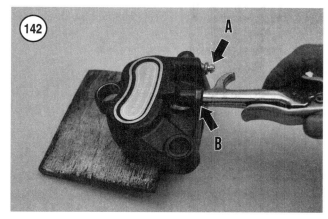

(142)

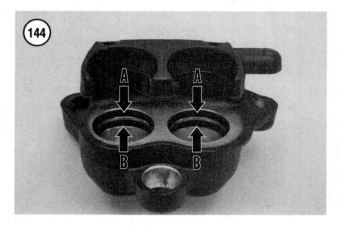

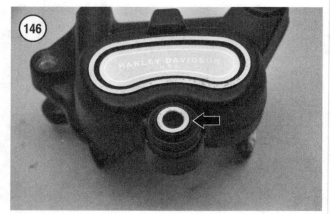

> *WARNING*
> *Compressed air will force the pistons out of the caliper bodies under considerable force. Do not block the piston by hand, as injury will result.*

6. Apply air pressure in short bursts to the hydraulic fluid passageway (B, **Figure 142**) and force out the pistons. Use a service station air hose if compressed air is not available.

7. Remove both pistons (**Figure 143**). Due to the tight fit of the piston in the bore, the use of padded pliers may be necessary.

> *CAUTION*
> *Do not use a sharp tool to remove the dust and piston seals from the caliper cylinders. Do not damage the cylinder surface.*

8. Use a piece of wood or plastic scraper and carefully push the dust seal and piston seal in toward the caliper cylinder and out of their grooves. Remove the dust (A, **Figure 144**) and piston (B) seals from both cylinders.

9. Unscrew and remove the bleed valve (A, **Figure 142**).

10. Remove the lower bushing (**Figure 145**) from the rubber boot.

11. Inspect the caliper assembly as described in this section.

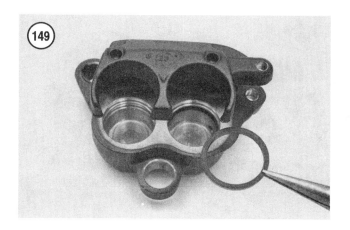

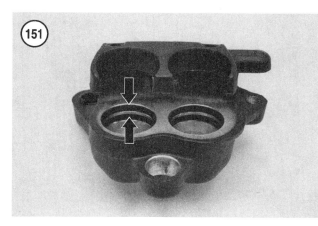

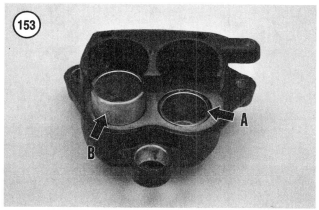

Assembly

CAUTION
Do not use DOT 4 brake fluid for lubrication.
If used, it will result in increased brake lever
travel.

NOTE
Never reuse old dust seals or piston seals.
Very minor damage or age deterioration can
make the seals ineffective.

1. Apply a light coat of Versilube silicone grease (G.E. part No. GE233L), disc brake caliper lube (Permatex part No. 20356), or an equivalent, to the following parts:
    a. Inside diameter surfaces of both piston and dust seals.
    b. Caliper bores.
    c. Outside surfaces of pistons.
    d. Closed end of pistons.
2. All remaining surfaces must remain dry.
3. Install the lower bushing (**Figure 145**) into the rubber boot. Push it in until it is centered in the rubber boot (**Figure 146**).
4. Carefully install a *new* piston seal (**Figure 147**) into the lower groove. Ensure the seal is properly seated in its respective groove (**Figure 148**).
5. Carefully install a *new* dust seal (**Figure 149**) into the upper groove. Ensure the seal is properly seated in its respective groove (**Figure 150**).
6. Repeat procedure to install the seals in the remaining cylinder (**Figure 151**).
7. Position the piston with the open end facing out and install the piston (**Figure 152**) into the piston bore. Push the piston in until it bottoms (A, **Figure 153**).
8. Repeat procedure to install the remaining piston (B, **Figure 153**).
9. Check that both pistons (**Figure 154**) are bottomed in their respective piston bore.
10. Install the phenolic insulators (**Figure 155**) into the pistons, if removed. Push them in until they are completely seated within the piston bore.

13

11. Install the anti-rattle spring into the caliper body. Ensure the positioning foot is located as shown in **Figure 156**.

12. Install the bleed valve (A, **Figure 142**), if removed, and tighten to 80-100 in.-lb. (9.0-11.3 N•m).

13. Install the caliper as described in this section.

14. Install the rear brake pads as described in this chapter.

15. Bleed the brake as described in this chapter.

Inspection

1. Clean both caliper body halves and pistons in clean DOT 4 brake fluid or isopropyl alcohol and dry with compressed air.

2. Ensure the fluid passageways (**Figure 157**) in the piston bores are clear. Apply compressed air to the openings to ensure they are clear. Clean out, if necessary, with fresh brake fluid.

3. Inspect the piston and dust seal grooves (**Figure 158**) for damage. If they are damaged or corroded, replace the caliper assembly.

4. Inspect the threaded banjo bolt hole (A, **Figure 159**) in the caliper body. If it is worn or damaged, clean out with a thread tap or replace the caliper assembly.

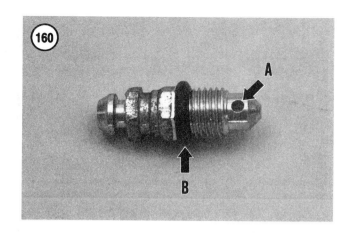

160

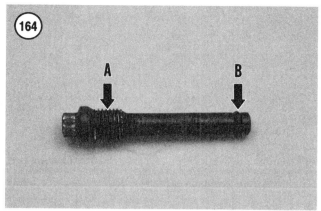

164

161

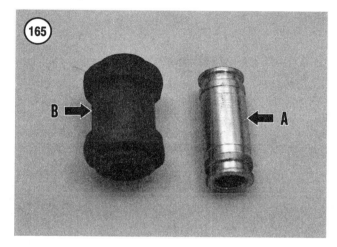

165

162

5. Inspect the threaded bleed valve hole (B, **Figure 159**) in the caliper body. If it is worn or damaged, clean out with a thread tap or replace the caliper assembly.

6. Inspect the banjo bolt passage. Apply compressed air to the opening and ensure it is clear. Clean out with new brake fluid.

7. Inspect the bleed valve. Apply compressed air to the opening (A, **Figure 160**) and ensure it is clear. Clean out if necessary with new brake fluid. Install a *new* O-ring (B, **Figure 160**). Install the bleed valve and tighten to 80-100 in.-lb. (9.0-11.3 N•m).

8. Inspect the caliper body (**Figure 161**) for damage.

9. Inspect the cylinder walls and pistons (A, **Figure 162**) for scratches, scoring or other damage.

10. Inspect the phenolic insulators (B, **Figure 162**) for wear

11. Check the anti-rattle spring (**Figure 163**) for wear or damage.

12. Inspect the pad pin threads (A, **Figure 164**). If worn or damaged, clean out with a thread die or replace. Install a *new* O-ring (B, **Figure 164**).

13. Inspect the lower bushing (A, **Figure 165**) for wear or damage; replace if necessary.

14. Inspect the rubber boot (B, **Figure 165**) for damage or deterioration; replace if necessary.

163

13

REAR MASTER CYLINDER (ALL MODELS)

Read *Brake Service* in this chapter.

Removal

1. Support the motorcycle on level ground using a swing arm stand.

2. Block the front wheel so the motorcycle will not roll in either direction.

3. Remove the right side saddlebag, models so equipped.

4. Remove the exhaust system as described in Chapter Four.

5. Remove the mounting bolts (A, **Figure 166**) and nut (B) securing the muffler rear bracket (C) to the crankcase. Remove the bracket if necessary.

6. At the rear brake caliper, perform the following:
   a. Insert a hose onto the end of the bleed valve (**Figure 167**). Insert the open end of the hose into a container.
   b. Open the bleed valve and operate the rear brake pedal to drain the brake fluid from the master cylinder and rear brake line. Remove the hose and close the bleed valve after draining the assembly. Discard the brake fluid properly.

7. Remove the screws (A, **Figure 168**) securing the cover. Then, remove the cover (B, **Figure 168**) and diaphragm.

8. Remove and/or release any clips or ties securing the rear brake line to the chassis. Create just enough slack in the brake line to allow removal of the brake line from the rear of the master cylinder fitting.

9. Disconnect the connector (**Figure 169**) from the brake light switch.

10. Hold the hex nut (A, **Figure 170**) and remove the brake light switch/banjo bolt (B) securing the brake hose to the rear of the master cylinder cartridge body. Place the loose end of the brake hose in a plastic bag to prevent the entry of debris and prevent any residual brake fluid from leaking out.

11. Remove the circle cotter (A, **Figure 171**) and pivot pin (B) from the rear brake pedal. Disconnect the brake rod (C, **Figure 171**) from the pedal.

12. Loosen the jam nut (A, **Figure 172**) on the brake rod (B).

13. Unscrew the push rod (A, **Figure 173**) from the master cylinder push rod (B).

14. Use an open end wrench, and unscrews the 28-mm hex nut (A, **Figure 170**) securing the rear of the master cylinder assembly to the frame boss. Pull the master cylinder free from the square hole in the frame boss.

15. Service the master cylinder as described in this section, if necessary. If the master cylinder is not going to be serviced, place it in a plastic bag to keep it clean.

Installation

1. Carefully insert the piston end of the master cylinder fitting into the square hole in the frame boss. Ensure that the fitting is fully engaged within the frame boss square hole.

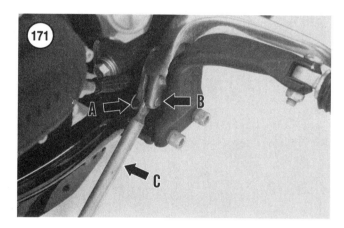

2. Apply Loctite Threadlocker 243 (blue), or an equivalent threadlock, to the hex nut threads prior to installation. Install the 28-mm hex nut (A, **Figure 170**) and tighten to 30-40 ft.-lb. (40.7-54.2 N•m).

3. Thread the push rod (A, **Figure 173**) onto the master cylinder pushrod (B). Do not tighten the jam nut at this time.

4. Install *new* sealing washers against each side of the hose fitting.

5. Move the brake hose into position and install the brake light switch/banjo bolt (B, **Figure 170**) through the hose fitting and *new* sealing washers, and into the rear of the master cylinder body. Then, tighten the brake light switch/banjo bolt to 21-25 ft.-lb. (28.5-33.9 N•m).

6. Connect the connector (**Figure 169**) onto the brake light switch.

> *WARNING*
> *To avoid the brake rod coming apart from the master cylinder push rod, never allow more than nine threads exposed between the brake rod and jam nut.*

7. Adjust the brake rod so there are less than nine threads visible (C, **Figure 172**). Securely tighten the jam nut (A, **Figure 172**).

8. Connect the brake rod (C, **Figure 171**) onto the pedal and insert the pivot pin (B). Install the circle cotter (A, **Figure 171**) securing the pivot pin. Make sure it is secure on the pivot pin.

9. Ensure the rubber boot (D, **Figure 172**) drain hole is located at the bottom. Readjust if necessary.

10. Secure the rear brake line to the chassis using new ties or clips, where removed.

11. Bleed the rear brake as described in this chapter.

12. Install the right side saddlebag, models so equipped.

13. Install the exhaust system as described in Chapter Four.

Disassembly

Refer to **Figure 174**.

1. Remove the rear master cylinder as described in this section.

2. Clean the master cylinder housing with clean DOT 4 brake fluid or isopropyl alcohol and dry.

3. Store the master cylinder components in a divided container, such as an egg carton, to help maintain their correct alignment position.

4. If still installed, remove the master cylinder cover and diaphragm.

5. Press down on the washer (A, **Figure 175**) and hold it down.

6. Remove the small snap ring (B, **Figure 175**) from the pushrod (C).

7. Carefully release the spring, and remove the washer, rubber boot (A, **Figure 176**), retainer, return spring (B) and washer (C).

13

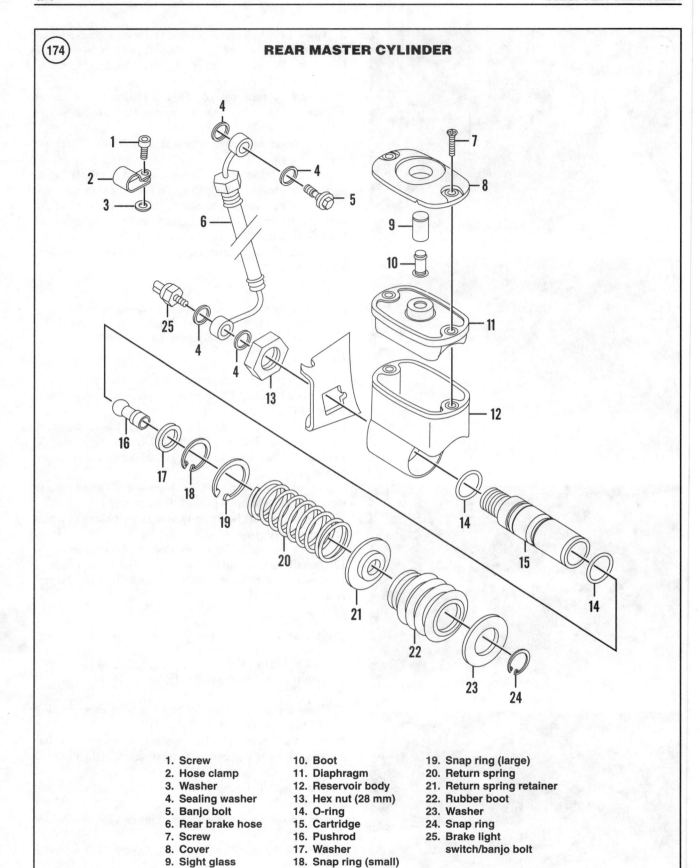

REAR MASTER CYLINDER

1. Screw
2. Hose clamp
3. Washer
4. Sealing washer
5. Banjo bolt
6. Rear brake hose
7. Screw
8. Cover
9. Sight glass
10. Boot
11. Diaphragm
12. Reservoir body
13. Hex nut (28 mm)
14. O-ring
15. Cartridge
16. Pushrod
17. Washer
18. Snap ring (small)
19. Snap ring (large)
20. Return spring
21. Return spring retainer
22. Rubber boot
23. Washer
24. Snap ring
25. Brake light
switch/banjo bolt

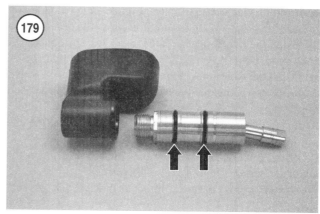

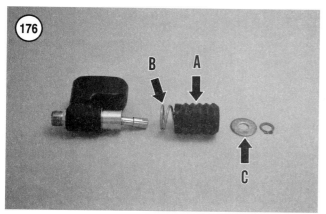

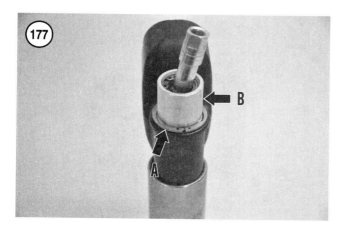

8. Remove the large snap ring (A, **Figure 177**) from the cartridge (B).

9. Place the reservoir (A, **Figure 178**) and cartridge assembly into a deep socket (B).

10. Use a soft-faced mallet and carefully drive cartridge assembly (C, **Figure 178**) out of the reservoir body (A), if necessary.

11. Inspect the components as described in this section.

Assembly

1. If removed, soak the cartridge in clean DOT 4 brake fluid for at least 15 minutes to make the O-rings (**Figure 179**) pliable. Coat the inside of the reservoir with clean brake fluid prior to the assembly of parts.

2. Install the cartridge as follows, if removed:

    a. Position the notch on cartridge body (**Figure 180**) to align with the notch in the reservoir.

    b. Use hand pressure only, carefully push the cartridge part way into the reservoir. Push it in until it bottoms. If necessary, place the reservoir body (A, **Figure 181**) on wood block and place a deep socket (B) over the end of the cartridge. Use a soft-faced mallet and carefully tap it into place until it is seated (**Figure 182**). Ensure that the notch on cartridge body (**Figure 180**) is aligned with the notch in the reservoir body.

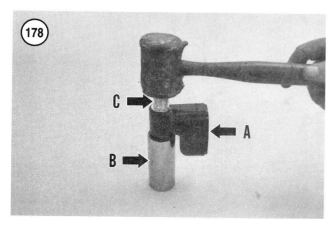

13

3. Install the large snap ring (A, **Figure 177**) onto the cartridge body (B), and make sure it is correctly seated.

4. Install the return spring (B, **Figure 176**), spring retainer and rubber boot (A) onto the pushrod and cartridge.

5. Install the washer (A, **Figure 175**) onto the boot.

6. Press down on the washer, compress the spring, and hold it down.

8. Install the small snap ring (B, **Figure 175**) onto the end of the pushrod (C). Make sure it is correctly seated.

9. Install the diaphragm and reservoir cover. Tighten the cover screws to 6-8 in.-lb. (07-0.9 N•m).

10. Install the rear master cylinder as described in this section.

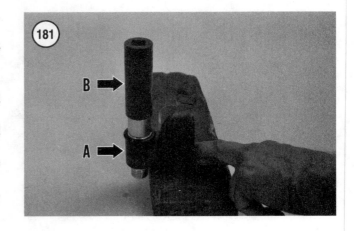

Inspection

1. Clean all parts in clean DOT 4 brake fluid or isopropyl alcohol and dry with compressed air. Replace worn or damage parts as described in this section. It is recommended that a new cartridge rebuild kit assembly be installed every time the master cylinder is disassembled.

2. Inspect the cartridge body cylinder bore surface (A, **Figure 183**) in the reservoir body for signs of wear and damage. Do not hone the cartridge bore to clean or repair it. If there is any visible wear or damage, replace the reservoir.

3. Inspect cartridge, O-rings and pushrod (**Figure 184**) for damage. Replace the O-rings if necessary.

4. Check the return spring (B, **Figure 176**) for bending, unequally spaced coils or corrosion.

5. Inspect the boot (A, **Figure 176**) for tears or deterioration.

6. Check the pushrod, washer and small snap ring (**Figure 185**) for bending, wear or damage.

7. Check the reservoir body (B, **Figure 183**) for corrosion or other damage. Ensure the opening (**Figure 186**) in the base is clear.

8. Check the reservoir body cover (**Figure 187**) and diaphragm (**Figure 188**) for damage.

BRAKE HOSE AND LINE REPLACEMENT

A combination of metal brake pipes and flexible brake hoses connect the master cylinder to the brake caliper(s). Banjo fittings connect brake hoses to the master cylinder and brake calipers. At each connection, the banjo bolt is sealed with a combination steel/rubber sealing washers. Replace the sealing washers every time a fitting is disassembled, or whenever a line is replaced.

Replace the brake line assembly if the flexible portion is swelling, cracking or other damaged, or if the metal brake pipes leaks or if there are dents or cracks. When replacing a new brake line assembly, ensure the length and angle of the steel pipe portions are correct.

Read *Brake Service* in this chapter.

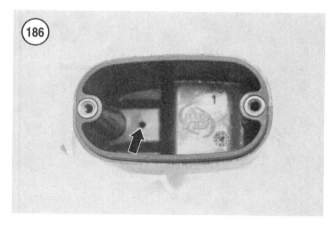

Front Brake Line Removal/Installation

Refer to **Figure 189** or **Figure 190**.

1. Support the motorcycle on level ground using a swing arm stand.

2. Block the front wheel so the motorcycle will not roll in either direction.

CAUTION
Cover the fuel tank and front fender with a heavy cloth or plastic tarp to protect them from accidental brake fluid spills. Wash brake fluid off painted, plated, or plastic surfaces immediately as it will damage most surfaces it contacts. Use soapy water and rinse completely.

3. Cover the fuel tank to protect it from any accidental brake fluid spills.

4. Drain the front brake system as described in this chapter.

5. Before removing the brake line assembly, note the brake line routing from the master cylinder to the caliper(s). In addition, note the number and position of any metal hose clamps and/or plastic ties used to hold the brake lines in place. Install the brake hose assembly along its original path. The metal clamps can be reused.

6. Cut any cable ties securing the brake line assembly and discard them.

7. Remove the bolt (**Figure 191**) securing the brake hose mounting plate, or clamp to the lower steering stem. On models so equipped, do not lose the guide plate between the hose mounting plate and the steering stem.

8A. On single-disc models, remove the screw and washer securing the metal clamp to the base of the lower fork bridge. Spread the clamp and remove it from the brake line.

8B. On dual-disc models, remove the screw securing the brake line assembly to the base of the lower fork bridge.

9. Remove the banjo bolt (**Figure 192**) and sealing washers securing the hose to the caliper(s).

10. Remove the banjo bolt (**Figure 193**) and sealing washers securing the hose to the front master cylinder.

11. Cover the ends of the brake hoses to prevent brake fluid leakage.

12. Carefully remove the brake hose assembly from the frame.

13. If the existing brake hose assembly is going to be reinstalled, inspect it as follows:

   a. On single-disc models, check the pipes where they enter and exit at the flexible hoses. Check the crimped clamp for looseness or damage.

   b. Check the flexible hose portions for swelling, cracks, cuts or other damage.

   c. Check the banjo bolt fittings at each end of the brake hose for damage.

   d. If any wear or damage is found, replace the brake hose assembly.

14. Install the brake hose, sealing washers and banjo bolts by reversing the removal steps. Note the following:

13

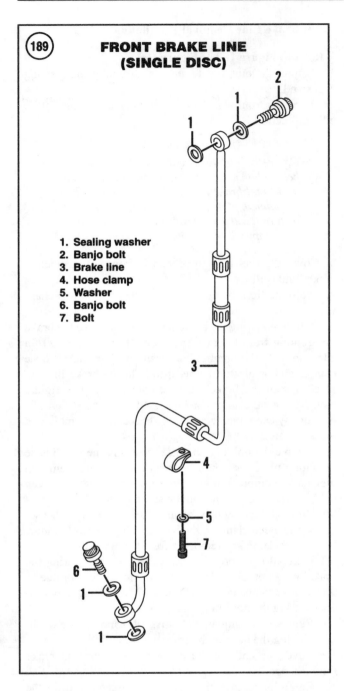

FRONT BRAKE LINE (SINGLE DISC)

1. Sealing washer
2. Banjo bolt
3. Brake line
4. Hose clamp
5. Washer
6. Banjo bolt
7. Bolt

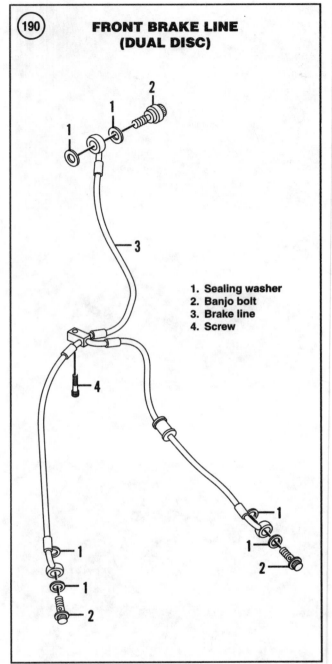

FRONT BRAKE LINE (DUAL DISC)

1. Sealing washer
2. Banjo bolt
3. Brake line
4. Screw

a. Install *new* sealing washers against each side of the hose fitting.
b. Carefully install the clip to hold the brake hose in place. Tighten the screws securely.
c. Tighten the banjo bolts to 17-22 ft.-lb. (23.1-29.9 N•m) on 2006-2007 models and to 21-25 ft.-lb. (28.5-33.9 N•m) on 2008-2011 models.
d. Refill the front master cylinder with clean brake fluid clearly marked DOT 4. Bleed the front brake system as described in this chapter.

Rear Brake Line Removal/Installation

Refer to **Figure 194**.

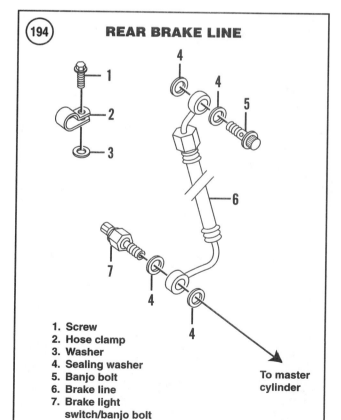

REAR BRAKE LINE

1. Screw
2. Hose clamp
3. Washer
4. Sealing washer
5. Banjo bolt
6. Brake line
7. Brake light switch/banjo bolt

To master cylinder

CAUTION
Take precautions so brake fluid will not spill on the swing arm, frame or rear wheel. Brake fluid will damage most surfaces. Immediately wash off spilled brake fluid with soapy water and rinse the area completely.

1. Support the motorcycle on level ground using a swing arm stand.

2. Block the front wheel so the motorcycle will not roll in either direction while the rear wheel is off ground.

3. Remove the right side saddlebag as described in Chapter Fourteen, models so equipped.

4. Remove the exhaust system as described in Chapter Four.

5. Drain the rear brake system as described in this chapter.

6. Before removing the brake line assembly, note the brake line routing from the master cylinder to the caliper (**Figure 195**). In addition, note the number and position of the metal hose clamps, plastic clips and plastic ties used to hold the brake line in place. Install the brake hose assembly along its original path. The metal clamp and plastic clips can be reused. However, new plastic ties must be installed.

7. Remove the bolt (**Figure 196**), star washer and clamp securing the brake hose to the rear swing arm.

13

8. Disconnect the brake light switch connector (**Figure 197**).

9. Hold the hex nut (A, **Figure 198**) and remove the brake light switch/banjo bolt (B) securing the brake hose to the rear of the master cylinder cartridge body.

10. Remove the banjo bolt (**Figure 199**) and washers securing the brake hose to the rear caliper.

11. Carefully remove the rear brake line assembly from behind the shock absorber. Then, remove it from the motorcycle.

12. If the existing brake line assembly is going to be reinstalled, inspect it as follows:

    a. Check the banjo bolt fittings at each end of the brake hose for damage.

    b. Check the flexible hose portion for swelling, cracks, cuts or other damage.

    c. If any wear or damage is found, replace the brake hose.

13. Install the brake hose by reversing the removal steps. Note the following:

    a. Install *new* sealing washers against each side of the hose fitting.

    b. Carefully install the clips and guides to hold the brake hose in place.

    c. Tighten the banjo bolt to 17-22 ft.-lb. (23.1-29.8 N•m) on 2006-2007 models and to 21-25 ft.-lb. (28.5-33.9 N•m) on 2008-2011 models.

    d. Apply Loctite 565 thread sealant, or an equivalent, to the brake light switch/banjo bolt threads prior to installation.

    e. Tighten the brake light switch/banjo bolt to 21-25 ft.-lb. (28.5-33.9 N•m).

    f. Refill the master cylinder with clean brake fluid clearly marked DOT 4. Bleed the rear brake system as described in this chapter.

BRAKE DISC

Inspection

The brake disc can be inspected while attached to the wheel. Small nicks and marks on the disc are not important, but radial scratches deep enough to snag a fingernail reduce braking effectiveness and increase brake pad wear. If these grooves are present and the brake pads are wearing rapidly, replace the disc.

A warped disc may be caused by a faulty caliper due to the brake pads dragging on the disc and overheating it. Overheating can also be caused by unequal pad pressure on the disc. Check for worn or damaged caliper piston seals and/or master cylinder cups, or plugged master cylinder's small relief port.

The brake disc cannot be machined to remove warp or damage. Each disc is also marked (**Figure 200**) with the minimum (MIN) thickness.

1. Support the motorcycle with the wheel (front or rear) off the ground.

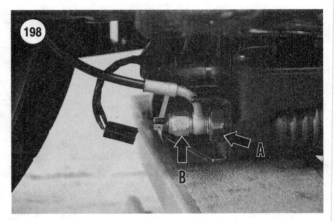

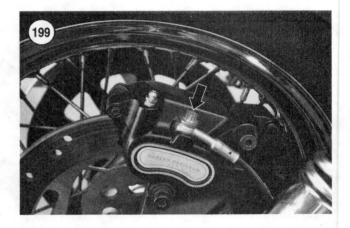

2. Measure the thickness of the brake disc (**Figure 201**) at several locations around the disc. Replace the disc if the thickness in any area is less than the minimum allowable specification stamped on the brake disc.

3. Ensure the disc mounting bolts are tight prior to checking disc runout.

4. Position the dial indicator stem against the brake disc (**Figure 202**). Zero the dial gauge and slowly turn the wheel and measure the runout. If the runout is excessive:

    a. Check for loose or missing fasteners.

    b. Remove the front and/or rear wheel and check the wheel bearing condition.

5. Clean the disc of any brake fluid drips or corrosion. Wipe it clean with a rag dampened with brake parts cleaner. Never use an oil-based solvent that may leave an oily residue on the disc.

Removal/Installation

1. Remove the front or rear wheel as described in Chapter Ten.

2. Mark the disc with a R (right side) and L (left side) prior to removal.

3. Remove the Torx bolts (**Figure 203**), and washers on models so equipped, securing the brake disc to the hub and remove the disc. Discard the bolts as they cannot be reused.

4. Check the threaded brake disc bolt holes in the wheel hub for thread damage. Clean out with a tap if necessary.

5. Clean the disc and the disc mounting surface thoroughly with brake parts cleaner or contact cleaner. Allow the surfaces to dry before installation.

NOTE
The dual front brake discs are symmetrical and can be installed on either side. During installation, they should be installed on the same side as noted during removal.

6. Install the disc onto the correct side of the wheel hub.

7. Install the washers onto the bolts, on models so equipped.

8. Install *new* brake disc Torx bolts and tighten to the following:

    a. Front wheel Torx bolt: 16-24 ft.-lb. (21.7-32.5 N•m).

    b. Rear wheel Torx bolt: 30-45 ft.-lb. (40.7-61.0 N•m).

9. Install the front or rear wheel as described in Chapter Ten.

REAR BRAKE PEDAL

Removal/Installation
(FXD, FXDC, FXDL, FXDB and FXD35 Models)

Refer to **Figure 204**.

1. Remove the exhaust system as described in Chapter Four.

2. Remove the circle cotter (A, **Figure 205**) and pivot pin (B) from the rear brake pedal. Disconnect the brake rod (C, **Figure 205**) from the pedal. Lower the brake rod.

3. Remove the bolts (D, **Figure 205**) and lockwashers securing the foot rest (E) to the mounting bracket. Remove the foot rest, and do not lose the spring washer.

4. Remove the snap ring and remove the brake pedal from the footrest mounting bracket pivot post.

13

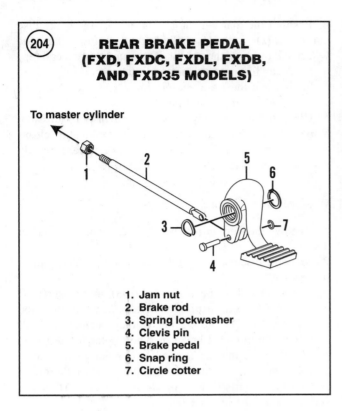

204 REAR BRAKE PEDAL
(FXD, FXDC, FXDL, FXDB,
AND FXD35 MODELS)

To master cylinder

1. Jam nut
2. Brake rod
3. Spring lockwasher
4. Clevis pin
5. Brake pedal
6. Snap ring
7. Circle cotter

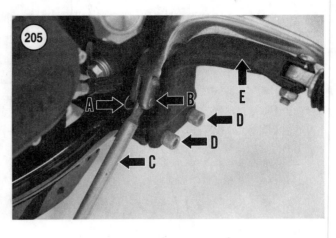

205

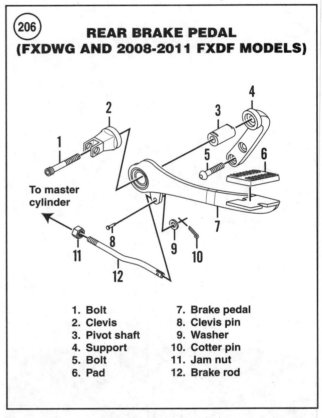

206 REAR BRAKE PEDAL
(FXDWG AND 2008-2011 FXDF MODELS)

To master
cylinder

1. Bolt	7. Brake pedal
2. Clevis	8. Clevis pin
3. Pivot shaft	9. Washer
4. Support	10. Cotter pin
5. Bolt	11. Jam nut
6. Pad	12. Brake rod

5. Remove the spring lockwasher from the pivot post.

6. Lubricate the brake pedal bearing and the pivot post with multipurpose grease.

7. Install the spring lockwasher onto the pivot post.

8. Install the brake pedal onto the footrest mounting bracket pivot post and install a *new* snap ring.

9. Install the footrest onto the mounting bracket. Install the bolts and lockwashers. Securely tighten the bolts.

10. Connect the brake rod onto the brake pedal. Insert the clevis pin from the outside and install a *new* circle cotter. Ensure the cotter is snapped correctly into place.

11. Apply the brake pedal to ensure correct movement without binding.

12. Install the exhaust system as described in Chapter Four.

Removal/Installation (FXDWG, FXDWG Anniversary, FXDSE, FXDSE2, FXDF and FXDFSE Models)

Refer to **Figures 206-209**.

1. Remove the exhaust system as described in Chapter Four.

2. Remove the circle cotter, or cotter pin, and pivot pin from the rear brake pedal. Disconnect the brake rod from the pedal.

3. Remove the bolt and nut securing the foot rest to the mounting bracket. Remove the foot rest, and do not lose the spring washer. Lower the brake rod.

4. Remove the bolt securing the brake pedal to the support.

5. Remove the clevis and brake pedal assembly from the support on the frame.

6. Remove the pivot shaft from within the brake pedal.

7. Remove the bolts securing the support to the frame, if necessary.

8. Lubricate the brake pedal bushing and the pivot shaft with multipurpose grease.

9. Install the rear brake pedal support and mounting bolts onto the frame, if removed. Tighten the support bolts to 25-35 ft.-lb. (33.9-47.5 N•m).

NOTE
The flats on the pivot shaft must be indexed correctly onto the flats in the support and brake pedal. If not aligned correctly there will be a gap on each side of the brake pedal pivot area.

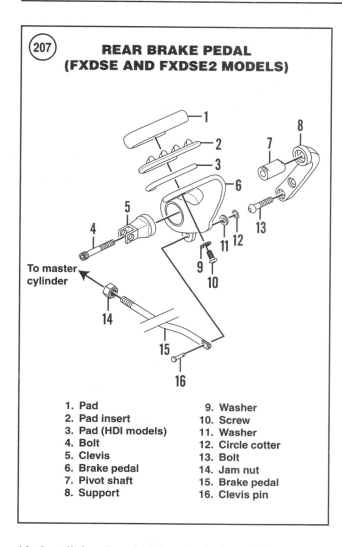

REAR BRAKE PEDAL (FXDSE AND FXDSE2 MODELS)

1. Pad
2. Pad insert
3. Pad (HDI models)
4. Bolt
5. Clevis
6. Brake pedal
7. Pivot shaft
8. Support
9. Washer
10. Screw
11. Washer
12. Circle cotter
13. Bolt
14. Jam nut
15. Brake pedal
16. Clevis pin

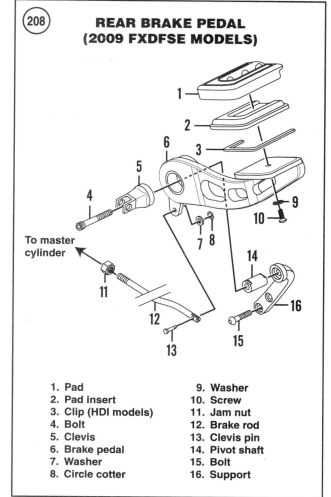

REAR BRAKE PEDAL (2009 FXDFSE MODELS)

1. Pad
2. Pad insert
3. Clip (HDI models)
4. Bolt
5. Clevis
6. Brake pedal
7. Washer
8. Circle cotter
9. Washer
10. Screw
11. Jam nut
12. Brake rod
13. Clevis pin
14. Pivot shaft
15. Bolt
16. Support

10. Install the pivot shaft into the brake pedal. Rotate the pivot shaft so the small flats at each end face up.

11. Install the brake pedal assembly onto the frame support. Ensure that the flat on the pivot shaft is indexed correctly onto the support.

12. Install the clevis onto the brake pedal. Ensure that the flat on the pivot shaft is indexed correctly onto the clevis.

13. Install the bolt securing the brake pedal to the support and securely tighten.

14. Connect the brake rod onto the brake pedal. Install the washer and *new* cotter pin Ensure the cotter is snapped correctly into place.

15. Install the exhaust system as described in Chapter Four.

Inspection (All Models)

1. Inspect the bearing or pivot bushing within the pivot bore for wear or damage.

2. Carefully press out the old bushing and install a new bushing if necessary.

3. Inspect the pivot shaft for wear or distortion, models so equipped.

4. Inspect the rear brake pedal and support (on models so equipped) for wear, cracks or damage. Replace part(s), if necessary.

5. Replace the brake pedal pad, if necessary, on models so equipped.

BRAKE BLEEDING

General Bleeding Tips

1. Clean the bleed valves and the surrounding area of all dirt and debris. Ensure the passageway in the end of the bleed valve is open and clear.

2. Use a box-end wrench to open and close the bleed valves. This prevents damage to the bleed valve hex-head. Replace bleed valves with damaged hex-heads. These are difficult to loosen and cannot be tightened fully.

3. Install the box-end wrench on the bleed valve before installing the catch hose. This allows operation of the wrench without having to disconnect the hose.

4. Use a clear catch hose to allow the visual inspection of the brake fluid as it leaves the brake caliper. Air bubbles visible in the catch hose indicate there still may be air trapped in the brake system.

13

5. Depending on the amount of play present in the bleed valve when it is loosened, it is possible to see air exiting through the catch hose even though there is no air in the brake system. A damaged catch hose also caused air leaks. In both cases, air is being introduced into the bleed system at the bleed valve threads and catch hose connection and not from within the brake system itself. This condition can be misleading and cause excessive brake bleeding when there is not air in the system.

6. Open the bleed valve just enough to allow fluid to pass through the valve and into the catch bottle. The farther the bleed valve is opened, the looser the valve becomes. This allows air to be drawn into the system from around the bleed valve threads.

7. If air is suspected of entering from around the bleed valve threads, remove the bleed valve. Wrap a small amount of Teflon tape around the bleed valve threads to seal them and install the bleed valve.

8. If the system is difficult to bleed, tap the banjo bolt on the master cylinder several times; it is not uncommon for air bubbles to become trapped in the hose connection where the brake fluid exits the master cylinder. When a number of bubbles appear in the master cylinder reservoir after tapping the banjo bolt, it means air was trapped in this area. Also tap the other bolt and line connections or joints at the caliper and other brake units.

Vacuum Bleeding

Vacuum bleeding can be accomplished by using either a hand-operated pump (**Figure 210**) or a compressed air tool. The tools described in this section can be used by one person to drain and bleed the brake system.

Hand-operated vacuum pump

1. Connect the catch hose between the bleed valve and catch bottle. Connect the other hose between the catch bottle and vacuum pump. Refer to the tool manufacturer's instruction for additional information.

2. Secure the vacuum pump to the motorcycle with a length of stiff wire so it is possible to check and refill the master cylinder reservoirs without having to disconnect the catch hose.

3. Remove the dust cap from the caliper bleed valve.

4. Place a clean shop cloth over the caliper to protect it from accidental brake fluid spills.

5. Clean the top of the master cylinder of all dirt and debris.

6. Remove the screws securing the master cylinder top cover. Then, remove the cover and diaphragm.

7. Fill the reservoir almost to the top with new DOT 4 brake fluid and reinstall the diaphragm and cover. Leave the cover in place during this procedure to prevent the entry of dirt.

8. Operate the vacuum pump to create a vacuum in the catch hose connected to the bleed valve. Then, open the

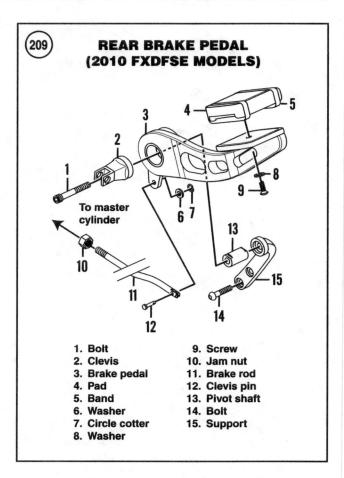

REAR BRAKE PEDAL (2010 FXDFSE MODELS)

To master cylinder

1. Bolt
2. Clevis
3. Brake pedal
4. Pad
5. Band
6. Washer
7. Circle cotter
8. Washer
9. Screw
10. Jam nut
11. Brake rod
12. Clevis pin
13. Pivot shaft
14. Bolt
15. Support

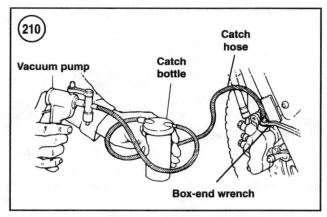

Vacuum pump   Catch bottle   Catch hose

Box-end wrench

bleed valve with the wrench to allow the brake fluid to be drawn through the master cylinder, brake hoses and lines. Close the bleed valve before the brake fluid stops flowing from the system (no more vacuum in the line) or before the master cylinder reservoir runs empty.

NOTE
Do not allow the master cylinder reservoir to empty during the bleeding operation or more air will enter the system. If this occurs, the procedure must be repeated.

9. Continue the bleeding process until the fluid running through the vacuum hose is clear and without any air bub-

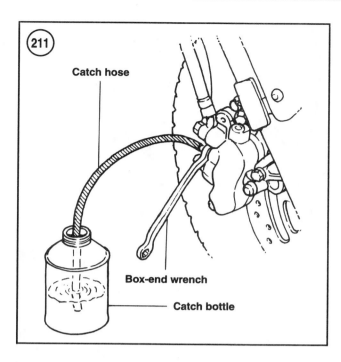

(211)

Catch hose

Box-end wrench

Catch bottle

bles. Tighten the bleed valve to 80-100 in.-lb. (9.0-11.3 N•m). Remove the brake bleeder assembly and reinstall the bleed valve dust cap.

10. If necessary, add fluid to correct the level in the master cylinder reservoir. When topping off the front master cylinder, turn the handlebar until the reservoir is level. Add fluid until the level is even with the reservoir gasket surface. The fluid level in the rear master cylinder must be slightly below the upper gasket surface. Refer to Chapter Three.

11. Reinstall the reservoir diaphragm and cover. Install the screws and tighten to 6-8 in.-lb. (0.7-0.9 N•m).

12. Test the feel of the brake lever or pedal. It should be firm and offer the same resistance each time it is operated. If it feels spongy, there is probably still air in the system. Bleed the system again. After bleeding the system, check for leaks and tighten all fittings and connections as necessary.

Compressed-air vacuum pump

1. Assemble the tool, following the tool manufacturer's instructions.

2. Connect the box-end wench onto the bleed valve. Connect the vacuum hose onto the bleed valve.

3. Connect a compressed-air source to the vacuum tool.

NOTE
Always close the bleed valve before releasing the lever on top of the pump.

4. Depress the lever on top of the pump and open the bleed valve slightly. As long as the lever is depressed, a vacuum is created in the canister and brake fluid will evacuate from the brake line. Releasing the lever stops the vacuum. Because this tool will drain the master cylinder rapidly, check the master cylinder fluid level often.

5. Continue until the brake fluid running through the vacuum hose is a clear and steady stream without bubbles. Air drawn in around the bleed valve will cause bubbles to form in the vacuum hose. While this is normal, it is misleading as it always appears there is air in the system, even when the system has been bled completely. If necessary, remove the bleed valve and wrap a small amount of Teflon tape around the valve threads to seal the threads. Install the bleed valve.

Manual Bleeding

This is a one-person procedure that requires a reservoir bottle, a length of clear hose (catch hose), a box-end wrench and the specified brake fluid. Refer to **Figure 211**.

1. Connect the catch hose to the bleed valve on the caliper. Submerge the other end of the hose into a bottle partially filled with the specified brake fluid. This prevents air from being drawn into the catch hose and back into the brake system.

2. Apply the front brake lever or rear brake pedal until it stops and hold in this position.

3. Open the bleed valve with the wrench and let the lever or pedal move to the limit of its travel. Then, close the bleed valve and ensure it is closed before releasing the brake lever or pedal. This prevents air from being drawn back into the system on the lever's or pedal's return stroke if the bleed valve was left open.

4. Release the lever or pedal slowly,. Repeat this process until the brake fluid exiting the system is clear and air-free.

Brake Fluid Draining

Before disconnecting a brake hose from the front or rear brake component, drain the brake fluid as described in this section. Doing so reduces the amount of brake fluid that can spill out when disconnecting the brake hoses and lines from the system.

Front brake lever line

1. Support the motorcycle on level ground using a swing arm stand.

2. Block the front wheel so the motorcycle will not roll in either direction while on the swing arm stand.

3. Turn the handlebars to level the front master cylinder.

4. Remove the screws (A, **Figure 212**) securing the cover (B), and remove the cover and diaphragm.

5. Connect a brake bleeder to the front brake caliper bleed valve (**Figure 213**). Open the bleed valve and operate the brake bleeder until the fluid stops flowing. Tighten the bleed valve tp 80-100 in.-lb. (9.0-11.3 N•m).

6. Repeat procedure to drain the other caliper, on models so equipped.

7. Disconnect the brake bleeder.

13

Rear brake pedal line

1. Support the motorcycle on level ground using a swing arm stand.
2. Block the front wheel so the motorcycle will not roll in either direction.
3. Remove the screws (A, **Figure 214**), cover (B) and diaphragm from the reservoir.
4. Connect a brake bleeder to the rear brake caliper bleed valve (**Figure 215**). Open the bleed valve and operate the brake bleeder until the fluid stops flowing. Tighten the bleed valve to 80-100 in.-lb. (9.0-11.3 N•m).
5. Disconnect the brake bleeder.

Bleeding The System

Front brake lever line

1. Support the motorcycle on level ground using a swing arm stand.
2. Block the front wheel so the motorcycle will not roll in either direction while on the swing arm stand.
3. Turn the handlebars to level the front master cylinder.
4. Remove the screws (A, **Figure 212**) securing the cover (B), and remove the cover and diaphragm.
5. Connect a brake bleeder to the front brake caliper bleed valve (**Figure 213**). Open the bleed valve and operate the brake bleeder to bleed the brake line. Repeat until the brake fluid exiting the catch hose is clear and free of air. Tighten the bleed valve to 80-100 in.-lb. (9.0-11.3 N•m).
6. Repeat the procedure to bleed the other caliper, on models so equipped.
7. Continue the bleeding process as necessary until the front brake lever feels firm when applying it there are not air bubbles in the catch hose.
8. After bleeding and making sure there are no air bubbles appear in the catch hose, test feel of the brake lever. It should be firm and should after the same resistance each time it is operated. If the brake lever feels spongy, air is trapped in the system and the bleeding procedure must be repeated.
9. Tighten the bleed valve to 80-100 in.-lb. (9.0-11.3 N•m).
10. Remove the brake bleeder.
11. If necessary, add the new DOT 4 brake fluid to correct the level in the master cylinder reservoir. The brake fluid level should be 1/8-1/4 in. (3.2-6.4 mm) from the top edge of the master cylinder body.
12. Install the diaphragm and cover. Install and tighten the cover screws to 6-8 in.-lb. (0.7-0.9 N•m).

Rear brake pedal line

1. Support the motorcycle on level ground using a swing arm stand.
2. Block the front wheel so the motorcycle will not roll in either direction while on the swing arm stand.
3. Remove the screws (A, **Figure 214**), cover (B) and diaphragm from the reservoir.

4. Connect a brake bleeder to the rear brake caliper bleed valve (**Figure 215**). Open the bleed valve and operate the brake bleeder to bleed the brake line. Repeat until the brake fluid exiting the catch hose is clear and free of air. Tighten the bleed valve to 80-100 in.-lb. (9.0-11.3).

5. Repeat the procedure as necessary until the rear brake pedal feels firm when applying it there are no air bubbles in the catch hose.

6. After bleeding the rear brake system so no air bubbles appear in the catch hose, test feel of the brake pedal. It should be firm and should after the same resistance each time it is operated. If the brake pedal feels spongy, air is trapped in the system and the bleeding procedure must be repeated.

7. Tighten the bleed valve to 80-100 in.-lb (9.0-11.3 N•m).

8. Remove the brake bleeder.

9. Refill the master cylinder reservoir, if necessary, to maintain the correct fluid level of 1/8-1/4 in. (3.2-6.4 mm) from the top surface of the master cylinder body. Install the diaphragm and the cover. Tighten the cover screws to 6-8 in.-lb (0.7-0.9 N•m).

FLUSHING THE BRAKE SYSTEM

When flushing the brake system, use the recommended brake fluid as a flushing agent. Flushing consists of pulling new brake fluid through the system until the new fluid appears clear exiting the caliper and without the presence of any air bubbles. To flush the brake system, follow one of the bleeding procedures described in *Bleeding The System* (this chapter).

Table 1 BRAKE SPECIFICATIONS

Item	Specification
Brake fluid	DOT 4
Brake fluid height	
Front and rear reservoir	1/8-1/4 in. (3.2-6.4 mm) from the top edge of the master
Brake disc	
Lateral runout, maximum	0.008 in. (0.2 mm)
Warp, maximum	0.008 in. (0.2 mm)
Minimum thickness	Stamped on side of the disc
Brake pad minimum thickness	
Front and rear pads	0.04 in. (1.02 mm)

Table 2 BRAKE TORQUE SPECIFICATIONS

Item	ft.-lb.	in.-lb.	N•m
Banjo bolts			
2006-2007 models	17-22	–	23.1-29.8
2008-2011 models	21-25	–	28.5-33.9
Bleed valve	–	80-100	9.0-11.3
Brake disc Torx bolts			
Front wheel	16-24	–	21.7-32.5
Rear wheel	30-45	–	40.7-61.0
Front brake caliper (2006-2007 models)			
Pad pin bolts	–	180-200	20.3-22.6
Mounting bolts	28-38	–	38.0-51.5
Body assembly bolts	28-38	–	38.0-51.5
Front brake caliper (2008-2011 models)			
Assembly bolts	28-38	–	38.0-51.5
Mounting bolts	28-38	–	38.0-51.5
Pad pin bolts	15-16	–	20.3-21.7
Front brake master cylinder clamp bolt	–		
2006-2007 models	–	70-80	7.9-9.0
2008-2011 models	–	60-80	6.8-9.0
Master cylinder reservoir top cover screws			
(front and rear)	–	6-8	0.7-0.9
Rear brake caliper (2006-2007 models)			
Caliper mounting bolts	28-38	–	38.0-51.5
Pad pin bolts	15-16	–	20.3-21.7
Rear brake caliper (2008-2011 models)			
Mounting bolt (to caliper mounting bracket)	10-14	–	13.6-19.0
Pad pin bolt	–	80-120	9.0-13.6
Slider pin	10-14	–	13.6-19.0
Rear brake light switch/banjo bolt	21-25	–	28.5-33.9
Rear brake master cylinder 28-mm hex nut	30-40	–	40.7-54.2
Rear brake pedal support bolt	25-35	–	33.9-47.5

13

CHAPTER FOURTEEN

BODY AND FRAME

This chapter describes the removal and installation of the body and frame components. Most body panels are fragile and must be handled carefully. Protect the finish when handling them. Once the component is removed, attach all loose mounting hardware to avoid misplacing them. If a component is going to be left off for a period of time, wrap it with a blanket or towels and place it in a safe location.

Refer to **Table 1** at the end of this chapter for specifications.

SEATS

Removal/Installation

Refer to **Figure 1** and **Figure 2**.

1. Support the motorcycle on level ground using the jiffy stand.
2. Remove the bolt (A, **Figure 3**) securing the back of the seat to the top of the rear fender. Slightly lift up on the rear of the passenger seat (B, **Figure 3**), slide it toward the rear

and disengage the front bracket from the slot in the frame backbone. Remove the rider seat.

3. Check the tightness of the screws securing the seat strap, on models so equipped. Tighten securely if necessary.
4. Check the tightness of the screws securing the seat rear mounting tab. Tighten securely if necessary.
5. Place the seat on the frame. Firmly push down on the front of the seat and push it forward. Engage the seat front bracket under the frame backbone bracket (**Figure 4**).
6. Push the seat down and install the bolt (A, **Figure 3**) securing the rear of the rider seat to the top of the rear fender. Tighten the bolt securely.
7. Pull up on the front of the seat to ensure the seat front hook is secured in place in the frame backbone.

FRONT FENDER

Removal/Installation

Refer to **Figure 5**.

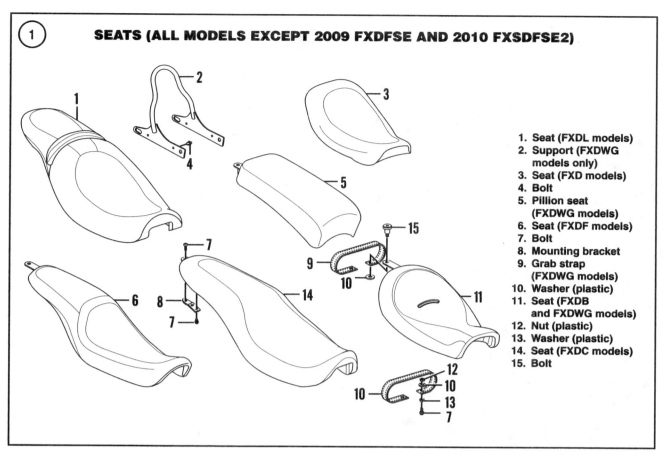

SEATS (ALL MODELS EXCEPT 2009 FXDFSE AND 2010 FXSDFSE2)

1. Seat (FXDL models)
2. Support (FXDWG models only)
3. Seat (FXD models)
4. Bolt
5. Pillion seat (FXDWG models)
6. Seat (FXDF models)
7. Bolt
8. Mounting bracket
9. Grab strap (FXDWG models)
10. Washer (plastic)
11. Seat (FXDB and FXDWG models)
12. Nut (plastic)
13. Washer (plastic)
14. Seat (FXDC models)
15. Bolt

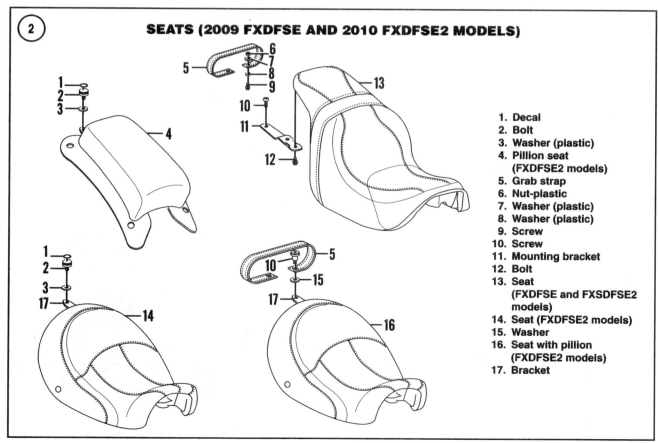

SEATS (2009 FXDFSE AND 2010 FXDFSE2 MODELS)

1. Decal
2. Bolt
3. Washer (plastic)
4. Pillion seat (FXDFSE2 models)
5. Grab strap
6. Nut-plastic
7. Washer (plastic)
8. Washer (plastic)
9. Screw
10. Screw
11. Mounting bracket
12. Bolt
13. Seat (FXDFSE and FXSDFSE2 models)
14. Seat (FXDFSE2 models)
15. Washer
16. Seat with pillion (FXDFSE2 models)
17. Bracket

14

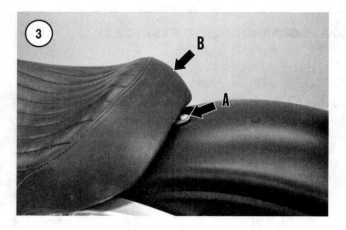

1. Remove the front wheel as described in Chapter Ten.

2A. On all models except FXDSE and FXDSE2, remove the screws (A, **Figure 6**) and nuts (B) securing the fender (C) to the fork slider brackets.

2B. On FXDSE and FXDSE2 models, remove the screws and washers securing the fender to the fork slider brackets.

3. Rotate the left-side fork slider 180°, moving the brake caliper out of the way for removal clearance.

4. Slowly slide the fender down the fork assembly and off the forks. Protect the paint and the inside surface of both forks.

5. Install by reversing the removal steps. Tighten the front fender screws and nuts to 15-21 ft.-lb. (20.3-28.5 N•m).

REAR FENDER

Removal/Installation

Refer to **Figures 7-11**.

NOTE
Elevate the rear of the motorcycle sufficiently to allow the rear fender to roll back and over the rear wheel, as well as clear the frame rear cross member.

1. Support the motorcycle on level ground using a swing arm stand.

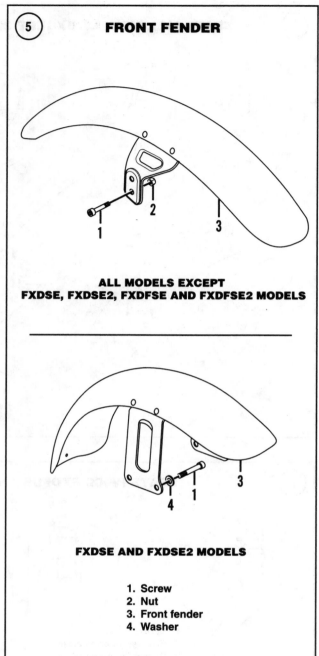

FRONT FENDER

**ALL MODELS EXCEPT
FXDSE, FXDSE2, FXDFSE AND FXDFSE2 MODELS**

FXDSE AND FXDSE2 MODELS

1. Screw
2. Nut
3. Front fender
4. Washer

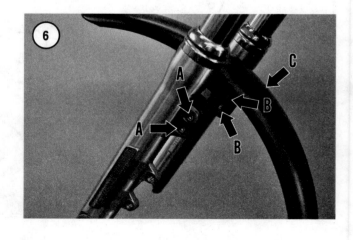

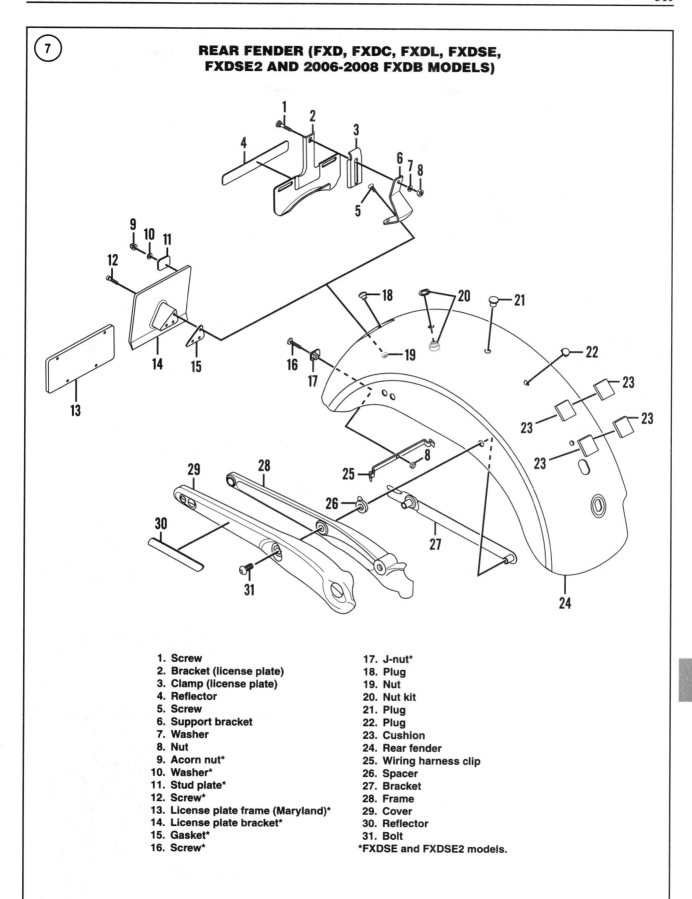

⑦ **REAR FENDER (FXD, FXDC, FXDL, FXDSE, FXDSE2 AND 2006-2008 FXDB MODELS)**

1. Screw
2. Bracket (license plate)
3. Clamp (license plate)
4. Reflector
5. Screw
6. Support bracket
7. Washer
8. Nut
9. Acorn nut*
10. Washer*
11. Stud plate*
12. Screw*
13. License plate frame (Maryland)*
14. License plate bracket*
15. Gasket*
16. Screw*

17. J-nut*
18. Plug
19. Nut
20. Nut kit
21. Plug
22. Plug
23. Cushion
24. Rear fender
25. Wiring harness clip
26. Spacer
27. Bracket
28. Frame
29. Cover
30. Reflector
31. Bolt
*FXDSE and FXDSE2 models.

14

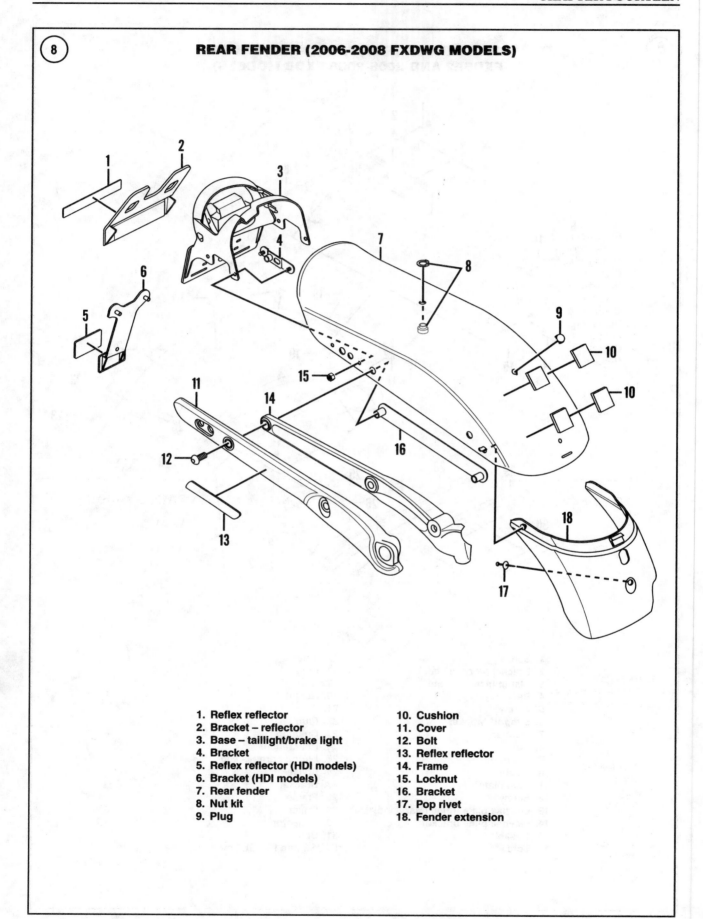

REAR FENDER (2006-2008 FXDWG MODELS)

1. Reflex reflector
2. Bracket – reflector
3. Base – taillight/brake light
4. Bracket
5. Reflex reflector (HDI models)
6. Bracket (HDI models)
7. Rear fender
8. Nut kit
9. Plug
10. Cushion
11. Cover
12. Bolt
13. Reflex reflector
14. Frame
15. Locknut
16. Bracket
17. Pop rivet
18. Fender extension

⑨ **REAR FENDER (2010 FXDWG MODELS)**

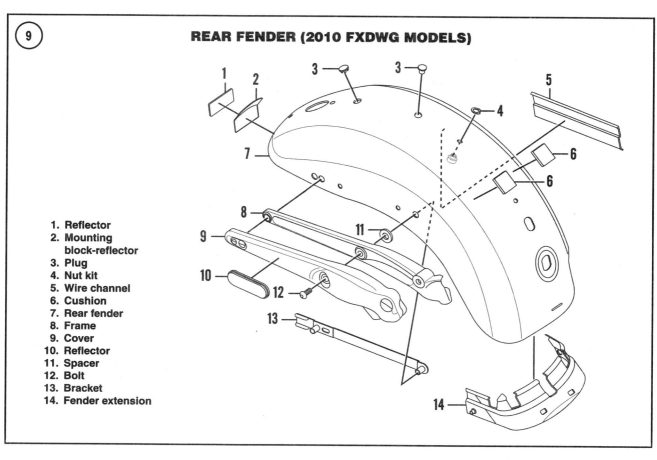

1. Reflector
2. Mounting block-reflector
3. Plug
4. Nut kit
5. Wire channel
6. Cushion
7. Rear fender
8. Frame
9. Cover
10. Reflector
11. Spacer
12. Bolt
13. Bracket
14. Fender extension

⑩ **REAR FENDER (2008-2011 FXDF, 2009 FXDFSE AND 2010 FXDFSE2 MODELS)**

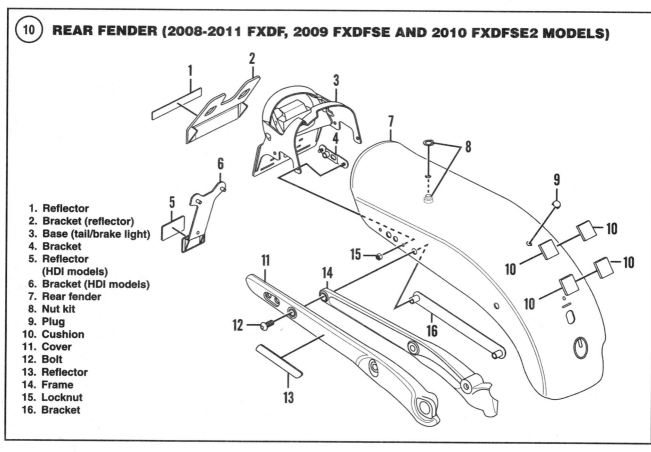

1. Reflector
2. Bracket (reflector)
3. Base (tail/brake light)
4. Bracket
5. Reflector (HDI models)
6. Bracket (HDI models)
7. Rear fender
8. Nut kit
9. Plug
10. Cushion
11. Cover
12. Bolt
13. Reflector
14. Frame
15. Locknut
16. Bracket

14

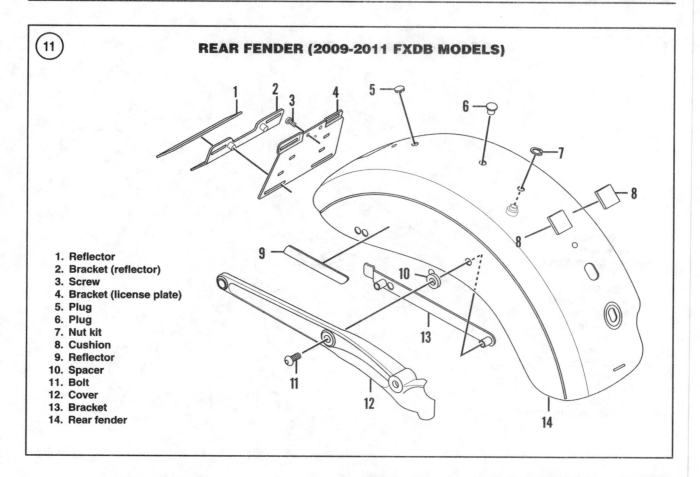

11 **REAR FENDER (2009-2011 FXDB MODELS)**

1. Reflector
2. Bracket (reflector)
3. Screw
4. Bracket (license plate)
5. Plug
6. Plug
7. Nut kit
8. Cushion
9. Reflector
10. Spacer
11. Bolt
12. Cover
13. Bracket
14. Rear fender

NOTE
Always disarm the optional TSS/TSSM/ HFSM security system before disconnecting the battery or pulling the Maxi-Fuse so the siren will not sound.

2. Disconnect the negative battery cable as described in Chapter Nine.

3. Remove the seat as described in this chapter.

4. Remove both saddlebags, on models so equipped.

5. Remove both shock absorbers (A, **Figure 12**) as described in Chapter Twelve.

6. Follow the tail light and rear turn signal wiring harness from the leading edge of the rear fender (A, **Figure 13**) and under the frame backbone (B).

7. Move the HFSM antenna (C, **Figure 13**) out of the way and disconnect the 8-pin rear lighting connector (D, **Figure 13**) under the HFSM antenna.

8. Disconnect the terminals from within the 8-pin connector socket housing as described in Chapter Nine. Note the wire color location within the connector as they must be installed in the correct location.

9. Remove the clip(s) securing the wiring harness to the frame. Carefully pull the harness out through the fender opening.

10. Carefully withdraw the wiring harness (A, **Figure 13**) out through the hole in the rear fender.

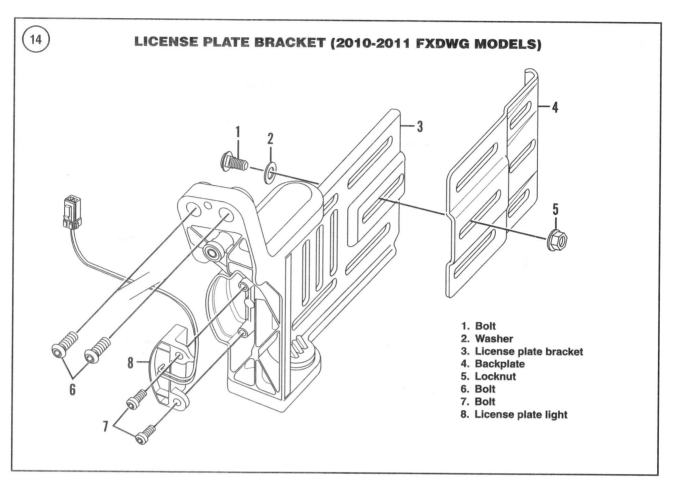

LICENSE PLATE BRACKET (2010-2011 FXDWG MODELS)

1. Bolt
2. Washer
3. License plate bracket
4. Backplate
5. Locknut
6. Bolt
7. Bolt
8. License plate light

11. On 2006-2008 FXDWG models, drill out and remove the pop rivet securing the fender extension to the frame.

12. Remove the bolts (B, **Figure 12**) securing the cover to the rear fender on each side. Remove both covers (C, **Figure 12**).

13. Carefully pull up and remove the rear fender (D, **Figure 12**) from the frame.

14. Install by reversing the removal steps. Tighten the cover bolts to 12-18 ft.-lb. (16.3-24.4 N•m).

LICENSE PLATE BRACKET (2010-2011 FXDWG MODELS)

Removal/Installation

Refer to **Figure 14**.

1. Disconnect the negative battery cable as described in Chapter Nine.

2. Disconnect the 2-pin license plate light connector.

3. Remove the bolts securing the license plate bracket to the rear fender mounting bracket.

4. Remove the license plate bracket, being careful to not scratch the rear fender.

5. Remove the bolt, washer and locknut, and then remove the backplate from the mounting bracket, if necessary,

6. Install by reversing the removal steps. Tighten the bolts securely.

JIFFY STAND

Cleaning

1. Park the motorcycle on level ground.

2. Support the underside of the motorcycle frame with a suitable size jack with both wheels off the ground.

3. Wipe all road debris and old grease from the catch and pivot block area.

4. If the debris cannot be removed, remove the bolt and catch. Clean the bolt, catch and the pivot block mating surface with solvent and dry with compressed air.

5. Position the catch so it engages the flats on the jiffy stand leg and secure the catch with the mounting bolt. Tighten the jiffy stand bolt to 19 ft.-lb. (25.8 N•m).

6. Spray the catch area, jiffy stand leg pivot area and the pin with Loctite aerosol anti-seize lubricant. Move the jiffy stand leg back and forth while applying the lubricant. Wipe off any excess lubricant.

7. Move the jiffy stand all the way up and down and ensure that it stays in that position.

8. Lower the motorcycle to the ground and ensure that the jiffy stand still operates correctly with the full weight of the motorcycle applied to it.

14

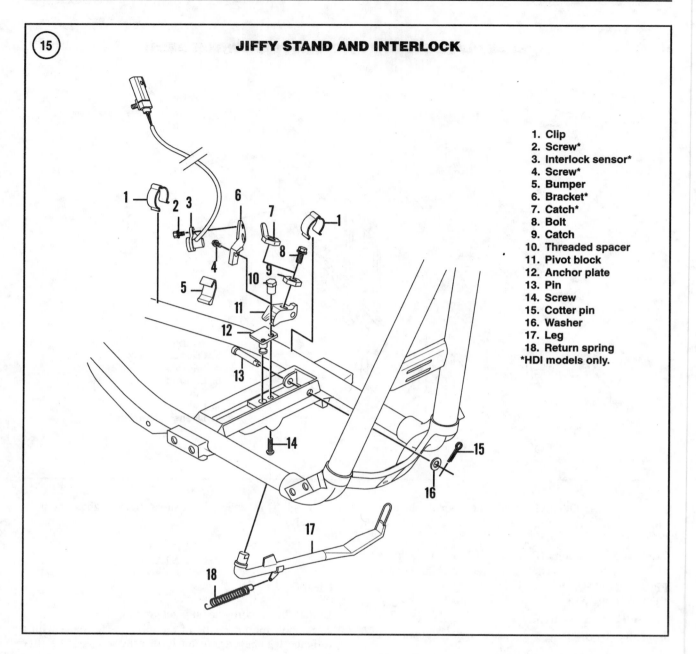

JIFFY STAND AND INTERLOCK

1. Clip
2. Screw*
3. Interlock sensor*
4. Screw*
5. Bumper
6. Bracket*
7. Catch*
8. Bolt
9. Catch
10. Threaded spacer
11. Pivot block
12. Anchor plate
13. Pin
14. Screw
15. Cotter pin
16. Washer
17. Leg
18. Return spring
*HDI models only.

Removal

Refer to **Figure 15**.

1. Support the motorcycle with the front wheel off the ground as described in Chapter Ten.

2. The motorcycle must be raised sufficiently to allow room for full movement of the jiffy stand.

3. Move the jiffy stand up with the spring fully relaxed.

4. Remove the return spring from the jiffy stand leg and from the hole in the frame weldment.

5. Remove the cotter pin and washer from the pivot pin.

6. Withdraw the pin from between the frame cross-brackets.

7. Lower the jiffy stand and pivot block from the frame as an assembly

8. Inspect the jiffy stand leg and pivot block as described in this section.

Installation

1. Insert the jiffy stand and pivot block as an assembly between the frame cross-brackets.

2. Install the pin between the frame cross-brackets and pivot block from the rear. Push it in until it bottoms.

3. Install the washer and *new* cotter pin. Bend the ends of the cotter pin over completely.

4. Position the return spring so the hook faces toward the rear and hook the return spring onto jiffy stand leg.

5. Hook the spring into the frame weldment hole.

6. Extend and retract the leg several times to ensure proper operation. The jiffy stand must move freely from the fully-extended to the fully-retracted positions.

7. Remove the motorcycle from the stand as described in Chapter Ten.

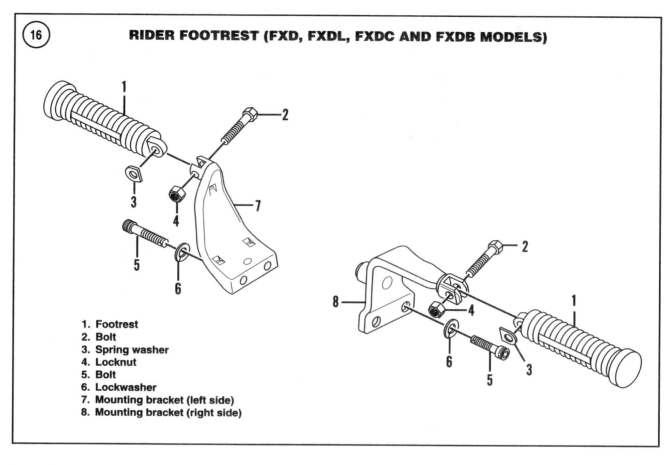

16 **RIDER FOOTREST (FXD, FXDL, FXDC AND FXDB MODELS)**

1. Footrest
2. Bolt
3. Spring washer
4. Locknut
5. Bolt
6. Lockwasher
7. Mounting bracket (left side)
8. Mounting bracket (right side)

Inspection

1. Thoroughly clean all old grease and road debris from the pivot point in the bracket and the pivot post of the leg.
2. Inspect the leg for cracks or other damage; replace if necessary.
3. Inspect the bracket mounting holes for elongation or other damage; replace if necessary.

Interlock Sensor Replacement (HDI Models)

1. Remove the seat as described in this chapter.
2. Disconnect the 3-pin interlock sensor electrical connector.
3. Note the routing of the electrical harness through the frame. The harness must be installed in the exact same locations throughout the frame.
4. Note the exact location of the clips securing the harness in place, and release them.
5. Remove the screw securing the sensor.
6. Remove the screw and catch, if necessary. Then, remove the sensor and harness from the frame.
7. Install by reversing the removal steps. Note the following:
   a. Be sure to route the harness inside the left lower frame member and under the engine rear mount casting.

b. Tighten the interlock sensor mounting screw to 96-144 in.-lb. (10.8-16.3 N•m).

FOOTREST

Rider Footrest Removal/Installation

FXD, FXDL, FXDC and FXDB models

Refer to **Figure 16**.
1. Place the motorcycle on level ground using the jiffy stand.
2. To remove only the footrest, perform the following:
   a. Remove the bolt (A, **Figure 17**) and nut (B), and then remove the footrest (C) to the support. Do not lose the spring washer.
   b. Install by reversing the removal steps. Tighten the bolt and nut securely.
3. To remove the left-side mounting bracket, perform the following:
   a. Remove the bolt(s) and lockwasher(s) securing the footrest mounting bracket (D, **Figure 17**) to the frame. Remove the assembly from the frame.
   b. Apply a small dab of Loctite 243 (blue) threadlock, or an equivalent, to the bolt.
   c. Install the support bracket and tighten the bolts to 25-35 ft.-lb. (33.9-47.5 N•m).

14

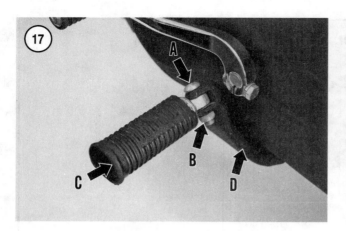

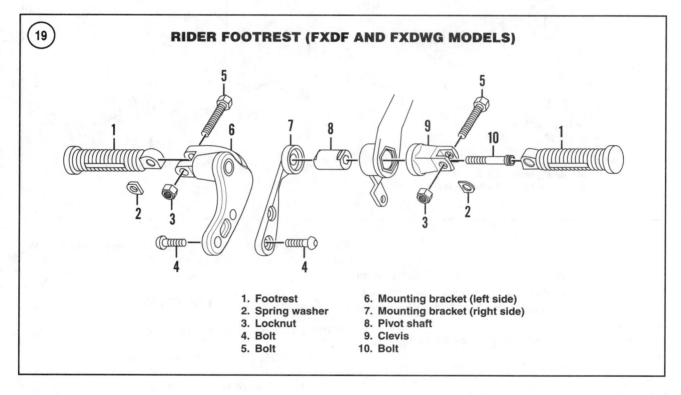

RIDER FOOTREST (FXDF AND FXDWG MODELS)

1. Footrest
2. Spring washer
3. Locknut
4. Bolt
5. Bolt
6. Mounting bracket (left side)
7. Mounting bracket (right side)
8. Pivot shaft
9. Clevis
10. Bolt

NOTE
*The right-side mounting bracket (**Figure 18**) also includes the rear brake pedal assembly.*

4. To remove and install the right-side mounting bracket (**Figure 18**), refer to *Rear Brake Pedal* in Chapter Thirteen.

FXDWG and FXDF models

Refer to **Figure 19**.
1. Place the motorcycle on level ground using the jiffy stand.
2. To remove only the footrest, perform the following:
   a. Remove the bolt and nut, and then the footrest. Do not lose the spring washer.
   b. Install the bolt, spring washer and nut, and tighten securely.

3. To remove the right side clevis and pivot shaft, perform the following:
   a. Remove the footrest as described in this section.
   b. Remove the bolt securing the clevis and pivot shaft and remove the parts from the frame and mounting bracket.

NOTE
The flats on the pivot shaft must be indexed correctly onto the flats in the mounting bracket and clevis. If not aligned correctly there will be a gap on each side of the pivot area.

   c. Install the pivot shaft into the receptacle in the mounting bracket. Rotate the pivot shaft so the small flats at each end face up.
   d. Install the clevis onto the pivot shaft. Ensure that the flat on the pivot shaft is indexed correctly onto the clevis.

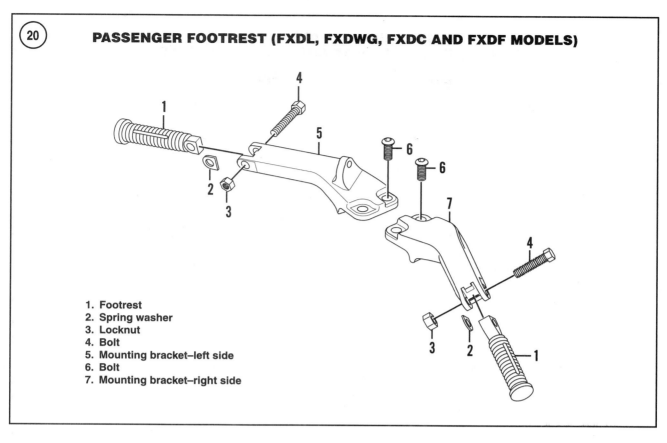

(20) PASSENGER FOOTREST (FXDL, FXDWG, FXDC AND FXDF MODELS)

1. Footrest
2. Spring washer
3. Locknut
4. Bolt
5. Mounting bracket–left side
6. Bolt
7. Mounting bracket–right side

e. Install the bolt securing the clevis and tighten securely.

4A. To remove the right side mounting bracket, perform the following:

   a. Remove the bolt(s) securing the mounting bracket to the frame, and then remove the bracket.

   b. Apply a small amount of Loctite 243 (blue) threadlock, or an equivalent, to the bolt(s).

   c. Install the bolt(s) and tighten to 25-35 ft.-lb. (33.9-47.5 N•m).

4B. To remove the left side mounting bracket, perform the following:

   a. Remove the bolt(s) securing the mounting bracket to the frame, and then remove the bracket.

   b. Index the mounting bracket onto the raised pad on the frame.

   c. Apply a small amount of Loctite 243 (blue) threadlock, or an equivalent, to the bolt(s).

   d. Install the bolt(s) and tighten to 25-35 ft.-lb. (33.9-47.5 N•m).

Passenger Footrest Removal/Installation

FXDL, FXDWG, FXDC and FDXF models

Refer to **Figure 20**.

1. Place the motorcycle on level ground using the jiffy stand.

2. To remove only the footrest and mounting bracket, perform the following:

   a. Remove the bolt and nut, and then remove the footrest from the mounting bracket. Do not lose the spring washer.

   b. Install the bolt, spring washer and nut. Tighten the bolt and nut securely.

3. To remove the mounting bracket, perform the following:

   a. Remove the bolts securing the mounting bracket to the frame, and then remove the bracket.

   b. Apply a small amount of Loctite 243 (blue) threadlock, or an equivalent, to the bolt.

   c. Install the bolt and tighten to 25-35 ft.-lb. (33.9-47.5 N•m).

Screamin' Eagle and CVO models (left-side)

Refer to **Figure 21**.

1. Place the motorcycle on level ground using the jiffy stand.

2. To remove only the footrest and support, perform the following:

   a. Remove the end bolt and slide the housing and pad assembly off the support.

   b. Separate the pad from the housing, if necessary.

   c. Remove the pivot bolt and nut and remove the support. Do not lose the spring washer.

   d. Install by reversing the removal steps. Install the end bolt and pivot bolt and tighten securely.

14

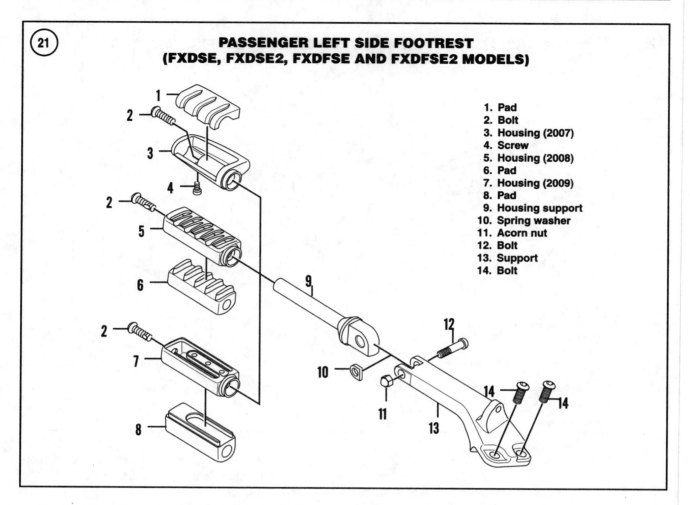

21

**PASSENGER LEFT SIDE FOOTREST
(FXDSE, FXDSE2, FXDFSE AND FXDFSE2 MODELS)**

1. Pad
2. Bolt
3. Housing (2007)
4. Screw
5. Housing (2008)
6. Pad
7. Housing (2009)
8. Pad
9. Housing support
10. Spring washer
11. Acorn nut
12. Bolt
13. Support
14. Bolt

3. To remove the mounting bracket, perform the following:

 a. Remove the bolts securing the mounting bracket to the frame, and then remove the bracket.

 b. Apply a small amount of Loctite 243 (blue) threadlock, or an equivalent, to the bolt.

 c. Install the bolt and tighten to 25-35 ft.-lb. (33.9-47.5 N•m).

HIGHWAY FOOTREST

Removal/Installation

All models except Screamin' Eagle and CVO

 Refer to **Figure 22**.

1. Place the motorcycle on level ground using the jiffy stand.

2. To remove just the footrest and support, perform the following:

 a. Remove the bolt and nut, and then remove the footrest from the support. Do not lose the spring washer.

 b. Remove the nut, lockwasher, and washer. Then, remove the support from the support plate.

 c. Install by reversing the removal steps. Tighten the bolts and nuts securely.

3. To remove the support plate, perform the following:

 a. Remove the bolts, lockwashers and washers securing the footrest support bracket to the frame. Remove the assembly from the frame.

 b. Apply a small amount of Loctite 243 (blue) threadlock, or an equivalent, to the bolt.

 c. Install the support bracket and tighten the bolts to 25-35 ft.-lb. (33.9-47.5 N•m).

Screamin' Eagle and CVO Models (right-side)

 Refer to **Figure 23**.

1. Place the motorcycle on level ground using the jiffy stand.

2. To remove just the footrest and support, perform the following:

 a. Remove the end bolt and slide the housing and pad assembly off the support.

 b. Separate the pad from the housing, if necessary.

 c. Remove the snap ring and washer from the end of the pivot pin.

 d. Remove the pivot pin and support from the mounting bracket. Do not lose the spring washer.

 e. Install by reversing the removal steps. Install the end bolt and tighten securely.

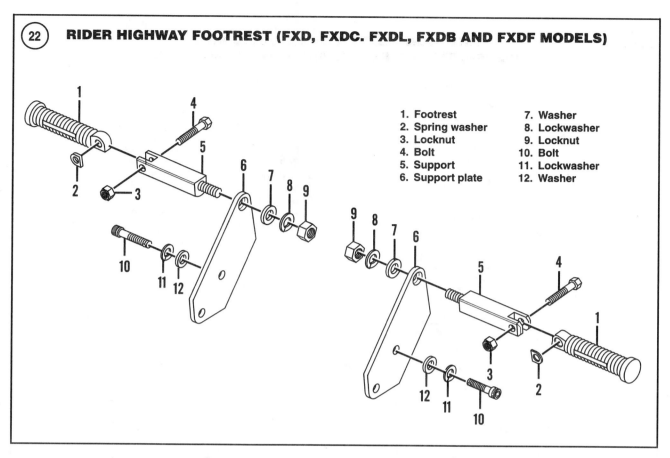

(22) RIDER HIGHWAY FOOTREST (FXD, FXDC. FXDL, FXDB AND FXDF MODELS)

1. Footrest
2. Spring washer
3. Locknut
4. Bolt
5. Support
6. Support plate
7. Washer
8. Lockwasher
9. Locknut
10. Bolt
11. Lockwasher
12. Washer

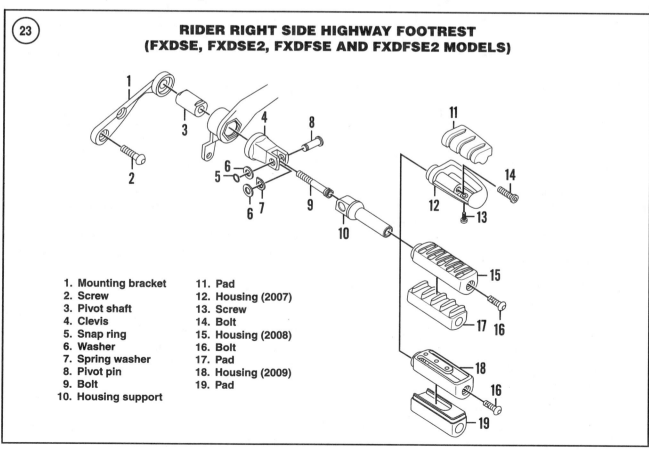

**(23) RIDER RIGHT SIDE HIGHWAY FOOTREST
(FXDSE, FXDSE2, FXDFSE AND FXDFSE2 MODELS)**

1. Mounting bracket
2. Screw
3. Pivot shaft
4. Clevis
5. Snap ring
6. Washer
7. Spring washer
8. Pivot pin
9. Bolt
10. Housing support
11. Pad
12. Housing (2007)
13. Screw
14. Bolt
15. Housing (2008)
16. Bolt
17. Pad
18. Housing (2009)
19. Pad

14

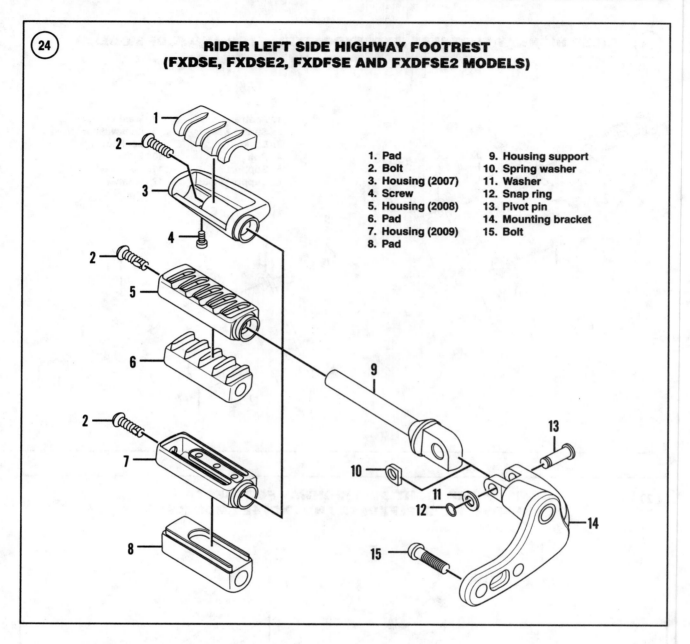

(24)

**RIDER LEFT SIDE HIGHWAY FOOTREST
(FXDSE, FXDSE2, FXDFSE AND FXDFSE2 MODELS)**

1. Pad
2. Bolt
3. Housing (2007)
4. Screw
5. Housing (2008)
6. Pad
7. Housing (2009)
8. Pad
9. Housing support
10. Spring washer
11. Washer
12. Snap ring
13. Pivot pin
14. Mounting bracket
15. Bolt

3. To remove the clevis and pivot shaft, perform the following:

   a. Remove the footrest and support assembly as described in this section.

   b. Remove the bolt securing the clevis and pivot shaft and remove the parts from the frame and mounting bracket.

NOTE
The flats on the pivot shaft must be indexed correctly onto the flats in the mounting bracket and clevis. If not aligned correctly there will be a gap on each side of the pivot area.

   c. Install the pivot shaft into the frame receptacle and onto the mounting bracket. Rotate the pivot shaft so the small flats at each end face up.

   d. Install the clevis onto the pivot shaft. Ensure that the flat on the pivot shaft is indexed correctly onto the clevis.

   e. Install the bolt securing the clevis and tighten securely.

4. To remove the mounting bracket, perform the following:

   a. Remove the bolt(s) securing the mounting bracket to the frame and remove it.

   b. Apply a small amount of Loctite 243 (blue) threadlock, or an equivalent, to the bolt(s).

   c. Install the bolt(s) and tighten to 25-35 ft.-lb. (33.9-47.5 N•m).

Screamin' Eagle and CVO Models (left side)

Refer to **Figure 24**.

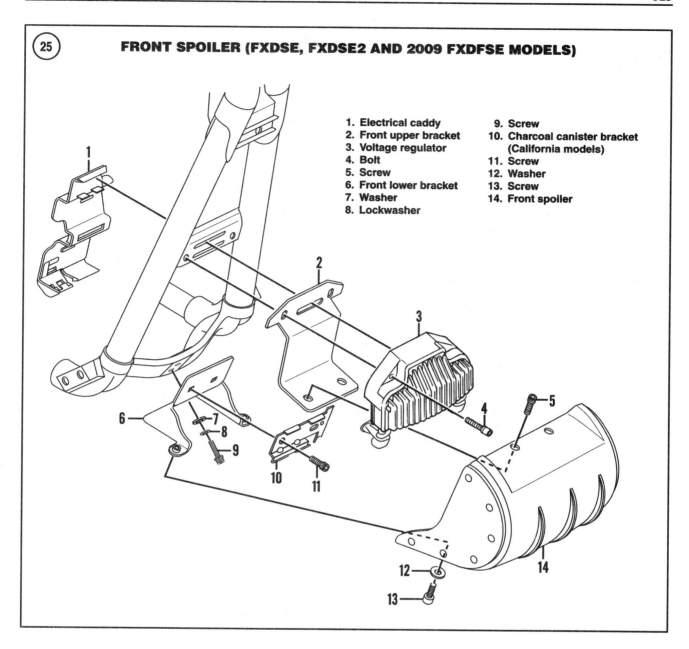

FRONT SPOILER (FXDSE, FXDSE2 AND 2009 FXDFSE MODELS)

1. Electrical caddy
2. Front upper bracket
3. Voltage regulator
4. Bolt
5. Screw
6. Front lower bracket
7. Washer
8. Lockwasher
9. Screw
10. Charcoal canister bracket (California models)
11. Screw
12. Washer
13. Screw
14. Front spoiler

1. Place the motorcycle on level ground using the jiffy stand.

2. To remove just the footrest and support, perform the following:

   a. Remove the end bolt and slide the housing and pad assembly off the support.

   b. Separate the pad from the housing, if necessary.

   c. Remove the snap ring and washer from the end of the pivot pin.

   d. Remove the pivot pin and support from the mounting bracket. Do not lose the spring washer.

   e. Install by reversing the removal steps. Install the end bolt and tighten securely.

3. To remove the mounting bracket, perform the following:

   a. Remove the bolt securing the mounting bracket to the frame and remove it.

   b. Index the mounting bracket onto the raised pad on the frame.

   c. Apply a small amount of Loctite 243 (blue) threadlock, or an equivalent to the bolt.

   d. Install the bolt and tighten to 25-35 ft.-lb. (33.9-47.5 N•m).

SPOILER (SCREAMIN' EAGLE AND CVO MODELS)

Refer to **Figure 25** and **Figure 26**.

1. Place the motorcycle on level ground using the jiffy stand.

2. Remove the voltage regulator as described in Chapter Nine.

3. Remove the two lower screws and washers securing the spoiler to the lower bracket.

14

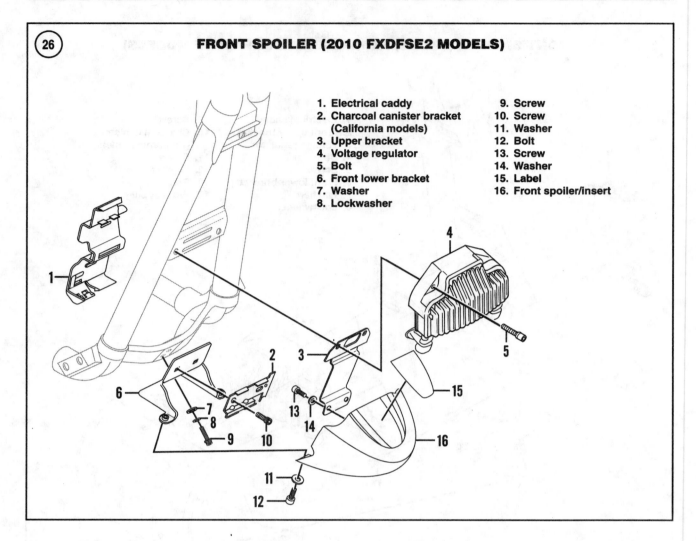

㉖　**FRONT SPOILER (2010 FXDFSE2 MODELS)**

1. Electrical caddy
2. Charcoal canister bracket (California models)
3. Upper bracket
4. Voltage regulator
5. Bolt
6. Front lower bracket
7. Washer
8. Lockwasher
9. Screw
10. Screw
11. Washer
12. Bolt
13. Screw
14. Washer
15. Label
16. Front spoiler/insert

4. Remove the spoiler and front upper bracket from the frame.

5. Remove the screws securing the upper bracket to the spoiler, and separate the two parts, if necessary.

6. Remove the screws, lockwasher and washer securing the front lower bracket, if necessary. Remove the bracket and canister bracket (California models only).

7. Remove the screw securing the canister bracket (California models only) to the front lower bracket, if necessary.

8. Install by reversing the removal steps, noting the following:
   a. Tighten screws securing the front lower bracket to the spoiler to 69-84 in.-lb. (7.8-9.5 N•m).
   b. Tighten screws securing the front upper bracket to the spoiler to 69-84 in.-lb. (7.8-9.5 N•m).

Table 1 BODY PANEL TORQUE SPECIFICATIONS

Item	ft.-lb.	in.-lb.	N•m
Footrest support bracket bolt	25-35	–	33.9-47.5
Front fender screw/nut	15-21	–	20.3-28.5
Jiffy stand			
Mounting bolt	19	–	25.8
Sensor screw (HDI)	–	96-144	10.8-16.3
Rear fender cover bolts	12-18	–	16.3-24.4
Seat strap nut	–	60-90	6.8-10.2
Spoiler screws (Screamin' Eagle and CVO models)			
Front lower bracket to the spoiler	–	69-84	7.8-9.5
Front upper bracket to the spoiler	–	69-84	7.8-9.5

INDEX

A

Active exhaust module 140-141
Air filter
  backplate. 256-264
  element 75-82
Alloy wheels, changing. . . . 407-409
Alternator 312-314
Automatic compression release
  (ACR) solenoid 347-348

B

Bank angle (BAS) sensor 321
Battery. 306-310
  charging rates/times 378
  tray 310
Bleeding, brakes 503-507
Body and frame
  fender
    front 508-510
    rear 510-515
  footrest 517-520
    highway 520-523
  jiffy stand 515-517
  license plate bracket 515
  seats 508
  specifications, torque 524
  spoiler. 523-524
Brake rotor protection. 381
Brake
  bleeding 503-507
  caliper
    front 459-470

    rear 481-491
  disc 500-501
  flushing the system 507
  hose and line
    replacement. 496-500
  master cylinder
    front 470-476
    rear 492-496
  pad replacement
    front 455-459
    rear 476-480
  pedal, rear 501-503
  service. 69-70, 454-455
  specifications 507
    torque 507
  troubleshooting. 50-51
Bulbs, specifications 378-379

C

Caliper, brakes
  front 459-470
  rear 481-491
Camshaft
  sprocket spacers specifications . 180
  support plate 154-166
Charging system 310-312
  troubleshooting. 44-47
Clutch
  assembly. 186-192
  cable replacement 203-204
  hydraulic hose replacement, . . 216
  lever assembly 204-205

  master cylinder 209-213
  pushrod and release plate
    inspection, ... 192-193
  release cover 206-208, 213-215
  secondary actuator 215-216
  service, hydraulic 208-209
  shell, hub and sprocket . . . 198-201
  specifications
    sprocket sizes 218
    torque 218-219
  system. 70-73
    bleeding 216-218
    draining 216
    flushing. 216
  troubleshooting. 49
Compensating sprocket. 203
Compression test. 82-83
Control cables, lubrication . . . 66-67
Conversion formulas. 25-26
Crankcase
  and crankshaft. 166-173
  bearing replacement 174-179
Crankshaft position (CKP)
  sensor 320
Cylinder. 123-128
  head. 109-114
    leak test. 112

D

Decimal and metric
  equivalents 24-25
Depressurizing the fuel system . . 265

Device part numbers 59
Diagnostic trouble codes 56-58
  flowcharts . . . . See CD
  multiple DTC priority 58-59
  symptoms that do not
    set DTC codes 58
  troubleshooting . . . . See CD
Dimensions, general 23-24
Drive
  belt 400-401
    deflection and alignment . . 68-69
Driven sprocket 400
DTC flowcharts . . . . See CD

E

Electrical system
  alternator 312-314
  automatic compression release
    (ACR) solenoid 347-348
  bank angle (BAS) sensor 321
  battery 306-310
    tray 310
  charging system 310-312
  component replacement 304
  connector service 359-377
  crankshaft position (CKP)
    sensor 320
  electronic control module
    (ECM) 318
  engine temperature (ET)
    sensor 320-321
  equipment and switches 75
  fuel gauge 345-346
  fuel tank console mounted
    instruments 342
  fundamentals 16
  fuses 304-305
  ground wires and studs 306
  handlebar mounted
    instruments 343-345
  headlight 332-335
  horn 356
  ignition
    coil 315-318
    system 315
  indicator lamps 343
  jiffy stand interlock sensor
    (HDI) 355-356
  lighting system 332
  maxi-fuse 306
  relays 359
  side electrical caddy 318-319
  specifications 54-55, 377-378
    battery charging rates/times . . 378
    bulbs 378-379
    fuses 378
    general 377-378

torque 379-380
  troubleshooting 54-55
starter 321-332
starting system 321
switches 348-355
tail/brake light 339-342
testing and troubleshooting . . 35-38
turn signal security modules (TSM,
  TSSM and HFSM) 357-358
turn signals 335-339
vehicle speed (VSS) sensor . . . 321
voltage regulator 314-315
wiring diagrams . . . . See CD
Electronic
  control module (ECM) 318
  diagnostic system,
    troubleshooting 51-54
  fuel injection (EFI) 284-287
Engine
  lower end 146-151
    break-in 179
    camshaft, support plate . . 154-166
    crankcase
      and crankshaft 166-173
      bearing replacement . . 174-179
    oil pump 151-154
  lubrication, troubleshooting . 48-49
  mounts and stabilizer inspection 74
  oil and filter, maintenance . . . 61-64
  scan values, typical 56
  specifications
    general 142
    lower end 179-180
      torque 180
    oil 91
    top end 142-144
      torque 144-145
  temperature (ET)
    sensor 299, 320-321
  top end
    active exhaust module . . 140-141
    cylinder 123-128
      head 109-114
    exhaust system 134-140
    pistons and piston rings . 128-134
    rocker arms, pushrods
      and valve lifters 94-109
    service precautions 93-94
    valves and components . 114-123
  troubleshooting
    noises 34-35
    performance 33-34
    starting 31-33
Evaporative emission control
  system 301-302
Exhaust system 134-140
  inspection 74
  torque specifications 144-145

External shift mechanism . . 220-223

F

Fasteners 3-6
  inspection 74-75
Fender
  front 508-510
  rear 510-515
Flowcharts, troubleshooting . See CD
Flushing the brake system 507
Footrest 517-520
  highway 520-523
Fork 421-432
  oil 66
    capacity and level 440
  stem lower bearing
    replacement 437-438
Fuel system
  air filter backplate 256-264
  depressurizing 265
  electronic fuel injection
    (EFI) 284-287
  engine temperature (ET)
    sensor 299
  evaporative emission
    control system 301-302
  filter 272-276
  gauge 345-346
  idle air control (IAC) 298-299
  induction module 290-295
  injectors 295-296
  inlet strainer 276
  intake air temperature (IAT)
    sensor 296-298
  level sending unit 272
  line inspection 74
  manifold absolute pressure
    (MAP) sensor 299
  oxygen (O$_2$) sensor 299-301
  pressure
    regulator 277
    test 277-278
  pump 276-277
    assembly 272
  specifications 302
    engine and drive fluid
      capacities 91
    torque 303
  supply check valve 268-268
  tank 265-268
    console 278-284
    mounted instruments 342
  throttle
    and idle cables 287-290
    position (TP) sensor 298
  top plate 269-272
  troubleshooting 48

Fuses 304-305
    specifications 378

G

Ground wires and studs 306

H

Handlebar 413-420
    inspection 421
    mounted instruments 343-345
    wiring 420-421
Headlight 332-335
Highway foot rest 520-523
Horn 356
Hubs 388-400
Hydraulic
    clutch service 208-209
    hose replacement, ... 216

I

Idle
    air control (LAC) 298-299
    speed adjustment 86
Ignition
    coil 315-318
    system 315
        troubleshooting 47-48
    timing 86
Indicator lamps 343
Induction module 290-295
Inlet strainer 276
Intake air temperature (IAT)
    sensor 296-298

J

Jiffy stand 515-517
    interlock sensor (HDI) . . . 355-356
    lubrication 67-68

L

Laced wheels
    changing 405-407
    service 401-403
License plate bracket 515
Lighting system 332
    troubleshooting 50
Lower clamp rubber
    bushing replacement 421
Lubricants and fluids
    recommendations 91
Lubrication
    control cables 66-67
    engine oil and filter 61-64
    fork oil 66

jiffy stand 67-68
primary chaincase oil 65-66
schedule 89-90
Screamin' Eagle and CVO
    models 61
throttle control grip 67
transmission oil 64-65

M

Main drive gear 246-250
Maintenance
    brake system 69-70
    clutch system 70-73
    electrical equipment
        and switches 75
    engine mounts
        and stabilizer inspection 74
    exhaust system inspection 74
    fastener inspection 74-75
    fuel line inspection 74
    motorcycle alignment 86-88
    pre-ride inspection 60-61
    primary chain and
        drive belt 68-69
    schedule 89-90
    shock absorber inspection 74
    specifications 91-92
        torque 92
    steering play inspection 74
    swing arm pivot bolt
        inspection 74
    throttle cable adjustment . . . 73-74
    tires and wheels 61
Manifold absolute pressure (MAP)
    sensor 299
Master cylinder
    front 470-476
    rear 492-496
Maxi-fuse 306
Model designations 23
Motorcycle
    alignment 86-88
    stands 381
    weight 24

O

Oil
    pan 253-254
    pump 151-154
Operating requirements,
    troubleshooting 31
Oxygen (O2) sensor 299-301

P

Pistons and rings 128-134
Pre-ride inspection 60-61

Primary
    chain
        and drive belt 68-69
        and tensioner inspection 202
        case oil 65-66
    chaincase
        cover 181-183
        housing 183-186
    drive
        assembly 193-198
        compensating sprocket,
            inspection 203
Push rod and lifter location,
    specifications 144

R

Rear fender 510-515
Relays 359
Rocker arms, pushrods and valve
    lifters 94-109

S

Safety 2-3
Seats 508
Service methods 16-21
Serial numbers 3
Shift
    arm assembly 224-225
    assembly 220
    forks and cam 225-228
Shock absorbers 441-447
    adjustment 447
    inspection 74
    swing arm 447-453
Shop supplies 6-7
Side door
    assembly 228-234
    bearings 243-246
        specifications 255
Side electrical caddy 318-319
Spark plugs 83-85
Specifications
    battery charging rates/times . . . 378
    brakes 507
    bulbs 378-379
    camshaft sprocket spacers 180
    clutch and sprocket sizes 218
    conversion formulas 25-26
    decimal and metric
        equivalents 24-25
    device part numbers 59
    diagnostic trouble codes 56-58
        multiple DTC priority 58-59
        symptoms that do not set
            DTC codes 58
    dimensions, general 23-24

15

Specifications (continued)
electrical system . . . 54-55, 377-378
engine
and drive fluid capacities 91
general 142
lower end 179-180
oil recommendations 91
scan values, typical. 56
top end 142-144
fork oil capacity and level 440
fuel system 302
fuses 378
laced wheel offset 411
lubricants and fluids 91
maintenance 91-92
and lubrication schedule. . . 89-90
model designations 23
motorcycle weight 24
push rod and lifter location. . . . 144
side door bearings. 255
special tools 28-30
tap and drill sizes
metric 28
U.S. standard 27-28
technical abbreviations 26-27
tire inflation pressure (cold) 90, 411
torque
body panel 524
brakes 507
clutch and primary
chaincase 218-219
electrical system 379-380
engine
lower end 180
top end 144-145
fuel system 303
maintenance 92
general recommendations. 25
suspension
front 440
rear 453
wheels. 411-412
transmission 254
service 254-255
torque 255
wheel, tire and hub 411
Spoiler. 523-524
Starter 321-332
Starting system
troubleshooting. 38-44
Steering
head
and stem 432-436
bearing race
replacement 436-437
play inspection 74
and adjustment 438-439
Storage 21-22

Suspension
fork 421-432
lower bearing
replacement 437-438
handlebar 413-420
inspection 421
wiring 420-421
lower clamp rubber bushing
replacement. 421
specifications,
torque
front 440
rear 453
steering
head, and stem 432-436
bearing race
replacement. 436-437
play inspection and
adjustment 438-439
troubleshooting. 50
Swing arm 447-453
pivot bolt inspection 74
Switches, electrical 348-355

T

Tail/brake light 339-342
Tap and drill sizes
metric 28
U.S. standard 27-28
Technical abbreviations. 26-27
Throttle
and idle cables 287-290
adjustment 73-74
control grip lubrication. 67
position (TP) sensor 298
Tires
and wheels, maintenance 61
changing
alloy wheels 407-409
laced wheels 405-407
inflation pressure (cold) . . . 90, 411
motorcycle stands. 381
repairs 409-410
runout 410
Tools 7-12
measuring 12-16
special 28-30
Torque specifications
body panel 524
brakes 507
clutch and primary
chaincase. 218-219
electrical system 379-380
engine
lower end 180
top end 144-145
fuel system 303

general recommendations. 25
maintenance 92
suspension
front 440
rear 453
transmission 255
wheels. 411-412
Transmission
case. 251-253
drive sprocket 250-251
external shift mechanism . 220-223
main drive gear. 246-250
oil 64-65
pan 253-254
shafts. 234-243
shift assembly 220
arm assembly 224-225
forks and cam 225-228
side door assembly 228-234
bearings 243-246
specifications 254-255
torque 255
top cover 223-224
troubleshooting. 49-50
Troubleshooting
brake system 50-51
charging system 44-47
clutch 49
device part numbers 59
diagnostic trouble codes 56-58
multiple DTC priority 58-59
symptoms that do not set DTC
codes. 58
electrical system
specifications 54-55
testing 35-38
electronic diagnostic system. 51-54
engine
lubrication 48-49
noises 34-35
performance 33-34
scan values, typical. 56
starting 31-33
operating requirements 31
flowcharts . . . . See CD
fuel system 48
ignition system 47-48
lighting system 50
starting system 38-44
suspension and steering 50
transmission 49-50
vibration 50
Tune-up. 75
air filter element 75-82
compression test 82-83
idle speed adjustment 86
ignition timing 86
spark plugs 83-85

Turn signals. 335-339
  security modules (TSM, TSSM
    and HFSM). 357-358

V

Valves and components. . . . 114-123
Vehicle speed (VSS) sensor 321
Vibration, troubleshooting 50
Voltage regulator. 314-315

W

Wheels
  balance 404-405
  brake rotor protection 381
  drive
    belt 400-401
    sprocket 400
  front 381-384
  inspection 387

laced service 401-403
rear 384-387
specifications
  laced wheel offset. 411
  tires and hubs 411
  torque 411-412
Wiring diagrams . . . . See CD
WOW test 54

15

NOTES

NOTES

NOTES

MAINTENANCE LOG

Date	Miles	Type of Service

BMW

M308	500 & 600cc Twins, 55-69
M502-3	BMW R50/5-R100GS PD, 70-96
M500-3	BMW K-Series, 85-97
M501-3	K1200RS, GT & LT, 98-10
M503-3	R850, R1100, R1150 & R1200C, 93-05
M309	F650, 1994-2000

HARLEY-DAVIDSON

M419	Sportsters, 59-85
M429-5	XL/XLH Sportster, 86-03
M427-3	XL Sportster, 04-11
M418	Panheads, 48-65
M420	Shovelheads, 66-84
M421-3	FLS/FXS Evolution, 84-99
M423-2	FLS/FXS Twin Cam, 00-05
M250	FLS/FXS/FXC Softail, 06-09
M422-3	FLH/FLT/FXR Evolution, 84-98
M430-4	FLH/FLT Twin Cam, 99-05
M252	FLH/FLT, 06-09
M426	VRSC Series, 02-07
M424-2	FXD Evolution, 91-98
M425-3	FXD Twin Cam, 99-05

HONDA

ATVs

M316	Odyssey FL250, 77-84
M311	ATC, TRX & Fourtrax 70-125, 70-87
M433	Fourtrax 90, 93-00
M326	ATC185 & 200, 80-86
M347	ATC200X & Fourtrax 200SX, 86-88
M455	ATC250 & Fourtrax 200/250, 84-87
M342	ATC250R, 81-84
M348	TRX250R/Fourtrax 250R & ATC250R, 85-89
M456-4	TRX250X 87-92; TRX300EX 93-06
M446-3	TRX250 Recon & Recon ES, 97-07
M215	TRX250EX, 01-05
M346-3	TRX300/Fourtrax 300 & TRX300FW/Fourtrax 4x4, 88-00
M200-2	TRX350 Rancher, 00-06
M459-3	TRX400 Foreman 95-03
M454-4	TRX400EX 99-07
M201	TRX450R & TRX450ER, 04-09
M205	TRX450 Foreman, 98-04
M210	TRX500 Rubicon, 01-04
M206	TRX500 Foreman, 05-11

Singles

M310-13	50-110cc OHC Singles, 65-99
M315	100-350cc OHC, 69-82
M317	125-250cc Elsinore, 73-80
M442	CR60-125R Pro-Link, 81-88
M431-2	CR80R, 89-95, CR125R, 89-91
M435	CR80R & CR80RB, 96-02
M457-2	CR125R, 92-97; CR250R, 92-96
M464	CR125R, 1998-2002
M443	CR250R-500R Pro-Link, 81-87
M432-3	CR250R, 88-91 & CR500R, 88-01
M437	CR250R, 97-01
M352	CRF250R, CRF250X, CRF450R & CRF450X, 02-05
M319-3	XR50R, CRF50F, XR70R & CRF70F, 97-09
M312-14	XL/XR75-100, 75-91
M222	XR80R, CRF80F, XR100R, & CRF100F, 92-09
M318-4	XL/XR/TLR 125-200, 79-03
M328-4	XL/XR250, 78-00; XL/XR350R 83-85; XR200R, 84-85; XR250L, 91-96
M320-2	XR400R, 96-04
M221	XR600R, 91-07; XR650L, 93-07
M339-8	XL/XR 500-600, 79-90
M225	XR650R, 00-07

Twins

M321	125-200cc Twins, 65-78
M322	250-350cc Twins, 64-74
M323	250-360cc Twins, 74-77
M324-5	Twinstar, Rebel 250 & Nighthawk 250, 78-03
M334	400-450cc Twins, 78-87
M333	450 & 500cc Twins, 65-76
M335	CX & GL500/650, 78-83
M344	VT500, 83-88
M313	VT700 & 750, 83-87
M314-3	VT750 Shadow Chain Drive, 98-06
M440	VT1100C Shadow, 85-96
M460-4	VT1100 Series, 95-07
M230	VTX1800 Series, 02-08
M231	VTX1300 Series, 03-09

Fours

M332	CB350-550, SOHC, 71-78
M345	CB550 & 650, 83-85
M336	CB650, 79-82
M341	CB750 SOHC, 69-78
M337	CB750 DOHC, 79-82
M436	CB750 Nighthawk, 91-93 & 95-99
M325	CB900, 1000 & 1100, 80-83
M439	600 Hurricane, 87-90
M441-2	CBR600F2 & F3, 91-98
M445-2	CBR600F4, 99-06
M220	CBR600RR, 03-06
M434-2	CBR900RR Fireblade, 93-99
M329	500cc V-Fours, 84-86
M349	700-1000cc Interceptor, 83-85
M458-2	VFR700F-750F, 86-97
M438	VFR800FI Interceptor, 98-00
M327	700-1100cc V-Fours, 82-88
M508	ST1100/Pan European, 90-02
M340	GL1000 & 1100, 75-83
M504	GL1200, 84-87

Sixes

M505	GL1500 Gold Wing, 88-92
M506-2	GL1500 Gold Wing, 93-00
M507-3	GL1800 Gold Wing, 01-10
M462-2	GL1500C Valkyrie, 97-03

KAWASAKI

ATVs

M465-3	Bayou KLF220 & KLF250, 88-10
M466-4	Bayou KLF300, 86-04
M467	Bayou KLF400, 93-99
M470	Lakota KEF300, 95-99
M385-2	Mojave KSF250, 87-04

Singles

M350-9	80-350cc Rotary Valve, 66-01
M444-2	KX60, 83-02; KX80 83-90
M448-2	KX80, 91-00; KX85, 01-10 & KX100, 89-09
M351	KDX200, 83-88
M447-3	KX125 & KX250, 82-91; KX500, 83-04
M472-2	KX125, 92-00
M473-2	KX250, 92-00
M474-3	KLR650, 87-07
M240-2	KLR650, 08-12

Twins

M355	KZ400, KZ/Z440, EN450 & EN500, 74-95
M360-3	EX500, GPZ500S, & Ninja 500R, 87-02
M356-5	Vulcan 700 & 750, 85-06
M354-3	Vulcan 800 & Vulcan 800 Classic, 95-05
M357-2	Vulcan 1500, 87-99
M471-3	Vulcan 1500 Series, 96-08
M245	Vulcan 1600 Series, 03-08

Fours

M449	KZ500/550 & ZX550, 79-85
M450	KZ, Z & ZX750, 80-85
M358	KZ650, 77-83
M359-3	Z & KZ 900-1000cc, 73-81
M451-3	KZ, ZX & ZN 1000 &1100cc, 81-02
M452-3	ZX500 & Ninja ZX600, 85-97
M468-2	Ninja ZX-6, 90-04
M469	Ninja ZX-7, ZX7R & ZX7RR, 91-98
M453-3	Ninja ZX900, ZX1000 & ZX1100, 84-01
M409	Concours, 86-04

POLARIS

ATVs

M496	3-, 4- and 6-Wheel Models w/250-425cc Engines, 85-95
M362-2	Magnum & Big Boss, 96-99
M363	Scrambler 500 4X4, 97-00
M365-4	Sportsman/Xplorer, 96-10
M366	Sportsman 600/700/800 Twins, 02-10
M367	Predator 500, 03-07

SUZUKI

ATVs

M381	ALT/LT 125 & 185, 83-87
M475	LT230 & LT250, 85-90
M380-2	LT250R Quad Racer, 85-92
M483-2	LT-4WD, LT-F4WDX & LT-F250, 87-98
M270-2	LT-Z400, 03-08
M343-2	LT-F500F Quadrunner, 98-02

Singles

M369	125-400cc, 64-81
M371	RM50-400 Twin Shock, 75-81
M379	RM125-500 Single Shock, 81-88
M386	RM80-250, 89-95
M400	RM125, 96-00
M401	RM250, 96-02
M476	DR250-350, 90-94
M477-3	DR-Z400E, S & SM, 00-09
M384-4	LS650 Savage/S40, 86-07

Twins

M372	GS400-450 Chain Drive, 77-87
M484-2	GS500E Twins, 89-02
M361	SV650, 1999-2002
M481-5	VS700-800 Intruder/S50, 85-07
M261-2	1500 Intruder/C90, 98-09
M260-2	Volusia/Boulevard C50, 01-08
M482-3	VS1400 Intruder/S83, 87-07

Triple

M368	GT380, 550 & 750, 72-77

Fours

M373	GS550, 77-86
M364	GS650, 81-83
M370	GS750, 77-82
M376	GS850-1100 Shaft Drive, 79-84
M378	GS1100 Chain Drive, 80-81
M383-3	Katana 600, 88-96 GSX-R750-1100, 86-87
M331	GSX-R600, 97-00
M264	GSX-R600, 01-05
M478-2	GSX-R750, 88-92; GSX750F Katana, 89-96
M485	GSX-R750, 96-99
M377	GSX-R1000, 01-04
M266	GSX-R1000, 05-06
M265	GSX1300R Hayabusa, 99-07
M338	Bandit 600, 95-00
M353	GSF1200 Bandit, 96-03

YAMAHA

ATVs

M499-2	YFM80 Moto-4, Badger & Raptor, 85-08
M394	YTM200, 225 & YFM200, 83-86
M488-5	Blaster, 88-05
M489-2	Timberwolf, 89-00
M487-5	Warrior, 87-04
M486-6	Banshee, 87-06
M490-3	Moto-4 & Big Bear, 87-04
M493	Kodiak, 93-98
M287	YFZ450, 04-09
M285-2	Grizzly 660, 02-08
M280-2	Raptor 660R, 01-05
M290	Raptor 700R, 06-09

Singles

M492-2	PW50 & 80 Y-Zinger & BW80 Big Wheel 80, 81-02
M410	80-175 Piston Port, 68-76
M415	250-400 Piston Port, 68-76
M412	DT & MX Series, 77-83
M414	IT125-490, 76-86
M393	YZ50-80 Monoshock, 78-90
M413	YZ100-490 Monoshock, 76-84
M390	YZ125-250, 85-87 YZ490, 85-90
M391	YZ125-250, 88-93 & WR250Z, 91-93
M497-2	YZ125, 94-01
M498	YZ250, 94-98; WR250Z, 94-97
M406	YZ250F & WR250F, 01-03
M491-2	YZ400F, 98-99 & 426F, 00-02; WR400F, 98-00 & 426F, 00-01
M417	XT125-250, 80-84
M480-3	XT350, 85-00; TT350, 86-87
M405	XT/TT 500, 76-81
M416	XT/TT 600, 83-89

Twins

M403	650cc Twins, 70-82
M395-10	XV535-1100 Virago, 81-03
M495-6	V-Star 650, 98-09
M281-4	V-Star 1100, 99-09
M283	V-Star 1300, 07-10
M282-2	Road Star, 99-07

Triple

M404	XS750 & XS850, 77-81

Fours

M387	XJ550, XJ600 & FJ600, 81-92
M494	XJ600 Seca II/Diversion, 92-98
M388	YX600 Radian & FZ600, 86-90
M396	FZR600, 89-93
M392	FZ700-750 & Fazer, 85-87
M411	XS1100, 78-81
M461	YZF-R6, 99-04
M398	YZF-R1, 98-03
M399	FZ1, 01-05
M397	FJ1100 & 1200, 84-93
M375	V-Max, 85-03
M374-2	Royal Star, 96-10

VINTAGE MOTORCYCLES

Clymer® Collection Series

M330	Vintage British Street Bikes, BSA 500–650cc Unit Twins; Norton 750 & 850cc Commandos; Triumph 500-750cc Twins
M300	Vintage Dirt Bikes, V. 1 Bultaco, 125-370cc Singles; Montesa, 123-360cc Singles; Ossa, 125-250cc Singles
M305	Vintage Japanese Street Bikes Honda, 250 & 305cc Twins; Kawasaki, 250-750cc Triples; Kawasaki, 900 & 1000cc Fours